HISTORY OF PSYCHOLOGY

AN OVERVIEW

HISTORY OF PSYCHOLOGY

AN OVERVIEW

BY

HENRYK MISIAK
Fordham University

AND

VIRGINIA STAUDT SEXTON
*Hunter College of the City University
of New York*

GRUNE & STRATTON   New York and London

Copyright © 1966
GRUNE & STRATTON, INC.
381 Park Avenue South
New York, New York 10016

Printed in U.S.A.
(M-A)

Table of Contents

Part I

ROOTS OF PSYCHOLOGY

CHAPTER

Part II

THE BEGINNINGS AND GROWTH OF SCIENTIFIC PSYCHOLOGY IN VARIOUS COUNTRIES

Part III

THEORETICAL PSYCHOLOGY

Preface

THIS BOOK IS INTENDED TO BE a textbook for students of psychology, both undergraduate and graduate, particularly for those enrolled in courses such as "History of Psychology" and "Systems of Psychology." Its aim is practical and didactic: to provide a basis and stimulation for further study of the history and systems of psychology. The book does not aspire to be either a novel conception or an exhaustive presentation of the history of psychology. It rather seeks to provide an unbiased overview of basic facts and concepts related to the roots of scientific psychology, to the development of psychology in various countries, and to psychological theories.

Special attention was given to topics and areas of recent origin which are not treated systematically in other historical textbooks. Thus relatively special consideration is given to psychology as a profession, to clinical psychology, to psychology in Asia, and to the phenomenological-existential approach in psychology. For various reasons, it was not possible to cover the development of psychology in all countries.

The authors are indebted to many colleagues in psychology and in allied disciplines who read portions of the manuscript and offered criticisms and suggestions. They are also grateful to their students for the stimulation which their interest, queries, and comments provided. Special appreciation is expressed to Fordham University Professors: Ewert H. Cousins for reading the chapters on phenomenological and existential psychology, and the section on Carl Jung, and for his helpful suggestions and advice; Alan Grey for his critical comments on the chapter on psychoanalysis; and J. Quentin Lauer, S.J., for his comments on the chapter on phenomenological psychology. For their encouragement and for their graciousness in providing essential information we wish to thank Professors James F. Adams, of Temple University, Philadelphia, Pa.; Johannes von Allesch, of Göttingen University, Germany; Jaime Bulatao, S.J., of Ateneo de Manila, Philippines; Heiner Erke, of University of Münster, Germany; James Filella, S.J., of St. Xavier's College, Bombay, India; J. E. Jayasuriya, University of Ceylon, Ceylon; Ivan D. London, of Brooklyn College, New York; P. H. Müller, University of Neuchâtel, Switzerland; Lamaimas Saradatta, Bangkok Institute for Child Study, Thailand; Koji Sato, of Kyoto University, Japan; H. Y. Su, of National Taiwan University, China; Frank Wesley, of Portland State College, Oregon; and S. M. Hafeez Zaidi, of University of Karachi, Pakistan. We thank Mr. James M. Smith, graduate assistant in the Department of Psychology of Fordham University, who was most helpful in the final preparation of the manuscript. Our very special thanks and gratitude are owed to Professor Richard Sexton, Department of English, Fordham University, who generously read the entire manuscript and made numerous constructive and valuable textual suggestions. Responsibility for any flaws or omissions that remain is assumed by the authors.

Henryk Misiak
Virginia Staudt Sexton

Acknowledgments

THE AUTHORS WISH TO THANK the following publishers and persons for their permission to cite from their publications. The exact sources from which excerpts were taken are given in the References at the end of each chapter.

Publishers: American Journal of Psychology; American Psychological Association; Appleton-Century-Crofts; Barnes & Noble, Inc.; British Journal of Psychology; British Journal of Statistical Psychology; Clark University Press; Duquesne University Press; E. P. Dutton & Co. Inc.; Fordham University Press; Grune & Stratton, Inc.; Harcourt, Brace & World, Inc.; International Universities Press, Inc.; The Journal Press; The Psychology Press; Journal of Humanistic Psychology; Liveright Publishing Corp.; McGraw-Hill Book Co.; Thomas Nelson & Sons; W. W. Norton & Co., Inc.; Philosophical Library Publications Universitaires de Louvain; Random House, Inc.; Julius Stubman, Publisher; Ronald Press; Science; Charles Scribner's Sons Publishers; University of Chicago Press.

Persons: Gordon W. Allport; F. C. Bartlett; Edwin G. Boring; Richard W. Coan; Herbert Feigl; Maurice Friedman; Thomas W. Harrell; Ross Harrison; L. S. Hearnshaw; Donald O. Hebb; Ernest R. Hilgard; Sigmund Koch; Wolfgang Köhler; Abraham H. Maslow; Rollo May; Gardner Murphy; Carl R. Rogers; Michael Scriven; David Shakow; Mary Rose Sheehan; Thorne Shipley; B. F. Skinner; Gary A. Steiner; James Strachey; Anthony J. Sutich; Adrian L. van Kaam; Robert I. Watson; Henry Winthrop.

Introduction

PSYCHOLOGY, LIKE ALL OTHER BRANCHES OF SCIENCE in the twentieth century, has been expanded and refined to great depth and precision. The American Psychological Association—the national professional organization in the field—has recognized its variety and complexity, by grouping its membership into 24 separate divisions. In the colleges and universities, both undergraduate and graduate curricula have offered constantly more expansive programs for the psychology student. Under the circumstances of such widespread growth, the choice of study areas becomes a pressing consideration in the economy of scholarship in psychology. Among the competitive demands of various areas, what special claim does the history of psychology have upon the time and energy of the psychology student?

A general answer to this question is provided by a committee of the American Psychological Association. The committee surveyed chairmen in graduate departments of psychology in American universities, asking what courses would compose "an ideal undergraduate curriculum for prospective graduate students." The results of this survey, based on answers from 149 chairmen and published in the *American Psychologist* for October 1958, reveal that "History of Psychology" and "Schools and Systems" are rated among the top ten ideal courses for preparing prospective graduate psychology students. Student surveys by the authors over the years indicate that undergraduates find two principal values in the historical study of psychology: improved understanding of the scope of the entire field; and a familiarity with outstanding contributors to its development. Characteristically, students regard a knowledge of the history of psychology as an important phase of their professional orientation.

The basic function of the history of psychology is to record the facts of its past. But regarding the past for its own sake limits, unrealistically, the vital purpose of the study of history. George Sarton, the historian of science, has observed that "The past interests only because of the future, and acquires all its real significance only in the light of the present." This dynamic conception of history is the ultimate justification of historical study. When a knowledge of the basic facts in the history of psychology helps us to know the relation of the past to the present and, in the possession of such knowledge, to build for the future, it has achieved in the fullest measure its dynamic possibilities.

The particular values of the study of the history of psychology, when they are considered dynamically, are those of the history of any science. When such a study is a research of the successes and progress in the work of the great men of the past, it can provide powerful inspiration to the neophyte. Moreover, as a source of information on past misconceptions, errors, and deficiencies, it can have the constructive effect of preventing their repetition. A knowledge of the historical progress of the science of psychology—in both its accomplishments and deficiencies—may reveal what can and should be done in the years ahead and may, indeed, point the way to future progress. Perhaps most importantly, by comprehensive projecting of the continuous growth of psychology, the study of the history of psychology provides for its students a source of wisdom.

REFERENCES

American Psychological Association, Division 2, Committee on the Role of Psychology in Small and Large Institutions, Subcommittee of Curriculum Differences. Undergraduate training for psychologists. *Amer. Psychologist,* 1958, *13*, 585–588.

Crutchfield, R. S., & Krech, D. Some guides to the understanding of the history of psychology. In L. Postman (Ed.), *Psychology in the making: histories of selected research problems.* New York: Knopf, 1962. Pp. 3–27.

Latham, A. J. Guides to psychological literature. *Amer. Psychologist,* 1954, *9*, 21–28.

Nance, R. D. Student reactions to the history of psychology. *Amer. Psychologist,* 1961, *16*, 189–191.

Nance, R. D. Current practices in teaching history of psychology. *Amer. Psychologist,* 1962, *17*, 250–252.

Watson, R. I. The history of psychology: a neglected area. *Amer. Psychologist,* 1960, *15*, 251–255.

1

Genealogy of Psychology

SCIENTIFIC PSYCHOLOGY originated in the last quarter of the nineteenth century. Psychological inquiries, however, began in the very dawn of philosophy. For more than 24 centuries—from ancient Greek philosophy until that of the late nineteenth century—psychological thought was a phase of philosophy and grew in its womb. Contemporary scientific psychologists refer to this psychology as philosophical or rational psychology. Under the influence of science—particularly physiology—and of scientific methodology, psychology was separated from philosophy and began to develop as an independent science. In the first part of this book, we shall examine briefly the roles that philosophy, physiology, and scientific methodology played in the origin of psychology and its subsequent growth. Before details of these influences are given, it will be useful to explain first the meaning of the word "psychology," and then to make a few general statements about the genealogy of psychology.

The Term "Psychology." The word "psychology," like many scientific terms, has a Greek source. It is composed of two words, *psyche*—the soul or mind, and *logos*—knowledge or study. Literally, it meant the study, knowledge, or science of the soul. That is what psychology was when the word was coined. Philip Melanchthon (1497-1560), the collaborator of Martin Luther, is credited with this coinage. But the term came into general use only about 100 years later. Christian von Wolff (1679-1754) popularized it when he distinguished between *empirical* and *rational* psychology and wrote separate treatises on each of them (1732, 1734).

There were also other names for this science in simultaneous use, in the eighteenth and nineteenth centuries. Mental philosophy, autology (science of one's self), and pneumatology (science of spirits or "created intelligences") were some of them.

Philosophical, Physiological, and Methodological Roots. Philosophy, throughout its long history, endeavored to understand and explain human nature and man's mental life. All the ideas and solutions which philosophers offered to explain human nature, mind, consciousness, mental processes and activities—such as sensation, perception, learning, cognition, reasoning, willing, and feeling—these constitute the psychological thought of philosophy. Since it was developed by philosophical, rather than experimental methods, it is called *prescientific psychology*. This psychological thought in philosophy, particularly as it was formulated by

1

certain philosophical schools—especially by associationism—was absorbed by the new *scientific psychology* and was greatly responsible for its early character and orientation. In this sense we speak of philosophy as one of the roots of psychology.

Physiology also had an important part in the making of the new psychology. It was chiefly the influence of physiology that led to psychology's separation from philosophy and emergence as an independent science. Men interested in psychology began to realize that the exclusively philosophical treatment of psychological problems was incomplete and inadequate. Physiological discoveries about the brain, the nature of nervous activity, and the functions of sense organs were found relevant to psychology. Not infrequently these discoveries contradicted some notions about man and psychological functions handed down by philosophy. The need for a new treatment and a new approach in psychological inquiries became strikingly apparent to people both interested in psychology and familiar with the achievements of physiology. The vital role of physiology in the establishment of psychology is clearly reflected in the name first adopted for the new psychology, *physiological psychology*.

Entering the modern phase of its development, psychology utilized scientific methodology which was being developed by physiology and other sciences in the nineteenth century. Without methods suitable for its specific investigations, psychology could not have made progress as a science. The most useful methods were furnished by Gustav Theodor Fechner (1801-1887) and presented in his 1860 book, *The Elements of Psychophysics*.

Other Influences.   Scientific interest in the nineteenth century was extended to areas previously neglected, such as hypnotism, reaction time in astronomy, mental diseases, and educational questions. Because of their psychological nature, these new scientific interests called for study and explanation by psychology. Moreover, biological theories—such as the theory of evolution—ethnological and anthropological studies, the rise of the new science of genetics, interest in sociology, and animal experimentation all had a share in arousing psychological interests and affected in greater or lesser degree the development of the young science.

Wilhelm Wundt, Founder of Scientific Psychology.   The numerous philosophical and varied physiological and methodological influences coincided and merged effectively in one person: Wilhelm Wundt, professor—first of physiology and later of philosophy—at the University of Leipzig, Germany. He was well trained in both fields and highly productive in research and writing. At the same time he was well acquainted with psychophysics and used psychophysical methods in his experiments. In 1873 Wundt published a book entitled *Principles of Physiological Psychology*. In the preface he announced: "The work which I here present to the public is an attempt to mark out a new domain of science." This book was the most important textbook of the new science of psychology for decades. Six years after its publication, in 1879, Wundt established a psychological laboratory at Leipzig University—the first laboratory of this kind in the world. This event has been acclaimed the beginning of scientific psychology, and the year 1879 has since been regarded as the birth year of the new science.

Diagrammatic Presentation of the Genealogy of Psychology. The accompanying diagram summarizes the genealogy of psychology. In it are specified the roots of psychology and the contributions from other sciences to its growth. Later sections of this first part of the book will deal with them in greater detail.

THE GENEALOGY OF SCIENTIFIC PSYCHOLOGY

AND THE MAIN SOURCES OF INFLUENCE ON THE GROWTH OF PSYCHOLOGY

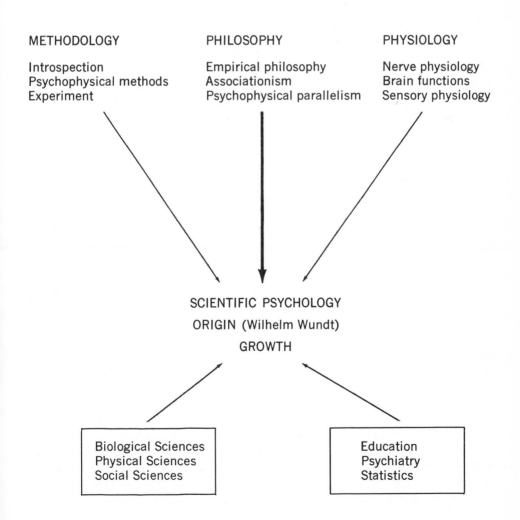

METHODOLOGY

Introspection
Psychophysical methods
Experiment

PHILOSOPHY

Empirical philosophy
Associationism
Psychophysical parallelism

PHYSIOLOGY

Nerve physiology
Brain functions
Sensory physiology

SCIENTIFIC PSYCHOLOGY

ORIGIN (Wilhelm Wundt)

GROWTH

Biological Sciences
Physical Sciences
Social Sciences

Education
Psychiatry
Statistics

2

Psychological Thought in Ancient and Medieval Philosophy

THE LONG HISTORY OF PSYCHOLOGY, similar to the history of philosophy of which it was a part, can be conveniently divided into two main periods. The first extended from the ancient Greek philosophy until the end of the Middle Ages, a span of over 2000 years, during which psychology's main theme was the soul, its nature, and its relation to the body. This was the period of metaphysical psychology. During the second period—from Descartes to the nineteenth century—the focus of interest shifted from the soul to the mind. Psychology became empirical and was preoccupied chiefly with mental processes, especially with sensation, perception, and association of ideas. Psychology began to be increasingly influenced at that time by natural sciences, by physics, biology, and physiology. In the first period, the *remote* philosophical roots are to be found. The second period provided the concepts which constituted the *immediate roots* and the philosophical foundation of the new psychology of the last quarter of the nineteenth century.

Development of Philosophy. Because of the close and long association of psychology with philosophy, and because of the dependence of psychological thought on philosophical thought, acquaintance with the main philosophical doctrines, even if superficial, is in order. The development of philosophy can be briefly and cursorily summarized like this. Western philosophy, with which psychology was associated, begins in ancient Greece in the seventh century B.C. The great syntheses of ancient thought were achieved by Democritus (ca. 460-370 B.C.), Plato (427-347 B.C.), and Aristotle (384-322 B.C.). Democritus represents materialism; Plato, idealism; and Aristotle, realism. These three systems remained fonts of philosophical thought for centuries after. Thomas Aquinas (1225-1274) revived Aristotelian philosophy and built on it his philosophical system, which was the epitome of Medieval Christian philosophy. A critical turn in the history of philosophy occurs in the seventeenth century when Descartes (1596-1650) disregards the entire philosophical past and develops a new system. This is the beginning of the modern era of philosophy. Reaction and opposition to Descartes' philosophy (Cartesianism) led to a new and different orientation—the empirical philosophy—and to the related systems developed under the aegis of empirical thought. At the end of the eighteenth century came Kant's revolution against existing philosophies. After him two powerful systems arose in the nineteenth century—namely, positivism and idealism. Keeping this historical framework in mind, we can proceed now to describe it in more detail.

4

Greek Philosophy. The earliest traces of psychological thought in the Western world are to be found in ancient Greek philosophy—which then embraced all fields of knowledge—and in medicine. It is noteworthy that the range of psychological inquiry in Greek philosophy included virtually all the fundamental problems of modern psychology: sensation, perception, learning and memory, emotions, motivation, sleep and dreams, the temperament and its physiological basis, differences in personality, even the role of the mind in health and sickness of the body. These problems were not always formulated clearly nor were they exhaustively studied, but they were posed and invited study.

The Greek approach to them was sometimes metaphysical and purely speculative, sometimes biological or physiological and based on observations. In the fifth and fourth centuries B.C., Greek philosophy introduced the consequential body-mind problem when it distinguished between the material and the spiritual worlds and applied this dichotomy to the nature of man. The first philosopher in Greece to suggest a differentiation between the spiritual and material elements in man, animal, and plant is believed to be *Anaxagoras* (ca. 500-428 B.C.).

Ancient Cosmology. In the earliest period of Greek philosophy, from the seventh to the fifth century B.C., the focus of attention was on *cosmology* —that is, on the material world and nonliving matter. The only psychological problem considered by the early cosmologists was that of sensation and sensory organs, particularly of vision. Empedocles, in the fifth century B.C., maintained that sensation is possible because of the material contact between the effluxes or emanations naturally produced by both the sense organ and the external object. Historically, the first psychological question raised and studied was probably "How can man see distant objects?"

The final and most complete product of the cosmological tradition was *atomism*. This is the first great synthesis of the ancient philosophy and at the same time the main form of ancient materialism. This synthesis was achieved by *Democritus* (ca. 460-370 B.C.). He taught that the whole universe—the body and the soul included—is made of the same matter and that this matter is composed of small indivisible particles, the atoms. Their motions produced thought and mental operations, in his view.

Plato. Whereas atomism was the first materialistic and monistic system, the second great synthesis of Greek thought, embodied in the philosophy of Plato (427-347 B.C.), was an idealistic, spiritualistic, and dualistic system. The starting point of this philosophy was the analysis of man's knowledge. In his knowledge two levels could be distinguished, the sensory and the intellectual. From this distinction Plato derived a differentiation between the spiritual world and the material world and, together with this distinction, the concept of the human soul. To him the soul was a complete substance, of divine origin, spiritual, immortal, and eternal. It lived independently before coming to dwell in the body. It is imprisoned by the body, but only temporarily until the body's death.

Plato's idealism affirms that ideas are the only reality. Ideas, such as beauty, are not merely creations of the mind. They exist and they make up the world of ideas—a world which is real, absolute, unchangeable, and eternal. The world that we perceive around us is merely a passing shadow and copy of the world of ideas.

A direct extension of Plato's philosophy, with some modifications, was the system called *Neoplatonism*—popular from the third to the sixth century. The Platonic tradition was powerful until the thirteenth century. At that time Thomistic philosophy—based on Aristotle's realism—overshadowed it. But some elements of Platonic philosophy were revived again in certain systems of modern philosophy. No other philosophical system ever matched the Platonic influence, and none has made an equal imprint on Western culture.

Aristotelian Psychology.   The first strong opponent of Platonic philosophy was Plato's famous disciple Aristotle (384-322 B.C.). His system avoided the extremes and partiality of the preceding materialistic and spiritualistic doctrines. It was a synthesis of the idealistic and materialistic elements of these doctrines on a new and original basis. Aristotle has been called the greatest philosopher of all times, and his philosophy has never ceased to interest thinking men.

Aristotle declared that psychology—which he defines as "the study of the soul"—is among his first interests. If any philosopher deserves the title of the originator of psychology, it is Aristotle. It is he who presented the first complete systematic discussion of fundamental psychological issues. This is contained in *De anima* ("On the Soul") often said to be his best work—and in a body of smaller treatises called collectively *Parva naturalia* ("The Short Physical Treatises"). In *De anima*, Aristotle expounds his views on the nature and properties of the soul. In this work he is also the first historian of psychology, since he records and reviews the opinions of others who wrote on the soul before him. In *Parva naturalia*, Aristotle is a physiological psychologist rather than a metaphysician, for he devotes his attention mainly to biological aspects and physiological processes of man. This attitude is revealed in the titles of the treatises which comprise this work: "On Sensation and That Which Is Sensed," "On Memory and Forgetting," "Concerning Sleep and Awakening," "Concerning Dreams," "Interpretation of Dreams," "About a Long Life and a Short Life," "Concerning Youth and Old Age," "Concerning Life and Death," and "About Respiration."

Aristotelian psychology and its influence on psychology in general were acknowledged by such psychologists as Külpe, Ebbinghaus, and C. S. Myers, to mention just a few. Külpe states that "the first truly complete systematic psychology comes from Aristotle." Ebbinghaus says of Aristotle that his amazing genius constructed a psychology which surpassed all other sciences of his epoch. Myers says that the experimental psychology of the late nineteenth century cannot be called new because "experiment in psychology is at least as old as Aristotle."

Aristotle's Hylomorphism.   Unlike Plato—who begins with the differentiation of the spiritual and the material elements in man and then proceeds to explain how these two elements are united—Aristotle takes the unity of man as his starting point. Upon analysis of man's nature, however, he discovers its complexity and is led to recognize in it two principles, the soul and the body. How the two are related to each other is the subject of Aristotle's discourse in *De anima*. The explanation he offers is in harmony with the fundamental and critical concept of his entire philosophy. This concept is the metaphysical dichotomy of potency and act embodied in the distinction of matter and form.

According to Aristotle, all existing things are composed of matter and form. Neither element is complete nor can it exist by itself; each must complement the other. Matter must have form, and form must be related to matter. Both are interdependent and when united, make one substance. Form determines all the characteristics of the substance. To illustrate this point Aristotle cited the example of a piece of bronze. The bronze must have some shape in order to exist. This shape may be a sphere, or a statue of Apollo, or a misshapen mass. Without some kind of shape, the bronze cannot possibly exist. On the other hand, the shape has no existence of its own. This formulation is known as the hylomorphic (*hyle*: matter; *morphe*: form) doctrine of Aristotle. Applied to man, this doctrine regards the soul as the form of man—that is, his vital principle, and the body as his matter. Both make one complete substance, one organism, which exists and acts as an integrated unit. Not only man but also other living beings—animals and plants—have their own soul, which, as their form is the source of all their properties and of their unity and integration. The human soul is the highest kind of soul because it is endowed with ability to think. Aristotle distinguished three levels of functioning in man, the vegetative, sensory, and rational, all of which he discussed in detail. He recognized a fivefold division of the senses, but pointed out the variety of tactual sensations. Intellect is uniquely human and is the highest capacity through which man can grasp the essence of things, in Aristotle's system.

After Aristotle.   After Aristotle there was no other original system of psychology in the ancient world. There was, to be sure, much psychological material in the writings of Greek and Roman philosophers. But there was no exposition which approached the scope or originality of the Aristotelian system. The treatment of psychological matters was eclectic. The Stoics and Epicureans were concerned with practical life, principally with a way of life which would secure the maximum of pleasure and happiness and a minimum of suffering. Theirs was a practical psychology of everyday living.

The Christian Era.   Christian philosophy concentrated on the religious and moral aspects of human life. The Christian authors of the first seven centuries—called Fathers of the Church—and later, the Christian theologians and philosophers, were concerned principally with the spiritual nature of the soul, man's relation to God, and his eternal salvation. The psychological processes as such were of secondary interest to them. In their writings, however, we frequently come across profound analyses of man's inner experiences, spiritual development, and affective life. A good example of this kind of analysis is *Confessions*, the famous autobiography of *Augustine* (354-430 A.D.), Bishop of Hippo. This autobiography gained for him the title, "First Modern Psychologist," because in it Augustine presented a penetrating and sincere self-analysis of his own emotions, thoughts, memories, and motives. These inner experiences modern man easily understands and, despite a lapse of fifteen centuries, finds them familiar and similar to his own.

Medieval Philosophy. The lack of systematic treatment of psychology continues until the Middle Ages. Much psychological material, however, can be found scattered in philosophical writings. In the twelfth century, a great scholar, *Moses Maimonides* (1135-1204), effecting rapprochement of Greek and Hebrew intellectual traditions, offered a system of rational psychology. In Christian thought, a radical change occurred when scholastic philosophy was developed. The majority of Christian philosophers in the Middle Ages abandoned the Platonic orientation and turned instead to Aristotle. The hylomorphic doctrine of Aristotle was restudied and amplified, particularly by *Thomas Aquinas* (1225-1274). This philosopher examined all the philosophical thought of the past, as well as of his own time, and built a new system which incorporated elements from the Greek, Hebrew, and Arabic philosophies. The psychology of Thomas Aquinas is contained mainly in his *Commentary on Aristotle's De Anima*, and in the first part of his *Summa Theologica*. For Aquinas, psychology is a study of human nature, through the analysis of man's acts, powers, and habits. The basic characteristic of man's nature is the integration of the vegetative, sensory, and spiritual properties of man. The focal point of Aristotle's psychological inquiry is the soul. The emphasis of Thomistic psychology, however, is the nature of man, who, in Aquinas' interpretation, is the besouled body. Allied to this notion is the main characteristic of Aquinas' psychology: insistence on the unity of man, despite the presence in him of two elements, the bodily and the spiritual. A contemporary of Aquinas, *Peter of Spain* (ca. 1215-1277)—who near the end of his life was elected Pope John XXI—was the author of an original treatise, which was perhaps the first systematic treatment of psychology as a separate discipline since antiquity. He devoted one chapter of his book to the history of psychology. In general the psychological works of the Middle Ages were metaphysical and deductive, but occasionally they made reference to biology and physiology.

The Renaissance. Increasing interest in science and the gradual development of scientific methodology also made an impact on psychological thought. The realm of psychology began to be better differentiated and defined. *Francis Bacon's* (1561-1626) classification of sciences had as its point of departure the three faculties of the soul—namely, memory (history), imagination (poetry), and intellect (philosophy). Psychology was classified under philosophy as a part of anthropology.

One of the most original representatives of psychological thought during the Renaissance was *Juan Luis Vives* (1492-1540), an eminent humanist. Vives proposed social and educational reforms, which impress us even today for their progressiveness. In every book he wrote, he stressed the importance of the understanding of the human mind for education, philosophy, politics, and science, and he proved himself a master of introspection and observation. Vives has been described as the greatest psychologist not only of his own time but of the next three centuries. He is a distant forerunner of the dynamic psychology of the twentieth century. His claim to fame in psychology is his most significant book, *De anima et vita* ("About the Mind and Life," 1538). It has three parts—the first devoted to association of ideas, learning, memory; the second, to the rational soul and its faculties; and the third, to feelings and emotions. The book contains a wealth of keen observation about human nature in general. The most original part of the book is that which pertains to the association of ideas.

PHILOSOPHICAL ROOTS OF PSYCHOLOGY
600 B.C.—1550 A.D.

PHILOSOPHICAL DOCTRINES	CHARACTERISTICS	TIME
1. Early Greek	Main interest is cosmology. Speculation about sensation.	7th to 5th century B.C.
2. Anaxagoras	Early distinction between the soul and the body.	ca. 500–428 B.C.
3. Democritus	Materialistic and atomistic interpretation of the soul, its nature and operations.	ca. 460–370 B.C.
4. Plato	Spiritualistic and dualistic psychology. Gulf between the soul and the body.	427–347 B.C.
5. Aristotle	The first system of psychology. The soul is the vital principle of the body. Both substantially united.	384–322 B.C.
6. Early Christian Philosophy	The soul is considered from religious and moral viewpoints.	1st to 9th century
7. Scholasticism	The soul is studied in its nature and relation to the body. Aristotelian psychology is revived by Thomas Aquinas.	9th to 15th century
8. Vives	Forerunner of modern psychology. He stresses the importance of understanding human mind for philosophy, education, science, and politics.	1492–1540

REFERENCES

ANCIENT PHILOSOPHY

Beare, J. I. *Greek theories of elementary cognition from Alcmaeon to Aristotle.* Oxford: Clarendon Press, 1906.

Chaignet, A. E. *Histoire de la psychologie des Grecs.* Paris: Hachette, 1887–93 (5 volumes).

Hammond, W. A. *Aristotle's psychology: De anima and Parva Naturalia.* London: Macmillan, 1902.

Hicks, R. D. *Aristotle De anima.* Cambridge, England: Cambridge Univer. Press, 1907.

Nuyens, F. J. *L'évolution de la psychologie d'Aristote.* Louvain: Institut Supérieur de Philosophie, 1948.

Nuyens, F. J. The evolution of Aristotle's psychology. *Proc. Xth Int. Cong. Phil.* Amsterdam, 1948, 1101–1104.

Sarton, G. *A history of science: ancient science through the golden age of Greece.* Cambridge, Mass.: Harvard Univer. Press, 1952.

Shute, C. *The psychology of Aristotle.* New York: Columbia Univer. Press, 1941.

Siwek, P. *La psychophysique humaine d'après Aristote.* Paris: Alcan, 1930.

Stratton, G. M. *Theophrastus and the Greek physiological psychology before Aristotle.* New York: Macmillan, 1917.

Strong, C. A. A sketch of the history of psychology among the Greeks. *Amer. J. Psychol.,* 1892, *4,* 177–197.

MEDIEVAL

Brennan, R. E. *Thomistic psychology, a philosophic analysis of the nature of man.* New York: Macmillan, 1941.

Gilson, E. *The spirit of medieval philosophy.* New York: Scribner, 1936.

Grabmann, M. *Thomas Aquinas: his personality and thought.* London: Longmans, 1929.

Husik, I. *A history of mediaeval Jewish philosophy.* New York: Meridian, 1958.

Onians, R. B. *The origins of European thought: about the body, the mind, the soul, the world, time and fate.* Cambridge, England: Cambridge Univer. Press, 1951.

Watson, F. The father of modern psychology. *Psychol. Rev.,* 1915, *22,* 333–353.

3

Psychological Thought
in Modern Philosophy

THE SEVENTEENTH CENTURY brings a definite change in the treatment of psychological problems. Observation and induction now supplant metaphysical analysis and deduction. Psychology decidedly ceases to be the science of the soul. Instead, the mind and its operations become the main interest. This change is largely due to Descartes. Psychology now assumes also a more important role within philosophy. Virtually every philosopher from this time forward will discuss psychological problems, and the philosophical systems will analyze issues of psychological relevance. In the two and a half centuries, from 1600 to 1850, philosophy formulated concepts, ideas, and theories which became the philosophical foundation for modern psychology. This chapter reviews both the systems and the particular issues which contributed to that philosophical foundation. The philosophical systems most significant for psychology were: the philosophy of Descartes, empirical philosophy, and associationism. Among the problems essential for understanding—both of the early character and orientation of psychology and its subsequent transformation in the twentieth century—are: the body-mind problem, the question of sensation and perception, and the association of ideas. Principally, it was the philosophy of Descartes which posed the body-mind problem. Empirical philosophy furthered the study of sensation and perception. The school of associationism developed the concept of association of ideas and stressed the process of association as the most important one for understanding the mind.

DESCARTES

René Descartes (1596-1650; Latin name: Cartesius) was a philosopher, mathematician, and a natural scientist. He revolted against the whole philosophical past and developed a new system. It was a rationalistic system based solely on deduction. The subject of psychology, according to him, is not man but the spiritual mind of man and its contents. The mind has three functions: intellectual cognition, volition, and sensation. The only method of studying the mind is by analysis of consciousness. Mind does not comprise anything but conscious states. Knowledge is possible because man is richly endowed from his birth with innate ideas.

Innate ideas constitute an indispensable basis and prerequisite for acquiring knowledge. These ideas are not necessarily actual knowledge of things. Rather they are intuitive knowledge of principles, or inclinations and potentialities which the soul possesses for knowing things. The idea of infinity is such an innate idea. So is, "I think, hence I exist." Innate ideas exist in every mind regardless of experience. They are to be recognized, uncovered, and used in man's thinking. Where do they come from? They are implanted in the mind—or more exactly in the soul, since Descartes equated mind with the soul—by God, the Creator of the soul. Sensory experience is secondary in the acquiring of knowledge. It is only an occasion, a stimulus, for awakening the innate ideas. The latter were rejected by empirical philosophy which held the opposite position—namely, that the human mind is completely blank at birth and that all acquired knowledge comes through senses. The question whether the human mind is furnished with any inherited knowledge or acquires all knowledge through experience is a psychological problem still studied today. In the late nineteenth century the different solutions divided psychologists and physiologists into nativists (nativism) and empiricists (radical empiricism). Currently the question is studied in psychology under the heading: past experience, or learning, versus innate organizing processes.

The imprint of Cartesianism on subsequent generations has been extensive and profound. Many trends and doctrines which appeared after Descartes can be traced to him. The dual aspect of his system—which was both spiritualistic and materialistic—became the source of two opposite streams of philosophical thought, the idealistic and the mechanistic. The doctrine of Descartes' philosophy which is of special interest to us here is the Cartesian dualism. This conception became strongly embedded in psychological thought and can still be detected in contemporary psychology and physiology. Since the issue of body-mind has been a crucial one for psychology, it merits special attention.

THE BODY-MIND PROBLEM

The new psychology of the nineteenth century viewed mán as a composite of body and mind. Hence, consistently, it distinguished in him, if not the soul and the body, at least the bodily and the mental, the somatic and the psychic. It was a *dualistic* psychology.

The term *dualism* (*duo*, two) has been defined in various ways. In a metaphysical sense, it means a theory which admits in any given realm two distinct and independent substances. In a psychophysical sense, applied to man, it means a theory which holds that man is composed of two different and mutually irreducible elements. It is contrasted with *monism* (*monos*, one) which denies such a distinction and asserts complete homogeneity of human nature. Depending on their fundamental philosophical viewpoint, either spiritualistic or materialistic, the adherents of monism may be divided into two classes: those who regard man as a purely material entity, not different essentially from other beings of the universe, and those who view man as an entirely spiritual substance. The former view has been called materialistic monism, the latter spiritualistic. Materialistic monism, spurred by the progress of the natural sciences and the theory of evolution, has become particularly strong—both as a theory and method—in the nineteenth and twentieth centuries.

The body-mind problem has been the perennial problem of philosophy. Ever since man came to be viewed as composed of two elements—the bodily and the mental, or as displaying two classes of phenomena—the problem of their relationship has been the most persistent one both in philosophy and psychology.

The Forms of Dualism.   As a concept, dualism is as old as human thought, both philosophical and theological. Philosophy was predominantly dualistic until the nineteenth century. Two main forms of dualism can be distinguished in the various philosophical systems. One—the extreme form introduced by Plato—postulated the existence of two completely different entities in man, the soul and the body, which remain permanently separated as distinct substances. This notion flourished in the Neoplatonic philosophy of the first centuries of the Christian era and in all later systems built on Platonic philosophy. The other form, the moderate, was conceived by Aristotle. It distinguished in man the two principles, body and soul, but saw them united, forming one complete substance. Philosophies which followed Aristotle—Scholasticism in particular—preserved this form of dualism. Descartes reverted to the extreme dualism of Plato and made it even more explicit and radical.

Cartesian Dualism.   Descartes' philosophy of human nature may be summarized as follows: Man is a composite of a material body and a spiritual soul. The body is like a machine or automaton governed by the laws of mechanics. Its functions and movements are executed by material energies or forces called *animal spirits*. Produced in the brain, moved by the heat of the heart, these animal spirits travel along the nerves and blood vessels, reach the muscles, and put them into action. The soul is spiritual and independent of its material body. It is the ultimate source of life in man. Its influence reaches the body through the pineal gland in the center of the brain.

The interrelation between soul and body had to be explained. Descartes' own explanation gave rise to the *doctrine of interaction*, which regarded soul and body as directly acting on each other. But this doctrine was abandoned even by his ardent disciples because it presented insurmountable difficulties. It was always hard to conceive how a spiritual and inextended substance could act upon a material and extended substance, and vice versa. In the nineteenth century, especially, the interactionism of Descartes appeared incapable of reconciliation with physics. The influence of the soul on the body through the pineal gland was the influence from outside, from another world, the immaterial world. This implied a constant influx of *material* energy from an immaterial source. Such a new influx of energy clashed with the physicists' principle of the conservation of energy in the physical universe. Although the theory of interactionism did not find popularity in psychology, the essential Cartesian dichotomy of man persisted for some time. It can still be found, though usually not identified by name, in views of contemporary scientists—psychologists included.

Leibnitz and his Parallelism. Philosophical systems proposed various solutions of the body-mind problems consistent with their fundamental principles. Only one of these requires closer examination because it generated a theory embraced later by the majority of psychologists. This is the doctrine of *pre-established harmony* and *parallelism*, of Gottfried Wilhelm Leibnitz (1646-1716) which led to *psychophysical parallelism*. This is a conception formulated by Alexander Bain around 1860, and widely accepted by psychologists as their basic notion of the nature of man. Leibnitz believed that the world was composed of innumerable substances, the *monads*, which are independent of each other and without any mutual influence. The human soul is a monad, and the body is an aggregate of monads which the soul dominates. Both the soul and the body act together for the same purpose. How this cooperation is possible, Leibnitz explains by the harmonious order established among the monads by God. Spiritual and bodily activities are independent but exist in perfect parallel, thanks to this pre-established harmony. Body and soul are like two clocks, Leibnitz illustrates, which although completely independent, show exactly the same time because they were wound and regulated by the same hand. This concept of parallelism, rendered more explicit with regard to the psychological study of man, is known as *psychophysical parallelism*.

Psychophysical Parallelism. The body-mind issue became much more important in the nineteenth century when functions of the nervous system —the brain especially—and the sense organs were studied in relation to psychological functions. Psychologists were concerned with the question of the "connexion of mind and body," as Bain put it. Alexander Bain (1818-1903) considers this issue in his book, *Mind and Body, The Theories of Their Relation* (1872). As a physiological psychologist, he saw the need for a doctrine which would integrate the facts of physiology with psychology. In his opinion, the study of the nervous system and sensory processes—in fact, of all biological data—are relevant to psychology. Psychophysical parallelism appeared to him the most suitable theory for the reconciliation of psychology with physiology, hence a sound theoretical basis for physiological psychology.

This theory assumes the existence of two realms, one spiritual or mental, the other material or physical. There is no causal relationship between the two realms; they do not influence each other, yet the events in one realm are paralleled in the other. In other words, bodily and mental events, the physiological and psychological processes, are coincidental and correlated. Every mental activity, such as perceiving or thinking, has its bodily counterpart. But the latter is neither the source nor the cause of the former, yet one could not exist without the other. For psychologists whose relations with philosophy were still close, and whose interest in philosophical issues was strong, psychophysical parallelism represented a solution which avoided the difficulties inherent in extreme dualism.

Psychophysical parallelism was found useful and convenient and was widely accepted among pioneers of the new psychology. When the Third

International Congress of Experimental Psychology convened in Munich in 1896, the body-mind issue was vigorously debated. The majority of the 450 participants expressed support for the psychophysical parallelism. Eventually, however, as the ties with philosophy grew looser and those with science closer, interest in this theory and in other theories of body-mind relation gradually waned. The dichotomy of man, implicit in parallelism, was to be replaced by a developing notion of the unity of man as an organism. Psychological thought leaned toward monism and away from dualism. Moreover, the focus of psychology was changing from the mind to behavior. Retained, for some time—before behaviorism banned even this remnant of philosophy—was the distinction without any dualistic implications between two aspects of man—the mental and the bodily. This position, that one can distinguish in man two kinds of activity, mental and bodily or physical, is called the *double-aspect theory*. Nevertheless, the body-mind issue has not vanished from psychological discussions. With good reason Edna Heidbreder termed it the "bugbear of psychology." The body-mind issue has recurred with persistence in new formulations and in different frames of reference. In the last two decades it seems to have generated renewed interest and again provoked much discussion. One example of this renewed interest is Ludwig von Bertalanffy's article *The Mind-Body Problem: A New View* (1964), in which he calls for "modern reconsideration of the mind-body problem" in the light of recent developments in sciences.

THE BODY-MIND PROBLEM

NAME	THEORY	FORM	VIEW	REPRESENTATIVES
Monism	Existence of only *one* principle in man: body *or* soul	Idealism	*Spiritual soul* is the only reality	Berkeley, idealists of the 19th century
		Materialism	*Material body* is the only reality	Democritus, Hobbes, de La Mettrie, Cabanis
		Hylomorphism	Body and soul form *one substance*	Aristotle, Thomas Aquinas, Neoscholastics
Dualism	Existence of *two* different principles in man: body *and* soul	Interactionism	Body and soul are *two substances interacting*	Plato, Descartes
		Parallelism	Body and soul are *two substances acting independently*	Leibnitz
		Psychophysical parallelism	Body and mind are *two different aspects* of man	Bain, Wundt

DIAGRAMMATIC REPRESENTATION OF THE MAIN BODY-MIND THEORIES

INTERACTIONISM:

Body and mind are different and
   separate but influence each other.

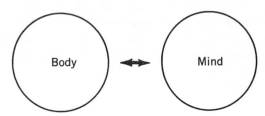

PARALLELISM:

Body and mind are distinct and
   separate, do not influence each
   other but bodily and mental
   activities are perfectly correlated.

HYLOMORPHISM:

Body and mind make one complete
   entity (substance).

DOUBLE-ASPECT THEORIES:

Man is an organism which manifests two
   different aspects: bodily and mental.

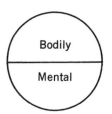

(Adapted from H. Misiak. *The philosophical roots of scientific psychology.* New York: Fordham Univer. Press, 1961. P. 51. By permission of the publishers.)

EMPIRICAL PHILOSOPHY

The development of empirical philosophy in England in the seventeenth and eighteenth centuries opens a new phase in the history of philosophy. Empirical philosophy abandoned rationalism, with its deductive method, and turned to experience as a source of knowledge. Thereby was started a trend of great significance for psychology. Empirical philosophy had a twofold emphasis: experience and its main source, the senses; and exploration of the human mind. Psychology, developed in empirical philosophy, became oriented towards the study of sensation and perception on the one hand, and analysis of mental states on the other. Its methods were observation and introspection. By its emphasis on experience and on the value of observation, empirical philosophy prepared ground for the use of experiment in psychology. The main representatives of empirical philosophy were Thomas Hobbes, John Locke, George Berkeley, and David Hume.

John Locke (1632-1704). John Locke laid the foundation of empirical philosophy by insisting that experience is the only means of attaining knowledge. He declared that "all the materials of reason and knowledge" come from experience. His principal work is *Essay Concerning Human Understanding* (1690). It was the reading of Descartes' works which aroused Locke's interest in philosophy. But ironically, the system which Locke subsequently built was strongly opposed to Cartesian philosophy. He particularly opposed, as the whole empirical school did, the Cartesian notion of innate ideas.

Locke argued that the human mind is like a "white sheet," and that all its ideas are acquired by the senses or through *reflection*. Sensations furnish the ideas of objects outside ourselves, such as their color, taste, or temperature. Reflection accounts for the ideas which do not come directly from senses but originate within the mind. In Locke's definition, reflection is "the perception of the operations of our own mind within us, as it is employed about the ideas it has got." Reflection is not used by children who rely solely on their senses. It comes only with maturity, Locke said.

The *idea* occupies an important place in Locke's philosophy, as it does in all British empirical philosophy. But its definition differs widely. For Locke, ideas are the objects of thinking and have essentially the same meaning as "logical concepts" in present terminology. Our knowledge, according to him, is composed of ideas which are expressed by words such as whiteness, hardness, man, army, and elephant. Association of ideas, as Locke understood it, was a simple combination of two or several ideas. It was not yet a well-developed doctrine. As will be seen, it received much attention and assumed greater importance in subsequent British philosophical doctrines.

Locke concentrated on analysis of the human mind. His whole system evolved from psychological analysis carried out systematically. This analysis not only formed the basis of his philosophy, but was its core. This kind of psychological philosophy inaugurated a tradition which eventually matures into experimental psychology. For this reason, some refer to Locke as the "founder of experimental psychology."

George Berkeley (1685-1753). George Berkeley studied man's mental world and its relation to the material world. His thesis, which is the distinctive characteristic of his system, was that the material world is made or generated by the mind. "To be," he declared, "is to be perceived," which means that something exists only if it is perceived. In his major work, *An Essay towards a New Theory of Vision* (1709), Berkeley proposed "to show the manner wherein we perceive by sight the distance, magnitude, and situation of objects: also to consider the difference there is betwixt the ideas of sight and touch, and whether there be any idea common to both senses." This same inquiry will be pursued by other philosophers. The problem of perception, and perception of space specifically, was intensively studied by Berkeley. Up to the present, it has never ceased to be an object of psychological investigation.

David Hume (1711-1776). David Hume probed more deeply and more critically than Locke and Berkeley into the possibility and validity of knowledge through experience. He denied that knowledge of universal truths is either possible or valid. In his conception, we cannot know anything of the universe, the nature of things, causes, the soul, or the self. We can only know what is in our consciousness, that is, its phenomena. There are only two sources of knowledge, namely, *impressions* and *ideas*. The impressions are the sensations and feelings; they are always the first. The ideas are the subsequent mental copies, which are preserved unchanged in memory, are used in thinking, and may be transformed in imagination. "An impression," says Hume, "first strikes upon the senses, and makes us perceive heat or cold, thirst or hunger, pleasure or pain of some kind or other. Of this impression there is a copy taken by the mind, . . . this we call an idea." The difference between them, Hume said, "consists in the degrees of force and liveliness with which they strike upon the mind, and make their way into our thought or consciousness." Here is a first clear distinction between what psychology now calls sensation and perception. The ideas may be simple or complex—simple if they are copies of simple impressions; complex if they come from complex impressions or result from the combination of simple ideas. This combination, or association, of ideas can be explained by resemblance, contiguity in time or space, or by cause and effect relationships. These explanations are the laws of association proposed by Hume. Hume's system is expounded in his *Treatise of Human Nature* (1739-1740) and *Essays*, of which the most notable is *An Enquiry Concerning Human Understanding* (1748).

Sensationism. Sensationism, the teaching of the empirical school, is the theory that the principal source of knowledge is sensation. The interest in sensation, however, and thus in sense organs, was always strong in philosophy. As early as the sixth century B.C. a Greek physician, *Alcmaeon*, studied the structure and function of the sense organs and their connections with the brain. He distinguished between the physiological processes in the sense organs and the mental processes resulting from them. In the fourth century B.C. there was a treatise *On Sense Perception and the Sensory Objects* by *Theophrastus* (372-287 B.C.), whose critical survey of earlier opinions about sensation attests to the concern of ancient philosophers with this function. *Aristotle* devoted much attention to sensation. He established the fivefold division of the senses, although he realized fully, it is worth noting, that there are more than five sensations. He raised the question whether touch should be considered a single sense, or rather a composite of senses.

Sensation was studied by philosophers through the centuries, but it was the empirical philosophy which added special significance to the study of senses. For this school, as mentioned, rejected the Cartesian notion of innate ideas and taught instead that all knowledge comes from the senses. A large part of the empiricists' works was devoted to the analysis of sensation and mental contents derived from it. The most typical exponent of sensationism was *Etienne de Condillac* (1715-1780), a French empiricist. He carried the sensationist doctrine to the extreme, making the senses and sensations the source of consciousness and all its phenomena. Mind was generated by sensations, he maintained. He illustrated this by his famous example of an inanimate marble statue which becomes alive, and becomes a thinking, feeling, and willing individual simply through sensations. Condillac's position and prestige were strong in France, and subsequent psychological writers made frequent reference to him. The philosophical tradition which he initiated prepared ground for the acceptance of the new psychology in that country. Sensationism was not strong in German philosophy, but the contributions of that country to sensory physiology were outstanding. In Germany, the philosophical treatment of sensation and the physiological investigations merged together in physiological psychology.

The Effect of Empirical Philosophy on Psychology. This effect is evident in several ways. Empirical philosophy raised the prestige of psychology when it used psychological analysis of consciousness in its study of human knowledge. It stressed experience as the source of knowledge and emphasized the value of empirical data. Under this influence, psychology advanced closer to experimentation and to natural sciences. Following the empirical tradition, psychology became sensationist—that is, principally devoted to the study of sensation and perception. It also became associationist because it adopted the association of ideas, a product developed and handed down by empirical philosophy, as the theoretical principle for understanding the nature of mind.

Opposition to Empirical Philosophy. Empirical philosophy found opposition in the land of its origin, in the *Scottish school*, founded by *Thomas Reid* (1710-1796). This new group recognized the value of the empirical method, but did not want to be drawn too far into the dangerous—as they called them—exaggerations of empirical philosophy, which could destroy

the notions of the soul and conscience. These notions were valid and necessary, in their opinion. Reid was the first in the history of psychology to
distinguish clearly between sensation and perception and to define these
processes. To illustrate the difference between the two processes, he used
the perception of a rose—in which several sense modalities, such as visual,
tactual, and olfactory, are combined. Subsequently, this example was
often cited by psychological writers. He is also credited with the introduction of the muscle sense into psychology. Reid advocated the notion of
mental faculties, or active powers of the mind, such as reason, memory,
emotion, and will. Psychology, developed around the notion that the mind
has distinct and independent powers, came to be called *faculty psychology*.
It has been discredited and vigorously opposed by modern psychologists.
The idea that the mind is a composite of faculties was given a physiological
flavor by the founder of phrenology, *Franz Joseph Gall* (1758-1828), who
assigned sites in the brain to the various faculties.

The philosophy of Reid was carried on and its influence spread by his
disciple, *Dugald Stewart* (1753-1828). Stewart's collaborator, *Thomas
Brown* (1778-1820), departed from the position of the Scottish school and
approached associationism. He represents the transition from the empirical school to associationism. The Scottish tradition, it is to be noted,
dominated psychology in the United States for the whole century before
William James. Its last representatives were two professors of psychology
(or of mental philosophy, as psychology was then called in America).
These men were presidents of two universities, Yale and Princeton, respectively: *Noah Porter* (1811-1882) and *James McCosh* (1818-1894). They
were the last great exponents of the "old" psychology on American soil.

ASSOCIATIONISM

Of all the philosophical systems, it was the school of associationism
which exerted the strongest and most direct influence on scientific psychology. Originated in Britain and developed by British philosophers in
the eighteenth century, it was called British associationism or the English
school of associationism. As a doctrine, associationism represented the
culmination of psychological thought within empirical philosophy. It had
followers in other countries. By the mid-nineteenth century it was ready
to be absorbed by the new psychology as the most appropriate doctrine
to explain the mind and its operations. The origin and the early character
of scientific psychology are much more readily understandable in the light
of the development of associationism.

The Meaning of Association. The concept of association is almost as old
as philosophy. As soon as men began to analyze the human mind, they
readily observed that thoughts come in succession, that one thought evokes
another, or that some thoughts always appear together. Moreover, it was
noticed, that certain events, if experienced at the same time or in succes-

sion, are consequently remembered together. Thus when one of these events is recalled, the others easily and promptly come to mind. We experience association of ideas when, for example, the thought of Christopher Columbus brings readily to our minds the discovery of America. Whenever one thought or idea evokes another, when two or more of them tend to appear in our mind together, or when the same external event is succeeded by the same sensation, we say that they are associated. The process or operation by which they are bound or linked together is called association. With the progress of philosophy which further analyzed association, its meaning broadened.

Association in Philosophical Psychology. Association came to be regarded as the basic process of the human mind. Initially its application was limited to a single area, to memory. It was Aristotle who first explained memory in terms of association. He and after him many others, particularly the great associationists of the eighteenth and nineteenth centuries, tried to discover the laws of association, to explain why ideas became associated. Various laws were suggested. But the most persistent one, reiterated by many philosophers, was the law of contiguity. It meant that events or ideas contiguous in time or space—that is, occurring either simultaneously, or successively, or in the same place—tend to become associated in the mind and thus are apt to recur together.

A systematic application of association, not only to memory but to other aspects of mind, had to await the advent of empiricism. Association began then to be explored to the best advantage of empirical philosophy. It was to be extended from memory to other mental processes—cognitive as well as affective. Finally it became, in British associationism, the basic psychological principle applied to all mental life. The most complex mental processes, indeed the nature of mind, were explained by association.

The application of association was extended in still another direction. Physiologically minded associationists, of whom David Hartley is an example, used association to account for the relationship between the functioning of the brain and mental processes. Some, in the spirit of parallelism, considered mental events to be parallel to brain activity or to be merely its correlates. But others considered mental events to be identical with neural events. According to the latter view all mental events can be simply reduced to neural events. This view came to be called *reductionism*.

The Associationistic Program. The lines along which British associationism proceeded can be briefly summarized by a few points. British associationism sought: (1) to find and formulate the laws of association; (2) to analyze all facts of conscious life and to demonstrate how all can be explained by the associative process; (3) to break down the complex material of the conscious mind into the simplest elements possible; (4) to refer mental phenomena to the facts of anatomy and physiology, and to any other pertinent science; and finally (5), to apply association and the empirical findings of associationism to other branches of human knowledge, and to build upon them the systems of ethics, logic, epistemology, juris-prudence, sociology, esthetics, and education. The following pages present the views of the chief representatives of British associationist thought.

British Associationists.   The ancient concept of association, handed down by various philosophers, was modernized by *Thomas Hobbes* (1588-1679). It was subsequently discussed by *Locke*, who was the first to use the term "association of ideas," and by *Berkeley*. But only *Hume* gave it full for-mulation within empirical philosophy. It was, however, *David Hartley* (1705-1757) who made association a consistent systematic principle and the very core of his philosophy. He is the true founder of the school of associationism. *Thomas Brown* (1778-1820) of the Scottish school was an associationist and added new laws of association. British association-ism reached its culmination in the nineteenth century in the thought of *James Mill* (1773-1836) and of his son *John Stuart Mill* (1806-1873). In the second half of the nineteeenth century, *Alexander Bain* (1818-1903) marks the transition from associationist-philosophical psychology to sci-entific psychology.

David Hartley, Founder of Associationism.   A practicing physician—and a philosopher only by avocation—David Hartley (1705-1757) published his *Observations on Man* (1749), in which he made a vigorous attempt to integrate the facts of both anatomy and physiology with the ideas of phi-losophy. On one hand he made use of anatomy as it was known in his day. In addition, he applied Newton's physics, especially *vibratory action*, to explain not only nervous activity, but also mental activity.

Hartley was the first to abandon completely the then prevalent notion of animal spirits residing in the brain and moving along the nerves, which were thought to be hollow tubes. For him the brain, the spinal cord, and the nerves contained small (called by Hartley: "infinitesimal") particles which could be set in longitudinal motion. He considered sensations the result of small vibrations in the nerves. But images and ideas, mental phenomena of a higher order, consist of still smaller and more delicate vibrations ("vibratiuncles") in the brain. The vibrations in the brain are the effect and the replica of the vibrations in the nerves. This correspond-ence between these two sets of vibrations is the reason why images and ideas are similar to the original sensations. Seeing a tree is one set of vibrations; having a mental image of a tree is another set of vibrations. But, because these two sets of vibrations are correlated, the image of a tree is a faithful copy of the sensation of a tree. If sensations and their accompanying vibrations are repeated often, they leave vestiges or traces in the nervous system.

Hartley's idea of vibrating particles is obsolete now, although it was original and progressive then. But his juxtaposition of physiological and mental events, his search for physiological counterparts or substrates of mental processes, and his localization of mental functions in the brain have become the characteristic subject of subsequent physiological psychology.

Hartley is rightly called a physiological psychologist and his system, properly termed, a system of physiological psychology.

In itself, the whole Hartleyan interpretation of association would perhaps not have much importance had he not consistently applied association to all psychological matters. He explained perception, emotion, language, memory, recall, and imagination in terms of association. Emotions, for instance, are experiences of pleasure or pain habitually associated with certain sensations; memory is simply an accurate association. Hartley demonstrated more convincingly than other philosophers the usefulness of association for psychology and its potential as the fundamental psychological law. Other associationists after Hartley tried to develop the laws of association further and to find additional applications of association. In later psychology, for example, learning is the field where association will be used most extensively.

The Two Mills. The immediate successors of Hartley in associationism were James Mill and John Stuart Mill. The father, *James Mill* (1773-1836), and his son, *John Stuart Mill* (1806-1873), mark the culmination of British associationism. James Mill's *Analysis of the Phenomena of the Human Mind* (1829) sought to explain the human mind by treating it as a sort of machine and by consistently applying association to all mental activity and contents. His was the first complete system of psychology constructed solely on the associationistic doctrine. The mind, which is like a blank sheet at birth, records all the experiences received through the senses. Sensations and their copies, ideas, are bound together into complex ideas by association. The function of association is merely to bind and not to transform or modify anything in the elements which are bound. Thus complex ideas, the result of the associative process, contain all the single elements which enter into their formation without any change. This form of psychology has been called *mental mechanics*.

The son, John Stuart Mill, represents what has been termed *mental chemistry*. He reworked his father's system by applying to it a different conception of the association process. He made this substitution in the notes which he added to his edition of his father's *Analysis of the Phenomena of the Human Mind* (1869). Association, in J. S. Mill's view, is not a simple combination of elements analogous to, let us say, a mixture of coffee and milk, but it is like a chemical process by which something completely different is made. It is analogous to water in which the characteristics of oxygen and hydrogen are fused in a distinctly new substance. Simple ideas *generate* complex ideas which do not have to bear recognizable resemblance to their sources.

The concept of mental chemistry should be kept in mind because scientific psychology at first adopted this concept. In its initial phase, psychology was conceived literally as a chemistry of the mind. That is, it treated mind and its states like chemical substances which had to be broken down to their constituents. No doubt the science of chemistry—which originated at the end of the eighteenth century—gave impetus to such a conception. It should be noted that the first writer to use the idea of mental chemistry before John Stuart Mill was Thomas Brown.

The Psychological System of Bain. We have already referred to Alexander Bain (1818-1903) in discussing his psychophysical parallelism. Bain belongs partly to the prescientific period of psychology and partly to the new scientific psychology. His system of psychology is built on the principle of association. This principle is extended by him to new problems of psycholcgy like movement, habit, and will, which were not treated to any extent by his predecessors.

Bain's greatest single contribution to psychology was his systematic treatments, *The Senses and the Intellect* (1855) and *The Emotions and the Will* (1859). These two works were abridged in 1868 as *Mental and Moral Science*. For almost 50 years this was the textbook of psychology in Britain. Moreover, it had a marked influence on American psychologists, including William James. The characteristics of this work, which signals the approaching scientific psychology, are its inclusion of physiological material (nervous system), its effort to integrate physiology with psychology, and its emphasis on the senses.

First Experiments with Association. The associationist psychology was the result mainly of armchair speculation—of philosophical presuppositions and introspection. Only occasional and unsystematic use of observation was made. No serious effort was given to submitting associationist theories to experimental verification. But one of the first investigations the new psychology undertook was to experiment with association.

The experimental approach to association was initiated by *Francis Galton* around 1879. In this first experiment on association, Galton presented 75 stimulus words and recorded the ideas (expressed in words) that were spontaneously elicited by them. He also measured the time between the stimulus word and the response word (associative reaction time). This pioneer experiment inspired a series of experiments at the Leipzig laboratory, conducted with improved techniques. *James McKeen Cattell*, an American student of Wundt and the first American to obtain the doctorate in the new psychology at Leipzig (1886), refined the association experiment both methodologically and technically.

Opposition to Associationism. As powerful as associationism had become, it did not by any means find universal acceptance. There was a current in philosophical thought which not only ran counter to associationism as a philosophical school, but which opposed association as a basic psychological principle. The hostile reaction to associationist doctrine gained strength soon after the turn of the twentieth century and gave rise to an entirely different orientation in psychology.

Early opposition to associationism came from the Scottish school—especially from Thomas Reid who had followers in other countries. The idealistic philosophy of the nineteenth century, stressing the unity of the mind, also opposed associationism. Later associationist psychology, descended from philosophical associationism and represented in Germany chiefly by Wilhelm Wundt and in America by E. B. Titchener, was attacked by various individuals for its atomistic conception of mind. It was criticized early by Franz Brentano and by others who, like him, adopted *act psychology*. James reacted against it vigorously, denying that mind is merely a storage of images and ideas. Instead he presented mind as a constant change, a *stream of consciousness*. *Gestalt psychology*, whose origin was the result of the rebellion against the elementism of associationist psychology, fought this psychology on experimental grounds, showing that perception and other functions have a unitary character. It demonstrated that various perceptual phenomena cannot be explained in terms of associationist theory.

PHILOSOPHICAL INFLUENCES IN THE NINETEENTH CENTURY

We have thus far followed the main stream of philosophical thought relevant to psychology. This stream included the doctrine of dualism and the body-mind problem. It included also empirical philosophy, the philosophical study of sensation and perception, and the school of associationism. These several theories constitute the most significant and most direct philosophical influences. Yet, it must be realized many other influences and currents of thought of consequence for psychology were superimposed on the main philosophical traditions.

German Philosophy. German philosophers of particular historical significance for psychology were *Immanuel Kant* (1724-1804), *Johann Friedrich Herbart* (1776-1841), and *Hermann Lotze* (1817-1881). The philosophy of Kant was familiar to all the builders of psychology in the nineteenth century, and many of them were under its influence. It not only tempered the strength of associationism in Germany, but it also resisted the tendency to reduce mind to mere brain processes and to make psychology a chapter of physiology.

Herbart's interest was much livelier, his treatment more extensive, and his influence on psychology in Germany more direct and more tangible than Kant's. Psychology was defined by Herbart as a precise empirical science, based not on physics or physiology but derived from metaphysics and aided by mathematics. There were previously undiscovered psychological problems, to which Herbart called attention, such as *attitude* and *set*. Herbart, who was interested in pedagogy and had personal teaching experience, demonstrated the need and value of psychology in education and called upon educators to use the findings of psychology. For that reason, he deserves credit as the originator of *educational psychology*.

The two influential philosophers in the critical period of the emancipation of psychology, Herbart and Lotze, complemented each other in their contributions. Just as Herbart was a champion of the scientific character of psychology, so Lotze furthered the cause of experiment and the significance of physiology for psychology. The period of German psychology in which Lotze lived—so important for the future of psychology—owes much to him as a spiritual parent and protector of many a leading psychologist. From a historical point of view, Lotze probably did more for psychology as a teacher than as philosopher or writer. Among the men who came under his direct supervision, and whom he helped in various ways, were Brentano, Stumpf, and G. E. Müller. Müller succeeded him in Göttingen, and also became the director of its laboratory—the second important center of psychological research and training after Leipzig.

Ernst Mach (1838-1916). An Austrian philosopher and a physicist, a thinker and an experimentalist, Ernst Mach made many specific theoretical and experimental contributions to the study of vision, hearing, and to time and space perception. Mach tried to make psychology less philosophical and more quantitative and objective than it had been formerly. There is a link between Mach's ideas and American *operationism*, which claims Mach in its ancestry.

Herbert Spencer (1820-1903). In England the philosopher who influenced psychology the most, besides J. S. Mill and Bain, was Herbert Spencer. His compendium, *Principles of Psychology*, appeared as early as 1855. William James used it for his course in psychology at Harvard for many years. Spencer influenced psychology largely by his *evolutionary theory* and its application to mental life. Evolution, a word which originated with Spencer, was his theme since 1852, seven years before Darwin's *Origin of Species*. Most characteristic of Spencer's view is the notion that mind is a product of the endless process of evolution.

Positivistic Philosophy. This system was founded by *Auguste Comte* (1798-1857). It held that the sensible comprises the whole sphere of knowledge and that anything that cannot be reached by the senses is unknowable. Consequently, *positivism* radically rejected all metaphysics—that is, the inquiry into the ultimate causes and nature of things. The object of science is to discover facts, their relations and the laws governing them. The positivistic current, which is strongly reflected in the nineteenth century science, reinforced the antimetaphysical, antimentalistic and anti-introspectionist tendencies in psychology. The *behaviorist* tenets in American psychology were much in agreement with positivistic thought.

Scholasticism. This Christian philosophical system of the Middle Ages received its complete form in the thirteenth century in the works of Thomas Aquinas who, as was previously mentioned, based his philosophy on Aristotle. Scholastic philosophy flourished in the thirteenth and fourteenth centuries but began to decay in the fifteenth century. In the middle of the nineteenth century, scholastic philosophy was revived under the name of *neoscholasticism* or *neothomism*. Psychology based on this system was faithful to Aristotelian principles, attacked Cartesian dualism, and reiterated the hylomorphic doctrine. The pioneer of this psychology was *Desiré Mercier* (1851-1926) in Belgium.

Marxism. The philosophical writings of *Karl Marx* (1818-1883) were contemporaneous with the beginnings of experimental psychology. However, his main work, *Das Kapital* ("Capital," 1867), made no immediate impression on the psychology of the period. When Marxism became the official doctrine of Soviet Russia, psychology had to conform to its principles. One of the first to construct a system of psychology consistent with *dialectical materialism* was *K. N. Kornilov* in the mid-1920's. Current Russian psychology continues to reflect that country's prevalent political and economic ideology of Marxism.

PHILOSOPHICAL ROOTS: AN OVERVIEW

In the last two chapters the remote and immediate philosophical roots of psychology have been presented in historical sequence. Psychological thought first began in *ancient Greece* with the problem of sensation. In the fourth century B.C. the range of psychological topics was wider. It already comprised all the basic issues of modern psychology, though in a rudimentary form. Cognitive processes, ideas, association, memory, learning, sensation, and perception were particularly discussed. The physiological approach to psychological problems was also practiced. But the predominant problem of general interest was the relation between the soul and the body. This problem, in various forms, remained in the focus of philosophical psychology until the nineteenth century. In Greece and Rome, there was also a practical psychology of how to live happily.

The *Christian era* brought forward the notion of an immortal soul created by God and destined for eternal happiness. In the *Middle Ages* psychology was metaphysical, preoccupied with the body-soul relationship and the nature of the soul and its faculties.

Descartes departed from the preoccupation with the soul and turned to the mind and mental processes. His psychology was rationalistic, as was the psychology of his followers. After Descartes, attention was fixed on the mind, but its rationalistic treatment was soon replaced by the empirical analysis introduced by empirical philosophy.

The *empirical school* initiated a radical change in psychological thought. It abandoned rationalism and held that experience is the source of knowledge. Empirical philosophy made psychological problems its main object of inquiry and studied them more seriously and intensively than did previous philosophical schools. It gave psychological thought a new direction, which eventually led to psychology's emancipation and establishment as a science.

Associationism analyzed the process of association of ideas and adopted the concept of association as a general principle for understanding the mind. This system tried to account for all mental content and activity in terms of the combination of mental elements such as ideas. Associationist psychology, the product of the empirical-associationist tradition, accepted the notion that the mind is constituted of elements. It proceeded to identify the constituent mental elements through introspection, and to establish the laws governing their combination.

When psychology became a separate domain, with the intention of developing further as a science, it rejected philosophical affiliations and, as Binet said, cut the rope which hitherto bound it to metaphysics. However, while the conduct of modern psychological research has generally been free of philosophical influences, psychological theories, especially global conceptions of psychology represented by the schools of psychology, have often been inspired or influenced by past or contemporary philosophical thought. The various approaches and orientations in psychology also frequently stemmed from philosophical theories or were based on philosophical assumptions. Gordon W. Allport, in his *Becoming*, expresses the opinion that "virtually all modern psychological theories seem oriented toward one of two polar conceptions," which he calls the Lockean and the Leibnitzian traditions. The former—said to predominate in Anglo-American psychology—views man's mind as passive. The latter, predominant in Continental European psychology, conceives of its nature as essentially active. These contrasting conceptions were consequential in determining the character of these psychologies.

The degree and extent to which philosophical thought has exerted influence on modern psychology varies with countries. In general, European psychology has been more philosophical and more sensitive to philosophical currents than American psychology. German theoretical psychology in particular has consistently kept close relations with philosophy and has borne the imprint of philosophical influences. American psychology, on the other hand, has intentionally resisted communication with philosophy and avoided philosophical discussions. Nevertheless, as Herbert Feigl, a philosopher, said in his 1959 article "Philosophical Embarrassments of Psychology," "important philosophical issues keep bothering the psychologists; and many significant developments in psychology have baffled the philosophers." And now, as Feigl stated further, "that the divorce is fully accepted by both parties, and remarriage is clearly out of question, there are signs that a good friendship may be mutually profitable." In the second part of this century this "friendship" is being practiced as evidenced by the dialogue taking place between psychologists and philosophers here and abroad. For a few decades already scientists and philosophers, having found mutual need for discussing issues of common interest, have been developing a discipline which has come to be known as philosophy of science. In its framework a *philosophy of psychology* is also now developing. A book of 1965, *Scientific Psychology*, composed of 30 chapters written by psychologists and philosophers, has precisely as its aim, according to its preface, "to bring about a *rapprochement* between scientific psychology and the philosophy of science." But even closer association between philosophy and psychology is being realized in the field of *philosophical psy-*

chology. A division of Philosophical Psychology (24th), organized in 1962 within the American Psychological Association, provides a platform for discussion of various theoretical issues of psychology from the philosophical viewpoint. According to the bylaws of this division, its purpose is "to encourage and to facilitate the active and informed exploration and discussion of (a) the relationships of psychology and psychological theory to the problems of philosophy and (b) the philosophical issues that arise as psychology develops as a science, as a profession, and as a means of promoting human welfare." At the first official function of the Division, one of its organizers, Joseph R. Royce, of the University of Alberta, delivered a speech in which he called the beginning of the Division a celebration of "the official remarriage of psychology and philosophy after almost 100 years of legal separation." His thesis was that "psychology and philosophy were divorced in name only." The increasing number of publications in philosophical psychology—both textbooks and special studies—affirms the existence of a trend toward a closer friendship between the two fields, a trend which apparently is going to persist and perhaps to grow.

THE ROOTS OF PSYCHOLOGY IN MODERN PHILOSOPHY

PHILOSOPHICAL DOCTRINES	CHIEF REPRESENTATIVES	TIME
1. Cartesianism *Sharp distinction between body and soul. The subject of psychology is mind, which possesses innate ideas.*	Descartes	1596–1650
2. Parallelism *Mind and body act harmoniously but independently of each other.*	Leibnitz	1646–1716
3. Empiricism *Experience is the sole source of knowledge.*	Hobbes Locke Berkeley Hume	1588–1679 1632–1704 1685–1753 1711–1776
4. Sensationism *All knowledge is derived from sensation.*	Condillac	1715–1780
5. Associationism *Mind and its content are explained by combination of simple elements.*	Hartley, founder Brown James Mill John S. Mill Bain	1705–1757 1778–1820 1773–1836 1806–1873 1818–1903
6. Various philosophies of the 19th century *The degree of their influence differed in various countries.*	Kant Herbart Lotze Mach Spencer Comte Marx Mercier	1724–1804 1776–1841 1817–1881 1838–1916 1820–1903 1798–1857 1818–1883 1851–1926

REFERENCES

The following references have been selected for their particular interest to psychology students and are recommended as additional readings. Very helpful in the study of the philosophical roots will be the three volume *A History of Psychology* by G. S. Brett or its abridged edition by R. S. Peters. Books or special studies on modern philosophy and its various phases can easily be found in standard textbooks on the history of philosophy.

DESCARTES

Pirenne, M. H. Descartes and the body-mind problem in physiology. *Brit. J. Phil. Sci.*, 1950, *1*, 43–59.

Wallon, H. La psychologie de Descartes. *Pensée*, 1950, *32*, 11–20.

BODY-MIND PROBLEM

Feigl, H. The "mental" and the "physical." In *Minnesota studies in the philosophy of science.* Vol. II. Minneapolis: Univer. Minnesota Press, 1958. Pp. 370–497.

McDougall, W. *Body and mind.* New York: Macmillan, 1911. Reprinted in paperback with preface by J. S. Bruner. Boston: Beacon, 1961.

Reeves, Joan W. *Body and mind in Western thought.* Glasgow, Scotland: Penguin, 1958.

Ryle, G. *The concept of the mind.* London: Hutchinson, 1949.

Scher, J. (Ed.) *Theories of the mind.* New York: Free Press of Glencoe, 1962.

Von Bertalanffy, L. The mind-body problem: a new view. *Psychosom. Med.*, 1964, *26*, 29–45.

Weber, C. O. Theoretical and experimental difficulties of modern psychology with the body-mind problem. In P. L. Harriman (Ed.), *Twentieth century psychology.* New York: Philosophical Library, 1946. Pp. 64–93.

EMPIRICAL PHILOSOPHY

Hochberg, J. E. Nativism and empiricism in perception. In L. Postman (Ed.), *Psychology in the making: histories of selected research problems.* New York: Knopf, 1962. Pp. 255–330.

King, C. D. The Lockean error in modern psychology. *J. gen. Psychol.*, 1948, *38*, 129–138.

Rasmussen, E. T. Berkeley and modern psychology. *Brit. J. Phil. Sci.*, 1953, *4*, 2–12.

SENSATIONISM

Boring, E. G. *Sensation and perception in the history of psychology.* New York: Appleton-Century-Crofts, 1942.

Crombie, A. C. Early concepts of the senses and the mind. *Sci. Amer.*, 1964, *210*, 108–116.

ASSOCIATIONISM

Warren, H. C. *A history of association psychology.* New York: Scribner, 1921.

PHILOSOPHIES OF THE NINETEENTH CENTURY

Denton, G. B. Early psychological theories of Herbert Spencer. *Amer. J. Psychol.*, 1921, *32*, 5–15.

OVERVIEW OF PHILOSOPHICAL ROOTS

Allport, G. W. *Becoming.* New Haven: Yale Univer. Press, 1955.

Feigl, H. Philosophical embarrassments of psychology. *Amer. Psychologist*, 1959, *14*, 115–128.

Gustafson, D. (Ed.) *Essays in philosophical psychology.* Garden City, N.Y.: Doubleday, 1964.

Misiak, H. *The philosophical roots of scientific psychology.* New York: Fordham Univer. Press, 1961.

Royce, J. R. Pebble picking vs. boulder building. *Psychol. Rep.*, 1965, *16*, 447–450.

Wolman, B. B., & Nagel, E. (Eds.) *Scientific psychology: principles and approaches.* New York: Basic Books, 1965.

4

The Physiological Roots

THE STUDY OF PHYSIOLOGY in the nineteenth century was the most important single factor in the development of a distinct science of psychology. The influence of physiology was evident to, and readily recognized by, the pioneers of psychology, many of whom were physiologists before they became psychologists. The two founders of the new science of psychology— Wilhelm Wundt in Germany and William James in America—both had medical degrees, and both were professors of physiology before they turned to psychology. The new psychology was named *physiological psychology* and its first textbook in Europe was entitled *Principles of Physiological Psychology* (W. Wundt, 1873-74), and in America *Elements of Physiological Psychology* (G. T. Ladd, 1887). The present meaning of physiological psychology is not the same as it was then. Currently, "physiological psychology" refers to the special branch of psychology which studies the physiological correlates of behavior. But in the latter part of the nineteenth century "physiological" denoted not just a part or one aspect, but the whole new psychology. When the First International Congress of the new science convened in 1889, it adopted the title "The Congress of Physiological Psychology."

Physiological seemed the most appropriate title for the new psychology at that time, principally because psychology was concerned then with the relationship between the psychological and physiological processes, and because most of its scientific data and methodology came from physiology. Moreover, it was largely to physiology that psychology owed its independence, and it was the physiologists who made the most significant contributions to psychology.

Three Great Physiologists and Psychology. Among the physiologists of the nineteenth century, three who directly and significantly influenced psychology were Weber, Müller, and Helmholtz. *Ernst Heinrich Weber* (1795-1878) will be remembered in the history of psychology for his research on the sense of touch, his methods employed in measuring sensitivity, and for his findings about the relationship between stimulus and sensation (Weber's law). *Johannes Müller* (1801-1858), called the "father of experimental physiology," gave prominence to psychological matters in his encyclopedic *Handbook of Physiology* (1834-1840) in which he formulated the story of specific energies of nerves. *Hermann von Helmholtz* (1821-1894), Müller's student, was particularly esteemed by psychologists for studies of sight and hearing and for numerous scientific achievements which had much psychological significance. Indeed, for these accomplishments he is regarded as one of the founders of psychology.

31

Specific Contributions of Physiology. The role of physiology in the emancipation and orientation of psychology is made evident by a review of the progress and discoveries of physiology in the nineteenth century. The most relevant studies for psychology related to (1) the nervous system, and the brain in particular; (2) the nature of nerve impulses; (3) the reflex action; (4) the localization of functions in the brain; (5) the sense organs and their functions—especially vision, hearing, and touch; (6) the theory of specific energies of nerves; and (7) the concepts of internal environment. We shall discuss these points in sequence.

NEUROLOGY

That the mind and the brain may be related in some fashion had been the subject of speculation since the early period of philosophy. Descartes, who located the point of communication between the soul and the body in the brain; associationists, who attempted to correlate cerebral events with psychological processes; and materialistic philosophers, who identified the mind with the brain—all formed the background for psychologists' interest in the brain study of the nineteenth century. A knowledge of the nervous system was considered indispensable for the understanding of both sensation and motion. All new discoveries about the nervous system were readily noted and promptly related to psychological matters. Such discoveries were abundant in the nineteenth century. Many of them contradicted traditional philosophical notions and called for revision and correction of some old concepts. They frequently suggested new interpretations of psychological problems. It was not surprising that new textbooks of psychology appeared with illustrations and descriptions of the nervous system.

The Structure and Functions of the Nervous System. The *gross anatomy* of the nervous system was already well known at the end of the eighteenth century. Thanks to the invention of the microscope in the early nineteenth century, and its improvement about 1830, the microscopic structure of the nervous system could now be learned. Understanding of the function of the spinal cord, of the brain, and of the nerves soon increased. Physiologists were greatly aided by experiments made on animals, as well as by studies of clinical cases of neurologic pathology.

A British anatomist, *Charles Bell*, in 1811, and a French physiologist, *François Magendie*, in 1822, independently discovered that the dorsal root of the spinal nerve carries only sensation, whereas the ventral root mediates only motor action. Cutting the former, they found, eliminated sensation in the experimental animal; severing the latter induced paralysis of those muscles which were innervated by the fibers of this root. This finding was expressed in the form of a law, known as the law of roots or the *Bell-Magendie law*. Later Bell also showed that some cranial nerves transmit sensation exclusively, some are entirely motor, and others are mixed, having both the sensory and motor fibers. These discoveries dispelled the notion that nerves can transmit both motor and sensory impulses promiscuously. Psychological distinction between the motor and sensory functions was thus confirmed on anatomical and physiological grounds.

The study of the *brain* by anatomists resulted in a better understanding of the functions of some of its parts. *Luigi Rolando* (1770-1831) and *Pierre Flourens* (1794-1867) were the outstanding anatomists of the brain in the early part of the nineteenth century. Although some of their findings and theories were not correct, they made many spectacular discoveries and stimulated further research. Flourens used animals for his studies and, by systematic removal of various parts of the brain, was able to demonstrate their major functions. He came to realize, that in spite of the diversity of functions of these parts, the nervous system is "a unified system."

Nervous Impulse.   Up to the beginning of the nineteenth century, nervous impulse was believed to be a process or energy which moved along the nerves instantaneously. What kind of energy this was remained a matter of speculation. Spiritual properties were commonly attributed to it. When physicists furnished physiology with the electric battery, faradic current, and galvanometer, a number of discoveries by such early investigators as du Bois-Reymond and J. Bernstein in the middle of the nineteenth century were made which shed new light on the nature of nerve impulse. It was found that electric phenomena were associated with the nerve impulse. Moreover, it was observed that when an electric current was applied to a nerve, the latter responded in the same way as when activated by a natural stimulus. Many other new facts were learned. One of the most significant was the finding that the nerve impulse is propagated along the nerve at a certain speed which is relatively slow and measurable—contrary to the belief that the communication between the mind and the sense organs and muscles was instantaneous. Some physiologists who suspected that the propagation of the nerve impulse requires time thought this time was too fast to make its measurement feasible.

Reflex Action.   The existence of reflex action which can take place without consciousness and without any act of will—and even despite will—was already recognized in antiquity. The pupillary constriction in response to light and the knee jerk, when the knee cap is struck, are examples of such action. Experiments on living animals in the eighteenth and nineteenth centuries brought a better understanding of reflex action, but at the same time posed a question about the nature of the will and consciousness and their relations to the organism. Physiologists of the nineteenth century, like Marshall Hall and Johannes Müller who made the important experiments on reflexes, were aware of this question and of the possible philosophical implications of their findings. *Marshall Hall* (1790-1857), whose neurological experiments and interpretations provoked great interest, demonstrated that a decapitated animal such as a snake responds to a sensory stimulus. It was an action, he held, which was mediated solely by the spinal cord; it was unconscious and involuntary. Müller later pointed out similar reflexes mediated by the brain. Up to this time it was assumed that every function of the nervous system is part of the mind. In 1853, in view of this assumption, the prominent physiologist Pflüger asked how can reflexes, which are controlled by the nervous system, be called unconscious?

The animated controversy that surrounded conscious and unconscious functions involved many prominent physiologists and philosophers of that time. This controversy, lasting several years, illustrates the great importance to psychology of strictly physiological findings. The discovery of neural activity, independent of the brain, involuntary, mechanical-like, and yet purposive, was a real challenge for psychological theory. It is noteworthy that the discussion of the reflex arc by John Dewey in 1896 signaled the beginning of American functionalism. Half a century after the controversy about reflex action, came Pavlov's discovery of the conditioned reflex with all its repercussions in psychology. Around the reflex concept a whole psychological system was developed, Bekhterev's *reflexology*. The conditioned reflex also found a significant role in American behaviorism.

LOCALIZATION OF FUNCTIONS IN THE BRAIN

The brain—its structure and its connections with the sense organs and the muscles—was intensively studied by physiologists of the nineteenth century. One of their most fascinating problems was the functional significance of the various parts of the brain. Hypotheses and theories about the localization of functions in the brain were offered—frequently ahead of factual evidence. Philosophers, following this trend of interest, speculated about the relationship between mental faculties and functions and various parts of the brain.

Phrenology. There were some who believed that all mental abilities and individual characteristics either depended on certain definite parts of the brain or were centralized in some specific brain areas. This belief found its strongest expression in phrenology, a movement which arose at the turn of the nineteenth century, spread rapidly, and gained many adherents on both sides of the Atlantic. Phrenologists claimed that the intellectual and affective faculties had their organs in the brain. Since they thought that the form of the skull corresponded exactly to the formation of the brain, they contended that it was possible to assess one's personal characteristics from the shape of the head. The fallacies of phrenology were exposed, and the system was discredited in scientific circles. However, interest in the relationship of the brain to mental functions, which phrenologists incited, remained unabated. Further research in cerebral physiology led to discoveries, many of which had psychological implications. Some of the more important discoveries are mentioned below.

Motor and Sensory Function in the Brain. Research in cerebral physiology disclosed localization of motor and sensory functions. In 1870 *Gustav Fritsch* and *Eduard Hitzig* discovered that the precentral region of the brain is directly related to bodily movements. When they applied electric current to this region in a dog, they were able to elicit discrete movements. Subsequently, other neurologists and physiologists demonstrated the existence of cortical areas associated with functions such as sight, hearing, and touch.

Localization of Speech. One of the most interesting discoveries—and one of consequence for both neurological and psychological theories—was the location of the so-called "speech area" in the brain by the French physician *Paul Broca* in 1861. After the death of his patient, who had been unable to speak although all his speech organs were normal, Broca performed an autopsy and discovered a lesion in the left precentral gyrus of the patient's brain. This area, he concluded, must be the center of speech. It now bears his name, "Broca's area." Thirteen years later another neurologist in Germany, *Carl Wernicke*, described a patient with a lesion in the temporal lobe, which resulted in his inability to understand spoken language. Wernicke concluded that this particular convolution was the center for the comprehension of speech ("Wernicke's area"), and that any form of aphasia can be associated with a specific cortical area. Subsequent studies revealed that speech functions are not localized in this simple fashion. Nonetheless, neurological studies of this type strongly suggested that functions—even those as complex and as specific to man as speech—may be related to circumscribed cerebral areas, injury to which may result in permanent impairment or loss of such functions.

Localization of Mental Functions. Hitzig, after his successful localization of motor functions, ventured a hypothesis that possibly all mental functions are localized in the brain in a discrete fashion similar to that of the motor and sensory functions. While the localization of certain sensory and motor functions could not be doubted, Hitzig's theory of localization of mental functions lacked corroboration. Scientific opinion with regard to such localization was divided and oscillated between one extreme and the other. At one time, the view in favor of strict localization of all functions was prevalent; at another time, the opinion against such parceling of the brain was more popular. However, as the evidence for localizing bodily functions accumulated, the opinion in favor of specific cerebral localization of mental functions such as memory, learning, and thinking appeared more plausible. But attempts to demonstrate loci in the brain for such functions failed. Views were expressed that complex functions are mediated by the whole brain rather than by its specific portions. The participation and cooperation of all brain structures and the functioning of the brain as a whole began to be recognized. Some time later this view received substantiation in the research of *Shepherd I. Franz* (1902 and later) and *Karl S. Lashley* (from 1917 on) and in their theories of *equipotentiality* and *mass action* of the brain.

Brain Research and Psychology. Brain research established a large body of facts of considerable significance for psychology. Ebbinghaus, writing about this significance in 1908, observed that psychology owes to the investigations concerning the physiology of the brain two fundamental conceptions: (1) that the search of centuries for the exact seat of the soul in the brain is without an object; (2) that even those mental functions which have always been regarded as comparatively simple are enormously complicated. Moreover, since sensation, movement, and speech are related to the brain and depend on its functioning, he said, psychology ought to explore this relationship. In time, the study of the relation between brain functioning and psychological processes and of the degree and manner in which human behavior is dependent upon the brain has become one of the major problems and tasks of physiological psychology. Such a study brought about a closer association between psychology and neurology. The realization of the mutual scientific benefits in knowledge to be derived from such an association has grown stronger in the twentieth century. This association is evidenced in the development of a new discipline, neuropsychology.

SENSORY PSYCHOPHYSIOLOGY

Intensive study of the senses by physiology began around 1850 after other sciences had amassed data fundamental and essential to physiological investigations. Anatomy, in possession of the microscope, provided information with ever increasing detail about the structure of the sense organs —the eye and the ear in particular. Physics explained the physical characteristics of the visual and auditory stimulus, the light and the sound. It showed that sound is the result of vibration of air particles and that air is a necessary medium for sound to be heard. It knew that frequency of vibrations determines pitch, and intensity determines the loudness of the sound. A large mass of observations was also available in the literature on the subjective sensory phenomena. Visual functions and visual phenomena were best known, hearing less known, and touch relatively poorly known. Taste and smell were even less understood; their study began much later, after 1880. The next two paragraphs briefly indicate some of the highlights of studies in vision and audition before 1850.

Vision. How much there already was to report about vision in 1759 is shown in the fact that *William Porterfield* required 885 pages in his *A Treatise on the Eye, the Manner and Phenomena of Vision* to relate all he knew about the subject. In this volume he discussed such topics as the retinal image, accommodation and convergence of the eye, perception of distance, binocular vision, adaptation, the nature of color, and the like. These topics show that the range of interest and knowledge in vision was already extensive at this early date.

A theory of color vision was proposed by *Thomas Young* in the first years of the nineteenth century. Helmholtz took up this theory half a century later and developed it further. Various and numerous color phenomena were studied and described by the poet *Goethe* in two volumes of his *Zur Farbenlehre* ("On Colors," 1810), and later they were effectively investigated by *J. E. Purkinje* (1819, 1825). Color blindness was known, thanks to the accurate description of his own deficiency by the chemist *John Dalton* (1794).

Audition. While the physics of sound was highly advanced by 1800, some anatomical details about the ear were still obscure. Therefore, it was not yet possible to understand thoroughly how this organ functioned. The inner ear and the function of the semicircular canals particularly had to await studies in the latter part of the century. The phenomena of hearing, however, were well described. Known were the limits of hearing, difference tones, and beats. Attempts were made to explain more complex phenomena like the localization of sound, but not with much success at this early date.

Psychology's Interest in Sensory Physiology. It was to be expected that scientific psychology—the offspring of empirical philosophy—would be highly interested in sensation and all the pertinent facts which science was providing in that field. As already discussed, the question of how and through what media we know the external world has always been the object of philosophical interest and study. While Aristotle had already devoted much attention to the senses, and while pre-empirical philosophy was not neglecting this matter either, it was only in empirical philosophy that sensation became the chief topic. Psychology, being developed from this philosophy, continued to regard the study of sensation as its foremost task. It turned for information about the sense organs and their functions to physiology, because from physiology it could learn more on the subject than from the works of its philosophical ancestors. Psychology was not only prompt to incorporate in its textbooks the findings of physiology, but it also started to experiment on its own, using the methods which had brought so much success to physiologists.

Main Contributors. Men who made the greatest contributions to sensory physiology in the nineteenth century, and who by these contributions enriched psychology, were the already mentioned trio: Weber, Müller, and Helmholtz. Of these *E. H. Weber* (1795-1878), professor of anatomy and physiology at Leipzig, was the first to experiment with touch and to shed light on this sense. His treatise on the sense of touch, *Der Tastsinn und das Gemeingefühl* ("The Sense of Touch and Common Sensibility"), in 1846, was the most prominent single contribution on this subject in the nineteenth century. Psychologists were also indebted to Weber for his measurement of sensitivity, and for devising new methods which constituted the foundation of psychophysics. The two greatest merits of *Johannes Müller* (1801-1858), the famous professor of physiology at Berlin, lie, from a historical viewpoint, in his organization and systematization of all physiology and in his formulation of the theory of specific energies of nerves.

Theory of Specificity of Nerve Energies. This theory of Müller revolutionized the concept of sensation, and was a turning point in the understanding of the process of sensation. It inspired and stimulated further research in sensory psychophysiology. The theory stated that the specificity of sensation is not primarily the result of the external stimulus acting upon sense organs, but of the specific energy residing in a given nerve and peculiar to this nerve. We see not because it is light that stimulates the visual system, but because specific energy possessed by the optic nerve is activated by the light stimulus. Any stimulus capable of activating the optic nerve can produce a visual sensation. Touching the eyeball, or applying an electric current or some chemicals, can produce visual sensations as long as they stimulate the optic nerve and the energy residing in it. Müller cited many such examples demonstrating that different physical stimuli can elicit the same sensation, and that one and the same stimulus when applied to different sense organs can produce different sensations.

It was not then the object itself which was directly perceived but the effects of its stimulation in the nerves. When neurophysiology later found that the nerves do not have different energies but only one kind, common to all of them, and that the nature of the nerve process is identical from nerve to nerve, the theory was reformulated. The specificity of sensation was ascribed not to the nerves themselves and their energies, but primarily to their place of termination in the brain. We must note that Müller himself saw this possibility. In fact the whole idea of projection of function in the brain was already foreseen by Müller.

Müller's "Of the Mind." In his *Handbook of Physiology* Müller devoted one chapter to psychological problems and entitled it "Of the Mind." It was a small chapter, merely 82 pages, constituting two per cent of the volume. But the array of topics was extensive: association, memory, imagination, thought, feeling, passion, the problem of mind and body, phantasms, action, temperament, and sleep. The inclusion of such topics in this authoritative work, the standard textbook of physiology of that time, is worth noting. It showed both the interest in such problems and the recognition that there are areas common to physiology and psychology. Müller made other references to psychological processes to explain physiological processes, which pointed again to the value of cooperation between the two disciplines.

Hermann von Helmholtz. The name of Helmholtz is more often mentioned in psychology textbooks than that of the founder of psychology, Wundt. The history of science credits Hermann Helmholtz (1821-1894) with contributions to many scientific fields, ranging from anatomy and biochemistry to physics and physiology, and calls him one of the greatest scientists of the nineteenth century. After teaching at the universities of Königsberg, Bonn, and Heidelberg, he was named professor of physics at

Berlin (1871), a great academic distinction in Germany. His research in physiological optics and acoustics, which resulted in two monumental works, *Physiological Optics* (1856-1866) and *On the Sensations of Tone* (1863), began when he was at Königsberg and continued over a period of 16 years. Much of his research, many of his discoveries and theories, were of great consequence for psychology. He gave a thorough account of the function of the eye, filling in many gaps in the knowledge of this organ. Various phenomena of vision, such as *afterimage* and *parallax*, for example, were studied and explained by him. Where knowledge was incomplete or proof missing, Helmholtz offered hypotheses and theories. Thus in order to account for color vision, he suggested the *three-component theory*, based on Young's hypothesis. As to the field of audition, Helmholtz was able to describe the role of the "Organ of Corti" in the inner ear and the roles of other parts of this organ. Coordinating various findings, his own and others', he proposed the resonance theory of hearing.

In the study of perception Helmholtz was an avowed empiricist. Opposed unequivocally to the nativism and apriorism of Kant, he believed experience and learning to be the main factors in perception. Together with other psychological processes, particularly with the one which he called the "unconscious inference," experience and learning can account for all perception, including the controversial perception of space. There was no need to invoke innate intuition to explain perception. The "inference" was a process based on data of experience. He called it "unconscious," because it occurred without apparent conscious reasoning and without awareness of the individual.

We should also mention Helmholtz's earlier studies on the speed of nerve impulse and reaction time. It was he who determined for the first time, by a simple but ingenious procedure, the velocity of nerve transmission in the frog's nerve. When he turned to measuring nerve transmission in man, using man's reaction time, he was faced with such wide individual differences in reaction time that he abandoned his investigation. Reaction time was obviously not the appropriate method for measuring speed of nervous impulse in the human nerve. But this attempt of Helmholtz makes him one of the earliest experimenters in reaction time.

Helmholtz and Psychology. Like his teacher Müller—though more frequently—Helmholtz referred in his works to psychological processes, recognizing that they are indispensable in the understanding of certain aspects of sensation and perception. He affirmed that the problem of sensation "can be solved entirely by scientific methods," but "at the same time," he stated, "we cannot avoid referring to psychic activities and the laws that govern them." "We cannot altogether avoid speaking," he declared in *Physiological Optics*, "of the mental processes that are active in the sense-perceptions, if we wish to see clearly the connection between the phenomena and to arrange the facts in their proper relation to one another."

In the critical stage of psychology's gradual separation from philosophy, Helmholtz's contributions to sensory physiology were of considerable significance. They epitomized the value and necessity of joint efforts of both psychologists and physiologists in the study of sensation and perception. They demonstrated how in this study contributions of psychology and physiology can complement each other. The service rendered to psychology by Helmholtz was direct and important and was matched by no other scientist of his time. Not only could many of his findings in sensory physiology be directly appropriated by psychology, but his methods and his attitude in scientific inquiry set an example and model for the young psychology. The emancipation of psychology from philosophy, and psychology's very appellation, "physiological," were in no small degree the effect of the scientific spirit which Helmholtz so well represented. In view of the role that Helmholtz had in this period of psychology's history it is not surprising that he has been regarded as a cofounder of scientific psychology, along with Wundt and Fechner.

Ewald Hering.   Examination of another important figure in sensory psychology, Ewald Hering (1834-1918), acquaints us with a different approach to the psychology of sensation. Ewald Hering, a pupil of E. H. Weber, and professor of physiology at Leipzig University, differed in many respects from Helmholtz with whom he was in controversy on several issues. Like Helmholtz, he also made researches and wrote extensively on vision and visual space perception. But, unlike Helmholtz, he was an avowed nativist in his theory of space perception, believing the ability to perceive space to be part of one's inborn endowment and not the result of learning. Another difference between him and Helmholtz was his phenomenological approach to the study of sensation. The phenomena of vision and subjective sensory experiences, their observation and description, were the primary interests and objects of his study. This is the same approach which was previously followed, as noted above, by Goethe and Purkinje. With Hering the tradition of phenomenology in psychology strengthened. It found many followers, particularly in Europe. Gestalt psychology belongs to this tradition. Color theory affords still another example of difference between Hering and Helmholtz. Hering proposed a six-component theory and suggested the operation of some extra processes in color vision, like the dissimilation and assimilation reactions in the retina.

To Hering, psychology owes valuable accounts of visual phenomena and astute analysis of visual space perception. To him belongs also the honor of being the first to establish the distinction between the sense of pressure and sense of temperature. He devised numerous ingenious instruments and apparatus for his studies of color phenomena. Some of them can still be found in modernized versions in psychological laboratories.

INTERNAL ENVIRONMENT

In the early part of the second half of the nineteenth century physiology advanced considerably in the understanding of the living organism and its functioning when, as a result of systematic physiological experimentation, a new concept of internal environment emerged. This concept not only threw a new light on organismic processes, but initiated a novel approach in physiological studies, leading to the creation of new disciplines.

Claude Bernard. It was the French physiologist Claude Bernard (1813-1878), the pupil of Magendie, who first formulated the concept of internal environment (1859). He was an ingenious experimentalist, a keen observer, and a profound thinker with a gift for synthesis and generalization. He has been called the founder of experimental medicine and the greatest experimental physiologist of all time. His studies included the digestive system, vasodilation and vasoconstriction, sugar metabolism, activity of muscles, and carbon monoxide poisoning. He made several outstanding advances of which the most important was the discovery of internal secretion. Bernard found that certain organs, like the liver, for example, secrete certain substances directly into the blood stream through which they can affect other organs and tissues. With this discovery Bernard became the founder of endocrinology.

In the course of his studies Bernard found that all the cells of the organism live in a medium consisting of humors, the blood, and the lymph. This medium he called *milieu intérieur* or internal environment. Bernard established that this internal environment remains constant in its composition despite changes within or outside the organism. The level of sugar in blood, for example, is practically the same, deviating only within a very narrow range and for a short duration in a healthy organism. Many tissues and organs of the body regulate the internal environment and contribute to its constancy. If some conditions of the body upset the balance of the internal environment, appropriate organs go to work immediately to restore the sound balance. Thus the numerous and basic discoveries of Bernard opened an entirely new field for physiology. They resulted in a better understanding not only of the functions of single organs, but of the integration of various biological processes benefiting the whole organism. The concept of internal environment was paramount in this understanding, and thus has been acclaimed one of the most useful and fundamental concepts of modern physiology.

According to a French historian of psychology, M. Reuchlin, Bernard's *Introduction to the Study of Experimental Medicine* (1865) "incontestably" influenced the introduction of the experimental method in French psychology. It is worthy of note that several eminent French psychologists, such as G. Dumas, P. Janet, P. Guillaume, and H. Piéron, had studied physiology under Bernard's disciples.

Homeostasis. The concept of internal environment and its constancy amid changing conditions of the organism was further developed by the American physiologist *Walter B. Cannon* (1871-1945). He termed the regulation of the internal environment *homeostasis*. His studies and discoveries enabled him to describe some of the physiological mechanisms which maintain and regulate the internal environment of the organism.

The implications for psychology of Bernard's findings and concept of internal environment were not realized at the time of their promulgation. Moreover, not much attention was given to Bernard's works by psychologists of the nineteenth century. Not until Cannon's work did they fully awaken to the significance of homeostasis and the endocrine glands in the study of behavior. The book which Cannon published in 1915, *Bodily Changes in Pain, Hunger, Fear, and Rage,* presented emotions, and their role in animal and human behavior, in new light. Cannon conducted extensive experiments on the autonomic nervous system and its activity in emotions, which led him to propose the so-called *emergency theory of emotions.* According to this theory, emotions, through the activation of the sympathetic nervous system, mobilize resources of the organism in emergency situations. It was Cannon's work which inspired intensive research on the neurophysiological basis of emotions.

The above review of the contributions of physiology to psychology is by no means complete. The list of these contributions can be considerably extended to include the contributions made in the twentieth century, such as the neurohistological discoveries of Ramon y Cajal, the researches of Sherrington and Adrian, electroencephalography, and, more recently, Penfield's study of cerebral localization, Selye's adaptation syndrome, and cybernetics. But the aim of this chapter is to emphasize particularly those contributions which were critical in the rise of scientific psychology and which gave it its initial direction.

PHYSIOLOGY AND PSYCHOLOGY

While philosophy gave psychology its conceptual and theoretical foundation, physiology, as well as other branches of biology, increased the knowledge of man's biological nature and the understanding of the intimate relationship between the mental and bodily processes. Some notions about psychological functions and about man as a living organism—which philosophy had held for centuries—received a lethal blow from physiological discoveries, and had to be abandoned in favor of radically new ones. For example, the energy which moved the muscles, called animal spirits, was found to be not a mysterious immaterial energy, but a material bodily process, the nervous impulse, which could be studied and measured in a laboratory. In the light of physiology's progress and discoveries, it became obvious that philosophy alone could not achieve a complete understanding of the human mind and its processes, and consequently psychology could no longer remain merely a branch of philosophy.

The methods of philosophy, moreover, were found no longer adequate to ensure the progress of psychology. It became clear that laboratory experimentation is a much more effective method for studying at least some psychological processes than centuries of armchair speculations could be. Furthermore, as was seen in the second half of the nineteenth century, it was necessary to seek correlation of physiological and psychological data because they were often complementary. The "psyche" and its processes had to be investigated in reference to the brain, nerves, sense organs, and their functions.

On the other hand, the role of physiology in the origin of scientific psychology and the strong emphasis on the relevance of physiological data for psychology created a situation which seemed to lead to the absorption of psychology by physiology. Johannes Müller's statement, often cited, "Nemo psychologus nisi physiologus"—no one can be a psychologist unless he is a physiologist—was interpreted to mean that there could not be psychology without physiology. Thus some philosophers and psychologists of the late nineteenth century voiced a concern that psychology—if its subject matter be limited merely to psychophysiological relations—might lose its identity and become simply a branch of physiology. They argued that there are aspects of psychology which lie beyond the reach and scope of physiology, and that there are problems which defy physiological methodology—in other words, that there exists a strictly psychological realm. G. S. Fullerton in 1895 cautioned his colleagues in psychology: "Let us not . . . grow too interested in the study of the body as to forget that we are psychologists," and "let us not take up physiological work which has no psychological aim." As it developed, psychology was able to transcend the narrow confines of psychophysiology and to grow as a science of wider scope and aims than physiology could provide.

Psychology, then, owed to physiology its separation from philosophy, its acquisition of a scientific status, and its initial impetus as a science. Having attained its own identity, however, it proceeded on its own power. After ceasing to be *philosophical,* psychology became *physiological,* but only for a brief period. It was later called *experimental,* to mark its basic methodology, but eventually "experimental" was confined to only one aspect of psychology. Now, we do not designate psychology by any qualifying term, unless we refer to its branches—physiological, experimental, clinical, social. We use the qualifier *scientific,* when we wish to emphasize the nonphilosophical psychology, the psychology which originated at the end of the nineteenth century as a separate discipline.

The association between psychology and physiology has continued, as has, although to a lesser degree, its association with its other parent, philosophy. Where the biological orientation in psychology predominates, the physiological association is obviously closer. Where the attention is directed to understanding the biological bases of behavior, there is a greater collaboration with physiology and other biological disciplines and greater dependence on their progress. In America the biological orientation has always been strong; thus, physiological psychology has flourished in this country. It will be remembered that one of the earliest American texts was G. T. Ladd's *Elements of Physiological Psychology* (1887). This book was revised by Robert S. Woodworth in 1911, after his studies with Sherrington and remained a standard text in physiological psychology for 25 years. Another significant and extensive American work in physiological psychology in America was L. T. Troland's four volume *The*

Principles of Psychophysiology (1930-1932). Physiological psychology also held a prominent place in France, represented eminently in that country by Henri Piéron.

SUMMARY OF THE PHYSIOLOGICAL ROOTS

Physiology was a major factor in psychology's separation from philosophy and its becoming a separate science.

Specifically physiology:

1. Provided a body of facts essential to the understanding of the physiological basis of psychological functions.
2. Demonstrated the need and value of scientific procedures in the acquisition of knowledge. Provided new effective methodology, such as laboratory experimentation.
3. Demonstrated that the physiological data have complementary significance for psychology.

CONTRIBUTIONS OF PHYSIOLOGY

AREAS OF PHYSIOLOGICAL RESEARCH	SPECIFIC PROBLEMS	PRINCIPAL INVESTIGATORS	TIME
1. Neurology	Structure and functions of the nervous system	Bell, Magendie	First half of 19th century
	Reflex action	Marshall Hall	Around 1850
	Specific energies of nerves	Johannes Müller	1838
	Nature of nerve impulse	du Bois-Reymond, Bernstein	1843–1849 1866
2. The brain	Structure and function	Rolando, Flourens	First half of 19th century
	Localization of functions	Broca	1861
		Fritsch and Hitzig	1870
		Wernicke	1874
3. Sensory physiology	Sensory threshold Touch	Weber	First half of 19th century
	Vision	Weber Helmholtz, Hering	1850's and 1860's
	Audition	Helmholtz	1860's
4. Internal environment	Internal environment	Bernard	1859
	Homeostasis	Cannon	1932

REFERENCES

Brazier, Mary A. B. The historical development of neurophysiology. In J. Field (Ed.), *Handbook of physiology*: Section 1: Neurophysiology, Vol. 1. Baltimore: Williams & Wilkins, 1959. Pp. 1–58.

Davis, R. C. Physiological psychology: a view of fifty years. In Georgene S. Seward and J. P. Seward (Eds.), *Current psychological issues; essays in honor of Robert S. Woodworth*. New York: Holt, 1958. Pp. 249–277.

Donaldson, H. H. On the relation of neurology to psychology. *Amer. J. Psychol.*, 1888, *1*, 209–221.

Fearing, F. *Reflex action: a study in the history of physiological psychology.* Baltimore: Williams & Wilkins, 1930.

Fullerton, G. S. Psychology and physiology. *Psychol. Rev.*, 1895, *3*, 1–20.

Krech, D. Cortical localization of function. In L. Postman (Ed.), *Psychology in the making: histories of selected research problems.* New York: Knopf, 1962. Pp. 31–72.

Lachman, S. J. *History and methods of physiological psychology: a brief overview.* Detroit: Hamilton, 1963.

Nichols, N. Psychology and physiology. *Amer. J. Insan.*, 1897, *54*, 181–200.

Poynter, F. N. L. (Ed.) *The history and philosophy of knowledge of the brain and its functions.* Oxford: Blackwell, 1958.

Riese, W., & Hoff, E. C. A history of the doctrine of cerebral localization: sources, anticipations, and basic reasoning. *J. Hist. Med.*, 1950, *5*, 49–71.

Stumpf, C. Hermann von Helmholtz and the new psychology. *Psychol. Rev.*, 1895, *2*, 1–12.

Yerkes, R. M. Walter Bradford Cannon: 1871–1945. *Psychol. Rev.*, 1946, *53*, 137–146.

5

Scientific Methodology

AFTER PRESENTING the philosophical and physiological roots of psychology, we shall now consider its third major root of origin and growth: methodology. The history of science demonstrates that the origin and progress of science are conditioned by methods, techniques, or instruments appropriate for its problems. It is methods which spur science's advance. As methods develop or improve, the perimeter of science expands. No problem can be scientifically investigated if there is no method available to attack it. Astronomy's progress was accelerated by the invention of the telescope and other optical instruments. Biology advanced rapidly when the microscope was made available for its use. The cathode-ray tube was the decisive factor in the invention of radio and television. Psychology, as a rising new science, also required methods and instruments which would allow it to attack its problems. Wundt aptly stated in the introduction to his *Contributions to the Theory of Sense Perception* in 1862: "It is a maxim, impressed upon us from all sides, by the history of the natural sciences, that advances in science are intimately linked with advances in the methods of investigation. The entire natural science of recent years owes its origin to a revolution in methodology, and where great results are achieved, we may be sure that they were preceded by an improvement in previous methods or by discovery of new ones." Wundt did not think, however, that this statement applied to psychology. But from the perspective of a century we find that what he said of science in general was also true of psychology. To assert its independence from philosophy, to rise to the level of a scientific discipline, and to assure its growth as such a discipline, psychology had to find methods, techniques, and instruments which, while suited to its subject matter, would also comply with the criteria of modern science. What these methods were, how they originated, and what role they played in the rise and progress of psychology are the subjects of this chapter. Two kinds of methods are discussed: first, methods which were merely adopted by the new psychology; second, those which were developed by psychology itself.

INTROSPECTION

The first, and at the beginning the most prominent method of psychology, was introspection. Introspection, or in Wundt's terminology *Selbstbeobachtung* or literally "self observation," was defined by J. R. Angell as the direct observation of one's own mental processes. This method was employed in different ways by philosophers long before psychology made extensive use of it. When the great empiricists and associationists

46

of the British school concentrated on the study of the human mind, they used introspection and showed how it could be employed to the advantage of psychology. Scientific psychology, born in this philosophical tradition, inherited the practice of introspection. Since the subject matter of early psychology was consciousness, introspection was its essential and paramount method. Because of its insistence and dependence on introspection, this early psychology is referred to as "introspectionistic." Its data were obtained mostly through the introspective method. The staunchest exponents and defenders of introspectionistic psychology were Wundt in Leipzig, and, in America, Titchener at Cornell.

Different Forms of Introspection. With the progress of psychology and its new orientation, the inadequacies of introspection were realized. As a result, introspection underwent certain modifications. The kind of introspection which prevailed in Leipzig and Cornell was rigorous and pedantic, with strict rules and well-defined procedures. The subjects used in laboratory experiments had to be thoroughly trained in it, and their reports supplemented by measurements with instruments such as the chronoscope. This type of introspection is referred to as *classical*.

The first significant deviation from classical introspection and standard methodology in general was introduced by Külpe and his Würzburg school in the early 1900's. He and his students set out to investigate higher mental processes, such as thought and will. These were more elusive than the sensations and feelings studied at Leipzig and Cornell and harder to describe and to analyze. Finding classical introspection unsuitable for their purpose, they refined the introspective technique to obtain more accurate and reliable reports from their subjects. The Würzburg group introduced *systematic experimental introspection*, a name proposed by N. Ach (1905), a member of the school. In this method the psychological experience under study was divided into discrete parts or units, each of which was separately described by the subjects (fractionation). The Gestalt school, which objected to the Wundtian "brick and mortar psychology," regarded introspection in general as a futile method. They were interested in the variety of perceptual experiences—that is, in the perceptual phenomena. Under controlled conditions, they used what is called *phenomenal observation and description*. This phenomenological method eventually became more popular. More will be said about it in the chapter on phenomenological psychology.

Difficulties with Introspection. In spite of various improvements and safeguards, introspection had inherent defects and insurmountable limitations. It was often found unreliable. The results based on introspection in various laboratories were conflicting, and at times the findings of one laboratory were exactly opposite to those of another, even when the conditions of experimentation were identical. Woodworth's subjects failed to confirm Titchener's subjects, and Titchener's own students reported results different from those of their master. The controversy about "imageless thought" provided another striking case of the unreliability of introspection. The problem under study was: Do we always have images when we think, are images necessarily present in our consciousness in the thinking process? While the Würzburg laboratory insisted on finding cases of thought without images, and other laboratories confirmed this, the subjects in Wundt's and Titchener's laboratories failed to confirm the existence of "imageless thought."

Moreover, some unconscious mental states, although exerting a strong effect on behavior, could not be detected by introspection. Sometimes even perceptions escaped the scrutiny of the best trained introspectionist. It was demonstrated, for example, that subjects, instructed to imagine a familiar object such as an apple on a screen, failed to notice the appearance of a real though faint picture projected on the same screen, and thought it to be their mental image. These subjects in another experiment, looking at the screen on which a faint picture had been projected, reported that they still saw the picture even when it was gradually extinguished and was no longer visible. Because of the defects and limitations of introspection, psychologists restricted its use and put greater trust in more objective methods, particularly when they began to focus their attention more sharply on performance and overt behavior than on conscious states.

Behaviorism and Introspection.   The most vigorous attack against introspection was launched by the leader of *behaviorism*, J. B. Watson, in 1913. Behaviorism denied any value to introspection and eliminated it completely from psychology. It admitted only a subject's "verbal report" as one of the manifestations of response. The behaviorists held that nothing that comes from introspection can be accepted by the science of psychology. They rejected all prior conclusions based on either introspection or on the assumption of consciousness. They felt that the subjectivity of introspection must be replaced by the objectivity of experimentation and measurement. Some behaviorists went so far as to replace such terms as "sensation," because these terms implied consciousness and introspection. They offered instead a more objective term: "physiochemical response of the organism." However, this radical denouncement of introspection has not been supported, not even by other behaviorists.

Though considerably restricted in its use and application, introspection has survived in contemporary psychology, and is being employed as a complementary method in some areas. For example, it has been retained in psychophysics in the subject's report of sensory experience, in clinical psychology as part of the patient's protocol, and in psychopharmacological studies as an additional and useful source of information in the evaluation of drug effects on humans.

PSYCHOPHYSICS

A system which holds a special place in the history of psychology is *psychophysics*. This system provided useful and precise methods, furnished valuable new concepts, and became a powerful stimulus and inspiration for psychological research. In L. L. Thurstone's definition, psychophysics is "that branch of psychology which deals with measurement in the subjective or experiential continuum." Its chief object has been to find what the minimum magnitude of the physical stimulus must be to be perceived by the subject at all (absolute threshold), and how far apart two stimuli must be to be noticed as different (differential threshold). Special methods devised for the determination of these thresholds are known as the psychophysical methods. However, psychophysics when it made its appearance in 1860 was more than just methodology. According to its founder, G. T. Fechner, it was a philosophical system concerned with "the functional relation or relations between body and mind." This system and its author will be the subject of this section. As a preliminary stage in the development of psychophysics, the work of E. H. Weber, already mentioned in the preceding chapter, will be considered. His experiments constituted the beginning of psychophysics.

Weber's Experiments and His Law. The principal object of Weber's study was the sense of touch. The experiments which he painstakingly performed resulted in many discoveries and systematization of tactual sensations. He offered hypotheses to explain various observed phenomena, such as the two-point threshold and tactual localization. Particularly valuable from the historical viewpoint was his study of the just noticeable difference between sensory stimuli, and the formulation of the principle operating in the perception of this difference. Weber's experimentation on the just noticeable difference included not only touch, but also temperature, visual, and auditory discrimination. Working on the perception of differences between weights, the length of lines, and the pitch of tones, he found that in order for a subject to notice a change in the stimulus, this change must constitute a certian proportion of the stimulus. Thus, it is not just any increase or decrease in the stimulus that is noticed, but only a change which is proportional to the stimulus already acting on the sense organ. He found this proportion or ratio (Weber's ratio) to be 1/30 for weight; 1/50 or even 1/100 for lines; and 1/160 for tones.

These findings, confirmed—as he said—"in several departments of sense," led him to state a general principle. This principle is that: "in comparing objects and observing the distinction between them, we perceive not the difference between objects, but the ratio of this difference to the magnitude of the objects compared." This principle was later called by Fechner "a law," and has become known as Weber's law. It was expressed in mathematical terms, in the formula $\frac{\Delta R}{R} = C$, in which R is the stimulus, ΔR is the just noticeable difference, and C is the constant.

Needing special methodology in his work on the threshold of sensation, Weber devised a method called the just noticeable difference (j.n.d.) method. This method later became better known as the method of limits. Further refined by Fechner, this first psychophysical method was incorporated into the latter's system of psychophysics. By systematizing the order of presentation of the stimulus and using all of the subject's responses for the determination of the threshold, the j.n.d. method was the true beginning of psychophysical methodology.

G. T. Fechner.   Fechner's interest in Weber's law, and his search for new methods, were motivated by his philosophical theory. At the time when philosophical thought was divided between materialism, growing in strength, and idealism, then blossoming, Gustav Theodor Fechner (1801-1887) took a middle stance. Fechner was a religious man and a strong believer in the spiritual world. But he was also a scientist, well aware of the material aspect of nature. He sought to bridge the two views by proclaiming that reality is both spiritual and material at the same time, either aspect being perceptible depending on the point of view. Reality is like a circle which appears concave from the inside, but looks convex from the outside. Fechner's aim was to achieve a full understanding of the relation between the spiritual and the material world, and of the laws governing this relationship.

Since the spiritual world is not directly accessible to our senses, it can only be learned through the material world. To achieve this knowledge of the spiritual via the material world Fechner founded psychophysics. It was a philosophical program, but Fechner was not merely a philosopher. His background was both extensive and complex, and his talents and activities were varied. Besides his training and writing in philosophy, he studied medicine and physics. He held a medical degree, had an excellent background in mathematics, and was a professor of physics. Theology was also familiar to him. His writings included creative literature, both poetry and novels.

Fechner studied Weber's work because it was concerned with the relationship between physical and psychical phenomena. Weber's findings revealed that, while psychical events do not follow exactly the physical events, there is some regularity in their relationship. In Weber's conclusion, Fechner saw the first step toward a complete understanding of the relation of the psychical world to the physical. The inquiry into the arrangement existing between the psychical and physical worlds was to be the object of psychophysics, as Fechner understood it. He hoped to continue on the path opened by Weber, and, through psychophysics, to achieve a complete knowledge of the relationship between body and mind.

Elements of Psychophysics.   The system of psychophysics was expounded in Fechner's *Elemente der Psychophysik* ("The Elements of Psychophysics," 1860), a book hailed by some as the actual beginning of scientific psychology. This work was quickly noted by those concerned with the new psychology. It evoked many comments favorable as well as unfavorable and inspired new research. Almost every psychologist of the second half of the nineteenth century took part in the controversy concerning Fechner's psychophysics and its various issues. Psychophysical writings were particularly abundant in the 1880's. Wundt gave immediate attention to the *Psychophysics* and studied all of Fechner's philosophy thoroughly. After Fechner's death, Wundt sponsored a new edition of the *Psychophysics* and added to it notes and bibliography. Fechner wrote other works on psychophysics, arguing with and answering his critics, and also adding new material.

Fechner's Law and His Psychophysical Methods. Fechner conducted extensive experiments both before and after the publication of his *Psychophysics*. These experiments were laborious, requiring considerable time and patience on the part of both experimenter and subjects. They consisted mainly of comparison judgments of various stimuli, such as weights, brightness, distances, and tones. They aimed at finding the thresholds of sensation, absolute or differential. Fechner's experiments provided him with the foundation for his law, Fechner's law, as it came to be called. This law stated that the strength of sensation is proportional to the logarithm of the stimulus. It was expressed by the formula $S = C \log R$ in which S is the sensation, C a constant, and R the stimulus (R from the German *Reiz*, stimulus). Fechner regarded this principle as the first law of the mind, in that it explained in mathematical form the relationship between the stimulus (a physical event) and sensation (a mental event). One of the goals of science at the time of Fechner's work was to find the laws of nature, and the discovery of such laws was considered a mark of progress. Therefore, Fechner's law brought prestige to psychology, which was separating from philosophy and was claiming the status of a distinct science. It also strengthened the hope that additional similar laws would be found in the course of time.

Fechner's most valuable and lasting contributions to psychology were his new methods of psychological measurement, the so-called psychophysical methods. For this work alone, Fechner deserves the title of cofounder of psychology. Although these methods were not invented by Fechner, they were described by him in detail, systematized, and presented in a form readily usable in psychological research. They were: (1) the method of just noticeable differences, known also as the method of minimal changes or of limits; (2) the method of right and wrong cases, or the method of constant stimuli; (3) the method of average error, or the method of adjustment, or of reproduction. Each of these methods comprised a procedure to be followed in the experiment and a mathematical treatment of the collected data. Psychologists have made extensive use of these methods.

Fechner's Other Contributions to Psychology. Prior to his special interest and work in psychophysics, Fechner, always an avid experimentalist, made extensive experiments on visual phenomena, on complementary and subjective colors, and on afterimages (1838-1840). It was in that period that visual phenomena, now known as Fechner's colors and Fechner's paradox, were discovered and described. After the publication of *Psychophysics*, Fechner explored the field of esthetics for over ten years (1865-1876). He was interested in finding the general principles involved in judging objects as beautiful, or in other words, in the objective character-

istics of esthetic objects. For this study Fechner used both the laboratory
and the empirical approach, thus founding *experimental esthetics*. In the
first approach he studied esthetic judgments and preferences under controlled conditions. In the second he examined the existing works of art,
trying to find the fundamental elements common to all of them.

Further Development of Psychophysics.   Psychophysics—not its theory,
but its methodology—was adopted, improved, and expanded. The most
notable contribution toward its development was made by *Georg Elias
Müller* (1850-1934), who for this reason has been called "the most eminent psychophysicist after Fechner." One of the leading psychologists of
the early era in Germany, G. E. Müller was a professor for 40 years at
Göttingen University, where he had an excellent laboratory. His research
and writing were focused on three areas: psychophysics, vision, and memory. Müller's fruitful work in psychophysics extended over three decades
(1878-1903). His first publication in this field was *Zur Grundlegung der
Psychophysik* ("Foundation of Psychophysics") in 1878. In 1903 appeared
Die Gesichtspunkte und die Tatsachen der psychophysischen Methodik
("The Viewpoints and Data of Psychophysical Methodology"). In these
two works Müller discussed the fundamental concepts of psychophysics,
presented his own laboratory findings concerned with Weber's law, and
gave an improved version of the psychophysical methods. The method of
constant stimuli, the most involved of all the psychophysical methods in
procedure and mathematical treatment, was the main object of his study
and was most improved by him. *Die Gesichtspunkte* was a critical review
of the whole field of psychophysics, and a most comprehensive compendium
of psychophysical methodology. After almost 30 years, Müller published
another major work in psychophysics, this time on the psychophysics of
color. In two volumes of 647 pages, the work was entitled *Ueber die
Farbenempfindungen: psychophysische Untersuchungen* ("On the Perception of Color: Psychophysical Investigations") in 1930.

Third in importance in psychophysics was the Belgian psychologist
J. L. R. Delboeuf (1831-1896), author of *Eléments de psychophysique*
("The Elements of Psychophysics") and *Examen critique de la loi psychophysique* ("Critical Examination of the Psychophysical Law"), both
published in 1883. He met the objection raised by critics of Fechner's
measurement of sensation. Whereas the stimuli could be measured easily,
these critics pointed out, sensations could not, for introspection does not
reveal them as magnitudes or compositions of discrete units or steps. To
answer this objection, Delboeuf developed the concept of sense distance
and the method of sense distances (also called the method of gradations
or of equal-appearing intervals). He admitted that sensations in any sense
modality make a continuum, but he showed how, with the use of his method,
distances in this continuum can be established. One can tell, for example,
that the difference between weight A and B is the same, smaller, or greater
than between weight B and C. Using this type of judgment, one can
arrange sensations as to their intensities from weaker to stronger, without
any reference to the absolute limen, or to the actual units of sensations.

Students of psychology are usually familiar with "Müller-Urban weights and products" to which they refer when computing and graphing the results of their psychophysical experiments. The first of this pair of names is G. E. Müller and the second *F. M. Urban*, an Austrian, who spent several years in the United States teaching and doing research. He has written extensively on psychophysics.

American Contributions. Americans also made their imprint on psychophysics. *G. S. Fullerton* and *J. McK. Cattell* experimented in psychophysics together, and in 1892 published a joint monograph *On the Perception of Small Differences.* In this work they discussed various psychophysical problems, and on the basis of their experimental results suggested some methodological improvements. *E. B. Titchener* thoroughly reviewed the field of psychophysics, and his experimental manual contained a series of experiments in psychophysics. *E. Culler*, in his articles in 1926 and 1927, proposed further refinement of the method of constant stimuli. *L. L. Thurstone* in the years 1925-1927, and also in his later writings, broadened the scope of psychophysics to scale making, and to the study of attitudes and preferences, in which modern psychology became interested. Thurstone was one of the first to bridge psychophysics and psychometrics, which thus far had grown independently of each other. He proposed the *law of comparative judgment*, which is the third law in psychophysics after Weber's and Fechner's laws. It is concerned with the judgment made by a subject when he is presented with two stimuli and asked to compare them and judge which of them is greater or lesser, stronger or weaker with respect to some criterion of comparison. *R. S. Woodworth* included two extensive chapters on psychophysics in his well-known *Experimental Psychology* (1938). There he introduced numerous modifications of existing methods and proposed new procedures of his own, many of which have been widely accepted. *J. P. Guilford* wrote *Psychometric Methods* (first edition in 1936, second in 1954), a practical textbook on the quantitative methods of psychology, in which much attention was devoted to psychophysical methodology.

Psychophysics Today. As a result of a century-long experience in psychophysics, some of Fechner's original notions had to be rejected or corrected. His idea that just noticeable differences are equal over the entire range of intensities, for instance, was not verified, nor could his law be universally applied. Consequently, various psychophysical concepts have been reformulated, and methods have been modified and improved. *S. S. Stevens* (b. 1906) is to be given much credit for reexamining the field of psychophysics. Since the 1930's, he and his students have done much experimentation which led him to repeal Fechner's law and to propose a new formulation of the stimulus-sensation relationship in the form of the *power law*. According to this law, the relation between the magnitude of sensation and the intensity of the stimulus is not logarithmic, but a power relation. That is, the sensation grows as the stimulus is raised to a power n. The psychophysical law could be rewritten by the equation $S = kI^n$

in which S is the sensation magnitude, I the intensity of the stimulus, k a constant, and n a constant power varying with the sense modality and conditions of stimulation. Stevens defined psychophysics in his *Handbook of Experimental Psychology* (1951) as "the science of the response of organisms to stimulating configurations." Psychophysics is useful in many fields of psychology, predominantly in sensation and perception, but it has been found useful elsewhere as well. "In the middle of the twentieth century," says Stevens, "psychophysics like mathematics, finds itself incorporated into the applied disciplines of science, industry, and government." After Stevens, the problems with which psychophysics is concerned now can be divided into the following seven categories: absolute thresholds, differential thresholds, equality, order, equality of intervals, equality of ratios, and stimulus rating. In the 1960's psychophysics is being applied to new areas opened by our technological progress, areas in which the question of detection and recognition of signals is of utmost importance for personal safety or national defense. Psychophysics, as can be seen, has remained an indispensable tool in psychological research, from Weber's and Fechner's times to the present day.

LABORATORIES

The establishment of psychological laboratories was psychology's most distinctive mark of separation from philosophy. It also signaled the goal of the new science: to study the processes of the mind experimentally. At the same time, psychological laboratories augured well for psychology's progress. James McKeen Cattell remarked in 1888, in his article on the psychological laboratory at Leipzig, that "whenever experiment has been introduced into science, a rapid and almost sudden advance has followed, and there are good grounds for hope that methods which have been so fruitful in physics will not prove barren for psychology." Although the rapid progress of psychology cannot be credited exclusively to laboratories, its initial advance in various countries was usually proportional to the number of laboratories and the extent of laboratory research. For it was in laboratories that new findings were made and psychologists received their training. It is understandable then that the year 1879, when the first laboratory was established—the Leipzig laboratory of Wundt—has been universally accepted as the birth year of psychology.

The Origin of Laboratories. The trend of establishing scientific laboratories attached to the universities was very strong in Germany. The most remote ancestry of the laboratory as an adjunct to scientific research should probably be sought in the rooms used for anatomical dissections of the animal and the human body. The first laboratories created specifically for research purposes, however, were the chemistry laboratories. It was the famous German chemist Justus von Liebig, who opened such a laboratory for the first time in Giessen in 1824. Then came physics laboratories, followed by biological, and finally by physiological laboratories. These scientific laboratories abounded in Germany. Thus it was quite natural for Germany to be the country of the first psychological laboratory, and of the many other psychological laboratories which sprang up in fast succession and took the lead in psychological research.

Principal Psychological Laboratories. Soon after the founding of the Leipzig laboratory, universities in Germany and in other countries, impressed by its success and realizing its importance, followed the example of Leipzig and began to open their own laboratories. Almost every prominent experimental psychologist made an effort to have a laboratory at the university where he lectured. Each of these various laboratories, in Europe and America, specialized in some particular field, usually following the predilections of its founder. They also tended to attract different groups of students. The differences between Würzburg and Göttingen laboratories in Germany, discussed below, illustrate this point. In America the differences between laboratories at Cornell and Clark Universities serve also as examples of the imprint made by the founders of these laboratories on the type of research conducted in them.

In Germany in those early days the most influential, after the Leipzig laboratory, was the laboratory at Göttingen, directed by G. E. Müller. Here problems and methods differed from the ones that occupied the Leipzig investigators who followed the direction of Wundt, the founder of that laboratory. Göttingen's investigations centered around psychophysics, learning, and visual sensation, in a more permissive atmosphere and with an openmindedness which readily took up and tested novel ideas. In the 1900's the laboratory at Würzburg, under the leadership of Oswald Külpe, gained prominence when it set out to subject higher mental processes to rigorous laboratory experimentation. There new methods were developed, and discoveries were made which stirred up the psychological world. The Würzburg studies marked a significant advance in experimental psychology.

Many laboratories on the continent were opened by Wundt's students: Hugo Münsterberg founded a laboratory at Freiburg, Alfred Lehmann at Copenhagen, and Friedrich Kiesow at Turin. The first laboratories in America were also established by Leipzig students: at Johns Hopkins by Hall, at the University of Pennsylvania by Cattell, at the Catholic University of America by Pace, and at Cornell by F. Angell. Psychologists from all countries, planning to open laboratories at their universities, traveled mainly to Leipzig for inspiration and information, and for laboratory equipment as well. Most of the early experimental equipment was usually manufactured in Leipzig and patterned after the apparatus devised and used by Wundt and his students. Made of brass, these instruments gave the appellation "brass psychology" to psychology based on laboratory experiments conducted in the spirit of the Leipzig laboratory.

Laboratories in Other Countries. England was tardy in establishing laboratories, and France was even slower. There were few Englishmen and Frenchmen among Wundt's earliest students. Americans predominated among the foreign students at Leipzig. The first laboratory in England, with W. H. R. Rivers in charge, was opened in Cambridge in 1897. In France, the Sorbonne had the first laboratory in 1889. The subjoined table lists the early laboratories in various countries.

America did not have to wait long for its first laboratory. After his arrival from Leipzig, the energetic Hall promptly founded the laboratory at Johns Hopkins in 1883, only four years after the establishment of Wundt's laboratory. Soon afterwards laboratories were set up at the University of Pennsylvania, Clark, Indiana, Brown, Stanford, Columbia, Harvard, Chicago, and other colleges and universities.

A novelty introduced in the United States was the animal laboratory. The laboratories were very active and were soon to affect the course of American psychology noticeably. The laboratory at the University of Pennsylvania, founded by Cattell, had the distinction of being the first laboratory to be used for training undergraduates in experimental methods.

THE EARLY LABORATORIES OF PROMINENCE IN VARIOUS COUNTRIES*

COUNTRY	UNIVERSITY	FOUNDER OR DIRECTOR	YEAR OF ESTABLISHMENT
Germany	Leipzig	W. Wundt	1879
	Göttingen	G. E. Müller	1881
	Berlin	H. Ebbinghaus	1886
	Munich	C. Stumpf	1889
	Würzburg	O. Külpe	1896
	Breslau	H. Ebbinghaus	1894
	Halle	expanded by H. Ebbinghaus	1905
United States	Johns Hopkins	G. S. Hall	1883
		reactivated by J. M. Baldwin	1903
	Pennsylvania	J. McK. Cattell	1888
	Wisconsin	J. Jastrow	1888
	Indiana	W. L. Bryan	1888
	Clark	G. S. Hall and E. S. Sanford	1889
	Harvard	W. James	1890
		H. Münsterberg	1892
	Michigan	J. H. Tufts	1890
	Columbia	J. McK. Cattell	1891
	Catholic	E. A. Pace	1891
	Wellesley	Mary Calkins	1891
	Cornell	F. Angell	1891
	Yale	G. T. Ladd and E. W. Scripture	1892
	Brown	E. B. Delabarre	1892
	Princeton	J. M. Baldwin	1893
	Stanford	F. Angell	1893
	Minnesota	J. R. Angell	1893
	Chicago	J. Dewey and J. R. Angell	1893–1894

* The exact year of the establishment of laboratories is often difficult to determine. The dates in this table are based on reliable historical sources, but in some cases reliable information could not be obtained. The sources do not always agree on the definition of a "laboratory." Laboratories differed in size, equipment available, extent of activities, and other features —and some of these laboratories were small and relatively insignificant, while others were of particular historical consequence.

THE EARLY LABORATORIES OF PROMINENCE
IN VARIOUS COUNTRIES (*continued*)

COUNTRY	UNIVERSITY	FOUNDER OR DIRECTOR	YEAR OF ESTABLISHMENT
Argentina	Buenos Aires	H. G. Pinero	1900
Austria	Graz	A. Meinong	1894
Belgium	Louvain	D. Mercier	1891
		J. F. Heymans	
		A. Thiéry	
	Brussels	G. Dwelshauvers	1897
Canada	Toronto	J. M. Baldwin	1889
	Montreal, McGill	W. D. Tait	1910
Denmark	Copenhagen	A. Lehmann	1886
France	Sorbonne	H. Beaunis and A. Binet	1889
	Rennes	B. Bourdon	1896
	Montpellier	M. Foucault	1906
Great Britain	Cambridge	W. H. R. Rivers	1897
	London	W. H. R. Rivers	1897
	Edinburgh	W. G. Smith	1906
	Oxford	W. Brown	1936
Holland	Groningen	J. F. Heymans	1893
India	Calcutta	N. N. Sengupta	1916
Italy	Rome	G. Sergi	1885
	Turin	F. Kiesow	1895
	Reggio Emilia	A. Tamburini	1896
	Florence	F. de Sarlo	1903
Japan	Tokyo	M. Matsumoto	1903
Poland	Cracow	W. Heinrich	1897
Russia	Kazan	V. Bekhterev	1886
	St. Petersburg (now Leningrad)	V. Bekhterev	1895

STATISTICAL METHODS

Francis Galton stated about science that "until the phenomena of any branch of knowledge have been submitted to measurement and number it cannot assume the dignity of a science." From the beginning, psychology consistently has striven to attain "the dignity of a science" by submitting its data to measurement and quantification. Its success in this regard represented progress, but at the same time it also constituted a new stepping stone to further achievements. Success in quantification of psychological data both signaled and conditioned progress. The principal pioneers of quantification in psychology were Herbart, Fechner, Galton, and Ebbinghaus. J. F. Herbart was the first to make a strong case for the use of mathematics in psychology in 1824. Those psychologists who came under his influence looked to mathematics to bolster the scientific value of their inquiries. One of those influenced by Herbart was Fechner, who said of himself that in the ashes of Herbart's fire he had found some coals for his own hearth. Another great innovator was Galton, as will presently be seen. Ebbinghaus, who founded the experimental study of learning, provided the first quantitative analysis of the process of learning in 1885.

This work opened a new era for psychology as a whole. Henceforth all fields of psychology sought to measure and quantify their data. Because of Ebbinghaus' spectacular success the volume of research in learning increased rapidly and new methods were constantly devised. Thirty years after Ebbinghaus, according to Boring, there were 15 new standardized methods for measuring learning and memory. Adoption and development of statistics in psychology was a logical consequence of the trend toward quantification.

The Introduction of Statistics to Psychology. Statistical methods were introduced into psychology by *Francis Galton* (1822-1911). It was he who demonstrated their usefulness for psychology and developed techniques directly applicable to psychological problems. He turned to statistical methods when he became interested in problems of human heredity and in psychological differences existing among people. At that time statistics had developed sufficiently to be effective in this kind of study (1869-1889).

The development of statistics was the result of many divergent lines of study. It grew mainly out of the mathematics of probability and the discovery of the normal curve. The mathematician and astronomer *Karl B. Gauss* (1777-1855) pointed out the practical value of the normal curve (which is still sometimes called the Gaussian curve) in scientific measurements. Gauss devised formulas for computing the mean, standard error, probable error, and the like. *Adolphe Quetelet* (1796-1874), also a mathematician and astronomer but with broad interests in other sciences, showed that the normal curve and statistical methods can be applied to biological and social data. He soon became the most enthusiastic propagator of statistics on the continent. His use of the normal curve for anthropometric measurements coincided with Galton's interest in such measurements. It was natural then for Galton to draw on Quetelet's work. But Galton's research faced problems for which Quetelet's methods were not sufficient. Therefore, when he studied the problems of heredity, Galton developed new methods and concepts—such as the concept of regression and the scatter diagram of frequencies. His next innovations were the method and the coefficient of correlation. Other statistical measures followed: the median, percentile rank, standard scores, and such methods as the order-of-merit and the rating scale. In this work Galton was greatly helped by the statistician *Karl Pearson* (1857-1936), his associate and friend, and later his biographer. Pearson, for example, developed the mathematical procedure for finding the correlation coefficient. This is the procedure which we now use to find the "Pearson r."

British Statistics. Through Galton psychology came to appreciate the usefulness of statistics and acquired the first statistical methods. This was Galton's great contribution to psychology, in addition to his study of individual differences. Psychology in England has been statistically oriented to the present time. British psychologists have lived up to Galton's tradition by emphasizing and further developing psychological statistics. The outstanding among them were *Charles E. Spearman* (1863-1945),

Cyril L. Burt (b. 1883), and *Godfrey H. Thomson* (1881-1955). They initiated factorial analysis, a method which was to become one of the most widely used in modern psychological research on abilities and personality. To another British statistician, *R. A. Fisher* (1890-1962), successor in Pearson's chair at the Univeristy College in London, psychology owes statistical procedures for small samples and the analysis of variance.

Statistics in America. American psychology adopted statistics enthusiastically. To a considerable degree it was through psychology that statistics became known in the United States. In this activity *James McK. Cattell* played the important role in introducing statistics to psychology. After working with Galton, with whom he shared the interest in individual differences, he quite naturally adopted statistics and transplanted it here in 1887. While professor at the University of Pennsylvania, Cattell was the first in America to include statistical methods in a psychology course. When he moved to Columbia University, he continued to emphasize statistics, taught the subject in a special course, "Mental Measurement," and used it in his research and writings. Cattell's work was the strongest single factor responsible for popularizing statistics among American psychologists. By 1896 three departments of psychology had courses in statistics, Clark, Columbia, and Yale. The first formal exposition of statistics in a textbook of psychology was given by *E. W. Scripture* in his book *The New Psychology* (1897), in which he had a chapter entitled "Statistics" and one entitled "Measurement."

Extensive use of statistics in education and educational psychology was made by *E. L. Thorndike*, at one time Cattell's student at Columbia. After 1899, he gave regular courses in statistical methods in education for many years. Factor analysis had its exponent in *L. L. Thurstone*, already mentioned in connection with psychophysics. Through the methods of measurement and tests which he developed, through his research in psychometrics, and through his books, such as *Vectors of Mind* (1935), *Multiple Factor Analysis* (1947), and *The Measurement of Values* (1959), he considerably advanced both statistics and psychometrics.

The Contribution of Ebbinghaus. There was still another door through which statistical concepts and procedures entered psychology. It was the work of Hermann Ebbinghaus, in quantitative analysis of the data obtained in his research on memory, which we mentioned above, that demonstrated the usefulness of statistics in a different field of psychology. His application of the law of error was one of the earliest attempts of this kind made in a purely psychological study (1885). He made it with full awareness that it was an innovation. Ebbinghaus was the first psychologist to make use of statistics in a field other than psychophysics, although it was psychophysics which gave him the idea of using mathematical treatment for data collected in his study of memory.

Historical Significance of Statistics. The quantitative approach to psychological data began first with the use of mathematical methods in psychometrics. Statistical methods were adopted when they were found useful for the study of individual differences. Once their usefulness and practical value were discovered in this field their application to other, and eventually to all psychological, experimental research readily followed. The adoption of statistics, and its extensive use, which allowed the presentation of research findings in quantitative terms, strengthened the status of psychology as a quantitative science and gave substance to its aspirations for objectivity. Like experimentation, the use of statistics meant for psychology another stride away from philosophical speculation toward the ideal of science. Since "the progress and maturity of a science are often judged by the extent to which it has succeeded in the use of mathematics," as J. P. Guilford said, psychology, by making statistics its indispensable tool, has made progress toward this ideal. As the developments in mathematical psychology in the second half of the twentieth century show, the statistical methods of psychology are becoming ever more refined and complex. The use of mathematical models in certain areas of psychology is an example of the increasing refinement of quantification in scientific psychology.

PSYCHOMETRICS

Psychometrics is defined as "the theory and methods of psychological measurement." Mental testing, such as testing and measurement of intelligence or personality traits, constitutes a large part of psychometrics. This branch of psychology developed as a result of the interest in individual differences and the tests devised to measure them. Since psychometrics was an expression of this new orientation in psychology, and because it played a role in psychology's expansion to practical applications and in the origin of clinical psychology, a historical sketch of its origins and growth is in order here.

The Origin of Psychometrics.   The inspiration for psychometrics did not originate in Leipzig or in the orbit of Wundt's influence. Wundt's psychology studied only the psychological processes and traits which were general and common to all men. It could only come from those circles which focused their attention on men as individuals, and on the factors which accounted for differences among them. This inspiration came originally from Francis Galton and his book *Inquiries into Human Faculty and Its Development* (1883). In America, psychometrics was introduced formally by J. McK. Cattell in his article *Mental Tests and Measurements* (1890) ; in Germany by Wilhelm Stern in his work *Uber Psychologie der individuellen Differenzen* ("On the Psychology of Individual Differences," 1900). Since differential psychology found its strongest support in America, the progress of psychometrics was fastest here. The interest in individual differences called for tools and measures to assess such differences. If one wants to know what makes individual "A" different from "B", or how individual "C" differs from the rest of the population, one must have some yardstick by which to determine in what respect, and by how much, one differs from another. It was the need of such a yardstick that created psychometrics.

Pioneers of Psychometrics. Undoubtedly *J. McK. Cattell* stands out as the foremost figure, if not the actual originator of psychometrics. He started mental testing in 1890, and the term "mental test" was his invention. He had this to say about mental testing at that time:

> Psychology cannot attain the certainty and exactness of the physical sciences, unless it rests on a foundation of experiment and measurement. A step in this direction could be made by applying a series of mental tests and measurements to a large number of individuals. The results would be of considerable scientific value in discovering the constancy of mental processes, their interdependence, and their variation under different circumstances. Individuals, besides, would find their tests interesting, and perhaps, useful in regard to training, mode of life or indication of disease.

Faithful to this program, Cattell devised numerous tests and used them on large samples of population. Thereafter mental testing was on its way in America, gaining momentum and spreading to new fields as it moved along. We shall have occasion later to say more about Cattell's activities in this respect.

Europe was less active and not as productive in psychometrics, but nevertheless a number of psychological tests were developed there. The most outstanding was the individual test of intelligence devised by *Alfred Binet* in collaboration with Théodore Simon in 1905. It was an achievement of great historical consequence for psychology in general, and for psychometrics especially.

Subsequent years witnessed not only the development of other intelligence tests but tests of various types such as personality, achievement, and aptitude tests. These types were both individual and group tests. They were used first in schools for educational purposes. Subsequently, they were used in fields such as vocational guidance, industry, business, personality, and in clinical psychology. The two World Wars spurred the use of tests for the selection of military personnel. Success of testing programs in the wars, such as group intelligence testing, demonstrated to governments the practical value of psychological testing in general, and in national emergencies especially. Another major spur to psychometrics came from factor analysis, which has been mentioned above. It helped in analysis of abilities and development of better tests for them.

CONCLUSION

The development of methods suited for the problems which the new psychology proposed to study contributed considerably to psychology's emancipation and scientific status. Development of methods and progress of psychology were interdependent. As new interests accrued and new problems were incorporated, new methods had to be developed or the old ones improved and expanded. New and better methods, on the other hand, contributed to further progress and wider applications.

Introspection was a method inherited from philosophy. It was systematized, improved, and refined to make it suitable for psychological research. Its use was gradually reduced when psychology, striving for objectivity of its data, gave preference to observation and measurement. *Psychophysical methods* were the first true and appropriate psychological methods. Developed by Weber and Fechner, and systematized by G. E. Müller, they found wide use in psychological research and rendered great service, especially in sensory psychology. The *psychological laboratory* was the distinctive mark of psychology's emancipation from philosophy and of its experimental character. It became the center of psychological training and research. When individual differences began to be seriously studied, the need for their measurement brought *statistics* into psychology and led to the development of *psychometrics*. Galton initiated both statistics and psychometrics. The use of mathematics and statistics was a major factor in psychology's growth as a quantitative science.

SUMMARY OF THE METHODOLOGICAL ROOTS

1. INTROSPECTION. The oldest method. Inherited from philosophy and adapted to psychological study by:
   Wundt and Titchener—the classical introspection (1879–1927).
   Külpe and the Würzburg school—the systematic experimental introspection (1900's).
   Gestalt school—phenomenological observation (from 1910).

2. PSYCHOPHYSICS. Major methodology in the study of sensation and perception. Through it the laws of Weber and Fechner were established.
   The foundation: E. H. Weber (1830's and 1840's).
   G. T. Fechner—*Elements of Psychophysics* (1860).
   Further development and systematization: G. E. Müller (1878–1903).
   Teaching and textbook: E. B. Titchener (1901–1905).
   New practical application: L. L. Thurstone (1925–1927).
   Systematic presentation: J. P. Guilford in his *Psychometric Methods* (1936; 2nd ed., 1954).
   Re-examination: S. S. Stevens (1950's).

3. LABORATORIES. Distinctive mark of psychology's separating from philosophy and assuming experimental character. Early centers of research and training.
   The first laboratory: Leipzig, Germany (1879).
   First laboratory in America: Johns Hopkins (1883).

4. STATISTICS. Factor in psychology's becoming a quantitative science.
   Introduction into psychology: F. Galton (1869).
   Development: K. Pearson (1896).
   C. Spearman (1912).
   New techniques: R. A. Fisher (1930's).
   Factorial analysis: C. Burt
   G. H. Thomson   } (1930's)
   L. L. Thurstone

5. PSYCHOMETRICS. Result of interest in individual differences. Factor in psychology's becoming an applied science.
   Pioneers: J. McK. Cattell (1883).
   A. Binet (1905).
   L. L. Thurstone (1930's).

REFERENCES

INTROSPECTION

Bakan, D. A reconsideration of the problem of introspection. *Psychol. Bull.*, 1954, *51*, 105–118.

Bennett, C. C. The drugs and I. In L. Uhr & J. G. Miller (Eds.), *Drugs and behavior*. New York: Wiley, 1960. Pp. 596–609.

Boring, E. G. A history of introspection. *Psychol. Bull.*, 1953, *50*, 169–189.

Gottschalk, L. A. Introspection and free association as experimental approaches to assessing subjective and behavioral effects of psychoactive drugs. In L. Uhr & J. G. Miller (Eds.), *Drugs and behavior*. New York: Wiley, 1960. Pp. 587–595.

McKellar, P. The method of introspection. In J. M. Scher (Ed.), *Theories of the mind*. New York: Free Press of Glencoe, 1962. Pp. 619–644.

PSYCHOPHYSICS

Boring, E. G. Fechner: inadvertent founder of psychophysics. *Psychometrika*, 1961, *26*, 3–8.

Galanter, E. Contemporary psychophysics. In *New directions in psychology*. New York: Holt, Rinehart & Winston, 1962. Pp. 89–156.

Stevens, S. S. On the psychophysical law. *Psychol. Rev.*, 1957, *64*, 153–181.

Stevens, S. S. To honor Fechner and repeal his law. *Science*, 1961, *133*, 80–86.

Thurstone, L. L. Psychophysical methods. In T. G. Andrews (Ed.), *Methods of psychology*. New York: Wiley, 1948. Pp. 124–157.

Titchener, E. B. *Experimental psychology*. Vol. II. Parts I and II. New York: Macmillan, 1905.

Woodworth, R. S. Professor Cattell's psy-. chophysical contributions. *Arch. Psychol.*, 1914, *4*, 60–74.

Fechner's first volume of *Elements of Psychophysics* is available in English translation with introduction by E. G. Boring, published by Holt, Rinehart & Winston, New York, 1966.

LABORATORIES

Cattell, J. McK. Early psychological laboratories. *Science*, 1928, *67*, 543–548.

Garvey, C. R. List of American psychological laboratories. *Psychol. Bull.*, 1929, *26*, 652–660.

Krohn, W. O. Facilities in experimental psychology at the various German universities. *Amer. J. Psychol.*, 1892, *4*, 585–594.

Krohn, W. O. The laboratory of the Psychological Institute at the University of Göttingen. *Amer. J. Psychol.*, 1893, *5*, 282–284.

Stratton, G. M. The new psychological laboratory at Leipzig. *Science*, 1896, *4*, 867–868.

Titchener, E. B. A psychological laboratory. *Mind*, 1897, *7*, 311–331.

STATISTICS

Atkinson, R. C. The use of models in experimental psychology. In B. H. Kazemier & D. Vuysje (Eds.), *The concept and the role of the model in mathematics and natural and social sciences*. Proceedings of the Colloquium sponsored by the Division of Philosophy of Sciences organized at Utrecht, January 1960, by Hans Freudenthal. New York: Gordon & Breach, 1961.

Boring, E. G. The beginning and growth of measurement in psychology. *Isis*, 1961, *52*, Part II, 238–257.

Ramul, K. Some early measurements and ratings in psychology. *Amer. Psychologist*, 1963, *18*, 653–659.

Walker, Helen M. *Studies in the history of statistical method*. Baltimore: Williams & Wilkins, 1931.

Walker, Helen M. The contributions of Karl Pearson. *J. Amer. Stat. Ass.*, 1958, *53*, 11–22.

PSYCHOMETRICS

Anastasi, Anne. *Psychological testing*. (2nd ed.) New York: Macmillan, 1961. Chapter I: Functions and origins of psychological testing. Pp. 3–20.

Cattell, J. McK. Mental tests and measurements. *Mind*, 1890, *15*, 373–380.

Goodenough, Florence L. *Mental testing: its history, principles, and applications*. New York: Holt, Rinehart & Winston, 1949.

Guilford, J. P. *Psychometric methods*. (2nd ed.) New York: McGraw-Hill, 1954.

Historical perspective of the study of individual differences and a selection of readings relevant to the history of psychometrics are presented in: Anastasi, Anne. *Individual differences*. New York: Wiley, 1965.

6

Contributions of Other Sciences

ALTHOUGH THE PRINCIPAL ROOTS of psychology are philosophical, physiological, and methodological, there have been numerous other influences on the science of psychology. To understand the development of psychology one has to keep in mind the entire intellectual and scientific atmosphere of the period being studied. If this is done, it becomes apparent that psychological concepts and theories are often reflections of trends existing in the other sciences or in the whole culture of an era. For example, the search for laws of nature, which characterized the physical science of the nineteenth century, gave impetus to the search for mental laws that would prove as absolute and stable as physical laws. It is no surpise to find, therefore, that the discovery of such laws of the mind was one of the principal objectives of nineteenth century psychologists. This was especially true in Germany.

That psychology more than any other science has been affected by concurrent philosophical, scientific, and cultural patterns seems to be without question. Any branch of knowledge, any problem, or finding, or theory related to man as an organism, as an individual, or as a member of society is bound sooner or later to interest psychology and be reflected in it. In all countries psychology has been sensitive to prevalent trends in the natural sciences. Biology, for example, has had a most pronounced influence on Anglo-American psychology. European continental psychology, on the other hand, responded more readily and directly to philosophical currents. A compilation of all such influences would produce a long list, including biology, social sciences, anthropology, education, child study, jurisprudence, psychiatry, and psychopathology, as well as political, social, and cultural movements contemporary with the growth of psychology. The discovery and evaluation of these influences is one of the most complex and fascinating tasks of historians of psychology. Of these many influences, only four have been selected for discussion in some detail here, because of their direct historical role in the development of psychology: the theory of evolution, psychiatry, hypnotism, and reaction time. Some other influences will be touched upon briefly in subsequent parts of the book.

THEORY OF EVOLUTION

The theory of evolution brought a radical change in psychological thought. Its impact was not peculiar to psychology alone. In fact, the theory of evolution, although a biological theory, had a much more dramatic effect on human thought and culture than it had on biology. Full of implications for science in general, for social life, religion, and philosophy, it incited a real revolution in man's thinking, not dissimilar to the revolution created by the Copernican theory. The promulgation of biological evolution aroused the whole intellectual world and stirred up one of the greatest scientific debates in the history of mankind, which raged for over half a century.

The Initial Effect of the Theory.   There is no need to recount the history of the evolutionary theory here. The concept of evolution, together with the idea of continuous progress, had been enunciated repeatedly by philosophers and scientists from antiquity to modern times. The concept of *biological* evolution took shape in the theory of J. B. P. Lamarck (1744-1829). Subsequently it was forcefully formulated and supported by evidence laboriously assembled over many years by Charles Darwin (1809-1882). The publication of Darwin's *The Origin of Species* (1859) is accepted as one of the greatest events in the history of science. Man and his mental life were encompassed in Darwinian evolution. Darwin spoke not only of the evolution of anatomical structure of animals, and the continuity of the organism from animals to man, but also of evolution of mind. This idea was expressed explicitly in Darwin's *Expression of the Emotions in Man and Animals* (1872). Such an idea, having the prestige of the great naturalist behind it, pronounced at the time the new psychology was formed, could not but awaken interest and attention. Indeed evolutionary theory created a new orientation in the thinking of those who were constructing this new psychology. The effect upon psychology ranged from mild to strong, from a mere mention of evolution to a complete reorientation and revision, resulting in a new concept of human nature and methods of studying man. The latter effect is the reason why some authorities classify psychology as pre- and post-Darwinian.

Psychology and Evolution.   The first clear application of the theory of evolution to the human mind was made by Herbert Spencer in his *Principles of Psychology* (1855). Spencer said that since man's mind is a product of evolution, and since its achievements are the result of the accumulation of all the experiences and events of the past, psychology should study primitive men and animals and go even to the lowest forms of animal life—to protozoa.

Another evolutionary psychology was constructed by physiologist George Henry Lewes (1817-1878) in his five volume *Problems of Life and Mind* (1873-1879). Numerous other works dealing specifically with the evolution of the mind appeared both in this period and later. Authors of psychological textbooks, particularly British and American, considered the theory of evolution in their works, and often interwove it into their systems with varying degrees of success and consistency.

What was actually new in the character of the post-Darwinian psychology? What were the concrete effects of evolutionary theory in psychology? As far as the character of psychology was concerned, evolution introduced the idea, which began to permeate the whole of psychology, that man is not essentially different from animal and that any actual difference between man and animal is only a difference of degree of development. Coincidentally with this idea, psychology saw itself as part and continuation of the biological study of the organisms. Consequently it allied itself with the biological sciences. Such a change resulted in emphasis upon the organismic viewpoint—namely, that man should be studied as an organism. This change in turn inevitably led to de-emphasis of consciousness and mentalism. It stressed instead an orientation toward behavior as the primary and sole object of psychological study. The most obvious difference between pre-Darwinian and post-Darwinian psychology—noticeable particularly from the point of view of the philosophical tradition—was a definite abandonment of the concept of the soul. Evolution "played a considerable part," as McDougall puts it, "in establishing the 'psychology without a soul'." Evolution seemed, in his words, to undermine the last prop of animism—namely, the notion of the soul. Functionalism, so characteristic of American psychology, was also a natural consequence of evolution. Adaptation to environment and survival of the fittest—essential concepts in Darwinian evolution—were extended from purely biological functions to psychological matters. Psychological processes were studied now in reference to the adaptive role they played in man's accommodation to his environment. The "why" and "what for" of psychological processes, and eventually of behavior, came to be the fundamental questions posed by a large body of psychologists.

New Branches of Psychology. Evolution suggested to psychology new areas of study and thus inspired new psychological disciplines. The study of individual differences, considered in the framework of heredity and evolutionary principles, developed into differential psychology. The study of the animal mind and emotions initiated animal and comparative psychology. Genetic psychology was also a product of this trend. Its initiators and propagators in America were G. S. Hall and J. M. Baldwin. The latter was one of the foremost American advocates of evolutionary doctrine in psychology. Francis Galton, who was Darwin's cousin, and who was much impressed by evolutionism, was prompted by the new theory to undertake the study of heredity and inheritance of traits. Through Galton the foundations of differential psychology can be traced directly to evolutionary theory. As to comparative psychology, it was George Romanes (1848-1894), author of *Animal Intelligence,* and of two books on mental evolution of animals and man, who started this new branch of psychology and was the originator of the term "comparative." C. Lloyd Morgan (1852-1936) made this discipline more scientific, and E. L. Thorndike, by his extensive experimentation with animals, raised it to a prominent position in psychology. Research in comparative psychology covered the whole range of the animal kingdom, from the higher primates down to invertebrates and protozoa.

The above survey shows that Britain, the birthplace of Darwinism, was the birthplace of new psychological disciplines—that is, of differential, genetic, animal, and comparative psychology. Further development and popularity of these disciplines, however, is owed to America. This country, because of its past, its temperament, and its vigorous historical growth from a colony to a powerful nation, was well disposed towards evolutionism. It fitted America's way of thinking and living and consequently strongly affected American science in general and psychology in particular. In American psychology, evolutionism was applied with greater consistency than elsewhere.

PSYCHIATRY

A clear and full understanding of the development of psychology cannot be gained without considering psychiatry, a branch of medicine concerned with the treatment of mental diseases, and psychopathology, the scientific study of psychological abnormalities associated with mental disorders. The latter was to become an integral part of psychology. Its concepts and findings were soon to assume a significant role in the growth of psychology. This role was not equally important in all countries. German, British, and American psychology in the early period were not as directly influenced by psychopathology as, for example, was Italy or, especially, France. In these latter countries psychopathology was the main inspiration, and leadership in psychology was often in the hands of psychiatrists.

The Influence of Psychopathology. How effective psychopathology's inspiration was can be realized from a few examples. Théodule Ribot, the pioneer of French psychology, started his psychological career with studies in psychopathology. So too did Alfred Binet, the director of the first French laboratory. Binet continued to be interested in psychopathology, while promoting experimental psychology. His intelligence test grew out of this interest, specifically from his concern with the problem of mental deficiency in French schools. Pierre Janet, the dean of French psychology for half a century, was primarily a psychopathologist. French psychologists were inclined to work in clinics with patients, rather than in experimental laboratories with experimental subjects. In Italy the two pioneers of scientific psychology, Francesco de Sarlo (1864-1937) and Sante De Sanctis (1867-1935), were eminent psychiatrists. In Germany, Theodor Ziehen (1862-1950), professor of psychology and author of systematic books in psychology, gained prominence first in clinical psychiatry and continued to cultivate both fields, psychology and psychiatry. In Britain, the work of neurologists such as John Hughlings-Jackson (1835-1911) and Henry Head (1861-1940), and especially the writings of psychiatrist Henry Maudsley (1835-1918), influenced psychology in that country.

Mental Illness. Mutual recognition and influence of psychology and psychiatry developed gradually in the late nineteenth century. The interrelation between the two disciplines is better appreciated if viewed in the light of the concept of mental illness held by psychiatry at different times.

Mental abnormality has been recognized at all times. The scholars of antiquity and the Middle Ages regarded it as a disease. But their views on the causes of mental illness and on methods of treatment differed greatly. Popular views about mental derangement, however, were often based on superstitions. The insane were regarded sometimes as bedeviled, to be punished or executed; sometimes, as victims of their own immoral life, to be isolated and unworthy of any help. If the insane were put into institutions and were treated, this treatment was for the most part inhumane, cruel, or senseless. Living in unsanitary conditions, often chained and abused, they were a most pitiful lot. In the seventeenth century their fate was much ameliorated when some religious communities, motivated by the ideals of Christian charity, took as their sole purpose the care of the insane and opened asylums where the insane were cared for with patience and kindness.

Psychiatric Revolution. A complete change in the treatment of the mentally ill and in the whole concept of mental illness was effected by the activities and writings of *Philippe Pinel* (1745-1826). A physician of thorough education in the sciences and in psychology, with many years of experience with the mentally ill, Pinel tried, with great courage, to improve 'the lot of the insane. He is known as the one who liberated the insane from their chains, but it was not only chains that he succeeded in casting away. In the two large asylums in Paris which he headed in succession, Bicêtre and Salpêtrière, he changed the whole regimen of these institutions. This new method was imitated both in other cities of France and in other countries. Pinel discussed the whole problem of mental disease and therapy in his writings. For the first time, someone tried to understand and classify mental diseases without philosophical preconceptions and solely on the basis of observations and study. Because Pinel was the first to treat the subject of insanity on a scientific basis, he is called the founder of psychiatry. Pinel's main thesis on the nature of mental disease is somatic. In his judgment mental illness was the result either of heredity or of brain pathology. His thesis of the organic origin of mental illness survived in France for a long time and markedly influenced French psychology.

In the following century the predominating interest of French psychopathologists shifted from insanity—that is, from the psychoses—to the neuroses. The study of hypnotism was a strong factor in arousing this new interest. The work of Charcot and Janet exemplifies the preoccupation with neuroses and neurotics. The contributions of French psychiatry attracted the attention of *Sigmund Freud*, as they were akin to his own interest. In America the studies of *Morton Prince* (1854-1929) followed a trend similar to that of the French.

Psychiatry in Germany. The emphasis of German psychiatry was directed at severe mental diseases, the psychoses. One of its main interests was nosology (classification and nomenclature) of mental diseases. In this field the name of *Emil Kraepelin* (1855-1926), author of the monumental *Lehrbuch der Psychiatrie* ("Textbook of Psychiatry"), stands out. His aim was to make psychiatry a branch of medicine, based on the same principles as other medical disciplines. After a detailed study of numerous cases, of all the symptoms manifested by patients, and of the course of the disease, he classified all mental diseases into two major groups: the dementia praecox and the manic-depressive. The work of Kraepelin went beyond mere description and classification of mental diseases. Their nature and treatment were of equal concern to him. His view in both matters was somatic. Educated in the medicine which looked upon disease as the consequence of some fault in the cells of the organism, he regarded mental disease as resulting exclusively from some pathology of the brain—of faulty metabolism, of endocrine disturbance, or of heredity. Although Kraepelin studied and worked with Wundt, for whom he expressed great admiration, he did not attribute any role to psychological factors in the etiology of mental illness. His extreme organic view of insanity, which regarded insanity as resulting from pathology neither ascertainable nor curable, offered little basis for true treatment of mental disorders. Thus, Kraepelin's psychiatry did not propose any real therapeutic methods. Whatever the errors and deficiencies of Kraepelin, psychiatry made a considerable stride forward, thanks to his study of psychotic symptoms.

Psychiatry and Psychology. In general, psychiatry of the nineteenth and the early twentieth century showed little interest in psychology. Similarly, psychology—except for the circles where interest in psychopathology prevailed—had little contact at the beginning with psychiatry. The main reason for this lack of mutual interest or collaboration lay in the predominant somatic orientation of psychiatry. The need for psychology was expressly denied by many psychiatrists. Psychology had no value for them since they ascribed mental disease to purely organic factors. On the other hand, psychologists could not see how they could learn anything from the study of mental disorders since these were nothing but organic diseases; thus they should be studied and treated by medicine. Nevertheless, there were voices raised on both sides in favor of mutual assistance and collaboration.

Among the medical men, one of the first and most eloquent in pointing to the psychological factors in insanity was François Leuret (1797-1851) in his books *Psychological Fragments on Insanity*—which was studied by Janet and Freud—and *The Moral Treatment of Insanity*. In Germany Carl Wilhelm Ideler (1795-1860) and in Austria Ernst von Feuchtersleben (1806-1849) fought for the recognition of psychological factors in the etiology and treatment of mental disease. Their views came very close to those of modern psychiatry. In Britain, D. H. Tuke (1827-1895) recognized the importance of psychological factors in bodily diseases in his *Influence of the Mind upon the Body* (1872), one of the early books in psychosomatic medicine. Among psychologists, attention was directed to psychopathology by Friedrich Eduard Beneke (1798-1854), who made a strong plea for rapprochement of psychology, psychiatry, and biology. These were but sporadic voices easily drowned out amidst the enunciations of strictly organic orientation. Sigmund Freud was to change this situation in the twentieth century. But the story of the Freudian revolution will be treated later. Psychology eventually realized that much could be learned about the normal mind from the study of the abnormal, and thus abnormal psychology became one of its branches.

HYPNOTISM

Hypnosis and hypnotic states have been known from time immemorial. Scientists ignored hypnotism for a long time, but when reputable scientists turned attention to it and studied it, phenomena of hypnosis eventually were recognized as worthy of scientific investigation. The man most responsible for arousing interest in hypnosis was *Anton Mesmer* (1734-1815), a physician, who came from Vienna to Paris where he stirred up a controversy involving both the general public and scientists. Hypnotic manifestations were so strongly associated with his name for half a century that, before the term *hypnosis* was coined, they were called *mesmeric* phenomena. Mesmer believed that certain men could radiate an invisible power acting at a distance, analogous to magnetism in physics, and he named it *animal magnetism*. The various mesmeric phenomena were simply manifestations of this special kind of magnetism, he maintained. Since Mesmer obviously could not prove to scientists that there is *animal magnetism*, he was a charlatan in their eyes.

Scientific Study of Hypnotism. The issue of hypnotism was not forgotten after Mesmer's death (1815). Some medical men as well as laymen continued to practice mesmerism despite opposition and criticism. Some physicians used it for therapeutic or anesthetic purposes, laymen for amusement and entertainment—all equally fascinated by its mysterious aspects. Among medical men in the middle of the nineteenth century who decided to study hypnotism seriously and to use it were British medical practitioners: *James Esdaile* (1808-1859), *John Elliotson* (1791-1868), and *James Braid* (ca. 1795-1860). *Esdaile* used it to perform painless surgery. *Elliotson*, a prominent London physician and a university professor, believed in the therapeutic value of hypnotism. Despite ostracism by official medicine, he established mesmeric clinics and wrote on the subject. *Braid* was the first to make official medicine in England recognize hypnotism as worthy of scientific study. He convinced the medical profession of the genuineness of mesmeric phenomena and attempted to explain them in physiological and psychological terms. The present name, *hypnosis*, was derived from the terminology which he used. Braid opened the door to the medical use and study of hypnosis.

Psychiatry and Hypnotism. After Braid—that is, when the genuineness of hypnotic phenomena was no longer questioned—physicians and scientists did not have to be embarrassed when they wished to use hypnosis or study it. A number of prominent scientists published studies on hypnotism. In France, particularly, the issue of hypnotism became the subject of lively discussions. Hypnosis was used there for therapeutic purposes in neurological and mental disorders. *Hippolyte Bernheim*, professor of neurology at Nancy University, and *J. M. Charcot*, at the University of Paris, figured prominently in this field. In the 1880's an animated controversy arose between these two physicians about the nature of hypnosis. Bernheim and his followers (the Nancy school) maintained that hypnosis is a natural state in which suggestion is the main factor, and which can be induced in perfectly normal individuals. Charcot and his school (the Paris school) interpreted hypnosis as a fundamentally pathological state to which hysterics were mainly susceptible. The view of the Nancy school proved to be correct.

Psychology and Hypnotism. Hypnotism with its extraordinary phenomena, so numerous and varied, appealed to the imagination of the layman and intrigued the curiosity of the scientist. Psychologists took up the study of hypnotism. Wundt wrote on hypnotism. Binet and Féré published a volume on hypnotism, and other prominent psychologists made contributions to this study. Systematic experimental studies, however, were not undertaken until the 1920's. In 1933 C. L. Hull produced a work, *Hypnosis and Suggestibility*, which was the first extensive systematic investigation of hypnosis with experimental methods. This investigation dispelled several traditional misconceptions about hypnosis. When Freud, disappointed with hypnotism as a therapeutic procedure, abandoned it, hypnotism lost its prominence in psychiatry. But interest in the nature of the hypnotic state has continued. In recent years there has been a revival of interest in hypnotism among psychiatrists and psychologists. Several aspects of hypnosis, such as hypnotic age regression and posthypnotic suggestion, were subjected to experimental studies. There has also been increased use of hypnosis in medicine and psychotherapy.

REACTION TIME

A visitor to German and American psychological laboratories in the last two decades of the nineteenth century would have found them busy with experiments on reaction time, measured under various conditions. The subject of reaction time attracted much attention and stimulated a great deal of experimentation in that period. But the study of reaction time did not originate in psychology itself. It began, strange as it may seem, in astronomy.

Reaction Time in Astronomy. One of the tasks of astronomers was to establish the time of stellar transits. An observer looked at a moving star through a telescope provided with cross wires in the reticle. He had to watch the passage of the star through the midline of the telescope while he listened, at the same time, to a clock ticking every second. His task was to note the position of the star before the midline at the first tick of the clock and then the next position of the star after the midline at the second tick. Dividing the distance between the two positions of the star into ten sections, the observer could determine at which tenth of a second the star crossed the midline of the telescope. *F. W. Bessel,* an astronomer at Königsberg at the beginning of the nineteenth century, became concerned with the accuracy of such estimates. He discovered, to his and other astronomers' surprise, that there were appreciable differences between observers, amounting sometimes to over one second—a considerable error for astronomical observations. Bessel began to investigate this question in the 1820's. When he found that astronomers, exerting the greatest effort to be accurate, still differed in their estimates, he conceived a method to correct the time estimates. The method consisted of determining the difference in time measurements by various astronomers and using it for correcting time estimates. This method was called the *personal equation.*

Later, when the chronograph was invented, astronomers could determine their absolute personal equation—that is, the absolute error they made in marking the observed event. The device was simple. The event to be observed—for example, the passage of the star simulated by an artificial light—was recorded by a jag on the smoked paper moving at a known speed. The observer, as soon as he saw the event, pressed a key which also made a jag on the paper. The difference between the mark of the actual event and the observer's mark was the absolute personal equation, which, of course, was his reaction time. Astronomers and then physiologists, continuing their investigation of this phenomenon, discovered further that reaction time was not constant but variable. Reaction time changed as the conditions of the stimulus situation, or the observer's state, changed. Magnitude, brightness, or speed of movement were found to have appreciable effect on reaction time.

Psychological Experiments. The problem of reaction time was recognized as psychological. It was then up to psychologists and psychological laboratories to investigate it. These investigations were conducted in great number, between 1860 and 1900. They were aided by the invention and constant perfecting of chronoscopes and chronographs. How important such studies were in German physiological psychology can be judged from Ribot's book, *German Psychology of To-Day,* which devoted one of its seven chapters specifically to "the duration of psychological acts." In Italy, G. Buccola's experiments in mental chronometry reported in his *La legge del tempo mei fenomeni del pensiero* ("The Law of Time in the Thought Phenomena," 1883) were instrumental in winning approval for psychological research in that country. The American pioneer of psychology, J. McK. Cattell, figured prominently in reaction time study. The first textbooks of psychology devoted much space to reaction time and treated the subject in considerable detail.

Mental Chronometry. The study of reaction time eventually developed in two directions: first, finding the significant parameters of reaction time, such as the intensity of the stimulus or the subject's conditions; and, second, determining the duration of various mental acts. The latter line of investigation deeply absorbed many psychologists. It was instigated by a Dutch physiologist, *F. C. Donders*, who published his results in a work entitled *Die Schnelligkeit psychologischer Processe* ("The Speed of Physiological Processes," 1862). He and others—among them Wundt— were of the opinion that they could measure the duration of mental processes, such as choice, discrimination, and judgment. They found that reaction time increased when the subject had to make a choice or discrimination before reacting. They thought that by subtracting simple reaction time (mere reaction to a stimulus) from reaction time involving choice or other mental operation, they could determine how much time was required by the given mental operation. Proceeding on this assumption, psychologists, in Wundt's laboratory particularly, systematically added other processes in reaction time experiments. Finding an increase in reaction time by each process, they ascribed this increase to actual duration of the mental process which was introduced. These psychologists believed that an important accomplishment was achieved—namely, the measurement of duration of mental events, such as cognition, apperception, association, and judgment. They called this study psychometry or mental chronometry.

Mental chronometry was abandoned in a short time for compelling reasons. First of all, the times obtained in various situations were unreliable, since they changed from day to day or from subject to subject. Second, it was realized that complex mental processes were not just sums of simpler processes, and thus could not be fractionated. Külpe criticized mental chronometry on this ground in 1893. The failure of this study was a valuable lesson in the early history of psychology.

Historical Significance. As it has been described, reaction time was studied seriously and eagerly. Much was learned about reaction time itself, and about other processes through these studies. Reaction time experiments showed wide variations between individuals, and within individuals, in the speed of reaction to the same stimulus. In the course of these experiments new processes and their effect on reaction were discovered. They included such processes as set, predisposition, and attention. Furthermore, it came to be realized that what was learned about human reaction time could be applied and used not merely in astronomical observatories, but in many areas of practical life. But, historically speaking, the most significant effect of the discovery and experimentation with reaction time was on psychological theory. It was demonstrated that, contrary to existing beliefs, mental events were not instantaneous but temporal and measurable. The idea of an experimental psychology concerned with such processes as reaction time was thus reinforced. Reaction time remains a significant area of psychological investigation, which today still is being explored in new situations and new applications.

SUMMARY OF THE CONTRIBUTIONS
OF EVOLUTION, PSYCHIATRY, HYPNOTISM, AND REACTION TIME

EVOLUTION.   Applied to mental life by Spencer (1850's).
Initiated comparative psychology (Romanes, C. Lloyd Morgan, Thorndike).
Inspired differential psychology (Galton).
Strengthened biological orientation of psychology.

PSYCHIATRY.   Pinel, founder of psychiatry, author of psychiatric revolution in Franec (1795).
Charcot and Janet, representatives of French psychiatry (late nineteenth and early twentieth centuries). Emphasis on neuroses.
Kraepelin, representative and pioneer of German psychiatry (1855–1926). Emphasis on psychoses and their classification.
Initiated abnormal psychology.
Contributed to the development of dynamic psychology, and eventually to clinical psychology.

HYPNOTISM.   Became a controversial issue because of the activities of Anton Mesmer (1734–1815).
First scientific study by James Braid (1843).
Object of controversy between Nancy and Paris schools (last quarter of the nineteenth century).
First systematic experimental investigation by C. L. Hull (1933). Introduced new problems for psychological investigation.

REACTION TIME.   Problem in astronomy (beginning of the nineteenth century).
Studied by astronomers (from 1820)
  physiologists (from 1850)
  psychologists (from 1860); intensive experimentation in 1880–1900.
Mental chronometry—measurement of the duration of mental processes (1881–1894): Donders, Wundt, Buccola.
Demonstrated: temporal duration of mental events, individual variability, new psychological processes, and potentialities for practical applications

REFERENCES

EVOLUTION

Angell, J. R. The influence of Darwin on psychology. *Psychol. Rev.*, 1909, *16*, 152–169.

Boring, E. G. The influence of evolutionary theory upon American psychological thought. In S. Persons (Ed.), *Evolutionary thought in America.* New Haven: Yale Univer. Press, 1950. Pp. 267–298. Reprinted in R. I. Watson & D. T. Campbell (Eds.), *History, psychology, and science: selected papers.* New York: Wiley, 1963. Pp. 159–184.

Eiseley, L. *Darwin's century.* New York: Doubleday, 1958.

Howard, D. T. The influence of evolutionary doctrine on psychology. *Psychol. Rev.*, 1927, *34*, 305–312.

Warden, C. J. The historical development of comparative psychology. *Psychol. Rev.*, 1927, *34*, 57–85; 135–168.

Warden, C. J., & Warner, L. H. The development of animal psychology in the U.S. during the past three decades. *Psychol. Rev.*, 1927, *34*, 196–205.

PSYCHIATRY

Braceland, F. J. Kraepelin, his system and his influence. *Amer. J. Psychiat.*, 1957, *113*, 871–876.

Gerard, R. W. Biological roots of psychiatry. *Science*, 1955, *122*, 225–230.

Kahn, E. Emil Kraepelin. *Amer. J. Psychiat.*, 1956, *113*, 289–294.

Zilboorg, G., & Henry, G. W. *A history of medical psychology.* New York: Norton, 1941.

HYPNOTISM

Bramwell, J. M. *Hypnotism: its history, practice and theory.* Philadelphia: Lippincott, 1903.

Gill, M., & Brenman, Margaret. *Hypnosis and related states.* New York: International Univer. Press, 1959.

Hull, C. L. *Hypnosis and suggestibility: an experimental approach.* New York: Appleton-Century-Crofts, 1933.

Kline, M. V. *Freud and hypnosis: the interaction of psychodynamics and hypnosis.* New York: Julian Press, 1958.

Murray, J. B. Hypnosis: a review of research. *Cath. psychol. Rec.*, 1964, *2*, 9–32.

Sarbin, T. R. Attempts to understand hypnotic phenomena. In L. Postman (Ed.), *Psychology in the making: histories of selected research problems.* New York: Knopf, 1962. Pp. 745–785.

Shor, R. E., & Orne, M. T. (Eds.) *The nature of hypnosis: selected basic writings.* New York: Holt, Rinehart & Winston, 1965.

REACTION TIME

Garrett, H. E. Cattell's studies of reaction time. In H. E. Garrett, *Great experiments in psychology.* (3rd ed.) New York: Appleton-Century-Crofts, 1951. Pp. 312–330.

Sanford, E. C. Personal equation. *Amer. J. Psychol.*, 1888–89, *2*, 3–38; 271–298; 403–430.

SUMMARY OF PART I

In this first part, the roots of psychology have been outlined. It has been shown how philosophy, physiology, and methodology contributed to the emancipation of scientific psychology and to the formation of its character and orientation.

Philosophy was the main root because it was in philosophy that psychological thought originated and grew. Empirical philosophy and the school of associationism constitute the immediate philosophical ancestry which provided the initial theoretical basis for psychology.

Physiology was instrumental in psychology's separation from philosophy and in psychology's development into an independent experimental science. Physiology provided a body of facts about the nervous system, sense organs, and their functioning.

The development of psychophysical methods, and the establishment of psychological laboratories were also factors in psychology's emancipation and independence and contributed to its progress. The adaptation and use of mathematics and statistics (for psychometrical purposes) in analyzing psychological data was important in psychology's becoming a quantitative science.

The influence of the theory of evolution, of psychiatry, of hypnotism, and of reaction time has been discussed, and their place in the earlier history of psychology evaluated.

Part II. The Beginnings and Growth of Scientific Psychology in Various Countries

This part will describe how scientific psychology originated and how three elements, the philosophical, physiological, and scientific methodology, merged in the work of one person, Wilhelm Wundt. It will show how he gave the world its first system of psychology. The early psychology was overly philosophical and too physiological. Gradually, however, psychology grew more and more independent of its roots in philosophy and physiology, and at the same time became more scientific. Its subject matter and objectives were better defined. To show this maturation of psychology and the contributions various countries made to it, is also the purpose of this part. Since America had an important role in the development of psychology, special attention is given to the history of American psychology. However, the beginnings and growth of psychology in other parts of the world, including Europe and Asia, are also presented.

7

Wilhelm Wundt, The Founder
of Scientific Psychology

DESTINY SEEMS TO HAVE MARKED WILHELM WUNDT for the signal task of delivering the new science of psychology to the world. In him the synthesis and integration of existing trends toward a scientific psychology were realized. By him laboratory psychology was formally instituted. He is generally recognized as the originator of experimental psychology. The latter became known in the late nineteenth century as the *new* psychology in contrast to the older philosophical psychology.

Wundt named the new psychology, "physiological psychology," not because he regarded it as a province of physiology. Rather he meant to acknowledge thereby psychology's indebtedness for the methodology which physiology had furnished—namely, the experiment—and also to signify the new science's concern with the physiological substrata of mental life. However, he did not want to reduce mind to mere physical activity in the brain. Departing radically from German tradition, Wundt ruled metaphysics out of his psychology. This trend away from and against metaphysics initiated by Wundt seems to have had an enduring influence on psychology.

Life. One may quite naturally inquire how it happened to be Wundt by whom the union of philosophy and physiology was effected. Why did Wilhelm Wundt become the *first* psychologist? A brief résumé of his life reveals the elements in his personality, training, and habits of work that molded him and adapted him to his role as founder of experimental psychology.

Wundt was born in Neckarau, in Baden, Germany on August 16, 1832. He spent a rather quiet childhood and uneventful youth. In 1852, after one year's study at the University of Tübingen, he went to the University of Heidelberg. Although he had resolved while at Tübingen to make physiology his career, Wundt chose medicine instead because of financial stresses caused by his father's death. Research attracted him intensely. Accordingly in 1856, just prior to receiving his medical degree from Heidelberg, he went to Berlin where he studied physiology with Johannes Müller, "the father of experimental physiology," and with du Bois-Reymond. Wundt appreciated the scientific atmosphere of Berlin and found added inspiration there to enter academic life.

After receiving his medical degree from Heidelberg, Wundt worked in the medical clinic there. From 1857 to 1864 he served as Dozent. In the latter year he was appointed *aussordentlicher Professor*, a rank corresponding roughly to that of associate professor in America. While at

Heidelberg, from 1857 to 1874, he assisted Helmholtz who arrived there in 1858. During that time Wundt shifted from physiology to psychology and started to produce his first writings in experimental psychology.

In 1874, the year he published the second volume of his important *Principles of Physiological Psychology*, Wundt accepted the chair of inductive philosophy at Zürich, a change that paralleled his intellectual development. But he remained in Zürich for only one year. In 1875, he was named professor of philosophy at Leipzig. It is with Leipzig that Wundt is usually identified, for it was there that he formally began to offer instruction in the new scientific psychology. It was there that the first psychological laboratory was founded in 1879, and the first experiments were conducted. In the 1880's Leipzig became the object of world-wide attention and the training center for students from all over the world who wanted to learn the new science at its point of origin. It was at Leipzig and with Wundt that most famous psychologists who later founded laboratories and departments of psychology in many different countries studied in the late nineteenth and early twentieth centuries.

For 45 years, until his death on August 31, 1920 at the age of 88, Wundt remained at Leipzig. Here he nurtured the young science, protected it in its formative years, and defended it vigorously. During all this time Wundt labored ceaselessly at teaching, directing research, writing his numerous books and articles. By constant revision he achieved his vital objective of keeping his material up to date.

Wundt's Concept of Psychology. German psychology before Wundt had always been metaphysical. Metaphysics, together with observation and mathematics, had been regarded as basic to psychology by Herbart, who refused to acknowledge experimentation. In his psychophysics Fechner had offered the first practical demonstration of Herbart's "exact psychology." He introduced experimentation, but did not eliminate metaphysics. Employing Fechner's methodology, Wundt fashioned a new psychology which dealt with measurable stimuli and responses. Although he ruled out metaphysics, he always insisted on a close reciprocity between philosophy and psychology. Wundt was an experimentalist, but his experimentalism was a by-product of his philosophical views. All his life he steadfastly maintained that psychology should be cultivated in close contact with philosophy.

Wundt's own philosophical orientation was that of a dualist—more specifically that of a psychophysical parallelist and an associationist. Within this framework, with the help of physiology, he proceeded to study mind, not as metaphysical substance but as the logical subject of internal experience. The path to psychology, he believed, lay through anatomy and physiology of the nervous system. However, he also clearly affirmed of the new psychology: "It is not a province of physiology, nor does it attempt, as has been mistakenly asserted, to derive or explain the phenomena of the psychical from those of the physical life." Physiology was to furnish methodology and facts to the new psychology, but psychology was to analyze conscious processes.

From three fields—philosophy, physiology, and psychophysics—Wundt derived the subject matter of the new psychology. This psychology was to be the science of immediate experience (as differentiated from "mediate experience" studied by physics), and to analyze the contents of consciousness. In Wundt's conception psychology had a threefold purpose: (1) to analyze mental contents into elements, of which there are three classes: sensations, images, and feelings; (2) to find how these elements are connected; and (3) to discover the laws that determine their connection. "Physiological psychology," Wundt observed, ". . . ends with those questions with which the philosophical psychology of the older day was wont to begin,—the questions of the nature of the mind, and of the relation of consciousness to an external world, and with characterization of the general attitude which psychology is to take up, when it seeks to trace the laws of the mental life as manifested in history and in society."

Restriction of psychology's subject matter to immediate experience limited the scope of Wundt's science. All his laboratory studies were devoted to scrutinizing meticulously the various elements of consciousness. Although Wundt recognized child study and animal psychology, he accorded no more than passing consideration to them and did no research in these areas. To applied psychology, however, he was far from indifferent. Wundt wanted psychology to be a pure science. The applications of psychology, later so eagerly developed by his American students, evoked severe criticism and clear opposition from him. In this initial period of scientific psychology, Wundt believed that psychologists should concentrate on the study of consciousness, on the analysis of mental contents, and on the accumulation of facts, before attempting to develop an applied psychology. Try as he might, however, Wundt could not stem the tide of enthusiasm for applied psychology, as the history of psychology demonstrates.

What methods was the psychologist to use in studying consciousness and in analyzing mental contents? Wundt believed that psychology, following an inductive path, should employ introspection coupled with experiment. To secure a valid objective report of man's experience, pure self-observation—the type used by philosophers—was not sufficient. Experimentation must be used, for in the experiment consciousness can be modified by varying external stimuli, and the resulting modifications can be studied from the subject's introspective reports. Despite his enthusiasm for experimentation, Wundt felt that only mental phenomena directly accessible to physical influence could be made the subject of experiment. In his opinion, the higher mental processes, such as thinking and willing, demanded the use of historical methods. These historical methods included an analysis of man's language, laws, customs, art, and institutions—in short, man's "cultural products." Little wonder, then, that Oswald Külpe, a former student and assistant at Leipzig, was vehemently opposed by Wundt when he initiated investigations of the higher thought processes in his experimental laboratory at Würzburg.

In summary, we may say that Wundt's psychology was antimetaphysical, dualistic, elementistic, associationistic, and introspectionistic. It was a natural science of consciousness dedicated to introspective analysis of sensations and feelings, but refraining from experimental study of the higher mental processes and opposing applied psychology.

Atomistic Character of Wundt's Psychology.   In analyzing mental contents, Wundt adopted the point of view of mental chemistry originally described by Brown and later revived by John S. Mill. The contents are of a composite nature which, upon analysis and abstraction, yields those ultimate parts of the conscious contents, namely the elements which cannot be further broken down. The elements are processes, not static units.

One element of consciousness is the *sensation* which occurs when a sense organ is stimulated and contact is made in the brain. The neural excitations and the sensations are parallel phenomena. Another element is the *image*. Wundt felt that there was no basic difference between sensation and image, the image being associated simply with local excitation in the cortex. Sensations are the elements of the objective contents which tend to remain the same despite change of combinations. They are the "ultimate and irreducible elements of ideas." The sensations may be analyzed into their attributes of quality, intensity, duration, and extension. A combination of the elements into a pattern of more or less complicated consituation is an *idea,* which is the form of appearance in consciousness of something in the outside world. Sensations and ideas both have reference to the objective world. They represent the outside world in consciousness.

Complementing and accompanying these objective elements there is a third type of elements which are subjective, and which do not project themselves into the outside world. They seem to be part of us, to belong to us. They relate to our consciousness and not to things external. These subjective elements are the *feelings*—the feelings concomitant, for example, with seeing, hearing, tasting, and the like. Feelings depend not only on the impressions themselves but on the individual receiving the impressions. They may accompany sensations and ideas, but they are not identical with them. Feelings do not derive from any sense organ nor from a recurrence of sensory experience. In describing feeling (in his *Grundriss der Psychologie,* "Outline of Psychology," 1896) Wundt presented a tridimensional scheme with three continua ranging from tension to relaxation, from excitement to calm, and from pleasantness to unpleasantness. He observed that these forms of feeling seldom appear in isolation, as partial feeling. Several of them are usually joined together into a single feeling compound or aggregate feeling. Like sensations, feelings also have such attributes as quality and intensity.

Between partial feelings and aggregate feelings, the same relationship exists as between pure sensations and ideas. Sensations and feelings are fundamental, but they can combine into a variety of different patterns in experience. For example, feelings and bodily sensations may synthesize and produce an emotion which, therefore, is an affective and ideational process. Wundt considered the volitional process to be closely allied with emotion, the will being regarded as an affective process and not a specific psychical element. Combinations of feelings may thus be termed "complex feelings," "emotion," "volition."

Wundt's psychology was atomistic. Yet it did not concentrate exclusively on the analysis of the elements and overlook the totality. While Wundt assiduously dissected experience into its elements he also tried to see how these elements were synthesized in experience and to deduce the laws governing their combinations. Nonetheless, Wundt stressed analysis and imprinted his elementism upon the young psychology.

Association, Apperception, and Psychic Laws. The conscious elements, as we have just seen, are capable of combinations resulting in various ideational compounds, aggregate feelings, emotions, and volitional processes. Wundt tried to account for the manner in which these combinations were made. In view of the influence that British psychology had exerted upon him, it is not surprising that he invoked association as the basic explanatory principle for combination. Wundt described the passive combinations as *associations*, the active combinations, as *apperceptions*.

A feeling of activity differentiates apperception from mere association in experience. We can understand what is meant by apperception if we realize that only some mental processes are within the focus of our awareness. These are the processes that are said to be apperceived. The range of this focus of awareness is really the range of attention, and this range is always less than the total range of consciousness or awareness. Apperception, then, is that process which combines the elements in all cases by a union of a larger complex of elements. It arranges the manifold contents into a single organized whole. In Wundt's view, then, associations and apperceptions are always in a state of interaction.

Besides describing the elements of man's mental contents and their mode of connection and combination through association and apperception, Wundt also attempted to postulate the laws that determine their connection in experience. Earlier, the old association psychology had viewed association as a connection between ideas. The associationists utilized the primary laws of similarity, contiguity, and contrast and the secondary laws of frequency, recency, and intensity as explanations for associations. But Wundt felt that the associationists did not probe deeply enough into the laws underlying the association processes, and he proceeded to develop laws of psychical life—that is, a set of psychological principles having universal validity. He formulated several such laws, but they did not find much popularity with psychologists.

Wundt's Writings. Wundt was a prolific writer. His extensive bibliography includes articles and books on philosophy, physiology, and psychology. Wundt's first book on experimental psychology was *Beiträge zur Theorie der Sinneswahrnehmung* ("Contributions to the Theory of Sense Perception"). This work appeared in its entirety in 1862, although it had been published in parts, beginning with the first part in 1858. The *Beiträge* made a genuine appeal for an experimental psychology, and this appeal constituted in large measure the significance of the work. As a physiologist, Wundt was beginning to concentrate on psychological functions of the organisms—specifically on perception—and he was beginning to think in psychological terms. He was already recognizing the value of experiment and envisioning a new psychology in which experiment could be put to use. In the *Beiträge*, Wundt presented a threefold division of the new science—including experimental psychology, social psychology, and scientific metaphysics. It was this classification which Titchener later interpreted and referred to as the blueprint which Wundt had sketched for his future psychological endeavors.

From the standpoint of the history of psychology, Wundt's most important volume is the *Grundzüge der physiologischen Psychologie* ("Principles of Physiological Psychology"). Begun in 1867, the book's first half was published in 1873. The second half appeared in 1874, the year that Wundt left Heidelberg for Zürich. In the *Grundzüge* Wundt presented his system of physiological psychology. He explained how the methods of natural science could be employed in psychology, and he emphasized the relations between psychology and physiology. The subsequent six revisions of this historic volume—which launched psychology as an independent science—represented the further extension and modification of the original system.

Already world renowned as the founder of laboratory psychology, Wundt published in 1896 the *Grundriss der Psychologie* ("Outline of Psychology"). This less elaborate volume—which went through ten revisions by 1911—was a less detailed treatment than the *Grundzüge*. But it attracted attention because it presented Wundt's tridimensional explanation of feeling for the first time.

Concurrent with the last revision of the *Grundriss* in 1911, Wundt published his *Einführung in die Psychologie* ("Introduction to Psychology"), a popular presentation of his system. Between 1900 and 1920 the ten volumes of his comprehensive psychology of culture, *Völkerpsychologie* ("Folk Psychology"), appeared successively. These represented Wundt's attempt to understand man's higher thought processes by a study of the history of mankind through language, art, mythology, religion, customs, and law. Because of its psychogenetic approach to the total development of mental life, Wundt regarded his folk psychology as *genetic* psychology rather than as *social* psychology.

During his long career he also contributed numerous psychological articles to periodicals. Many appeared in *Philosophische Studien* ("Philosophical Studies"), the journal he began to publish in 1881, and which he renamed *Psychologische Studien* ("Psychological Studies") in 1903. Intended as a special medium for publication of Leipzig research, it was the first journal of the new experimental psychology. Over the years, Wundt contributed several theoretical papers to this journal.

In his writings Wundt presented his views on scientific psychology clearly and in detail. He described its relationship with its origins—philosophy and physiology. He defined the science, marking off its domain and indicating the methods by which its subject matter was to be studied.

The Leipzig Laboratory. The Leipzig Laboratory is significant in the history of psychology because it is the first experimental laboratory in which psychological research was conducted. Therefore, a closer examination of this laboratory, its procedures, and its fields of investigation affords us a better understanding of the beginning of experimental psychology. It also gives us an idea of the laboratory training of the world's first psychology students.

It will be recalled that in 1875 Wundt arrived at Leipzig. By this time he had achieved distinction as an author of books and articles in physiology, physics, and psychology. Plans for the establishment of his laboratory were instituted by Wundt and the university administrators in 1876. (This year the University apparently considered the founding year since it observed the laboratory's 50th anniversary in 1926.) By 1879, the year of its formal opening, research was already being done. Once the laboratory was opened, its fame spread and its growth was phenomenal.

Initially Wundt's laboratory—situated on the top floor of one of the University's buildings—occupied four rooms. In time, additional space was provided. In 1892, larger quarters were made available, and finally, in 1897 the laboratory was relocated in a building in which 14 rooms were allocated to psychology. Into this training center came not only German students, such as Kraepelin and Külpe, but students from all over the world—Americans, Frenchmen, Scandinavians, Eastern Europeans, Greeks, Japanese, and Englishmen—although the latter were conspicuously few. Most of the first generation experimental psychologists in America studied in the Leipzig laboratory before 1900. Among them were Hall, Cattell, Wolfe, Pace, Scripture, Frank Angell, Warren, Gale, Patrick, Stratton, Judd, and Tawney. Here they attended demonstrations and conducted their original researches in psychology. When the Leipzig students returned to their respective countries many of them founded laboratories patterned after this first laboratory.

Wundt was interested in the laboratory mainly as a system and method of introspection. He regarded it also as a useful adjunct to his teaching. Wundt was the first psychologist to introduce demonstrational apparatus into the lecture room. Ordinarily, after his lectures he would spend some time in the laboratory. He would supervise the research in progress, answer questions, and give help and encouragement to the students. Usually at the beginning of the semester he suggested research topics. After that he urged the students to work out their own problems and techniques independently, although the work proceeded according to certain conditions and regulations prescribed by him. The students generally worked in pairs, alternating as experimenters and subjects. No one was permitted to serve as a subject in the laboratory unless he had been trained in introspection.

Naturally the research at this laboratory attracted much attention. Now, one may inquire, what kind of experiments did these first psychology students perform at Leipzig? Recalling that Wundt's psychology was essentially the study of consciousness by introspection, and realizing that the laboratory was very much his creation, we can readily understand the course which research took there. The Leipzig experiments were divided into four major categories: (1) *Sensation and perception.* During the first two decades (1880's-1890's) much research was done on the analysis and measurement of sensation, particularly on vision, but also on hearing, taste, and touch. (2) *Reaction time.* This measurement also attracted much attention. Such studies, inspired partially by the personal equation problem—inherited from astronomy—and in part by the researches of Helmholtz and Donders in physiology, led to mental chronometry, an elaborate system of addition and subtraction for the calculation of the time required for judgment, cognition, willing, and the like. This method, as was mentioned earlier, did not fulfill its initial promise. (3) *Time perception and estimation* of certain time intervals. (4) *Attention, memory, feeling, and association.* Wundt borrowed the association experiment from Galton, the British pioneer of psychology, who was interested in the study of individual differences.

In all four areas, intensive, careful investigations were conducted by Wundt's students. Fechner's psychophysical experiments were fostered by Wundt, although he took exception to Fechner's contention that sensations could be measured. Wundt maintained that only stimuli could be measured. A record of the Leipzig research, its methodology, findings, and fields of concentration, is found in the *Philosophische Studien* and its successor, *Psychologische Studien.*

American Students and Their Reactions to Wundt. After the formal opening of Wundt's laboratory, as we have just seen, students came from many European countries, from America, and from the Orient for training in scientific psychology. Upon completion of their studies most of them returned to their native lands where they became the pioneers of the new science. Not all who studied at Leipzig subscribed to Wundt's approach. Many left his laboratory only to grow away from him and his psychology and to fashion a new kind of science in their own laboratories. In this connection, Müller-Freienfels has remarked, "It was the tragedy of Wundt's life that he attracted many pupils, but held only a few." In other words, there were not many who remained loyal followers of the master, despite the large numbers who trained at Leipzig. Hall attributed this lack of attachment, in part, to Wundt's failure to keep in touch with his former pupils.

The largest single group who effected radical changes in scientific psychology after leaving Leipzig were the American students. It is of interest, therefore, to see how they regarded the professor who gave them their first formal training in laboratory techniques. A tribute to Wundt, after his death, published in the *Psychological Review* in 1921, affords some interesting insights into Wundt as psychologist and as a personality. The tribute is composed of reminiscences of him by 17 of his American students. Diverse views are expressed, ranging from the harsh criticism of Hall to the enthusiastic devotion of Titchener.

G. S. Hall, the organizer of American psychology and founder of the psychological laboratories at Johns Hopkins and Clark Universities, was the first American student at Leipzig. By his own admission, he had limited contact with Wundt. Hall regarded Wundt as a compiler and digester, who made no significant contribution, except possibly his doctrine of apperception. Wundt's proneness to overlook the contributions of psychiatry particularly irritated Hall. In general, German psychology held little appeal for him. Hall was devoted to applied psychology which he vigorously promoted in America.

Hall's unfavorable criticism of Wundt was also expressed in his correspondence from Leipzig with William James, who had urged Hall to go to Leipzig. It should be pointed out here, however, that James, who was the first to publicize German psychology in America, was also critical of it. He opposed its elementistic nature and labeled it "microscopic psychology." James considered Wundt "not a first class ingenium, but only a rather ordinary man who has worked up certain things uncommonly well."

The American students who went to Leipzig after Hall almost unanimously praised Wundt's scholarship and his ability as lecturer and writer. He is fondly described by them for his "lack of ostentation" and "patience" (Pace), for his "geniality and fatherliness" (Tawney), for not being "objectionably dogmatic, like many other German professors," although he was "conscious of his leadership" (Warren).

Among the last Americans to study with Wundt were G. F. Arps (1906) and R. Pintner (1909-1911). The former regarded Wundt as "the modern Aristotle with respect to versatility if not with respect to originality." During Pintner's stay in Leipzig, Wundt had already reached advanced age and did little experimentation. Pintner describes Wundt as "very unemotional" and says that "as such he probably lacked the enthusiastic friendships of other great teachers. No student seemed to get very close to him. His cold intellectuality seemed to make them stand back." In this connection, Pintner states that when he had translated Wundt's *Einführung* and had considerable correspondence with Wundt, he never really got to know him any better.

From these American observations, Wundt emerges as a distinctly intellectual type, who shunned close attachments with people and who characteristically avoided association with professional colleagues. On the other hand, he is also described as humble, friendly, fatherly, and as a hard worker dedicated to his psychological studies.

Wundt's Role in the History of Psychology. Wundt's permanent and unique claim to fame in the history of psychology is not for his system or theories but as the founder of scientific psychology. From philosophy and physiology he derived the new science which he called "physiological psychology," and for which he cultivated the psychophysical methods. He produced the first system of psychology. Although it was harshly criticized by some of his contemporaries, like James and Hall, they learned about scientific psychology from Wundt and they had to acknowledge him as its creator and promoter.

Wundt founded the laboratory in which the first significant psychological researches were conducted, and he established the first psychological journal in which the laboratory's findings were published. Throughout his life Wundt made his influence felt as systematist, organizer, and encyclopedist. Painstaking by nature and dedicated to hard work, he wrote the first textbooks of psychology and then assiduously revised them to record faithfully the latest research findings and theoretical speculations. If, as some have claimed, he lacked the genius of Helmholtz and the scintillating personality of William James, perhaps these deficiencies were themselves assets for the task he had to perform. His extensive bibliography, an invaluable service to psychology in its initial stages of growth, remains a lasting testament to Wundt's scholarship and his indefatigability.

For almost three decades Wundt's personal influence on psychology was singularly potent. His prestige as physician, philosopher, author, and professor inspired attention to his strong plea for a scientific psychology. In his laboratory the early leaders of psychology in various countries were trained. As these students left Leipzig and established laboratories in their own lands, and did their own researches, psychological science developed in diverse directions. New fields, new methods, new theories, and new systems of psychology gradually emerged, some of the latter in direct opposition to Wundtian views. Such opposition was not to Wundt's discredit. It signified the progress of psychological science. Whether or not succeeding generations of psychologists followed Wundt's leadership, whether or not they liked his personal characteristics, agreed or disagreed with his theories and systems, they could never gainsay their debt to him. Wundt was the founder of scientific psychology and the first psychologist.

HIGHLIGHTS: WILHELM WUNDT, THE FOUNDER OF SCIENTIFIC PSYCHOLOGY

1856   Wundt studied for a semester with Johannes Müller at Berlin. Received his medical degree at Heidelberg.
1857   Wundt began teaching at Heidelberg.
1862   Completed his first volume in experimental psychology: *Beiträge zur Theorie der Sinneswahrnehmung* ("Contributions to the Theory of Sense Perception").
1873   Published first part of *Grundzüge der physiologischen Psychologie* ("Principles of Physiological Psychology").
1874   Second half of *Grundzüge* published.
       Left Heidelberg for chair of inductive philosophy at Zürich.
1875   Became professor of philosophy at Leipzig.
       Gave experimental demonstrations with his psychology lectures.
1879   Formally opened the first psychological laboratory at Leipzig.
       G. Stanley Hall, Wundt's first American student, arrived.
1881   Started journal, *Philosophische Studien* ("Philosophical Studies").
1886   Cattell, Wundt's first assistant, received doctorate.
1892   Titchener, loyal protagonist of Wundtian psychology, received doctorate at Leipzig.
1896   Tridimensional theory of feeling published in *Grundriss der Psychologie* ("Outline of Psychology").
1903   *Philosophische Studien* discontinued and replaced by *Psychologische Studien* ("Psychological Studies").
1920   Completed *Völkerpsychologie* ("Folk Psychology"), a ten volume comprehensive psychology of culture, begun in 1900.
       Wundt died.

WUNDT'S STUDENTS: PIONEERS OF PSYCHOLOGY IN VARIOUS COUNTRIES AND UNIVERSITIES

Germany:
A. Kirschmann.................Leipzig
E. Kraepelin....................Munich
F. Krueger......................Leipzig
O. Külpe.............Würzburg, Munich
L. Lange.....................Tübingen
K. Marbe.....................Würzburg
E. Meumann..................Hamburg
H. Münsterberg........Freiburg, Harvard
G. W. Störring...................Bonn
W. Wirth......................Leipzig

Belgium:
A. Thiéry.....................Louvain

Denmark:
A. Lehmann................Copenhagen

France:
B. Bourdon.....................Rennes
V. Henri.....................Sorbonne

Great Britain:
W. G. Smith........Aberdeen, Edinburgh
C. Spearman....................London

Greece:
Th. Voreas......................Athens

Italy:
J. Fröbes.....................Gregorian

F. Kiesow.......................Turin

Poland:
A. Mahrburg...................Warsaw
W. Witwicki...................Warsaw

Russia:
V. Bekhterev.......Kazan, St. Petersburg

Switzerland:
E. Dürr.........................Bern
G. F. Lipps....................Zürich

United States:
F. Angell...............Cornell, Stanford
J. McK. Cattell....Pennsylvania, Columbia
H. Gale......................Minnesota
G. S. Hall..........Johns Hopkins, Clark
C. H. Judd.....................Chicago
E. A. Pace....................Catholic
G. T. W. Patrick..................Iowa
R. Pintner....................Columbia
W. D. Scott................Northwestern
E. W. Scripture............Yale, Vienna
G. M. Stratton................California
G. A. Tawney.....................Beloit
E. B. Titchener................Cornell
H. C. Warren..................Princeton
L. Witmer..................Pennsylvania
H. K. Wolfe...................Nebraska

REFERENCES

WILHELM WUNDT
Accounts of Wundt's contribution to psychology may be read in:
Feldman, S. Wundt's psychology. *Amer. J. Psychol.*, 1932, *44*, 615–629.
Hall, G. S. *Founders of modern psychology.* New York: Appleton, 1912. Pp. 311–458.
Stratton, G. M. Wundt and Leipzig in the Association's early days. *Psychol. Rev.*, 1943, *50*, 68–70.
Titchener, E. B. Wilhelm Wundt. *Amer. J. Psychol.*, 1921, *32*, 161–178.
Accounts of Wundt's students can be found in:
Fernberger, S. W. Wundt's doctorate students. *Psychol. Bull.*, 1933, *30*, 80–83.
Tinker, M. Wundt's doctorate students and their theses, 1875–1920. *Amer. J. Psychol.*, 1932, *44*, 630–637.

The various tributes written by Wundt's American students at the time of his death may be found in:
In memory of Wilhelm Wundt. *Psychol. Rev.*, 1921, *28*, 153–188.
THE LEIPZIG LABORATORY
Boring, E. G. On the subjectivity of important historical dates: Leipzig 1879. *J. Hist. behav. Sci.*, 1965, *1*, 5–9.
Cattell, J. McK. The psychological laboratory at Leipzig. *Mind*, 1888, *13*, 37–51.

WUNDT'S WRITINGS
Listings of Wundt's books and articles are presented in *Amer. J. Psychol.*, 1908, 1909, 1910, and 1911. (Titchener, E. B. and Geissler, L. R.); 1912, 1913, and 1914, (Titchener, E. B., and Foster, W. S.); and 1922 (Titchener, E. B., and Feldman, S.).

8

Pioneers of Psychology in Germany

IN THE LATE NINETEENTH CENTURY the flurry of activity and excitement at Leipzig continued. Students kept coming from around the world to this first laboratory for training. Having received it, they returned to their own countries to institute scientific psychology. With the establishment of similar laboratories in many lands, Wundt's was no longer unique. The new science was developing and progressing rapidly.

Not only were Leipzig-trained psychologists altering and expanding the psychology that they had brought back from Wundt, but in Germany itself, concurrent with the developments of Wundt's psychology, certain lines of cleavage emerged. There were other German psychologists, like Ebbinghaus, working entirely independently. Other laboratories were also developed on German soil, some of which vied with Leipzig in quality of research and students. The contributions of these laboratories and of Wundt's German contemporaries were substantial. A history of the pioneering epoch of German experimental psychology would not be complete without consideration of men such as Brentano, Stumpf, Ebbinghaus, Külpe, and G. E. Müller.

FRANZ BRENTANO

Brentano merits particular consideration since his psychology was the first formal opposition to Wundt. Although predominantly a philosopher, Franz Brentano (1838-1917) won distinction in the new psychology largely because of his 350 page volume, *Psychologie vom empirischen Standpunkte* ("Psychology from an Empirical Standpoint") published in 1874. Brentano intended to write a second volume but never realized this ambition. In his published book, which Titchener called "a masterly and 'masterful work" and "one of the most logical products of the human mind," Brentano described his views on the subject matter and methodology of psychology.

Brentano and Wundt. The reader has probably noted that the year of publication of Brentano's *Psychology from an Empirical Standpoint*, 1874, was also the year in which Wundt's *Principles of Physiological Psychology* was completed. More significant than the simultaneous publication of these books was the divergent stands toward psychology which they assumed. Brentano's system, which considered psychic processes as acts, stood in sharp contrast to Wundt's content psychology. It was a functionally oriented psychology.

Both Brentano and Wundt wanted to establish psychology as a science. In spite of identical purposes, their approaches were markedly different.

In constructing his system Brentano offered logical proofs and arguments. He used the data of observation mainly, but he did not object to experimentation. Brentano's psychology is empirical. Wundt's is experimental. Empirical psychology's domain is vast, encompassing experimental psychology within it. The empirical psychologist can use casual observation, his own experience, or experimentation, separately or in combination. Using description and occasional logical argument, Wundt presented anatomical and physiological facts, and to these he added the findings of psychological and psychophysical experiments.

The types of exposition used by Wundt and Brentano also differed markedly. Brentano presented his views in dogmatic fashion, with an air of finality that left little room for alteration and modification. On the other hand, Wundt gave the impression that further modification was necessary and could be expected. The numerous revisions of his writings gave ample proof that he felt the need for continual change and modification. As a line of opposition to Wundt and in its own right, act psychology attracted attention and assumed a place of importance in the history of psychology.

Act Psychology. Brentano was an ardent disciple of Aristotle, for whom he had a keen appreciation as a result of his association with F. A. Trendelenburg (1802-1872), his philosophy professor at Berlin. The Aristotelian influence and the effect of his thorough training in Scholastic philosophy in preparation for the Catholic priesthood (which Brentano later abandoned) are reflected in his act psychology. The latter also bears the empirical and naturalistic mark of Trendelenburg's influence.

In his analysis of mental process, Brentano distinguished between act and content. For example, there is a distinction between the *act* of hearing and the thing heard, or the *content* of hearing. For Brentano, psychology is the science of psychical phenomena or acts. Acts are of three kinds: ideating acts, judging acts, and loving-hating acts. Into all of these acts, objects are intentionally incorporated. Brentano's act psychology is an intentionalism according to which mind is viewed as comprising mental acts, which are intentionally directed upon some object. For example, hearing is a mental act. It must have some object, like a tone. The hearing "intends" the tone, which "inexists" within the hearing. The tone is the "immanent object" of the hearing. This intentional inexistence was the "immanent objectivity" of Aristotle and the Scholastics. Brentano's "acts" always have objects or contents, and acts can become the objects of other acts.

In his system Brentano made a distinction between perception and observation. Mental experience can only be perceived, but reality can be both perceived and observed. Sensory stimulation offers the material aspect of psychic acts, but meaning is created by the mind in the form of an image or idea. For the mind, intentional existence is the only real existence. Physical phenomena are known only through intentional existence, and intentional creations—that is, perceptions—are the mind's view of reality.

In the sense that Brentano's act psychology studies acts logically, it can even be considered applied logic. Its affinity to logic made act psychology particularly attractive to philosophers. But probably for the same reason the experimentally minded psychologists were inclined to shun it. Brentano had a powerful influence in Austria and Germany. His influence also extended to British psychology, principally to James Ward who followed Brentano's leadership.

Brentano and the History of Psychology.   Although act psychology offered a challenge to him, Wundt continued to be the patriarch of German psychology in the early period. His literary output, for one thing, was enormous, and his writings kept him in the public eye. By comparison, Brentano's psychological writings were meager. With the exception of three papers on optical illusions, Brentano published no other significant psychological writings. In 1907 he wrote a volume on sensory psychology entitled *Untersuchungen zur Sinnespsychologie* ("Investigations in Sensory Psychology"). In 1911, *Von der Klassifikation der psychischen Phänomene* ("Concerning the Classification of Psychic Phenomena") was published as a supplement to his *Psychology from an Empirical Standpoint*. Ultimately, Brentano's psychology advanced the development of phenomenology in Germany.

By force of his personality, principally, Brentano attained prestige. He attracted to him many gifted students, some of whom figured prominently in the history of psychology. Among these were Edmund Husserl, who formally established phenomenology; Alexius Meinong, founder of the first Austrian laboratory at Graz in 1894; Christian von Ehrenfels, well known for his form-quality concept (Gestaltqualität), a precursor of Gestalt psychology; Sigmund Freud, the founder of psychoanalysis; and finally Carl Stumpf, who applied experimentation to act psychology.

CARL STUMPF

Life.   After coming under Brentano's influence at Würzburg, Carl Stumpf (1848-1936) went to Göttingen at Brentano's suggestion for further study in philosophy with Lotze. Here he received his doctorate (1868) and two years later went back to Göttingen where he remained as Dozent for three years. About this time he became acquainted with E. H. Weber and Fechner. In 1873 he returned to Würzburg as professor. Thereafter Stumpf made several changes in academic affiliation. Following six years at Würzburg, he held the chair of philosophy at Prague (1879) for five years. Thereafter, he spent five years each at Halle and Munich, beginning in 1884 and 1889, respectively. In 1894 he went to his last post, Berlin. Here he remained until his retirement in 1921, when he was succeeded by Wolfgang Köhler. During his period at Berlin, Stumpf also served as rector of the university (1907-1908).

At Munich, Stumpf acquired apparatus and set up his first experimental laboratory at which he was able to pursue investigations in acoustics. At

Berlin, on the other hand, when Stumpf arrived to accept the most coveted chair of philosophy in all Germany, Ebbinghaus was there as Dozent. The latter already had a modest laboratory which Stumpf further expanded into an institute. Not an enthusiastic experimentalist, Stumpf left the details of experimentation to his assistants, among the better known of whom were F. Schumann and N. Ach. During his early years at Berlin, Stumpf was active professionally serving, for example, as joint president with T. Lipps at the Third International Congress of Psychology at Munich in 1896.

Stumpf and the New Psychology. In several respects Stumpf opposed the dominant tendencies in the German psychology of his day. He preferred interactionism to the psychophysical parallelism supported by Wundt and Ebbinghaus. Stumpf recognized the limitations of the Darwinian interpretation of development. Child psychology and animal psychology he wholeheartedly endorsed. He did only incidental research in both fields, in one case a study of the language development of his own son; in the second, a study of Der Kluge Hans, the horse which could solve mathematical problems. But he promoted and encouraged research in these fields. He supported the founding of an association for child psychology, *Verein für Kinderpsychologie*, and gave valuable assistance to Köhler in the latter's research on the anthropoid apes in Tenerife.

Stumpf, always independently of Wundt, pursued his work in psychology, chiefly in language and music. In the latter area he produced his most important work, *Tonpsychologie* ("Psychology of Tone"), begun in 1875 and completed in 1890. By and large, Stumpf was basically a philosopher. He never abandoned the philosophical approach he learned from Brentano, but used psychology to explain philosophy. For him philosophy and psychology were in close relationship. Through him the influence of Aristotle on psychology was transported to Berlin from southern Germany. Early in his career Stumpf concerned himself with the study of phenomena, such as tones. Later his interests shifted to functions and acts, and in this later work the influence of Brentano became more pronounced. Stumpf distinguished between functions and contents—between the act of hearing and the thing heard. In his opinion, functions and contents could vary independently. The study of functions, he insisted, belonged to psychology; the study of content, to phenomenology. Although he did considerable work in the latter field, he never considered himself a phenomenologist.

Imbued with respect for act psychology, Stumpf subjected it to experimentation. Through him the functional approach found expression in the German laboratory. His work represents a transition of psychology from a philosophical discipline to an empirical science. Because of his prestige at Berlin, Stumpf's endorsement of act psychology made functional psychology a vigorous opponent of Wundt's content psychology. Unlike Wundt, however, Stumpf was not a voluminous writer, nor did he compile a systematic psychology. Perhaps because of his stress upon method in the laboratory rather than upon the substance of thought, he inspired no students to carry out his doctrines. He gave students considerable freedom, but demanded clear thinking and logical precision. Among his students who became well known were the Germans—Köhler, Koffka, Poppelreuter, and von Allesch—and an American, Langfeld.

At the time of Stumpf's death in 1936 his contribution was summed up in one necrology as follows: "Psychologists venerate Stumpf together with Brentano as the founder of the school of functional psychology. It was he who broke loose from the mechanistic psychology of associations. Going beyond phenomenological psychology (perceptions and concepts) he created a functional psychology which gave science a new perspective."

HERMANN EBBINGHAUS

Hermann Ebbinghaus (1850-1909), like Brentano, was taught by Trendelenburg. He obtained the doctorate in philosophy (1873) at the University of Bonn. Unlike Brentano, however, Ebbinghaus was an ardent advocate of experimentation, and thus was influential in the development of psychology in Germany. At all the universities at which he taught he sought either to found or develop laboratories.

In the history of psychology Ebbinghaus stands out as an independent worker. His interest in experimental psychology stems from his discovering a copy of Fechner's *Elements of Psychophysics* in a Paris bookstall. He was particularly attracted by Fechner's application of mathematics to psychology. Ebbinghaus acknowledges his indebtedness to the eminent psychophysicist, Fechner, when he says in the dedication of his *Grundzüge der Psychologie* ("Principles of Psychology"), "ich hab' es nur von Euch" (I've gotten it only from you).

In 1880 Ebbinghaus became Dozent at the University of Berlin. There he established a laboratory from which in 1885 he published his famous *Über das Dedächtnis* ("On Memory"). In 1886 he became professor. It appears that Ebbinghaus was experimenting at Berlin before there were formal laboratories elsewhere in Germany, except at Leipzig. Leaving Berlin in 1894, he became professor at Breslau and also founded a laboratory there. Later on, in 1905, Ebbinghaus went to Halle, where he remained as professor of philosophy until his death (1909). At Halle he expanded the small laboratory. It will be recalled that Stumpf had been at Halle from 1884 to 1889, but apparently had not developed any laboratory.

Ebbinghaus possessed a high degree of intellectual acumen and an attractive personality—which made him an excellent lecturer. Toward his students he displayed kindness and genuine interest. As an editor, too, he is said to have had unusual tolerance, remaining calm and unruffled in the face of sincere opposition. In fact, he anticipated and encouraged objections and differences of opinion, especially from younger men. Ebbinghaus readily became a leader in the German organization of professional psychologists, the *Deutsche Gesellschaft für experimentelle Psychologie*

("German Society for Experimental Psychology"), at whose meetings he participated actively. His ability to enlist the cooperation of others was in evidence when with A. König he founded a journal, the *Zeitschrift für Psychologie und Physiologie der Sinnesorgane* ("Journal of Psychology and Physiology of the Sense Organs") in 1890. Helmholtz, Hering, von Kries, and Preyer, all physiologists, as well as the psychologists, T. Lipps, G. E. Müller, and Stumpf supported him in this publication enterprise. Wundt's *Philosophical Studies* furthered the interests of Leipzig and its students. The newer publication represented German psychological views and researches outside of Leipzig, and independent of Wundt.

Ebbinghaus had few followers and no outstanding pupils. He seemed to have no desire to found a school or to attract disciples. He did not foster close professional attachments of the type that would bind others into a school of psychology. Ebbinghaus himself did not affiliate with any school but simply pursued his interests independently. His main concern was to establish psychology on a quantitative and experimental basis. Neither physics nor biology was his starting point. He took associationism and to it applied a scientific experimental methodology. He was impressed with Fechner's psychophysics and with Fechner's careful experimental investigations of the sensory processes. Yet he directed his attention to the quantitative study of the mental processes and, in particular, to memory.

Memory Experiments. The best known of Ebbinghaus' accomplishments was his experimentation on memory. His volume, *On Memory*, previously mentioned, embodies the results of painstaking experiments many of which he did on himself. Convinced that the higher mental processes could be studied experimentally—the reader will recall that Wundt had denied that they could be studied by experiment—Ebbinghaus undertook the study and measurement of memory. He did the preliminary research in 1879 and 1880. Five years were devoted to this research.

In applying quantitative methodology to the investigation of learning and forgetting, Ebbinghaus demonstrated originality. In an effort to get subject matter devoid of previous associations for use in his experiments, he invented nonsense syllables. These are combinations of three letters, usually two consonants separated by a vowel, such as *nuv* and *tup*. Altogether Ebbinghaus devised about 2300 such meaningless syllables which he employed in his studies. In his investigations of memory he concentrated his attention chiefly on the acquisition and recall stages.

In this research he sought to answer the following questions: (1) How does the length of a list of nonsense syllables affect the speed with which it can be memorized? (2) What influence does the number of repetitions of a particular list exert upon retention? (3) How does time affect forgetting? (4) What effect do repetition and review have upon the subject's retention of previously studied material? (5) What kinds of connections are established in learning and what is their strength? Rigorous experimentation ultimately yielded answers to these questions. Despite the fact that Ebbinghaus served as subject for almost all of his own experiments, his results have been verified and substantiated by subsequent research.

As a result of learning lists of nonsense syllables of varying lengths up to the point of one errorless reproduction, Ebbinghaus discovered that more reading and additional time were needed, the longer the list. The longer the list of syllables, the more time was required per syllable. Second, Ebbinghaus found that, up to a certain point, overlearning—that is, repetition beyond mere mastery—increases retention. Frequent repetitions insure greater retention. Third, in studying the effect of time on retention he derived the curve of forgetting—or "curve of retention" as it is often called—which shows the general pattern of forgetting. The curve is characterized by a rapid drop immediately following learning, with a less rapid loss as time elapses. This curve was one of the significant early attempts in psychology to express experimental findings in mathematical form. Fourth, Ebbinghaus discovered that frequent reviews improve retention. The more often connections are exercised, the more firmly they become imbedded. Last, both forward and backward associations may be made, and repetitions make them strong.

Significance of Ebbinghaus' Memory Research.   This memory research so diligently executed by Ebbinghaus has been significant not only in psychology but also in education. Prior to his work, exact experimentation had dealt mostly with sensory problems. In this research a basic central function, memory, was subjected to measurement. Here again, as in Stumpf's studies, functional psychology was being promoted, rather than the content psychology of Leipzig. The memory experiments were well received generally, and were lauded in America by James and Titchener. In his famous *Principles* (1890), James referred to the "heroic nature" of the experimentation. James apparently was impressed with the great diligence and persistence with which Ebbinghaus designed his experiments and then learned lists of nonsense syllables, being careful to check his results by learning meaningful material also. Later, in 1910, Titchener commented: "It is not too much to say that the recourse to nonsense syllables, as a means to study association marks the most considerable advance in this chapter of psychology, since the time of Aristotle." Modern memory research continues to employ Ebbinghaus' methodology, especially the nonsense syllable technique.

Without doubt, the memory experiments and especially the volume, *On Memory*, which reported their results, were Ebbinghaus' chief contributions to scientific psychology. The memory investigations offered a starting point for research not only in memory but in the acquisition of skill. When work on memory was abandoned by Ebbinghaus, it was expanded and developed by G. E. Müller.

Other Contributions.   Ebbinghaus also devised the completion test as a technique of mental measurement. In 1897 he used this device while investigating the effects of fatigue and arrangement of working hours on school children in Breslau. The completion test, like the nonsense syllable, has found wide application in psychology and education. Ebbinghaus also made certain other contributions to German psychology and to psychology in general. His volume, *Grundzüge der Psychologie* ("The Principles of Psychology"), should be mentioned. It was a well-written book presenting a concise survey of contemporary literature in a strikingly lucid style.

Furthermore, Ebbinghaus' founding and editing of the *Zeitschrift* advanced German psychology during the vital period of the two decades after its inception. Ebbinghaus' strong faith in laboratory psychology, which expressed itself in the founding of two laboratories (Berlin, Breslau) and the development of a third (Halle), stimulated research outside of Leipzig. Finally, the firm insistence on the quantitative approach helped to pry German psychology a little freer from its philosophical moorings. Ebbinghaus was notably less preoccupied with philosophy than Wundt, Brentano, or Stumpf.

Evaluation. Ebbinghaus' achievements, although not extensive, were significant. He was a systematist. He made no attempt to formulate any theory or rational basis for his significant experimental findings on memory. His own life was short, and he lacked devoted students who could continue his work. He had few publications. Compared to Wundt in this respect, Ebbinghaus seems like an amateur. His continual desire to check, recheck, and revise his work delayed its completion and may in part account for his dearth of publications. *On Memory* (1885) was his *magnum opus*. The other items in his bibliography include some noteworthy pieces: three papers (1887-1890) treating the revision of the Weber-Fechner law and presenting a physiological interpretation to explain the inadequacy of the law at the extremes; a publication presenting his *Theorie der Farbensehen* ("Theory of Color Vision"), which was not favorably received; his previously mentioned *Principles*, the first volume of which appeared in 1902 and the second volume of which was published posthumously (1913); and last, in 1908, *Abriss der Psychologie* ("A Summary of Psychology"), a 200 page survey of psychology which went through many editions after Ebbinghaus' death. At the beginning of the *Abriss*, the author sketched the history of psychology. In the introduction appears the oft-quoted classic: "Psychology has a long past, but only a short history."

What Ebbinghaus' contemporaries felt about him can perhaps best be grasped by restating Titchener's comments on the occasion of the twentieth anniversary celebration of Clark University in 1909—an event which Ebbinghaus had been scheduled to attend. His untimely death deprived the audience of the opportunity of hearing his address. In speaking of the German memory researcher, Titchener said: "There was about Ebbinghaus a sort of masterfulness; he never did violence to facts, but he marshalled them; he made them stand and deliver; he took from them, as of right all that they contained; and with the tribute thus exacted he built up his theories and his system. . . ."

Ebbinghaus' significance lies in large part in the fact that he represented a line of development independent of Wundt—even a kind of experimental psychology that Wundt opposed. His importance attaches to his concern for, and application of, controlled experimentation and experimental design. His model experiments have remained classics in the history of psychology.

OSWALD KÜLPE

The youngest of the early German psychologists was Oswald Külpe (1862-1915), and of all of these pioneers he also had the shortest life. Wundt, Brentano, Stumpf, G. E. Müller, and Ebbinghaus were all his seniors. Of these, only Ebbinghaus preceded him in death. In evaluating Külpe's role in German psychology one may well keep in mind, therefore, that his productive years and the years of his influence were considerably fewer than those of the previously discussed psychologists.

In the light of his chronology one can understand that when Külpe undertook the study of psychology there were laboratory facilities available. He had the advantage of studying with Wundt and with G. E. Müller, whom he rated second to Wundt in the formation of his career. As a student he had at his disposal textbooks of psychology such as Wundt's *Principles of Physiological Psychology* and Brentano's *Psychology from an Empirical Standpoint*. When he started his work in psychology, journals were available, such as the British *Mind* (1876), Wundt's *Philosophische Studien* (1881), the *American Journal of Psychology* a little later (1887), and then the *Zeitschrift für Psychologie und Physiologie der Sinnesorgane* (1890). Thus Külpe entered psychology at a time when the science had already progressed considerably. He therefore cannot be considered a pioneer in quite the same sense as the other German psychologists whom we have just been discussing.

First, in 1881, Külpe went to Leipzig for a year. In 1883, he undertook his studies of three semesters' duration at Göttingen, starting his dissertation on feeling under Müller's direction. In 1886 Külpe returned to Wundt and Leipzig, remaining there for eight years and taking his degree in 1887. At Leipzig, he became Dozent and also—following Cattell's return to America—Wundt's second assistant. Thoroughly interested as he was in the new psychology, Külpe demonstrated remarkable fitness for experimental work, participating in the Leipzig research, which at the time centered chiefly on mental chronometry. In the early part of his career as an experimentalist, Külpe devoted himself to content psychology. Later, his interests shifted to functional psychology.

In 1894 Külpe accepted the call to a full chair at Würzburg in Bavaria. There, in 1896, he founded a laboratory which became a close competitor to Leipzig. After his departure from Leipzig, Külpe's influence became more extensive. In fact, in view of his attainments, he earned the title of second founder of experimental psychology on German soil. Of all Wundt's students, Külpe was the foremost in promoting the new psychology in Germany.

Külpe and Functional Psychology. At Würzburg, the psychology of thought previously neglected was to become Külpe's chief concern. Here he perfected psychological methodology and developed systematic introspection. In moving to Würzburg, Külpe did more than simply sever himself physically from Leipzig. His interests and endeavors turned to an area of which Wundt did not approve—that is, the psychological study of the higher thought processes. Now *functions*, not contents, became Külpe's chief concern. From these studies there emerged the well-known school of imageless thought, the Würzburg school. At Würzburg, Külpe's thought psychology leaned heavily toward functionalism. Thus it became far removed from Wundt's content psychology and American structuralism.

Promoter of Laboratory Psychology. After 15 years (1894–1909) Külpe moved to Bonn where he founded a laboratory. Later in 1913, when he went to Munich, he further expanded the laboratory developed there earlier by Stumpf. Thus Külpe extended laboratory psychology in Germany. Würzburg, Bonn, and Munich were all in Külpe's debt. Of these, however, in the history of psychology his name is most frequently identified with Würzburg because of the research on thought psychology conducted there under his inspiration.

Külpe's kindness, amiability, and pleasantness of personality won friendship from his contemporaries. By some he has been ranked next to William James as the most approachable figure among the psychologists of his day. Well-known contemporary psychologists were visitors to his laboratories, among whom were Michotte, Spearman, Gemelli, Frank Angell, Lillien Martin, and Pillsbury.

Külpe's Writings. While at Leipzig, Külpe began to consider writing a textbook, which he published in 1893, the *Grundriss der Psychologie* ("Outline of Psychology"), a volume which he dedicated to Wundt. It was in this book that Külpe first outlined his concept of psychology as the science of the facts of experience. Psychology's task, as he saw it, was to describe adequately those properties of the data of experience that depend upon the experiencing individual. In writing his *Outline of Psychology* Külpe treated with fair adequacy the sensations, feelings, the connection of the conscious elements and, much more briefly, the problem of attention. Not a single comment was made about thought. Will and self-consciousness were accorded cursory treatment.

After the *Outline* Külpe wrote numerous other books and articles which revealed a pronounced shift in interest toward philosophy and esthetics, although he continued to publish in psychology too. During his Würzburg period he published his *Einleitung in die Philosophie* ("Introduction to Philosophy," 1895) and also wrote on the objectivity of esthetic laws and the role of association in esthetic impression. *Die Philosophie der Gegenwart in Deutschland* ("Contemporary Philosophy in Germany") appeared in 1902, followed in 1907 by a volume on Immanuel Kant. In his psychological publications he discussed attention (1897) and psychophysics

(1902). For the G. Stanley Hall commemorative edition of the *American Journal of Psychology* (1907) he wrote a paper on experimental esthetics. Although in the last decade or so of his life Külpe wrote on philosophy primarily, significant research was being reported from the Würzburg laboratory by his students. These students are usually referred to as the Würzburg school.

THE WÜRZBURG SCHOOL: EXPERIMENTAL STUDY OF THE HIGHER THOUGHT PROCESSES

The Würzburg school was the logical result of Külpe's emphasis in 1893 on the role that the preparation or disposition plays in all reaction experiments. Külpe maintained that in these experiments the subjects' reactions vary according to the preparation of the subjects. The problem of a motivational variable was thus introduced. Further experimentation was undertaken in Külpe's laboratory to explore this problem. These experiments brought the Würzburg school closer to Brentano's act psychology and furthered German functionalism. Chronologically, the members of the Würzburg school are Mayer, Orth, Marbe, Watt, Ach, Messer, and Bühler.

The Würzburg school began in 1901 with the publication of a paper on the qualitative nature of association by A. Mayer and J. Orth. These investigators concluded that their subjects' responses depended upon conscious attitudes (*Bewusstseinslage*), which often had an affective tone. That is, the subjects' responses were dependent upon internal as well as external stimuli. With their research, thought came to be regarded as a series of associations amenable to study by the introspective method. In a later paper on feeling (1903) Orth argued that many mental contents are unanalyzable, indescribable, conscious attitudes.

Marbe's Investigation of Judgment (1901). Simultaneous with the Mayer and Orth publication of 1901, Karl Marbe (1869-1953) published his experimental study of judgment, which showed that much conscious content in judging was revealed by introspection but "no psychological conditions of judgment." Marbe's subjects, when making right judgments, did not know how these judgments got into their minds. Accordingly, Marbe's results signified to him that judgment is not the result of a conscious process, since he could find nothing in his subjects' introspections to indicate that their judgments could be explained by introspection. In fact introspection seemed to prove that the mind was an irrational chain of mental contents that somehow arrives at a rational conclusion. Therefore, Marbe concluded that judging must be something more than mental content. It must be related to the subject's purpose (*Absicht*) or attitude, which is more like an act and not conscious mental content. Two criteria, Marbe decided, were essential for judgment: the palpable content and the impalpable purpose of the subject.

Watt and the Experimental Study of Thought (1904). While Marbe considered only the subject's conscious experience, which occurs in the interval between the stimulus presentation and the response of judgment, H. J. Watt (1879-1925) in 1904 began a study of thought itself. He set specific problems for his subjects such as naming parts for wholes and the like. He made careful recordings of associative reaction times on the Hipp chronoscope, and, using the method of fractionation, Watt had his subjects introspect on their conscious experiences during the four following periods: (1) preparatory; (2) the appearance of the stimulus; (3) the search for the reaction; and (4) the occurrence of the reaction word. Instead of finding, as he suspected, that the third stage was significant for the thought process, he discovered that the preparatory stage held the key to the thought process. When the subject undertook the task in the preparatory period, the thought process would flow freely when the stimulus was presented. Watt, therefore, emphasized the problem (*Aufgabe*) or task which furnished the set in the preparatory period. Thus there were no describable mental contents, but there was a psychological factor, a conscious task, which determined the subject's thought process. Watt, just as Marbe, found that an extra-introspective factor determined the sequence of the thinking process.

Ach's Studies of Volition and Thought (1905). Elaborating on Watt's fractionation procedure, Narziss Ach (1871-1946) perfected the methodology of the thought investigations by developing systematic experimental introspection. "Systematic" presumably referred to fractionation and experimental to the use of the chronoscope. Using association words, Ach questioned his subjects about their experiences when thought passed from the passive to the volitional stage—that is, when the subject made the choice. From his subjects' introspections, Ach concluded that an imageless component, an awareness (*Bewusstheit*) was the determiner of thought, and that this awareness might be an awareness of meaning or of relations.

Messer's Thought Research (1906). Unlike Marbe, Watt, and Ach, August Messer (1867-1937) had no specific purpose which systematically permeated his studies. He employed a variety of problems in his exploration of the thought process by means of introspection. Using the method of free and constrained associations, he concluded that certain psychic processes underlie mental content. Messer found that his subjects experienced both emotional and cognitive attitudes in addition to having certain mental impressions in their minds. Messer's conscious attitudes (*Bewusstseinslage*) are like the imageless thought of Külpe and are similar to Marbe's purpose (*Absicht*), Ach's awareness (*Bewusstheit*), and Watt's task (*Aufgabe*).

Buhler and the Imageless Thought Controversy (1907-1908). In 1907, Karl Bühler (1879-1963) came to Würzburg from Berlin and published three papers on thought. Bühler's studies represent the culmination of the Würzburg investigations. In studying the actual experience of thinking, Bühler introduced a special manner of questioning subjects for their introspections *(Ausfragemethode)*. He used six different types of questions to get every bit of introspectable data during thinking. From his researches Bühler discovered that thought lacked sensory factors, feelings, and attitudes. Thoughts were elements which were devoid of sensory quality or intensity, but did possess clearness, assurance, and vividness. In Bühler's estimation, images were too fleeting and spotty to be essential to thought. Thoughts could be accompanied by images or not. Even where images do occur, if they fade, thought does not become less lucid. Thought is goal directed and creative. It has a task and seeks a solution to a problem. Bühler observed that the laws governing the thought process are not identical with the laws of image association. He insisted that psychologists had to reckon with thought elements, in addition to other structural elements—sensations, images, and feelings—because the thought elements furnished the content of the thinking process.

Toward the end of the first decade of the twentieth century, after Bühler's studies on imageless thought were published, a real controversy raged. In France, Binet claimed priority for the initial observations on imageless thought (1903). In America, Woodworth made this same finding independently.

Imageless thought received a poor reception from Wundt. He criticized the Würzburg studies as mock experiments. Some of his criticisms were actually indictments of the introspective method, although he may have been justified in citing that suggestion was at work. It will of course be recalled that Wundt always objected to the experimental study of the higher thought processes. G. E. Müller also opposed the Würzburg school, criticizing particularly "the determining tendency" as mere perseveration. In America, Titchener likewise rejected the new thought elements. He argued that the subjects in the imageless thought studies reported their experiences, but did not really describe the contents of their experiences. Although Külpe answered the attacks of "imageless thought" critics, his own pronouncements on thought psychology were really few, except for a single somewhat popular article on modern psychology of thinking. In 1909, when Külpe moved to Bonn, the Würzburg school ended.

Significance of Külpe and the Würzburg School. Külpe and the Würzburg psychologists were important not only because they investigated subject matter untouched by Wundt—namely, the higher mental processes—but because by studying thought they were focusing attention on a function and a process. From the outset they employed a systematic methodology in their investigations which failed to find palpable content that could be considered thought. Their research, like that of Ebbinghaus and Stumpf, leaned heavily toward functionalism. The findings of Marbe, Watt, Ach, Messer, and Bühler stressed that thought processes are represented by psychological criteria other than mental content. These psychological criteria emphasize the process nature of thought and are analogous to Brentano's mental acts. Thus the Würzburg school helped to set up a clearer differentiation between the act and content psychologists in Germany, resembling the opposition between the functionalists and structuralists in America. Moreover, the Würzburg experiments stressed purposiveness and wholeness, rather than the elementistic, atomistic approach of Wundt and the associationists. In this emphasis on the synthetic rather than the analytic approach, they paved the way for Gestalt and field theories. The influence of the Würzburg school on psychological theory and on experimental research during the first quarter of the twentieth century was more significant than their actual research findings.

GEORG ELIAS MÜLLER

In considering German psychologists outside Leipzig, reference must again be made to one whose research and writings were described in an earlier chapter in connection with psychophysics and laboratories, Georg Elias Müller (1850-1934). He obtained his doctorate at Göttingen under Lotze, and after brief academic affiliations at Leipzig, Berlin, Göttingen, and Czernowitz, he succeeded Lotze at Göttingen, where he remained the guiding spirit for 40 years. What was probably more characteristic of Müller than of any of his German contemporaries was that he was highly systematic and exact in his investigations on memory, vision, and psychophysics. His rigorous experimental studies gained favor for him and easily made the Göttingen laboratory a close competitor to Leipzig.

Unlike Ebbinghaus, who was not surrounded by distinguished students, Müller attracted many students who later became prominent psychologists. The roster of Göttingen-trained students includes several distinguished psychologists: *Adolph Jost*, whose well-known research on the strength of association was reported from Göttingen in 1897; *David Katz*, whose early investigations on the perception of color and space emanated from Müller's laboratory; *E. R. Jaensch*, known for his work on eidetic imagery; *Lillien Martin*, his American student who became professor of psychology at Stanford University, and *E. Rubin*, celebrated for his study of figure, ground, contour, and visual perception. Müller gave his students inspiration and sound training. It is said of him that he himself served as subject in each and every investigation at Göttingen. Thus apart from his previously mentioned research on memory, vision, and psychophysics, Müller advanced psychology through the stimulation which he gave to his students and through the excellent laboratory which he directed.

For at least 20 years Müller managed the activities of the psychological organization, *Deutsche Gesellschaft für experimentelle Psychologie*, whose establishment he had promoted. His contemporaries respected him and had confidence in him because of his fairmindedness. After Wundt died (1920) and extensive inroads into German psychology had been made by the Gestalt school, Müller was looked to as the venerable custodian of the older introspective psychology.

EARLY GERMAN PSYCHOLOGY: A SUMMARY

In spite of their keen interest in experimentation, the German psychologists maintained a close proximity to philosophy. Of this affinity of German psychology to philosophy Kurt Lewin said, ". . . it seems to me that psychology in Germany never lost entirely the somewhat apologetic aspect, a kind of inferiority complex toward its master, philosophy." Although there was a strong attachment to philosophy, German psychology made rapid progress. Among the pioneering German psychologists there was a probing of more involved problems for which experimental techniques did not always yield answers. However, they had a great enthusiasm to establish a body of carefully proven facts.

Within the decade after the founding of the Leipzig laboratory, numerous other laboratories were either founded or projected. Actual laboratories were established at Göttingen by Müller, at Berlin and Breslau by Ebbinghaus, at Bonn by T. Lipps, at Freiburg by Münsterberg, and at Würzburg by Külpe. In the early nineties there was no formal laboratory at Munich, but apparatus was available for experimental research. Experimentation was done during the same period at Heidelberg, Halle, and Strassburg, although no real laboratories existed at these universities. So much research was conducted in Germany outside the Leipzig laboratory that several independent workers such as Ebbinghaus, G. E. Müller, Stumpf, Hering, Helmholtz, von Kries, and Preyer organized a second German psychological journal, the *Zeitschrift für Psychologie und Physiologie der Sinnesorgane*. Until the founding of this Journal in 1890, Wundt's *Philosophische Studien* was the only publication German psychology had. Literary productivity in psychology steadily increased as can be judged by the numerous books written during this period, such as Ebbinghaus' *On Memory* and *Principles of Psychology*; Stumpf's *Psychology of Tone*; Külpe's *Outline of Psychology*; and of course Wundt's many volumes.

The increasing diversity of interests in German psychology is reflected in the numerous articles which appeared in the journals during the eighties and nineties. In Wundt's laboratory the research concentrated mainly on sensation, perception, and reaction time. First at Prague, then at Halle, Munich, and Berlin, Stumpf pursued his psychological study of music. Early in the eighties Ebbinghaus performed his quantitative memory research which provoked considerable subsequent experimentation, especially that of G. E. Müller at Göttingen in the nineties. Finally, at the turn of the century and in the first decade of the twentieth century, thought psychology came into prominence at Würzburg under Külpe. Child study was fostered by Preyer, who earned the title of "father of child psychology," and was encouraged by Stumpf who assisted in the foundation of the *Verein für Kinderpsychologie*. The early twentieth century also witnessed organizational activity among professional psychologists. Especially significant was the founding of the *Deutsche Gesellschaft für experimentelle Psychologie* (1904).

With Müller's death in 1934, and Stumpf's in 1936, German psychology definitely came to the end of an era. Ebbinghaus, Külpe, Brentano, and

Wundt, all had passed away before. Each of them had been a frontiers-man, a pioneer in the task of subjecting mind to experimental investiga-tion. Each man in his unique way through qualities of intellect, person-ality, or both, made a singular contribution to the progress of psychology.

PIONEERS OF PSYCHOLOGY IN GERMANY: A SUMMARY

PIONEER	UNIVERSITY	AREAS OF STUDY	SIGNIFICANCE
Franz Brentano (1838–1917)	Würzburg Vienna	Empirical psychology	Developed *act* psychology in opposition to Wundt's *content* psychology; pre-cursor of phenomenology.
Carl Stumpf (1848–1936)	Göttingen Würzburg Prague Halle Munich Berlin	Psychology of music and tone	Psychological theorist who subjected act psychology to experimentation, promoting functional psychology.
Hermann Ebbinghaus (1850–1909)	Berlin Breslau Halle	Learning and memory	Initiated experimental study of learning and memory; employed quantitative methods; invented nonsense syllables and completion type test.
Oswald Külpe (1862–1915)	Leipzig Würzburg Bonn Munich	Psychology of thought	Studied higher mental pro-cesses experimentally; direc-ted Würzburg school fa-mous for studies of image-less thought.
Georg Elias Müller (1850–1934)	Czernowitz Göttingen	Memory Vision Psychophysics	Developed and systema-tized psychophysical meth-ods; second only to Wundt as a "power and institu-tion" in Germany.

REFERENCES

FRANZ BRENTANO

Barclay, J. R. Franz Brentano and Sigmund Freud. *J. Existentialism*, 1964, *5*, 1–36.

Barclay, J. R. Themes of Brentano's psychologi-cal thought and philosophical overtones. *New Scholast.*, 1959, *33*, 300–318.

Puglisi, M. Brentano: a biographical sketch. *Amer. J. Psychol.*, 1924, *35*, 414–419.

Sussman, E. J. Franz Brentano—much alive though dead. *Amer. Psychologist*, 1962, *17*, 504–506.

Titchener, E. B. Brentano and Wundt: empirical and experimental psychology. *Amer. J. Psy-chol.*, 1921, *32*, 108–120.

Titchener, E. B. Empirical and experimental psy-chology. *J. gen. Psychol.*, 1928, *1*, 176–177.

CARL STUMPF

Langfeld, H. S. Carl Stumpf: 1848–1936. *Amer. J. Psychol.*, 1937, *49*, 316–320.

Nadoleczny, M. Death of Carl Stumpf. *J. Speech Dis.*, 1938, *3*, 76–80.

Stumpf, C. Autobiography. In C. Murchison (Ed.), *A history of psychology in autobiography.* Vol. 1. Worcester, Mass.: Clark Univer. Press, 1930. Pp. 389–441.

HERMANN EBBINGHAUS
Ebbinghaus, H. *Über das Gedächtnis.* Leipzig: Duncker & Humblot, 1885. Trans. by H. A. Ruger & Clara E. Bussenius, *Memory: a contribution to experimental psychology.* New York: Teachers College, Columbia Univer. Press, 1913. Reprinted by Dover, New York, 1964.
Garrett, H. *Great experiments in psychology.* (3rd ed.). New York: Appleton-Century-Crofts, 1951. Pp. 101–126.
Shakow, D. Hermann Ebbinghaus. *Amer. J. Psychol.*, 1930, *42*, 505–518.

OSWALD KÜLPE AND THE WÜRZBURG SCHOOL
Humphrey, G. *Thinking.* New York: Wiley, 1951. Paperbound edition, 1963. Pp. 30–131.

Mandler, Jean M., & Mandler, G. *Thinking: from association to Gestalt.* New York: Wiley, 1964.
Ogden, R. M. Oswald Külpe and the Würzburg School. *Amer. J. Psychol.*, 1951, *64*, 4–19.

G. E. MÜLLER
Boring, E. G. Georg Elias Müller, 1850–1934. *Amer. J. Psychol.*, 1935, *47*, 344–348.
Katz, D. Georg Elias Müller. *Psychol. Bull.*, 1935, *32*, 377–380.

LABORATORIES
Cattell, J. McK. Early psychological laboratories. *Science*, 1928, *67*, 543–548.
Krohn, W. O. Facilities in experimental psychology at the various German universities. *Amer. J. Psychol.*, 1892, *4*, 585–594.
Krohn, W. O. The laboratory of the Psychological Institute at the University of Göttingen. *Amer. J. Psychol.*, 1893, 5, 282–284.

9

German Psychology
in the Twentieth Century

AFTER 1900 THERE WAS A STEADY DECLINE of scientific psychology in Germany, and a pronounced trend toward a qualitative psychology, concerned more with kinds of experience and qualitative study than with quantitative evaluation, appeared. During the first two decades of the twentieth century some significant researches, however, were conducted. In addition to the Würzburg studies were the studies of attention by *Wilhelm Wirth* (1876-1952) of Leipzig; the social and cultural psychological researches of the physician *Willy Hellpach* (1877-1955) at Heidelberg; and the experiments on the effects of the group on an individual's work performance by *Walther Moede* (1888-1958) of the Technische Hochschule in Berlin. Dissatisfaction with elementistic psychology patterned after natural science mounted steadily, and in the 1920's a crisis developed in German psychology. This crisis was created principally by two earlier currents of German psychological thinking: experience psychology (*Erlebnispsychologie*) and cultural science psychology (*geisteswissenschaftliche Psychologie*). Experience psychology, as we have seen, was cultivated by Stumpf and Külpe who took inspiration from Brentano and Husserl. It emphasized the subjective aspects in its study of experience: phenomena and psychical functions. On the other hand, cultural science psychology, promoted by Dilthey, emphasized the critical study of man in society. In its intuitive study of the works of humanity, cultural science psychology regarded man as a unit and as the expression of human character and led to a psychology of personality. Both currents of psychological thinking molded and produced a new kind of psychology radically different from the nineteenth century physiological psychology.

THE IMPACT OF CULTURAL SCIENCE PSYCHOLOGY

As the cleavage between natural science and cultural science psychology became more marked in the early twentieth century, a personalistic aspect, or totality aspect, became pronounced in German psychology. Typological and characterological studies flourished. Educational, vocational, and clinical applications of psychology were initiated. Experimental psychology was still represented in studies of sensation, perception, and the higher thought processes, but their findings were often related to typology and characterology. The influence of Wundt on method, problems, and solutions almost disappeared.

By the 1920's, natural science psychology lost its firm control and its status in German universities. Cultural science psychology gained prestige and vitality. A multiplicity of new theories appeared, but there was almost no concern for their experimental verification or validation. German psychology was infused with a romantic, nationalistic idealism which made it subjective, qualitative, and speculative. After 1933, scientific psychology in Germany virtually collapsed under the impact of Nazism. Although some psychologists tried to preserve their scientific integrity, others yielded to Nazi ideology. Furthermore, several prominent psychologists, especially the founders of the Gestalt school, left Germany. Germany's loss was a gain for those countries to which they retreated, notably the United States. Among those who left Germany and Austria at that time were many psychoanalysts and psychiatrists as well—including Freud who went to London. Freudian psychoanalysis had never been well received in Germany, and even after 1933 the campaign against Freud was perpetuated by Krueger and Ach.

Understanding Psychology and Wilhelm Dilthey. Although the philosopher Wilhelm Dilthey (1833-1911) announced his cultural science psychology in the 1880's, the principal effects of its impact were not felt until early twentieth century. Dilthey charged that laboratory psychology was inadequate to understand man. He was particularly opposed to the "new" psychology represented by Ebbinghaus, whose explanatory psychology he attacked as atomistic. Atomistic psychology simply could not perceive man as a whole—which Dilthey insisted was essential to a valid psychology. Dilthey cited the limitations of introspection in probing the inner life and motives of men, and in exploring cultural phenomena and history. Introspection's incapacity to study the higher thought processes had, it will be remembered, been acknowledged by Wundt. Wundt had sharply criticized Külpe's experiments on thinking as "mock experiments" because he believed that the higher thought processes had to be studied through the history of civilization in its social institutions, religion, art, and the like.

According to Dilthey, the proper method for psychology is understanding (*Verstehen*), since psychology must study the totality of mental life. Only through the process of understanding can one be made constantly conscious of the relation of parts to a whole. In 1894, Dilthey called for a descriptive or "understanding" psychology rather than an explanatory psychology in his *Ideen über eine beschreibende und zergliedernde Psychologie* ("Ideas Concerning a Descriptive and Analytical Psychology"). This cultural science psychology begins with an articulated whole (*Strukturzusammenhang*) and tries to describe the various aspects of the totality analytically; while natural science psychology begins with elements and establishes causal connections. Cultural science psychology *understands*, natural science psychology *explains*, was Dilthey's theme. Dilthey believed that if the human mind was to be understood by the psychologist, psychology had to be brought closer to history, art, literature, and ethics. Moreover, he regarded psychology as fundamental to all cultural sciences. Dilthey's sharp distinction between the natural science and cultural science approaches perplexed German psychologists for several decades. Nevertheless, Dilthey specifically prepared the way for those psychologies which made the dynamic unity—that is, the *structure* of mind—their concern. His "understanding" psychology emphasized the dynamic nature of this structure and the uniqueness of growth of each individual structure. Dilthey's psychology was implemented principally by Spranger. Moreover, its attack on elementism and mechanism paved the way for the psychologies of Krueger, Stern, and the Gestalt school, as well as for depth psychology, Klages' characterology, and Jaensch's typology, all of which are fundamentally organismic.

Spranger's Types. In the philosopher Eduard Spranger (1882-1963), Dilthey found an ardent disciple. At Berlin, Spranger assiduously dedicated himself to the "understanding" psychology. Using intuitive rather than laboratory methods, he studied the whole individual, the situation in which he lives, and his goals and values. He concerned himself with the study of personality of the individual as a whole in relation to his historical environment. Spranger named his psychology *Strukturpsychologie* (psychology of structure), in contrast to Wundt's elementistic psychology, because it treated each mental life as a unique structure without dissecting it.

In 1914, Spranger identified six human values or goals, apart from the biological goals of self-preservation and reproduction. His important volume, *Lebensformen: geisteswissenschaftliche Psychologie und Ethik der Persönlichkeit* ("Types of Men: The Psychology and Ethics of Personality"), lists these values or goals as: the theoretical or knowledge-seeking; the esthetic; the economic or practical; the religious; the social or sympathetic; and the practical or managerial. In discussing these goals, Spranger refers to types of men, such as the practical man or the religious man. These types are not construed by him as classes of distinct individuals. They are ideal type combinations which are blended in a given individual. Spranger's types have been criticized as arbitrary and as unrepresentative of the full range of human goals and motivation. His relation of the types to culture, however, makes them cultural types rather than personality types—and thus different from the typologies of Jaensch, Kretschmer, and Jung who concentrated on the empirical determination of types. Spranger's typology influenced the subsequent typologies of personality developed by G. W. Allport, Horney, and Lewin.

The Totality Psychology of Felix Krueger. Further implementation of Dilthey's psychology was expressed in the developmental psychology, or genetic holism, of Felix Krueger (1874-1948), Wundt's student and successor at Leipzig and a visiting professor at Columbia University (1912-1913). Krueger established the school of *Ganzheitspsychologie*, or totality psychology, which accepted the integrated whole as basic, but insisted that psychological facts be understood in the light of their development. The mental and physical must be studied as a unitary total. Furthermore, social conditions and cultural factors must be taken into account if the individual's development is to be thoroughly understood. The psychologist, Krueger contended, must keep in close relationship with the social sciences. He insisted that developmental psychology must furnish useful information to pedagogy, history, ethnology, and political economics. During his directorship of the Leipzig laboratory, Krueger did some experimental research on perception, but he extended his psychology beyond the laboratory to embrace the study of various cultural and social phenomena. Krueger's totality psychology has continued as a leading school in mid-twentieth century psychology and has contributed significantly to the scientific study of personality, in Germany. Well represented in the work of *Friedrich Sander* (b. 1889), recently retired from Bonn, and *Albert Wellek* (b. 1904), at Mainz, this "totality" school, also known as the Leipzig Gestalt School, went beyond the study of cognitive processes of the Berlin Gestalt School. It emphasized the totality of affective processes and the development of personality.

Personalistic Psychology—Stern's Synthesis.   At Hamburg, the scientist and humanist Wilhelm Stern (1871-1938) tried to bridge the gap between laboratory psychology and "understanding" psychology, between associationism and holism. In his three volume *Person und Sache: System der philosophischen Weltanschauung* ("Person and Thing: A Plan for a Philosophical World-View," 1906, 1918, 1924) Stern presented his synthesis. His personalistic psychology, which grew out of his recognition of the limitations of differential psychology, attempted to reconcile the scientific and philosophical approaches to the individual. For Stern, scientific psychology and personalistic philosophy necessarily belonged together. Personality presented a unit, a blending of the physical and mental, of heredity and environment. Stern regarded explanatory methods as essential to the study of the elements of personality, but thought that personality as a whole demanded description and understanding. The principal tenet of Stern's psychology is that every mental function is rooted in a *person*, and that person, not function, is the focus of personalistic psychology. The undivided totality (*unitas multiplex*) of person is of major importance in Stern's system.

Stern's versatile achievements illustrate the synthesis of natural science and culture science psychologies which he sought zealously to effect in Germany. From 1916 to 1933 Stern was director of the Hamburg Psychological Institute. He was the most influential psychologist in Germany at the time. His contributions were original, varied, and numerous. As a pioneer in differential psychology, he developed mental tests and devised the intelligence quotient for use with the Binet tests. He conducted systematic studies of the child and did researches in the psychology of testimony and clinical psychology. For many years Stern was Germany's chief authority in applied psychology. He organized the Hamburg Institute of Applied Psychology and also founded the *Zeitschrift für angewandte Psychologie* ("Journal of Applied Psychology") in 1907.

In 1933, this eminent German psychologist, president of the German Psychological Society at that time, was compelled under political pressure to resign his university post. Thereupon, Stern accepted an invitation to join the faculty of Duke University in the United States, where he died in 1938.

Gestalt Psychology.   Unlike Stern's personalistic psychology which concentrated on the person as a totality, Gestalt psychology focused on experience as a totality. Gestalt psychologists dealt primarily with perception, while Stern dealt with the perceiver. Since the Gestalt school is discussed more fully later, it is treated only briefly here.

Gestalt psychology originated in 1912 at the University of Frankfurt with the studies of apparent movement conducted by *Max Wertheimer* (1880-1943) and his observers, *Kurt Koffka* (1886-1941) and *Wolfgang Köhler* (b. 1887). Their emphasis on the Gestalt (whole), and on synthesis, emerged from their attempts to explain how an individual can perceive movement from the rapid projection of a series of still stimuli. Although the Gestalt principles were developed mainly in perception, they were later extended to learning and personality. After 1916, when Wertheimer went to the University of Berlin, which had nurtured Dilthey's "understanding" psychology and Spranger's typology, Berlin gradually became the center of Gestalt psychology. The new movement with its phenomenological approach to perception was encouraged by Stumpf who held the important chair of psychology at Berlin. Köhler became acting director of the laboratory in 1920, and upon Stumpf's retirement Köhler was named his successor in 1922. In the same year *Kurt Lewin* (1890-1947), famous for the psychology of personality and field theory which he subsequently developed, became Dozent at Berlin.

The tenets of Gestalt psychology stood in marked contrast to the earlier elementistic, analytic psychology. Naturally, the Gestalt school met with Wundt's opposition. With his passing they lost a vigorous opponent. In the 1920's Gestalt psychology gained prominence. By 1933 it was firmly established in Germany. With the rise of Nazism in the 1930's, however, its foremost leaders—Wertheimer, Köhler, and Lewin—left Germany and joined Koffka who had already gone to the United States in 1924. Thereafter, the scene of Gestalt psychological enterprises shifted to America.

Summary.   The psychologies of Spranger, Krueger, Stern, and the Gestalt school all emphasized the aspect of totality or wholeness. Spranger's psychology came closest to Dilthey's ideal of the "understanding" psychology. The Gestalt psychologists Krueger and Stern asserted that they were trying to preserve the best and the most vital of natural science psychology. Perhaps the interpenetration of physiology into Gestalt psychology lends some support for their claim, but the same cannot be said for Krueger or Stern. All were sympathetic to rigorous experimentation except Spranger, whose method was exclusively intuitive. The Gestalt psychologists did much experimentation; Krueger, a fair share, and Stern, a little. Generally speaking, these German psychologies of the first quarter of the twentieth century were characterized by a predilection for philosophy and a pronounced tendency to incorporate their speculations freely into their systems without experimental verifications.

Characterology.   The emphasis on structure or totality expressed itself in the development of a study of the structure of character, or characterology. Although the term characterology may be unfamiliar to many non-European psychologists, the field which characterology embraces corresponds roughly to what is known in America as the psychology of personality. Characterology views mind as a totality and as an expression of human character. It has been promoted in Germany as a psychology of individuality since the early twentieth century. Characterology emerged mainly from the experience of its proponents and not from the official psychology of the German universities, as did the previously discussed totality psychologies. Furthermore, there were two approaches—philosophical and scientific. The philosophical approach to characterology employed the cultural science methods of history, ethics, philosophy, and esthetics, while the scientific approach used natural science methods. For the total picture of human character both methods are essential. Philosophical characterology was developed by Klages and Spranger, whose work has already been described as a direct implementation of Dilthey's cultural science psychology. Scientific characterology emerged in the typologies of Jaensch, Kretschmer, and Jung.

Ludwig Klages and the Science of Expression.   *Ludwig Klages* (1872-1956) is generally acknowledged as the father of German characterology. Convinced of the worthlessness of physiological psychology for characterology, he attempted to cultivate a psychology or science of expression. More specifically, he tried to place the study of one type of expressive movement—handwriting—on a scientific basis, and to use graphology as a method of personality analysis.

Klages' interpretations of his findings stemmed largely from the unique intuitive philosophy which is basic to his science of expression. He regarded the soul as the meaning of the living body and the living body as the phenomenon of the soul. Personality is the singular locale where soul and body meet and fuse. The principle that personality is a system of dynamic relationships is fundamental to Klages' characterology. All actions of men are expressive, and the total and undivided personality is present in every action. To determine the individuality of expressive behavior, Klages maintained that one has to probe beyond the volitional aspects of the behavior, beyond conscious control, and beyond any evidence of skill or convention.

The type of expressive movement which Klages selected and developed as a psychodiagnostic tool was handwriting, because it afforded a permanent measurable record of volitional movement. Moreover, he was convinced that it necessarily carried the individual stamp of personality. Klages described his psychology of handwriting in several volumes. Among these are *Die Probleme der Graphologie* ("The Problems of Graphology"),

1910; *Handschrift und Charakter* ("Handwriting and Character"), 1928; and *Einführung in die Psychologie der Handschrift* ("Introduction to the Psychology of Handwriting"), 1928. As a result of Klages' inspiration and leadership, graphology became a significant psychodiagnostic method in Europe in the twentieth century. While graphology was originally ignored by the natural science psychologists, it gradually interested psychiatrists and applied psychologists. Eventually it found its way into German universities. Graphology was used in child guidance and vocational guidance, in industrial and clinical psychology. Characterological studies have been extended in other directions, too—such as physiognomy. Interest in graphology, however, continues to be strong in the second half of the twentieth century in Germany.

Typological Psychology. Parallel with this trend toward philosophical speculation about human nature and personality, there was a rise of interest in the description of personality types. Some prior inspiration for the systematic typologies derived from the classification of psychoses in Germany and of the neuroses in France, by Kraepelin and Janet respectively. In the 1920's two empirical typologies were developed, one by G. E. Müller's student, E. R. Jaensch, and the other by Kretschmer, a psychiatrist. We should also mention here the introvert-extrovert typology developed by Jung, although discussion of his analytical psychology, as well as of Adler's individual psychology and of Freud's depth psychology, is deferred until a later chapter.

At Marburg, *Eric R. Jaensch* (1883-1940), in collaboration with his brother, Walter Jaensch, investigated eidetic imagery, or perceptlike imagery. This research led to the postulation of two biotypes—the B-type and T-type—related to endocrine function. The B-type, a very vivid memory image subject to voluntary control, was associated with a hyperactive thyroid gland. The other biotype, resembling an afterimage and not under voluntary control, the T-type, was associated with underactivity of the parathyroid gland. Jaensch not only described the characteristics of eidetic types; he indicated their relation to clinical psychology and anthropology. Among his numerous publications there is a short book describing his typology: *Die Eidetik und die typologische Forschungsmethode* ("The Eidetic and Typological Method of Investigation," 1925, 2nd ed., 1927).

In subsequent revisions of this typology, the B-type and T-type were designated as integrate and disintegrate types. The integrate was plastic, concerned with the outer world, and characterized by an interpenetration of mental process. On the other hand, the disintegrate was rigid and had clearly differentiated mental processes. Although E. R. Jaensch did other research on visual perception, he is best known for the eidetic imagery investigation and for the typology to which it led. In its concern with the genetic interpretation of mental life, Jaensch's early research contributed to biological psychology rather than to the psychology of perception. However, whatever merit this typological system had in the 1920's, it was obliterated by the subsequent capitulation of the Jaensches to Nazism and by their accommodation of their typology to Nazi ideology.

In 1925, *Ernst Kretschmer* (1888-1964) described his typology in his book, *Körperbau und Charakter* ("Physique and Character"). Investigation of the physique and temperament of schizophrenic and manic-depressive patients led him to distinguish two psychotic personality types, the schizoid and the cycloid. The schizoid is quiet, reserved, serious, and humorless. The cycloid is good natured, friendly, and genial. When these traits are toned down and expressed normally, they are referred to as schizothymia and cyclothymia. The schizoid tends to have the leptosomic, or spindle-shaped, physique. The cycloid has the pyknic, or well-rounded, body build.

In both typologies, psychology and physiology were interrelated. Personality type was correlated with physiological or constitutional type. While the B- and T-types of the Jaensches emerged from experimental studies of eidetic imagery, Kretschmer's schizoid and cycloid types evolved from his clinical practice. Psychopathology found both typologies useful. However, as with all other typological systems before and since, these two suffered from obvious inability to account for the wide variability in human beings.

Decline of Scientific Psychology in the Universities.   Contemporaneous with the increased interest in cultural science psychology there was decreased interest in laboratory psychology in the 1920's and a decrease in academic recognition and support for psychological science in the German universities. In spite of the prestige of the pioneer German psychologists, several universities began to appoint philosophers and educators to vacant chairs of psychology. Psychology, as science, steadily lost prestige in the German academic world.

By 1929, a group of German psychologists including **Karl Bühler** (Vienna), **Wilhelm Stern** (Hamburg), **Narziss Ach** (Göttingen), **David Katz** (Rostock), **Johannes Lindworsky** (Prague), **Walther Poppelreuter** (Bonn-Aachen), and **Hans Volkelt** (Leipzig) pleaded for better academic consideration for psychology. Their formal statement was concomitant with their announcement of a name change for the *Gesellschaft für experimentelle Psychologie* to the *Deutsche Gesellschaft für Psychologie*. These distinguished psychologists called attention to the expanded activities of psychology and to the development of applied psychology in Germany. They insisted that pedagogy and pure philosophy had obtained the university chairs of psychology because of a complete misunderstanding of modern psychology. They cited experimental psychological research on higher mental functions, on character and temperament, on moral and religious life. They noted the behavioral, social, and genetic studies of man. Moreover, the increased significance of psychology for education, penology, industry, and medicine demanded, they felt, an increase in professional chairs of psychology to provide training for practical psychologists. These professional psychologists pointed to German psychology's close ties with the cultural sciences and its relations with the natural sciences. Failure to reinstate psychology in its proper position in the German university would ultimately damage German science, they predicted. But their zealous efforts to salvage scientific psychology in Germany could not ward off the devastating blow psychology was to suffer with the rise of the Nazi state.

After 1933, the tendency to ignore and condemn nineteenth century psychology grew. There was not only no encouragement of experimental psychology and research by the Nazi government; there was avowed and active hostility toward it. Moreover, in 1936, as we noted previously, Carl Stumpf, the last German pioneer of psychology, died. German scientific psychology was left without strong senior leadership. Consequently, Germany ceased to contribute to psychology with the advent of the Nazi regime.

PSYCHOLOGY UNDER THE NAZI REGIME

Psychology underwent pronounced changes in viewpoints and problems under the Third Reich. Psychology as science could not be freely pursued during the Nazi regime. At the universities some chairs of psychology were eliminated. Others were diverted to different academic disciplines. Free exchange of scientific information with other countries, such as the United States, was suppressed by rigid governmental control. From 1938 through the war years, German psychology was compelled to develop independently of outside influences. Subscriptions to foreign periodicals, for example, were discontinued. International travel was curtailed. During this period, German psychology mirrored the dominant Nazi social trends and ideology. The general effect of this distorted and artificially controlled atmosphere was a contamination of psychology with unscientific and irrational attitudes. Obviously more objective fields of psychology, like physiological psychology, were less influenced by Nazism than more theoretical areas. Test research, for example, was unable to flourish, since the results of objective psychological tests did not always support the Nazi doctrine of racial biological superiority. Personality study, too, was noticeably affected. Among German academic psychologists, graphology attained considerable popularity. After 1933, characterology and typology, with a definite political and nationalistic flavor, flourished. They bolstered Nazi political doctrine by reinforcing its cherished values concerning "born leadership" and racial superiority. Psychoanalysis, never well received in Germany, was vigorously opposed during the Nazi regime.

In general, German psychology in the Nazi period served practical governmental needs. Only those applications of psychology, which served political and pragmatic ends, were encouraged by the Nazi rulers of the Third Reich. A few psychologists tried desperately to pursue their scientific endeavors in spite of the political pressure. Some yielded. A few participated in the resistance movement. Several left Germany. Wertheimer, Lewin, and Köhler, as well as Stern, went to the United States. Katz went to Sweden, and Freud to England.

WORLD WAR II AND GERMAN PSYCHOLOGY

The complete disintegration of German psychology was probably averted by World War II. War activities demanded realistic attitudes and created needs for practical psychological services and personnel.

Psychological Services. Activities in the areas of military and industrial psychology were intensified for efficient conduct of the German war effort. Research was instituted on problems of fatigue, auditory acuity, noise, and the like. Selection and training procedures for military and industrial personnel were inaugurated. Both military and industrial psychology employed a variety of tests to measure intelligence, mechanical comprehension, manual ability, aptitudes, attention, and memory. Special tests were also constructed for the placement of foreign workers in industry. Throughout, however, military and industrial psychologists adopted a characterological orientation. Usually their approach was clinical rather than psychometric.

In the war years, as the manpower shortage became acute, industrial psychology attained a new prominence. Increased emphasis was accorded aptitude testing to insure the efficient placement of workers. In addition to the time and motion studies introduced in the thirties, industrial psychologists gave attention to job analyses and merit rating procedures. They devised industrial suggestion systems to capitalize on the talents and inventiveness of workers. The primary aim of such devices was to raise industrial morale.

Professional Training. The increased need for psychological services in industry and in the military created a demand for trained psychological practitioners. Accordingly, the German universities began in 1941 to offer an additional degree in psychology—namely, the diploma. The doctorate and the diploma required the same minimum training period of eight semesters. Both degrees were equivalent in respect to professional standards and admission to professional societies. In emphasis, however, the doctorate was academic; the diploma was professional. For the doctorate there were no required courses, no specific number of credits or specialized professional training. The diploma, which stressed the professional aspect in both requirements and in its examination, qualified its recipients for the practice of psychology. After World War II the German universities continued to offer the diploma.

POST-WORLD WAR II PSYCHOLOGY IN GERMANY

In 1945, when the Nazi power was overthrown, German psychologists encountered serious handicaps in rehabilitating their science and profession: (1) There was a shortage of trained personnel because of the loss of senior psychologists and the interruption of training programs during the war. (2) Laboratory facilities damaged by war had to be restored.

(3) German psychologists had to rejoin the psychological science field from which they had been isolated by Nazism. They had not received foreign books and journals. Most had not been in communication with psychologists of other lands or with German psychologists who had left their country. (4) New economic resources were required to restore psychology. For physical reconstruction and for employment of adequate qualified personnel in the universities, large sums of money were required.

Psychology's recovery in Germany has not been easily effected. Only gradually were university staffs and facilities reorganized. In 1947, the *Deutsche Gesellschaft für Psychologie* was re-established under the presidency of Stumpf's student *Johannes von Allesch* (b. 1882), now emeritus professor of Göttingen, who founded a journal, *Psychologische Rundschau* ("Psychological Review") in 1949. German journals, such as the *Zeitschrift für Psychologie* ("Journal of Psychology") and the *Zeitschrift für experimentelle und angewandte Psychologie* ("Journal of Experimental and Applied Psychology"), gradually re-established after the war, came back into circulation in other countries only very slowly. Various new journals, such as *Psychologische Beiträge* ("Psychological Contributions," 1953) were founded. While progress was slow, it was steady. In the following sections the status of contemporary German psychology will be discussed.

Trends in Contemporary German Psychology. Experimental psychology of the Wundtian type is practically unknown today. In fact, only a few universities are interested in laboratory experimentation as such. This experimentation is primarily directed toward studies of will, cognitive processes, clinical processes, and the like. The old German tradition of philosophical and theoretical consideration of human nature still persists. Despite this philosophical tendency, some purely empirical research is done. There is a growing tendency toward objectivity—in intersubjective agreement, actually—and toward explicitness of design. Elaborate and sophisticated designs are rarely used. Sharp criticism of German psychology for its lack of rigor, purity, and care in experimentation and for a tendency toward conclusions based on inadequate data has been made by some German psychologists, such as Wolfgang Metzger, a strong protagonist of experimental psychology and of Gestalt psychology in particular. Metzger has described German psychology in the 1960's as being characterized by a tendency toward phenomenology, by a deeply ingrained distrust of purely empiricist views, and by a disdain for elementism and for excessive objectivism.

The traditional topics of investigation—perception, characterology, and motivation—continue to attract attention. A strong interest in personality and its assessment, including various kinds of expression analysis, persists now, as it did in the past few decades. Contemporary German psychologists concern themselves particularly with personality theory. Serious consideration is given to the dynamics of personality, social adjustment, analysis of motivation, and to depth psychology. Social psy-

chology, particularly group dynamics, receives attention as it did prior
to World War II. Recently this field was given added encouragement and
stimulation from American activity in social psychology.

Applied psychology flourishes. Educational and industrial services,
child guidance, and vocational guidance are emphasized. Projective tests
enjoy particular prominence. The development and use of intelligence
tests and achievement tests, on the other hand, have been promoted most
enthusiastically by educators. German psychologists have tended to cultivate a global, intuitive approach to personality. On that account the
projective tests, expressive movements, and analysis of situational behavior are useful observational aids. They furnish data which can be
freely synthesized and interpreted. Various personality theories and diagnostic procedures have been developed, but their validation is still not a
pressing concern to German psychologists. Psychoanalytic concepts receive almost no attention from the academic psychologists except as subjects for occasional critical comments. German psychotherapy, as it is
practiced by medical and lay analysts, is based mainly on Adler and Jung.

Psychologists and Research Areas.   German psychologists today have a
rather heterogeneous background professionally. Some have taken their
psychological education outside Germany. Others have had their training
in Germany, but their major professional development has been gained in
other countries to which they went in the 1930's and where they remained
until the end of the war. Several have had brief study in, or visits to,
America and other lands on postwar exchange programs. British, French,
Russian, and American psychologists from the occupation forces also left
their impress on modern German psychology. Above all, re-establishment
of contact with the rest of the world through books and journals has
strongly stimulated contemporary German psychologists. All these imported influences explain the increased diversity of interests today in
contrast to the earlier period when Germany was largely an exporter of
psychology.

Analysis of the areas of specialization of contemporary German psychologists reveals certain groupings or clusters. *Wolfgang Metzger* (b.
1899), *Wilhelm Witte* (b. 1915), both of whom are at Münster, and *Edwin
Rausch* (b. 1906), at Frankfurt, constitute a "physiological physicalistic
group interested in perception and thinking." Their orientation is Gestalt,
as is that of *Johannes von Allesch* and of Köhler's former student at
Swarthmore, *Kripal Singh Sodhi* (b. 1911, in India), at the Free University in West Berlin, who has done extensive research in social psychology.
Kurt Gottschaldt (b. 1902), formerly of Humboldt University in East
Berlin and more recently at Göttingen, is also a Gestalt psychologist. He
has won distinction for his work in experimental social psychology and
personality theory.

Krueger's *Ganzheitspsychologie* or totality psychology tradition is represented at Heidelberg by *Johannes Rudert* (b. 1894), at Bonn by *Friedrich Sander* (b. 1889), retired director of the institute there, at Cologne
by *Udo Undeutsch* (b. 1917), and at Mainz by *Albert Wellek* (b. 1904).

They have been concerned with personality development, personality theory, and applied psychology. They use intuitive methods of studying human nature. The empirical, pragmatic approach characterizes applied and social psychologists, such as *Wilhelm Arnold* (b. 1911) of Würzburg, *Curt Bondy* (b. 1894) of Hamburg, and *Heinrich Düker* (b. 1898) at Marburg. They specialize in personality theory, perception, developmental and applied psychology. Others—like *Helmut von Bracken* (b. 1899), a psychologist-physician at Marburg, *Robert Heiss* (b. 1903), a philosopher turned projective tester, of Freiburg, and Ach's student, *Karl Mierke* (b. 1896) at Kiel, whose interests are psychology of will, experimental, educational, and social psychology—have singular orientations.

In the German Democratic Republic (East Germany) Otto Köhler's and F. J. J. Buytendijk's student, *Werner Fischel* (b. 1900) of Leipzig, has conducted extensive animal researches. Investigations of personality and social psychology are made at Jena by *Friedrich Winnefeld* (b. 1911), who studied with Lewin and Charlotte Bühler. The East German theoretical orientation tends toward Gestalt psychology. While the Gestalt trend runs counter to Russian psychology, the tribute paid to Pavlov reflects the Russian influence. In East Berlin, the Institute of Cortical-Visceral Pathology and Therapy of the German Academy of Science synthesizes clinical and experimental techniques within a Pavlovian framework. Pavlovian concepts are invoked to interpret physiological and psychological activities. These highly diverse research interests of contemporary German psychologists in the West and East—personality, perception, thinking, testing, applied psychology, social psychology, developmental and comparative psychology—are exemplified in their current periodical literature.

Psychological Training. In the Federal Republic of Germany (West Germany) there are 18 universities with departments of psychology. These departments are not independent, however. Since psychology deals with human problems and is a science, too, there has been some problem concerning just where psychology belongs in the university. Therefore, in some universities the psychological laboratory is under the science faculty and in others, under the faculty of arts and humanities. Because of the powerful, enduring influence of Diltheyanism there has been a reluctance in the universities to support scientific psychology in respect of its laboratory needs and psychological chairs. Psychology is also taught at technological institutes, theological seminaries, and teachers' colleges.

Most students at the 18 universities work for the diploma in psychology, which, as we previously indicated, was instituted in 1941. The diploma is regulated by state laws that are roughly the same in the ten states of the Federal Republic and in West Berlin. The diploma requires completion of eight semesters (four years) of academic study, writing of a scientific thesis, passing of oral and written examinations in a special area, and completion of three internships. Usually the diploma is a prerequisite for doctoral candidacy. In the 1950's and 1960's, about 20 per cent of the students—most of them aiming at academic careers—continued for the Ph.D.

degree. The Ph.D. demands two additional semesters beyond the diploma, acceptance and publication of a dissertation, and successful completion of a comprehensive examination in psychology and in two other sciences selected by the student.

In East Germany three institutes—East Berlin, Leipzig and Dresden—offer training for the doctorate and diploma. Five years are required for the diploma and an additional four years for the doctorate. Very few students pursue the doctorate. At the universities of Jena, Halle, Greifswald, and Rostock, at the teachers' college at Potsdam, educational psychology is offered for prospective teachers. Professional training in East Germany is offered in vocational psychology, medical psychology, and educational psychology. Considerable training for research is given. Generally speaking, however, applied psychology is popular in East Germany. Many psychologists are employed in industry and in rehabilitation centers. Psychology is closely coordinated with medical programs.

Since 1945 psychology has attracted a larger number of German students than previously, most of whom are interested in the practice of psychology rather than in experimental psychology. However, in Germany psychology has not been accorded as much recognition by university administrations and is not as popular among the student bodies as it has been in the United States. Moreover, psychology tends to be viewed with suspicion in German society. Attitudes of educators and physicians toward psychologists are not always cordial either. For these reasons, professional psychology has grown slowly in Germany, compared to other countries such as the United States, Sweden, Holland, and Denmark where there has been a large demand for psychological services.

Most German professional psychologists are employed in civil service or in industry. They do counseling with youth and the aged, act as consultants in government employment agencies, or serve as prison psychologists. In industry their activities include personnel selection, training, studies of efficiency, human relations, and human engineering. There has been a rising interest in market research and the psychology of advertising. Although professional psychology has attracted large numbers of students in Germany since 1945, its progress has been slow, principally because employment opportunities for applied psychologists are limited.

Clinical Psychology. The growth of clinical psychology in West Germany was stimulated by World War II and by the development of child guidance clinics. In comparison to applied psychology, generally, clinical psychology has made very slow progress. It has encountered considerable opposition from the medical profession which objects to the appellation "clinical" for nonmedical psychologists. In the clinics, the psychologist plays a role ancillary to the physician rather than that of professional colleague. Independent practitioners generally do psychodiagnosis for forensic or vocational purposes. Psychological tests and projective techniques, as well as graphology, find frequent use. Impressions and subjective interpretations are stressed, but there is a growing tendency toward increased objectivity.

Training for clinical psychology in Germany has been hindered by lack of clear definition of the field. Universities offer no special degree for clinical psychology. Formal organized clinical training was begun in 1950 when the first child guidance clinic was established at the University of Hamburg by *Curt Bondy* (previously mentioned). Trained at Hamburg under Stern, Bondy, a specialist in adolescent and social psychology, spent ten years (1940-1950) in the United States at the Richmond Professional Institute, College of William and Mary, in Virginia. In 1950, Bondy became director of the Psychological Institute at Hamburg. He and a collaborator, *Hans Priester* (b. 1924), who is now in the United States, prepared the Hamburg-Wechsler Intelligence Scales for use with German children and adults. Hamburg offers intensive training to third and fourth year students in diagnosis of emotionally disturbed children. Although not wholeheartedly endorsed in Germany, the team approach—psychiatrist, psychologist, and social worker—is emphasized at Hamburg. No provisions are made in the department, however, for training in psychoanalysis and psychotherapy. Students who want such training must arrange to take it elsewhere.

After 1950, the number of mental hygiene clinics and child guidance clinics increased steadily. Additional training programs at other universities also became available. In general, these programs are characterized by a theoretical orientation and limited practicum experience. Most practicum training is obtained in university-related clinics or hospitals because there are few nonuniversity training centers. Practicum training is usually taken for six months while students are doing their academic work. An additional year is advised but not required, after the student completes his course and receives the diploma.

Among the universities which offer clinical training are the following: *Freiburg* in Breisgau where *Robert Heiss*, a specialist in projective techniques and depth psychology, directs the Institute for Psychology and Characterology; *Munich*, where *Philip Lersch* (b. 1898), distinguished for his contributions to the study of personality and personality theory, directs the Psychological Institute; *Göttingen*, with which *Erna Duhm* (b. 1923), a specialist in learning theory, forensic psychology, and projective techniques, is associated; *Saarbrücken*, with which *Otfried Spreen* (b. 1926), a clinical psychologist interested in clinical theory and research, is identified; *Tübingen*, where for many years Kretschmer investigated the relationship of physique and personality. The program at Tübingen has been described by Henry David as "one of the few European examples of an integrated multidisciplinary research program with opportunities for advanced study and degrees for psychologists in a medical setting." Training in depth psychology is available to psychotherapists at *Munich*, *West Berlin*, *Heidelberg*, *Würzburg*, *Mainz*, and *Stuttgart*. Formal training in clinical research is offered at *Hamburg* where the institute is now directed by *Peter R. Hofstätter* (b. 1913), a specialist in the construction, standardization, and clinical application of tests; and at *Marburg* by *Heinrich Düker*, director of the Psychological Institute, who specializes in psychopharmacology.

Upon completion of university training, many psychologists in West Germany work at educational counseling centers where they do diagnostic studies of children and adults. Little opportunity for therapy or research is provided. Research is considered principally a university function. Although community mental health programs have been formulated, there are few nonuniversity clinical facilities. Psychological services are characterized by the absence of a dynamic approach. The strong predilection of German psychiatrists for an organic orientation has prevented the adoption of a dynamic viewpoint in clinical psychology. Psychotherapy, as it is practiced, is largely Jungian or Adlerian.

In East Germany, training in medical psychology can be obtained at Humboldt University in East Berlin, at Leipzig and at Dresden. The chief emphasis is on research. Humboldt University has modern laboratories and a kindergarten for disturbed children which provides facilities for experimental studies. After obtaining the diploma most psychologists in East Germany work in clinics or in industry. Some teach. Research continues to be an essential part of their work. There is almost no independent private practice of clinical psychology. Medical psychology is part of the state service. One type of therapy that is practiced extensively is sleep therapy, which has been developed according to Pavlovian principles.

Professional Organizations.   The number of psychologists in Germany has increased noticeably during the 1950's and 1960's. Membership in professional psychological organizations has also increased. The societies have become more active. German psychologists have participated more frequently and actively in international meetings. Moreover, in 1960, the Sixteenth International Congress of Psychology was held at Bonn. The late Karl Bühler, formerly of the University of Vienna but then in the United States, was honorary president of the Congress, and Wolfgang Metzger of Münster was the president. The general tone of the Congress indicated that German psychologists had become an active, international-minded group.

While in East Germany there is only one active psychological organization—the Association of Psychologists in the Public Health Service of the German Democratic Republic, two psychological organizations flourish in West Germany. These organizations are the *Deutsche Gesellschaft für Psychologie* ("German Psychological Society") and the *Berufsverband Deutscher Psychologen* ("Professional Association of German Psychologists"). The German Psychological Society, originally organized in 1903, was reactivated after the war in 1947. By the 1960's its membership was more than 2,000. Members of this group are mainly university professors and psychologists engaged in pure research. They are qualified to train and supervise doctoral candidates. The German Psychological Society has a subcommittee on clinical psychology which collaborates with the Professional Association to improve standards and to obtain legislation. More than 40 per cent of the practitioners have licenses in graphology. Attempts have also been made to develop ethical standards for clinical psychologists.

The *Berufsverband*, established in 1946, is an association of applied psychologists who have either the Ph.D. or the diploma. This organization includes in its membership those who teach below the university level. The ten divisions of the Berufsverband indicate a wide range of interests among German applied psychologists. These interest areas include clinical psychology, family and educational counseling, vocational guidance, school psychology, industrial psychology, market research and advertising, traffic psychology, forensic psychology, psychology in crime and delinquency, and graphology. The Berufsverband and the Gesellschaft cooperate closely with each other. In fact, a number of members of the academic group hold membership in this association of applied psychologists. Some members of these two major groups belong to a third with which the other two, however, in the past have had somewhat less cordial relations.

This third group, *Deutsche Gesellschaft für Psychotherapie und Tiefenpsychologie* ("German Society for Psychotherapy and Depth Psychology") is an amalgamation of Freudian, Adlerian, and Jungian groups which existed in pre-World War II Germany. Membership in this society is open to those who have had specialized training in psychotherapy and who have the Ph.D. or M.D. degrees. As the universities have gained some control over training in depth psychology and psychotherapy, which had previously been independent of them, academic psychologists and psychotherapists have been led to more amicable relations.

GERMAN PSYCHOLOGY: DECLINE AND RECONSTRUCTION

In the twentieth century, Germany lost hegemony in scientific psychology. Several factors—political and intellectual—contributed to the decline of German psychology. Politically, nationalism was fostered after Germany's defeat in 1918. This trend grew stronger in the twenties and ultimately culminated in Nazism, which not only contaminated but actually destroyed German psychological science. It stifled scientific methods and pursuits and encouraged only that psychology which could serve the purposes and ends of national socialism. Even more disastrous, however, was the fact that it drove out of Germany many prominent and productive psychologists. Furthermore, the nineteenth century cleavage between natural science psychology, with its laboratory method, and cultural science psychology, with its intuitive, philosophical approach, became increasingly wider. Objective psychology, marked by its concern for elements, introspective analysis, and the individual, gave way to a more subjective psychology which emphasized totality, synthesis, and the broad study of human nature. While cultural science psychology gained vitality and prestige, natural science psychology lost recognition, even in the universities where it had previously been honored.

In Germany, philosophy had perennially exerted a deep and direct influence on psychology. Many German psychologists were philosophers and wrote philosophical books. However, twentieth century German psychology became preoccupied with the philosophical inquiry into personality

SUMMARY OF GERMAN PSYCHOLOGICAL SCIENCE: 1860–1933

AREA	PROPONENT	ORIGINS	SIGNIFICANCE
Psychophysics (1860)	Gustav Fechner	Interest in mind-body problem: experimental physics and natural philosophy	Established method for foundation of psychology as an exact science.
Experimental Psychology (1874)	Wilhelm Wundt	Philosophy, physiology, psychophysics	Established scientific psychology: initiated laboratory approach.
Empirical Psychology (1874)	Franz Brentano	Aristotelian philosophy	Developed *act* psychology in contrast to Wundt's *content* psychology. Precursor of phenomenology.
Experience Psychology (1880's)	Carl Stumpf	Brentano's act psychology	Subjected acts to experimentation. Stimulated the experimental phenomenology of Göttingen and Würzburg.
"Understanding" Psychology (1880's)	Wilhelm Dilthey	Kant, Brentano, 19th century German Romanticism and historicism	Rejected natural science psychology. Emphasized understanding and holism.
Thought Psychology (1900's)	Oswald Külpe	Wundt's content psychology, Brentano's act psychology, Stumpf's experience psychology	Studied higher mental processes experimentally. Discovered "imageless" thought.
Gestalt Psychology (1912)	Max Wertheimer Wolfgang Köhler Kurt Koffka	Kant, Mach, von Ehrenfels	Stressed study of organized wholes in cognitive processes—perception. Rejected atomistic psychology.
Psychology of Structure (1914)	Eduard Spranger	Dilthey's cultural science psychology	Intuitive study of personality as a whole. Identified six ideal types of human values.
Totality Psychology (1915)	Felix Krueger	Dilthey, James, irrationalism—pre-classical period (*Sturm und Drang* of Herder and Tetens)	Created a psychology of wholeness which was developmental and evolutionistic. Emphasized the emotional and social rather than intellectualistic and individualistic.
Personalistic Psychology (1920's)	Wilhelm Stern	Attempts to effect synthesis of natural science and cultural science psychologies	Described the person as a unity of many parts (*unitas multiplex*).

SUMMARY OF GERMAN PSYCHOLOGICAL SCIENCE: 1860–1933—*Continued*

AREA	PROPONENT	ORIGINS	SIGNIFICANCE
Psychology of Expression (1920's)	Ludwig Klages	Goethe, Nietzsche, late Romanticism and early 20th century interest in mysticism	Established a philosophical system of characterology and a science of expression, particularly graphology.
Typological Psychology (1920's)	Ernst Kretschmer	Empirical static approach to personality, stressing influence of heredity on character	Related physique to personality. Developed empirical constitutional typology: schizoid–cycloid.
	E. R. Jaensch	Empirical static approach to personality through biological factors	Related eidetic imagery to endocrines. Empirical typology: B and T types.

PERIOD OF RECONSTRUCTION: 1945–1965*

FIELDS OF PSYCHOLOGY	REPRESENTATIVES
Personality	Arnold, von Bracken, Gottschaldt, Heiss, Hörmann, Lersch, Rudert, Sander, Thomae, Wellek, Winnefeld
Projective Techniques and Testing	Anger, Arnold, Bergius, Bondy, Duhm, Heiss, Hofstätter, Hörmann, Höhn, Lienert, Moers, Sander, Spreen, Undeutsch, Wellek, Wewetzer
Social Psychology	Anger, Bondy, Bornemann, Gottschaldt, Höhn, Hörmann, Mierke, Scharmann, Sodhi, Winnefeld
Clinical Psychology	Bender, Bornemann, Duhm, Görres, Moers, Schlosser, Schraml, Spreen, Wewetzer
Developmental Psychology	Boesch, Bondy, Metzger, Thomae, Undeutsch
Applied Psychology	Arnold, Heiss, Sander, Traxel, Undeutsch
Animal Psychology	Fischel, O. Köhler
Educational Psychology	Bondy, Bornemann, Höhn, Mierke, Wegener, Winnefeld
Industrial Psychology	Anger, Gottschaldt, Scharmann, Schorn, Spiegel
Learning Theory	Duhm, Düker, Hoffstätter, Höhn
Thinking	Bergius, Metzger, Rausch
Perception	Metzger, Rausch, Sander, Sodhi, Witte

*General patterns of psychological thought: (1) pronounced interest in personality and personality theory; (2) Tendency toward phenomenology and a philosophical approach; (3) Suspicion of empiricism; and (4) Disdain for elementism and extreme objectivism.

and human nature. This trend expressed itself in a variety of systems: Dilthey's "understanding psychology," Krueger's "totality psychology," Spranger's "psychology of structure," and Gestalt psychology. These systems condemned the elementistic, analytic approach and promoted psychologies of the whole man. A noteworthy attempt to integrate the elementistic and holistic approaches was made in Stern's personalistic psychology. The interrelatedness of the physical and mental in man was expressed in the eidetic imagery typology of Jaensch and the constitutional types of Kretschmer. Psychodiagnostics, or personality appraisal, was notably advanced by Klages, whose science of expression led him to graphology, or the scientific study of handwriting, as a clue to personality. These systems offered abundant and imaginative theories, but made no effective attempt to establish their validity.

As of 1933, the psychological institutes at the German universities carefully maintained their distinctive character and individual research domains. Thus German psychology tended to remain systematic, while it was also subjective, qualitative, and dedicated to understanding the individual rather than to making predictions about the group. It sought to achieve insight rather than to derive objective scores and amass facts. Concerned chiefly with totalities, German psychologists regarded a knowledge of fundamental type differences as basic to understanding of individual trait differences. On that account characterological and typological investigations flourished.

After 1933, with the rise of the Nazi state, Germany's contribution to scientific psychology ended. Thereafter, characterology became the favorite topic. The nature of characterology was such that it could accommodate itself readily to Nazi ideology. It seemingly substantiated Nazi theories of racial superiority and leadership. Applied psychology, which had never been enthusiastically endorsed in the early days, was cultivated during the Nazi era to achieve practical governmental ends. Educational, industrial, and military psychology were developed within the characterological framework. Where tests were employed, for example, the approach was clinical rather than psychometric. Increased psychological services required more psychologists with practical training. The universities met the demand for psychological practitioners by offering a new degree, the diploma degree, in 1941.

When World War II ended, the long period of intellectual isolation, the ravages of war in terms of personnel and property, and the peace terms posed numerous difficulties for the rehabilitation of psychology. But in the second half of the twentieth century, German psychologists have been steadily recreating their science. Depth psychology, social psychology, psychology of personality, phenomenology, and the applications of psychology to education, industry, and guidance flourish. Subjectivity permeates German psychology, however. Experimentation and especially quantitative methods have not been generally accepted. Current German psychological research leaves something to be desired as far as rigor and exactness of experimental method are concerned. Untested theories still abound. Professionally, German psychologists have revived many of their former journals and their organizations. They have also established new ones. Former lines of communication with foreign psychologists have been re-established through periodicals, international congresses, and travel to other countries.

In comparison to the United States where psychology has enjoyed a phenomenal growth in the twentieth century, German psychologists are fewer in number, relatively speaking, and less influential. The American public has been far more accepting of psychology as a profession than have the Germans, who have been slower to employ psychologists in the schools, in clinics, and in industry. Psychologists in Germany have not had the impact outside the university and in society that American psychologists have had.

REFERENCES

GERMAN PSYCHOLOGY IN THE 1920's

Bentley, M. Deutsche Gesellschaft für Psychologie. *Amer. J. Psychol.*, 1929, *41*, 689.

Wenzel, A. Contemporary German psychology. *Monist*, 1928, *38*, 120–157.

CHARACTEROLOGY AND TYPOLOGY

Klüver, H. An analysis of recent work on the problem of psychological types. *J. nerv. ment. Dis.*, 1925, *62*, 561–596.

Spearman, C. German science of character. I. Approach from experimental psychology. *Charact. & Pers.*, 1936–7, *5–6*, 177–201. II. Approach from typology. *Charact. & Pers.*, 1937–8, *6*, 36–50.

Stein-Lewinson, Thea. An introduction to the graphology of Ludwig Klages. *Charact. & Pers.*, 1937–8, *6*, 163–167.

IMPACT OF NAZISM

Watson, G. Psychology in Germany and Austria. *Psychol. Bull.*, 1934, *31*, 755–776.

Watson, G. Psychology under Hitler. *Sch. & Soc.*, 1933, *38*, 732–736.

Wyatt, F., & Teuber, H. L. German psychology under the Nazi System: 1933–1940. *Psychol. Rev.*, 1944, *51*, 229–247. See also Lerner, E. A reply to Wyatt and Teuber. *Psychol. Rev.*, 1945, *52*, 52–54.

PSYCHOLOGY AFTER WORLD WAR II

Adams, J. F. The status of psychology in the universities of Austria and Germany: 1955–1956. *J. gen. Psychol.*, 1957, *56*, 147–157.

Adams, J. F. The status of psychology in the universities of Austria and Germany: 1960–1961. *J. gen. Psychol.*, 1962, *67*, 337–347.

Adams, J. F. Current developments in Germanic academic psychology. *J. Hist. behav. Sci.*, 1966, *2*, 168–170.

Angermeier, W. F. Psychology in East Germany. *Amer. Psychologist*, 1964, *19*, 846.

Bracken, H. von Recent trends in German psychology. *J. gen. Psychol.*, 1952, *47*, 165–179.

David, H. P. *International resources in clinical psychology*. New York: McGraw-Hill, 1964. Pp. 28–32.

Dorsch, F. *Geschichte und Probleme der angewandten Psychologie*. Bern: Huber, 1963.

Gast, H. Deutsche Demokratische Republik. *Gawein*, 1956, *4*, 65–68.

Hehlmann, W. *Geschichte der Psychologie*. Stuttgart: Kröner, 1963.

Holzner, B. *Amerikanische und deutsche Psychologie: eine vergleichende Darstellung*. Würzburg: Holzner, 1958.

Hoyos, G. C. *Denkschrift zur Lage der Psychologie*. Wiesbaden: Steiner, 1964.

Metzger, W. The historical background for national trends in psychology: German psychology. *J. Hist. behav. Sci.*, 1965, *1*, 109–115.

Pfaffenbeger, H. G. On the training of psychologists in Germany. *Amer. Psychologist* 1952, 7, 98–99.

Schuetzinger, Caroline E. Post-war development of psychology in Germany. *Amer. Cath. Psychol. Ass. Newsltr.*, May 1957, Suppl. No. 27.

Wellek, A. Deutschland. *Gawein*, 1956, *4*, 55–65.

Wellek, A. (Ed.) *Gesamtverzeichnis der deutschsprachigen Psychologischen Literatur der Jahre 1942 bis 1960*. Göttingen: Hogrefe, 1965.

Wesley, F. Masters and pupils among the German psychologists. *J. Hist. behav. Sci.*, 1965, *1*, 252–258.

Wesley, F. Assessing German psychology—1965. *J. gen. Psychol.*, in press.

Zuckerman, S. B. Some notes on psychology in Germany, 1953. *J. clin. Psychol.*, 1954, *10*, 353–357.

10

American Psychology: Beginnings

IN THE LAST TWO DECADES of the nineteenth century Germany held hegemony in scientific psychology. Americans welcomed the new science enthusiastically and eagerly looked to Germany for their training during this period. A majority of the prominent American psychologists who in the 1890's were establishing laboratories, writing textbooks, founding journals, and expanding psychology in various directions had studied in Leipzig.

Scientific psychology had a phenomenal rise in the United States. Its ready acceptance was concomitant with late nineteenth century reforms in American higher education. The traditional classics curriculum in the colleges began to yield place to the sciences. Therefore, psychology as science readily won support from the colleges and universities along with chemistry and physics.

Moreover, the association with Johns Hopkins where Hall developed the first American psychological laboratory also gave prestige to psychology. Among American universities, Johns Hopkins had attained fame for its leadership in the formation of graduate schools. Other institutions were influenced by the fact that Johns Hopkins had fostered the study of the new psychology. Under these auspicious academic conditions psychology flourished and psychological laboratories were established rapidly at the leading universities.

Although America imported psychology from Germany enthusiastically, it did not adopt German psychology in its entirety. While, from the outset, in the 1880's and 1890's Americans borrowed the idea of an experimental psychology and its methods and concepts, they proceeded to fashion a kind of psychology different from that which originated in Germany.

Outside of Germany, psychology attained its most important development in America. Unlike the German psychology, which gradually evolved from a struggle of competing systems of speculative philosophy, the American scientific psychology was totally different from the psychology that immediately preceded it. Its course was unique. Early American psychology was successively nurtured in theology, moral philosophy, and mental philosophy.

The publication of the first American textbooks of psychology indicates the introduction of the subject into the college curriculum between 1800 and 1830. Thus, prior to the rise of experimental psychology in Germany, psychology was being taught in American colleges and universities and in some high schools and academies. It was taught, however, as mental philosophy, and mainly by theologians at most institutions. The differentiation of psychology from theology and philosophy in the United States was a process not uncomplicated by political, economic, social, and cultural struggles of a population striving to build a new nation.

In the latter half of the nineteenth century a more vigorous psychology emerged under British and German influence. Scientific psychology began to take its place as a distinct discipline in American institutions. Before one looks into this development, however, the prescientific antecedents must be examined.

PRESCIENTIFIC PSYCHOLOGY

The progress of American psychology in its prescientific period is characterized by three stages: (1) The beginnings in theology and moral philosophy during the colonial or pre-Revolutionary period; (2) the period of mental philosophy under the Scottish influence in the interval between the Revolution and the beginning of the Civil War; (3) the impact of British and German influence from the Civil War to the 1880's, when the first American students acquired training in scientific psychology, mainly in Wundt's laboratory in Leipzig.

Beginnings in Theology and Moral Philosophy. In the period from 1640 to 1714 the American colonists, isolated from European influence as they were, were hardly aware of such recent developments as the scientific ideas and views of Bacon and their influence. Under the pressure of everyday living they were more concerned with eking out a livelihood and warding off Indian attacks than with promoting scholarship. Since the colonists were a serious, religious-minded people, it is not surprising that theology occupied a prominent position in their intellectual life, and that philosophy was not neglected.

In the early eighteenth century (1714), *Samuel Johnson* (1696-1772), later the first President of Columbia University (King's College), wrote a youthful synopsis of the old scholastic systems in which he treated psychology as a part of physics. Later in the eighteenth century more immigrants came to America bringing with them the latest cultural and philosophical developments from Europe, as well as the reactions to Locke, Descartes, and the earlier philosophers. Then Berkeley, Hume, Hartley, and the other modern philosophers came to be known in America. The number of libraries and colleges increased. In spite of disrupting influences like the French and Indian Wars and the Revolution, there was more time for study and thinking. Scholarship began to develop.

By 1752 "the first textbook of philosophy published in America," *Elementa Philosophica*, was written by Samuel Johnson. Johnson's psychology presented in the *Elementa* treated such topics as sensation, cognition, affection, conation, and, in a more limited manner, the anatomy and physiology of the nervous system. In this prescientific period of American psychology, Johnson was already expressing an interest in genetic and comparative psychology. Among Johnson's contemporaries was *Jonathan Edwards* (1703-1758), a clergyman, who has been described as "the chief thinker in the Colonies prior to the Revolution." He concerned himself with psychological problems related to religion, freedom of the will, and the affections. Occasionally Edwards used psychotherapeutic techniques on disturbed individuals in his congregation. In their psychological thinking both Edwards and Johnson show the influence of Locke.

In the works of these men, the early nineteenth century psychology in America showed a lively interest in abnormal, social, and physiological psychology. Subsequent development of mental philosophy (1845-1885) dominated so powerfully that it tended to overshadow completely this earlier American psychology.

Mental Philosophy. In the post-Revolutionary period, under the influence of a burgeoning rationalism, American psychology weaned itself from theology and moral philosophy. Mental or intellectual philosophy then rose to importance, dominated by the Scottish realism which first came (1768) to America through *John W. Witherspoon* (1722-1794) at Princeton (then the College of New Jersey). As a reaction to the idealism of Berkeley and Hume, the Scottish realism, a common sense philosophy, sought by introspection to deduce principles that are "prior to, and independent of, experience." From the Revolutionary period until the early nineteenth century, the writings of the Scottish philosophers such as Reid, Stewart, and Brown served as the chief textbooks in American colleges and universities where psychology was taught. In 1827, *Thomas Upham* (1799-1872), a clergyman, produced the *Elements of Intellectual Philosophy* and, in 1831, *Elements of Mental Philosophy*. But even after the more distinctively American textbooks such as Upham's began to appear, they continued to reflect the Scottish influence.

In 1840 the first text in English bearing the title *Psychology* was written by the German-born *Frederick Rauch* (1806-1841), who tried to integrate German and American intellectual philosophy. His book was entitled *Psychology, or, a View of the Human Soul: Including Anthropology.* Thereafter, additional American volumes appeared which reflected scientific advances. Among these should be mentioned a two volume work by *James Rush* (1786-1869), entitled *Brief Outline of an Analysis of the Human Intellect Intended to Rectify the Scholastic and Vulgar Perversions of the Natural Purpose and Method of Thinking: by Rejecting Altogether the Theoretical Confusion: the Unmeaning Arrangement and Indefinite Nomenclature of the Metaphysician* (1865). Rush can be regarded as the most original American psychologist of the nineteenth century. Based on objectivism rather than on metaphysical principles, his system is a radical departure from his predecessors. Rush's volume, and *The Human Intellect* published in 1868 by *Noah Porter* (1811-1882), indicated that American psychology was moving slowly away from the philosophical toward the scientific orientation.

During this period, however, most works were really dilutions of the Scottish philosophers, Reid, Brown, and Hamilton, and were written in the interests of religious orthodoxy. Mid-nineteenth century philosophy was a kind of Protestant scholasticism which derived its psychology from theological dogma. Thus in spite of rising interest in science, there was a narrow range of perspectives. The earlier concern for abnormal, animal, and physiological psychology was conspicuously absent. Interest in phrenology and mesmerism was evident. Publications in both fields appeared in the 1820's and increased considerably in the mid-nineteenth century. The Scottish philosophical emphasis on intellectual processes persisted strongly in America until the Civil War. Finally, the influence of mental philosophy expired with *James McCosh* (1811-1895), whose book, *Psychology, the Cognitive Powers,* appeared in 1886. This volume was the last expression of the old mental philosophy type of psychology in America.

German and British Influence. Following the Civil War, in the 1870's and 1880's, Americans were more intensely scrutinizing trans-Atlantic intellectual developments. Improved means of transportation and communication after the Industrial Revolution were bringing the people of the world into closer proximity. American students began to travel abroad in greater numbers. Many studied at European universities and returned with enthusiasm for German philosophers such as Kant and Hegel. In the 1880's, the American shift from mental philosophy to scientific psychology was abrupt and radical. Americans did not look back to build upon their earlier psychology. Instead they directed their attention to the European developments in physiological psychology. Principal inspiration came naturally from the German psychology of Fechner, Helmholtz, and Wundt, and from the British associationism of James Mill, John Stuart Mill, and Alexander Bain. Americans were also profoundly influenced by Spencer's notions of development and by Darwin's evolutionary theory. The effect of the latter on American psychology merits detailed examination.

Impact of Evolutionism. Previously it was noted that evolution had reorientated the new psychology in a definitely biological direction. In England, the birthplace of evolution, it prompted Galton's investigation of individual differences and races and led to his development of tests, measurements, and statistical methods.

Evolutionism thus launched the study of individual differences and provoked the perennial nature-nurture controversy. It sparked an interest, too, in animal behavior and fostered a study of the infra-human species. This influence of evolution with its emphasis on biology was not confined to England. In America with its democratic spirit, the psychology of adaptation, survival, and usefulness, which evolution posed, easily captured attention. It is not surprising, therefore, to discover how much evolution shaped the character of American psychology.

Wundt's effect on Americans who came to study under him during the 1880's and 1890's was confined largely to methodology. The subject matter and the spirit which they created in turn in their universities were definitely not German. It seems no exaggeration to say that, in terms of content and spirit, Galton's influence on American psychology was actually greater than that of Wundt. American psychology was being developed toward practical ends. Subsequent developments have made this practical trend clear. It is also now evident that, although nineteenth century

American psychologists acted as if they were copying Wundt, unwittingly they were fashioning a different psychology from that taught at Leipzig. And yet few of them seemed to appreciate the influence of Galton, which in fact proved to be stronger.

Galton's influence was translated to American shores by an American who in 1886 had received his doctorate at Leipzig under Wundt—namely, *James McKeen Cattell* (1860-1944). Cattell had been interested in the psychology of individual differences even before going to Leipzig. There he received little sympathy for this interest. But he met Galton at Cambridge in 1888 and found him a kindred spirit. Galton encouraged Cattell in his early cultivation of differential psychology and in his construction of mental tests to measure individual differences. Cattell's pioneering efforts instituted an important practical application of psychology which American psychologists eagerly and significantly developed—namely, psychometrics.

The psychology of individual differences and mental testing, while important, were not the only derivatives of evolutionism in America. Animal psychology, given impetus by the work of E. L. Thorndike, also drew its share of attention and enthusiasm in the 1890's. Finally, genetic psychology, in which biology and psychology joined forces to investigate the growth and development of mental life, was fashioned out of evolutionary doctrine by G. Stanley Hall. The latter, one of the foremost American advocates of evolution along with J. M. Baldwin, publicized its significance and applied the theory to mental capacities.

Evolution thus set the stage for a kind of psychology in America different from the earlier mental philosophy. It helped to mold a science which studied mental functions and their usefulness to the organism—that is, a functional psychology. From the outset, American psychology was functional in spirit and approach, and this quality remains one of its distinctive characteristics.

WILLIAM JAMES

The American who best mirrored the late nineteenth century philosophical and psychological developments in Europe was William James (1842-1910). As early as 1875 he wrote to President Eliot of Harvard urging him to take cognizance of the new psychology: "A real science of man is now being built out of the theory of evolution and the facts of archeology, the nervous system, and the senses." With his broad background in physiology and philosophy, William James was a logical person to initiate an original American formulation of scientific psychology. He publicized the new science in America and achieved for it independence from philosophy and a place of honor in American universities.

Wundt and James. While in America James played a role similar to that of Wundt in Germany—namely, that of founding father of the new science—these men were quite different. Each had qualified for medical practice, had a good background in physiology and philosophy, and had used psychology as a means of satisfying the desire to be at once physiologist and philosopher. Both men had simple psychological laboratories as early as 1875. While Wundt developed his by 1879 into a world-renowned laboratory, James neglected his. Wundt was an experimentalist basically, although he stressed the limitations of experimentation in such areas as the higher thought processes. He exalted the introspective method. James was more empiricist than experimentalist. He believed that experimentation was important, but he did not want to have to do it himself. Above all James could not commit himself to a single method as Wundt did to introspection. James preferred ideas to laboratory results. Finally, James drifted from psychology and settled himself in philosophy in his later years, while Wundt remained with psychology until the end of his life.

Life.   Born in New York in 1842 into an illustrious family, William James enjoyed the advantages of some early education in, and frequent visits to, Europe. After abandoning his youthful ambition of becoming an artist, he went to Harvard Medical School from which he received his medical degree in 1869. He suffered recurrent physical illness which induced intermittent spells of depression and fits of restlessness. In an effort to recuperate, he made several visits abroad, which served to mold him into an international-minded scholar.

James's interest in psychology dates from 1867, when he went to Germany to study physiology and came to know the work of Helmholtz and Wundt at Heidelberg. Upon his return to America he taught physiology at Harvard, where in 1875 he offered a graduate course entitled "The Relations between Physiology and Psychology." It was about this time that he also introduced laboratory work into psychology.

Later (1880) James became assistant professor of philosophy, and then professor (1885). By 1889 he had his title changed to professor of psychology. In this same year he attended the International Congress of Physiological Psychology in Paris where he met other psychologists. This meeting, James acknowledged, was a source of inspiration for him. The following year he succeeded in finishing and publishing *The Principles of Psychology*. Thereafter, James's interest in psychology began to wane. The *Principles* remained his major psychological work, although he wrote other books and articles in the field. In 1894 he served as president of the American Psychological Association, an office to which he was re-elected in 1904.

In 1897, James again had his title changed to professor of philosophy. Upon his retirement from Harvard in 1907, James started to produce his famous philosophical volumes, *Pragmatism* (1907), *A Pluralistic Universe* (1909), and *The Meaning of Truth* (1909). Although in the last two decades of his life until his death in 1910 his concern was largely with philosophy, he kept active in psychology. In 1905, for example, he attended the Fifth International Congress of Psychology in Rome and read a paper entitled, "Does consciousness exist?" In 1909, he was present at the twentieth anniversary celebration of Clark University, where he met Freud and Jung. Here for the first time he also met Titchener, who had been at Cornell since 1892, and who had demonstrated a noticeably cool attitude toward James, probably because of James's views toward the German psychologists, whom Titchener respected highly.

James continued to encourage and foster psychological enterprises, as, for example, his support of Clifford Beers, a former mental patient who campaigned to improve asylum conditions of the early twentieth century. Beers described the wretched conditions in the institutions for the insane in a volume entitled *A Mind That Found Itself* and in 1908 inaugurated the well-known mental hygiene movement. In so bold and daring an adventure, Beers welcomed the approval, advice, and encouragement of the eminent William James. Beers asked him to become a member of the National Committee for Mental Hygiene. In accepting the invitation to serve as an honorary trustee of this organization, James wrote Beers that it was "not only a duty, but a privilege to promote so humane a cause."

Throughout his life James remained practical, tolerant, and alert to new movements and new developments. He had a keen mind and could communicate his ideas effectively and clearly whether by spoken or written word. He continually suggested new viewpoints in psychology, new topics and areas of research for others to develop. James conceived the ideas, but had no interest in subjecting them to experimentation. As a matter of fact, because of his own reluctance to teach experimental psychology, he induced Hugo Münsterberg to come from Europe to conduct that course at Harvard. He chose Münsterberg because the latter, although he was only 29 years of age, had already published two important volumes in psychology and had displayed much talent. When Münsterberg agreed to remain at Harvard, James relinquished his title of professor of psychology and resumed his original title of professor of philosophy.

Although this trend from science to philosophy has been characteristic of other scientists, too, the intellectual progress of William James deserves special notice here because of the vital role one phase of it played in the growth of the new science. Although psychology was not his exclusive interest, psychology profited immeasurably because James was attracted to it and gave years to teaching and writing about it.

Writings. It is James, the author of the *Principles*, to whom American psychology is indebted for its attainment of status as an independent science before the turn of the century. Written from a positivistic viewpoint—James's single self-admitted claim to originality in the book—this volume launched psychology on a scientific basis in America. Originally contracted for in 1878, *The Principles of Psychology* appeared in two volumes in 1890. Sections of it had been published at various intervals during the 1880's in *Mind*, the *Journal of Speculative Philosophy*, and *Popular Science Monthly*. The first volume covers such topics as the scope of psychology, the function of the brain, habit, methods of psychology, and such problems as the stream of thought, consciousness of self, attention, perception, association, perception of time, and memory. In the second volume, sensation, imagery, perception of space, reasoning, instinct, emotion, and will are discussed. James's inclusion of these topics set a precedent. A product of more than 20 years' study and writing, produced during the formative years of scientific psychology, the *Principles* furnished a pattern which textbook writers followed for about three decades. Thereafter, some topics treated by James, such as will, reasoning, conscience, and the like, receded from prominence in psychology and psychological textbooks.

In writing the *Principles*, James drew heavily from Spencer, Helmholtz, Wundt, and Bain. Spencer and Wundt were both used and rejected by the author. Among others to whom he referred were Hering, Delboeuf, Fechner, Stumpf, Lipps, Ward, Mach, and Münsterberg. James's psychology shows a catholicity. He was able to draw on the German, English, and French contributions without undue enthusiasm for any one line of development. Because of his interested detachment, James could work out his own independent concept of the new psychology.

From the *Principles* it becomes clear that for James psychology is a natural science whose subject matter is the mind in use. In his conviction that mental functions have survival value for the individual, the influence of evolutionary theory on James's thinking is readily detected. *Use* is the core of James's psychology: Mind has use and can be observed in use. James wanted his psychology to be practical, and he was willing to employ whatever methodology—introspection, experimentation, and the like— would throw light on man's mental life. He found a place for the unconscious, the psychical, animal behavior, religious experience, and the abnormal. When James expressed tolerance for these topics, he did not always win approval from his colleagues. However, his psychology—so practical and broad in scope—had a generally popular appeal.

William James was no ivory-tower psychologist. His books had a literary flavor, but they exuded a practical wisdom that captured the reader. Although the *Principles* was his greatest contribution to psychological literature, he produced other psychological works. In 1892, *Psychology: Briefer Course* appeared as an abridgment of the *Principles* designed mainly for classroom use. The *Talks to Teachers* appeared in 1899, and in 1901–1902, *The Varieties of Religious Experience*. While most of these works are today referred to mainly for their historical significance, they aroused considerable interest at the time of their publication. James's best known contributions include the theory of emotions and his views on consciousness, which are discussed in detail in the *Principles*.

Theory of Emotions. Originally published in 1884 in *Mind*, James's theory of emotions succeeded in provoking much inquiry into the nature of emotions. James viewed the emotions as stemming essentially from a physiological base. He believed that "the bodily changes follow directly the perception of the exciting fact, and that our feeling of the same changes as they occur *is* the emotion." Emotion then is the awareness of bodily and physical changes, especially visceral and muscular responses. Others such as Aristotle, Spinoza, Maudsley, Henle, Sergi, and Lotze had anticipated this kind of interpretation of emotion. James acknowledged the work of Carl Lange, the Danish physiologist who almost simultaneously with him promulgated a similar theory in which Lange stressed vasomotor changes.

The interpretations of James and Lange ran counter to the popular view that emotion preceded and caused bodily changes and overt manifestations. According to James, the common sense approach would argue: We lose a fortune, we are sorry, we cry. But James maintained the reverse sequence: We lose a fortune, we cry, we are sorry. He insisted that in emotion one mental state is not followed by another mental state, but that bodily changes intervene between them. These bodily changes follow the perception directly. If they did not occur, James argued, perception would merely be cognitive and devoid of any emotion. Because of James's insistence on peripheral activity as the initiator of emotion, his theory has often been called a peripheral theory of emotions.

It is not surprising that James's interpretation of emotion should have encountered difficulty. It challenged common belief. There were numerous criticisms. In a later paper (1894) James tried to clarify his theory further, differentiating between affective tone and emotion, and stressing the fact that the emotion-arousing stimulus is actually a "total situation" and not a mere object. In spite of his further clarifications, however, the theory continued to be criticized and disputed. In opposition to James's peripheral theory, Cannon and Bard developed the thalamic theory of emotion. This theory stresses the role of the central nervous system in emotions. According to it, both emotional experience and bodily changes, themselves independent of each other, are viewed as dependent upon thalamic discharges.

The Stream of Consciousness.   James's views of consciousness also attracted considerable attention. He argued that mental life must be studied as a whole, and not as a composite of individual elements after the fashion of Wundt. While he approved of analysis as a method, he protested against a purely analytic approach to mental processes and consciousness. James described the phenomena of consciousness existing as a continuous stream.

Starting with the fact that no individual could deny that "states of mind succeed each other in himself," James enunciated five characteristics of consciousness: (1) Every thought or state tends to be part of a personal consciousness. Every thought is had by someone. (2) Within each personal consciousness, states are always changing. James observes that "no state once gone can recur and be identical with what was before." Only objects, not sensations or thoughts, can recur. (3) Within each personal consciousness, thought is sensibly continuous—in spite of gaps as in sleep. (4) It always appears to deal with objects independent of itself. (5) Consciousness is always more interested in one part of its object than in another. It welcomes and rejects, or chooses all the while it thinks.

The fact that such choosing activity exists is demonstrated by selective attention and deliberation of the will.

James considered that the stream of consciousness was connected with, and due to, nervous activity—namely, to "currents and vibrations of the nerve cells of the human brain." Only the intervention of the will "switched the current or changed the vibration." To explain the facts of mental life James turned to biology, not to theology and metaphysics. This type of explanation departed radically from mental philosophy— that is, the American psychology just prior to James.

Influence as Writer and Teacher. That William James occupies a position of distinction in the history of American psychology is indisputable. He was, as his biographer Ralph Barton Perry has observed, "one of the first of the scientific psychologists and one of the last of the philosopher psychologists." Much of his influence may be attributed to his forceful, dynamic, tolerant personality, which made him an outstanding writer and teacher. As a writer he enjoyed a wide audience. His style was clear and powerful. His readers reaped enjoyment and inspiration from him. Phrased in a cogent style, his views and arguments compelled study and, more often than not, acceptance. Both John Dewey and William McDougall admitted that the early development of their own thinking could be attributed largely to having read James's *Principles*. E. L. Thorndike has said that "the influence of James on psychology means essentially the influence of *The Principles of Psychology*." Similarly Spearman has referred to the same work as "the most successful book ever written in psychology." Thousands of college students came under his influence, too, through his *Briefer Course*, a textbook widely used for many years. Beyond the United States, James's writings also made a mighty impact. In Europe his influence has persisted longer than in America, where his works are now usually presented as classics in psychology.

While James displayed his ability to teach chiefly and most effectively through his writings, those who came under his immediate influence in the lecture hall found much stimulation and inspiration from their professor. It has already been stated that James was not an experimentalist. It was not laboratory techniques which he taught his students. He gave them the spirit of the new developments in German psychology. He had read widely in the European literature and had been abroad. He had the background in physiology and in philosophy. All this was at his command in the lecture hall. He had a breadth, a world view in his psychology unsurpassed by his American contemporaries. He exuded a wealth of ideas, which his students seized upon to develop. During the years from 1875 to 1892 he taught psychology regularly at Harvard, but thereafter he taught only one or two courses for some years, much to the chagrin of the students. Many subsequently prominent psychologists came under his influence in their student days. Among them may be mentioned Hall, James Angell, Thorndike, Woodworth, Healy, and Calkins. The accomplishments of these students alone bear eloquent testimony to the inspiration of their professor.

Position in American Psychology. While James gained renown for his writing and his capacity to stimulate others, perhaps his greatest attainment was in charting the course of American psychology during its critical formative days. First of all, he directed Americans from their preoccupation with mental philosophy and its emphasis on religion and morals. In advocating a new psychology he took a precise stand against the German approach to psychology—namely, analysis. Although he presented and interpreted the German psychology to Americans, he vehemently opposed the elementism of Wundt and the latter's insistence on the sole use of introspection. He had an intense dislike for what he called "the humbugging pretense of exactitude in the way of definition of terms and description of states. . . ." James's criticisms carried weight since his comprehension of German psychology was recognized, and he was rated as a competent authority.

In a more positive way, James was influential because he was promulgating a new psychology in which he sought an explanation for mental process through biology. This psychology, the precursor of functional psychology, studied the mind in activity and the usefulness of mind to man. Such a psychology suited American temperament. It was the psychology which James's American colleagues were drafting in their own minds. James verbalized and clarified their ideas. His contemporaries spoke assent because his words stated precisely what they were feeling. James merely pointed the way to functionalism, which later became a formal school under Dewey and Angell at the University of Chicago. James never affiliated himself with this school or considered himself an adherent of it, although he supported the functional approach to psychology. In 1907 James wrote in the *Philosophical Review:*

> We habitually hear much nowadays of the difference between structural and functional psychology. I am not sure that I understand the difference, but it probably has something to do with what I have been privately accustomed to distinguish as the analytical and the clinical points of view in psychological observation . . . the clinical conceptions, though they may be vaguer than the analytic ones, are certainly more adequate, give the concreter picture of the way the whole mind works, and are of far more urgent practical importance. So the 'physician's attitude', the 'functional' psychology is assuredly the thing most worthy of general study.

James wanted psychology to embrace animal study, the abnormal, and a wide variety of subject matter. Later as psychology broadened its horizons, James was not always enthusiastic, as, for example, when psychologists started measuring intelligence. Perhaps the use of psychology in this fashion appeared excessive to him. Gradually as American psychology became more and more practical. James began to seem old fashioned in his insistence on such problems as will and reasoning, topics which most modern American psychologists have tended to shy away from in the twentieth century. Yet there is much in William James that is modern.

In assessing James's influence on psychology it must be acknowledged that he furnished the direction and inspiration, although he did not implement the blueprint which he sketched. On that account some may scorn his psychology as the armchair type. Armchair psychology, so called by

E. W. Scripture, came into disrepute in the late nineteenth century and has remained so in the eyes of the experimentally oriented psychologists. But, if he was an armchair psychologist, he was, as D. Klein observed, "an armchair psychologist with his chair planted in the pulsating world of experience and not in the arid atmosphere of wordy metaphysical abstractions." James never lost sight of the total man. He tried to comprehend man's mental life as it is actually experienced. With this approach perhaps he was able to learn more about man than his experimental colleagues. As an empiricist he utilized any method that would shed light on man. He welcomed psychoanalysis, for example, and saw its potentialities for creating a better understanding of man even though he distrusted its protagonists. On account of this totalistic approach his psychology won recognition and distinction.

G. STANLEY HALL

While William James was the foremost thinker in the beginning period of the new psychology in America, his student G. Stanley Hall was its organizer and promoter. Unlike his professor, Hall was a man of action. Unlike James, too, Hall actually studied at Leipzig. In fact, he was Wundt's first American student. A brief review of his life reveals that he had definite views regarding the kind of psychology that should be promoted in America. With the enthusiasm of a pioneer he set to work to implement his ideas.

Life. G. Stanley Hall (1844-1924) was born into a poor New England farm family and was reared in a stern Puritanical home. Having received his education in a village school, Hall at first taught for a short while. Then, intending to become a minister, he went to Williams College. After graduation he attended Union Theological Seminary in New York for a year, but theology failed to satisfy him. He yearned to be a professor and decided to go to Europe. Hall went to Bonn and then to Berlin, devoting himself to physiology, theology, and philosophy, as well as to mastery of the German language.

Returning to America, he obtained his divinity degree, served as a preacher for a short interval, then as a tutor with a private family. He also taught a variety of subjects, including philosophy, at Antioch College (1872-1876). Hall was interested in philosophy, although dissatisfied with the contemporary philosophy. In 1874 when Wundt's *Principles of Physiological Psychology* was published, Hall read it, was much attracted by the new psychology, and decided to go to Leipzig as soon as possible to study with Wundt. He wanted to leave Antioch directly but was urged to remain another year. After Antioch, his trip abroad was further delayed by a two-year teaching interlude at Harvard, where he studied philosophy and soon became absorbed in the new psychology which James was teaching. In 1878, after completing a thesis on the muscular perception of space, Hall received the first doctorate in the new psychology awarded in the Harvard philosophy department. Thereupon he left Harvard the same year, proceeding first to Berlin and then to Leipzig in the year that the laboratory was formally opened by Wundt. When he returned to America after two years in Germany, Hall delivered lectures at Harvard on education, which were eminently successful and drew much public notice.

In 1881 Hall was invited to lecture at Johns Hopkins, and in 1884 he obtained a professorship there. He remained there for seven years until he went to Clark University as its first president (1888). Hall fashioned the new Clark University as a graduate institution, with five science departments and with a psychological laboratory. His ambitious plans for Clark University were curtailed when the requisite funds were not forthcoming from the founder, Jonas Clark, who, as time went by, offered more opposition and less financial assistance to Hall. Disappointed and humiliated, still Hall remained with the institution for 32 years as its president. From his retirement (1921) until his death (1924) he continued to be a dynamic and active participant in psychology.

Hall, the Psychological Evolutionist.   Quite early Hall, a devotee of evolutionary theory, wanted psychology to take cognizance of evolutionary doctrine. In describing evolution's appeal to him, Hall used to say that the word evolution "was music to my ears and seemed to fit my mouth better than any other." Through the application of evolutionary principles Hall hoped to arrive at a better understanding of human behavior. He tried to work out comparisons between human and animal behavior. His efforts earned for him an appellation of which he was immensely proud, "the Darwin of the mind." His devotion to evolutionary doctrine approximated a devotion to religion, and the zeal with which he taught this doctrine was akin to the zeal of the most ardent religionists.

Influenced by evolution as he was, Hall could not tolerate the pre-Darwinian psychology. His object was to develop a kind of evolutionary psychology or, what is customarily called, genetic psychology. Hall's evolutionism is readily evident in his recapitulation theories of child development and of children's play activities. The recapitulation theory (ontogeny recapitulates phylogeny) endeavors to demonstrate that the individual's growth and development follow the pattern that the race has gone through in its evolution. Thus, for example, children's climbing activities are interpreted as reverting to the anthropoid. In other words, Hall's genetic psychology views man's mental life not as a succession or series of mental states but rather as a product of years of biological development.

Genetic Development.   With inspiration from evolution, Hall forged ahead to learn more about child behavior. His child studies attracted attention to him and to Clark University, which he made famous as a center for child study. In his investigations of the child, Hall made generous use of the technique employed by Galton—namely, the questionnaire method. One of Hall's early researches, published in 1883, concerned the content of children's minds on entering school, a study inspired by a similar one done in Berlin in 1869. A variety of questions was put to young children to discover just what and how much they knew by the time they presented themselves for formal schooling. Questions such as, "Have you ever seen a river?" and "Where does wool come from?" were asked. The answers to such questions were tabulated to appraise the child's knowledge at this early period.

As one might readily guess, this preoccupation with child study was certain to interest educators. Teachers began to seek out information relative to children, which might be useful to them. Hall demonstrated how psychology could help teachers acquire better understanding of their pupils. Thus psychological pedagogy, or a study of the psychological foundations of education, was initiated by Hall as a branch of psychological science.

In his contribution to genetic psychology, Hall treated the full gamut from childhood through old age. To its literature he made two major contributions besides numerous articles. The first, published in 1904 and entitled *Adolescence: Its Psychology and Its Relations to Physiology, Anthropology, Sociology, Sex, Crime, Religion, and Education* presented an encyclopedic treatment of youth. It appeared later (1906) in condensed form. His views on adolescence and his penetrating analysis of this period especially influenced secondary education. In 1922, Hall, an old man himself then, wrote a treatise entitled *Senescence*. Old age, which in the mid-twentieth century became an important concern, was scarcely given any attention in early scientific psychology. Hall's realistic appraisal of senescence and his appreciation of the problems of the aging, bear further testimony to his originality and vision.

In respect to content, Hall's contributions were clearly in genetic psychology. He did more than set up this special branch of psychology with its allied field of psychological pedagogy. He tried to promote child study by founding the National Association for the Study of the Child in 1893.

Hall as Organizer. Hall played an important role as organizer of American psychology generally. His principal organizational efforts were applied to the establishment of laboratories, the founding of journals, and the organizing of the American Psychological Association. The first real working laboratory in America was founded by Hall in 1883 at Johns Hopkins. Later he established the laboratory at Clark University. At both institutions Hall stimulated and inspired many psychologists who became the foremost leaders in twentieth century American psychology and also founders of laboratories. Dewey, Cattell, Sanford, Burnham, and Jastrow were students at Hopkins in Hall's time. At Clark he taught Terman and Gesell. Directly and indirectly, therefore, Hall contributed to the growth of laboratory psychology in America.

Not content with creating research facilities for psychology, Hall secured a medium for the publication of research results by founding in

1887 the first American psychological periodical, still in existence, the *American Journal of Psychology*. Thereafter, he founded other journals, some of which, however, did not survive more than a decade or so. At least two more should be mentioned here, since they are still being published and are considered important journals: *Pedagogical Seminary* founded in 1891, and renamed the *Journal of Genetic Psychology* in 1927, and the *Journal of Applied Psychology* founded in 1917. Such periodicals offered a clearing house for the interchange of ideas and results from laboratory to laboratory and from psychologist to psychologist.

To promote psychology as a science, Hall suggested the formation of an organization of psychologists. The planning meeting for this group was called by him in July 1892 in his study at Clark University. The new organization, the American Psychological Association, had 26 charter members. By the end of the year, in December 1892, it held its first annual meeting at the University of Pennsylvania. Hall was the first president and was re-elected to that office in 1924. Only he and William James have had the honor of re-election to the presidency of this association. The subsequent growth and development of the American Psychological Association will be treated in Chapter 12.

Hall and Psychoanalysis.   Hall must be cited for literally bringing psychoanalysis to America. In 1909, on the occasion of Clark University's twentieth anniversary, Hall arranged a symposium to which he invited Freud and his fellow psychoanalysts, Jung, Jones, and Ferenczi. At this celebration American psychologists, like James, Titchener, and Cattell, met the founder of psychoanalysis, Sigmund Freud, and heard the tenets of his system from him and his colleagues. Hall further sponsored the spread of psychoanalysis in America by translating Freud's *General Introduction to Psychoanalysis*. While the translator did not fully share Freud's view on pansexualism, he recognized Freud as "the most original and creative mind in psychology of our generation." The Clark University catalogue stated that psychoanalysis was included in the "complete course in psychology at Clark Univeristy." Sympathy with the system at this early period was quite radical because his fellow psychologists, Münsterberg, James, and Titchener, felt no such enthusiasm for the Viennese psychiatrist. James and Titchener distrusted Freud, and Münsterberg abhorred Freud's system intensely.

The Versatile Pioneer.   In summing up Hall's contributions to psychology: his founding of laboratories, journals, and associations; his promotion of psychoanalysis; his development of genetic psychology and psychological pedagogy, one is impressed with the versatility of this pioneer. A variety of projects and activities interested him, and many of his self-admitted "crazes" became permanent contributions to American psychology.

Although Hall founded no particular school or system of psychology, he did bring the influence of biology, especially evolution, to bear heavily upon American psychological science, which in turn laid the foundation for future systems. Hall more than achieved the goal he formulated for himself in these words: "To contribute ever so little to introduce concepts in psychology, where they were practically unknown, and to advance the view that there were just as many rudiments and vestiges in our psychic activity and make-up as in our bodies, and that the former was just as much a product of slow evolutionary tendencies as the latter."

Hall was principally an organizer and promoter. His biographer Lorine Pruette says of him:

> In all his long life of research he made no great discoveries—but he never faltered in his search for truth. His greatest service unquestionably lay in his capacity for stimulating others. His vigorous imagination cast off countless sparks, some of which tended by other hands, have developed into a steady flame.

Hall's ability to inspire others and to organize helped lay a solid foundation for American scientific psychology and for applied psychology. He exerted a deep personal influence on teachers and education. When the occasion demanded, he gave his opinions as a psychologist to educators. This he did in 1919 after World War I, when he suggested the course of study that should be established to meet the future demands of democracy. One by one, he treated subjects such as health, biology, physics, literature, and history, with a stress on patriotism and vocational guidance—all of which he considered requisites of education for democracy. In the list he also included religion, stating that: ". . . religion itself created schools and . . . the very root of the impulse to even science is religious, for 'it seeks to think God's thoughts after Him'." In this postwar period Hall also turned his attention to industry. He called for a rehumanizing of industry and an application of psychological principles in this field.

Hall had many loyal, devoted friends and admirers, but he was not without severe critics. Some of his contemporaries lauded him for his outstanding achievements, and others belittled him and minimized these same attainments. In spite of the diversity of opinions that have been expressed concerning Hall, however, he has won incontestable recognition as a versatile promoter of American psychology.

In the 1880's James and Hall were the two prominent figures in American psychology. With them also was *George Trumbull Ladd* (1842-1921), who had achieved distinction with the publication of his textbook, *Elements of Physiological Psychology* (1887), to which reference was made earlier. These men were the three first generation psychologists who trained and stimulated those who were to develop American psychology more fully in the twentieth century.

GEORGE TRUMBULL LADD

After graduation from Andover Theological Seminary (1869), Ladd served for ten years as a minister. Then he taught the subjects which theologians customarily taught at that time, first at Bowdoin College

(1879-1881) and then at Yale (1881-1905). At Yale he pursued his study of physiological psychology and wrote the *Elements of Physiological Psychology* (1887), which offered a digest of Wundt's psychology to Americans three years before James's *Principles* appeared. The *Elements* represented a careful synthesis of the existing scattered literature with considerable emphasis on the physiology of the nervous system. It received a hearty welcome in America and in England. The book was widely used and was revised in 1911 by R. S. Woodworth. An abridgment of this important textbook appeared in 1891, and was followed in 1894 by a *Primer of Psychology*. In 1894 Ladd also published *Psychology, Descriptive and Explanatory*, which was more vulnerable to criticism because there were then competing textbooks such as James's and Baldwin's. This later volume was less successful than Ladd's initial venture.

In addition to these books Ladd also established laboratory psychology at Yale. He brought E. W. Scripture to Yale to direct the formal laboratory when it was instituted in 1892. Thereafter, Ladd devoted himself more to philosophy than to psychology.

Ladd reflected the early American trend toward functional psychology by consistent stress in his writings on the usefulness of mind. As theologian and psychologist he helped to bridge the gap between the old and the new psychology in America. His election as second president of the American Psychological Association bears testimony to the high esteem in which he was held by his contemporaries. Although he left the psychological scene in 1905 when he retired from Yale, his contribution to the new science through his textbooks had already been substantial, so that he was given the title, "the Sully of America."

JAMES McKEEN CATTELL

Outstanding in the second generation of American psychologists was the Leipzig-trained *James McKeen Cattell* (1860-1944). Cattell took his undergraduate work at Lafayette College. He went to Europe to study philosophy and stayed there from 1880 to 1882. While abroad he heard the lectures of Lotze at Göttingen and of Wundt at Leipzig. This experience had a determining effect upon his future career. On receiving a fellowship in philosophy for a paper on Lotze, Cattell returned to America and went to Johns Hopkins for a year. There he became one of Hall's students. In 1883 he returned to Leipzig and literally thrust himself upon Wundt as an assistant. He remained there for three years.

During this period "reaction time" was an important topic of psychological investigation. Wundt used the reaction time experiment to measure the time required for such elementary processes as perception, choice, and association. Such measurement was called "mental chronometry." Cattell was more interested in using total reaction time as a tool to study attention, fatigue, and practice. This approach enabled him to pursue his interest in individual differences. For his doctoral thesis Cattell selected a topic for which Wundt showed no enthusiasm and which he described as "ganz Amerikanisch" ("typically American"). Originally published in five papers in *Philosophische Studien* in 1886, the thesis was also published the same year in the British *Mind* under the title, "The Time Taken Up by Cerebral Operations." Apparatus and method, reaction time, will time, and the influence of attention, fatigue, and practice on reaction time were carefully treated. All Cattell's Leipzig experiments dealt with time, but not merely with reaction time. He also measured, for example, the exposure time required for the perception of letters, words, colors, and pictures.

Awarded his doctorate at Leipzig in 1886, Cattell was appointed instructor at the University of Pennsylvania. After one year he returned to Europe, this time as lecturer at Cambridge (1888), where he associated with Galton. The latter, it will be recalled, was engrossed in his study of individual differences and had already established an anthropometric laboratory in which actual measurements and studies were made. This association with Galton encouraged and inspired Cattell's already strong interest in individual differences.

When Cattell returned to America in 1888, he was ready to inaugurate a psychology of individual differences. Back at the University of Pennsylvania, he established a laboratory. He was also nominated the first American professor of psychology. Three years later, in 1891, Cattell moved to Columbia University where he remained until 1917. He established the Columbia laboratory and did considerable research. After he was forced to resign because of his pacifistic stand during World War I, Cattell accepted no other academic posts. Instead he dedicated his executive talents to the business management and public relations of the profession of psychology until his death in 1944. His fellow psychologists appreciated his many contributions to their science. An example of their esteem for him was the invitation to Cattell to preside as America's senior psychologist at the Ninth International Congress of Psychology in New Haven in 1929, the first international congress held in America.

Contributions to Laboratory Psychology. At Leipzig Cattell had displayed ability and originality in laboratory research. In fact, he had found it difficult to limit his work to Wundt's rigid laboratory schedule. Frequently he worked after hours in his own room and with his own apparatus. At Columbia University, his skill and ingenuity expressed themselves in his invention of apparatus for studying vocal reactions— namely, the lip key and the voice key. Besides reaction time, Cattell conducted investigations on association, perception and reading, individual differences in mental abilities, and psychophysics. In the field of psychophysics, he developed in 1902 the order-of-merit method, a technique employed to advantage in his study of American men of science. Although Cattell published a considerable number of articles, his literary output was not impressive. He did not produce any textbook.

Through his teaching and experimental research Cattell stimulated his students and imbued them with research spirit. Among the students who received their doctorates from Columbia during his administration are such outstanding psychologists as E. L. Thorndike, R. S. Woodworth, S. I. Franz, E. K. Strong, A. T. Poffenberger, J. F. Dashiell, and A. I. Gates. Through his own work and the attainments of his students, Cattell advanced the techniques, apparatus, and statistical treatment of data in American laboratory psychology.

Mental Tests.   In conjunction with his laboratory work, Cattell initiated the mental test movement and coined the name "mental test." The testing movement is perhaps his greatest contribution, for it is in intensive and extensive development of psychological and educational tests that American psychology has achieved general attention. Cattell foresaw the future importance of mental tests in psychology.

Cattell developed a battery of mental tests at the University of Pennsylvania, which he later extended at Columbia. These Columbia Tests, known as the Freshman Tests, encompassed physical characteristics, vision, hearing, dermal and muscular sensations, time measurements, memory, imagery, and the like. Cattell hoped to discover an interdependence among these measures. Applying correlational techniques to his data, however, he found only low correlations. These results were disappointing to Cattell, but were subsequently attributed to attentuation by Spearman, the British statistician-psychologist. Cattell's scheme for analyizng discrete functions in this fashion was largely overshadowed by Binet's intelligence test. However, Cattell's investigation of individual differences contributed substantially to the development of correlational techniques.

Cattell's mental tests demonstrated how psychology could be quantified, and fashioned differential psychology, as a distinct branch of modern psychology. Cattell had imported the spirit of Galton to America. Americans liked that spirit though they were unaware, as was pointed out earlier, of their indebtedness, through Cattell, to Galton's inspiration. The psychology that Cattell fostered won support because it suited the American functional spirit so well. It had use. Cattell lived to see considerable attainment of the promise in the field of mental testing which he initiated. His promotion of the mental test movement brought attention and recognition to Columbia and particularly to his student E. L. Thorndike, whose work in this field he encouraged.

Applied Psychology.   Practicality was a primary consideration for Cattell. Whether he was dealing with mental tests or laboratory results, his concern, in true functional spirit, was with their usefulness, which he constantly strove to demonstrate. "We should be practical men and see to it that we have a practical psychology," Cattell admonished his colleagues. This was the recurrent and dominant theme in his writings and speeches. He exhorted his students to apply psychology to education, medicine, and industry. At the same time he urged the recognition of individual differences so that people could be trained for work which they could do best, and which would be most satisfying to them. Such applications, Cattell held, would promote better living and increase human happiness in society. Applied social psychology appealed to him too. Disturbed as he had been by the world conflict into which America had been plunged in the early twentieth century, Cattell felt that psychology could ameliorate international relations. He vehemently opposed war and was convinced that, through science, good will could be fostered between nations.

Psychology's Businessman. Academic life, with its laboratory work, teaching, and administration of a university department, was not sufficient to satisfy Cattell's energetic and aggressive nature. Possessed by a zeal—not unlike Hall's—to create channels for the dissemination of psychological information, with J. M. Baldwin he founded the *Psychological Review* in 1894. Later the two established and edited *Psychological Monographs* and *Psychological Index*. Cattell even took over *Science*, the organ of the American Association for the Advancement of Science, when that publication met financial reverses. The series known as *The American Men of Science* was instituted by him. Later he founded *Leaders of Education* and *The Directory of American Scholars*. Subsequently Cattell served as editor of *Popular Science Monthly* and, later, of one of its off-shoots, *The Scientific Monthly*. He also edited *School and Society* and the *American Naturalist*. Such an impressive list of "foundings" and editorships has not been excelled and would be difficult for anyone to surpass.

In addition to these publication enterprises, Cattell served remarkably well as public relations man for psychology. Through his numerous professional and scientific affiliations—for example, his participation in the American Association for the Advancement of Science—he brought wider attention to psychology. Cattell seized every opportunity to espouse the cause of psychology, which he insisted was not new, but really one of the older sciences. Such gentle but persistent propaganda for psychology, while it was still struggling for academic and public recognition, was invaluable.

In the years following his retirement from academic life, Cattell tried to extend further the application of psychology. To facilitate this extension Cattell actually put psychology into business. In 1921 he founded in New York the Psychological Corporation, a nonprofit organization having for its avowed purpose the "advancement of psychology and the promotion of the useful applications of psychology." Among the 20 original directors of the corporation were Hall, Ladd, and Titchener.

In the history of American psychology, Cattell stands out as an important link between the pioneers, James, Hall, and Ladd, and the prominent twentieth century psychologists. He extended the efforts of the pioneers in his advancement of laboratory psychology, development of mental tests, and promotion of psychological literature and applied psychology. To the succeeding generation of psychologists, he handed down a psychology which he had groomed as a profession, and for which both as science and profession he had won recognition among other American scientists.

JAMES MARK BALDWIN

Cattell's collaborator in publication ventures, James Mark Baldwin (1861-1934), was more the philosopher and theorist than an experimentalist. After undergraduate studies at Princeton, he went to Germany to study philosophy (1884-1885). While at Leipzig, he studied psychology with Wundt and later obtained his doctorate in philosophy with McCosh at Princeton. Thereafter, he founded laboratories at Toronto (1889) and at Princeton (1893). In 1903, going to Johns Hopkins, Baldwin reactivated the laboratory which had been discontinued after Hall's departure for Clark University in 1888. After he left Hopkins in 1908 Baldwin's activities were mainly outside of psychology. During the later years of his life he taught in Paris, where he died in 1934.

Baldwin is best known for his interest in psychological theory, for his promulgation of evolution, for his several publication enterprises, and for his writings. Among the latter are the two volume *Handbook of Psychology* (1889; 1891); and the two volumes in which he gave eloquent support to the evolutionary doctrine—*Mental Development in the Child and the Race* (1890) and *Social and Ethical Interpretations in Mental Development* (1897). In 1913, when he was no longer vitally interested in psychology, he wrote a brief *History of Psychology*. In addition to his cooperative publication enterprises with Cattell, he also published the *Dictionary of Philosophy and Psychology* (1901-1902), a two volume work to which European and American philosophers and psychologists contributed.

Baldwin's interests were always more theoretical and philosophical than experimental. In American psychology he played more a supporting than a leading role. Baldwin championed the work of Hall and Cattell by endorsing the functional approach to psychology and the psychology of individual differences. Such support, along with his textbooks and publications, helped to promote and advance American psychology in its formative stages.

REPRESENTATIVES OF WUNDTIAN PSYCHOLOGY IN AMERICA

In 1892 two European-born, Leipzig-trained psychologists were invited to America to assume charge of laboratories—*Hugo Münsterberg* (1863-1916) to Harvard and *E. B. Titchener* (1867-1927) to Cornell. These men represented completely divergent views. Titchener wanted psychology to be pure science. Münsterberg cultivated applied psychology.

Hugo Münsterberg. It will be recalled that Münsterberg was brought to Harvard by James to teach experimental psychology. In the early part of his career Münsterberg had dedicated himself to experimentation. He wrote in German *Willenshandlung* ("Treatise on the Will," 1888), *Beiträge zur experimentellen Psychologie* ("Contributions to Experimental Psychology," 1889-1892), and *Grundzüge der Psychologie* ("Principles of

Psychology," 1900). Münsterberg developed interest in applied psychology, especially the applications to law and industry. He contributed the volumes *On the Witness Stand* (1908), *Psychology and Industrial Efficiency* (1913) and *Psychology, General and Applied* (1914), and some aptitude tests. Because of his overzealous dedication to practical applications of psychology, Münsterberg incurred the scorn of those who abhorred such activity as a mere popularization. Psychotherapy was also in the sphere of his interest, and he practiced it (he had a medical degree).

Edward Bradford Titchener. Unlike Münsterberg, Titchener opposed applied psychology, sought to keep psychology pure science, and relentlessly insisted on the study of mental elements by means of introspection. In spite of the fact that around him he saw functionalism growing and flourishing with its concomitant applications of psychology, he continued to oppose functionalism and to insist on the structuralist approach. Like Wundt, Titchener studied consciousness through introspection. Very rigid training in introspection was demanded by him of participants in laboratory experiments. The latter consisted in careful analysis of the elements: sensations, images, and affective states.

Titchener was an important figure in American psychology at the turn of the century because of his experimentation and his books. He wrote many volumes, among them: *An Outline of Psychology* (1896); the four volume *Experimental Psychology: A Manual of Laboratory Practice* (1901-1905); *Lectures on the Elementary Psychology of Feeling and Attention* (1908); *Lectures on the Elementary Psychology of the Thought Processes* (1909); *A Textbook of Psychology* (1910); and *A Beginner's Psychology* (1915). Besides texts, Titchener published numerous notes, articles, and translations.

Many of the future leaders of American psychology had earned their doctorates with Titchener before the turn of the century. Among them were Margaret Washburn, W. Pillsbury, Madison Bentley, and Eleanor Gamble. Characteristically he demanded loyalty and devotion from his students. In the American Psychological Association, he took little part and showed little interest in participating with his fellow members. Instead he formed his own group, the Society of Experimental Psychologists, who met informally. Titchener served as editor of the *American Journal of Psychology*, in which, exclusively, the work of the Cornell laboratory was published.

Much controversy developed around Titchener and his views in America. His system of psychology—which will be described in more detail in Chapter 17—was unpopular in America. Titchener, British born and thoroughly attached to German psychology, refused to change with the times. American psychologists were unwilling to restrict their science to the introspective analysis of consciousness. While they pursued their studies of individual differences, Titchener continued his analysis of the generalized mind. Ultimately the structuralist system disappeared from the American scene.

EXPANSION OF AMERICAN PSYCHOLOGY
AT THE TURN OF THE CENTURY

By the turn of the twentieth century, American psychology was making rapid strides as science. Having abandoned its philosophical and theological entanglements, it forged ahead rapidly on its own course. Because of the vigorous and masterful efforts of the early pioneers, the science flourished. American psychologists started to repay the debt which they had incurred to German psychology. American works were being translated into German and French. Instead of traveling to Europe, most students were studying at American universities. Popular interest was aroused, too. In 1893 at the World's Fair in Chicago, psychology made its debut before the public through the efforts of Münsterberg and Jastrow. To demonstrate experimental psychology, they featured exhibits of laboratory apparatus. Services of a testing laboratory were available for those who wanted information about their abilities. Psychological articles in popular magazines appeared with increasing frequency at this time also. Further expansion of psychology was reflected in the establishment of new laboratories, new fields of interest, new publications, and new psychological organizations.

Laboratories. From about 1887 to 1893 there was a phenomenal growth in the number of laboratories, with their establishment at most prominent universities in the country. In rapid succession, laboratories were founded, after the first was organized at Hopkins by Hall (1883): at the University of Pennsylvania by Cattell (1887); at the University of Wisconsin by Jastrow and at Indiana University by Bryan (1888); at Clark University by Hall with E. C. Sanford (1889); at Toronto by Baldwin (1890); at Columbia by Cattell, at Wellesley by Mary Calkins, at Cornell by Frank Angell, and at Catholic University by E. A. Pace (1891); at Harvard University by James with Münsterberg, at Yale by Ladd with Scripture, and at Brown by E. B. Delabarre (1892); at Princeton by Baldwin, at Minnesota by James Angell, and at Stanford by Frank Angell (1893). By 1900 there were approximately 40 psychological laboratories in the United States.

Fields of Psychology. In these laboratories, research was conducted along varied lines. Different fields of psychology began to emerge as a result. Under Hall at Clark, *genetic* psychology progressed and foundations were laid for *educational* psychology, a field later to be more fully developed by E. L. Thorndike at Columbia. *Differential* psychology, together with *mental tests*, was cultivated at Columbia by Cattell. At Cornell, Titchener continued in the tradition of Wundt, while at Harvard Münsterberg promoted *applied* psychology with its specific applications to industry, law, and medicine. By 1896, *clinical* psychology was inaugurated by Lightner Witmer at the University of Pennsylvania, as a result of his initial efforts to help school teachers cope with poor spellers and readers. Although the clinic began with an educational orientation, it soon became obvious that often personality and emotional problems were at the root of these seemingly educational difficulties. With the introduction of psychoanalysis to America, clinical psychology was further advanced. In the same decade that saw clinical psychology inaugurated, Thorndike was busying himself with *comparative* psychology. Thus, by 1900, the major fields of psychology were already being marked off, and various areas of specialization were available to those entering psychology. With the increased interest in genetic, educational, differential, applied, clinical, and comparative psychology, enthusiasm for pure experimental psychology started to wane. Now practical studies began to supplant the older investigations of reaction time, sensation, and perception.

Increased Publication.   Besides the rapid growth in laboratories and in research, this period also witnessed much enterprise in psychological publications. American periodicals, such as the *American Journal of Psychology* (1887), *Pedagogical Seminary* (1891), *Psychological Review* (1894), *Psychological Index* (1894), and *Psychological Monographs* (1894) had their beginnings. Moreover, numerous textbooks were being published, most of which have been enumerated previously in the historical consideration of the various psychologists. The younger students entering psychology no longer had to confine their reading to foreign volumes in the original or in translation. They had American textbooks available such as Ladd's *Elements* (1887), Baldwin's *Handbook* (1889-1891), and James's *Principles* (1890). Throughout the last two decades of the nineteenth century the number of books and journal articles increased steadily.

Organizational Activity.   Since scientific psychology was new and presented considerable opportunity for development, it attracted many students. The number of psychologists began to increase rapidly. Gradually psychology was acquiring status and recognition. By 1892, it will be recalled, Hall had already organized the American Psychological Association. This group of psychologists began with 31 members, 26 charter members and 5 elected. A decade later in 1902 the membership was 127. Regional associations also began to be established, such as the Eastern Psychological Association in 1896. Professional contacts in these associations no doubt helped to stimulate activity in the various areas of psychological endeavor during this early period.

EARLY TWENTIETH CENTURY TRENDS

From 1900 to 1915 the number of laboratories almost doubled. The subject matter and methods of psychological investigation changed. Researches on consciousness declined. Sense perception, child development, feelings and emotions became topics of increased study. Although scientific methods were used, the research characteristically suffered from the limitations of small numbers of subjects, of artificial laboratory situations, and of an elementistic approach to human behavior. Interest was variously expressed in the application of psychology to education, law, business, and industry, but by no means received the universal endorsement of psychologists.

In the beginning of the twentieth century several new journals began publication: *Psychological Bulletin* (1904); *Journal of Philosophy, Psychology, and Scientific Method* (1904); *Archives of Psychology* (1906); *Journal of Abnormal Psychology* (1906); *Psychological Clinic* (1907); *Journal of Educational Psychology* (1910); *Psychoanalytic Review* (1913); and *Journal of Experimental Psychology* (1916).

From about 1902 to 1911, the schools of psychology arose. It was previously noted that from the outset American psychology had a functional character. The functional psychology first sketched by James and Ladd and fostered by Baldwin was implemented by Hall and Cattell. While these developments were taking place, Titchener at Cornell persevered in his study of mental elements and in the exclusive use of introspection. Despite his efforts to preserve the Wundtian tradition, the American enthusiasm for functionalism and for a psychology different from the Leipzig variety could not be curbed. The first formal collective opposition to German psychology, and to its counterpart headed by Titchener, found expression in the school of functionalism which originated at the University of Chicago under John Dewey and James Angell in 1896. In view of the long-standing definite trend toward functional psychology it remained simply for someone to state the functional position systematically. Dewey did this. He verbalized what many of his contemporaries felt and believed. He rejected Wundt's elementism and advocated the study of function or process. For at least a decade, a controversy raged between functionalism and Titchener's system—which then came into sharper focus as structuralism.

Psychologists in America became increasingly vocal in asserting their views on the content and methods of psychology. They began to scrutinize each other. The literature of the period reflects their critical attitude toward contemporary American research, textbooks, and journal articles. As considerable diversity of opinion developed, other systems and schools emerged. In 1913, Watson's famous paper, entitled *Psychology as the Behaviorist Views It*, introduced his new system. Behaviorism, with its mechanistic emphasis, stimulated exciting changes and significantly altered the course of American psychology. Watson's surging popularity as the founder of this challenging system temporarily dimmed the glory of William James. To the bold young behaviorists, James seemed armchairish and outmoded.

Immediately prior to World War I Americans concentrated on psychological science at home. While they were perfecting it, World War I summoned psychology to duty. Eventually American psychology, which had not commanded much respect in Europe previously, won recognition and attained world leadership in the twentieth century.

HIGHLIGHTS OF AMERICAN PSYCHOLOGY: BEGINNINGS

1883   First laboratory in America established at Johns Hopkins by Hall.

1886   Cattell, first American recipient of Leipzig doctorate in psychology.
       Publication of Dewey's *Psychology*.

1887   Hall founded first American journal, *American Journal of Psychology*.
       Publication of Ladd's *Elements of Physiological Psychology*.

1888   Laboratories founded at University of Wisconsin (Jastrow) and at Indiana University
       (Bryan).
       Cattell visited Galton at Cambridge and on return received first professorship of
       psychology and founded the laboratory at the University of Pennsylvania.

1889   Founding of Laboratory at Clark University by Hall with E. C. Sanford.

1890   Publication of James's *Principles of Psychology*.
       Cattell coined term "mental test."
       Laboratory founded at Toronto (Baldwin).

1891   Laboratories founded at Columbia (Cattell); at Catholic University (Pace); at
       Wellesley (Mary Calkins); and at Cornell (Frank Angell).
       Hall founded *Pedagogical Seminary*.

1892   Laboratories founded at Harvard (James with Münsterberg); at Yale (Ladd with
       Scripture); and at Brown (E. B. Delabarre).
       Founding of the American Psychological Association.

1893   Laboratories founded at Princeton (Baldwin); at Stanford (Frank Angell); at Minne-
       sota (James Angell).

1894   *Psychological Review*, *Psychological Index*, and *Psychological Monographs* founded
       by Cattell and Baldwin

1896   First psychological clinic founded at the University of Pennsylvania by Witmer.
       Publication of Dewey's paper, *The Reflex Arc Concept in Psychology*, which presented
       the functional viewpoint against elementism.

1898   First American doctorate in animal psychology obtained by E. L. Thorndike.

1904   Society of Experimental Psychologists established.
       Founding of *Psychological Bulletin* by Cattell and Baldwin.

1905   Titchener published last volumes of
       Experimental Psychology: A Manual of Laboratory Practice

1906   Founding of the *Journal of Abnormal Psychology* by Morton Prince.   James Angell
       gave his presidential address to the American Psychological Association entitled *The
       Province of Functional Psychology*, in which he stated the functionalist viewpoint.

1908   First American textbook on animal psychology: Margaret Washburn's *Animal Mind*.

1909   Twentieth anniversary celebration of Clark University: Freud and Jung visited
       America.

1910   William James died.
       Founding of *Journal of Educational Psychology*.
       Publication of Guy Whipple's *Manual of Mental and Physical Tests* (2nd ed., 2
       vols., 1914–1915).

REFERENCES

EARLY HISTORY OF AMERICAN PSYCHOLOGY

Albrecht, F. M. The new psychology in America: 1880–1895. Unpublished doctoral dissertation, Johns Hopkins, 1960.

Britt, S. H. European background (1600–1900) for American psychology. *J. gen. Psychol.*, 1942, *27*, 311–329.

Buchner, E. F. A quarter century of psychology in America: 1878–1903. *Amer. J. Psychol.*, 1903, *14*, 402–416.

Davis, R. C. American psychology, 1800–1885. *Psychol. Rev.*, 1936, *43*, 471–493.

Fay, J. W. *American psychology before William James*. New Brunswick, N. J.: Rutgers Univer. Press, 1939.

Garvey, C. R. List of American psychological laboratories. *Psychol. Bull.*, 1929, *26*, 652–660.

Jastrow, J. American psychology in the '80's and '90's. *Psychol. Rev.*, 1943, *50*, 65–67.

Ladd, G. T. On certain hindrances to the progress of psychology in America. *Psychol. Rev.*, 1899, *6*, 121–133.

WILLIAM JAMES

Allport, G. W. The productive paradoxes of William James. *Psychol. Rev.*, 1943, *50*, 95–120.

Allport, G. W. William James and the behavioral sciences. *J. Hist. behav. Sci.*, 1966, *2*, 145–147.

Harper, R. S. The first psychological laboratory. *Isis*, 1950, *41*, 158–161.

Perry, R. B. *The thought and character of William James*. 2 vols. Boston: Little, Brown & Co., 1935.

Pillsbury, W. B. Titchener and James. *Psychol. Rev.*, 1943, *50*, 71–73.

—— A list of the published writings of William James *Psychol. Rev.*, 1911, *18*, 157–165.

EVOLUTIONISM AND AMERICAN PSYCHOLOGY

Angell, J. R. The influence of Darwin on psychology. *Psychol. Rev.*, 1909. *16*, 152–169.

Boring, E. G. The influence of evolutionary theory upon American psychological thought. In S. Persons (Ed.), *Evolutionary thought in America*. New Haven, Conn.: Yale Univer. Press, 1950. Pp. 267–298. Reprinted in R.I. Watson & D. T. Campbell (Eds.), *History, psychology, and science: selected papers by Edwin G. Boring*. New York: Wiley, 1963. Pp. 159–184.

Davies, A. E. The influence of biology on the development of modern psychology in America. *Psychol. Rev.*, 1923, *30*, 164–175.

Howard, D. T. The influence of evolutionary doctrine on psychology. *Psychol. Rev.*, 1927, *34*, 305–312.

Morgan, C. L. Comparative and genetic psychology. *Psychol. Rev.*, 1905, *12*, 78–97.

G. STANLEY HALL

Burnham, W. H. The man, G. Stanley Hall. *Psychol. Rev.*, 1925, *32*, 89–102.

Fisher, S. C. The psychological and educational work of Granville Stanley Hall. *Amer. J. Psychol.*, 1925, *36*, 1–52.

Pruette, L. *G. Stanley Hall: A biography of a mind*. New York: Appleton-Century-Crofts, 1926.

THE AMERICAN PSYCHOLOGICAL ASSOCIATION

Cattell, J. McK. The founding of the association and of the Hopkins and Clark laboratories. *Psychol. Rev.*, 1943, *50*, 61–64.

Dennis, W., & Boring, E. G. The founding of the A.P.A. *Amer. Psychologist*, 1952, *7*, 95–97.

Fernberger, S. W. The American Psychological Association: a historical summary, 1892–1930. *Psychol. Bull.*, 1932, *29*, 1–89.

JAMES McKEEN CATTELL

Poffenberger, A. T. (Ed.) *James McKeen Cattell: man of science*. Vol. I. *Psychological research*. Vol. II. *Addresses and formal papers*. Lancaster, Pa.: Science Press, 1947.

Woodworth, R. S. J. McKeen Cattell, 1860–1944. *Psychol. Rev.*, 1944, *51*, 201–209.

11

American Psychology: Growth as a Science

IN THE 1880'S AND 1890'S, while they were importing German psychology and were struggling to develop their psychological laboratories and departments in the universities, American psychologists were a fairly cohesive group. Most of them were rather generally agreed on basic concepts and on a functional orientation for their science. At the turn of the century, however, the traditional American functionalism concerned with the powers and operations of the mind was attacked by Titchener's structuralism and, later more forcefully, by Watson's behaviorism. By the second decade of the twentieth century, the influences of Freud's psychoanalysis and of behaviorism were making an impact on American psychology.

Psychology in America gradually broke loose from its European moorings and acquired its own distinctive character. Less and less attention was paid to foreign literature as American psychologists produced their own. As it progressed, American psychology emphasized the biocentric and objective in contrast to the older anthropocentric, introspective psychology. It encouraged large-scale studies on practical problems. Philosophical terminology was gradually abandoned. Philosophical problems and traditional subjects of study, such as consciousness, yielded place to researches designed to increase man's personal happiness and his social efficiency. American investigations from 1900 to 1925 tended to group themselves into rather clearly differentiated subfields. These studies encompassed mental measurement (Cattell, Terman); child and adolescent psychology (Hall); educational psychology (Dewey, Thorndike, Judd); social psychology (Dewey, Hall, Baldwin); industrial psychology (Münsterberg, Scott); clinical psychology (Witmer, Healy, Goddard, Wallin); comparative and physiological psychology (Yerkes, Cannon, Carr, Franz, Lashley); and systematic psychology (J. Angell, Titchener, Watson, and McDougall). Stimulation for these investigations was furnished in large part by the rival schools of psychology, whose violent controversy was temporarily interrupted by World War I because of the participation of psychologists in the war effort.

PSYCHOLOGY IN WORLD WAR I

America's entry into World War I in 1917 gave significant impetus to American psychology. The national emergency created an opportunity for psychology to demonstrate its use and value potentials. Psychologists did war service in laboratories, in training camps, and in the field. They tried to solve certain technological problems of military importance in the areas of visual and auditory perception, military instruction, morale, and the like. American psychologists contributed significantly to the war effort in the air service, the medical service, and in personnel selection.

The principal immediate assignment in April 1917 was to devise valid, efficient, objective techniques by which civilian recruits could be selected and allocated to military assignments. To meet this challenge, the American Psychological Association appointed a committee of five psychologists, all specialists in mental testing, under the chairmanship of *Robert M. Yerkes* (1876-1956), who is distinguished also for his researches in comparative psychology. After careful study, the committee devised two group intelligence tests: verbal Army Alpha and nonverbal Army Beta. The former was used on literates and the latter on illiterates. Trade tests were also administered to those who claimed occupational skills. A personality inventory called *The Personal Data Sheet*, designed to detect emotional instability, was devised by Woodworth, who for almost three decades was the chairman of the department of psychology at Columbia University. Its completion, however, came too late to have its diagnostic value tested on recruits. It was used thereafter on civilians and became a prototype for subsequent personality questionnaires.

During the years 1917-1918 more than 1,700,000 men were examined in the service by psychologists. This mass testing made possible the efficient, speedy classification and selection of draftees. In addition, it offered psychologists their first chance to investigate the behavior and functioning of large numbers of individuals. After the war, group tests were adapted for civilian populations and used extensively in schools and industry. Moreover, these paper-and-pencil tests set the pattern for new group tests of intelligence, aptitudes, and personality.

In their military service, psychologists demonstrated that human factors and their effective use are as vital in war as are mechanical factors. Besides testing and classifying recruits, they analyzed various jobs to determine the personnel qualifications and the duties which these jobs demanded. The wartime services justified applied psychology and gained support for it. The concept of personnel specifications aroused particular attention. Most importantly, the efficient selection and allocation of manpower created a postwar market for personnel selection and testing procedures in education and in industry.

EXPANSION OF AMERICAN PSYCHOLOGY
IN THE 1920's AND 1930's

Between 1920 and 1940 American psychology expanded in different directions. Its academic status continued to improve. The number of psychologists, departments of psychology, publications, and the amount and variety of researches grew. Sparked by psychology's wartime accomplishments and contributions, public concern for what applied psychology could offer to education, business, and industry increased during the 1920's. Textbooks and college courses entitled "Applied Psychology" started to appear. Individuals and groups of psychologists began to offer professional services as consultants. Advances were made in clinical psychology, vocational guidance, and industrial psychology. Experimental interest was expressed in emotions, motivation, personality, religious and social psychology, and tests. Compared to these areas, there was a decrease in the number of individuals interested in pure experimental psychology, especially in the topics which were formerly popular—sensation, perception, language, and esthetics. An important factor stimulating psychology's postwar expansion was the renewal of the controversy between the competing schools of psychology.

Schools of Psychology.   The 1920's were characterized by interest in, and keen opposition among, the schools of psychology. An increasing sensitivity to the inadequacy of experimental introspection encouraged an emphasis on objective methodology. Under the powerful influence of Watson and his behaviorism, the study of mind and its operations yielded place to an objective mechanistic, physicalistic, and behavioristic psychology. The controversies of the early 1920's among structuralism, functionalism, and behaviorism were all within the framework of associationism. Although there was a steady increase of interest—particularly popular interest—in psychoanalysis because of the early efforts of Hall and A. A. Brill, Freud's renowned translator, no serious, and little favorable, attention was paid to Freud by most American psychologists at first. But by 1930 psychoanalysis gained recognition and planted its roots in American psychology.

About 1925 Gestalt psychology was introduced, too, chiefly through the availability in English of Köhler's *The Mentality of Apes* (1925) and Koffka's *The Growth of the Mind* (1st ed., 1924; 2nd ed., 1928). Although Gestalt psychology attacked associationist psychology and behaviorism, and introduced some interesting new theoretical formulations and researches, this German system encountered rugged opposition from its rivals. Its American adherents were few at this time, and therefore it did not significantly alter the course of American psychology.

In a report on the Ninth International Congress of Psychology—whose convening at Yale in 1929 signalized American psychology's growth and prestige—Boring, the eminent historian of psychology and now emeritus Harvard professor, noted that the program revealed the "increasing dominance of behavioral psychology in America." He also observed that behaviorism in America had achieved its goal and that its day was over. By the end of the third decade of the twentieth century, behavior, not mind, was the principal subject matter of psychology. The behavioristic movement had accomplished its purpose. After 1930 the controversies among the various schools gradually subsided. The narrow frames of reference of the schools began to disappear, and American psychology assimilated divergent viewpoints and facts, regardless of their origin. Most psychologists assumed eclectic or broad behaviorist positions.

During the early thirties, American psychology was also influenced by the arrival in the United States of European psychologists who sought refuge from political oppression abroad. Among them were Stern, Wertheimer, Köhler, and Lewin, all of whom received academic appointments in the United States. A considerable number of persons competent in mental health areas, such as psychoanalysis and psychiatry—Kurt Goldstein, Erich Fromm, Jacob L. Moreno—came from central Europe at this time, too, and started professional practice and research in America. Among this group also was psychoanalyst Karen Horney, author of *The Neurotic Personality of Our Time* (1937), who developed the neo-Freudian approach which stressed the role of social factors in the development and functioning of personality.

Broadened Scope. Changes in subject matter emphasis also occurred. While research on sensation and perception, on the nervous system, attention, and memory declined, relatively speaking, there was a marked stimulation of research on *childhood* and *adolescence* (Gesell, Goodenough, McGraw), enlivened by the "nature-nurture" controversy of the late twenties and early thirties. Gifted children received considerable attention, notably from Terman and Leta Hollingworth. The number of studies in *animal psychology* and in *educational psychology* and *testing* showed an upward trend.

In the 1920's and 1930's, a variety of *individual* and *group tests* of all types appeared. Among the performance tests which followed the Pintner-Paterson Performance Scale (1917) were the Goodenough Draw-A-Man Test (1922), the Arthur Point Scale of Performance (1933), and the Cornell-Coxe Performance Ability Scale (1934). Among the verbal group tests were the Otis Self-Administering Test (1922), the Henmon-Nelson Self-Scoring Tests (1931), and the California Tests of Mental Maturity (1937). Substantial psychometric progress was made with the two individual tests, the Terman-Merrill Revision of the Stanford-Binet (1937) and the Wechsler-Bellevue Test of Adult Intelligence (1939). The latter provided both verbal and performance scales.

Personality measurement was also promoted by American psychologists at this time. Various types of personality tests were published: extroversion-introversion tests (Laird, Marston); inventories (Humm-Wadsworth, Bernreuter, Bell, Brown); measures of values (Allport-Vernon); and performance tests of temperament and adjustment (Downey, Pressey, Kent-Rosanoff). In the 1930's, projective techniques came into prominence, when the Rorschach Inkblot Test was imported from Europe and the Thematic Apperception Test was published in the United States by Morgan and Murray (1935). Between 1920 and 1940 several vocational interest tests (Freyd, Strong, Cowdery, Brainard, Kuder) were devised, as well as a large number of aptitude and achievement tests.

Some research on *abnormal psychology* was done, notably by *Morton Prince* (1854-1929), American pioneer of abnormal psychology, founder of the Harvard Psychological Clinic (1927), and famous for his studies of personality dissociation. Prince criticized American psychologists as late as 1925 for their neglect of abnormal psychology, and for their preoccupation with the study of behavior and environment and of stimulus-response activity. Prince deplored the failure of American psychologists to develop experimental research and instruction in abnormal and dynamic psychology, which he considered essential for understanding the normal.

In the late 1920's, there was a sudden spurt of interest in motivation, methodology, and theoretical issues, while, in the 1930's studies of personality increased noticeably. About this time, too, the Institute of Human Relations at Yale (1933) was established to promote closer collaboration among sociologists, psychologists, and psychiatrists. The Institute, directed by Mark May and enthusiastically supported by Clark Hull, encouraged interdisciplinary studies such as that of Dollard, Miller, and their associates on *Frustration and Aggression* (1939). Recently arrived European psychiatrists and psychoanalysts contributed to the increase of interest in personality, personality measurement, and especially in psychoanalysis. Among the significant contributors was Kurt Lewin, author of *A Dynamic Theory of Personality: Selected Papers* (1935) and *Principles of Topological Psychology* (1936), which were the first reports in English of his theories and of his concepts of self and of life space.

After the heated controversy over the instincts in the late 1920's, *social psychology* rose to prominence. It broadened its horizons and adopted objective methods. Since the scope of their field was not sharply defined, social psychologists with these objective methods began to investigate a variety of specific topics, including the socialization of the child, public opinion, and propaganda. The economic depression of the 1930's precipitated increased study of social problems. In 1934, Moreno, author of *Who Shall Survive? A New Approach to the Problem of Human Relations*, described his technique—sociometry—for determining interpersonal relations within groups. By 1935, Muzafer Sherif, using the autokinetic effect, was conducting some of the first laboratory researches on the establishment and change of social norms.

During this period *statistical methods* found increased use in practically all areas of investigation. This trend was given added impetus by Thurstone's development of factor analysis in the early thirties, and by the publication of his books, *Vectors of the Mind* (1935) and *Primary Mental Abilities* (1938). In their 50 year survey (1890-1940) of American psychology, Bruner and Allport noted that empirical, mechanistic, quantitative, nomothetic, analytic, and operational trends were all observable in American psychology by 1940.

In the late 1920's American psychologists started to review the progress their science had made and to recapitulate the contributions of the various systems of psychology. Several volumes of the late 1920's and early 1930's on the *history of psychology* (Murphy, Warren, Pillsbury, Kantor, Heidbreder, Hulin, and Williams and Bellows) attest to the concern with historical perspective and analysis. E. G. Boring published the first edition of his well-known, comprehensive, and carefully documented *A History of Experimental Psychology* in 1929. Two years later Woodworth's *Contemporary Schools of Psychology* appeared. During this same era, Carl Murchison contributed to historical literature through his editorial efforts in the publication of *Psychologies of 1925* (1926), *Psychologies of 1930* (1930), *Foundations of Experimental Psychology* (1929), *Psychological Register* (1928), and the first three volumes of *A History of Psychology in Autobiography* (1930, 1931, 1936).

Publications. The expansion and progress of psychology were mirrored in the psychological literature—the books and the journals. Although all textbooks subscribed to some scientific ideal, few agreed on the nature of the science of psychology. They gave less emphasis to consciousness and simple mental processes and more to experimental work on testing, educational, and animal psychology.

In the two decades between World War I and World War II several significant books ushered in new important experimental and theoretical trends. Among these were the following: Lashley's *Brain Mechanisms and Intelligence* (1929), a quantitative study of injuries to the animal brain, shifted emphasis away from physiological theory in the study of human behavior, rendering more acceptable the aphysiological approaches in the behavioral analyses of Tolman and Skinner; Tolman's *Purposive Behavior in Animals and Man* (1932) turned attention to learning and instituted a new approach to construction of theory, by defining psychological concepts in objective terms; and Skinner's *The Behavior of Organisms* (1938) surveyed the research on operant conditioning. Written within the stimulus-response frame of reference, one of the first systematic treatments of social psychology was F. H. Allport's *Social Psychology* (1924), followed by the important volume of Gardner and Lois Murphy, *Experimental Social Psychology* (1931), and shortly thereafter by its revision with T. Newcomb (1937).

Up to World War II there was an accelerated output of textbooks in psychology. The widespread interest in the study of individual differences during this period was reflected, for example, in Anastasi's *Differential Psychology* (1937). In general psychology, Boring, Langfeld, and Weld published *Psychology: A Factual Textbook* (1935), whose title, as well as its contents, signified that psychological science had amassed a body of facts and tried to dispel the impression created by the various schools of psychology that psychology was a disorganized conglomeration of opinions.

Not until the mid-thirties did personality receive adequate attention except for popular volumes on psychoanalysis and case studies. The publication of Stagner's *Psychology of Personality* (1936), with its stress on social and cultural factors in the development of personality, initiated a new trend. The following year G. W. Allport produced his classic, *Personality: A Psychological Interpretation*. In 1938, H. A. Murray's *Ex-*

plorations in Personality, with a psychoanalytic orientation, presented results of experimental and clinical investigations. These volumes and the abundant periodical literature of the late 1930's signalized an emerging psychology of personality, which was showing its influence on clinical psychology. Although clinical work was largely confined to children at this time, it was becoming more systematized. Its systematic development of diagnostic and therapeutic procedures in the treatment of children's behavior problems was exemplified in Rogers' *The Clinical Treatment of the Problem Child* (1939).

One of the greatest publications of this period was the encyclopedic *Experimental Psychology* (1938) by Woodworth, author of numerous psychological textbooks. This compendium of research findings covered a broad scope of experimental literature including learning, memory, perception, feelings, and emotions. Several noteworthy handbooks of various psychological fields were also edited by Murchison in the 1930's: *A Handbook of Child Psychology* (1st ed., 1931; revised ed., 1933); *A Handbook of Experimental Psychology* (1934); and *A Handbook of Social Psychology* (1935). During the years from 1935 to 1940, C. J. Warden, T. N. Jenkins, and L. H. Warner presented a comprehensive coverage of the literature of animal behavior in their three volumes of *Comparative Psychology*.

Just as the production of books increased, so did the production of periodical literature. Moreover, several new journals were founded in the twenties and thirties. Among the more important of these which have survived are: *Genetic Psychology Monographs* (1925); *Psychological Abstracts* (1927); *Journal of General Psychology* (1927); *Journal of Social Psychology* (1929); *Child Development* (1930); *Journal of Psychology* (1935); *Psychometrika* (1936); *Psychological Record* (1937); *Journal of Consulting Psychology* (1937); and *Sociometry* (1937). These new journals reflected the newer emphasis on animal, social, developmental, applied, and statistical psychology. In general, the number and types of publications—books, handbooks, and periodicals—during the twenties and thirties testified to the scientific character and mature status of American psychology.

Facilities and Personnel. By 1928 there were already more than 100 laboratories in operation. Many new departments of psychology had been created. Graduate and undergraduate programs were expanded. Increased academic and professional opportunities in psychology attracted more students for training. In 1928 a national honor society in psychology, *Psi Chi*, was established. The number of psychologists increased steadily, as did the membership of the American Psychological Association (A.P.A.). This national organization, which had 31 members in 1892 at its founding, had 471 members in 1925, the year of its incorporation. After the establishment of an "associate" category of membership in 1926, A.P.A. membership rose rapidly to 1,101 in 1930 and to 2,739 by 1940. Its subsequent growth is described in the next chapter.

AMERICAN PSYCHOLOGISTS AND WORLD WAR II

In 1941 came United States' entry into World War II, and with the war came new, varied experiences for American psychologists. At home, in the wartime industries, the civilian psychologists engaged in the selection and training of personnel and in the study of the role of human factors in the design and operation of equipment. Approximately 1500 psychologists served in the United States armed forces, and of these about 25 per cent were in applied areas. More than 14 million men and women joined the armed services. They had to be assigned to various posts and technical positions. Therefore, just as in World War I, psychologists in World War II selected and classified military personnel at induction and reception centers. They had to devise selection and classification techniques and tests, such as the Army General Classification Test (A.G.C.T.), the Army Air Force (A.A.F.) Qualifying Examination, and the Aircrew Classification Tests. Psychologists also had to analyze military tasks, and design instruments according to the human specifications of the personnel operating them. While some wrestled with problems of morale and psychological warfare, others developed diagnostic and consultation procedures for coping with the maladjusted in the armed services.

Both the National Research Council and the Office of Strategic Services (O.S.S.) employed psychologists during the war. For the former, psychologists studied various specific military-centered problems. The O.S.S. engaged psychologists, psychiatrists, and army administrators to develop and administer a personality assessment program to select intelligence personnel for special assignments. These assignments included the establishment and training of resistance groups, the disruption of morale in enemy forces, and the procurement of information behind the enemy lines.

During the war there were limited numbers of psychology students and psychologists in the universities. Research and publications decreased markedly. Several important volumes, however, were published: *Counseling and Psychotherapy* (1942), in which Carl Rogers elaborated his client-centered therapy; Clifford Morgan's *Physiological Psychology* 1930; Hull's *Principles of Behavior* (1943), which set forth his mathe- (1943), a textbook surveying the vast literature on this subject since matico-deductive, theoretical system; and *Personality and Behavior Disorders* (1944), a two volume handbook based on experimental and clinical research, edited by J. McVicker Hunt. Although the war necessarily curtailed academic research, it provided new service and research opportunities in military, clinical, and industrial psychology. This wartime experience gave American psychologists increased confidence in the contributions which they could make to society. They demonstrated their usefulness in the areas of selection, training, morale, instrument design, and in psychological diagnosis and psychotherapy. Their distinguished performance, both in the armed services and at home, commanded attention and enhanced the prestige of psychology.

PSYCHOLOGY AS SCIENCE AFTER THE WAR

In 1945, World War II ended both in Europe and in Asia. The postwar period brought numerous problems to all nations, as they recovered from the war and resumed peacetime living. It also brought new challenges and problems to American psychologists. Their newly acquired prestige created an unprecedented demand for psychological services in the community, a demand at once gratifying and disturbing to them. Large numbers of students enrolled in graduate and undergraduate programs. Old curricula had to be revised and new curricula had to be developed. The changes came rapidly for psychology. One change stood out clearly—namely, that American psychologists could no longer afford to avoid facing the bifurcated character of their field—as science and as profession. This duality had been evident before the war but had not been met directly.

Postwar changes brought many benefits for psychology, not the least of which was generous government and foundation support for research of all types. Grants became available to students to help them finance their education. Generous grants enabled universities and colleges to develop and expand their psychology laboratories and research facilities. Grants to faculty enabled them to be released from heavy teaching schedules and to conduct research. In their researches, psychologists now collaborated with other scientists on interdisciplinary projects. Several universities have promoted and facilitated such collaboration, among them Yale with its Institute of Human Relations (established in 1933), and Harvard with its Department of Social Relations (established in 1945). All these developments opened up new horizons for American psychology in the 1950's and 1960's. Postwar America unmistakably supported psychology. The *Zeitgeist* clearly favored behavioral sciences. Therefore, after 1945 psychology made rapid progress both as science and as profession.

Experimental Psychology: The New Look. In spite of the many changes in American psychology at mid-twentieth century, the experimental method has remained the sine qua non of the science. Experimental psychology, however, has undergone change. Although the term may still be used in its narrow sense to refer to basic research, experimental psychology is no longer restricted to mere laboratory exercises, or to the traditional academic research on sensation, perception, and learning. These and other topics have gradually been studied from a more dynamic viewpoint in everyday life settings and situations. Moreover, new techniques have been introduced as progress in electronics and engineering has made available new, improved, and more refined apparatus and measurement devices.

Furthermore, the subject matter to which the experimental method is applied has been extended. Experimental psychology has acquired broader scope and more vitality. Social, child, industrial, and educational psychologists, as well as the "pure" research psychologists, use the experimental method. It has become commonplace to speak of experimental social and experimental child psychology, and of experimental research in personality. Moreover, an applied experimental psychology has also emerged, as laboratory methods have been put to use in industry and in the military to assist in design of equipment according to human specifications. Thus, in a sense, even experimental psychology is itself no longer exclusively academic. It, too, has become professionalized.

Models and Theories. The older topics of experimental investigation, particularly perception and learning, have become frequent testing grounds for rival theories. The traditional schools and systems of psychology have been supplanted by models, theories, and theoretical systems which have, in turn, precipitated research on varied topics. Although the idea of models is not new, in recent times models have been borrowed from various fields more frequently to represent certain relationships. Cybernetics, initiated by Norbert Wiener about 1938, has encouraged the adoption of the feedback model from communication engineering. Information theory has also been borrowed from communication and been effectively used by psychologists (Hovland, N. Miller). Feedback, information theory, the theory of games, all deal with sequential behavior, decision making, and uncertainty. Such models facilitate theory testing by representing various functions involved in highly complex behavior, and by providing simulated behavioral results which can then be analyzed by computer techniques. As psychological science advances, it appears likely that there will be increased use of mathematical models based on differential calculus and probability. In view of their limitations, however, it appears just as likely that other types of theorizing will continue to be used as well.

Although contemporary theorists have paid less and less attention to the traditional systems, some have borrowed heavily enough from them to be rapidly identified as neobehaviorist or organismic. Other theorists have developed their own miniature systems independently. These miniature systems are theoretical structures restricted to one particular segment of psychology. In contemporary American psychology, theories have become more plentiful, more elaborate, more sophisticated but less comprehensive than formerly. Interest in inclusive and highly formalized theory of the Hullian type waned, however, in the late 1950's, as interest in positivism, empiricism, and model building grew. Present-day theorists more and more prefer mathematical language to verbal schemata. The former is less ambiguous, more exact, and more adaptable to computer techniques. There has also been a revival of interest in the physiological correlates of behavior since the 1950's as a result of progress in physiology and, more particularly, as a result of Hebb's theoretical enterprises which link neurophysiology and psychology.

CONTEMPORARY RESEARCH AND THEORY

Contemporary research and theory cover a wide range of topics. Four principal areas—learning, perception, motivation, and personality—are discussed here. Developments in these areas offer a fairly good picture of the experimental and theoretical trends in contemporary psychology. Some of the topics discussed in the following sections are considered more fully in the chapters on the psychological schools.

Learning. Learning theory and research have been prominently emphasized by contemporary American psychologists. American psychologists have analyzed the behavior of organisms spanning the phylogenetic scale. They have created competing systems of psychology and have influenced all phases of theoretical and applied psychology. Learning theory has received more thought and attention than any other phase of contemporary psychological theory. The greater emphasis accorded learning in comparison to other areas, such as perception, motivation, and personality, is readily apparent from a review of the literature in these areas.

Learning has been a traditional subject of American theoretical interest and research endeavor since *Edward L. Thorndike* (1874-1949) first proposed his stimulus-response psychology of learning in his *Animal Intelligence* (1898). Thorndike's connectionism, or bond psychology, explained learning as trial and error (selecting and connecting) in terms of three associative laws—readiness, effect, and exercise—with no consideration of conscious influence or of intervening ideas. From 1898 to 1930, his system remained essentially the same. Only after 1930 did he substantially modify his theory, revising the laws of exercise and effect, and introducing the concept of "belongingness" as an organizing principle for stimulus-response bonds. For almost half a century Thorndike's learning theory prevailed, influencing American educational practice and inspiring learning research both here and abroad. Beginning in the third decade of the twentieth century, American psychologists gave increased attention to the learning process. Since that time, the major theoretical issues relative to perception, personality, and motivation have been treated largely within the framework of learning theory.

American learning theorists fall into two principal categories: the *S-R theorists*, who are neobehavioristic or associationistic in approach; and the *cognitive theorists*, who are organismic with a Gestalt-like approach. More specifically, S-R theorists, in contrast to cognitive theorists, offer peripheral (muscular) rather than central (brain processes) explanations of learning. They focus on the learning of habits (responses) through trial and error rather than on learning of cognitive structures through insight or the understanding of essential relationships. S-R theorists may be further differentiated in terms of their basic explanatory principles of the response-strengthening process—reinforcement, contiguity, or a combination of these factors. Even those who make reinforcement central to learning—the S-R reinforcement theorists—differ in the nature of the role they accord to reinforcement.

In S-R reinforcement theory, the name of *Clark Hull* (1884-1952) is well known. Prior to his research on learning Hull had distinguished himself for his contributions to aptitude testing, statistics, and experimentation on hypnosis and suggestibility. Adopting Thorndike's law of effect, he explained learning as the acquisition of contiguous S-R connections as a result of reinforcement. The essential conditon for reinforcement was drive reduction, which his theory accounted for in terms of intervening or intra-organismic variables—a concept borrowed from Tolman. In the 1940's, Hull's mathematico-deductive theory was much respected for its objectivism, quantification, and sophistication. With its exact postulates, theorems, and corollaries, however, this theory easily became a vulnerable target of attack. Gradually, Hull modified his views on reinforcement and drive reduction. The final version of his principles was presented in *Essentials of Behavior* (1951), as a supplement to his earlier *Principles of Behavior* (1943). His last volume *A Behavior System* (1952), completed shortly before he died, is an application of the principles to the behavior of single organisms.

Whether Hull's theory survives or not, his influence cannot be gainsaid. During his tenure at Yale he infused the Institute of Human Relations with inspiration and creative ideas. Among the many behavioral scientists associated with him in the 1930's and 1940's were John Dollard, Ernest Hilgard, Carl Hovland, Donald Marquis, Neal Miller, O. H. Mowrer, Robert Sears, Kenneth Spence, and John Whiting—an impressive roster of outstanding contributors to contemporary psychological research and theory. Of these *Kenneth Spence* (b. 1907) has probably adhered most closely to Hull. As an S-R reinforcement theorist, Spence differs from Hull, however, in de-emphasizing physiological speculation and, particularly, in rejecting Hull's stress on need reduction as essential to reinforcement. In 1956, Spence presented his own theory in *Behavior Theory and Conditioning*. As of that time, Spence gave more emphasis to contiguity and shifted his position closer to Tolman's.

Unlike Hull, the Harvard professor and positivist *B. F. Skinner* (b. 1904) prefers an empirical, atheoretical approach, and has constructed a system of descriptive behaviorism or operant conditioning. A staunch supporter of neobehaviorism in the 1930's, he devised the Skinner box for his operant conditioning studies, which he pursued enthusiastically. An S-R theorist, he concerns himself only with response (R) factors, opposes organismic (O) factors, and regards the analysis of stimulus (S) factors as nonessential. His researches on pigeons and rats in Skinner boxes— using them as single experimental subjects—focus on emitted responses (no external stimulation) or operants. Skinner, the radical operationist, ignores the stimuli, the conditions of the organism, and the C.N.S., or "conceptual nervous system," as he calls it. Reinforcement is considered necessary, but no attempt is made to account for its underlying structure. Like Spence, Skinner is aphysiological in outlook. Boring speaks of Skinner's psychology as the psychology of the "empty organism." Although he was violently criticized by many, Skinner attracted a large following. His books, *Science and Human Behavior* (1953) and *Verbal Behavior* (1957) provoked discussion and criticism. As Skinnerian psychology gained prestige, particularly with its applications in the use of teaching machines in the late 1950's, Hull's system lost popularity. Skinner's followers have continued to be numerous and strong enough to warrant publication of their own journal since 1958, the *Journal for the Experimental Analysis of Behavior*. We shall return to Skinner in a later chapter in which we discuss behaviorism.

Representing the second type of S-R theory—contiguity theory—is *Edwin Guthrie* (1886-1959), a behavioristically oriented proponent of conditioning. Guthrie's simple, direct, associationistic theory rejects reinforcement of the Pavlovian type and makes contiguity the basic learning principle. Another S-R contiguity theorist, *William K. Estes* (b. 1919), has put contiguity theory into a mathematical framework and has scrupulously avoided theoretical postulates and interpretations. Not only has he evolved a statistical association theory; he has also become a prominent proponent of mathematical models. Estes terms his models probabilistic rather than deterministic.

Besides the separate contiguity and reinforcement theories, there are S-R theories which combine reinforcement and contiguity. Such two-factor theories, so-called, have been numerous. Among those who have proposed such formulations are Schlosberg (1937), Skinner (1938), and Mowrer (1956).

Unlike the S-R theorists, the cognitive theorists stress understanding, expectancy, or "sign" learning. Most representative of this group is *Edward C. Tolman* (1886-1959), who combined behaviorist and Gestalt orientations and assumed a molar rather than a molecular view of behavior. Rejecting the narrow S-R formulation and protesting against the law of effect and the principle of reinforcement as essential to the response-strengthening process, Tolman recognized the necessity of inferring "inner" processes between S and R. Accordingly, he invented the concept of intervening variables (expectancy, cognition, sign Gestalt) which, as we have already noted, was adopted by Hull. Tolman tried to deal with these intervening variables objectively. Conducting his research principally on the rat—to whom he gave a respected place in the American psychological laboratory—Tolman developed his sign learning theory. According to this theory, the rat learns a cognitive map of a maze which is reinforced by expectancy (for example, of finding food) and confirmation. Repetition or practice provides opportunity for acquiring the sign Gestalt, but does not produce the learning. Reward regulates behavior but does not reinforce the right responses. Sign learning theory, therefore, contends that performance is correlated with expectancies.

In 1922, when Tolman first promulgated his purposive behaviorism, American psychologists were still too enthusiastic about Watsonian behaviorism to appreciate Tolman. Eventually, enthusiasm for Watson dimmed under the tempering influence of Tolman and others who decreased the narrow rigidity of behaviorism. Tolman's concepts and his system were broad, and less clearly defined than others. For about 20 years (1930-1950), Tolman's cognitive theory occupied a prominent position in American psychology as chief rival to Hull's need reduction theory.

Before concluding the discussion of learning theorists, we should mention another group of learning investigators who constitute a functionalist position. Functionalism is essentially experimentalism, but not a clearly defined system. Functionalist research has been conducted principally on human verbal learning, in areas such as transfer of training, retroactive inhibition, and the like. Melton, McGeoch, and Woodworth are representative functionalist theorists. Although they are not antitheoretical, the functionalists simply have preferred not to organize their results into any theoretical framework.

Up to 1930, behavior or learning theory was largely neurological, but thereafter almost no attention was paid to the nervous system by theorists. Lashley's *Brain Mechanisms and Intelligence* (1929) put an end to the possibility of explaining learning in terms of localized, fixed neural pathways. Both Skinner and Tolman considered discussion of the nervous system unnecessary, and even a hindrance to the analysis of behavior. In their opinion physiology was not essential to the psychologist. After the publication of Tolman's *Purposive Behavior in Animals and Men* (1932) and Skinner's *The Behavior of Organisms* (1938), physiological psychology had few advocates. In fact, there was a drop in the number of courses offered in this subject until a reaction set in during the late 1950's, after the promulgation of Hebb's neurophysiological theory in his *The Organization of Behavior* (1949). In 1956 Hilgard, in his *Theories of Learning,* deplored the ". . . blot upon our scientific ingenuity that after so many years of research we know as little as we do about the physiological accompaniments of learning."

Contemporary American learning theory has been based largely on animal research and has been behavioristically oriented. Increasingly the psychology of learning has been reduced to S-R activity, with particular focus on the subject's response. The most divisive problem has been reinforcement. Many contemporary theorists have focused on intervening variables—the latent nonbehavioral aspects of learning—in their desire to prove the *how* of learning. This focus on "how" tends to bring the S-R theorists and cognitive theorists to common ground, even if through different approaches of reinforcement and cognitive processes. As cognitive theorists strive to quantify their formulations, the likelihood of rapprochement among S-R theorists appears greater. Another interesting trend over the years has been the tendency for theorists to abandon the global approach and to restrict themselves to miniature systems and specific types of learning. Thus it has been stated that the era of grand system builders drew to a close in 1959 with the death of Tolman.

The literature on learning researches and theories is voluminous. Numerous comprehensive textbooks (Deese, Hilgard, McGeoch, Mowrer) have appeared. New specialized journals have been founded, such as the previously mentioned *Journal of Experimental Analysis of Behavior* (1958) and the *Journal of Verbal Learning and Verbal Behavior* (1962). Different types—perceptual and verbal—and different aspects—social and emotional—of learning have been subjected to investigation. Various applications haye been made to education in programmed instruction and teaching machines. Serious attempts have been made to relate learning to clinical psychology (Dollard and Miller, Mowrer, and Sears). In short, learning is an ever-expanding area in the 1960's, and the one with the best developed theories to date.

Perception. Like learning, perception has been a traditional, if not as frequent, subject of psychological study. In contemporary American psychology, perception has continued to attract much attention. Traditional approaches have been abandoned. Perception is no longer regarded as a mere combination of sensory impressions which get meaning from past experience or from the organization of stimuli. Inner determinants which affect the individual's perception have been assigned greater significance. With the broadening of perceptual theory and research there has been a pronounced tendency to emphasize intervening or intra-organismic variables—such as needs, values, attitudes, and personality variables.

Perceptual theory has been cultivated within Gestalt, behavioristic, and functionalist frames of reference. Gestalt psychologists emphasize innate organizing factors and minimize experience and interactions of stimuli and observer. Köhler, for example, explains learning and perceptual phenomena in terms of changing field effects in the cortex arising from nerve impulses. Studying figural aftereffects, Köhler and Wallach have related perception to underlying cortical mechanisms according to the principle of isomorphism. Support for the Gestalt position in perception has been adduced by the researches of Lewin, G. W. Allport, Postman, and Gibson.

Within a behavioristic framework, *D. O. Hebb* (b. 1904) has presented a neurological theory of perceptual processes based on associationist principles. For Hebb, perception is learned. Rejecting Gestalt field theory of cortical activity, Hebb asserts that there is specific localization of functions at some place in the cortex at some point in perceptual learning. His basic postulate is the cell assembly which is a group of cortical neurons. Through learning, neurons become functionally associated with each other. Through practice, cell assemblies develop. Assemblies of cell assemblies can also develop. When a series of cell assemblies is aroused, a phase sequence or thought process develops. The establishment of cell assemblies and their corresponding phase sequences is the initial step in learning. Adult learning, according to Hebb, is conceptual and possible only when stimulation arouses well-established phase sequences. Prior to Hebb, and particularly under Gestalt influence, perceptual theories based on learning principles had practically disappeared. Hebb's sophisticated associationist theory of perception reaffirmed the role of learning in perception.

Functionalist perceptual theories of varying types have been developed. The functionalists maintain that perception helps the organism adjust to its environment. The individual develops certain perceptual constancies and on the basis of these he interacts with his environment. *Egon Brunswik* (1903-1955), Karl Bühler's student, proposed a *probabilistic functionalism* which holds that we set up certain hypotheses or probabilities which we bring to perception unconsciously. We never have perfect representations of the physical world, and we never achieve perfect constancy. The *transactional functionalism* of *A. Ames, Jr.* and *William H. Ittelson* (b. 1920) maintains that perception is based on learning. Experience and the interactions between the organism and the stimuli are important in enabling the individual to make instantaneous, though unconscious, inferences in future actions. Thus perceptual constancies that have been helpful in the past become automatic and are useful in the future. Two other types of functionalist theory which should be mentioned here are Helson's "adaptation-level theory" and Gibson's "gradient theory."

The role of central determinants (attitudes, moods, emotions, and values) in perceptual selectivity has been investigated (Bruner, Goodman, Postman, McGinnies, Witkin). Attempts have also been made to relate perceptual and personality variables (Blake and Ramsey, Bruner and Krech, Piotrowski, and Witkin). Such relationships have special relevance in the use of projective techniques, like the Rorschach. While considerable emphasis has been placed on the internal or organismic (O) factors in recent perceptual research by prominent theorists, J. J. Gibson has urged closer collaboration between theorists interested in stimulus (S) factors and those concerned with organismic (O) factors. In general, the tendency over two decades from 1945 to 1965 has been in the direction of a functionalist approach to perception. Perception is gradually being acknowledged as basic to man's interaction with the world about him. This view has compelled recognition and study by applied psychologists as well as by theorists.

Motivation.   It will be recalled from the early history of psychology that more attention was focused on the cognitive aspects of man's behavior than on the affective or conative aspects. Philosophers had of course dealt with free will and determinism in various ways. Later, Brentano's "intentionality" and the Würzburg school's "determining tendencies" focused on the direction of thought and also emphasized motivation. Evolution, too, with its emphasis on adaptation, gave impetus to this field by focusing on biological drives. Psychoanalysis turned attention to unconscious motivation. In America, Thorndike's "hedonism," McDougall's "instinct" or "hormic" psychology, and the "dynamic" psychologies of Woodworth, and later of Lewin, underscored the necessity for considering the "why" of behavior. In spite of these early efforts and the practical importance of this area of behavior—motivation—theories of motivation have been far less developed than those of learning and perception. Much has been written on motivational concepts, and numerous researches on motivational phenomena have been conducted. But there is no general theory of motivation. Consistently disparate viewpoints and varying experimental approaches have deterred progress. Problems of terminology—need, purpose, drive, instinct, motive, urge—and problems of definition have further complicated the field.

Generally speaking, two systematic standpoints have characterized

American motivational theories: the neobehavioristic and the organismic. The neobehavioristic concentrates on the study of animal drives. C. T. Morgan's physiological theory of drive may be considered an example of this type. A central rather than a peripheral theory, it explains motivated behavior in terms of underlying physiological mechanisms. The second type, the organismic, explains how the organism attempts to realize itself. Maslow's hierarchical theory of motivation, an organismic theory, maintains that there is a basic ordering of human motives from physiological needs to esteem needs and self-actualization. Unless the basic needs are satisfied, they dominate behavior and higher-order motives will not appear.

Just as in the areas of perception and learning, so in motivation there are those theorists who develop miniature systems. They isolate a single motive or group of motives—some special problem area—as their subject of investigation. The work of McClelland and his associates on the achievement motive represents this type of motivational theory. Their theory, based on psychological hedonism, views motives as arising from affective states. However, since only a single motive has been explored by McClelland and his group, their findings do not apply to human motivation in general.

Of all contemporary psychological theory in the United States, motivational theory has made the slowest progress. Two possible sources of future progress have appeared, however. One of these lies in the fact that there is almost universal agreement among American psychologists concerning the impoverished state of motivational theory, coupled with a recognition of motivation as a central problem in psychology. Another hopeful sign is the fact that the learning theorists have become interested in motivation as part of learning behavior, and that perceptual and personality theorists have increasingly recognized motivational determinants in their work.

Personality.   Although personality theory was not cultivated in the traditional American schools of psychology, personality study has attracted numerous psychologists. As noted previously, psychoanalysis, especially, generated interest in personality, both normal and abnormal. As a result, theories of personality have proliferated in Europe and in America. In addition to psychoanalysis—Freudian, Jungian, and Adlerian—which became well known in the United States after the arrival of many European-trained psychologists, psychiatrists, and psychoanalysts in the 1930's, many diverse personality theories emerged. Because of their multiplicity, only a brief enumeration of the major theories can be presented here. For detailed exposition of these theories, the reader should consult the references in the bibliography at the end of this chapter.

Among contemporary American personality theories, the following merit mention here:

(1) *S-R theory* (Dollard and Miller, Mowrer, Kluckhohn): is essentially a synthesis of learning with concepts of psychoanalysis and social anthropology.

(2) *Neo-Freudian or social psychological theory* (Horney, Fromm, Sullivan) : emphasizes social and cultural determinants of, and influences on, personality rather than stressing biological determinants.

(3) *Constitutional psychology* (Sheldon) relates quantitative ratings of bodily and psychological characteristics. This theory postulates three somatotypes—endomorphy, mesomorphy, and ectomorphy, which correspond to temperamental components—viscerotonia, somatotonia, and cerebrotonia.

(4) *Personology or need press theory* (H. A. Murray) : emphasizes the physiological processes underlying behavior but does not overlook environmental influences. It is humanistic and holistic in approach and strongly psychoanalytic in its stress on the unconscious.

(5) *Factor theory* (R. B. Cattell) : presents a sophisticated, highly objective, trait-centered approach to personality. It offers an empirical rather than a subjective or intuitive approach.

(6) *Biosocial theory or personality synthesis* (G. Murphy) : is ecletic and includes most of the common and well-known postulates of modern psychology.

(7) *Psychology of individuality or trait theory* (G. W. Allport) : makes self a central concept and stresses ego functions. It emphasizes uniqueness, the multiple determinants of behavior, and the complex structure and organization of personality.

(8) *Self theory* (C. Rogers) : has as its central concept the self, a structure developed out of one's experience. This self-concept or self-awareness regulates the individual's behavior. To the individual, the phenomenal self is reality, no matter how distorted it actually is compared to objective environment. This phenomenological theory insists that the best way of understanding behavior is from the internal frame of reference of the individual himself.

(9) *Organismic theory* (K. Goldstein) : is holistic and phenomenologically oriented. It stresses intensive study of the individual as a totality and applies Gestalt principles of perception to the study of the whole individual.

(10) *Field theory* (K. Lewin) : has a core concept, life space—the individual's psychological or subjective representation of reality. To understand his behavior, one must reconstruct and describe the life space by systematic observation of an individual's behavior in the environment.

This cursory list of personality theories makes evident the marked diversity of approach. Some theories emphasize the biological, others, the social and cultural. Some stress conscious factors, others unconscious. Some are subjective or phenomenological, while others are highly objective. Generally speaking, biological or constitutional theories have fared less well in America than abroad. American psychologists tend to prefer environmental interpretations not only for personality but for intelligence as well. It is of historical interest, too, that within the twentieth century in America there was a decline and then a revival of self psychology.

Summary. Although our treatment of contemporary learning, perceptual, motivational, and personality theory is necessarily brief, this account should serve to illustrate the contemporary concern of American psychologists with theoretical considerations, and the variety of their approaches. American failure to develop theoretical psychology and American dependence on European theory have long been criticized by European psychologists. Compared to pre-1945 psychology, contemporary American psychology has paid more attention to theory. Psychologists have worked out principles, concepts, and constructs. They have developed models, theories, and miniature systems. They have employed mathematics and statistics. In sum, American psychologists have endeavored to create sound theoretical systems that should lead to fruitful results.

The contrast in American theoretical psychology between the 1950's and the 1960's is evidenced in the difference between Marx's *Psychological Theory* (1951) and his later work entitled *Theories in Contemporary Psychology* (1963). The latter volume reveals an increased sophistication in use of mathematical and statistical models and theoretical constructs, in theoretical emphases, and in fields of study. In the preface of his 1963 volume Marx summarizes the primary changes that have occurred in American psychological theory in the period between his two volumes: (1) There have been two retreats from theory: one, a decline of interest in highly formalized theory of the Hullian hypothetico-deductive type; and the other, an increase in highly positivistic and empirical types of scientific research which is, at worst, antitheoretical and, at best, atheoretical. (2) There have been two corresponding advances: one, the progress in use of the model, particularly the mathematical type; and the other, the increased emphasis on functionalist theory, which is rooted in empirical findings, and which is intended to be constructed cautiously.

PROGRESS OF AMERICAN PSYCHOLOGICAL SCIENCE: AN OVERVIEW

As the volume and significance of psychological contributions in America steadily grew after the turn of the century, and as America eventually outdistanced other countries in productivity, the history of psychology was actually being made in the United States, particularly after 1930. The British psychologist F. C. Bartlett, reviewing 50 years of psychology in 1955, said: ". . . during the next fifteen years or so (fifteen years after World War I, that is, 1933) . . . America unmistakably took the lead in scientific psychology in the whole world, probably for good and all. Certainly this was the case as regards quantity of work done and general internal status achieved."

Considering the prevailing interests of American psychology in the twentieth century, one is struck by the varied history of generative interests and theories. Some show growth from decade to decade, some a decline; some retain their relative positions; others are powerfully productive for a limited time, then subside. The changes in American psychological science have been so rapid and diffuse in the twentieth century that any attempt to recapitulate them is sure to be inadequate. As Bruner and Allport said in their 50 year survey of American psychology by decades (1940): "No one has yet discovered a method for representing an historical epoch with strict accuracy." Yet the chronological outline by decades is a practicable method of clear and analytical presentation of major aspects of development and major contributions. Accordingly, we summarize here the chief characteristics of American psychology since 1900 by decades.

First Decade of the Twentieth Century: 1900-1909. The study of learning came to the fore and became the predominant interest, including animal learning. Animal research became prominent in psychological experimentation. Other areas began to take shape and expand: child study, educational psychology, abnormal psychology, and mental testing. This decade was also marked by the formation of the psychological schools. Wundtian psychology began to be vigorously opposed, and alternative theories were proposed. The opposition of functionalism to structuralism grew stronger and their controversies germinated the seeds of behaviorism.

Second Decade: 1910-1919. The psychological schools stabilized and found their adherents and opponents. Psychologists were being differentiated by schools. Opposing groups engaged in spirited debate. The school of behaviorism had the strongest impact as it profoundly affected both the subject matter and methods of psychology. Psychology became the study of behavior. In this decade the first significant applications of psychology were made in education, industry, and war. World War I offered psychology an opportunity to demonstrate its value in a national emergency, notably in the areas of testing and classification. The varied and valuable service rendered by psychology increased its prestige. Clinical psychology was enriched by psychoanalysis, which stimulated interest in human dynamics and abnormal psychology.

Third Decade: 1920-1929. The theoretical disputes between various schools were foremost in this period. Some schools became more active and better known (Gestalt school). Some gained stronger support than others (behaviorism); some declined (structuralism). There was much controversy about heredity and environment—the nature-nurture problem. At the end of the decade the excitement about schools began to wane. Most psychologists preferred to remain eclectic or simply neutral with respect to the school issues in question. If differences continued, they were not as radical and all exclusive. The study of personality was intensified. Interest in motivation showed a marked upturn. As the practical uses of psychology widened, the appreciation and prestige of psychology grew.

Fourth Decade: 1930-1939. Some trends of the previous decade became more evident and gained strength: study and measurement of personality; motivation; growth of clinical psychology; wider practical applications in business and industry; and theoretical eclecticism. In methodology a new trend appeared—operationism—which gained widespread support. Greater differentiation of specialties among psychologists was taking place. Distinctions also became more apparent between experimental and clinical psychology, experimentalists and clinicians; between academic and professional psychology, psychology as a science and as a profession.

Fifth Decade: 1940-1949. World War II again demonstrated the indispensability of psychology. The selection of military personnel, design of military equipment, psychological warfare, and therapy for veterans with psychological disabilities were developed to a high degree of refinement. The wartime demonstration of the value of psychology resulted in greater recognition of psychology by both the government and the public at large. Such recognition led to substantial financial support for psychological research by both government and private institutions. The financial support made possible large research projects which had not been feasible in the past and inspired the growth of the science of psychology as a professional career field.

Sixth Decade: 1950-1959. An outstanding feature of this decade was the revived interest in physiological psychology, which developed a deeper understanding of physiological functions, of biochemical factors in behavior, and of developmental processes from the prenatal period to senescence. Postwar advances in physiology and endocrinology promoted this revival. There was also increased concern about scientific method. Laboratory equipment—largely electronic—became more elaborate. Experimental designs became more complex, as mathematics and statistics became indispensable to the psychologist. Quantitative methods, facilitated by the new computer techniques, were increasingly employed. Although extensive animal research was conducted, it was usually ancillary to experimental studies of learning and motivation. Comparative psychology did not develop substantially in its own right. Social psychology progressed from a study of attitudes to a valuable branch of science in the service of society. As it expanded its scope, it perfected its methodology. It gained prestige from the citation of social psychological research in the 1954 Supreme Court decision against racial segregation in the public schools. New fields and new practical uses of psychology emerged: space psychology, engineering psychology, and psychopharmacology. The latter stimulated much research and achieved spectacular successes. Theoretical and systematic issues, neglected for a long time, began to attract more attention. The number of publications and frequency of discussions devoted to such issues increased markedly. Phenomenology and existential psychology, long ignored by American psychologists, attracted attention. They have helped to advance a new humanistic psychology or "third force" in contemporary psychology which studies the whole man. Organizational growth in membership and influence was unprecedented in America, owing largely to psychology's phenomenal growth as a profession during this decade.

AMERICAN PSYCHOLOGY IN THE SIXTIES

In the early sixties there was an intensification of interest in the newer emphases of the previous decade, and to these were added renewed interests in philosophical, theoretical, and historical psychology. One of the most important events was the convening of the Seventeenth International Congress of Psychology in Washington, D.C. in 1963. The distinguished psychologist and emeritus Harvard professor *Edwin G. Boring* (b. 1886) was honorary president of the Congress. A student of Titchener's at Cornell where he obtained his doctorate (1914), Boring served as a psychologist in the armed forces during World War I and thereafter taught at Clark and Harvard. Former president of the American Psychological Association (1928) and well known for his numerous publications and editorships, including *Contemporary Psychology* (1955-1961), Boring was awarded the American Psychological Foundation Gold Medal in 1959 in recognition of his varied and distinguished service to psychology as "investigator, teacher, historian, theorist, administrator and statesman, popular expositor, and editor." An eminent historian of psychology, he has himself lived the history of American psychology. He has also lived to see the *Zeitgeist*, whose penetrating role in the history of science he has repeatedly stressed, favor his own lifelong interest—the history of psychology. Interest in psychology's history had mounted sufficiently among American psychologists to warrant establishment of Division 26, The History of Psychology, in the American Psychological Association in 1965.

By 1965, 75 years had passed since William James wrote his *Principles of Psychology*. Within that relatively short span of time American psychology achieved its independence from philosophy, struggled through its stormy adolescence, survived the controversies of the schools, and advanced to a healthy maturity and international recognition. Within that period the United States changed from an importer to an exporter of psychology. American publications—textbooks and periodicals—acquired international reputation and use. Foreign students and psychologists began to còme in substantial numbers to visit and study at American universities and laboratories. American psychologists traveled abroad to lecture and to participate in research. At home the American psychologist acquired prestige as his performance and services commanded respect and were in demand. Although American psychology has been adversely criticized both at home and abroad for its provincialism, overempiricism, quantitative emphasis, and excessive faith in method or technique, it has likewise been praised for its hard-headed empirical approach, freedom from philosophical prejudice, vitality, and practicality.

Seventy-five years ago it would have been impossible for the wise and brilliant William James to forecast the mid-twentieth century status of American psychology. It is similarly impossible to predict accurately its future course, even for the remainder of the twentieth century. We can, however, discern certain characteristics of contemporary American psychology. These characteristics have been pithily stated by Carl Rogers at the Rice University Symposium on "Behavorism and Phenomenology" (1963) as follows:

> . . . there are three broad emphases in American psychology. These resemble three ocean currents flowing side by side, mingling, with no clear line of demarcation, yet definitely different. Like the flotsam and jetsam which float on each ocean current, certain words and phrases identify, even though they do not define, these separate flowing trends. Associated with the first trend are such terms as "behaviorism," "objective," "experimental," "impersonal," "logical-positivistic," "operational," "laboratory." Associated with the second current are terms such as "Freudian," "Neo-Freudian," "psychoanalytic," "psychology of the unconscious," "instinctual," "ego-psychology," "id-psychology," "dynamic psychology." Associated with the third are terms such as "phenomenological," "existential," "self-theory," "self-actualization," "health-and-growth psychology," "being and becoming," "science of inner experience."

PSYCHOLOGY: SCIENCE AND PROFESSION

Psychology is unique in that it is both science and profession. This duality was evident almost from the beginning of American psychology. The profession grew out of the science. In this chapter we have discussed principally American psychology's growth as science. We have necessarily made occasional reference to its concomitant development as a profession.

To acquire a complete understanding of American psychology's progress and especially of its status in the 1960's we must examine its growth as a profession. Only then can we appreciate the bifurcated character of mid-twentieth century American psychology, and the issues which it raises for psychological scientists and for professional psychologists. Psychology's dual development has been both a help and a hindrance to the science and to the profession. At times the science and the profession have exhibited remarkable unity, as in periods of national emergency. At other times a sharp rift has been clearly discernible. In the following chapter we shall consider the growth of psychology as a profession generally, and some of the problems relative to its scientific-professional bipolarity. One of the chief areas of professional development has been clinical psychology. Because of its singular achievement of professional status, an entire chapter, Chapter 13, is devoted to clinical psychology.

HIGHLIGHTS OF AMERICAN PSYCHOLOGY: GROWTH AS A SCIENCE

1913 Behaviorism officially introduced with publication of Watson's paper: *Psychology as the Behaviorist Views It.*

1916 Founding of the *Journal of Experimental Psychology.*

1920 McDougall came to America.

1922 Tolman introduced purposive behaviorism.

1928 Psi Chi, national honor society in psychology, established.

1929   Ninth International Congress of Psychology convened at Yale.
Lashley published *Brain Mechanisms and Intelligence*.
Boring published first edition of *A History of Experimental Psychology*.

1932   Tolman published *Purposive Behavior in Animals and Men*.

1933   Wertheimer came to the United States and accepted an appointment at the New School of Social Research in New York.
Institute of Human Relations established at Yale.

1935   Thurstone published *Vectors of the Mind*.

1937   G. W. Allport published *Personality: A Psychological Interpretation*.

1938   Skinner published *The Behavior of Organisms* reporting researches on operant conditioning.
Woodworth published first edition of *Experimental Psychology*.

1943   Hull published *Principles of Behavior* elaborating his mathematico-deductive learning theory.

1945   Lewin established the Research Center for Group Dynamics at the Massachusetts Institute of Technology.

1946   Department of Social Relations established at Harvard.

1949   Hebb published *The Organization of Human Behavior*.

1951   Hull published a revision of his system: *Essentials of Behavior*.

1954   Citation of social psychological research in the 1954 Supreme Court decision against racial segregation in the public schools.

1956   Spence published *Behavior Theory and Conditioning*.

1963   Seventeenth International Congress of Psychology held in Washington, D.C.

REFERENCES

AMERICAN PSYCHOLOGY

Oberndorf, C. *A history of psychoanalysis in America*. New York: Grune & Stratton, 1953.

Roback, A. A. *A history of American psychology*. (Rev. ed.) New York: Collier, 1964.

Shakow, D., & Rapaport, D. *The influence of Freud on American psychology*. New York: International Univer. Press, 1964. *Psychological Issues*, 4, No. 1 (Whole No. 13).

Watson, R. I. The historical background for national trends in psychology: United States. *J. Hist. behav. Sci.*, 1965, *1*, 130–138.

PSYCHOLOGY IN WORLD WAR I

Bingham, W. V. Army personnel work. *J. appl. Psychol.*, 1919, *3*, 1–12.

Yerkes, R. M. (Ed.) Psychological examining in the United States Army. *Mem. Nat. Acad. Sci.*, 1921, *15*, 1–890.

EXPANSION OF AMERICAN PSYCHOLOGY IN THE 1920'S AND 1930'S

Bruner, J. S., & Allport, G. W. Fifty years of change in American psychology. *Psychol. Bull.*, 1940, *37*, 757–776.

Goodenough, Florence L. Trends in modern psychology. *Psychol. Bull.*, 1934, *31*, 81–97.

Maller, J. B. Forty years of psychology: a statistical analysis of American and European publications, 1894–1933. *Psychol. Bull.*, 1934, *31*, 533–559.

Roback, A. A. Psychology as an American science. *Monist*, 1926, *36*, 667–677.

Ruckmick, C. A. The development of laboratory equipment in the United States. *Amer. J. Psychol.*, 1926, *37*, 582–591.

Woodworth, R. S. The adolescence of American psychology. *Psychol. Rev.*, 1943, *50*, 10–32.

AMERICAN PSYCHOLOGISTS AND WORLD WAR II

Hunter, W. S. Psychology in the War. *Amer. Psychologist*, 1946, *1*, 479–492.

Marquis, D. G. Psychology in the war. *Trans. N.Y. Acad. Sci.*, 1944, 7, 43–44.

Marquis, D. G. The mobilization of psychologists for war service. *Psychol. Bull.*, 1944, *41*, 469–473.

Murphy, G. Psychology and the post-war world. *Psychol. Rev.*, 1942, *49*, 298–318.

Yerkes, R. M. Man-power and military effectiveness: the case for human engineering: *J. consult. Psychol.*, 1941, *5*, 205–209.

PSYCHOLOGY AS SCIENCE AFTER WORLD WAR II

Fischer, R. P., & Hinshaw, R. B. The growth of student interest in psychology. *Amer. Psychologist*, 1946, *1*, 116–118.

Hebb, D. O. The American revolution. *Amer. Psychologist*, 1960, *15*, 735–745.

Langfeld, H. S. The development of American psychology. *Scientia*, 1951, *86*, 264–269.

Roback, A. A. (Ed.) *Present-day psychology.* New York: Philosophical Library, 1955.

ROYCE, J. R. Psychology in mid-twentieth century. *Amer. Scientist*, 1957, *45*, 57–73.

CONTEMPORARY RESEARCH AND THEORY

Allport, F. H. *Theories of perception and the concept of structure.* New York: Wiley, 1955.

Bartley, S. H. *Principles of perception.* New York: Harper, 1958.

Blake, R. R., & Ramsey, G. V. (Eds.) *Perception, an approach to personality.* New York: Ronald, 1951.

Chaplin, J. P., & Krawiec, T. S. *Systems and theories of psychology* New York: Holt, Rinehart, & Winston, 1960.

Cofer, C. N., & Appley, M. H. *Motivation: theory and research.* New York: Wiley, 1964.

Hall, C. S., & Lindzey, G. *Theories of personality.* New York: Wiley, 1957.

Hilgard, E. R. *Theories of learning.* (2nd ed.) New York: Appleton-Century-Crofts, 1956.

Lindzey, G., & Hall, C. S. (Eds.) *Theories of personality: primary sources and research.* New York: Wiley, 1965.

Marx, M. H. (Ed.) *Psychological theory.* New York: Macmillan, 1951.

Marx, M. H. (Ed.) *Theories in contemporary psychology.* New York: Macmillan, 1963.

Marx, M. H., & Hillix, W. A. *Systems and theories in psychology.* New York: McGraw-Hill, 1963.

Wolman, B. B. *Contemporary theories and systems in psychology.* New York: Harper, 1960.

Woodworth, R. S., & Sheehan, Mary R. *Contemporary schools of psychology.* (3rd ed.) New York: Ronald, 1964.

AMERICAN PSYCHOLOGY IN THE SIXTIES

Albee, G. W. American psychology in the sixties. *Amer. Psychologist*, 1963, *18*, 90–95.

Kahn, T. C. Evaluation of the United States of America psychology by the "four-years-absent" method. *Amer. Psychologist*, 1962, *17*, 706–708.

Lockman, R. F. An empirical description of the subfields of psychology. *Amer. Psychologist*, 1964, *19*, 645–653.

Rogers, C. R. Toward a science of the person. In T. W. Wann (Ed.), *Behaviorism and phenomenology.* Chicago: Univer. Chicago Press, 1964. Pp. 109–140.

Tryon, R. C. Psychology in flux: the academic-professional bipolarity. *Amer. Psychologist*, 1963, *18*, 134–143.

Woods, P. J. Psychological organizations: their nature and membership patterns. *Amer. Psychologist*, 1964, *19*, 663–669.

12

American Psychology: Growth as a Profession

AT THE BEGINNING OF THE TWENTIETH CENTURY, academic psychologists were in the majority in America. By mid-century there was a radical shift toward professional psychology, which grew rapidly in number of practitioners and in diverse areas of practice. Consequently, in the 1960's less than half of the nation's psychologists were in academic employment, and a distinct cleavage between academic and professional psychology had become discernible.

BEGINNINGS OF PROFESSIONALIZATION

Professionl psychology or the application of psychology to solve practical problems of clients—individuals, business firms, or institutions—emerged in the United States at the beginning of the twentieth century. No academic-professional bipolarity divided psychology at the outset, because most of those who initiated and promoted the applications of psychology held academic positions and contributed to psychological science. Among such early applied psychologists were Hall, Münsterberg, and Cattell, to whom we have already referred in the previous chapter. To this list must be added the name of the first industrial psychologist, Scott.

After receiving his doctorate at Leipzig in 1900, *Walter Dill Scott* (1869-1955) became professor of psychology at Northwestern University. During his tenure in psychology there, he published the first book written by an American psychologist designed to aid business—*The Theory of Advertising* (1903)—as well as *The Psychology of Advertising* (1910) and *Influencing Men in Business* (1911). These books antedated Münsterberg's *Psychology and Industrial Efficiency* (1913), which described the contributions psychology could make to industry in the areas of personnel selection, employee efficiency, and public relations. These works also earned for Scott the appellation, father of applied psychology.

On leave from Northwestern during 1916-1917, Scott went to Carnegie Institute of Technology as the first American professor of applied psychology and as director of the Bureau of Salesmanship Research. In this capacity he joined the staff of *Walter V. Bingham* (1880-1952), "dean of American industrial psychologists" and director of the Institute's Division of Applied Psychology (organized in 1916). This was the first American organization dedicated to applying psychological principles. Scott did research on various phases of personnel selection, which enabled him to contribute effectively to the classification of personnel during World War I. In 1919 he organized The Scott Company, a consulting firm devoted to industrial psychology, which conducted extensive studies in numerous American cities and promoted varied applications of psychology in business. The company was dissolved in 1923 because the directors believed that "each business organization should have, as part of its executive staff, one or more trained personnel workers, without whose presence the work instituted by outside organizations is of no avail." Thereafter there was a striking increase in the number of personnel workers in industry. Although Scott served as president of Northwestern from 1920 to 1939, he continued his interest in applied psychology, collaborating on the volume, *Personnel Management* (1923), a fourth edition of which appeared in 1949.

Applied psychologists gradually increased in numbers and became an active group. They published their researches in the *Journal of Applied Psychology*, founded by Hall in 1917. They wrote textbooks and offered courses in their subject. Applied psychologists—clinical as well as industrial—tried to organize special interest groups to further their professional objectives. These early attempts, however, met with little success because the ranks of applied psychologists were still small compared to the exclusively academic group. World War I offered wider opportunities for applications of psychology. The wartime activities of selection, classification, and testing of recruits underscored the usefulness of psychology and enhanced the prestige of applied psychologists. In the 1920's, therefore, psychological services were valued more than they had been previously.

Increased Interest after 1920. After World War I, professional psychology started to flourish independently. The Psychological Corporation, established in New York City in 1921 by Cattell, served as a clearinghouse for information about applied psychology and applied psychologists. Educational, industrial, and clinical psychology made substantial gains in the community. Extensive psychological testing programs were instituted in the schools. The excessive enthusiasm for tests in the 1920's provoked criticism from the public and also from psychologists. There was a dearth of qualified examiners. Frequently in the schools amateur psychologists and inadequately trained examiners—for example, teachers who had taken a course in Binet testing—administered the intelligence tests. Qualified clinical psychologists were anxious to remedy such abuses. They were eager to set standards for practice and to improve training. Psychological clinics—child guidance clinics, especially—proliferated in the 1920's. During this period clinicians tried to extend their functions beyond mere testing. By the late 1930's, clinical psychologists were making notable gains in psychotherapy.

While clinical psychologists were strengthening their specialty, industrial psychologists zealously extended their services in business and industry. The construction of special tests for use in business and industry came into vogue after World War I. Studies in the psychology of advertising and salesmanship, personnel selection and evaluation, employee motivation and efficiency, and consumer psychology were conducted. The depression of the 1930's dimmed some of the enthusiasm and interest in industrial psychology. It accounted in part for industrial psychology's failure to progress as rapidly as clinical psychology before 1940. As American psychology advanced vigorously and steadily from 1920 to 1940, there was a slow, gradual shift of attention to psychology in the service of society.

A review of employment trends in the membership of the American Psychological Association reveals that while in 1916 the percentage of A.P.A. members in academic positions was 75.7 per cent, it dropped to 61.5 per cent in 1931, and to 50.1 per cent in 1940. Concomitantly, there was a steady rise in the percentage of non-academic positions from 7.8 per cent in 1916 to 22.1 per cent in 1931 and 32 per cent in 1940. Among the non-academic specialties, clinical psychology showed the most pronounced growth, with guidance and personnel work a fairly close second.

As the number of applied psychologists employed in the community increased, there emerged a sharp division between the academic and non-academic—that is, between scientific and professional psychology. Academic psychologists criticized their non-academic colleagues because the latter, they claimed, did less research and published less. At the same time professional or applied psychologists complained that the academic psychologists did not appreciate their problems and that they did not provide adequate training for the professional specialties. As a result, two opposing trends developed in the 1930's: an experimental trend promoting laboratory psychology; and the other, an applied trend, demanding concern with human values and social research.

Applied psychologists felt that the American Psychological Association with its predominantly college professor membership not only did not represent their specialties, but that it was, as well, unsympathetic toward their objectives. Increased concern for professional problems, especially for licensing and certification, spurred the growth of state psychological associations. The academic-professional rift culminated in the formation of three specialty organizations: the Psychometric Society (1935); the Society for the Psychological Study of Social Issues (SPSSI, 1936), and the American Association for Applied Psychology (A.A.A.P., 1937). While most members of these groups remained in the American Psychological Association, they founded the newer groups to help them achieve recognition for their specialties. The A.A.A.P. acquired a membership of more than 700 applied psychologists, principally clinical and industrial, and rapidly became a powerful association. It started its own journal, the *Journal of Consulting Psychology* (1937). It also provided for affiliation of the state organizations in the Conference of State Psychological Associations. In spite of these advances made by applied psychologists, psychology prior to World War II remained an essentially academic discipline.

RECOGNITION OF PROFESSIONAL PSYCHOLOGY

Formal recognition of psychology as a profession was not achieved until after World War II. Once again, as a result of wartime service at home and in the military, American psychologists won distinction for the contribution they made. Consequently, after the war, psychological services were in enormous demand in the community. It became imperative for psychologists—academic and professional—to unite and to institute some long-needed changes of attitude, of curricula, of training, and of standards. Their first step was in the direction of organizational unity, an objective essential, too, to creating and maintaining a proper public image for psychology.

Reorganization of the American Psychological Association. Prompted by the need for unity and the obvious inadvisability of continuing two national organizations in the postwar expansion period, the American Association for Applied Psychology (A.A.A.P.) was dissolved, and its objectives incorporated in the reorganized American Psychological Association in 1945. In this move, the A.A.A.P. also surrendered its publication, the *Journal of Consulting Psychology*, to the A.PA. The amalgamation of the A.A.A.P. with the A.P.A. was a major move to maintain psychology's newly acquired prestige in American society. The A.P.A. was now a unified organization dedicated "to advance psychology as a science, a profession, and as a means of promoting human welfare." As a single group it now became the official voice for psychology and psychologists in the United States.

Implementing its objective of being official spokesman for psychologists, the reorganized A.P.A. structure established 18 separate divisions to represent the various specialties in psychology. Each division was designed to have its own membership requirements, its own officers, and to hold its own meetings at the annual A.P.A. convention. This divisional plan further provided representation of the various divisions in the A.P.A. central governing body—the Council of Representatives—as well as for possible future divisional changes, when interest in the various specialties grew, overlapped, or waned. Affiliated state associations were also represented on the Council. One of the two other prewar specialty groups, the Society for the Psychological Study of Social Issues, voted to become a division of the new A.P.A. But the second, the Psychometric Society, retained its independent status.

To conduct and manage the business activities of the A.P.A., a central office was established under the direction of an appointed Executive Secretary. While the reorganized A.P.A. continued its previous publication enterprises, it added a new journal, the *American Psychologist*. Established in 1946, this journal publishes news and articles concerning the profession of psychology, its relation to other professions, the status of psychologists, and educational and training facilities. Probably the most widely read of all A.P.A. journals, the *American Psychologist* is a vital unifiying force among psychologists in America. Over the years, as the need has arisen, A.P.A. has founded additional publications. In 1956 it established a journal of book reviews, *Contemporary Psychology*, and in 1957 it began publishing an annual membership directory. It also acquired the *Journal of Educational Psychology* (1957). In 1965, because of the large volume of research in these areas, A.P.A. split the *Journal of Abnormal and Social Psychology* into two journals—*Journal of Abnormal Psychology* (original title, 1906) and *Journal of Personality and Social Psychology.*

When the reorganized A.P.A. began to function officially in 1945, it had 4,173 members. In the ensuing years such extraordinarily rapid growth occurred in the science and profession that by 1966 there were about 24,500 A.P.A. members and 24 divisions. During these years the A.P.A. continued to hold annual conventions. These national meetings featured reports of current psychological research as well as lectures and symposia on topics of special interest to psychologists. Increased attendance at these conventions made it impossible to accommodate them at the universities where they had traditionally met. Since the early 1950's, therefore, these conventions have been confined to hotel sites chiefly in the larger cities of the United States. Certain advantages have accrued to the membership because of its magnitude—among them group medical and life insurance and income protection plans. The A.P.A. has further concerned itself with the welfare and interest of its members through monthly publication of the *Employment Bulletin.* This bulletin publishes availability notices for A.P.A. members, and for employers of psychologists it lists nontrainee, full-time position openings.

Since its reorganization, and in spite of problems besetting a rapidly growing profession, the A.P.A. has, above all, continued to pursue its original stated objective: the improvement of standards for psychological training and service. It has continued to work closely with the universities, with government agencies, and with the allied professions in the community to advance psychology as a science, as a profession, and as a means of promoting human welfare. To assure A.P.A.'s continuing dedication to its objectives, its Policy and Planning Board—a deliberative body with advisory rather than executive functions—maintains vigilance over current and future needs.

In the immediate post-World War II period, A.P.A. had to concern itself primarily with standards for the education and training of psychologists to meet the new service demands. University departments needed assistance in developing adequate programs for the large numbers of students seeking psychological training. Criteria for evaluating programs had to be determined rapidly—particularly for the clinical programs sponsored by the Veterans Administration and the United States Public Health Service. Most psychology departments were without adequate precedent or experience in the institution of such programs, since little attention had been paid to professional psychology prior to 1945.

Revision of Psychological Training. Although the need for revision of psychological training was precipitated principally by clinical psychology, the entire graduate education program in psychology came under scrutiny. There was concern and debate about curricular offerings, particularly with respect to their basic orientation, whether academic or professional. The difficulties were further compounded by the fact that, at both the graduate and undergraduate levels, student enrollments had increased. The many and varied vocational opportunities in the community, and the generous financial assistance programs of the federal agencies, made psychology an attractive field of study. Thus the screening of students, the development of appropriate curricula, provisions for practicum training, and the recruitment of personnel qualified to instruct and, especially, to supervise professional programs, constituted serious problems for university administrators.

In 1947 the A.P.A. Committee on Training in Clinical Psychology offered the universities a recommended training program for clinicians. Since the specific details relating to clinical psychology are presented in the next chapter, they are not recounted here. In recognition of the need for continued stimulation, coordination, evaluation, and improvement of the university training programs, A.P.A. established the Education and Training Board. In 1949 the first conference on graduate education in clinical psychology was held at Boulder, Colorado. Thereafter there was a succession of such conferences on various phases of graduate preparation: the Northwestern Conference for Counseling Psychologists (1951); the Thayer Conference for School Psychologists' Training (1954); Stanford Conference on Psychologists' Careers in Mental Health (1955); Estes Park Conference on Training for Research (1958); the Miami Conference on Graduate Education in Psychology (1958); the Greyston Conference on the Professional Preparation of Counseling Psychologists (1964); and the Chicago Conference on the Professional Preparation of Clinical Psychologists (1965). These conferences have been uniformly dedicated to evaluating and improving training at both doctoral and subdoctoral levels and to the maintenance of high standards of recruitment and high quality of instruction in the various specialties. While the principal concerns of most conferences have been professional, all have consistently emphasized dedication to science and to the advancement of scientific knowledge in the different specialties of psychology.

As a service to the universities, to their prospective students, and to the profession generally, the American Psychological Association's Education and Training Board evaluates the doctoral programs in clinical and counseling psychology of the various universities and publishes an annual listing of approved doctoral programs. This A.P.A. accreditation is limited exclusively to clinical and counseling programs. For graduate students in these areas, considerable financial support is available by way of traineeships, assistantships, scholarships, and fellowships. Assistance is generally made available to graduate students in programs sponsored variously by the Veterans Administration, the National Institute of Mental Health, the Vocational Rehabilitation Administration, the National Science Foundation, and the United States Office of Education.

While the A.P.A. has been active in the improvement of graduate training in psychology since 1945, it has also had other serious concerns. Because the large community demand for psychological services and the paucity of qualified personnel quite naturally encouraged charlatanism, professional safeguards and protections for the public had to be devised. Since membership in the national organization itself does not signify competence in a specialty, the A.P.A. almost immediately recommended and supported other procedures to promote and endorse the professional competence of its members, and it has continued to do so. Among such procedures are: the formation of the American Board of Examiners in Professional Psychology (ABEPP); the framing of an ethical code; and the licensing and certification of psychologists in various states.

American Board of Examiners in Professional Psychology (ABEPP). Chronologically, the American Board of Examiners in Professional Psychology was the first major development in the move toward professionalization on a national scale. The Board was established in 1946 and incorporated in 1947. Its functions are two: to examine and to certify psychologists. It embraces three areas of professional psychology: clinical, industrial, and counseling. Although its members are subject to approval by the American Psychological Association, the Board is an independent agency. The independence of ABEPP from A.P.A. was deliberately established for two important reasons. First, it helped to emphasize the specific professional function of the Board—namely, professional qualification of psychologists. Second, the Board's independence made clear that competence in a specific professional practice is not automatically evidenced by membership in A.P.A. The Board established rigorous educational, experience, and personal qualifications for diplomate status. In summary, the Board was authorized to certify candidates who hold the Ph.D. degree; who have had five years of experience; and who, after completing the educational and experience requirements, passed oral and written examinations in their professional specialty. The first written examinations were held in the fall of 1949, and the first orals in the fall of 1950. These examinations are now conducted annually by ABEPP. As a guide to the identification of qualified clinical, industrial, and counseling psychologists, ABEPP publishes a directory of diplomates in each specialty.

ABEPP filled an immediate postwar need to identify qualified psychologists to a public which made heavy demands for psychological services. Under pressure to fulfill such burgeoning demand for professional help, the board was a necessary instrumentality not only to maintain by certification a high level of competence in practitioners, but to protect both the public and the profession from unqualified practitioners. ABEPP still considers its primary responsibility to be that "of defining realistically the contemporary status of professional psychology and, within that framework, of devising procedures for identifying competent practitioners." Although diplomas are still granted in only three areas, ABEPP will expand its examinations to other areas of specialization "'whenever it can be demonstrated that a large body of psychologists share training, experience, and practice that differs significantly from the existing professional models."

The chief reason for the diploma granted by ABEPP is protection of the public, but it is also a mark of distinction for the holder. Nonetheless, the influence of ABEPP has been less strong than was originally anticipated. Fewer psychologists have achieved diplomate status than one would expect, considering the numbers engaged in clinical, counseling, and industrial psychology. Up to 1965, 1,970 A.P.A. members had earned diplomas. Of these 1,470 were in clinical, 292 in counseling, and 208 in industrial psychology.

Ethical Standards. In the same year that ABEPP was incorporated, the A.P.A. turned attention to framing a code of ethics for psychologists. Five years were spent on empirical investigation of ethical problems related to psychology and its practice. From the review, evaluation, and revision of this material the ethical code was developed. The code was officially published by the A.P.A. in 1953. It included a proviso for revisions, one of which was made in 1963. The code is a comprehensive and detailed presentation of the ethical principles which should govern the profession of psychology. Its concerns are the conduct of the psychologist himself, his use of psychological tests and techniques, and his relationships with his clients, the public, and with his fellow professionals.

A.P.A. implements its ethical code through its Committee on Scientific and Professional Ethics and Conduct. An additional control is exercised by the Committee on Scientific Responsibility, which is charged with vigilant observance of changes in the role of psychology in society and with the responsibility of formulating social controls required by these changes. While the ethical code and the ABEPP diploma are attempts to insure proper conduct and competence of psychologists, they do not have legal power to compel enforcement. Such power resides in the states where appropriate legislation has been passed.

Licensing and Certification. Although some interest in securing legal safeguards had been expressed before World War II, there was no formal legal regulation of the title "psychologist" or of the practice of psychology. Since the end of World War II, legislation has been the chief practical concern. The A.P.A., the regional, state, and local associations, and other groups have been deeply involved in drafting licensing and certification bills. Complex problems of defining psychology and psychotherapy have often produced violent disputes. Numerous direct conflicts have occurred throughout the country among psychiatrists, social workers, and psychoanalysts on issues regarding conflict of interests. The establishment of adequate educational and experience criteria has been a continuing challenge.

The purposes of legislation, broadly considered, are twofold: (1) social—to safeguard the public against malpractice and charlatanism; (2) professional—to establish by law the identity of the psychologist and to specify the scope of his specialty as a psychologist. In the light of these purposes, it is understandable that the chief impetus toward legislation should have come from professional psychologists, rather than from academic or experimental psychologists. Legal safeguards are most vital in professional practice of psychology because, in the community, assurance is needed by both practitioners and their clients that only the qualified are permitted to practice. Of course, many clinicians function in schools, clinics, hospitals, and allied institutions which maintain their own safeguards. However, the independent practitioners—much more numerous since the 1950's—have felt a great need for the status and protection conferred by legislation. In general, the majority of contemporary professional psychologists in America regard legal regulation of practice as highly beneficial and essential. At the end of 1965, seven states had licensing laws, 21 had certification laws, and 17 (16 plus the District of Columbia) had nonstatutory certification programs. Ordinarily, the doctoral degree in psychology is the educational requirement, while one or two years of appropriately supervised experience are also generally required.

NEW HORIZONS AT MID-CENTURY

After 1945, American psychology underwent drastic changes. Old areas expanded. New specialties developed. Professionalization of psychology proceeded at a rapid rate. Large numbers of students applied for graduate training in psychology, and their vocational goals were predominantly professional rather than academic. This professional trend was encouraged by the generous assistance available to students in clinical programs. Meanwhile, although academic and clinical psychologists debated the advisability of a new professional degree and new training programs, the traditional Ph.D. degree continued to be required of clinical students, together with academic and research requirements and some practicums.

In the community, psychologists found expanding employment opportunities—in universities, clinics, mental hospitals, prisons, schools, in government agencies, in business and industry, and in private practice. There was a noticeable decrease in the number of psychologists available for teaching in the colleges and universities. In the competition for staff, colleges and universities were forced to advance salaries and to provide research time. Frequently they had to permit their professors to engage in private practice or do consulting work. Government and foundation support for research became available in large supply.

Specialties Old and New. After 1945, applied psychology, particularly the clinical and industrial specialties, showed an unprecedented growth. Whereas psychologists had previously been called upon only for occasional jobs in industry and had done a moderate amount of work in clinics, they were now in heavy demand. The growth and development of various fields, old and new—industrial psychology, clinical psychology, engineering psychology, and space psychology—were rapid. Data from the 1960 National Register of Scientific and Technical Personnel indicate the trends. They reveal the percentages of psychologists distributed in the various subfields. These data are presented in Figure 1.

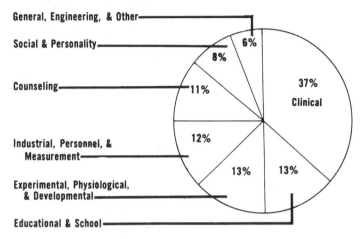

Figure 1. Subfields of Psychology.

Reproduced and adapted from Ross, S., & Lockman, R. F. *A career in psychology.* Washington, D.C.: American Psychological Association, 1963. P. 8.

From Figure 1 it is readily observable that clinical psychology has become the largest specialty, and that what may be considered "pure" science—experimental, physiological, and developmental—attracts only a small number, 13 per cent. The activities of psychologists in these various subfields include teaching or training, consulting, behavior modification, assessment and evaluation, and basic and applied research.

Expanded World of the Psychologists. Prior to 1945 most psychologists worked in an academic setting—in colleges and universities—and their principal function was teaching and research. After World War II so many opportunities for psychologists became available in all types of applied work, and in research too, that large numbers of psychologists were drawn from the colleges and universities. Many students seeking graduate degrees in psychology tended to shun the academic for more lucrative employment opportunities. Figure 2 indicates that in 1960 a little more than one-third of the nation's psychologists were employed by colleges and universities in teaching and in student personnel services.

Inspection of Figure 2 reveals that an equal percentage is employed by schools as school psychologists and counselors, by business as industrial psychologists, and by the Federal government in civil service positions—research and applied. Local governments and clinics—public and private—also employ psychologists. Psychologists' activities in the community

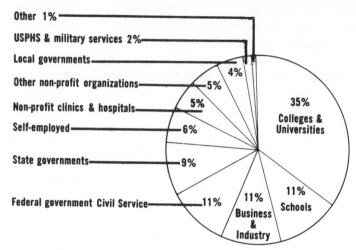

Figure 2. Employers of Psychologists.

Reproduced from Ross, S., & Lockman, R. F. *A Career in psychology*. Washington, D.C.: American Psychological Association, 1963. P. 12

range from personnel selection and training, consumer psychology, teaching, engineering psychology, diagnosis and therapy of the maladjusted, to military and space psychology. A small but growing number of psychologists—principally clinical psychologists—are engaged in private practice. In general, the employment activities of psychologists indicate a pronounced trend toward the professionalization of psychology in the 1960's. This trend has significant implications for American psychology as science, and especially for the training of psychologists in the future.

Academic vs. Professional Psychology: The Persistent Problem. Most American psychologists have been concerned about the trends their science has taken. There has been a deepening cleavage between the academic and professional psychologists in the 1960's, just as there was three decades before. Unlike the earlier period, however, the academic psychologists who train future psychologists in the colleges and universities are in the minority at present. While most psychologists pay lip service to the basic principle that psychological science and psychological service are interdependent and that a functional unity must be preserved between the two, integration of academic and professional interests has not been satisfactorily effected. There are extremists on both sides. Among academic psychologists there are the "purists"—represented, for example, by the membership of the Society of Experimental Psychologists and of the Psychonomic Society (organized in 1959)—who have made clear their dedication to scientific psychology and who avoid professional enterprises. Many academic experimental psychologists criticize the applied psychologists for their exclusive concern with application and their failure to produce more research. They cite the low publication rate of recently trained professional psychologists. On the other hand, the professional psychologists and, in particular, the clinical psychologists, who are in the majority, are not fully satisfied. They maintain that the academic psychologists, the traditional directors of university training programs in clinical and other applied areas, have been too research-oriented and have not provided adequate professional training. Professional psychologists aspire to greater involvement of psychologists in professional enterprises. Toward that end numerous local clinical societies, institutes, therapeutic centers, workshops, and seminars have been established by them. They have created their own opportunities for postdoctoral training in psychotherapy and psychoanalysis without university affiliation. They have concerned themselves with professional issues such as confidentiality, liability, and particularly with legislation. These activities they consider essential for training, and for safeguarding professional psychology.

While the complaints resemble those made chiefly by the clinicians in the 1930's, they have a new urgency and seemingly sounder basis in the 1960's. Although clinical psychologists were the first to grapple with the problems of professionalization after World War II, they are not alone. Psychologists have gone into the community as school psychologists, industrial psychologists, counseling psychologists, military psychologists, and space psychologists. It is only natural, therefore, that their professional training programs should have come under closer scrutiny. Professional curricula for the different specialties seem essential and inevitable because of the interdisciplinary character the specialties have acquired. Knowledge is required in allied areas such as engineering, medicine, sociology, political science, and economics. The bifurcated character of psychology as science and as service remains a pressing problem to psychologists. As ever-expanding service-oriented employment opportunities develop, academic psychologists find themselves a minority group with a steady flow of students more interested generally in service than in science —or at least, in basic research.

Trends in Professional Psychology: 1945-1965. Besides clinical psychology, to which the entire next chapter is devoted, other branches of professional psychology expanded after World War II. Both *school* psychologists and *counseling* psychologists became professionalized and gained stature, as schools and colleges instituted and extended their student personnel services. There was a growing awareness of the need to improve diagnostic methods and techniques which was stimulated, too, by the criticism of testing in social, political, and educational circles. Attempts were made at new methods of evaluation, including culture-free and culture-fair tests. *Educational* psychology, one of the oldest branches of applied psychology, was enriched by introduction of teaching machines and programmed instruction. Valuable use of psychological science has been made in teacher training, in the development of improved teaching techniques, and in promoting the social and emotional adjustment of pupils. *Industrial* psychology has developed from personnel selection and classification activities to more complex assessment programs, to applied experimental activities involving design of equipment according to human specifications, to market research and consumer psychology. Some industrial psychologists are affiliated with consulting firms which do research for industry and the government on a contract basis. Because of the unsettled world conditions since World War II, and the necessity of continuing the draft and larger armed forces, *military* psychology has been expanded in all branches of the service. Psychological activities include selection, classification, training, management, clinical practice, and human engineering.

A complete survey of the developments of each branch of professional psychology is beyond the scope of this book. The reader is referred to the references at the end of this chapter for more extended treatment of these and other subfields of professional psychology. Here we delineate only the general trends of American psychology as a profession in the period from 1945 to 1965. They may be summarized as follows:

(1) After World War II, psychology gained prestige in the community. The public, generally, became more psychology-oriented, as was evidenced by their unprecedented demand for psychological services. (2) Employment opportunities for psychologists were expanded in industry, the schools, social agencies, and hospitals. Some psychologists began independent private practice, and others established consulting firms. (3) Student enrollment in undergraduate and graduate training programs ran consistently high. Professional preparation, generously underwritten by government agencies—particularly for clinical psychology—attracted many students. (4) The number of American professional psychologists increased steadily, as evidenced by the rise in membership of the American Psychological Association and the establishment of many new professional groups to pursue professional objectives—improvement of professional training, legislation, ethical standards, and public relations. (5) Despite newer professional emphases in university education and training, experimental psychology has remained the core of most training curricula—undergraduate and graduate—but it is no longer all-important. The experimental method, however, has been extended to a broader subject matter. It is no longer confined to the academic laboratory. (6) While there has been an accelerated output of psychological publications, the increased production reflects the increased numbers of psychologists rather than increased per capita productivity. Multiple authorship has become more frequent. Recently trained psychologists have published less than those who entered the field earlier, probably because fewer of them now work in the universities where traditionally much research essential to psychology's scientific progress has been conducted. (7) Increasingly psychologists have participated with other professionals and scientists—behavioral, natural, and social—on interdisciplinary research projects. In some respects this trend has itself been divisive because psychologists often find more compatibility with these colleagues than with their own highly specialized fellow psychologists. (8) Psychologists have demonstrated a greater sensitivity to, and concern about, current social and political issues: international tensions, nuclear warfare, cold war, and civil rights. Society

has continued to enlist the aid of psychologists toward the solution of problems and on projects, such as national programs to promote mental health, to combat mental retardation, and to salvage the disadvantaged. (9) With its recently acquired scientific and professional interests and enterprises, American psychology has acquired a multifarious character. But American psychology is acutely bifurcated. The academic-professional division, with its concomitant conflict of interests, has constituted a major persistent challenge during the two postwar decades. It gives every indication of continuing to do so.

PSYCHOLOGY AS A PROFESSION ON THE INTERNATIONAL SCENE

Compared to psychology in other countries, psychology in the United States has had a phenomenal growth since 1945. However, professional psychology with its clinical and industrial applications also arose in other countries in the early twentieth century and has increased steadily since World War II. In many parts of the world the demand for psychological services has mounted in mid-twentieth century. The need has been met in different ways in different countries.

In most countries, as in the United States, academic traditions and local interests have shaped the development of psychology both as profession and as science. However, in no country has professional psychology attained the prestige and made the substantial progress in university training programs, practicums, internships, and legislation that it has achieved in the United States. In no other country have the social and economic conditions so favored psychology's growth as a profession. In Europe, for example, few universities have professional training programs in psychology or offer practicums and internship training. In many instances professional societies and private schools offer the only practicum training available to psychologists. Marked differences make strict comparisons of professional psychology from country to country difficult. Moreover, in different lands, there are varying degrees of receptivity to psychological services among the people. The American public has been remarkably psychology oriented.

International cooperation and interest in professional psychology have grown steadily over the years. Since 1920, when Edouard Claparède organized the first International Conference on Psychology as Applied to Vocational Guidance, an international conference of applied psychology has convened regularly. At the fourth international conference in 1927, an International Association of Applied Psychology was established, with membership available to workers in all branches of applied psychology. In 1952 this Association began publication of the *Bulletin*, which appears twice a year in English and French. Other international organizations have also been established. The International Council of Psychology (originally organized as the International Council of Women Psychologists during World War II), whose aim is "to promote psychology as science and as a profession throughout the world," includes male and female membership from all over the world. The Council publishes the ICP *Newsletter,* which offers a valuable medium for the international exchange of ideas. International communication is also encouraged among mental health personnel by two organizations—the World Health Organization and the World Federation for Mental Health. Thus applied psychology in all of its branches is promoted internationally as well as within individual nations.

How professional psychology has fared in a given country is discussed in this volume in connection with psychology's growth in that particular country. Of all phases of professional psychology, however, it seems that clinical psychology has attracted most attention, both within individual countries and internationally. On that account the following chapter is devoted exclusively to its rise and growth.

HIGHLIGHTS OF AMERICAN PSYCHOLOGY: GROWTH AS A PROFESSION

1903   Scott published the first book to aid business, written by a psychologist—*The Theory of Advertising.*

1913   Münsterberg published *Psychology and Industrial Efficiency*, in which he described the possible applications of psychology.

1916   Bingham organized the Division of Applied Psychology at Carnegie Institute of Technology; Scott headed its Bureau of Salesmanship Research.

1917   World War I—testing and classification of recruits.
Journal of Applied Psychology established by Hall.

1919   Establishment of the Scott Company, the first American consulting firm devoted to industrial psychology.

1920   First International Conference on Psychology as Applied to Vocational Guidance.

1921   The Psychological Corporation established by Cattell.

1927   International Association of Applied Psychology established.

1935   Psychometric Society founded.

1936   Society for the Psychological Study of Social Issues (SPSSI) established.

1937   American Association for Applied Psychology (A.A.A.P.) organized.
Journal of Consulting Psychology established.

1945   Reorganization of the American Psychological Association.

1946   *American Psychologist* established.
Establishment of American Board of Examiners in Professional Psychology (ABEPP).

1953   A.P.A. officially published its Ethical Code.

1956   *Contemporary Psychology* founded by A.P.A.

1959   Psychonomic Society founded.

REFERENCES

BEGINNINGS OF PROFESSIONALIZATION

Cattell, J. McK. Retrospect: psychology as a profession. *J. consult. Psychol.*, 1937, *1*, 1–3.

Finch, F. H., & Odoroff, M. E. Employment trends in applied psychology. *J. consult. Psychol.*, 1939, *3*, 118–122.

Finch, F. H., & Odoroff, M. E. Employment trends in applied psychology. II. *J. consult. Psychol.*, 1941, *5*, 275–278.

Fryer, D. The proposed American Association for Applied and Professional Psychologists. *J. consult. Psychol.*, 1937, *1*, 14–16.

Goodenough, Florence L. Trends in modern psychology. *Psychol. Bull.*, 1934, *31*, 81–97.

Symonds. J. P. Toward unity. *J. consult. Psychol.*, 1937, *1*, 23–24.

Wallin, J. E. W. History of the struggles within the American Psychological Association to attain membership requirements, test standardization, certification of psychological practitioners, and professionalization. *J. gen. Psychol.*, 1960, *63*, 287–308.

RECOGNITION OF PROFESSIONAL PSYCHOLOGY

Bingham, W. V. Psychology as a science, as a technology, and as a profession. *Amer. Psychologist*, 1953, *8*, 115–118.

Ericksen, S. C. Legislation and the academic tradition in psychology. *Amer. Psychologist*, 1963, *18*, 101–104.

Kelley, N. H., Sanford, F. H., & Clark, K. E. The meaning of the ABEPP diploma. *Amer. Psychologist*, 1961, *16*, 132–141.

Poffenberger, A. T., & Bryan, Alice. I. Toward unification in psychology. *J. consult. Psychol.*, 1944, *8*, 253–257.

Wolfle, D. The reorganized American Psychological Association. *Amer. Psychologist*, 1946, *1*, 3–6.

Wyatt, F. On the expansion of professional psychology. *Amer. Psychologist*, 1954, *9*, 522–528.

NEW HORIZONS AT MID-CENTURY

Clark, K. E. *America's psychologists.* Washington, D. C.: Amer. Psychol. Ass., 1957.

Poffenberger, A. T. Psychology: academic and professional. *J. consult. Psychol.*, 1945, *9*, 1–7.

Rodgers, D. A. In favor of separation of academic and professional training. *Amer. Psychologist*, 1964, *19*, 675–680.

Ross, S., & Lockman, R. F. Survey of graduate education in psychology: some trends for the last decade. *Amer. Psychologist*, 1964, *19*, 623–628.

Ross, S., & Lockman, R. F. *A career in psychology.* Washington, D.C.: Amer. Psychol. Ass., 1963.

Schwartz, E. K. Some trends in the development of psychology as a profession in the United States of America. *Int. J. soc. Psychiat.*, 1956, *2*, 51–58.

Tryon, R. C. Psychology in flux: the academic-professional bipolarity. *Amer. Psychologist*, 1963, *18*, 134–143.

AREAS OF APPLIED PSYCHOLOGY: THEIR DEVELOPMENT AND PROBLEMS

Brewer, J. M., *et al. History of vocational guidance: origins and early development.* New York: Harper & Row, 1942.

Corsini, R. J., & Miller, G. A. Psychology in prisons, 1952. *Amer. Psychologist*, 1954, *9*, 184–185.

Cutts, Norma E. (Ed.) *School psychologists at midcentury: a report of the Thayer Conference on the functions, qualifications, and training of school psychologists.* Washington: Amer. Psychol. Ass., 1955.

Daniel, R. S., & Louttit, C. M. *Professional problems in psychology.* New York: Prentice-Hall, 1953.

Dubno, P. The role of the psychologist in labor unions. *Amer. Psychologist*, 1957, *12*, 212–215.

Ferguson, L. W. *The heritage of industrial psychology.* Vol. 1. Hartford, Conn.: Finlay, 1963.

Grether, W. F. Psychology and the space frontier. *Amer. Psychologist*, 1962, *17*, 92–101.

Hahn, M. E. Counseling psychology. *Amer. Psychologist*, 1955 *10*, 279–282.

McCollom, I. N. Psychologists in industry in the United States. *Amer. Psychologist*, 1959, *14*, 704–708.

Melton, A. W. Military psychology in the United States of America. *Amer. Psychologist*, 1957, *12* 740–746.

Ogg, Elizabeth. *Psychologists in action.* New York: Public Affairs Comm., 1955.

Rees, J. R. The psychologist and world affairs. *Amer. Psychologist*, 1954, *9*, 613–616.

Rogers, L. S. Psychologists in public service and the public. *Amer. Psychologist*, 1956, *11*, 307–313.

Stevens, S. S. Human engineering. *Amer. Psychologist*, 1957, *12*, 222.

Taylor, F. V. Psychology and the design of machines. *Amer. Psychologist*, 1957, *12*, 249–258.

13

Clinical Psychology

CLINICAL PSYCHOLOGY is the branch of psychology which deals with the diagnosis and treatment of individuals who have intellectual and personality disorders, as well as with research on clinical techniques, on procedures, and on the disorders themselves. In America this branch of applied psychology dates from the establishment of Lightner Witmer's clinic at the University of Pennsylvania in Philadelphia. The year was 1896. Hence the history of clinical psychology in America has been, substantially, a twentieth century development. In the early years the development of clinical psychology was slow, but nonetheless constant. Yet this fact has at times been overlooked, because in those years academic psychologists dominated the field in America. As a result, the progress of psychology was frequently measured by the number and by the work of college and university laboratories rather than by clinical developments. In 1946, its fiftieth anniversary, clinical psychology emerged dramatically as an important field, primarily in consequence of its vital services to the armed forces in World War II. Two decades later clinical psychologists had substantially increased their numbers and extended their professional domain to include mental hospitals, community clinics, schools, prisons, courts, industry, government agencies, the armed services, and independent practice.

ANTECEDENTS

Since 1946, developments in the clinical field and expansion of clinical practice have been both comprehensive and rapid. This marked growth is due in part to the U.S. Government sponsored Veterans' clinical training program and to generous grants by the U.S. Public Health Service for clinical research. However, the vital antecedents of modern clinical psychology are to be found in the work of the late nineteenth and early twentieth centuries. These antecedents, most notably, are to be seen in four evidences: (1) the functional approach in psychology; (2) psychometrics; (3) the dynamic approach in psychiatry; and (4) the mental hygiene movement. It is worth noting that the first two evidences are developments within scientific psychology itself. The latter two, conversely, are in medicine and originate in the widespread twentieth century efforts to promote mental health. Each of these four factors contributed in a special way to the development of clinical psychology.

The Functional Approach. A functional approach emerged rather early in the history of scientific psychology, especially in America. This approach derives from an ideal and specific objective of service. To satisfy this aim, it works to apply laboratory findings to life situations and to employ psychological science to further human welfare. These interests are to be seen in early psychological literature, where the theme of service appears and is frequently emphasized and reiterated. Even though some psychologists—Titchener, for example—opposed the initial applications of psychology, the functional spirit prevailed.

In 1896, when Lightner Witmer first offered clinical services to Philadelphia school children, there was some immediate recognition of service possibilities. Yet there was counterbalancing opposition. At this time, American psychology was struggling to build a solid scientific foundation and to earn recognition among the sciences. In addition, many psychologists who advocated applied psychology were convinced that the most important strategic objective for the rapidly developing psychology was to implant it firmly in academic and scientific circles. Undoubtedly, the relatively unenthusiastic reception of clinical psychology by academic psychologists is explainable in terms of the latter group's commitment to a more thorough and systematic foundation for psychological science. A sign of this disinterest by the academicians is the record of Witmer's experience. When he made his first presentation of clinical psychology, and of his clinical program, to the membership of the American Psychological Association, it was received indifferently. In fact, the 50 year history of clinical psychology, following its initiation in 1896, was a continual struggle to achieve recognition. Rigorous development was required before the new offshoot would be accorded the status of respectability by the "pure" psychologists. A most vitally significant contribution to such development, and thus to the ultimate acceptance of clinical psychology, was psychometrics.

Psychometrics. Psychometrics emphasized quantification. The importance of such emphasis will be clear, when it is recalled that the pioneer laboratory psychologists patterned their techniques after physics, and were dedicated to measurement. The presence of such a vital historical link makes readily understandable the importance of psychometrics to the growth of clinical psychology, in that through this link could come, not only identification of clinical psychology with the science of psychology, but recognition as well. Thus, insofar as psychometrics helped to make their professional activity more objective and scientific, it was widely adopted by clinicians as an instrument in their practice.

Wundt and Fechner had initiated and used measurements to derive general and uniform principles underlying psychological functions. Galton and Cattell, taking an opposite tack, concentrated on differences, rather than similarities in human behavior. It was Galton's and Cattell's emphasis in measuring the individual as an individual that prevailed in clinical practice, where it superseded early the more generalized approach of

Wundt and Fechner. Galton's early use of measurements at his anthropometric laboratory in London, in effect, created differential psychology and led to the eventual widespread use of statistics in psychological research. It was Galton who first demonstrated that human psychological traits distribute themselves according to the normal probability curve. It is to be noted that his main interest was in the central portions of the normal curve, whereas Cattell, his American colleague and admirer, concerned himself primarily with the extremes.

1. Individual Tests. The great importance of the research of Galton and Cattell was that they focused attention on the clinical significations of individual differences. Possibly the greatest single psychometric contribution to clinical psychology, however, was Alfred Binet's test of intelligence. At the direction of the French Minister of Education, Alfred Binet and Théodore Simon composed the first individual test of intelligence in 1905. Its purpose was to screen out feebleminded children from the Paris schools. In this test, Binet furnished the first effective psychometric tool to clinicians. This archetypal individual intelligence test—and its subsequent revisions—was received with world-wide praise. The reception of Binet's test in America was enthusiastic. It was translated and revised by various American psychologists, notably by Lewis Terman at Stanford in 1916. In a relatively short time, the administration of intelligence tests became a principal technique in the practice of clinical psychology. In fact, intelligence testing became so essential to the work of the clinician that there was a long period during the first quarter of the twentieth century when "intelligence testing" and "clinical psychology" were practically synonymous. Perhaps because of the naturally limited applicability of intelligence tests to the broad field of clinical psychology, the clinicians of that period were criticized severely for excessive emphasis on mental tests.

2. Group Tests. The impact of Binet's test on American clinical psychology generated numerous tests of intelligence, both individual and group, both verbal and nonverbal. World War I presented a special challenge to the growing psychometric competence and initiative of psychologists. They developed the Army Alpha and Army Beta tests, which proved highly useful, both in the classification of men on a large scale and in their assignment to appropriate military duty. Woodworth devised a personality inventory, *The Personal Data Sheet*. Various aptitude tests were also devised. After World War I, these group tests were modified and standardized for civilian use in schools and in industry. Although it must be recognized that enthusiasm for tests was at times exaggerated in the first quarter of the present century, still such tests established beyond question the value of their use.

3. Projective Techniques. Following World War I, another development of significance in clinical psychology was the publication in Switzerland in 1921 of the inkblot test of Hermann Rorschach. This test, a projective technique, incorporated both a test approach and the dynamic viewpoint. It was based on the principle that an individual subject—by his interpretation of the blots—projected his own personality into his perception of them. While this technique was quantitative in a sense, it provided opportunity for qualitative appraisal as well. Such a test had an original feature that attracted clinicians. It seemed to overcome the somewhat confining character of the inventory-type of personality measurement, in that the latter required a self-understanding and complete honesty not always present in the examinee. Since the twenties, and especially since the thirties when the Rorschach Inkblot Test was popularized in America, numerous additional projective tests were developed, including those based on sentence completion, human figure drawing, and techniques such as finger painting and play therapy. An outstanding example is the Thematic Apperception Test (TAT) of Morgan and Murray (1935). At the beginning of World War II, clinicians had a sizeable repertoire of intelligence, personality, and aptitude tests. It is worthy of special note that tests were no longer used exclusively. While tests provided one of the major bases for clinical practice—namely, diagnosis—clinicians now paid more attention to therapeutic skills—particularly to psychotherapy, a mode of treatment that evolved from the dynamic point of view in psychiatry.

The Dynamic Point of View in Psychiatry. Psychiatry, both in Europe and America, had marked and significant influence on psychology. This influence was particularly important in the development of clinical psychology in the twentieth century.

Europe. Psychiatric interest in Europe in the nineteenth century was focused early on the problem of insanity—up to then, perhaps the most universally intriguing aspect of formal psychiatric interest. In Germany Emil Kraepelin had a most powerful interest in the development of nosology—the classification of mental diseases as to etiology, course, and outcome. The characteristic French concern, on the other hand, was with the mentally ill individual and with his care as a person. Such an approach evidenced itself in France early in the nineteenth century, when Pinel and Esquirol urged that the insane be recognized as sick people and advocated that more humane treatment and care be given them than had been available in the past. They stressed better housing for the mentally ill. In the late nineteenth century in France, there was concern for a better understanding of the mentally ill subject as a person with individual problems. At this time, physicians aimed and worked to know the patient, and to learn in detail his personality, his motivations, his feelings, and his emotions. Regarding his personality as a product of growth and experience, they sought means of understanding the adjustment of the individual to his environment. A significant development in this period in France was the interest of Charcot and Janet in neurotics, that is, people suffering from mild personality disorders. When treating neurotic cases, they used psychological techniques such as hypnotism and suggestion—rather than the traditional medical methods—to probe the dynamics of the patient's behavior.

The dynamic approach was used in England by Maudsley, in America by S. Weir Mitchell, and in Austria by Sigmund Freud. Freud, more than any other psychiatrist or psychologist, stressed the unconscious in human motivation. Emphasizing his theory of infantile sexuality, he directed the focus of psychiatry away from somatic factors and toward the psychic causes of personality disturbance. In Freud's view, personality is the result of a genetic process in which the forces of environment frequently are more powerful than those of heredity, and in which the emotions play a powerful role. Academic psychology had previously preoccupied itself with man's intellectual life. Freud's new approach was a concern to appreciate fully man's feelings, emotions, and motivations. His emphasis on the psychic produced an original diagnostic technique—a search in the life history of the patient for the cause of his disturbance. In addition, his method required a new mode of treatment—namely, psychotherapy, a treatment which employed psychological procedures such as mental catharsis, rather than medicine.

America. In America, the work of Charcot and Janet—with its dynamic approach to human maladjustment—strongly impressed William James. Morton Prince, James's colleague at Harvard, furthered the use of the dynamic approach in studies of dissociated personalities. Moreover, the initial promulgation of psychoanalysis in America by G. Stanley Hall— then president of Clark University—gave powerful impetus to the dynamic approach to personality study. Prince founded—and was first editor of— the *Journal of Abnormal Psychology* (1906), later (1922) renamed the *Journal of Abnormal and Social Psychology*, and restored to its original title in 1965. In founding this journal, Prince provided a medium for publishing research in psychopathology.

Freud visited America in 1909, at Hall's invitation. In that same year a new type of clinic, operating on the dynamic principle, was founded by William Healy in Chicago. Healy's clinic, organized in a court setting, was established to study delinquency. Witmer's clinic in Philadelphia, with its university background, was chiefly concerned with the intellectual characteristics of the school children who were its clientele. Healy's clinic, on the other hand, was mainly concerned with the affective aspects of personality and with social pathology. Its clients were delinquents. Healy's clinic probed the causes of antisocial behavior. His was a dynamic, total approach, in contrast to Witmer's static, segmented approach. Witmer was working in the tradition of Wundt and Kraepelin. Healy followed the pattern of Freud and the French school.

The importance of Healy's clinic was that it demonstrated how a dynamic approach in psychiatry could be applied with success in psychological practice. It was an exemplar and incentive for the founding and developing of child guidance clinics both in the United States and abroad. The experience of the Healy clinic made it evident that testing was only a partial basis for sound clinical diagnosis. Additionally—and importantly—qualitative evaluation of the individual's life history, and of the multiple and complex factors involved in the formation of the personality under treatment, had to be considered carefully.

Dynamic psychiatry and psychoanalysis focused on the individual *as a person*. The dynamic approach to clinical procedure was therefore unlike laboratory psychology, which, for the most part, had been impersonal. Such a dynamic approach forced the clinician and clinical psychology to assess man's affective nature—his emotions and drives—as well as his cognitive and intellectual powers on an individual basis.

The Mental Hygiene Movement. While psychologists and psychiatrists were developing their capacities to diagnose and treat the problems of the mentally disordered, an obstacle to their work was inadequate awareness of these problems on the part of the public. Obviously, mental health and mental disease are the concern of society as well as of patients. It was apparent, therefore, that public education in these matters was essential. Only by such education could the practical support of citizens be enlisted. By a program of education, the public would appreciate the need for improved psychiatric and psychological services for the nation's mental patients and would be willing to campaign for reform and improvement of both knowledge and facilities. The mental hygiene movement began to meet this need at the start of the twentieth century, by enlightening the public on current methods of treating mental patients, and by campaigning for needed improvements.

Clifford Beers—himself a former mental patient—was the spearhead of the mental hygiene movement. While he was institutionalized, Beers resolved that, upon his discharge, he would dedicate himself to propagandizing improved care for the mentally ill. In 1908, he aroused national opinion in behalf of more humane treatment of the mentally ill by publishing his own story in the book, *A Mind That Found Itself*. Beers' message reached a large audience of average citizens because he spoke to them in their own language—he was neither psychologist nor psychiatrist. Within a year he successfully established the National Committee of Mental Hygiene (1909). Beers also persuaded the legislature of his own state, Connecticut, to establish mental hygiene facilities to investigate and to improve existing conditions in mental hospitals. An additional and important provision of the Connecticut program was an educational campaign directed at the public on the facts of mental disease and its prevention. Other states soon followed the example of Connecticut. Beers emphasized prevention; to him, cure was a secondary objective. It was this primary emphasis on a prophylactic aim that inspired Adolf Meyer, an advocate of the movement, to suggest the name *mental hygiene*. Endorsement by William James spurred Beers' campaign for the promotion of activity on behalf of mental health. An additional and influential aid to the movement was the foundation in 1917 of the quarterly journal, *Mental Hygiene*. The movement spread internationally.

Emphasis on prevention alerted the public to the need for early diagnosis and treatment of behavior problems, especially in children. Inevitably the public became aware of the lack of adequate community facilities for such diagnosis and treatment. Thus the mental hygiene movement promoted the establishment and development of psychiatric and psychological services, particularly of child guidance clinics. Moreover, the public were urged to adopt hygienic measures to avert and control mental illness, just as they were doing for physical illness. The mental hygiene campaign was markedly successful. Yet it brought difficulties, in that it created a somewhat sudden demand for services which exceeded the capacities of available personnel, techniques, and facilities.

From this survey, it is readily seen that clinical psychology has multiple roots. Principal among them are: the functional approach; psychometrics; the dynamic approach in psychiatry; and the mental hygiene movement. Clinical psychology thus emerged from a succession of developments which enabled psychologists to render a special service, that of identifying and helping individuals suffering from intellectual, personality, and behavioral disorders. This service was rendered by them in various clinical settings as their specialty progressed.

THE DEVELOPMENT OF PSYCHOLOGICAL CLINICS

The development of psychological clinics, as has been pointed out, began with the opening of a clinic by Lightner Witmer (1867-1956) in Philadelphia. Witmer was introduced to psychology as an undergraduate at the University of Pennsylvania, where he studied under Cattell and served as his assistant. To Cattell, Witmer ascribed the most profound influence on his thinking and professional growth. After completing his doctoral studies at Leipzig in 1892, Witmer returned to America to succeed Cattell at Pennsylvania, when Cattell moved to Columbia University in New York.

Witmer's Clinic. The establishment of this first clinic at Philadelphia was more or less fortuitous. In 1894-1895, Witmer conducted a seminar on children's behavior problems at the University of Pennsylvania. In the spring of 1896, as a direct result, a local schoolteacher asked Witmer's help with a pupil who had a pronounced spelling deficiency. This chronically poor speller became the first formal clinic case in the history of American clinical psychology. For his second referral—a child with a speech disorder—Witmer sought the help of a specialist in remedial speech. It is to be noted, then, that the first clinic in America originated in a university setting, and that its orientation was educational in character— a trait that remained more or less distinctive of this clinic under Witmer's direction.

Witmer made a formal report on the operation of this clinic to the American Psychological Association in the autumn of 1896. He described the clinical approach in detail, making clear how the findings of clinical psychology were based on data revealed in individual examinations of many people. In addition, Witmer demonstrated how, by application of analytic and postanalytic diagnosis, classifications of behavior could be derived. Finally, he showed the potential of a psychological clinic as a service agency in the community—both as a research center and as a training ground for specialists in psychological services. As is often the case with pioneer work, Witmer's initial report of his activity in clinical psychology elicited no strong response. Despite the indifference of his professional colleagues, however, Witmer persevered in his clinical work.

Historians of psychology have tended to depreciate Witmer's work. One apparent reason for this is the narrow scope of the field to which his early work was confined. Yet his contributions are historic. It was Witmer who coined the terms *clinical psychology* and *psychological clinic*. From the beginning, he stressed a quantitative study of the individual patient, both for diagnosis and for therapy. In developing his clinical method, he incorporated the efforts of specialists—physicians, neurologists, social workers, and remedial teachers—in diagnostic and therapeutic practice. Yet, in dealing with the medical aspects of a clinical problem, his approach was concentrated on the physical or neurological traits, rather than on the psychiatric. Unaffected both by French psychiatric thinking and by psychoanalysis, he omitted almost entirely the dynamic approach; his medical associates were neurologists, rather than psychiatrists. Despite these limitations in perspective, however, Witmer's accomplishments in clinical psychology are substantial: (1) He founded the first service-oriented clinic. (2) He concentrated on the problems of the individual. (3) He enlisted the aid of specialists for both diagnosis and treatment.

Witmer was interested primarily in clinical problems related to education, with particular attention to mental retardation and superiority. Still he believed that the clinical method was applicable to the normal child, as well as the problem child. In his view, the schoolroom, the juvenile court, and the streets were all components of the larger laboratory of psychology. In defining clinical psychology, he saw its affiliations with medicine and sociology, as well as with pedagogy. Details of the work of the Philadelphia clinic are recorded in the *Psychological Clinic*, a journal founded by Witmer in 1907 and edited by him until 1935, when it ceased publication.

Another of Witmer's accomplishments was his founding of a hospital school at the University of Pennsylvania in 1907. This institution—which he later named the *Orthogenic School*—was a clinical operation in which cases could be accommodated for extended periods of observation and training. Under his auspices and direction, professional personnel in education, in medicine, and in social work were offered practical experience in training both normal and retarded children. The Orthogenic School was envisioned by Witmer as a training school for a new profession, which he termed that of *psychological expert*.

Witmer, of course, was aware of the opposition to a service-oriented psychology—especially in academic circles. To such opposition, he answered that in reality the pure and applied sciences of psychology were necessarily interpenetrating; that, actually, they proceed as a single developing field of knowledge. When scientific discoveries are applied, new problems for investigation continually emerge and proliferate. Clinical psychology, Witmer believed, could help to perpetuate psychology. As a clinician, Witmer was himself interested in research. He developed both techniques and instruments for diagnostic testing out of his own experience and practice. His clinical interest and enthusiasm endured until his retirement in 1937. In the remaining years of an unusually long life, he saw the clinical psychology which he initiated grow far away from him. Yet, the evidences of the pioneer spirit and work of Witmer endure in the history of clinical psychology.

Other University-Related Clinics.   Essentially Witmer's clinic at the University of Pennsylvania was psycho-educational, and, in this character, it became the prototype of psychological clinics which developed rapidly in the following decade. Twelve years after Witmer's clinic was established Jacob Heilman, who had obtained his doctorate at the University of Pennsylvania, directed the psychological clinic at State Teachers College, Greeley, Colorado. In 1909, during his tenure at the University of Minnesota, James B. Miner established and directed the Free Clinic in Mental Development at the university. In the same year, Clark University opened a clinic for exceptional children and accepted referrals from the public schools for free diagnosis. About 1910, too, Carl Seashore founded a clinic at the University of Iowa. J. E. W. Wallin organized a psycho-educational clinic at the University of Pittsburgh in 1912. It was Wallin who diverted the aims of the clinic to an educational rather than a purely psychological objective, and who urged that such clinics should be founded and operated in conjunction with departments of education. Thus, what with Witmer had been a somewhat fortuitous association of psychology and education, became a master-type for the specialized psycho-educational clinic. When Wallin reported a survey in 1914, he stated that 26 such clinics were operating in the United States at that time. In the years immediately following, especially after World War I, the number of psycho-educational clinics increased and with them university courses in clinical psychology.

Clinics for the Mentally Ill.   Clinical interest, rooted by Witmer in an academic setting and tending to psycho-educational focus, soon was directed to the mentally ill. In 1897, William O. Krohn established a laboratory for the study of the insane at the Eastern Hospital for the Insane at Kankakee, Illinois. Having become engrossed in this work, Krohn left the post in 1899, studied medicine, and became a psychiatrist. In 1904, Shepherd Ivory Franz established a psychological laboratory at McLean Hospital in Waverly, Massachusetts, an institution with a reputation for interest in research. This McLean laboratory, while it effected some integration of psychology and psychopathology, was preponderantly physiological in its approach. Two other Massachusetts hospitals were prominent in the early twentieth century: Worcester State, where David Shakow developed an internship program and was director of psychological research for almost 20 years (1928-1946), and where Grace Kent, well known for her various clinical tests, served from 1922 to 1926; and Boston Psychopathic Hospital where F. Lyman Wells, author of *Mental Tests in Clinical Practice* (1927), was the chief psychologist from 1921 to 1938. Research in these Massachusetts hospitals, and also at St. Elizabeth's Hospital, in Washington, D.C., was conducted along more or less traditional lines in the pattern of academic experiments. They are historically important, however, in that they helped define the functions of the clinical psychologist in a mental hospital. In these hospitals, psychologists had their first close association with psychiatrists, an association markedly different from that in the university clinic. When Franz went to St. Elizabeth's (Wells succeeded him at McLean), he instituted the practice, in 1907, of a routine psychological examination for all patients newly admitted to the mental hospital. In 1913, under the initial supervision of Yerkes, and later under Wells, the first internship for psychologists in a mental hospital was established at Boston Psychopathic. There was a gradual extension of these clinical services to mental hospitals throughout the country.

Clinics for the Mentally Deficient.   Psychological testing of the mentally deficient was begun as early as 1898 in the state institution for the feeble-minded at Faribault, Minnesota. This program was under the direction of R. T. Wylie, a physician. In 1906, a laboratory for the study of the feeble-minded was established at the Training School for the Feebleminded at Vineland, New Jersey. Under H. H. Goddard, a psychologist and former student of G. Stanley Hall's, this operation at Vineland became the first real laboratory of clinical psychology; it offered instruction in clinical psychology as well as research facilities. After two years at Vineland, during which he administered tests such as the Seguin Formboard, Goddard made a trip to Europe. While in Brussels, he met Decroly, who introduced him to Binet's method of intelligence measurement. When Goddard returned to America, he translated (1908) the Binet scale, revised it, and promoted its use in the United States. Under his direction, during the first two decades of the present century, and under the subsequent direction of Edgar A. Doll and Stanley Porteus, the Training School at Vineland was an exemplary exponent of the problems of mental deficiency.

The Behavior Clinic in Juvenile Court Work.   Thirteen years after the founding of Witmer's university clinic, in 1909, William Healy, a psychiatrist, established a behavior clinic in Chicago, in conjunction with the Cook County Juvenile Court, with Grace Fernald as psychologist. The specific purpose of this clinic was to probe the dynamics of delinquent behavior. This gave the psychologist in the clinic a new role. His function now became one of trying to understand human behavior and human relationships in terms of motivation. Healy, as has been pointed out above, was influenced by functional psychology. In particular, he was influenced by the dynamic approach of Freud and of French psychiatry in a way that had not touched Witmer. Healy's direction of approach was through the affective, rather than through the cognitive aspects of personality. Since he was operating in a court rather than in a university, Healy's clinic had to cope with different problems. His subjects were different from those of the academic clinics, and, perforce, he had contacts with a wide variety of social agencies and institutions. Moreover, the problems he treated were far more complex than the educational problems of retardation and learning difficulty. For Healy, social pathology was the chief focus of interest. On this account, Healy's clinic may be said to be more directly related to the present-day psychological clinic than was Witmer's. Like Witmer, he maintained contact with other specialists—particularly psychologists and social workers—but the scope of his work was necessarily broadened by the more complex problems of his clientele. Healy's clinic was initially supported by private endowment and was called the Juvenile Psychopathic Institute. Cook County assumed its operation in 1914, and in 1917 it was taken over by the State of Illinois. In 1920, the name of the clinic was changed to Institute for Juvenile Research. In its beginnings, this clinic was primarily concerned with the problems of juvenile offenders, but the work was gradually extended to include all kinds of behavior problems in children. For this reason, the Healy clinic became a model for subsequent child guidance clinics. It was the first clinic to regard the child's behavior in totality—physical, mental, emotional, moral, and social. Here diagnosis was regarded, not as a matter of mere classification, but rather as the beginning of the therapeutic program. About 1920, child guidance clinics were established and encouraged both in the United States and abroad by the support of the Commonwealth Fund.

BEGINNINGS OF PROFESSIONALIZATION

From the founding of Witmer's clinic to the outbreak of World War I, clinical psychology advanced from an original concern with the educational problems of school children to the more complex problems of the mentally ill, the mentally deficient, and of delinquents. Witmer established the first journal for this new branch of psychology, *Psychological Clinic*, in 1907. Whipple prepared and published, in 1910, a valuable compendium of available tests for clinicians, *Manual of Mental and Physical Tests*. Trained psychologists were now beginning to concern themselves with professional standards and procedures, such as the qualifications of examiners, tests to be used, and the organization of internship programs. During World War I, as we have already observed, psychologists developed tests and ably assisted the military in the screening and placement of draftees. By providing such vital services to the government in a time of national crisis, psychology was able to demonstrate convincingly the vast potential of psychological techniques. However, before clinical psychology could achieve its full professional status, many problems arising from its expansion had to be resolved.

When the first clinics, such as Witmer's and Healy's, had demonstrated their capacities for constructive and important psychological services, clinical psychology expanded. Universities, school systems, schools for mental defectives, hospitals for the mentally ill, courts, and private and public social service agencies began to develop clinical services. As the number of psychological clinics increased and the scope of their services widened, clinical psychology was drawn into closer association with other fields, such as medicine and social work. Naturally, the ramifications and complexity of integrating a growing clinical psychology with established fields and mores brought forth both criticisms and challenging problems.

Criticisms. Rapid growth in the new profession of clinical psychology stimulated sharp scrutiny. The importance of the work to the individual and to society, and the serious implications of its many concerns to individual and social well-being, made clinical psychology an open target for criticism and attack. The charges were various. According to some, it overemphasized testing. Others charged that it was overconcerned with diagnosis, and underconcerned with therapy. While some critics chided clinical psychology for inadequate scientific foundation, others attacked it for an orientation too heavily based in academic, experimental psychology. Still others insisted that clinical psychology was the proper domain of medicine.

Clinical psychologists recognized the soundness of some of these criticisms. Yet they held fast to the position that they had a distinct and valuable service to render. Those who were trained adequately saw the need for improvement in their knowledge and methods, and a careful control of their practices. They were necessarily as anxious as their critics to establish and to implement standards for clinical practice. Many were dissatisfied with the inadequate qualifications of their fellow psychologists who administered tests, especially with the exclusive devotion of many examiners to mental testing. They were eager to dispel the erroneous notion that the only tool of the clinician was the Binet scale. Sound and well-trained clinicians recognized the error of those who thought that tests could be administered with little or no professional training or who relied upon them exclusively for their diagnosis. Wallin reported in 1931 that 63 per cent of 115 psychological examiners in public schools were special class teachers, supervisors, or grade teachers, most of whom had the minimal qualification of a two year normal school course. Thus a majority would have had no training in clinical psychology. A report such as Wallin's made clear that the demand for clinical services far exceeded the capacities of trained personnel. Moreover, the criteria for sound training had not as yet been set.

Professional Problems. The time was clearly at hand for clinical psychologists to organize themselves professionally. They had several challenges to face immediately. Most fundamental was their obligation to define and precisely delimit their own field. They would have to determine the professional qualifications for the clinical psychologist. They would have to decide how the practice of clinical psychology was to be controlled and supervised. Not the least of their concerns with respect to practice was protecting the public from charlatans. Interest in these issues appeared early in the history of clinical psychology. Yet some of them were not resolved until mid-century.

1. Professional Identity.   The pioneer clinical psychologists were members and active participants in the American Psychological Association. One clinical paper was presented on the program of the organization's first annual convention in 1892. In the ten years following, twelve such papers were given. As has already been mentioned, Witmer reported to the Association in 1896 on the operations of the first clinic. During the next decade there was limited yet persisting interest in clinical psychology. After 1910, there was a pronounced increase in clinical papers at A.P.A. conventions, until a maximum of 22 papers was reached in 1916. The majority of papers in the 1920's concerned the development and validation of clinical tests.

Although the clinical psychologists were active members of A.P.A., they realized the limited capacity of the national organization to promote their special interests and objectives. The A.P.A. was dedicated to the development of psychology as a science. The specific needs and problems of clinical psychology required more precisely delimited attention. Toward that end, at the A.P.A. convention in Pittsburgh in 1917, a small group of clinicians, including Leta Hollingworth, F. N. Maxfield, J. B. Miner, D. Mitchell, R. Pintner, Clara Schmitt, and J. E. W. Wallin, organized the American Association of Clinical Psychologists. The aims of this association were as follows: (1) to establish a bond of unity among professional psychologists; (2) to furnish media for the exchange of ideas; (3) to aid in the establishment of standards of professional competence in clinical psychology; and (4) to promote research in mental hygiene and corrective education. The time—wartime—was inauspicious for establishing the new association. At that time many psychologists were in military service. The public at large were distracted and preoccupied by the war and its problems. Moreover, training facilities for psychologists were not adequate. Perhaps most important of all, some psychologists viewed the new association as separatist and as a threat to the A.P.A. In consequence of these several circumstances, the association's program could not be implemented effectively. By 1919 the organization was dissolved. However, it had pointed up the unique character of clinical psychology, and a clinical section with similar purposes was established within the A.P.A. Wallin has observed that thereafter several divisions of specialized interest were formed, and the applied aspects of psychology were given added emphasis.

2. Clinical Psychology: The Definition.   Wallin attempted to define the field in 1913. To him, the clinical psychologist had four principal functions: (1) diagnosis and classification of patient; (2) analysis of the etiological background—mental, physical, social, moral; (3) determination of the changes which the disorder had produced in the individual; (4) determination of the degree of modifiability of such behavioral changes as have been found. This functional delimitation of the clinical field thus attempted to meet its complexity and clearly indicated that it was much more than a mere testing operation. Indeed, Wallin protested vehemently against the notion that testing was synonymous with clinical phychology. Testing was simply one phase—a limited phase—of diagnosis. The clinician had to probe the patient's background and behavior as well. Wallin, like other qualified clinicians of this early period, saw the need for a systematized training beyond that of learning testing techniques. Some efforts were being made to provide this training. Yerkes, for example, had established the first clinical internship in a mental hospital for adults at Boston Psychopathic in 1913—the same year that Wallin had proposed his definition of the field. Other institutions thereafter offered similar training under professionally qualified supervision.

3. **Control of Clinical Tests.** The first real attempts at regulating clinical psychology were in the direction of establishing standards for controlling tests and test administration. In 1895, at the urging of J. M. Baldwin, "The Committee on Physical and Mental Tests" was organized within the American Psychological Association, under the direction of Cattell. The efforts of this committee in proposing a standard test battery and attempting to obtain norms for it met with little success. By 1899 the committee was defunct. A similar committee, designed to organize testing procedures, functioned from 1907 to 1919 and sponsored some research on the Woodworth-Wells Association Tests, but generally failed to achieve its goals. Thus, these initial attempts within the A.P.A. to regulate testing did not provide the needed support for clinicians.

4. **Qualifications for Psychological Examiners.** In 1915, Guy Whipple warned the A.P.A. against the inroads that charlatans and otherwise unqualified practitioners were making into clinical psychology. At Whipple's instigation, the Association expressed official disapproval of the use of mental tests by unqualified persons in that same year. By 1917, a committee was formed to review the qualifications of psychological examiners. In 1919, a committee was organized to consider certification of consulting psychologists. This committee, after long and serious deliberation, proposed an acceptable procedure in 1921. The first certificates were issued by A.P.A. shortly thereafter. However, there were no enforcement provisions. Moreover, since only about 25 psychologists applied for the certificates, the certification procedure was abandoned by an A.P.A. membership vote in 1927. Generally speaking, the A.P.A. efforts to control professional clinical work in this early period were a failure. In fact, more adequate regulation of professional psychologists was not effected until mid-century.

CLINICAL PSYCHOLOGY: BETWEEN TWO WORLD WARS

During the first quarter of the twentieth century, clinical psychology had a predominantly psychometric role. The development of the field followed closely the perfecting of clinical tests and measurements and the professionalizing of such psychological services. World War I produced the first mass applications of clinical psychology, particularly of psychological testing. The success of these activities encouraged a rapid extension of the use of standardized tests, especially intelligence tests. The initial upsurge in psychological tests in the period immediately following the war reached a plateau in the later twenties, however.

Clinical tests were increasingly subjected to close scientific analysis and evaluation. Some claims of their overenthusiastic protagonists were shattered. Since the duties of clinical psychologists were largely confined to testing, they bore the brunt of attacks by opponents of testing itself. Within the professional ranks of psychology, clinicians were adversely criticized by some of their academic colleagues as mere "testers." Even among clinicians themselves there was adverse criticism. An instance of this is Wells, author of *Mental Tests in Clinical Practice* (1927), who opposed the narrowness of the psychometric approach and encouraged a broader scope for clinical psychology. On the other hand, the excellent researches of Pintner, Porteus, Wallin, Paterson, and Thorndike gave prestige to testing and status to psychometrics.

Between 1920 and 1940, clinical psychology advanced moderately but steadily in scope and excellence. Its historic emphasis on work with children and on juvenile problems of a predominantly educational nature continued. But clinical psychology extended its frontiers to clinics, hospitals, courts, and prisons. This expansion of services created a growing demand for clinical psychologists, and they were graduated from universities in increasing numbers. Yet their functions remained limited, and their status and prestige failed to be enhanced significantly. In large measure, this failure of clinical psychologists to achieve growing recognition stemmed from lack of proper and adequate professional preparation for their specialty. Their training in the 1920's was largely on-the-job and haphazard. An apparent limitation was the fact that professional training for clinical psychology—with the exception of courses in testing and abnormal psychology—was essentially the same as that for academic-experimental psychology. Thus, ordinarily, professional experience was acquired after graduate training. Few clinical internships were available, and most of them were postdoctoral. A very limited number of schools had their own full-time and fully organized clinics where graduate students could receive practical training.

Revisions and improvements of tests, techniques, and professional standards marked the history of clinical psychology in the 1930's. Notable among the revisions was the Terman-Merrill Revision of the Stanford-Binet (1937). Among the many new tests was the Wechsler-Bellevue Intelligence Scale for adults (1939). Projective techniques—the Rorschach and the Thematic Apperception Test (TAT) came to the fore in America. These tests were adopted as important clinical tools, even though projective psychology differed radically from traditional American psychology. Moreover, the thirties were characterized, by serious attempts at rapprochement between clinical psychology and experimental psychology, especially in the late years of the decade. Experimental studies of conflict and frustration were reported in papers at the annual conventions of the American Psychological Association. Abnormal psychology—previously top-heavy with theory—began to fortify its subject matter by experimental investigations in many hospital laboratories. However, integration of the experimental-theoretical and the clinical-practical was not effected in the university training programs for clinical psychology. The majority of professors who offered instruction in clinical psychology had but limited experience in actual clinical practice. The inadequate training which they consequently provided resulted in wide variations in background for the clinicians they produced. Hence there was a wide diversity in clinical practice. Most clinical psychologists trained before World War II received or gleaned their clinical concepts chiefly from their co-workers, usually psychiatrists and social workers. Many concepts so adopted were not only untested, but essentially invalid.

Considerable self-evaluation developed in the thirties by clinical psychology in consequence of increasing self-awareness among clinicians. They protested vigorously that clinical psychology was more than psychometrics and more than mere classification in terms of specific traits. Instead, they argued that it was a total appraisal of the individual person. This total appraisal included all factors affecting a person's behavior and adjustment, together with an interpretation of his present status in the light of his past history and development. A limited number of clinicians were beginning to assume responsibility for therapy, in addition to their testing and diagnostic functions.

In 1931, the Clinical Section of A.P.A. named a special committee to consider the standards of training for clinical psychologists. Internships to provide essential supervised practice in psychometrics began to be formally organized about 1934. These internships were established chiefly in state mental hospitals, although some were located in private clinics and other institutions as well. In 1936, under the leadership of A. T. Poffenberger, the Psychology Department of Columbia University proposed a tentative curriculum for clinical psychology. But the final revision of this program—which provided two years of graduate work and one year of internship—was rejected by the Graduate Committee of Columbia University. However, the New York State internship program, providing experience in various types of institutions and sponsored by Elaine Kinder —she had participated in the Columbia plan—is an alleged outgrowth of that plan. A program similar to the Columbia plan was recommended in 1937 by the Boston Society of Clinical Psychology, but was apparently never carried out. Most of the plans and programs for standardized clinical training, regardless of merit, did not materialize.

Finally, in 1937, a great impetus was given in clinical psychology when the American Association for Applied Psychology (A.A.A.P.) was founded. This independent organization, while affiliating itself with A.P.A. absorbed both the Clinical Section of A.P.A. and the Association of Consulting Psychologists. It opened its membership to applied psychologists from a variety of fields including industrial, consulting, and clinical. The A.A.A.P. aimed to guarantee professional competence and to control professional standards through strict membership qualifications. It pressed vigorously for improved preparation of clinical psychologists and, in particular, for internships. Although the organization was solidly organized and dynamic, and alerted psychologists to their professional problems, World War II intervened to curtail much of its campaign. In 1945, it was united with A.P.A. The A.A.A.P. made a permanent contribution by establishing the *Journal of Consulting Psychology.* This journal remains a medium for publishing research and theoretical discussions of interest to clinical psychologists and to other applied psychologists.

The total number of psychological clinics almost doubled during the 1930-1940 decade, reaching about 150 by 1941. A substantial number of these were child guidance clinics. In the same period there was a 210 per cent increase in nonteaching psychological positions, most of them clinical in character. Such marked progress brought into sharper focus the function of clinical psychologists in relation to other professions. This notable advance in clinical psychology prompted Woodworth to express his optimism about its future in the first issue of the *Journal of Consulting Psychology* in 1937. In the same statement he urged that clinicians—as specialists in personal service psychology—compete, on terms of mutual respect, with other professional groups similarly dedicated.

THE FORTIES

Just as World War I had produced a breakthrough for clinical psychology, especially in psychometrics, so World War II produced a similar critical turning point in its history. Again, heavy demands were placed upon psychologists to assist in the selection, classification, and assignment of draftees in various military services. Numerous classification techniques were devised for all branches of military service. Diagnostic and consultation procedures were also developed to cope with problems of maladjustment in the armed forces. The influx of psychologists into the armed forces and its ancillary services produced a counterbalancing efflux from the schools. An inevitable consequence was a marked curtailment of academic research, but new research and service opportunities were made available in the armed forces.

War Service. Available estimates indicate that about 1,500 psychologists served in the armed forces during World War II, and that, of these, some 25 per cent worked in applied areas. Psychologists did much of the selection and classification of military personnel at induction and reception centers. A high percentage of draftees were judged unfit for military duty because of psychological and emotional problems. Among the top ten causes of rejection were mental disease and mental deficiency. These findings called to national attention the seriousness of the mental health problem in America.

Despite initial screening, there was a high incidence of personality disorders and mental illness among military personnel, both as a result of combat and of other experience. At the end of the war, more than 50 per cent of the patients in Veterans Administration hospitals were neuropsychiatric patients. During the war, demands for psychological treatment and rehabilitation far exceeded the capacity of available medical personnel. Consequently, clinical psychologists were called upon to assist. In the fall of 1944, the United States Army commissioned more than 200 clinical psychologists from the ranks for duty in military hospitals and rehabilitation centers. Clinical psychologists were now called upon to perform services, from which previously they had been restricted. These included the taking of case histories, assisting in the evaluation and diagnosis of patients, designing and participating in research studies, and administering individual and group therapy to several types of patients. The importance of these newly assumed functions is noteworthy. Their assumption represented official status and recognition for clinical psychologists. At the same time, they extended the scope of clinical psychology.

Trends in Research and Practice. Several trends mark the history of clinical psychology outside the armed services during the early forties, in both research and practice. Principal among these trends are the following developments:

(1) There was an almost exclusive emphasis on diagnostic functions; an exception was the interest in psychotherapy by a few individual clinicians, such as Frederick Allen, author of *Psychotherapy with Children* (1942), and Carl Rogers, who promulgated his nondirective client-centered approach in *Counseling and Psychotherapy* (1942). (2) Projective techniques, especially the Rorschach and the T.A.T., had decreased enthusiasm for paper-and-pencil questionnaires in the study of personality by 1940. However, the effective use of two new questionnaires in military processing—The Cornell Selectee Index and the Shipley Personal Inventory—revived interest in this type of measurement. An important, new clinical inventory—The Minnesota Multiphasic Personality Inventory—appeared in 1942. (3) Considerable research was conducted on test patterning, with special attention to its implications for determining personality disorders. (4) Factor analysis became a significant technique in the evaluation of test batteries. (5) Attention was given to devising group techniques, short effective tests, and abbreviated forms of existing intelligence and projective tests. (6) Clinical psychology now began to emphasize adult adjustment problems, that is, educational and pathological problems. Previously, children's problems, usually school related, had received major consideration. Such work brought clinical psychologists into closer con-

tact than previously with psychiatrists, under whose supervision they generally worked. In this setting they could demonstrate their usefulness, both in psychological diagnosis and in psychotherapy.

Postwar Expansion. The growing impact of these trends, particularly of the move toward adult adjustment problems, led to an improved status and wider professional recognition for clinical psychologists. Its distinguished contribution to the war effort led to an unprecedented development of clinical psychology after the war. The demands of military service had given status previously lacking to personality testing. Moreover, a therapeutic role had been created for clinicians by burgeoning demands in the armed services. These developments led to improved prestige and produced an unprecedented social demand for psychological services in the postwar period.

It will be recalled that an important development in postwar American psychology was the amalgamation of the American Association for Applied Psychology and the American Psychological Association. One of the prominent sections in the reorganized A.P.A. was the Division of Clinical and Abnormal Psychology, which later (1954) became known simply as the Division of Clinical Psychology. With the reorganization, too, the A.A.A.P.'s *Journal of Consulting Psychology* became the clinical journal of the A.P.A. Another significant development in the evolution of clinical psychology was the appearance of a new and independent publication, the *Journal of Clinical Psychology*, in 1945. This journal, established and edited by F. C. Thorne, was designed, in his words, "to serve as loyal opposition and 'needler' to the necessarily more conservative publications." Examination of these two journals for the two decades since World War II gives a good indication of the trends of clinical practice and clinical research. There is continued lively interest in the projective techniques. Many new ones have been developed. Wechsler developed a second form of the Wechsler-Bellevue (1946), a scale for children—the Wechsler Intelligence Scale for Children (WISC, 1949)—and a revision of the adult test—the Wechsler Adult Intelligence Scale (WAIS, 1955). A third revision of the Stanford-Binet was also produced in 1960. Besides the development of these and many other clinical tests, much attention was given to psychotherapeutic procedures. Considerably more energy was directed to clinical research than during the prewar period. Such research included evaluation of various types of therapy, validation of diagnostic techniques, and investigation of the causes of mental disorders. There was also an increasing concern with basic research designed to integrate clinical and experimental psychology.

Laboratory and Clinic. The unity evidenced by the amalgamation of the A.P.A. and A.A.A.P. in 1945 was more apparent than real. From the outset of this new phase of expansion in clinical psychology, alarm was felt that the traditional psychology and basic research were threatened and that, ultimately, they might be neglected. A cleavage had already existed between experimental-theoretical and clinical-practical psychology before World War II. The former dealt with segments of generalized behavior, while the latter concentrated on the problems of the individual person. Over the years, experimentalists viewed clinical psychology with suspicion, questioning the validity of both its techniques and procedures. In the postwar years, the threat of a rift between academic—that is, experimental psychology—and professional or clinical psychology intensified. Clinical psychology became more attractive in terms of employment and compensation, not only for experienced practitioners, but also for beginners and graduate students. Many university psychologists were attracted from their laboratories into clinical psychology, which offered greater advancement and higher salaries. Some, though inadequately qualified, began to engage in psychotherapy and personality diagnosis. Others, aware of their inadequate training for practice, devoted themselves to research.

The Fiftieth Anniversary. Clinical psychology celebrated its fiftieth anniversary in 1946, a half-century after the establishment of Witmer's first clinic. The occasion was commemorated by the A.P.A. at its first postwar convention. This meeting was held, appropriately, at the University of Pennsylvania, birthplace of clinical psychology. At the 50 year mark, the enduring problems of clinical psychology were still much in evidence. Qualifications for clinical practice, clinical training programs, ethics, certification, and the definition of clinical psychology itself were still in debate, even though they had been recognized, discussed, and wrestled with from the earliest days.

For half a century, American clinical psychology had worked unsuccessfully to clearly identify, establish, and accept itself as a profession. In 1946, American psychology, when regarded as a unit-field of knowledge, was still primarily a laboratory science dedicated to experimentation. In the 50 year period from 1896 to 1946, the field had expressed but minimal interest in a clinical science devoted to individual cases and to the scientific study of psychodiagnosis and psychotherapy. In effect, it had failed to integrate the laboratory science and the clinical profession. In the post-World War II period, efforts were intensified by clinical psychology to firmly establish itself as a profession. The prewar clinical psychology had overlooked or avoided direct confrontation with internal problems of the practice of psychology. Now, however, these problems had to be met, if wartime advances were to be maintained.

POST-WORLD WAR II STATUS

Of the many and complex postwar demands upon clinical psychology, perhaps the greatest demand was for therapy. That clinicians had accepted therapeutic responsibility in the armed services and had carried out their duties creditably, greatly increased their stature in the profession. But postwar demands for various clinical services exceeded both the qualified personnel and the validated clinical techniques available. Historically, clinical practice had evolved in a highly individualized and haphazard manner. As a result, clinical psychology was disorganized and unsystematic in its present state. Yet there was immediate and extensive need for clinical psychologists, and they had to be trained as quickly as possible. But before training could be effected, decisions had to be made concerning the type of training to be offered. Also, training facilities had to be established at the universities, and provisions made for practicums, which had been considered essential for decades. In this state of emergency for clinical psychology, two United States Government agencies came forward to sponsor the first training programs—namely, the Veterans Administration (V.A.) and the United States Public Health Service (U.S.P.H.S.).

Veterans Administration Program.   At the close of World War II, there were approximately 44,000 neuropsychiatric patients in V.A. hospitals, compared to some 30,000 patients suffering from all other ailments combined. These mentally disturbed patients were distributed throughout the United States in mental hygiene centers, neuropsychiatric hospitals, and also in general and specialized medical and surgical hospitals operated by the Veterans Administration. Care and rehabilitation of this sizable patient population required large numbers of psychiatrists and clinical psychologists. Consequently, the V.A. rapidly became the largest single employer of clinical psychologists. As such, it provided a principal impetus to development of standards for the profession of clinical psychology. Thus the V.A. did much to establish the identity and achieve the recognition for which the clinical field had been struggling for several decades.

In 1946, in conjunction with universities where facilities were available, the V.A. instituted a four year clinical program approved by the American Psychological Association. This program effected, for the first time, the integration of course work, research, clinical practice, and practical experience. It offered not only a complete plan for training in clinical psychology through the doctorate, but required that the trainee acquire practical experience at V.A. installations during the course of his graduate studies. In addition, the V.A. arranged a graduated stipend plan for the trainee, to be paid as he progressed in his four year program. Although this integrated program was a major breakthrough in the history of clinical psychology, it had some limitations. V.A. installations were often located in areas remote from universities qualified to co-administer the program. The practicum experience which such installations made available was mainly restricted to institutionalized adult males. A further limitation was the hampering effect of a paucity of qualified supervisory personnel.

In general, however, the V.A. program was a great constructive force in the professionalization of psychology. It helped the universities to develop and standardize their own training programs. Besides making funds available for trainees, it provided consulting funds for qualified personnel. The practicum facilities in V.A. hospitals and clinics created a long-needed setting for integrating scientific and professional activities. Definite advantages accrued to the profession of clinical psychology from the institution of this first large-scale standardized training program of the Veterans Administration. It established rigorous standards for education, experience, and personality. It incorporated theoretical and practical components of the clinical field. It extended and enriched the close wartime association of psychologists with psychiatrists, whose respect psychologists valued and sought to preserve by the maintenance of high performance standards. This furthered the growing reputation of the profession of psychology. In 1950, the professional character of the program was enhanced by the V.A., when it made the Ph.D. degree a requirement for employment as clinical psychologist. Employed clinical personnel lacking the degree were offered the opportunity for doctoral training as V.A. trainees.

The U.S. Public Health Service Program. In 1947, one year after the V.A. training program was inaugurated, the National Institute of Mental Health of the United States Public Health Service established its own program. The objective, by sponsored training in clinical psychology and allied professions, was an increase in the ranks of better-qualified mental health personnel. Generous grants were offered to universities to help improve and expand their training programs, to procure staff, and to develop their facilities. Additional funds were offered in the form of well-paying fellowships to selected students for graduate study in clinical psychology. Grants to the mental health professions were also made available so that conferences might be held at which staff members from various centers in the country could convene to discuss training policies and future plans.

Challenge to University Departments. Consequent upon the establishment of the V.A. and U.S.P.H.S. programs, as well as upon the normal growth of interest in clinical psychology, large numbers of graduate students were attracted to the field. Lively interest in mental health problems, the financial assistance programs of the Federal agencies, and increased employment opportunity for clinicians were principal factors in increased applications to graduate departments of psychology. The prospect of earning while learning had special appeal. Selecting graduate students and screening applicants for clinical programs became increasingly demanding. Not only were the rigorous standards of the V.A. and U.S.P.H.S. programs a factor, but the simultaneous need to accommodate increased enrollments spurred by veterans' educational benefits offered its own challenges to improved standards. The organization of curricula, and the recruitment of personnel qualified to instruct and supervise in clinical programs placed special burdens on university administrators. In the circumstances, it soon became clear that A.P.A. should offer university psychology departments some guiding principles for development and operation of clinical training programs. At the same time, the V.A. and U.S.P.H.S. called upon the national association for appraisal of programs.

A.P.A. Committee on Training. In March, 1947, the A.P.A. "Committee on Training in Clinical Psychology" was established. Its members included E. R. Hilgard, E. L. Kelly, Bertha Luckey, R. N. Sanford, L. F. Shaffer, and D. Shakow, Chairman. After careful study of the issues, and a review of existing facilities and programs at various universities, the Committee presented its "Recommended Graduate Training Program in Clinical Psychology" at the A.P.A. Convention in September, 1947. Facing the dangers of rigidity and over-regulation in making proposals, the Committee refrained from setting down a specific, detailed program. They worked from the proposition that "A clinical psychologist must first and foremost be a psychologist," and urged the establishment of a broad but vigorous four year doctoral program, directed toward research and professional goals. Preparation was to focus on three functions: diagnosis, research, and therapy, with special emphasis on the psychologist's contribution as a researcher.

The curriculum suggested by the Shakow Committee included courses in general psychology, psychodynamics, diagnostic methods, research methods, related disciplines, and therapy. Stress was to be placed upon mastery of basic principles, rather than on proficiency in technical skills. Thus a conceptual preparation was seen as a prime concern of the university. The Committee asserted that the dissertation, as a doctoral requirement, was essential to developing "the research-orientated professional," the ultimate goal of the training program. Moreover, the internship was strongly endorsed to provide "extended practical experience of gradually increasing complexity under close and competent supervision." In 1950, the Committee published tentative recommendations of standards for practicum training in clinical psychology. Despite some negative criticisms, the 1947 Shakow Report has remained the classic statement of recommended graduate education in clinical psychology.

Boulder Conference on Graduate Education. In 1949, after training programs had been in operation for about three years, some 1,500 students were enrolled in doctoral programs in about 60 institutions. Training was generally adequate, but diversity was marked from one institution to another. Thus, it seemed imperative that training activities be reviewed. There was need to reconsider in greater depth and detail the specifics of training for competent clinicians, as well as of the types of service required. Accordingly, an A.P.A. sponsored conference, under a grant from the United States Public Health Service, was scheduled at Boulder, Colorado. Leaders in clinical training at universities, field agencies and government agencies, and from related disciplines were invited. Seventy-one participants attended. Among the many topics considered were the following: social needs and clinical psychology; kinds and levels of training; professional ethics; background of preparation; core curriculum; training for research and psychotherapy; field training; student selection and evaluation; staff training; relations with other professions and with government agencies; accreditation of training programs; licensing and certification; current issues in clinical psychology.

Principal among the recommendations made by the Boulder Conference were the following:

(1) An academic-clinical division is apparent. Clinical psychology students should not be prepared, exclusively, for either service or research, but should be trained for both fields and become proficient in both.

(2) Diversity in university programs is evident, but it is preferable to concentration upon a single-approach curriculum. However, a basic core, combining general psychology and clinical psychology, is necessary to furnish some uniformity of background.

(3) There is need for a comprehensive approach to field training. Probably the least standardized aspect of existent programs was in the kind and amount of practicum training required for clinical psychologists.

The Boulder Conference made clear that clinical psychology had developed much self-awareness. The clinical field had become highly conscious of its professional and ethical obligations, both to society and to related professions.

Continuing self-study in the form of conferences was recommended by the Boulder Conference. In subsequent years several conferences on clinical psychology and allied specialities have been organized through the continuing support of the United States Public Health Service. Notable among such recent conferences was the Princeton Conference (1962) and the Chicago Conference on the Professional Preparation of Clinical Psychologists (1965). The latter, the only conference since Boulder to focus exclusively on graduate training in clinical psychology, considered functional specializations and their training needs, as well as training patterns. The former—the Princeton Conference on Manpower and Psychology: Joint Responsibilities of State and Universities—brought together coordinators from university clinical training programs and state-level psychologists in ten Northeastern states, with colleagues from the V.A. and U.S.P.H.S., and invited consultants to consider joint responsibilities, with special emphasis on internships. They offered several suggestions to meet the large demand for well-trained clinical psychologists. Among these were: (1) expansion of present doctoral programs; (2) additional programs, including the reorganization of Master's programs; (3) experimental development of professional schools that could focus on the clinical doctorate with sound training in basic psychology.

Standards and Regulation of Practice. Clinical psychologists, whose numbers have increased far more rapidly than those in any other area of applied psychology, intensified their efforts in the 1950's to establish professional and ethical standards and to institute legal controls for psychologists. Standards were of vital concern to all psychologists. However, the movement toward licensing and certification was spearheaded by clinical psychologists. Not only were they concerned with preserving their own professional integrity among allied professions, such as psychiatry and social service. They were also anxious to protect their field against incursions by charlatans. Three developments in the postwar professionalization of clinical psychology, previously discussed in Chapter 12, need only be enumerated here:

(1) The incorporation of the American Board of Examiners in Professional Psychology (ABEPP); (2) development of ethical standards by A.P.A.; (3) state certification and licensing of psychologists—with considerable variation, however, from state to state. As of November, 1965, seven states had licensing laws; 21 had certification laws; 17 (16 plus the District of Columbia) had nonstatutory certification programs.

CRITICAL ISSUES: 1950-1965

Despite the complexity of its problems at mid-century, it is clear that, primarily, clinical psychology was in the throes of a struggle for professional status. The rapidity with which professionalization proceeded in the postwar period reflects both the unprecedented public demands for psychological services and the assiduous concern of clinicians with professional matters. During this period, clinical psychology was definitely and firmly established as a practicing profession. The marked increase in legal certification of psychologists, and the substantial increase of service agencies and independent practitioners, attest to the flourishing state of the clinical field. Despite their great advances in status through newly established educational, ethical, and legal standards, clinical psychologists were still faced with knotty problems.

The gap between clinical science and clinical practice remained a considerable one. Clinical psychology had serious needs—for basic facts; sounder methods; more valid measures; improved criteria for diagnosis; new skills for clinical practice; more scientific validation for psychotherapeutic techniques. Too often functions and practices were justified simply on the basis of public demand. Demand for projective techniques, for example, far exceeded the knowledge of their validity. Most validation studies on the Rorschach and TAT during the late 1940's and the early 1950's showed consistently that these techniques are highly personal instruments, whose usefulness and validity depend on the clinician's skill. Personality inventories, particularly the MMPI, used on applicants for Government service in the Peace Corps and in the State Department, came in for heavy, if not exaggerated, criticisms. In 1965 there was a Congressional inquiry into accusations that these personality tests violated the privacy of the examinees. Intelligence tests fared only a little better. Over the years, intelligence tests were perfected and revised. Among the revisions in this period was that of the Wechsler-Bellevue Test, which appeared in 1955 as the Wechsler Adult Intelligence Scale (WAIS). However, the use of intelligence tests was banned in some school systems—such as that of New York City—during the 1960's because the tests allegedly discriminated against disadvantaged groups. Popular criticism of tests at this time hit hard at the clinician's tools.

Furthermore, many psychiatrists felt that some psychologists had over-extended their competence in the practice of psychotherapy. Conflicts between clinical psychologists and psychiatrists over psychotherapy, especially in private practice, often reached a violent stage during the discussions on the legal status of psychologists. Even now, the professional relationship of clinical psychology to psychiatry has not been determined; the clinicians have not resolved their own role in this relationship. That is, they have not decided whether to be professionally autonomous or to be subordinate to psychiatrists. Clinical psychologists, however, have done a creditable job in improving their skills through postdoctoral training in psychodiagnosis, research, and psychotherapy, particularly. Increased numbers have availed themselves of such postdoctoral training, which has been generously underwritten by the National Institute of Mental Health.

Clinical psychology has been criticized sharply for proneness to accept currently fashionable theories, even though they are inadequately tested and though they are at times ephemeral. Among the most urgent needs of the clinicians in the immediate future are theory construction and the development of a systematic science of personality. E. R. Guthrie in discussing the status of systematic psychology in 1950 called attention to this need:

> The recommendation here presented, that psychology be recognized as a basic science and not as a field of practice, may sound like evidence of a hostile attitude toward the new development of clinical work and clinical training. That is not correct. The new activities are not only good in themselves; they are in the last analysis the good served by a science of psychology which, if it has any proper end or purpose, aims at the understanding of human behavior which is in turn good only for its contribution toward the prediction and control of human behavior. In fact clinical work is the pay-off. It is the fruition of the science. But if there is to be a science that will ultimately bear such fruit, we . . . must take our start with theory and by the light of theory collect our facts. The facts must be public facts. Without systematic theories there are no scientific facts.

Some indication of the strides which clinical psychology has taken, both as basic and applied area, can be immediately observed by inspection of Wolman's *Handbook of Clinical Psychology*, which appeared in 1965. This monumental volume presents a comprehensive coverage of information on clinical psychology as science and profession. It recapitulates clinical psychology's progress in research methods, theoretical foundations, diagnostic methods, and methods of treatment. As a milestone in the history of clinical psychology, the publication of this volume fulfills its aim "to represent the profession of clinical psychology and to demonstrate its vitality, its vigorous pursuit of scientific truth, and its willingness and capacity for serving those who need it." This volume also strongly confirms the observation made by Shakow (1965) in discussing the status of clinical psychology 17 years after the 1947 Committee on Training in Clinical Psychology Report that ". . . clinical psychology is important both because of the contribution it has made and is making to basic psychology, and because of the potential social significance of its practical contribution."

THE INTERNATIONAL PROSPECT

Before World War II there was little concern for clinical psychology. After 1945 there was increased interest in psychology generally and, with it, a greater international demand for clinical psychological services. Although clinical psychology has emerged and expanded in Europe, Asia, Africa, and Australia, strict comparisons between countries are impossible because of varying educational systems and local conditions. The progress of clinical psychology in any given country must be studied individually. Excellent sources are available, among them H. P. David's *International Resources in Clinical Psychology* (1964), and his comprehensive chapter on the subject in Wolman's *Handbook*.

From a general survey of clinical psychology's international progress, it is obvious that in no country has clinical psychology prospered as it has in the United States. The scope of clinical development in this country is evidenced by its doctoral programs, approved internships, generous government and private support, and general public interest and acceptance. Clinical psychology in Great Britain, principally a post-World War II development, has been fostered by government support. In France, on the other hand, although interest in psychopathology dates back to an early period, clinical psychology is underdeveloped. There are restrictive pressures from the medical profession which similarly retard the growth of clinical psychology in West Germany. Less surprising is the slow progress of clinical psychology in Latin America and Italy, where psychology in general has progressed slowly. In Italy and in Spain, clinical psychology is practiced chiefly by physicians.

Considerable diversity in training standards for clinical psychologists is also apparent. The requirements range from the doctorate in the United States and Egypt, for example, to subdoctoral training in many European nations including the Scandinavian countries and the U.S.S.R. Generally, there is universal need for increased practicum training. In most countries psychodiagnosis is the acknowledged function of clinical psychologists whatever the diverse settings in which they function—child guidance clinics, mental hospitals, schools, courts, industry. Psychotherapy, on the other hand, proves to be a more controversial and debated function of clinicians. In Italy, France, Austria, and Turkey, the practice of psychotherapy is jealously guarded by physicians. But in Canada, Great Britain, United States, Switzerland, Sweden, Norway, Denmark, Belgium, and Japan, psychotherapy is part of the clinician's accepted professional role, although in varying degrees. In most countries independent private practice of clinical psychology is unknown. Where it does exist, the members involved are relatively small.

Clinical psychology as a basic science is almost universally respected. The importance of research is stressed in training programs and in psychological service centers in many countries. Among them are Great Britain, Canada, U.S.S.R., and East Germany, as well as the United States. Despite the variations in research, training, and practice from country to country, certain common international trends are discernible: the growing demand for clinical psychological services; improvement of training, especially practicum training; concern with clinical research and improvement of clinical techniques and procedures; definition of the functions of the clinical psychologist; legal protection of his position in the community; and, in general, the advancement of clinical psychology as a profession.

HIGHLIGHTS OF CLINICAL PSYCHOLOGY'S HISTORY

1896   Witmer founded first clinic at University of Pennsylvania, Philadelphia.

1904   First psychological laboratory in a mental hospital established at McLean Hospital (S. I. Franz, director).

1906   Laboratory for the study of the feebleminded opened at Vineland Training School, N.J. (H.H. Goddard, director).

1907   Witmer founded the journal, *Psychological Clinic*.

1908   First internship training at Vineland Training School under the supervision of Goddard.

1909   Healy founded a clinic at Cook County (Chicago) Juvenile Court.
Psychological clinic for the study of exceptional children was established at Clark University.
James B. Miner established and directed the Free Clinic in Mental Development at the University of Minnesota.
Clifford Beers inaugurated the mental hygiene movement.

1912   Publication of a manual of clinical psychology, *The Conservation of the Child* by A. Holmes.
J. E. W. Wallin established a psycho-educational clinic at the University of Pittsburgh.

1913   First internship in a psychiatric hospital for adults established at the Boston Psychopathic Hospital under the supervision of R. M. Yerkes.

1916   Terman's Revision of the Binet-Simon Scale—the Stanford-Binet.

1917   American Association of Clinical Psychologists organized. Appointment of a committee to consider qualifications of psychological examiners.

1918   Committee on qualifications reported favorably on certification of examiners by American Psychological Association.

1919   Section on Clinical Psychology formed within the American Psychological Association to replace American Association of Clinical Psychologists.

1920   Certification Committee of the American Psychological Association appointed.

1921   First certification instituted.
Rorschach devised the inkblot test of personality.

1927   Harvard Psychological Clinic founded by Morton Prince.

1931   Clinical Section of American Psychological Association appointed a special committee on Standards of Training for Clinical Psychologists.

1935   Morgan and Murray published the Thematic Apperception Test (TAT).

1937   Formation of the American Association for Applied Psychology.
Terman-Merrill Revision of the Stanford-Binet Intelligence Scale.

1939   Wechsler-Bellevue Intelligence Scale, Form I, published (II, 1946).

1942   Minnesota Multiphasic Personality Inventory published by S. R. Hathaway and J. C. McKinley.
Carl Rogers developed client-centered therapy.

1945   Amalgamation of the American Association for Applied Psychology and the American Psychological Association.
Founding of Division of Clinical and Abnormal Psychology in the American Psychological Association.
Journal of Clinical Psychology founded by F. C. Thorne.

1946   Veterans Administration Training Program for Clinical Psychologists instituted.

1947   United States Public Health Service Training Program inaugurated.

1949   Boulder Conference on Graduate Education in Clinical Psychology.
Wechsler Intelligence Scale for Children (WISC) published.

1954   Division of Clinical and Abnormal Psychology became Division of Clinical Psychology of American Psychological Association.

1955   Wechsler published revision of his adult scale—Wechsler Adult Intelligence Scale (WAIS).

1960   Revision of the Stanford-Binet Intelligence Scale.

1962   Princeton Conference on Manpower and Psychology: Joint Responsibilities of States and Universities.

1965   *Handbook of Clinical Psychology* published by B. Wolman (Ed.).
Chicago Conference on the Professional Preparation of Clinical Psychologists.

REFERENCES

GENERAL

Braun, J. R. (Ed.) *Clinical psychology in transition.* Cleveland, Ohio: Allen, 1961.

David, H. P. *International resources in clinical psychology.* New York: McGraw-Hill, 1964.

Mensh, I. N. *Clinical psychology: science and profession.* New York: Macmillan, 1966.

Morrow, W. R. The development of psychological internship training. *J. consult. Psychol.,* 1946, *10,* 165–183.

Sexton, Virginia S. Clinical psychology: an historical survey. *Genet. Psychol. Monogr.* 1965, *72,* 401–434.

Smith, T. L. The development of psychological clinics in the United States. *Ped. Sem.,* 1914, *21,* 143–153.

Thorne, F. C. The field of clinical psychology: past, present and future. *J. clin. Psychol.,* 1945, *1,* 1–20.

Wallin, J. E. W. *The mental health of the school child.* New Haven, Conn.: Yale Univer. Press, 1914.

Watson, R. I. A brief history of clinical psychology. *Psychol. Bull.,* 1953, *50,* 321–346.

Wolman, B. (Ed.) *Handbook of clinical psychology.* New York: McGraw-Hill, 1965.

CLINICAL PSYCHOLOGY: ORIGINS AND GROWTH (1896–1946)

Brotemarkle, R. A. Clinical psychology, 1896–1946. *J. consult. Psychol.,* 1947, *11,* 1–4.

Brown, F. The crisis in clinical psychology. *Psychol. Exch.,* 1935, *4,* 18–20.

Colvin, S. S. The present status of mental testing. *Educ. Rev.,* 1922, *64,* 196–206; 320–337.

Crane, L. A plea for the training of psychologists. *J. abn. & soc. Psychol.,* 1925, *20,* 228–233.

Davies, A. E. The training of psychologists. *J. abn. & soc. Psychol.,* 1926, *20,* 344–348.

Hutt, M. L., & Milton, E. O. An analysis of duties performed by clinical psychologists in the Army. *Amer. Psychologist,* 1947, *2,* 52–56.

Krugman, M. Recent developments in clinical psychology. *J. consult. Psychol.,* 1944, *8,* 342–353.

Kuhlmann, F. Retrogressive trends in clinical psychology. *J. consult. Psychol.,* 1941, *5,* 97–104.

Louttit, C. M. The nature of clinical psychology. *Psychol. Bull.,* 1939, *36,* 361–389.

Rogers, C. R. Needed emphases in the training of clinical psychologists. *J. consult. Psychol.,* 1939, *3,* 141–143.

Wallin, J. E. W. The new clinical psychologist and the psychoclinicist. *J. educ. Psychol.*, 1911, *2*, 121–132; 191–210.

Wallin, J. E. W. The establishment of the clinical section of the American Psychological Association. *Sch. & Soc.*, 1938, *48*, 114–115.

Wallin, J. E. W. PhDs in psychology who functioned as clinical psychologists between 1896 and 1910. *Psychol. Rec.*, 1961, *11*, 339–341.

Witmer, L. Practical work in psychology. *Pediatrics*, 1896, *1*, 462–471.

Witmer, L. Clinical psychology. *Psychol. Clinic*, 1907, *1*, 1–9.

Woodworth, R. S. The future of clinical psychology. *J. consult. Psychol.*, 1937, *1*, 4–5.

PROFESSIONAL DEVELOPMENT AFTER WORLD WAR II

Blank, L., & David, H. P. The crisis in clinical psychology training. *Amer. Psychologist*, 1963, *18*, 216–219.

Fine, H. J. The status of clinical psychologist. *J. clin. Psychol.*, 1961, *17*, 107–110.

Garfield, S. L. Clinical psychology and the search for identity. *Amer. Psychologist*, 1966, *21*, 353–362.

Harrower, Molly. *The practice of clinical psychology*. Springfield, Ill.: Thomas, 1961.

Holzberg, J. D. The role of the internship in the research training of the clinical psychologist. *J. consult. Psychol.*, 1961, *25*, 185–191.

Jacobsen, C. F. Clinical psychology as related to legislative problems. *Amer. Psychologist*, 1950, *5*, 110–111.

Kahn, M. W., & Santostefano, S. The case of clinical psychology: a search for identity. *Amer. Psychologist*, 1962, *17*, 185–189.

Levy, L. H. The skew in clinical psychology. *Amer. Psychologist*, 1962, *17*, 244–249.

Loevinger, Jane. Conflict of commitment in clinical research. *Amer. Psychologist*, 1963, *18*, 241–251.

Louttit, C., & Browne, C. G. The use of psychometric instruments in psychological clinics. *J. consult. Psychol.*, 1947, *11*, 49–54.

Miller, J. G. Clinical psychology in the Veterans Administration. *Amer. Psychologist*, 1946, *1*, 181–189.

Rogers, C. R. The interest in the practice of psychotherapy. *Amer. Psychologist*, 1953, *8*, 48–50.

Rosenzweig, S. Bifurcation in clinical psychology. *J. Psychol.*, 1950, *29*, 157–164.

Schwartz, E. K. The development of clinical psychology as an independent profession. In D. Brower & L. E. Abt (Eds.), *Progress in clinical psychology*. Vol. III. New York: Grune & Stratton, 1958. Pp. 10–21.

Shakow, D. Seventeen years later: clinical psychology in the light of the 1947 Committee on Training in Clinical Psychology Report. *Amer. Psychologist*, 1965, *20*, 353–362.

Small, L. Toward professional clinical psychology. *Amer. Psychologist*, 1963, *18*, 558–562.

Wolfle, D. Legal control of psychological practice. *Amer. Psychologist*, 1950, *5*, 651–655.

Zimet, C. Clinical training and university responsibility. *J. clin. Psychol.*, 1961, *17*, 110–114.

14

Psychology in Great Britain,
France, and Italy

THE CONCERN OF THIS AND THE NEXT TWO CHAPTERS is with psychology in countries other than Germany and the United States. In some of these countries the ideas proposed by Wundt and other builders of psychology were accepted readily. In others, the concept of a scientific psychology was received less readily—either because of continuing domination by philosophical psychology or from lack of interest. In some countries it took several decades for any real signs of a scientific psychology to appear.

In a general survey such as this it is not practicable to present a detailed account of the historical development of psychology in all countries. The three chapters following will simply survey the beginnings of psychology in a few selected countries, will note their main trends and characteristics, and will mention their leading psychologists. It is notable that both the historical antecedents of psychology, as well as the cultural differences in these countries, are reflected in the character and orientation of their psychologies. These differences are more evident in psychology than in philosophy or other sciences. As one compares and interrelates the psychologies of countries such as Germany, America, Great Britain, France, Italy, Russia, and Asian countries, one is impressed by the unique imprint that the national and cultural characteristics of each of these countries have left on psychology. This imprint is noticeable in the methodology, in the topics of interest, and in the emphases of psychology in these countries.

However, with the passage of time, this national imprint has become less distinct. Greater and faster communication in the modern era has led to a coalescence of ideas, so that psychologies in various countries tend now to lose their distinctive national features and acquire a more cosmopolitan character. Contemporary American psychology, by the assimilation of many trends of European psychology and by its vigorous productivity in all fields, embodies, perhaps to the highest degree, this cosmopolitan characteristic. What L. S. Hearnshaw said, in his book, *A Short History of British Psychology: 1840-1940*, about British psychology and the young generation of British psychologists is probably true also of other countries: ". . . since 1940 British psychology has become much more fully merged with international, particularly American, movements, and the special characteristics which previously marked it have diminished in importance. Today the young British student of psychology is brought up largely on American textbooks, and his gods, if he has any, are probably American."

GREAT BRITAIN

In Great Britain—the native country of empiricism and associationism —and the country described in 1870 by the French psychologist T. Ribot as the one "which has done most for psychology"—the new psychology ought to have found a fertile soil and have flourished. Actually, however, Britain's rich psychological tradition—reflected in its philosophy from Hobbes through Locke, Hartley, the Mills, and Bain—found strong opposition. This opposition is evidenced in the thinking of James Ward and George F. Stout at the end of the nineteenth century. As a result, psychology in the form of mental philosophy tended to linger at the British universities, and to make room for laboratories and chairs of experimental psychology very slowly. British psychology of the twentieth century was not the product of associationist philosophy, as would be expected. Rather, it derived from the combined influences of idealistic philosophy (Ward), of biology, especially the theory of evolution (Darwin), and of the study of individual differences (Galton).

Transition. It will be remembered that the man who prepared the ground for the new psychology in Britain, and who served as a link between the old psychology and the new, was *Alexander Bain* (1818-1903). His service to psychology consisted chiefly in his recognizing the relevance of physiology to psychology, of his formulation of psychophysical parallelism, of his founding the first journal of psychology, *Mind* (1876), and of his systematic books, *The Senses and the Intellect* (1855), and *The Emotions and the Will* (1859). These two volumes, abridged in 1868 as *Mental and Moral Science,* were the leading textbooks of psychology in Britain until G. F. Stout's *Manual of Psychology* (1898) took their place.

Establishment of Scientific Psychology. The men most instrumental in establishing the new psychology in Britain were Galton, Spencer, Sully, and Rivers—each in a different way and to a different degree. *Francis Galton* (1822-1911), the most original of them, left the strongest mark on British psychology. *Herbert Spencer* (1820-1903), the author of *Principles of Psychology* (1855) and of the improved two volume second edition of 1870-1872, introduced evolutionism into psychology. *James Sully* (1842-1923), a professor at the University College, London, holds a special position in the history of psychology because he wrote the first textbook for the new science in the English language—namely, *Outlines of Psychology* (1884), a scholarly and comprehensive work. Two years later he published a simplified version, *The Teacher's Handbook of Psychology.* In 1892, Sully revised and expanded his *Outlines* and published *The Human Mind,* a two volume work which was well received in Britain as well as in America. The introduction of child psychology was another of Sully's contributions. In addition, he played an important part in founding an experimental laboratory at the University College, London, in the fall of

1897. *William H. R. Rivers* (1864-1922) was the first true British experimentalist. Trained as a physician, Rivers turned to psychology. He not only lectured on experimental psychology, but directed the first psychological laboratory in Britain, established at Cambridge in 1897. There he trained the first generation of British experimental psychologists. He was also put in temporary charge of the laboratory at University College, London. As a result of his Cambridge and London associations, many future leaders of British psychology were Rivers' students. Although Rivers' interest shifted to anthropology in his later years, he continued to publish in psychology as well.

The first true textbook of experimental psychology with a manual for laboratory experiments was *The Text-Book of Experimental Psychology* (1909) by Charles S. Myers, Rivers' former student and his successor at Cambridge. This book had several editions and was subsequently revised by F. Bartlett, Myers' successor. Other psychological textbooks widely used in Britain in areas such as physiological, abnormal, and social were written by William McDougall.

Ward and Stout. Concurrent with the growth of scientific psychology, there was a growth of philosophical psychology embodied in the work of two influential philosophers. These were *James Ward* (1843-1925) at Cambridge, and his student, *George F. Stout* (1860-1944). Stout held several academic positions in England, and then went to St. Andrews in Scotland, where he remained for 33 years until his retirement. Ward and Stout represented the philosophical tradition in psychology by treating psychology as a field of philosophy. Ward presented his view of psychology in an article in the *Encyclopaedia Britannica* in 1885, which came to be regarded as the representative British view on psychology. Revised later, it was published separately as *Psychological Principles* (1918). This work was the last presentation of the old philosophical psychology in Britain, perhaps the final version of a system which had been long outmoded elsewhere. Stout detailed this system of philosophical and speculative psychology in a textbook, *Manual of Psychology* (1898), which became the standard textbook of psychology in British schools for a quarter century. Ward and Stout, although philosophers, were well disposed toward the new psychology and recognized its values. In fact, Ward helped to establish the first British psychological laboratory at Cambridge. But their philosophical conception of psychology, which had persisted in Britain from the end of the eighteenth and the beginning of the nineteenth century, actually hindered wider acceptance and advance of scientific psychology. Ward's philosophical ancestors were not Locke or the associationists, but rather the Scottish philosophers, such as Thomas Reid, and the German philosophers, Leibnitz and Kant. Following this philosophical tradition, Ward introduced into British psychology a stream of thought which was closer to Brentano than to Wundt. This thought has persisted in Britain, and its echoes can still be detected in British theoretical psychology.

Influences on Scientific Psychology. The principal initial source of inspiration for British scientific psychology was German experimental psychology. Almost all the builders of the new psychology in Britain—men such as Sully, Rivers, Watt, McDougall, and Spearman—either studied psychology at German universities or became acquainted with it during their visits to Germany. But there were also indigenous and more direct sources of inspiration, among them principally, Darwin and Galton. Largely because of Galton's prevailing influence, British scientific psychology was not a mere replica of German psychology, but had a character of its own.

Francis Galton (1822-1911). British psychology cannot be understood without Galton, because he has left the strongest characterizing mark upon it. Galton was discussed earlier as the initiator of statistics and mental testing in psychology. He was not a psychologist and was not affiliated with a university. Nevertheless, Galton, by his study of individual differences and the introduction of statistics, profoundly altered not only the course of British psychology but of psychology as a whole.

The basic stimulus for Galton's work was Darwin's theory of evolution. He began with the study of heredity, especially inheritance of abilities. His first book on this topic, *Hereditary Genius*, was published in 1869. Galton's interest in various forms of genius—scientific, literary, artistic— each of which he believed was inherited, led him logically to the study of individual differences, to the use of tests, and to statistics. Individual differences, mental measurement, and statistics were interrelated in Galton's mind and stemmed from his dominant interest, heredity; and all Galton's books deal primarily with this subject. Experimental psychology will remember best his *Inquiries into Human Faculty and Its Development* (1883), for in it Galton presented the procedure and results of his experiments on association and imagery. This work stimulated subsequent investigations of association, associative reaction time, and imagery.

Galton's most valuable and lasting contribution was the study of individual differences—a study which introduced a new era in psychology. Individual variations in mental and physical capacities, although occassionally noted by psychologists, were not previously thought to be proper subjects for the science of psychology. Hence there was no attempt to explore them systematically. The psychology practiced in Germany was concerned with what was common and general in men. Galton focused on the individual. Thus his work became the principal root of differential psychology. American interest in the psychology of individual differences and in their measurement is attributable in large measure to Galton and later to Cattell.

British Psychology in The Twentieth Century. In contrast to American psychology, the progress of British psychology was slow. There were several reasons for this slowness. First, the general conservatism of

British universities made them unwilling to incorporate new disciplines into their curricula. There was the enduring influence of philosophical psychology, already mentioned. Finally there was the skepticism—or even hostility—of philosophers toward the new psychology. When James Ward proposed a laboratory of psychophysics at Cambridge in 1877, the senate rejected the project because such a laboratory would "insult religion by putting the human soul in a pair of scales." The resistance of the academic senates toward psychology was assuredly difficult to overcome. At the outbreak of the Second World War in 1939, there were only six chairs of psychology in all Britain—three at London—and only about 30 university teachers of psychology in all Britain. It was largely practical considerations—the need for psychological services in education, industry, in mental health, and in war—that gained wider acceptance for psychology. Thus educational, industrial, and—after the Second World War—clinical psychology have been the fields which fared best. On the other hand, animal or comparative psychology—an original British product and a consequence of Darwin's evolutionary theory—practically disappeared from the British scene. Established on the basis of *C. Lloyd Morgan's* (1852-1936) observations, experiments, and writings, particularly of his *Animal Life and Intelligence* (1890-1891), animal psychology was vigorously pursued in America. After 50 years the study of animal psychology resumed in Britain. However, this revived study took its form from ethology, which had been initiated on the European Continent.

The strongest influence in British psychology in the first two decades of the twentieth century was *William McDougall* (1871-1938). L. S. Hearnshaw in his *A Short History of British Psychology* (1964) says of McDougall, that ". . . his influence on British psychology and educational thought in the generation prior to the Second World War was immense, and he was unquestionably one of the most striking and forceful figures in the psychology of his day." However, McDougall's influence in Britain declined after his departure for America in 1920. More attention is devoted to McDougall in the latter part of this book in connection with the schools of psychology. Other figures of enduring influence have been Spearman and Bartlett.

Charles E. Spearman (1863-1945). The originality of Spearman, the breadth and depth of his ideas, his achievements, and the effect which his work has had on psychology make him one of the greatest British pioneers in psychology and one of the greatest figures in the history of psychology. Spearman's first interest was philosophy.

He was 34 when he transferred his attention to psychology, marking this change by study under Wundt in Leipzig. There he took his Ph.D. degree in 1904. Although he had deep admiration for Wundt as a man and a scientist, he could not be satisfied with Wundt's psychology, especially Wundt's preoccupation with sensation. The desire to broaden his knowledge of psychology made Spearman study physiology and took him to other psychological centers—Würzburg, Göttingen, and Berlin. Spending seven years in Germany and gaining unusually extensive background and experience, Spearman returned to England. In 1906, he accepted a teaching appointment at the University College, London. There he remained until 1931. In the latter year he visited the United States and lectured at several universities. Of all the British psychologists, Spearman is the best known and most influential among Americans.

Most characteristic of Spearman's psychology was his dedicated effort to understand the whole man and his nature. Although his efforts were concentrated on the study of cognition and intelligence, the dynamic aspects of man also interested him profoundly. Spearman's thorough familiarity with philosophy, physiology, and history of ideas added breadth and depth to his views and theories. He hoped to provide psychology with a system of fundamental laws, a number of which he postulated. But Spearman is more widely known for his specific contributions to statistics and for his study of human abilities, particularly, of the nature of intelligence. Spearman's Rho, the Spearman-Brown prophecy formula, and his correction for attenuation, are widely familiar to students of psychology. His study of correlation laid the groundwork for factorial analysis.

As early as 1904, after having tested school children, Spearman published an article, *General Intelligence, Objectively Measured and Determined*, in which he proposed for the first time his famous two-factor theory of intelligence. This theory stated that in human capacities it is possible to distinguish one general factor g, identified with intelligence, and several independent special factors s, called "special abilities." This theory was a turning point in the history of mental testing and became a topic of heated discussion for decades. Spearman had more to say about intelligence in his later works: *The Nature of Intelligence and the Principles of Cognition* (1923), a book, and an article, *G and After—A School to End Schools* (1930). Another important Spearman publication, regarded as a classic of psychological literature, is *The Abilities of Man, Their Nature and Measurement* (1927), in which he summarized his views on human mind and psychological laws. In *Creative Mind* (1930) he applied his principles to creative work in art and science. *Psychology Down the Ages* (1937), Spearman's last book, is a two volume study of the philosophical ancestry of psychological thought from the Greek thinkers to modern times.

Centers of Psychological Research. The birthplace and stronghold of British experimental psychology was *Cambridge*. Even before the actual introduction of experimental psychology, Cambridge was an important center of psychological teaching. James Ward had been there since 1875, attracting to his lecture hall the future leaders of British psychology. Stout, McDougall, and Bartlett were Ward's students. Since 1877 Ward had tried, as we have mentioned, to establish a laboratory in psychophysics. But the laboratory did not materialize until 20 years later (1897). When it was established, it was put in the care of W. H. R. Rivers. Later it was directed and greatly expanded by C. S. Myers. The Cambridge laboratory contributed significantly to the development of experimental psychology in Britain. For decades it was the place where most British experimental psychologists received their training and where most experimental research was conducted. The early research was largely on perception, special senses, and higher mental processes. But in recent years physiological and comparative psychology have been strongly emphasized. Currently associated with the Cambridge department of psychology are two large research units, the Nuffield Foundation Unit for Research into Problems of Ageing (since 1946) and the Applied Psychology Unit. The latter unit is sponsored by the Medical Research Council, a governmental agency.

Two men were chiefly responsible for Cambridge's notable achievements. They were Myers and Bartlett who—jointly and in succession—directed the Cambridge laboratory and department for over half a century. *Charles S. Myers* (1873-1946) was there almost from the founding of the laboratory until 1921, when he became director of the National Institute of Industrial Psychology. At Cambridge for more than 20 years, Myers demonstrated versatility and in diverse ways affected British psychology. He conducted research. He published articles and books, among them *The Text-Book of Experimental Psychology* (1909), which he revised several times. Cofounder of the British Psychological Society (1901), Myers was its first president. Cofounder of the *British Journal of Psychology*, he was its editor for many years. After 1921 he devoted himself to applied psychology, particularly to industrial psychology.

Myers' successor at Cambridge, *Frederic C. Bartlett* (b. 1886), directed the department and the laboratory for 30 years. He has been an influential psychologist in Britain, not so much through his research or writings—though his two principal books, *Remembering* (1932) and *Thinking* (1958), received wide recognition—as by his teaching and administrative work. In 1960, more than two-thirds of the chairs of psychology in Britain were held by Bartlett's former students. He was editor of the *British Journal of Psychology* for 24 years, an officer of the British Psychological Society, and a principal promoter of support for psychological research by the British government. Bartlett always represented the forces that, in the span of 50 years, brought about the change in psychology. This change he summed up in the concluding remarks of his 1951 presidential address before the British Psychological Society: "But above everything else, as I see it, the old puppet subjects of the early German psychologists have had their time. They have played many a good play. Their strings are broken. Their commendatory epitaphs can be written and they can be put away in their boxes. In their places we will have real people." Although Bartlett retired one year after this address, and his post was filled by his former student O. L. Zangwill, he has remained active and still very much a part of the British psychological scene.

A professor who had a substantial part in the growth of psychological studies at Cambridge between the World Wars was *James T. MacCurdy* (1886-1947). Born in Canada, educated in the United States, with a degree in medicine from Johns Hopkins, he accepted a university appointment at Cambridge in 1922 and remained there until his death. His main field of teaching and study was psychopathology. His major work was *Common Principles in Psychology and Physiology* (1928), an attempt to integrate psychology and physiology by a unitary concept of "patterns." He defined "patterns" as "the immaterial agencies that guide and control the physico-chemical processes involved in all living."

The *University College of London* became a highly productive and influential training and research center in Britain. An experimental laboratory was founded there in 1897, the same year—presumably only a few months later—as the Cambridge laboratory. In 1900 McDougall assumed charge of the laboratory and lectures there. In 1906 Spearman was appointed and retained this post for 25 years. Under the directorship of Spearman—and because of the intense research on problems of human ability and personality initiated by him—the "London School," as the center has been called, enjoyed wide recognition both in Britain and abroad. Cyril Burt succeeded Spearman and held the position for 20 years (until 1950). He preserved the same main focal interest of the department. Also associated with the London school—for almost half a century —was J. C. Flugel (1884-1955). His interest lay in psychoanalysis and the application of psychoanalytic themes to a wide range of social, moral, and psychological problems. He is also known for his history of psychology, *One Hundred Years of Psychology* (1933, updated by D. J. West in 1964). In 1950 the department, then headed by Roger W. Russell, was reorganized and expanded, and its programs made more diversified. When the Institute of Psychiatry at Maudsley Hospital was attached to the University College, it added a new dimension to the department.

Oxford differed from other British universities by its indifference, perhaps even hostility, to scientific psychology, and by its tardiness in establishing study in experimental psychology. McDougall—who succeeded Stout in 1904 and remained at Oxford until his departure for America in 1920—lectured on psychology, but did not have a laboratory at the university. He conducted his experiments in a private laboratory. His successor was William Brown (1881-1951), a physician, who specialized in clinical psychology. Partly because of his efforts, Oxford's Institute of Experimental Psychology was created in 1936, with Brown as its director. The chair of experimental psychology was not instituted until 1947, when it was assumed by George Humphrey (b. 1889).

At the *University of Edinburgh* a laboratory was organized fairly early (1907) by W. G. Smith (1866-1918), who had been appointed lecturer of experimental psychology one year earlier. In 1919, when a separate department of psychology was opened, James Drever, Sr. (1873-1950) became its director and the first holder of the chair of psychology. This department grew in size and influence under Drever's and Mary Collins' (b. 1895) leadership. Drever wrote texts and other books, of which *The Psychology of Everyday Life* was particularly successful. Drever was succeeded by his son, James Drever, Jr., in 1944.

At *Glasgow University* psychology was represented in succession by Henry J. Watt (1879-1925), appointed in 1908; Robert H. Thouless (b. 1894); P. E. Vernon (b. 1905); and R. W. Pickford (b. 1903). Each of these psychologists is noted for some special work: Watt, for his participation in and contributions to the Würzburg school, and for his books on memory, sound, music, and cognition; Thouless, for psychology of religion, social psychology, and psychical research; Vernon, for mental testing (the Allport-Vernon-Lindzey *Study of Values*) and study of expressive movement; Pickford—a psychologist of broad interests and achievements in several fields—mainly for the work on individual differences in color vision.

Besides these centers of special significance in Britain, there have been other universities with departments, chairs, or lectureships of psychology which contributed to the development of British psychology. Among them have been Aberdeen—where Bain lectured for 20 years and Stout for two years; St. Andrews—where Stout taught for 33 years and where C. A. Mace established a laboratory in 1927; Bristol, where Lloyd Morgan held a chair of psychology; Liverpool, with whose university were associated at some time Charles Sherrington, and, in succession, psychologists W. G. Smith, H. J. Watt, and Cyril Burt; Manchester, distinguished by being the first university to establish the first full-time, exclusively psychological chair in Britain (1919). *C. A. Mace* (b. 1894) moved from St. Andrews to Bedford College of the University of London in 1932. In 1944 he accepted the first chair of psychology established at Birkbeck College, University of London. Now professor emeritus at Birkbeck College, Mace represents a wide range of psychological interests, from philosophical psychology to industrial psychology. He has been the editor of the *Pelican Psychology Series* and *Methuen's Manuals of Modern Psychology* and, as such has been responsible for a score of valuable additions to psychological literature, some of which have been highly successful.

Educational Psychology. A prominent field of interest in British psychology has been that of educational psychology and child study. Associationists, like the Mills, had already shown much interest in education and often sought to explain the educational process in terms of association. Bain reflected this interest in his *Education as Science* (1878). Sully turned to child study and organized the British Association for Child Study (1895). Almost all psychologists of the succeeding generations at one time or another, or in some degree, were concerned with problems of educational psychology. Work in psychometrics and statistics, for which Britain is noted, was stimulated largely by this concern. American educational psychology seems to have had a particularly strong effect in Britain.

One of the early significant events in this area was the opening of a laboratory of educational psychology at the teacher training college, the Moray House, in Edinburgh in 1912, with James Drever, Sr., as its first director. From that time forward, British interest in educational psychology has continued unabated. A survey in Britain in 1949-1951 revealed that the ratio of educational to experimental psychologists was approximately 100:1, and to those in abnormal and clinical psychology 7:1.

The most outstanding contributors to British educational psychology were Cyril Burt, Godfrey H. Thomson, and Charles W. Valentine. The first two are identified with the history of factorial analysis. *Cyril L. Burt* (b. 1883) was associated successively with the universities of Cambridge, Liverpool, and London. The bibliography of Burt is extensive and covers a wide range of topics. His books on testing, a volume on juvenile delinquency—*The Young Delinquent* (1925)—and a book on factorial statistics—*The Factors of the Mind* (1940)—won wide acclaim. *Godfrey H. Thomson* (1881-1955), author of a fundamental work, *The Factorial Analysis of Human Ability* (1939), was director of Moray House for over 25 years. During this time, he developed or directed the construction of school tests known as the Moray House tests. Thomson supervised testing programs and conducted huge population surveys in the country. He had many successes in these activities, but his greatest enjoyment, he said, was teaching applications of mathematics to psychology. *Charles W. Valentine* (1879-1964) was the recognized leader in British educational psychology. He was a professor of education at Birmingham University from 1919 to 1946. In 1931 he founded the highly regarded *British Journal of Educational Psychology* and was its editor for 25 years. In 1942 he published the *Psychology of Early Childhood*, a genetic study of the child from birth to five years. His most widely circulated volume was *Psychology and its Bearings on Education* (1950), a current standard text at colleges for teachers. His last book, completed when he was 82 years old, was *The Experimental Psychology of Beauty* (1962).

Clinical Psychology.   The rapid development of clinical psychology, which followed the Second World War, resulted from increasing demand for psychological clinical services and from financial support by the governmental National Health Service, created in 1948. Chief training and research centers in clinical psychology, sponsored by the National Health Service, are the *Tavistock Clinic* in London and the *Institute of Psychiatry at Maudsley Hospital,* associated with the University of London. The Institute includes a department of psychology with training and research facilities and a chair of clinical psychology. Several units and sections of the Hospital—such as the Children's Development Research Unit—have close relations with the psychology department.

The director of the department of psychology at Maudsley Hospital has been *Hans Jurgen Eysenck* (b. 1916), a German-born, British-trained psychologist, who within 20 years has become Britain's leading figure in clinical psychology. His extensive research in personality, his novel approach in this research, and his writings of prodigious scope have made him widely known. His methodology and his views on the dimensions of personality have become a subject of controversy on both sides of the Atlantic. His basic view on personality structure—expressed in *The Sci-*

entific Study of Personality (1952) and *The Structure of Human Personality* (1953)—follows the traditional lines of British thinking: personality is composed of four sectors or areas, cognitive, conative, affective, and somatic. Eysenck's research strategy consists of applying a large variety of tests, which measure as many levels of man's functioning as possible, and of submitting their results to factorial analysis. On the basis of this method, Eysenck tries to determine the fundamental dimensions or general underlying factors of personality. He has proposed the dimension of neuroticism-normal for the conative area; and for the affective, the extroversion-introversion polarity. Eysenck's intensive interest in abnormal personality is reflected in the voluminous *Handbook of Abnormal Psychology* (1961), which he edited.

Evaluation. Psychology in Britain in the twentieth century did not follow the empiricist-associationist tradition of Locke, Hartley, the Mills, and Bain. The major influences were Ward and Stout, on one hand, and Galton and the evolutionary theory, on the other. These two influences give rise to two different orientations or emphases in British psychology. One—more philosophical and theoretical, holistic, and qualitative—stresses man's cognitive functions. The other—more experimental, analytic, and quantitative—is interested in individual differences and their measurement and is practical. The first trend neither affected much, nor was it affected by, American psychology. The second, however, significantly influenced American psychology and reciprocally, it seems, was influenced by America.

Psychology is indebted to Britain for Darwin's theory of evolution, Galton's study of individual differences, and Spearman's initiation of interest in the measurement of human abilities. British interest in individual differences constituted a counterbalance to Wundtian psychology and prepared the ground for applied and clinical psychology. The other outstanding British contributions have been in psychological statistics, psychometrics, and educational psychology. British experimental psychology progressed slowly. Yet its contributions have also been numerous and substantial. British psychologists, in general, have been neither anti- nor aphilosophical. They have been less compartmentalized and not so highly specialized as their American colleagues. They are interested in all fundamental problems of psychology rather than in merely a few, and they usually extend their research to several fields rather than staying in narrow areas. The behavioristic approach did not find strong support in Britain before World War II.

In the second half of the century, psychology in Britain gained prestige and won effective support from the universities, the public at large, and the government. Many new institutions of psychological research and training were established. A number of others included psychology in their programs or employed psychologists on their staffs. Psychology has gone beyond university campuses. It has, moreover, joined hands with the medical and social sciences, in training, research, and applications. At the Festival of Britain in 1951 the psychological section of the British

Association for the Advancement of Science presented a series of 20 papers, entitled collectively "Current trends in British psychology." Ten of these papers—devoted to different applied fields—and ten others—related mostly to the concepts and methodology of applied psychology—signaled clearly British psychology's strong turn toward practical applications. This trend is also discernible in the swift growth of clinical psychology in contemporary Britain.

FRANCE

French psychology differed much from the psychologies of other countries—especially from American psychology—in background, origin, development, and in general character. The sources of the uniqueness of French psychology are to be sought in the particular roots from which this psychology developed. They included, on one hand, an uninterrupted and strong sensationist philosophical tradition and, on the other hand, close ties with psychiatry. Thus it is appropriate to review, if only briefly, the philosophical foundation and the impact of psychiatry on psychology in France. After this background is discussed, the beginnings and development of French psychology will be outlined.

Philosophical Background. The fact that Descartes was French, and that his philosophy was so influential in his own country, can in a way, and by itself, explain the intense interest of France in psychological problems. But French philosophers in their psychological writings, and the great French psychiatrists in their treatises, ignored both the metaphysics and spiritualism of Descartes. They were more impressed by Descartes' mechanistic interpretation of the organism. They proceeded to explain *l' âme*, which carried the meaning of both the soul and the mind, not in the spiritualistic tradition, but in terms of the brain, the nerves, and the senses. Consequently the general course followed by French psychology was oriented toward the physiological explanation of mind.

The highlights of the philosophical tradition which molded French psychology are represented in the eighteenth century in the writings of Condillac, La Mettrie, and Cabanis, and in the nineteenth century by Maine de Biran and Taine. The first three of these philosophers advanced the mechanistic thought in psychology, whereas the last two took a more moderate position and endeavored to modify or correct the views of their predecessors. The true initiator of the philosophical tradition consequential to psychology was *Etienne de Condillac* (1715-1780), already mentioned in the first part of this volume. *Julien Offray de La Mettrie* (1709-1751) proposed an extremely mechanistic conception of man's nature, clearly expressed in the very title of his famous work, *L'Homme machine* ("Man a Machine," 1748). *Pierre Jean Georges Cabanis* (1757-1808), a physician like La Mettrie, was particularly interested in consciousness and its phenomena. His views can be regarded as the culmination of

French psychological thought in the eighteenth century. The writers of this century differed in their views on psychological matters in many ways; but they had one common denominator, sensationism, and shared one tendency, namely, to reduce mind to brain processes. This tendency characterizes Cabanis' chief book, *Rapports du physique et du moral de l'homme* ("The Relations between the Bodily and the Moral in Man," 1802).

But *Maine de Biran* (1766-1824) departed from the position of his predecessors. Dissatisfied with their physiological and mechanistic orientation, he sought to establish psychology as a science of consciousness, based on idealistic or spiritualistic principles. Activity and will, previously neglected by French psychology, became the central issues in Biran's system. Biran's spiritualism, however, was too extreme for the majority of physiologically minded French psychologists and thus did not find much support. *Hippolyte Taine* (1828-1893), although primarily a literary critic and a historian, is regarded as the immediate precursor of the new psychology, mainly on account of his work on intelligence, *Théorie de l'intelligence* (1870). In it he pointed to John Stuart Mill and Bain whose ideas he recommended and followed. Taine viewed psychology as a necessary basis of moral and social science.

Other philosophical currents which affected psychological thought in the late nineteenth and twentieth centuries were the *positivism* of *Auguste Comte* (1798-1857), and the philosophy of *Henri Bergson* (1859-1941), two systems as radically different in their tenets as in their spheres of influence. Although Comte denied psychology any scientific status, his rejection of metaphysics and his fundamental tenet that only the sensible is knowable, corresponded rather well with the general direction of French psychological thought. Bergson, one of the most original philosophers of the modern era and the most eminent in the last hundred years in France, attacked, in his words, "the mechanistic intoxication" of his day, and revived an interest in a spiritual conception of man. His emphasis on the dynamic unity of mind and the ego as the substratum unifying the everchanging psychological states, as well as his other ideas, had an effect on psychology and psychiatry.

Psychopathology. The second root of French psychology was psychiatry. Psychiatry and psychology have always been closely related in France, psychopathology being their common ground. Many of the pioneers of French psychology had medical degrees and practiced psychiatry. Psychiatrists frequently held chairs of psychology and wrote books in psychology.

Interest in mental illness and mental aberrations was traditional in France. Modern psychiatry was born in that country, and humane treatment of the insane was first officially instituted in a mental hospital in Paris in 1795. Subsequently France led the world in psychiatry until the end of the nineteenth century. Suggestion, hypnotism, hysteria, and neuroses were widely and intensively studied. The psychiatric writers from *Philippe Pinel* (1745-1826), the founder of modern psychiatry, to *Jean-Martin Charcot* (1825-1893), the leader of French psychiatry at the end of the nineteenth century, constituted the basic inspiration for the new psychology in France. Charcot had a particularly powerful influence on the originators of French psychology, Janet, Ribot, and Binet.

The orientation of the French psychopathology was distinctly organic. Mental disorders were regarded simply as disorders of the brain. This orientation stemmed from the combined influence of the mechanistic philosophy and neurology. There was no real distinction made between neurology and psychiatry in France at the time of Charcot. Psychiatry was then considered a special application of neurology, which also was highly developed in France.

Ribot, Founder of French Psychology.   The men who made the first and most direct contributions to French psychology were Théodule Ribot, Alfred Binet, and Pierre Janet. Representing three different spheres of interest and different approaches, these men complemented one another and enriched French psychology in their own individual ways. Of these three, Théodule Ribot (1839-1916) was the earliest. He was the first to take the inititive to steer psychology away from philosophy and to launch it as a new science. He also formulated the first theoretical principles for the new psychology.

Ribot was the first teacher of experimental psychology in France, originally at the Sorbonne (1885-1889) and subsequently at the Collège de France (1889-1896). It was at the latter school that he taught Janet, his successor in the chair, and Georges Dumas, future prominent professor, writer, and editor in psychology. Ribot's work, which showed considerable logical consistency and continuity, can be divided into three periods. In the first period, from 1870 to 1880, he studied the psychology of England and Germany and was concerned with the theoretical problems of the new science. He acquainted his compatriots with psychology in England and Germany in his two books, *English Psychology* (1870, translated into English in 1874) and *German Psychology of To-Day* (1879, translated in 1886). The second period, 1881-1890, was dominated by his interest in problems of psychopathology and resulted in such books as *Les Maladies de la mémoire* ("The Disorders of Memory," 1881), *Les Maladies de la volonté* ("The Disorders of the Will," 1883), and *Les Maladies de la personnalité* ("The Disorders of Personality," 1885). Ribot's preoccupation with psychopathology grew from his belief that, as he expressed it, every mental phenomenon should be studied not only in its "biological evolution" but also in its "morbid dissolution." The last period, from 1890 on, was dedicated to psychology of affective states and problems which we would now classify as *dynamic psychology*. Several of Ribot's volumes appeared during this time, on the psychology of sentiments (1896), creative imagination (1900), logic of sentiments (1905), passions (1907), problems of affective psychology (1910), and in 1914, two years before his death, a book on "the unconscious life and movements."

When one examines all of Ribot's works in chronological sequence, one can observe the gradual evolution of his ideas which he continuously revised. But to one of his earliest views, expressed in the preface to *English Psychology*, he adhered with steadfast consistency. He said then (1870):

> The psychology in question here will then be purely experimental; it will have no other object than phenomena, their laws, and their immediate causes; it will concern itself neither with the soul nor its essence, for this question, being above experience and beyond verification, belongs to metaphysics.

This was the view which later French psychologists generally followed. It is worthy of note that, although well trained in philosophy and interested in philosophical questions, and although he was a founder and editor of a philosophical journal, *Revue Philosophique*, Ribot always stressed the independence of psychology from philosophy. Opposed as he was to philosophical meddling in psychology, his psychological system is clearly permeated by monistic and materialistic concepts. This was possibly due to his dissatisfaction with the spiritualistic and idealistic tendencies of the preceding psychology.

From the very start Ribot insisted that psychology go beyond the mere study of "adult, civilized, and white man." He advocated the broadening of its subject matter to encompass the study of the child, the animal, and the abnormal. Not venturing into these domains, himself, he remained principally a theorist. Neither did Ribot do any appreciable experimental research or base his writings on experimental evidence. Many of his works were clinical in character, but even these were not the result of his clinical experience. Ribot realized this shortcoming and acknowledged it, when he advised his students, Janet and Dumas: "I treated of psychopathology without seeing the sick. Do better than I did: study the sick."

What particularly characterizes Ribot's psychology is its stress on the significance of affective and emotional factors in psychological processes and behavior. It is notable that the unconscious also received an important place in his system. It was thus natural that Ribot was interested in Freud. His appreciation and persistent study of emotional factors as fundamental to human motivation, and his eagerness to understand them, made Ribot one of the founders of dynamic psychology, to whose establishment and development French psychology contributed prominently. Ribot enjoyed prestige and respect in France. His influence was unrivalled. In 1939 French psychologists, celebrating the centenary of Ribot's birth, emphasized his unique role in French psychology. However, as important as he was for French psychology, Ribot left no enduring mark on psychology equal to that of his contemporaries, notably Binet and Janet. Among the reasons for his lesser influence on psychology as a whole was the speculative character of his work unsupported by experimentation.

First Psychological Laboratories. France was relatively slow to establish psychological laboratories. It was in 1889—ten years after Wundt's opened in Leipzig—that the first experimental laboratory in France was founded at the Sorbonne. Its foundation coincided with the first International Congress of Psychology held in Paris in the same year. The direction of the Sorbonne laboratory should have fallen into the hands of Ribot.

But Ribot, then 50 years old, declined the honor. Instead Henri Beaunis (1830-1921), professor of physiology and an older man, took temporary charge. Alfred Binet was entrusted with the laboratory in 1891, but it was not until three years later that he took full charge as director. Binet retained this office until his death in 1911. However, his later activities were concentrated in another laboratory for whose foundation in 1904 he was directly responsible and to which he devoted most of his attention. This was the laboratory of experimental pedagogy, attached to an elementary school of the Rue Grange-aux-Belles in Paris. Here Binet gathered the necessary experience for the construction of his famous individual intelligence scale.

The second in importance was a laboratory established under the auspices of the mental asylum in Villejuif. In 1901 this laboratory became part of École des Hautes Études in Paris. It was there that Henri Piéron, one of the subsequent leaders of French psychology, began his career as an experimentalist. In 1907 he started a course in psychology which was the first given anywhere in France in association with a laboratory. Five years later Piéron was appointed director of the Sorbonne laboratory to succeed the deceased Binet. This first psychological laboratory of France had been so much neglected in the immediately preceding years that when Piéron came to head it in 1912, he had to reorganize it. Through his efforts, the University of Paris established a separate Institute of Psychology in 1920, and this historic laboratory was made an integral and vital part of it. When Piéron retired, Paul Fraisse assumed its directorship.

After the Sorbonne, laboratories were created successively in other parts of France: at Rennes, founded in 1896 by Benjamin Bourdon (1860-1943), one of Wundt's students; at Montpellier, founded in 1906 by Marcel Foucault; and at the Catholic Institute of Paris, organized in 1925 by Georges Dwelshauvers (1866-1937). There were also laboratories devoted to research in psychopathology, such as the laboratory at Salpêtrière under the direction of Pierre Janet. In 1925 a psychotechnical laboratory was opened in Paris by J. M. Lahy (1872-1943).

Laboratories have not played an important role in the development of French psychology. There have been only a few of them, their funds were meager, their personnel and equipment modest, their activities limited. The French were not interested in laboratory research as their German and American colleagues were, and they did not attach much importance to it. They had more interest and more confidence in clinical methods than in laboratory experimentation. Preoccupied with clinical problems, as they were, they preferred clinics, asylums, and hospitals, and even libraries, as the places of research. Thus, unlike Germany, Britain, and America, where laboratories were a major factor in the growth of psychology, the laboratory in France had much less influence.

Alfred Binet (1857-1911). From the standpoint of the general history of psychology, Alfred Binet was one of the chief founders of psychometrics and particularly of intelligence measurement, through his highly successful scale of intelligence. In the history of French psychology he was one of its great builders. Binet's research and writings strengthened the position of objective psychology and opened new pathways for its growth in France. From the very beginning of his career, Binet was a champion of scientific psychology. He did not enter psychology by way of philosophy like Ribot, Janet, and some other French psychologists. Hostile to any alliance between psychology and metaphysics, he insisted on the experimental basis of psychological data. His own experimental work was as extensive as it was intensive, embracing a wide range of functions and phenomena. He felt that any view regarding mental processes or human nature had to be submitted to experimental test and scientific verification. If a view was found untenable in face of scientific findings, Binet did not hesitate to change or reject it. Binet's readiness to accept facts and his eagerness to search for new ones explain his prodigious intellectual growth. The rejection of associationism is an illustration of his scientific integrity.

As a disciple of Taine, Binet initially accepted associationism as his theoretical springboard. Faithful to associationist doctrine, he regarded association as the fundamental process and the laws of association as the most general laws of psychology. In his first book on the process of reasoning, *La Psychologie du raisonnement* (1886), his approach was associationistic. But when he turned to abnormal psychology—to the study of dissociated personalities and hypnotic phenomena—he came to the conclusion that associationism was incapable of helping him in the solution of these problems. He encountered the same difficulty in the study of memory and character. As a result of this dissatisfaction, he repudiated associationism. Moreover, and as a consequence, Binet rejected Wundt's system of psychology. This system clashed with both his interest in higher mental processes and his functional approach. Neither Wundt's elementism nor his methodology was suitable for the study of problems such as judgment, imagination, memory, reasoning, and sentiments, which Binet considered the most important in psychology. He was closer to the school of Külpe, whose imageless thought found his support, and to the orientation which has been called functional. In fact, Binet can be counted as the chief representative and promoter of European functional psychology.

Binet's intelligence scale appeared in 1905. It was preceded by ten years of research and testing trials. Two years before, in 1903, Binet's *L'Étude expérimentale de l'intelligence* ("Experimental Study of Intelligence") appeared. Binet and his collaborator Théodore Simon revised the scale in 1908 and 1911. Binet realized that his tests measured only single faculties of the mind and could not, as he said "make us know the totality of an intelligence." Outside of France, the close association of Binet's name with intelligence testing tended to dim his other achievements and overshadow his general historical role. In France the intelligence scale passed unnoticed. Even after its success in the United States, the test was not used much until World War II. It was as late as 1959 that Simon learned that in America "Stanford-Binet" is the more common appellation of the test in America than "Terman-Merrill." But the French did not fail to recognize and value the other contributions of Binet.

Four books and numerous articles were produced by Binet in his relatively short life. He liked to work and write. Writing was one of his greatest pleasures in life, he stated. His plan to write a large treatise to show how "the mental machine functions" never materialized because of his untimely death at the age of 54. Throughout his life Binet never held any teaching position. However, as editor of *L'Année Psychologique*, the first French psychological journal, founded by him in 1895, Binet made his voice heard.

Abnormal and Dynamic Psychology. Psychiatry and psychology seemed inseparable in France. Many who were classified as psychologists held medical degrees and could just as well be called psychiatrists. The opposite is also true, psychiatrists often held degrees in philosophy and were engaged in psychological research. An example of France's characteristic combination of psychology and psychiatry is Pierre Janet. Emphasis on psychopathology has been the earliest and most persistent feature of French psychology. Initiated by Ribot, eminently represented by Janet for almost half a century, this trend is continued in the work of psychologists such as Daniel Lagache.

Pierre Janet (1859-1947). One can almost say that Janet personified all the characteristics of French psychology. His influence in France was unparalleled and was powerful in other European countries. In America, although not influential, he was well known. According to a survey conducted in 1953-1954, Janet was the fourth best known foreign psychologist to American psychology students (after Wundt, Ebbinghaus, and Spearman).

Janet's training was both philosophical and medical, and he held degrees in both fields. He was a professor at the Sorbonne from 1895 and successor to Ribot's chair at the Collège de France in 1902, a position which he held for over 40 years. He was, however, always in contact with patients and clinics. Besides numerous articles, he wrote 16 books. They were devoted to psychopathology, psychotherapy, and dynamic aspects of personality. Several of his books were repeatedly re-edited and translated into other languages. Most of his works have never been translated into English. The ones which were published in English are: *The Major Symptoms of Hysteria* (1907, second edition 1929); *Principles of Psychotherapy* (1924); and the two volume *Psychological Healing* (1925). Best known of his accomplishments are Janet's contributions to the study of hysteria.

Janet was also a systematist. He developed his own original system of psychology and psychopathology. Throughout his career he kept on improving his theories and never thought of them as complete and final. "Without doubt," he stated, referring to his theories, "these systematic constructions are very hypothetical and temporary." He considered "the numerous observations . . . gathered on both the normal and ailing man" the most interesting part of his work. The psychological system of Janet is referred to as *psychologie de la conduite* (psychology of conduct), which is to be distinguished from *psychologie du comportement* (psychology of comportment). "Conduct" means to imply direction and purpose and applies only to man and human activities. On the other hand, "comportement" is understood as behavior more in the sense of American behaviorism.

The central view of Janet's system is that the essential feature of mind and personality is the power of synthesis or integration. By this power all the elements of human personality are bound together in a harmonious unity. In the normal personality the integration is relatively stable and constant. If the power of synthesis is weakened, dissociation and disintegration result, lead to split personality, and to all kinds of neurotic or psychotic symptoms. The word "tension" is used to express the force or strength by which the various elements of personality are synthesized and maintained in balance. Mental health depends on the state of the tension. The nature of tension is not to be stable, but to fluctuate constantly. To the problem of tension and its variations, Janet devoted several studies. Janet's efforts to enrich psychology through psychiatry, and psychiatry through psychology, and to base psychotherapy on sound psychological principles made him one of the first clinical psychologists in the modern sense. Yet, Janet's ideas have not found wide support in America. The only follower of importance in America of Janet's interest and theories was Morton Prince (1854-1929), a physician, who became the founder of the Harvard Psychological Clinic in 1927, as was mentioned previously. There have been, however, American psychologists—and psychiatrists—who thought highly of Janet's theories. One of them was E. R. Guthrie who acknowledged the value of Janet's contributions.

Psychology of conduct, conceptualized first by Janet, was further crystalized and developed by one of the most prominent contemporary psychologists in France, *Daniel Lagache* (b. 1903), Ph.D. and M.D., professor of psychology at the Sorbonne since 1947, the year of Janet's death. He worked in a spirit similar to Janet's, but in a different theoretical framework, namely, psychoanalytical. He developed and popularized the concept of clinical psychology in his country, becoming the leading advocate of clinical applications of psychology. Lagache has also been interested in social psychology. A more experimental and organic approach to psychopathology has been pursued by *Jean Delay*, a psychiatrist, a professor at the University of Paris, and author of psychiatric books. Delay has relied heavily on elaborate laboratory techniques and neurosurgical procedures. His endeavor has been to explain clinical symptoms in terms of neurophysiological mechanisms. He has also been engaged in psychopharmacological research.

Henri Wallon (1879-1962), a philosopher and a physician, began his career as a psychiatrist but gradually turned to genetic psychology, particularly to child psychology. In the latter field he gained prominence and has many volumes to his credit. One of them, published in 1950, treats the origins of thought in the child. Wallon founded a laboratory for the psychobiological study of the child in Paris in 1927. Contemporary child psychology in France is represented prominently by *René Zazzo* (b. 1927).

Experimental Psychology. An experimental trend, although not as strong and popular as psychopathology, nevertheless always had a number of ardent followers in France. The area in which it was best expressed has been psychophysiology or physiological psychology. Most outstanding in this field has been Henri Piéron, a man equaled in influence and prestige only by Janet.

Henri Piéron (1881-1964) decided early to pursue experimental psychology, which he learned first from Ribot, and laboratory research. His academic association was with both the Sorbonne and Collège de France. There is hardly a parallel in the history of psychology for the diversity of activities, the scope of research, and the literary productivity combined in one man, as they were in Piéron. His research was concentrated in three fields: general experimental, animal, and physiological psychology. The latter absorbed most of his attention and energy, especially the psychophysiology of the senses, which was his specialty for more than 50 years. French psychotechnic (or psychotechnology)—a form of practical applied psychology, covering at once industrial and school psychology as well as personnel selection and vocational guidance—regards Piéron as its promoter. He made several significant contributions to this field, among which was the creation of the Institute of the Study of Work and Professional Guidance in Paris in 1928, which is headed at present by M. Reuchlin (b. 1920).

Facts, not theories, were Piéron's principal aim. Although he had no ambition to found any systems, he is regarded as the initiator of the French school of *psychologie du comportement*, which corresponds to American behaviorism. Psychology, Piéron declared in 1908, cannot have as its object the facts of consciousness. To be scientific it must study only the behavior of organisms. *Psychologie du comportement* postulates strict parallelism between the physiological and psychological processes and aims at an explanation of psychological data in terms of physiological mechanisms without any reference to consciousness. Congruent with this concept is Piéron's psychic evolution, which envisages a psychological continuum from unicellular animals to man. He sought to provide evidence for this theory by his studies of the crustacea, mollusks, ants, and higher mammals. The bibliography of Piéron contains about 500 items, but only two of his numerous books have been available in English—*Thought and the Brain* (1927), now obsolete, and *The Sensations* (1952). International recognition of Piéron's position in modern psychology is manifest in his election as president of the International Union of Scientific Psychology and in the numerous honors that universities of many countries bestowed upon him over the years. From 1913 until his death he was editor of *L'Année Psychologique*, a highly regarded psychological journal, distinguished among other things by its extensive review of world wide psychological literature and its chronicle of important events in psychology. His last major work was a seven volume book on applied psychology and testing, *Examens et docimologie* (1963).

Other prominent French experimentalists were Benjamin Bourdon, Georges Dumas, and Paul Guillaume. *Benjamin Bourdon* (1860-1943) was an early pioneer of experimental psychology. He was described as "a man of *his* laboratory, which he had founded on his own initiative at the Faculté des Lettres at Rennes, in 1896, and for whose development he dedicated his whole career and his whole life." Most of his research was centered around sensation and perception, especially the visual perception of space. *Georges Dumas* (1866-1946), a professor of psychology at the Sorbonne, is well known as the author of a large two volume treatise on psychology and editor and coauthor of a monumental multivolume new treatise, *Nouveau traité du psychologie. Paul Guillaume* (1878-1962)— a professor at the Sorbonne until 1947 and author of a significant book on Gestalt psychology—represented French behaviorism (psychology of comportment). His main research was with children and monkeys, the latter in collaboration with Ignace Meyerson. In his book, *Introduction à la psychologie* (1943), Guillaume's theme was the similarity between psychology and physics and the study of man by the same procedures as those used in the study of the natural world. An active experimentalist, *Paul Fraisse* (b. 1911) succeeded Piéron as director of the Sorbonne Laboratory in 1952. He distinguished himself by his studies on time perception, presented in *Les Structures rhythmiques* ("Rhythmic Structures," 1956) and in *La Psychologie du temps* (1957), which was translated into English as *The Psychology of Time* (1963), and which is probably the most important extant work on this subject.

Other Fields.   A field which has grown steadily and rapidly in France is psychotechnology and testing. In the postwar period, other new fields have appeared and the development of the old ones has accelerated. Among the new ones are, for example, psychopharmacology, psychosomatics, and ethology; among the older ones are genetic, child and social psychology.

Characterology, a discipline traditionally popular on the Continent, has also been pursued in France. Its chief exponent has been *René La Senne*, author of a treatise on characterology. By "character" he means the permanent structure of innate attributes or traits which constitute the psychological makeup of the human being. Largely owing to the example of America, the French now accord more value to statistics, factorial analysis, and mathematical models. One of the postwar developments in France has been existential psychology and existential psychiatry, whose rise and success is recounted in a later chapter.

Evaluation.   French psychology has been more independent of foreign influences than has the psychology of other nations. In the beginning, the theoretical framework of the new psychology in France came from British associationism, and experimental psychology got its inspiration from Germany. But soon French psychology severed itself from the school of associationism mainly because associationism was repudiated by Binet and Janet. Moreover, French experimental psychology departed from the German model and pursued a course which corresponded better to its views and interests. The indigenous forces were the strongest ones in shaping the character and orientation of France's psychology. As to American psychology, its influence on French psychology prior to 1940 was minimal. For the French in general had neither interest in, nor respect for, the kind of psychology that was developing in the United States. Janet seems to have summed up French opinion about American psychology when he said: "The Americans, they have magnificent edifices, impressive laboratories, but no psychology."

The predominant emphasis in France was on psychopathology. Laboratory psychology occupied a modest place. Its scope and achievements were relatively limited. The close union of psychology and psychiatry, so characteristic of France, proved to be harmful in its consequences for psychology. Psychiatry dominated psychology too long and prevented it from venturing beyond psychopathology. Associated with neurology and organically oriented, psychiatry hampered the development of clinical and counseling psychology as independent spheres of operation. The result is that despite the French intense interest in psychopathology, clinical psychology is not developed on a par with that of other countries. Little has been done to train clinical psychologists, and the practice of psychotherapy without a medical degree is legally forbidden in France.

If American psychology prior to the Second World War did not have much appeal for the French, so too the Americans on the whole were not interested in French developments. Binet's intelligence test was a notable exception. Ignored in France, it was enthusiastically received here for its usefulness, and, although modified substantially and standardized, it consistently acknowledged its author in the title even after several revisions. But perhaps, as some authors have observed, Americans could have learned more from the French. Piéron, reviewing an American book on the senses, noted the complete omission of French contributions, in particular, and European in general. He remarked: "It seems, that it is intended to give the impression that America alone contributes to the development of science, an attitude symmetrical to that of Russia." However, after World War II, the situation is different. Franco-American relations in psychology are improving. Unless we are misreading the signs, it appears that the doors are opened wider now to a livelier traffic of ideas between the two countries—in France, to the American objectivistic and quantitative approach in psychology and, in America, to the French subjectivistic and phenomenological-existential approach.

FRENCH-SPEAKING PSYCHOLOGISTS IN SWITZERLAND

There is still another group of European psychologists whose principal works are written in the French language, although they themselves are not French but Swiss or Belgian. A prominent Belgian psychologist, Albert Michotte, is discussed in Chapter 21. Among the Swiss French-speaking psychologists, three—Flournoy, Claparède, and Piaget—have attained international recognition. *Théodore Flournoy* (1854-1920) was the initiator of scientific psychology in Switzerland. After attending Wundt's lectures at Leipzig, he taught psychology and opened a laboratory (1892) at the University of Geneva. Here one of his first students was his cousin, *Edouard Claparède* (1873-1940), with whom he founded the *Archives de Psychologie* (1901). Flournoy did research on perception and hypnosis and made Geneva an active psychological center. In 1909 the Sixth International Congress of Psychology convened in Geneva, and Flournoy was its president. For many years Claparède served as secretary of the International Congress.

At Flournoy's death (1920) Claparède received his chair and assumed charge of the laboratory. In the beginning of his career Claparède had a biological orientation. Later he became a functionalist, studying psychical phenomena in terms of their usefulness in meeting the individual's needs and interests. Claparède promoted animal psychology and above all encouraged child study. To improve teacher training and to advance the scientific study of children, he established the J. J. Rousseau Institute. This institute became well known for its researches in child psychology and for the development of progressive methods of teaching.

A psychologist who has brought much distinction to the Institute is Claparède's successor in the chair of experimental psychology, and director of the psychological laboratory at Geneva, *Jean Piaget* (b. 1896). Piaget is a developmental psychologist, logician, educator, and philosopher. For more than 40 years Piaget and his associates—notable among them *B. Inhelder* (b. 1913), professor at the University of Geneva—have developed original studies of children and broad theories of intellectual and perceptual development. From the standpoint of genetic epistemology, Piaget has studied children's language and thought, intelligence, moral judgment, and reasoning. He has described his findings in numerous articles and books, including *The Language and Thought of the Child* (1924), *The Moral Judgment of the Child* (1932), and *The Psychology of Intelligence* (1950). A systematic thinker, critical of Gestalt psychology, Piaget distinguishes sharply between the functions of intelligence and perception and maintains that perceptual organization changes with mental development. Piaget's influence has extended beyond the psychology of child and adolescent to the general area of perception, cognition, intelligence, personality, and motivational theory. Although for a long time Piaget was relatively unknown in America, more recently his works have been translated into English, and his ideas have stimulated much research.

ITALY

Italy took early cognizance of scientific psychology and joined other countries in developing the new science. The attainments of Italian psychologists, while of consequence, were not equal in importance to those made by contemporary Italian scientists in allied areas like psychiatry and neurology. The contributions of Italy in these latter fields have attracted world-wide attention. For example, the first homes for the insane were established in Italy as early as the fourteenth century. The psychiatric hospital, Santa Maria della Pietà in Rome, founded in 1548 and still functioning, is the oldest in the country. The reforms in the treatment of patients, effected by Chiarugi (1759-1820), actually antedated those of the French physician Pinel. Chiarugi was also the author of the first Italian text in psychiatry. Therapeutic methods used in Naples in the middle of the nineteenth century were strikingly progressive.

Beginnings and Pioneers. Materialistic positivism had a strong hold on early Italian psychology. This was due to the powerful and enduring influence of Roberto Ardigò, professor at Padua University, who in 1870 published *La Psicologia come scienza positiva* ("Psychology as a Positive Science") and in 1898 *Unità della coscienza* ("Unity of Consciousness"). In these works Ardigò identified all mental life with cerebral physiology. The idealist opponents of the positivism of Ardigò and his followers regarded psychology as an offspring of positivism and as a pseudo-philosophy. As a result of the idealistic reaction, psychology was greatly reduced or entirely eliminated in the university curricula. During the early period of development of psychology in Italy, the centers of study were the Universities of Rome, Florence, and Turin.

The pioneer Italian psychologist was *Giuseppe Sergi* (1841-1936), a professor at the University of Rome. His book *Principi di psicologia* ("Principles of Psychology"), published in 1873—the same year as Wundt's first volume of *Grundzüge der physiologischen Psychologie*— marks the beginning of Italian psychology. In 1885 Sergi established the first Italian psychological laboratory as a section of the Institute of Anthropology in Rome.

Another pioneer was *Francesco de Sarlo* (1864-1937), Brentano's devoted disciple at the University of Florence. Through his efforts, the first institute of psychology was opened in Florence in 1903. De Sarlo was a philosopher, psychiatrist, surgeon, and psychologist. His views in psychiatry anticipated the psychobiological concept—later to become so popular—but without violation of the traditional dualism. De Sarlo received his training from the director of the Psychiatric Hospital in Reggio Emilia, *Augusto Tamburini*. Tamburini was greatly interested in psychology and influenced its development in Italy through his students, especially De Sarlo, G. Buccola, and C. G. Ferrari. It was Tamburini who first popularized the concept of mental hygiene among the Italians. Buccola (1854-1885) was the author of *La Legge del tempo nei fenomeni del pensiero* ("The Law of Time in the Thought Phenomena," 1883)—a work which provided an impetus to psychological research in Italy. Ferrari (1869-1932) contributed substantially to the development of psychology. With Tamburini, he founded both a psychological laboratory in Reggio Emilia in 1896 and the magazine *Rivista di Psicologia*. In 1901, Ferrari translated William James's *Principles of Psychology*, which stirred up further interest and activity in psychology.

In Turin, psychological problems were introduced into physiology by *Angelo Mosso* (1846-1910) and into criminal anthropology by *Cesare Lombroso* (1835-1909). The former is known to psychologists for his ergograph and for his pioneering research on work and fatigue. His books, *La Paura* ("Fear," 1884) and *La Fatica* ("Fatigue," 1891), were translated into many languages, including English. Lombroso became known for his *L'Uomo delinquente* ("The Delinquent Man," 1876) and was hailed as the forerunner of constitutional psychology. In general, Italians have done much research in an attempt to establish the relationship between physique and personality on the basis of anthropometric techniques. In 1895 Mosso's laboratory was turned over to *Friedrich Kiesow* (1858-1940), a disciple and former assistant of Wundt and a friend of Külpe. Kiesow brought from Leipzig to Turin not only the knowledge of experimental techniques, but also an enthusiasm for experimentation in psychology. For many years he was the foremost experimentalist in Italy. His own work was mainly in the field of sensation, in taste and touch especially. Among Kiesow's students were Gemelli and Ponzo. Another experimentalist imported from abroad was *Vittorio Benussi* (1878-1927), who, although born in Italy, lived in Austria for many years and became an outstanding experimentalist there. After World War I he went to Padua, taught psychology at the university, and opened a laboratory. His studies on perception, respiration, suggestibility, and hypnosis received recognition both in Italy and abroad.

A special place among Italy's pioneers in psychology is held by *Sante De Sanctis* (1863-1935), an eminent figure not only in psychology, but also in psychiatry. Through his enthusiasm for the new science, his versatile activities, and his writings, he left a deep impression on Italian psychology. He succeeded his teacher, Sergi, as head of the school of Rome and became the first graduate teacher of experimental psychology in Italy. While practically all fields of theoretical and applied psychology were explored by De Sanctis, his best energies were devoted to child study and to understanding and helping the mentally deficient and the abnormal. His publications were numerous, original, and influential. Interested in sleep and dreams, De Sanctis published several studies on the subject in 1896. He wrote a lengthy monograph, *I Sogni* ("Dreams"), in 1899, which preceded the work of Freud in that area. Other important writings of De Sanctis include *La Mimica del pensiero* ("The Imitation of Thought," 1904), *Psicologia sperimentale* ("Experimental Psychology," vol. I, 1929; vol. II, 1930), and *La Conversione religiosa* (1924; translated into English as *Religious Conversions: a Bio-Psychological Study*, 1927).

Progress after 1905. In 1905, the Fifth International Congress of Psychology was held in Rome and proved to be one of the most provocative psychological congresses. At this congress, the first scale of intelligence, the Binet-Simon, and William James's paper, "La Conscience existe-t-elle?" ("Does consciousness exist?") were given prominence. In general, the congress found psychology in Italy firmly established. The work of Italian psychologists and of their laboratories was already well recognized. There was lively interest in child study. Studies in this field conducted in Britain, Germany, and France were matched by Italian medical and biological studies of the child. De Sanctis and Ferrari had already distinguished themselves in that field, and Maria Montessori was about to launch her new educational movement. Two currents of psychological thought were dominant in the country—one stemming from Wundt, the other from Münsterberg.

One significant practical outcome of the congress for Italy was that in 1906 the ministry of education formally instituted three autonomous chairs of psychology on the university level. These were located in Rome, Turin, and Naples and were awarded, respectively, to De Sanctis, Kiesow, and Cesare Colucci. De Sanctis was later succeeded by Mario Ponzo, Kiesow by Alessandro Gatti, and Gatti, after his premature death, by Angiola Massucco Costa. Gradually other centers of psychological research and teaching were developed in Florence, Padua, Milan, and Genoa.

The initial interest and the creation of new chairs of psychology did not generate any significant scientific contributions from Italy, however. No doubt, Italian political and social conditions contributed to this lack of productivity. Principally, however, it was the prevailing ideological climate of the country which was responsible for holding Italian psychology back. This climate was clearly averse to the scientific orientation of modern psychology then taking shape in other countries in the 1920's and 1930's. Despite such unfavorable atmosphere, Italian psychology scored a few notable successes during this period. These include the formation of the Italian Psychological Association; the establishment of a modern psychological laboratory at the Catholic University in Milan; the opening of an experimental center for applied psychology in the National Research Council; and the scholastic reform of 1935, which made psychology a required subject in certain academic curricula.

Maria Montessori (1870-1952). The application of psychology to the education of both normal and mentally defective children was successfully made by Maria Montessori, world-renowned educational reformer. Her life was devoted entirely to the study and education of children. Italy's first woman doctor of medicine (1894), she was also probably the first woman student of experimental psychology and pedagogy at the University of Rome. After several years of experience in a psychiatric clinic and in a hospital for defective children, she founded the Orthophrenic School for feebleminded and defective children. Later, in 1907, in the slum district of Rome, she opened the first Montessori school under the name Casa dei Bambini ("House of Children"). Here she developed and applied her own method, later known as the Montessori system. This system was at first used with children of preschool age (three to six years) and then extended to older children. The main characteristics of this system were "free discipline" of children, individual attention, and emphasis on training of the senses.

Maria Montessori lectured and wrote extensively on both her own method and education in general. Leading educational centers throughout the world invited her to lecture. She also visited and lectured in the United States. Her major works have been translated into 14 languages. In English, there are *The Montessori Method* (1912), *Pedagogical Anthropology* (1913), *The Advanced Montessori Method* (1917), and *The Child in the Church* (1930).

Trends in Italian Psychology.   Following the period of interest in psychophysics, perception, and child study—so prominent prior to 1920—the emphasis in contemporary Italian psychology shifted to applied fields. A number of private and public centers for psychotechnical research were opened, and almost all leading psychologists were engaged at some time or other in applied psychology. Aptitude testing and vocational guidance received special attention. Strong efforts were made to extend psychology to education through the development of new methods based on the findings of child psychology. These efforts were realized by instituting projects for school reform, by training teachers in psychology, and by similar means. The psychology of personality, or characterology, attracted many adherents. However, psychoanalysis both as a doctrine and as a method has had more opponents than followers.

Leading Schools and Psychologists.   The important centers of psychology have been the University of Rome, the Catholic University in Milan, the University of Florence, and the National Institute of Psychology in Rome. Almost invariably, leading Italian psychologists have been identified with these places.

University of Rome.   As mentioned above, the teaching and the laboratory of psychology were begun there by Sergi. Under the subsequent direction of Sante De Sanctis, student and collaborator of Sergi, the school of Rome flourished and gained prestige. It became the most important and most influential center under the leadership of De Sanctis' successor, *Mario Ponzo* (1882-1960), who for many years was the representative psychologist of Italy.

Ponzo studied in Turin, where he received the doctorate in medicine and later taught psychology, from 1905 to 1931. He was Kiesow's student and subsequently his colleague and collaborator. In 1931 he went to Rome to take the chair of psychology and to head the Institute of Psychology until his death. Ponzo was president of the Italian Psychological Association, which after many years of inactivity was revived in 1951. He was also a member of the Executive Committee of the International Union of Scientific Psychology.

An indefatigable worker and an unusually prolific writer, Ponzo was for a long time concerned with psychophysical problems, especially with touch and taste. Later he extended his research to other fields. After 1940 he devoted himself particularly to applied psychology. With a profound conviction in the usefulness and possibilities of applied psychology, Ponzo fought strenuously for its recognition in education, in industry, in vocational guidance, and in personnel selection. His own studies are valuable contributions to aptitude testing and professional selection. According to Ponzo, vocational guidance should not be based solely on the assessment of aptitudes or intelligence, but on the general personality characteristics. Personality, character, and the natural inclinations of the individual were frequently stressed by Ponzo as primary considerations, whether in vocational guidance, personnel selection, or accident prevention. Recognition and growth of applied psychology and emphasis on the problems of applied psychology in contemporary Italian psychology were to a great degree the result of Ponzo's work. His writings and activities also produced practical effects in various spheres of the national life of Italy.

Leandro Canestrelli (b. 1908) succeeded Ponzo as the head of the Institute. He distinguished himself by original studies of psychomotor activity and by his development and use of a special technique for photographing the trajectories covered during movement in the study of voluntary acts.

Catholic University in Milan. One of the best equipped and most active laboratories in continental Europe has been that at the Catholic University in Milan. It was established and directed by *Agostino Gemelli* (1878-1959), the most prominent Italian psychologist, and a priest, whose influence changed the attitude of Catholics towards psychology in this traditionally Catholic country. Gemelli's work marks a new era in Italian psychology.

Gemelli first studied medicine. After earning his doctorate in medicine and surgery, he continued research as an assistant to professor Camillo Golgi (1844-1926), great anatomist, physician, and a Nobel Prize winner. During this period he also studied philosophy and engaged in social and political activities. Abandoning religion, he embraced materialism and Marxism but gradually became dissatisfied with these systems. After returning to the Church, Gemelli entered the Franciscan order and was ordained a priest in 1906. From 1907 to 1911 he studied biology, physiology, and philosophy at various universities in Bonn, Frankfurt, Munich, Cologne, Vienna, Louvain, Amsterdam, and Paris. In 1911, he completed his doctorate in philosophy at the University of Louvain.

The man who gave Gemelli his initial training in experimental psychology was Kiesow. Gemelli also studied with Külpe at Bonn, then went with him to Munich, working in Külpe's laboratories there. Gemelli renewed his association with Kiesow in 1914 when he accepted an appointment by the Italian government to teach psychology at the University of Turin. There, with Kiesow, he founded the journal *Archivio di Psicologia, Neurologia e Psichiatria.*

During World War I, Gemelli became known for his work in the selection of pilots. After the war his efforts were directed toward founding a

Catholic university. This school was officially opened in 1921 in Milan as "The Catholic University of the Sacred Heart in Milan." From its founding Gemelli was rector of the university and did much to promote teaching and research in psychology there. In later years, Gemelli conducted a large number of original researches and published many books and articles. His bibliography comprises several hundred items. Among them, *Introduzione alla psicologia* ("Introduction to Psychology," first edition in 1947, fourth edition in 1957), written in collaboration with Giorgio Zunini, has been acclaimed as the most complete theoretical work of modern Italian psychology. The work of the Laboratory of Psychology at the Catholic University has been fruitful. Its productivity is demonstrated in the numerous volumes of a special series, *Contributi del Laboratorio di Psicologia* (now over 25 volumes). The research at the Laboratory is diversified. It is now under the direction of Gemelli's successor, *Leonardo Ancona* (b. 1922), author of several experimental studies and a survey of social psychology in the United States (1954). Ancona directs also a postgraduate training program—probably at present the best of its kind in Italy—in clinical psychology for candidates already holding M.D. or Ph.D. degrees.

University of Florence. De Sarlo, founder and director of the first institute of psychology in Italy at Florence, was succeeded by *Enzo Bonaventura* (1891-1948). Bonaventura demonstrated the significance of empirical factors in perception, especially in the perception of time and space. Of several volumes that he published, the most successful was his book on psychoanalysis, *La Psicoanalisi* ("Psychoanalysis," last edition in 1950).

Bonaventura's successor in 1938 was *Alberto Marzi* (b. 1907), a prominent figure in contemporary Italian psychology. In addition to studies in his native country, he studied in England, France, and the United States. His research has included a variety of fields such as attention, eidetic imagery, intelligence of deaf mutes, endocrinopathies, and psychotechnical problems. Marzi's projects include translation of foreign psychological tests. In his book *Problemi ed esperienze di psicologia del lavoro* ("Problems and Experiments of the Psychology of Work," 1957) he presents the status of Italian psychotechnology.

The National Institute of Psychology in Rome was founded in 1940. Administratively it is part of the governmental "Consiglio Nazionale delle Ricerche" (abbreviated C.N.R.) or National Research Council. The Institute and its 14 collaborating laboratories throughout Italy furnish scientific counsel and guidance to public and governmental agencies on a variety of psychological problems. The Institute also sponsors the development and standardization of psychological tests.

The organizer of the National Institute was *Ferruccio Banissoni* (1888-1952). After studies in Vienna and Rome, he received the doctorate in medicine and later assumed the professorship of psychology at the University of Rome. His work, broad in scope, original and progressive in character, left its mark on many fields of experimental and applied psychology. As head of the psychological section of the National Research

Council, Banissoni inspired and directed several research projects in applied psychology. The directorship of the National Institute of Psychology, after Banissoni's death, was turned over to L. Canestrelli. The current director is Luigi Meschieri (b. 1919), one of the most active and influential psychologists in the country.

Psychology at the Gregorian University in Rome.   The Pontifical Gregorian University in Rome merits attention because of its role in the training of the Catholic clergy from all over the world.   Tracing its origin to the sixteenth century, the Gregorian University, administered and staffed by the members of the Society of Jesus (Jesuits), is now an international institution.   In the scholastic year 1960-1961 it had 2,860 registrants from 70 nations.   Its primary aim is to provide students with training in theology, philosophy, and canon law.   Many professors of these subjects at American religious institutions have been graduates of Gregorian University.   The Gregorian initiated instruction in scientific psychology by appointing *Joseph Fröbes* (1866-1947)—a psychologist and author of a successful two volume textbook of experimental psychology in German— to give a course in experimental psychology.   This appointment was a step of special significance because it was a formal recognition of psychology as separate and independent from philosophy in circles which traditionally regarded psychology as an integral part of philosophy.   Among professors of scientific psychology appointed to the faculty at the Gregorian University were well-recognized scholars—among them Johannes Lindworsky, Alexander Willwoll, Paul Siwek, André Godin, and Francesco Gaetani. One of the present psychology professors is Francis Nowlan, whose doctorate in psychology is from Harvard University.   The university offers a wide variety of courses in various fields of psychology, some of which are obligatory for all philosophy and theology students.

Clinical Psychology.   An event of significance for the development of clinical psychology in Italy was the first "Symposium of Clinical Psychology," organized by Gemelli in Milan in 1952 and attended by prominent psychologists and psychiatrists.   Considering the prestige Gemelli enjoyed in the country, his concern with clinical problems and active support of clinical psychology gave strong impetus to the growth of this field. Gemelli viewed clinical psychology as "a complex of diagnostic methods, clinical interpretations and therapeutic techniques."   To Gemelli, psychotherapy represented clinical psychology's "principal instrument."   Another historical event, which had repercussions in the clinical field in Italy and elsewhere as well, was the address of Pope Pius XII to the Fifth International Congress of Psychotherapy and Clinical Psychology in Rome in 1953.   In this address, the Pope stressed the importance of clinical psychology and various forms of psychotherapy and outlined the complex moral, social, and religious problems facing psychotherapy.   In Italy, whose traditions and life are so closely tied with the Catholic Church, the "warm interest" and "best wishes" of the Church for the research and clinical practice, as expressed in the Pope's statement, could not but considerably strengthen the cause of clinical psychology.

It has been estimated that about one-fifth of all Italian psychologists are engaged in full-time, and one-third in part-time, clinical activities. Training in clinical psychology is at the postgraduate level after receipt of the Ph.D. and usually the M.D. degree. Italian clinical psychologists generally have the doctorate in medicine. Qualified clinical psychologists work (in order of decreasing frequency) in: child guidance clinics, juvenile courts and prisons, mental hospitals, university teaching, public schools, armed forces, and research centers. Their work is psychodiagnostic for the most part. Psychotherapy is done rarely at these institutions. But there is private practice of psychotherapy. Most of the qualified psychotherapists are Freudian psychoanalysts. The legally recognized "specialists in psychology" are those who either received specialized postgraduate training at schools of psychology approved by the state or who, after passing a state examination and meeting certain requirements of research, received the title "Libero Docente."

Evaluation. In comparison to other countries, psychology in Italy developed slowly. Progress of psychology in Italy was hindered by resistance to accepting the scientific character of psychology. Even when psychology was generally accepted as an experimental and independent science in the 1920's, its popularity was not great and its influence was limited. University chairs of psychology were few, and the number of laboratories small and their work narrow in scope. After World War II, Italian psychology showed greater strength and vitality. Teaching and research have expanded, writing has greatly increased, new journals have appeared, and the Italian Psychological Association has become more active. Currently some courses in psychology are taught at 18 universities in various departments spread from psychology to law and medicine, but permanently appointed professors of psychology are still few. There are about 300 qualified psychologists recognized by the Italian Psychological Association. Bologna, the oldest university in Europe, has instituted the teaching of psychology for the first time in its history. Research has extended to almost all fields of psychology, the most active being perception, developmental, clinical, social, and industrial psychology. The National Institute of Psychology in Rome concentrates on testing programs, selection and training of personnel for the armed forces, and other government agencies. There is an increasing demand for industrial psychologists. They receive training in special postgraduate courses. Much effort has been exerted toward developing clinical psychology and providing clinical training.

Italian psychologists are well acquainted with psychology in the United States and with current American psychological literature. Many of the prominent Italian psychologists studied at American universities or spent some time at psychological centers in America. Several standard American intelligence, personality, projective, and personnel selection tests have been translated into Italian and used for practical and research purposes.

SUMMARY

GREAT BRITAIN

Major influences. Philosophical: British associationism (James Mill and John Stuart Mill; A. Bain); and J. Ward and G. F. Stout.

Biological: theory of evolution (Darwin).

Pioneers. H. Spencer (1820–1903), J. Sully (1842–1923), F. Galton (1822–1911).

Experimental psychology: W. H. R. Rivers (1864–1922).

Comparative: C. L. Morgan (1852–1936).

First laboratories. Cambridge (1897), London (1897).

Leaders. W. McDougall (1871–1938).

Experimental: C. S. Myers (1873–1946), James Drever, [Sr.] (1873–1950), F. Bartlett (b. 1886).

Differential, psychometrics: C. Spearman (1863–1945), C. Burt (b. 1883), P. E. Vernon (b. 1905).

Educational: G. H. Thomson (1881–1955), C. W. Valentine (1879–1964).

Clinical: H. J. Eysenck (b. 1916).

Main emphases. Cognitive functions, learning, thinking.

Educational psychology, educational tests.

Statistics, factorial analysis.

Industrial.

FRANCE

Major influences. Philosophical: E. Condillac; P. J. G. Cabanis; H. Taine; A. Comte; initially, also British associationism.

Others: psychiatry, neurology, J. M. Charcot.

Pioneers. T. Ribot (1839–1916), A. Binet (1857–1911).

Experimental psychology: B. Bourdon (1860–1943).

First laboratory. Sorbonne (1889).

Leaders. Psychopathology: P. Janet (1859–1947), D. Lagache (b. 1903).

Experimental: H. Piéron (1881–1964), G. Dumas (1863–1946), P. Fraisse (b. 1911).

Genetic: H. Wallon (1879–1962).

Main emphases. Psychopathology, neuroses.

Psychophysiology.

ITALY

Major influences. Philosophical: positivism, R. Ardigo.

Others: psychiatry.

Pioneers. G. Sergi (1841–1936), F. de Sarlo (1867–1937), S. De Sanctis (1863–1935).

Experimental: F. Kiesow (1858–1940).

First laboratory. Rome (1885).

Leaders. A. Gemelli (1878–1959), M. Ponzo (1882–1960), E. Bonaventura (1891–1948), F. Banissoni (1888–1952), A. Marzi (b. 1907).

Main emphases. Child guidance, personnel selection, industrial psychology, clinical psychology.

REFERENCES

GREAT BRITAIN

Bartlett, F. C. Cambridge, England: 1887–1937. *Amer. J. Psychol.*, 1937, *50*, 97–110.

Bartlett, F. C. Changing scene. *Brit. J. Psychol.*, 1956, *47*, 81–87.

Broadhurst, P. L., & Martin, Irene. Comparative and physiological psychology in Britain: 1960. *Bull. Brit. Psychol. Soc.*, 1961, *45*, 41–55.

Burt, C. Francis Galton and his contributions to psychology. *Brit. J. stat. Psychol.*, 1962, *15*, 1–49.

Carver, Vida (Ed.) *C. A. Mace, A symposium.* London: Methuen & Penguin, 1962.

Denton, G. B. Early psychological theories of Herbert Spencer. *Amer. J. Psychol.*, 1921, *32*, 5–15.

Drever, J. The historical background for national trends in psychology: on the non-existence of English Associationism. *J. Hist. behav. Sci.*, 1965, *1*, 123–130.

Flugel, J. C. A hundred years or so of psychology at University College, London. *Bull. Brit. Psychol. Soc.*, 1954, *23*, 21–31.

Hearnshaw, L. S. *A short history of British psychology 1840–1940.* New York: Barnes & Noble, 1964.

Mace, C. A. The permanent contribution to psychology of George Frederick Stout. *Brit. J. educ. Psychol.*, 1954, *24*, 64–75.

Mace, C. A., & Vernon, P. E. (Eds.) *Current trends in British psychology.* London: Methuen, 1953.

Monchaux, Cecily & Keir, Gertrude H. British psychology 1945–1957. *Acta Psychol. (Amst.)*, 1961, *18*, 120–180.

Ribot, T. A. *English psychology.* New York: Appleton-Century-Crofts, 1874.

Russell, R. W., & Summerfield, A. British psychologists, their training and placement, 1949–1951. *Bull. Brit. Psychol. Soc.*, 1956, *28*, 29–50.

Summerfield, A. Clinical psychology in Britain. *Amer. Psychologist*, 1958, *13*, 171–176.

Zangwill, O. L. The Cambridge psychological laboratory. *Bull. Brit. Psychol. Soc.*, 1962, *48*, 22–24.

Autobiographies of eminent British psychologists have been published in *A history of psychology in autobiography.* Worcester, Mass.: Clark Univer. Press, 1930–1952. 4 vols. The first three volumes edited by C. Murchison, the fourth by E. G. Boring, *et al.* Carl Spearman and William McDougall in Vol. 1, James Drever and C. Lloyd Morgan in Vol. 2, Frederic C. Bartlett and Charles S. Myers in Vol. 3. Cyril Burt and Godfrey H. Thomson in Vol. 4

FRANCE

Bailey, P. Janet and Freud. *A.M.A. Arch. Neurol. Psychiat.*, 1956, *76*, 76–89.

Bertrand, F. L. *Alfred Binet et son oeuvre.* Paris: Alcan, 1930.

Beuchet, J. Benjamin Bourdon, pionnier de la psychologie expérimentale. *Bulletin de Psychologie*, 1962, *16*, 162–175.

Beuchet, J. L'oeuvre de Benjamin Bourdon. *Bulletin de Psychologie*, 1962, *16*, 176–227.

Cardno, J. A. Auguste Comte's psychology. *Psychol. Rep.*, 1958, *4*, 423–430.

Centenaire de Th. Ribot, *jubilé de la Psychologie scientifique française.* Agen: Imprimerie moderne, 1939.

Fraisse, P. L'oeuvre d'Alfred Binet en psychologie expérimentale. *Rev. Psychologie française*, 1958, *3*, 1–8.

Fraisse, P. Psychologie expérimentale d'hier et d'aujourd'hui. *Bulletin de Psychologie*, 1962, *16*, 238–242.

Mayo, E. *The psychology of Pierre Janet.* London: Routledge & Kegan Paul, 1951.

Meyerson, I. Paul Guillaume. *J. Psychol. norm. path.*, 1962, *59*, 1–13.

Piéron, H. Cinquante ans de psychologie française. *Année psychol.*, 1951, *51*, 552–563.

Reuchlin, M. The historical background for national trends in psychology: France. *J. Hist. behav. Sci.*, 1965, *1*, 115–122.

Richard, J. F. Les recherches expérimentales de Bourdon sur l'association et les phénomènes intellectuels. *Bulletin de Psychologie*, 1962, *16*, 228–236.

Silverman, H. L., & Krenzel, K. Alfred Binet: prolific pioneer in psychology. *Psychiat. Quart., Suppl.*, 1964, *38*, 323–335.

Taylor, W. S. Pierre Janet, 1859–1947. *Amer. J. Psychol.*, 1947, *60*, 637–645.

Wolf, Theta H. An individual who made a difference. *Amer. Psychologist*, 1961, *16*, 245–248. (On T. Simon)

Wolf, Theta H. Alfred Binet: a time of crisis. *Amer. Psychologist*, 1964, *19*, 762–771.

Woods, Evelyn A., & Carlson, E. T. The psychiatry of Philippe Pinel. *Bull. Hist. Med.*, 1961, *35*, 14–25.

Zazzo, R. Portrait d'Henri Wallon (1879–1962). *J. Psychol. norm. path.*, 1963, *60*, 386–400.

Autobiographies of eminent French psychologists have been published in C. Murchison

(Ed.), *A history of psychology in autobiography*. Worcester, Mass.: Clark Univer. Press, 1930–1952. 4 vols. Pierre Janet in Vol. 1, Benjamin Bourdon in Vol. 2, Henri Piéron in Vol. 4.

SWITZERLAND

Flavell, J. H. *The developmental psychology of Jean Piaget*. Princeton, N. J.: Van Nostrand, 1963.

Müller, P. Suisse. *Gawein*, 1956, *4*, 68–76.

Tuddenham, R. D. Jean Piaget and the world of the child. *Amer. Psychologist*, 1966, *21*, 207–217.

Autobiographies of Edouard Claparède and Jean Piaget have been published in C. Murchison (Ed.), *A history of psychology in autobiography*. Worcester, Mass.: Clark Univer. Press, 1930–1952. 4 vols. Edouard Claparède in Vol. 1 and Jean Piaget in Vol. 4.

ITALY

Appicciafuoco, R. *La psicologia sperimentale di Sante De Sanctis*. Rome: Orsa Maggiore, 1946.

Benussi, V. Die Psychologie in Italien. *Arch. Gesam. Psychol.*, 1906, *7*, Literaturbericht, 141–180.

Canella, M. F. La psicologia sperimentale in Italia. *Riv. Psicol. norm. patol.*, 1933, *29*, 149–153.

Canestrelli, L. (Ed.) Current developments in applied psychology in Italy: a general review

to mark the Thirteenth International Congress to be held at Rome, April 9–14, 1958. *Bull. Ass. Int. Psychol. Appl.*, 1958, *7*, 2–77.

De Sanctis, S. Psychological science in Italy. *Scand. Sci. Rev.*, 1923, *2*, 114–118.

Lazzeroni, V., & Marzi, A. Psychology in Italy from 1945 to 1957. *Acta Psychol.* (*Amst.*), 1958, *14*, 54–80.

Manoil, A. *La psychologie expérimentale en Italie: Ecole de Milan*. Paris: Alcan, 1938.

Marzi, A. La psicologia in Italia dal 1939 al 1943. *Riv. Psicol.*, 1944–45, *40–41*, 193–207.

Misiak, H., & Staudt, Virginia. Psychology in Italy. *Psychol. Bull.*, 1953, *50*, 347–361.

Saffiotti, F. V. La evoluzione della psicologia sperimentale in Italia. *Riv. Psicol.*, 1920, *16*, 129–153.

Standing, E. M. *Maria Montessori: her life and work*. New York: New American Library, 1962.

Titchener, E. B. Experimental psychology in Italy. *Amer. J. Psychol.*, 1921, *32*, 597–598.

Autobiographies of eminent Italian psychologists have been published in C. Murchison (Ed.), *A history of psychology in autobiography*. Worcester, Mass.: Clark Univer. Press, 1930–1952. 4 vols. Friedrich Kiesow in Vol. 1, Giulio Cesare Ferrari in Vol. 2, Sante De Sanctis and Joseph Fröbes in Vol. 3, Agostino Gemelli in Vol. 4.

15

Psychology in The Soviet Union

WUNDTIAN PSYCHOLOGY WAS INTRODUCED INTO RUSSIA about the same time as it was introduced into other countries. It was, however, more short lived in Russia than elsewhere for political reasons, namely, the Bolshevik Revolution in 1917, the advent of Communism, and, with it, the promulgation of dialectical materialism. The development of Russian psychology after 1917 cannot be understood without reference to Marxist-Leninist doctrine. Since that time there has been an unending struggle to fashion dialectical psychology and to make dialectical psychology *the* Soviet psychology.

In considering the growth of psychology in Russia one cannot overlook the development of an allied science, psychophysiology, which traces its immediate historical roots to Sechenov and Pavlov. Their researches established the physiological bases of psychological science as it has been cultivated in the Soviet Union since 1950. After 1917 Pavlov had been regarded as a physiologist, and was therefore of secondary interest to psychologists. In 1950, however, Soviet psychology was Pavlovianized and thereafter Pavlov's psychophysiology, or "study of higher nervous activity," furnished the basic pattern for contemporary Soviet psychological investigations.

SECHENOV, THE FATHER OF RUSSIAN PHYSIOLOGY

The beginnings of Russian psychophysiology can be traced to Sechenov's study of reflexes. Sechenov's views and researches have formed the framework within which Pavlov began his researches and within which contemporary Soviet psychologists pursue their studies.

Life. After obtaining his medical degree at Moscow University (1856), the distinguished father of Russian physiology, Ivan M. Sechenov (1829-1905), went to Berlin (1856-1857) where he studied comparative anatomy with Johannes Müller shortly before that eminent German physiologist's death. He also attended lectures on animal electricity given by du Bois-Reymond under whose surveillance the young Russian conducted several electrophysiological researches. During 1857-1859 Sechenov visited Leipzig and Vienna studying the effects of acute alcoholic intoxication on the organism. In Vienna, he met Carl Ludwig, another world-renowned physiologist, who became Sechenov's lifelong friend. At Heidelberg in 1859, Sechenov studied optics with Helmholtz and the analyses of gases with Bunsen.

Returning to St. Petersburg (now Leningrad) in 1860 as assistant professor of physiology at the Medico-Surgical Academy, Sechenov lectured on bioelectrical phenomena—a phase of physiology scarcely known in mid-nineteenth century Russia. He presented simply and clearly the latest findings of Western European science and stimulated interest in independent scientific research. Convinced that the university should not only teach science, but that it should develop science, Sechenov opened a laboratory. This laboratory was soon swarming with eager, energetic young physiologists—including female students, whom Sechenov, the ardent protagonist of education for women, welcomed. Through his researches, lectures, and his daring, refreshing views, Sechenov's reputation grew in Russian intellectual circles and in the scientific world.

In 1862 Sechenov went to Paris to the laboratory of Claude Bernard, the French physiologist distinguished for his concern with the "internal environment." Sechenov attended Bernard's lectures and conducted researches on the nervous centers which inhibit reflex movements. Sechenov's findings on the central inhibition of reflex activity in the frog were hailed as interesting and convincing by Ludwig and du Bois-Reymond. But above all, his own researches convinced Sechenov of the need to assume a mechanistic, deterministic approach to psychology. Returning to St. Petersburg, he remained at the Academy until his resignation in 1870 (occasioned by the Academy's failure to appoint a candidate whom Sechenov had sponsored). After a six year interlude at Odessa, Sechenov became professor of physiology at St. Petersburg for another 12 years. In 1888, he took a lectureship at Moscow, and after three years was given a chair of physiology. Sechenov stayed there until his retirement, just four years before his death in 1905.

Throughout his life, because of his writings and teaching, and particularly after the publication of his *Reflexes of the Brain* (1863), Sechenov was a controversial figure. Philosophers criticized his materialism. They accused him of corrupting morals, because he attempted to reduce all physical manifestations to muscular action and because he was skeptical about man's ability to select his own mode of action. Russian medical men and scientists, on the other hand, lauded his work. Thus, Sechenov became the center of debates and bitter ideological battles.

Philosophical and Scientific Origins of Sechenov's Orientation. Unlike earlier years—when European scientists came to Russia to develop science at the invitation of Peter the Great—in Sechenov's day Russia was educating her own scientists. Many Russians, however, pursued their postgraduate work in other countries. As we have already noted, Sechenov himself trained in the two principal schools of nineteenth century physiology—the German and the French. Generally speaking, the German approach—mechanistic and materialistic—fragmented the living body and analyzed each separate element or structure in terms of the basic physical and chemical features of its functions. In marked contrast to their professor Johannes Müller, and his vitalism, du Bois-Reymond and Helmholtz represented a radical mechanistic and materialistic orientation in their studies of peripheral nerves and receptors. The same orientation also characterized Ludwig's researches on the heart.

The French approach in Bernard's laboratory was deterministic and was committed to the belief that vital processes follow fixed laws derivable by investigation. This approach sought to explain the performance of the total living organism and to establish broad principles that could account for the totality of vital processes. Through Sechenov these German and French influences worked their way into Russia. Finding neither school completely satisfactory, however, Sechenov developed his own formulation. He fashioned a new concept of psychology, an objective psychology which emerged from the following sources: sensory physiology and biology, particularly evolutionary theory; a materialistic trend in associationism; and the study of reflexes.

Design for an Objective Psychology. Sechenov regarded the emerging scientific psychology in Germany of the 1860's and 1870's as a significant and fascinating branch of knowledge. Yet he saw it as an inexact science requiring a solid scientific foundation. He wanted to construct this foundation on a physiological basis. As a physiologist, he attempted to establish a psychology that would investigate, from a psychological viewpoint, the development of individual elements of psychical processes, their manner of combination, and the underlying mechanisms involved. In his essay, *Who Must Investigate the Problems of Psychology and How* (1873; the same year that Wundt's first volume of the *Principles* appeared) Sechenov demonstrated that the only solution was to study psychological problems as if they were new and to explain the complex in terms of the simple. To him, reflexes were the things to study, and physiologists were the ones to study psychological problems. Animals were to be used as subjects of investigation since there was no proven difference between man and animals. Phenomenological methods were to be avoided because the nature of psychical states was unknown. On the other hand, statistics and mathematics were regarded as valuable tools.

Sechenov's objective psychology was based on five specific theses: (1) Its philosophical orientation was psychophysiologic, materialistic monism, reducing bodily and psychical phenomena to muscular movement. In Sechenov's own words:

> All the endless diversity of the external manifestations of the activity of the brain can be finally regarded as one phenomenon—that of muscular movement. Be it a child laughing at the sight of toys, or Garibaldi smiling when he is persecuted for his excessive love of his fatherland; a girl trembling at the first thought of love, or Newton enunciating universal laws and writing them on paper . . . everywhere the final manifestation is muscular movement.

(2) It equated reflex action to physiological and psychical reactions. Moreover, it considered both conscious and unconscious acts reflex, from the point of view of their mechanisms.

(3) It viewed the reflex as the mechanism of association. Sechenov says:

> An association is . . . an uninterrupted series of contacts of the end of every preceding reflex with the beginning of the following one. The end of a reflex is always a movement; and a movement is always accompanied by muscular sensations. Therefore, if we regard the association as a series of central activities, we may define it as an unbroken series of sensations.

(4) The psychic is associative in genesis and central-neural in mediation. Not only simple associations, but their total integration, are reflex in nature and origin. Association is a precondition of concrete elementary knowledge and its neural mediation is central.

(5) Finally, Sechenov's objective psychology was characterized by extreme environmentalism. While he admitted that individual peculiarities and differences of the central nervous system were present at birth—differences that stem from immediate family and racial influences—he stated:

> It is impossible, however, to ascertain these peculiarities, for in the majority of the cases, 999/1000 of the contents of the mind depend on education in the broadest sense of this word, and only 1/1000 depends on individuality. Of course, I do not ascertain that you can make a wise man out of a fool. This would be the same as to say that you can develop hearing in a man born without the acoustic nerve. What I really mean is that bringing up a clever Negro, Lap, or Bashkir in European society and in the European fashion, a person will be produced whose mentality hardly differs from that of the educated European.

In sum, Sechenov's psychology was materialistic, reflexological, associationistic, and environmentalistic.

Impact of Sechenov. Outside of Russia, and particularly in America, little notice was paid to Sechenov by psychologists in his lifetime, although his work was known abroad and he attended international congresses, such as the First International Congress of Psychology in 1889 at Paris. In France, his researches were commented upon favorably by Ribot, Dumas, Richet, and Piéron. Sechenov's theories have been regarded by some as influential in the development of materialistic theory in French psychology.

One reason why Sechenov was not better known in Anglo-American circles was that his works were not available in English. Only in mid-twentieth century, for example, were his essays, *Reflexes of the Brain* (1863), *Who Must Investigate Psychology and How* (1873), and *The Elements of Thought* (1878) translated into English. The first of these works generalized his research on frogs to the conclusion that all mental processes in man were reflex in nature and affirmed his materialistic position that psychology should study the external expressions of psychic life. The second essay, as we noted earlier, described the role of the physiologists in the development of psychology. *The Elements of Thought* presented Sechenov's mature, mechanistic formulation of the nature of intellectual, mental process. Sechenov's influence as pioneer of reflexology, and as the founder of an indigenous Russian system of objective psychology, was significant for the growth of scientific psychology in Russia.

Through his writings and his teaching, Sechenov established and promoted objective psychology and the deterministic approach to the analysis of behavior in Russia, during the period when Western psychologists were occupied with the study of consciousness through introspection. Modern commemoration of Sechenov has been made in the naming of the Physiological Institute at the University of Moscow in his honor and in the establishment of the *Sechenov Physiological Journal.* Sechenov paved the way for the reflexology of Pavlov and Bekhterev and for the study of higher nervous activity, or psychophysiology, by Russian physiologists.

PSYCHOPHYSIOLOGY: PAVLOV AND THE STUDY OF HIGHER NERVOUS ACTIVITY

The influence of Sechenov's *Reflexes* was frequently acknowledged by the most distinguished of all Russian scientists, Ivan P. Pavlov—a physician and physiologist—who brought together physiology and psychology and created a new field—psychophysiology.

Life.   Best known internationally for his discovery of the conditioned reflex, Ivan P. Pavlov (1849-1936) was born in Rjasan, Russia and received his secondary education in a religious seminary. He entered St. Petersburg University at a time when Sechenov's influence pervaded the atmosphere there. After getting his medical degree at the Military Medical Academy (1879), Pavlov devoted himself to research. During 1884-1886, on a fellowship in Germany, he studied with Ludwig at Leipzig and Heidenhain in Breslau. At the St. Petersburg clinic, which he organized to integrate medical theory and clinical practice, Pavlov discovered the secretory nerves of the pancreas (1888) and began the researches on digestion which earned him the Nobel Prize in 1904.

In 1890 Pavlov became professor of pharmacology at the Military Medical Academy of St. Petersburg, and a year later was named professor of physiology, a post which he held until 1924. Elected to the Russian Academy of Sciences in 1907, Pavlov later became director of its Physiological Institute, a position he retained until his death in 1936.

Conditioning.   By early twentieth century Pavlov had become one of the world's leading physiologists. In his researches on digestion before 1900, Pavlov had noted that salivary and gastric secretions appeared not only when food was put into a dog's mouth, but even when the dog saw food or heard the sound of the attendant's footsteps. Food, the natural, biologically adequate, or unconditioned stimulus, elicited salivation, a natural or unconditioned response. At the outset, Pavlov referred to the salivary secretions to indifferent stimuli as "psychical secretions" and only later called them "conditional reflexes" (1901). The meaning of Pavlov's Russian term was "conditional." In translation it came to be called "conditioned," and this latter term became the customary designation. Under

the inspiration of his predecessor, Sechenov, Pavlov after some t
decided to subject these conditioned responses, despite their psych.
nature, to physiological inquiry with strictly objective methods. He explored the various phenomena of conditioning—extinction, reinforcement,
spontaneous recovery, generalization, discrimination, and higher order
conditioning. As a result of his studies Pavlov concluded that in contrast
to true reflexes with a subcortical basis, the conditioned reflexes were
cortical activities. On the basis of his researches he developed a theory of
cortical excitation and inhibition which explained his findings in physiological terms.

In the course of studying excitation and inhibition, Pavlov noted that
certain dogs became seriously disturbed when the excitatory and inhibitory
conditioned stimuli closely resembled each other. Thus when a dog was
confronted with one bell which signified food and another similar-sounding
bell which signified no food, he became so upset that he could no longer
produce his regular reactions. After studying these phenomena in many
experiments Pavlov coined the term "experimental neurosis" for this condition in 1923. He regarded the confrontation of excitation and inhibition
as the cause of psychological disturbance and "protective inhibition" as
a cure. Pavlov amplified his animal studies by clinic visits and clinic
demonstrations. He also acknowledged the role of internal factors, as
well as of external environmental factors, in the production of break-
downs. Thus Pavlov extended his conditioning research to application in
psychiatry.

During the years from 1902 to 1936 Pavlov devoted himself to psychophysiology, the field of knowledge which he called the "study of higher
nervous activity." Essentially he studied three aspects of higher nervous
activity of animals (principally dogs): (1) unconditioned special reflexes
and the basal ganglia as a foundation for the overt behavior of the organism; (2) the activity of the cortex; and (3) the method of connection and
interaction of these ganglia and the cortex. Pavlov's researches—inspired
by the psychological objectivism of Sechenov—thus merged physiology
and psychology. Even after the 1917 Revolution with its accompanying
ideological turmoil, Pavlov pursued his psychophysiological research undaunted. He accepted and acknowledged government support of his research, but did not permit prevalent political views to be insinuated into
his psychophysiology.

Influence before Mid-twentieth Century. Although his investigations
had psychological significance, Pavlov protested that they were studies of
brain processes—that is, physiological processes—not psychological studies.
Furthermore, early in his career he held out little hope for psychology as
a truly independent science. Even toward the end of his life after he had
established an experimental basis for psychology and when he had taken
a less dim view of psychology, he still insisted on the importance and
primacy of physiology. For this reason, and also because of political
developments in Russia, Pavlov's findings exerted little constructive influ-

ence on Russian psychology before 1950. In the United States, on the other hand, Pavlov became well known to psychologists in the early twentieth century. His *Lectures on Conditioned Reflexes: Twenty-five Years of Objective Study of Higher Nervous Activity (Behavior) of Animals* was translated in 1928 by W. Horsley Gantt, an American physician, who spent seven years working in Pavlov's laboratory. In 1929 Pavlov himself visited America, attending the Ninth International Congress of Psychology in New Haven. Pavlov's conditioning had been well received by Watson and the behaviorists, principally because of its endorsement of objective psychology. Conditioning techniques yielded objective data in terms of stimuli, neural activity, and responses without reference to consciousness and introspection. Conditioning accounted for the modification of the organism's behavior, demonstrating how new responses were acquired, how responses were lost, and how recovered.

While Pavlov did most of his research on dogs, he made an important contribution to the psychology of humans in the development of his concept of the second signal system—language—in addition to the primary or sensory signal system. Pavlov realized that language was not only important for communication between individuals. He knew it was also important for the ability to generalize, since language symbols—words—represent both concrete and abstract things. This ability to represent things through words—language—Pavlov described as a peculiarly human function. Another fruitful concept for research on humans as well as on animals was that of the orienting reflex. The term orienting reflex referred to adjustive or investigatory behavior evident at the beginning of conditioning and usually conducive to the process; for example, perception, attention, or expectancy. Both concepts—verbal conditioning and the orienting reflex—are useful to a psychology which is objective, since they provide an indirect approach to consciousness and facilitate research on human cognition.

For 35 years the work of Pavlov and his associates furnished substantial support for objective psychology generally and in particular for the subsequent development of psychophysiology in Russia. However, it was not until 1950, as we shall see, that Pavlov achieved special recognition from psychologists in his own country. A dedicated scientist, skillful in the use of objective, experimental methods, Pavlov is esteemed, more in the 1960's than he was in his own lifetime, for creating a natural science foundation for psychology.

REFLEXOLOGY: BEKHTEREV

Pavlov and Bekhterev headed two early Russian schools of objective psychology which derived from common sources—Sechenov's physiology and the rationalistic, materialistic philosophy characteristic of the Russian intellectuals of their time. A pragmatic realist, Pavlov was always the dedicated physiologist. Bekhterev, the idealistic materialist, was at once a psychiatrist, experimental psychologist, anatomist, physiologist, sociologist, and politician. While their lives were parallel, their approaches to objective psychology were different and frequently at odds. Pavlov's system was neural—primarily psychophysiological; Bekhterev's was behavioral—primarily psychological.

Life. Vladimir M. Bekhterev (1857-1927) was born in the province of Viatka and received his medical degree in 1881 from the Medico-Surgical Academy of St. Petersburg. In 1882, he published *The Nerve Currents in Brain and Spinal Cord* (a second edition of which—1896—was translated into German and French). In 1884 Bekhterev visited Charcot's clinic and attended the lectures of du Bois-Reymond, whose antivitalistic teaching appealed to him. He spent the year 1885-1886 in Leipzig with Wundt, whose influence on Bekhterev was considerable.

While in Leipzig, Bekhterev was named professor of psychiatry at the Univeristy of Kazan. During his tenure at Kazan from 1886 to 1894, he established the first psychophysiological laboratory in Russia (1886), organized a psychiatric clinic, and founded the first brain institute, which combined clinical research on mental diseases and practice. In 1893, Bekhterev returned to the Military Medical Academy in St. Petersburg, where he organized a second laboratory in 1895 and in 1905-1906 was named its director. He founded the Russian Society of Normal and Abnormal Psychology in 1896, and also organized a journal, the *Review of Psychiatry, Neuropathology, and Experimental Psychology*, the first periodical in any country to bear the title, *experimental psychology*. At St. Petersburg, he established a psychoneurological institute in 1907. This institute was supported by private funds until 1917, when another brain institute was established and the control of both was assumed by the government. From 1913 on, until his death in 1927, Bekhterev devoted his time to the institute, especially when the regime later made his tenure at the Academy unpleasant. At the institute he conducted neurological research and produced many publications.

Objective Experimental Psychology. Bekhterev was the Russian pioneer of objective experimental psychology. Although Wundtian psychology was brought to Russia by him, he himself outgrew the traditional psychology. He did not consider it objective. In 1904 he wrote an article entitled, *Objective Psychology and Its Subject Matter*, which set forth his views. Later he offered a fuller exposition in his three volume *Objective Psychology* (1907-1910), which was translated into French and German (1910).

In fashioning his psychology Bekhterev preserved the philosophical orientation of psychophysical parallelism and the Wundtian principle of physiological objectivation of subjective experience. But he diligently threw out introspection and language from the study of behavior. Yet he did not want to study mere physiology. Bekhterev wanted to subject psychical processes, or the accumulation of nervous current energy, as he viewed them, to objective scrutiny. Moreover, he wanted to discover the materialistic bases of these processes. He tried to extend the objective method to all branches of psychology, including child study.

To distinguish his experimental psychology from the traditional psychology, Bekhterev called it psychoreflexology and later simply, reflexology. By 1917 Bekhterev described his system in *General Principles of Human Reflexology: An Introduction to the Objective Study of Personality*. This volume was revised and extended in 1923 and 1925. It is perhaps through this work that Bekhterev is best known in the United States.

Scope and Method of Reflexology. Reflexology, the outgrowth of Bekhterev's objective psycholgy, was the study of the whole of human behavior. As a biosocial discipline, it studied the objective correlations existing between personality and the inorganic, the organic, and the social environment—or what Bekhterev called "correlated activity." In his experimental and clinical work he searched for a method of studying the biological and social elements of human behavior in their ontogenesis. He did not want a method objective only in the sense that it eliminated all subjective interpretations. Well aware of Pavlov's method of salivary conditioned reflexes, Bekhterev recognized its inadequacy for the study of human reactions. He insisted that men and animals relate themselves to their environment principally through bodily movements. Recordings of such movements, he believed, were more objective than counting drops of saliva. Therefore, the method Bekhterev finally selected was that of associative motor reflexes or individually acquired responses to social or collective stimuli, that is, "psychical reflexes."

In contrast to Pavlov's work on conditioned reflexes in animals, Bekhterev investigated associative reflexes both in animals and men. Furthermore, in later experiments (1908), Bekhterev developed avoidance conditioning, using a nociceptive unconditioned stimulus (shock) rather than a natural unconditioned one (food). For example, he employed electric shock as the unconditioned stimulus and reflex withdrawal of the shocked limb as the unconditioned response. He measured the contractions of the skeletal muscles rather than visceral secretory responses. In his clinical psychiatric practice, Bekhterev applied his reflexological concepts. His reflexology integrated knowledge of personality and its correlation with nature and society.

Various aspects of reflexology were studied by Bekhterev's students and associates. Among these were (1) *general* reflexology, which attempted to establish laws of correlated activity of individuals (A. Schniermann); (2) *collective* reflexology, which studied the sociogenetic elements of behavior (M. V. Lange); (3) *individual* reflexology, which investigated the individual variations of correlated activity and attempted to relate these variations to constitutional and behavioral characteristics (V. N. Myasishchev); (4) *genetic* reflexology, which studied the development of correlated activity and its ontogenesis and phylogenesis (N. M. Shchelovanov); and (5) *age* reflexology, which examined the general mechanisms of correlated reflex activity in their development and children's reflexological typology (V. N. Osipova).

In 1921 Bekhterev wrote a volume entitled *Collective Reflexology*. He also published several articles on the various branches of reflexology. In 1925 he wrote a small brochure, *Psychology, Reflexology, and Marxism*. Bekhterev saw no conflict between reflexology and dialectical materialism and in fact sought to strengthen the bond between them. Between 1920 and 1926, reflexology enjoyed wide popularity and dimmed interest in psychology. Until his death in 1927 Bekhterev continued to extend his system. Although his system succeeded in creating a neurological basis for psychology, it too gradually lost favor because of the ideological struggle in the Soviet Union for a more dialectical psychology.

TRADITIONAL PSYCHOLOGY AND POSTREVOLUTIONARY TRENDS

While Pavlov and Bekhterev were busy with their objective psychology, traditional Wundtian psychology was also being cultivated in Russia. Among the several Russian psychologists who had studied in Leipzig— A. Nechaev, I. N. Spielrein, and D. Uznadze—G. I. Chelpanov (1862-1936) was the chief exponent of Wundtian and Titchenerian psychology in pre-Soviet Russia. Chelpanov had visited German and American laboratories and had served as the first director of the psychological institute of the University of Moscow when it opened in 1911. He wrote several books on psychology and philosophy including the *Introduction to Experimental Psychology* (1915), noteworthy for its special attention to statistics. He also founded a Russian *Psychological Review* (1917), publication of which was curtailed shortly after the Revolution.

While traditional psychology was developed at the universities, a practical experimental psychology was developed in the laboratories of the psychiatric clinics of Bekhterev, S. S. Korsakov, and G. Rossolimo, well known for the first professional application of mental testing. Chelpanov, like N. N. Lange, favored the development of university laboratories and the curtailment of practical experimental psychology in laboratories ancillary to psychiatric clinics. As early as 1893, Korsakov vehemently opposed Lange, claiming that the excellent work of medical laboratories should not be discarded or disregarded simply because the laboratories were not affiliated with philosophical or historical faculties.

A prominent spokesman for a practical psychology during this period was *A. F. Lazursky* (1874-1917), who urged that psychology, like natural science, should be based on concrete facts. Desirous of making psychology a more practical science, he devised original methods of clinical observation and "natural experiments" so that personality could be studied under natural, rather than artificial conditions. Lazursky, Korsakov, and Bekhterev were leading natural scientists who helped to establish experimental psychology in Russia before 1917.

After the 1917 Revolution in Russia, there was an ideological revolution among the educated classes which condemned all the previously allegedly idealistic ideology and which created a materialistic ideology. There were lengthy discussions about the status of psychology and about the significance of Marxist philosophy for psychological theory. During the 1920's Marxist thinking began to dominate Russian intellectual life. The government instituted reforms in the universities. In an attempt to accommodate their psychology to Communist thinking, some Russian psychologists fashioned a new Marxist psychology. Chelpanov tried to save Wundtian psychology by arguing that it was not inconsistent with dialectical materialism. But Wundtian psychology was denounced as a "metaphysical conception of empiric psychology," and Chelpanov's school was overthrown because it was "exceedingly idealistic." Some research topics of this traditional psychology—sensation and perception—survived. Bekhterev vehemently opposed psychology and substituted reflexology for it, as we have already pointed out. On the other hand, Pavlov, less militant, maintained that psychology was useful for the study of subjective experience, but that physiology really explained the behavior of organisms.

The Marxist approach to psychology—based on the principles of dialectical materialism—replaced the study of consciousness with a material study of personal behavior. It also sharpened the distinction between psychology and psychophysiology—the study of higher nervous activity. To understand the new psychology of the Soviet era one must have some familiarity with the tenets and practical consequences of dialectical materialism, its philosophical basis.

Dialectical Materialism.   This philosophy was first set forth in mid-nineteenth century by Karl Marx and Friedrich Engels and was later amplified by Nikolai Vladimir Lenin. Marx and Engels became dissatisfied with mechanistic, deterministic materialism which, they believed, enslaved man and forced him to accept his fate and existing conditions. It failed to give mental processes a dynamic function in life. Dialectical materialism, on the other hand, allowed for change and provided for thesis, antithesis, and synthesis. It viewed the world as a conglomerate of processes in which all things arise, have their existence, and pass away. It denied the existence of anything but matter in motion and its products.

According to dialectical materialism, mental processes are brain processes and are real—whether physiological or mental. Brain activity reflects objective reality—the environment. This reflection is not merely passive and sensory. The human mind is a co-determinant in molding human destiny. The human mind can change world process, alter its environment, and improve human conditions. Knowledge is valuable and must be used by man in controlling his environment. Theory and practice must be one. Philosophy must be practical—a way of life. Applied science is the only worthwhile science. Dialectical materialism and the sciences which it promotes must be useful, applied knowledge. Furthermore, dialectical philosophy and sciences demand the collective effort and knowledge of all men. The essential human unit is society, not the individual. There-fore, public interest must obliterate individual ambition. The goal is classless society without distinctions, inequalities, and class struggle.

Dialectical materialism—the foundation of the social and economic revolution in Russia—has had less effect on the physical sciences and mathematics than on psychology. It has generated a succession of Soviet psychologies quite different from the psychology of other countries, where philosophical and political pressures have been less direct and less influ-ential. Opposing the traditional concept of psychology as a science of mind and consciousness—and also rejecting the extremely objective psy-chology which denied consciousness or identified it with mechanical move-ment of matter—Soviet psychology assumed that the psychic life and the objective world constitute a unity. From this unity several other unities follow, namely, the unity of brain and mind; of organic and psychic life; of structure and function; of capacity and ability; and finally, the unity of the innate and the acquired.

REACTOLOGY: KORNILOV

Since the 1920's, with varying degrees of success, Soviet psychologists have worked to perfect their dialectical psychology. The history of Soviet psychology has been said by B. M. Teplov, a contemporary Soviet psychol-ogist, to be the history of the Soviet psychologists' mastery of Marxist-Leninist methodology. The principal link between pre-Soviet and Soviet psychology was K. N. Kornilov, a theoretical and experimental psychol-ogist who opposed Chelpanovian psychology and Bekhterev's reflexology. Kornilov established the first formal school of dialectical psychology—reactology.

Life. Born in Siberia and graduated from Moscow University (1910) where he was Chelpanov's assistant, Konstantin N. Kornilov (1879-1957) became director of the State Institute for Experimental Psychology (1923) in Moscow, Russia's foremost scientific institute of psychology. Although Marx and Engels had little to say about psychology, Kornilov worked out a formulation which he described in *Modern Psychology and Marxism.* Rejecting reflexological interpretations of behavior, Kornilov created a science of reactions or reactology, the tenets of which he set forth in *The Study of Man's Reactions or Reactology* (1922). Between 1926 and 1931 his *Textbook of Psychology from the Standpoint of Dialectical Materialism* (1926) went through five Russian editions and was translated into several languages. In 1928 Kornilov became editor of Russia's first truly psycho-logical journal, *Psychology.* During the 1920's Kornilov remained the leading psychologist in Russia, and reactology, along with pedology (the science of the growing organism), psychotechnics, and pedagogical testing, flourished. Moreover, the State Institute for Experimental Psychology, organized in 1923 to promote dialectical psychology and headed by Kornilov, prospered—with sections on general psychology (Kornilov), child psychology (N. A. Rybnikov), zoöpsychology (V. M. Borovski), and psychotechnics (I. N. Spielrein).

Reactology had a rapid rise, but it was short lived. By 1931, it was denounced as undialectical and not sufficiently Marxist-Leninist and disappeared from Soviet literature. Although Kornilov himself remained prominent, he lost his post as director of the Institute and was no longer considered the leading psychologist. He continued as editor of *Psychology*, later became head of the psychology department of the Moscow State Institute of Pedagogical Sciences, and was elected vice president of the Soviet Academy of Pedagogical Science. During his entire life, Kornilov dealt with the fundamental issues of Soviet psychology. Razran has observed of Kornilov, "He somehow managed at all times to keep afloat, in fact to be most of the time in the forefront, untoward and adverse trends to the contrary notwithstanding." His reactology was the first milestone toward a dialectical psychology. As such, it served to bridge the gap between pre-Soviet and Soviet psychology. A review of its tenets indicates how this school made the transition.

Reactology: The Science of Reactions. Taking as the starting point man's interaction with environment, Kornilov approached psychology as the science of behavior of the living concrete individual in concrete social conditions. It was a social science, not a branch of natural science. Although it assumed the unity of the subjective and the objective, reactology insisted that this synthetic view did not preclude the analysis of the elements of behavior, that is, reactions or the responses of living organisms to stimuli in their environment. Kornilov's reactology was then the science of the reactions of man as a whole. Reactions were considered biosociological in nature. They ranged from the simplest to the most complicated forms of human behavior in man's social life. They were classified into seven types: natural; muscular; sensory; discriminatory; selective; reactions of recognition; and reactions of logical order. On the basis of their predominant reactions, individuals were classified into four types: muscular active; muscular passive; sensorial active; and sensorial passive.

Reactology was not interested in mere physiological reactions, however, but in the subjective content of reactions and in voluntary behavior. While its methods were mainly objective—including simple objective observation, experimentation and statistics, and tests—reactology also included study of the subject's verbal report. With these methods, three elements of simple reactions were analyzed—the rate, intensity, and form—as well as their contents or social importance, and their inter- and intra-individual variability. In sum, reactology combined behavior and consciousness, holism and atomism, the qualitative and the quantitative. It postulated the principles of wholeness and socioeconomic prepotency. The former affirmed that total behavior dominates the individual reaction and that social behavior dominates individual behavior. The latter principle maintained that the form of reactions is biologically determined, but that their content is social—in fact economic—and that man is a function of a specific economic class.

Kornilov's reactology discredited traditional psychology as exemplified by Chelpanov and also Bekhterev. In spite of its dialectical advances, however, it was attacked soon after the publication of Lenin's *Philosophical Notebooks* (1929-1930), which claimed that man was active not simply reactive. Reactology was denounced because it failed to give consciousness the determining role in changing man and his environment. Furthermore, by 1930-1932 behaviorism in all its forms, including reactology and reflexology, was completely rejected.

Kornilov's school, whatever its limitations, inspired experimental research. Among Kornilov's students were the prominent psychologists, *Leo Vigotsky* (1896-1934) and *Alexander R. Luria* (b. 1902). The former, author of *Thought and Speech* (1934), studied the genesis of psychological functions in the child and insisted that instruction must keep ahead of development. Severely critical of Piaget, Vigotsky affirmed the "social" nature of children's allegedly "egocentric" speech. Vigotsky's researches in pedology and defectology (work with the handicapped) paved the way for development of Soviet psychology in these two areas and found practical application in the care and training of children.

Luria, currently professor of psychology at the State Institute of Psychology in Moscow, is a leading contemporary Soviet psychologist. Author of *The Nature of Human Conflicts* (1932), Luria originally applied reactological methodology to the study of affective reactions. From this work, as a psychiatrist and psychologist, he evolved an objective methodology to investigate, diagnose, and treat psychological phenomena and to shed light on the mechanisms underlying the disorganization of human behavior. Throughout his career Luria has been interested in "exact methods" of experimentation "to put the diagnosis of nervous and mental ailments on a scientific basis and to elaborate scientific methods of restoring impaired function." Psychopathology has continued to be an important branch of Soviet psychology, although it has been pursued principally by medical men. Luria's most recent volume—published in 1963 and translated into English in 1966 by Basil Haigh of Cambridge, England—is *Human Brain and Psychological Processes*, a product of 25 years of neuropsychological research on lesions of the anterior parts of the human brain.

SOVIET PSYCHOLOGY: 1920-1950

From 1920 to 1950 Soviet psychology developed under precarious conditions as it strove to become more dialectical. In the 1920's the influence of the Communist Party was not as direct and specific as it later became. The impact of American behaviorism, of German holistic psychologies— particularly Gestalt psychology—and even of psychoanalysis was felt in psychology and psychiatry. Pavlov was sharply critical of these psychologies—and, in particular of Janet, Claparède, Lashley, Woodworth, and

Köhler—at his Wednesday seminars in his laboratory, during which he discussed scientific problems with his associates. These criticisms were part of his systematic struggle against those who, in his opinion, digressed from the exact methods of natural science in probing the essence of consciousness. However, at the time Russian psychologists paid little attention to Pavlov because of his almost exclusive concern with physiology.

The Twenties. Soviet psychology in the 1920's was behavioral—concerned with the objective study of man's overt actions rather than with the study of consciousness. The influence of American behaviorism was obvious in the researches of P. Blonsky in child and educational psychology and of V. M. Borovski in animal psychology. Western influence was particularly discernible in the emphasis on applied psychology, particularly industrial and educational psychology. Industrial psychology was cultivated by S. G. Gellerstein, and also by Spielrein, who was influenced by German psychology, principally by the work of Stern. In spite of little or no progress during World War I, compared with other countries, psychotechnology in Russia developed in the 1920's. The Central Institute of Work, established in 1920, conducted job analyses and promoted industrial efficiency. Attention was focused on selection of workers and on analysis of the work process. Mental testing was prominent in psychotechnology as it was also in pedology.

Behavioral psychologists played a particularly important role in the development of pedology. This science of the growing child integrated the findings and techniques of medical psychology, pedagogy, physiology, and sociology concerning children. Testing programs were established in the schools, and training in child development was required of teachers. Besides Blonsky, others prominent in this field included Vigotsky and his students, notably *A. N. Leontiev* (b. 1903) and *L. V. Zanov* (b. 1901), who developed methods for studying thought, speech, and memory. New methodology for studying children also included the method of objective systematic observation of M. Basov for use with preschool children and the biographical method employing diaries and autobiographies developed by N. A. Rybnikov. The works of Vigotsky, Luria, and Leontiev on the cultural development of the child during this period were later cited as "the progressive tendencies" in Soviet psychology of the mid-1920's.

By the end of the twenties it began to seem as if psychology were recovering from the reverses it had suffered because of the pre-eminence of Pavlov and Bekhterev who tended to place the behavioral psychologists in the same category as the traditional subjective psychologists. K. N. Kornilov was the chief psychologist of this period. He encouraged educational and industrial psychology. Researches in these fields warranted publication in 1928 of three periodicals entitled "Psychology," "Pedology," and "Psychotechnics." But within a short time perspectives changed.

The Thirties. Political pressures mounted and weighed heavily on Soviet psychology in the 1930's. The publication of Lenin's *Philosophical Note-*

books (1929-1930) called attention to his theory of psychic life as a reflection of reality. This theory stimulated interest in the psychological study of sensation and provoked much theoretical discussion. Consciousness now became an important subject of psychological consideration. Kornilov's reactology was denounced for failing to emphasize man's active nature and neglecting to stress the role of consciousness in changing man and his environment. Psychology was put on trial and under fire by the Communist Party. By 1935 no psychological journals were published any longer in the Soviet Union, and none appeared again for two decades.

By 1936 a decree of the Central Committee of the Communist Party forbade mental testing. Testing was opposed because it called attention to individual differences and emphasized inequalities. The study of individual differences through tests—testology—was banned. The industrial psychology of the twenties with its stress on analysis of the work process shifted now to improving performance of the worker and to training. In conformity with the economic policy of the government the training of large numbers of unskilled workers became the important task. Industrial psychology virtually vanished. Psychology and psychologists were clearly under attack in this period. Amidst the barrage of criticism the principal directive given to psychologists was to make Soviet psychology different from "bourgeois" psychology.

The psychologist yielded place to the educator. Training became more important than heredity or "immutable" environment. The primary task now was to develop new Soviet citizens. Stress was put upon the social environment as the molder of personality and on the solution of concrete problems in life. The classroom was viewed as society in miniature where superior, mediocre, and inferior had to learn to adjust to each other.

In the midst of the denunciations of previous psychology as "bourgeois," S. L. Rubinstein (1889-1960), in a more positive vein, wrote *The Bases of Psychology* (1935). This volume presented a new approach to the study of the basic problems of development and personality, and of consciousness in its relation to activity—an approach conforming to his theory of the "formation of the psyche in the process of activity." This proposition was amplified in his *Foundations of General Psychology* (1940), a book which, in spite of limitations, defined the line for psychology and remained a standard text of Soviet psychology until 1947. According to the new approach, pedagogical psychology, for example, was to be studied in the concrete pedagogical process itself, in the way B. G. Ananiev (b. 1907) described in his book, *The Psychology of Pedagogical Evaluation* (1935). The distinctive feature of Soviet psychology in the late thirties was the disappearance of divergent viewpoints and schools and the consolidation to one school of Soviet psychology.

The Forties. Soviet psychology in the early forties was principally military. It included psychophysiological researches on sight and hearing, training of aviators, retraining of the disabled, and studies of morale. Findings of perceptual studies were used in intelligence and espionage

Studies of neurological impairment, work therapy, and rehabilitation received attention. After World War II the staffs and the number of experimental laboratories in psychiatric clinics and hospitals were reduced. For the first time, in 1947, the universities of Moscow, Leningrad, Kiev, and Tbilisi created special departments for training psychologists. But there was a growing desire in the late forties to infuse new life into psychology and to inspire new research efforts on the part of psychologists. Dissatisfaction with Rubinstein's system was violently expressed. He was cited as too reliant on Western psychologists, too sophisticated for the masses, and too abstract for concrete study of Soviet citizens in school and on the job.

PAVLOVIANIZATION: 1950

The attempt to establish a pure Soviet psychology—without "bourgeois" psychology and with relegation of studies of conditioning and related phenomena to physiology—had met with little success. While Soviet psychology declined, Soviet physiologists continued undaunted with their studies of conditioning. After World War II new inspiration was sought for all Soviet science. Stalin ordered a reorganization of science and culture along party lines. A new hero was needed around whom scientists could rally and build their new approaches. The one hundredth anniversary of Pavlov's birth in 1949 offered the occasion for renewed attention to Pavlov and the opportunity of making a national hero for Soviet scientists.

For one week, from June 28 through July 4, 1950, the Soviet Academy of Sciences and the Soviet Academy of Medical Sciences met jointly and discussed Pavlov's teachings. At these meetings—attended by hundreds of physicians, biologists, physiologists, and philosophers—extensive discourses on Pavlov's concepts were delivered by his two most active and orthodox disciples, K. M. Bykov and A. G. Ivanov-Smolensky. The purpose of these sessions was to stimulate and plan for the reconstruction of physiology, psychology, medicine, and allied fields along Pavlovian lines. Pavlovianization involved two essential steps: (1) Reprimanding, and directing to Pavlovianism, Soviet scientists who had not been dedicated to such research and thinking before 1950; and (2) insuring the correct interpretation of Pavlovian thinking and research, together with reprimanding Pavlovian researchers who failed to give "correct," that is, official interpretations. Among those cited for deviant interpretations and denounced for violating Pavlovian orthodoxy (that is, being contaminated by Western physiology) were: the outstanding neurophysiologists, second only to Pavlov—I. S. Beritov; L. A. Orbeli, Pavlov's principal student; P. K. Anokhin, a student of both Pavlov and Beritov; and P. S. Kupalov with whom the Americans W. H. Gantt and H. S. Liddell worked. All ultimately acknowledged their "errors" and joined the orthodox fold. Continuing criticism and Pavlovianization were assured by the establishment of a committee to pursue the objectives of these sessions held in 1950. The year, 1950, thus marked a turning point in the history of Soviet psychology because of the decisive shift of prescribed theory to Pavlovian objectives.

After 1950 Soviet psychophysiology acquired status because of the official return to Pavlov as an authority. There seemed to be little encouragement of the bold scientific spirit and empiricism characteristic of Pavlov. Pavlov was merely added to the prior list of authorities—Marx, Engels, Lenin—with whose theories Pavlov's theories were correlated and interwoven. In spite of state controls, Soviet psychophysiology has tended to be fact-finding and has accumulated a wealth of experimental data. Important research is conducted on the neurology of learning, higher nervous activity, language—or Pavlov's second signal system—psychopathology, psychopharmacology, sensory interaction, evolutionary physiology, and practical animal training. Such research is done principally by Soviet physiologists, however, rather than by Soviet psychologists. Much research that in the United States would be included under experimental psychology —physiological, animal, and conditioning studies—is in the domain of physiology in the Soviet Union.

CONTEMPORARY SOVIET PSYCHOLOGY

Unlike Soviet psychophysiology, Soviet psychology has been under sharper Communist scrutiny and state control throughout its history. Testing, social psychology, and industrial psychology have long been frowned upon. Freud is banned. Clinical psychology is underdeveloped, since psychopathology is an almost exclusive concern of psychiatry. Furthermore, in their research, Soviet psychologists have felt a persistent need to reaffirm their Marxist-Leninist loyalties. After 1950, Soviet psychology, which had been especially castigated for its failure to develop Pavlovian concepts, turned to Pavlov, particularly to the contents of his Wednesday seminars conducted late in his life. The reintroduction of Pavlov had a stimulating effect on Soviet psychology. Psychologists began to cite Pavlov in their textbooks to a degree hitherto unknown. Scientific and professional periodical literature also reflected this drastic shift of emphasis. Furthermore, a new psychological periodical, *Problems of Psychology*, was founded in 1955—the first in 20 years. Several others also appeared, including the *Journal of Higher Nervous Activity* and *Soviet Pedagogy*. About 1957 a *Society of Psychologists* was established with A. A. *Smirnov* (b. 1894) as president. Once again Soviet psychologists began to participate actively, too, in international conferences and congresses.

Training. While all Soviet universities and pedagogical institutes are said to have psychology departments, most do not have laboratories. The principal research and training centers are Moscow, Leningrad, Kiev, and Tbilisi. The basic undergraduate program for psychology students has a heavy concentration of biological sciences, plus courses in sociology and philosophy, and requires approximately five years. During the fourth year theoretical and experimental work· is taken, followed by a fifth year devoted to the diploma thesis which usually has to be defended at department assemblies. The diploma entitles the graduate to practice psychology professionally. Three specialties are available at Moscow, for example—clinical, educational, and engineering psychology.

After completion of the diploma program some students pursue an additional three or more years, preparing for the degree of candidate of science. This degree, which requires research in a specific laboratory and a dissertation, entitles them to teach at the university below the level of full professor. The Federal doctorate, which has a public character, may be awarded later in life to distinguished psychologists who have fulfilled certain research and publication requirements. This doctorate carries with it the rank of full professor and the right to obtain a chair. Psychologists, like other workers in the Soviet Union, must follow official directives and are compensated at rates fixed by the state.

Research Areas.   Within the decade from 1955 to 1965 Soviet psychologists have continued to be productive, although many areas are still relatively untouched. Only a few broad categories of their research can be mentioned here, but a thoroughgoing, comprehensive review of Soviet research can be found in the two volumes of *Psychological Science in the U.S.S.R.* (1959, 1960). Among the prominent research areas and researchers are the following: (1) *developmental* psychology—which focuses on mental development as one of the central problems of Soviet psychology with special emphasis on children (Elkonin, Leontiev); (2) *applied* psychology—largely applied·educational, which treats of concrete learning and training situations (Ananiev, Dobrynin, Menchinskaya, Leontiev); (3) *comparative* psychology—which concentrates on evolutionary aspects and the development of psychic processes (Ladygina-Kots, Roginsky); (4) *speech* development and its role in mental processes (Artemov, Luria, Sokolov, Zhinkin); (5) *memory, thinking,* and *problem solving* (Galperin, Smirnov, Zanov, Zinchenko); (6) *sensation* and *perception* (Ananiev, Sokolov, Shevarev, Elkin); (7) *sport* psychology—or psychology of physical culture (Rudik, Puni); (8) *individual differences*, with physiological emphasis (Teplov); (9) *defectology*—or the study of handicaps and various clinical conditions (Luria, Solovyev); (10) *labor* psychology—which studies work methods, skills, occupational and industrial training, human factors, and preparation of children for occupations (Oshanin, Lomov).

In contrast to contemporary psychology elsewhere, particularly in the United States, testing and statistics receive little favorable notice, and *clinical* psychology, as was mentioned previously, is underdeveloped. Known as pathophysiology, it is the province of physicians—among the most outstanding of whom is Luria, who is both M.D. and Ph.D. A senior clinical psychologist who works in pure psychology is *Bluma V. Zeigarnik* (b. 1900), a former student of Lewin, well known for her studies of memory for interrupted tasks ("Zeigarnik effect"). She directs the laboratory of the Institute of Psychiatry and also teaches psychopathology at the University of Moscow. Her principal research is on psychoses. Two of her recent books are *Disturbances of Thought in Mentally Ill Individuals* (1958) and *Pathology of Thought* (1962).

Psychotherapy, which was introduced into medical schools about 1956, has developed slowly. It has acquired considerable favor recently as an application of Pavlov's second signal system. Based on the concepts of Pavlov—who became interested in mental illness in his later career—psychotherapy in the Soviet Union is employed in the treatment of neuroses, alcoholism, and certain behavior problems. Systematic psychotherapy combined with medication has been tried in the treatment of psychotics. Increasing attention has been paid to hypnosis, suggestion, and speech therapy in the treatment of various problems. Psychologists have been urged to study the uses of hypnotherapy, brief rational therapy, and work therapy. Although there is strong predilection for a physiological interpretation of the etiology of mental diseases, the possibility of psychogenic disorders is admitted. Unconscious motivation finds little support in comparison to the support it gets in Western psychotherapy.

One feature of Soviet psychology which one cannot fail to notice is its socio-political involvement. Regardless of their specialty, Soviet psychologists work within the same theoretical and philosophical framework. Repeated references are made to Lenin or Stalin, and the omnipresence of the dialectical materialism of Marx and Engels is always evident.

Soviet Psychological Theory. Soviet psychology has been defined by Luria as "the science of voluntary behavior in man." This psychology is based on six principles which were summarized by P. A. Rudik, a Soviet psychologist, in 1958:

1. *Materialistic monism.* The psychologist **must understand** the physiology of higher nervous activity, since physiological processes are basic to psychological processes. Mental processes and phenomena are cerebral processes.

2. *Determinism.* Mental phenomena result from the interaction of higher nervous activity and the external environment.

3. *Reflection.* Consciousness is an internal or subjective reflection of external or objective reality.

4. *Unity of consciousness and activity.* Man's consciousness is fashioned by activity as well as expressed in activity. Therefore, mental processes must be studied by the psychologist in the concrete and not in the abstract.

5. *Historicism.* Human consciousness has developed in the historical process of man's social development. Psychologists must explore the development of mental phenomena and discover the social foundations of human consciousness and personality.

6. *Unity of theory and practice.* This principle indicates that psychologists must influence as well as study man. They must help to build the socialist state by improving the education and training of the young, by

improving working conditions and production, and by safeguarding the health of Soviet citizens.

Thoroughly committed to these basic principles, Soviet psychologists have pursued their researches and have displayed fervor for their work.

Evaluation. Although scientific psychology was imported to Russia from Germany, as it was in other countries, its history is entirely different from that in other countries for two main reasons. First, concomitant with the cultivation of Wundtian psychology there developed independently in Russia an objective experimental psychology which focused on behavior. It began with the physiological researches of Sechenov and with Pavlov's conditioning and culminated in the reflexology of Wundt's student Bekhterev, a psychologist and physiologist. Second, in Russia, as in no other country, psychology has been directly influenced for a long period by political conditions, beginning with the 1917 Revolution. Communism and the dialectical materialism of Marx, Engels, and Lenin successively overthrew Chelpanovian traditional psychology, Bekhterev's reflexology, and Kornilov's reactology. After 1936 all Western psychological influences—or "bourgeois" psychology—were eradicated, including testing, pedology, and industrial psychology. All psychological periodicals were discontinued. Attempts were made to establish a new theoretical framework for psychology and to develop a Soviet psychology. The entire history of Soviet psychology has been a persistent struggle from the 1920's to make Soviet psychology dialectical. This struggle produced a general sterility in Soviet psychology during the 1930's and 1940's.

Since 1950 and the Pavlovianization of psychology, new life has been injected into Soviet psychology. Soviet psychologists have become more active and productive, taking as the focus of their research higher nervous activity. Despite the narrowness of the concept of Pavlov's second signal system—language—fruitful research has been conducted on speech, thinking, and psychotherapy. There is increased interest in personality, social psychology, engineering psychology, and information theory. Soviet psychophysiology—which is pursued principally by physiologists and includes studies of conditioning, animals, and physiological psychology—has produced valuable studies on cerebral processes. Increasingly, Soviet psychologists have participated in international conferences and congresses. They have also been hosts to the psychologists of many other countries for the XVIII International Congress of Psychology, which convened in Moscow in 1966. The Western world has come to know more of the Soviet work in recent years as translations have become more readily available. Furthermore, in the Soviet Union translations have been made of American books, such as Stevens' *Handbook of Experimental Psychology*. Such intercommunication is valuable. However, in spite of the greater interchange of ideas, Soviet psychological science still tends to cling to its own framework, is restricted, and seems to deny itself the enrichment that it might otherwise derive from less intense commitment to its own closed system. Psychology as a profession—in the clinical or consulting sense—does not exist in the Soviet Union.

SUMMARY OF SOVIET PSYCHOLOGICAL SCIENCE

Major influences. Philosophical: dialectical materialism (Marx, Engels, Lenin)
Physiological: psychophysiology (Sechenov, Pavlov)
Political: Communism

Pioneers. Wundtian psychology: G. I. Chelpanov (1862–1936)
Objective experimental psychology: V. M. Bekhterev (1857–1927)
Reactology: K. N. Kornilov (1879–1957)

First laboratories. Kazan (1886), St. Petersburg (1895)

Leaders. I. P. Pavlov (1849–1936)
Developmental: L. Vigotsky (1896–1934); A. N. Leontiev (b. 1903)
Defectology: A. R. Luria (b. 1902)
Comparative: Nadezhda Ladygina-Kots (b. 1889)
Individual differences: B. M. Teplov (1896–1965)
Higher mental processes: P. Galperin (b. 1902); G. S. Kostiuk (b. 1899); A. A. Smirnov (b. 1894).
Clinical: Bluma V. Zeigarnik (b. 1900)

Main emphases. Cognitive functions, learning, thinking; developmental and pedagogical psychology; higher nervous activity.

Three periods of Soviet psychology after the Revolution.
1917–1936: Efforts to develop a system consistent with dialectical materialism; widespread use of standardized tests for selection of technical workers and for appraising intelligence of school children.

1936–1950: Tests banned in 1936; stagnation and lack of purpose among Soviet psychologists; period of searching for valid areas of research.

1950–1965: Stalin's aim to revive and improve Soviet science produced the Pavlovianization of psychology in 1950. Psychologists turned to the works of Pavlov and, after a period of study, reorganized their science along lines of Pavlov's researches, especially higher nervous activity. Soviet psychology in the 1960's is a rather narrow discipline bordered on one side by psychophysiology—the domain of physiologists and psychiatrists—and on the other by the dictates of the Communist Party. Principal areas of research are education and child development. There are signs of increasing interest in social, clinical, and industrial psychology.

REFERENCES

GENERAL

Ananiev, B., *et al.* (Eds.) *Psychological science in the U.S.S.R.* 2 Vols. (Trans. of the books *Psikhologicheskaya nauka v SSSR.* 2 Vols. Moscow: RSFSR Academy of Pedagogical Sciences, 1959, 1960) Washington, D.C.: U.S. Joint Publ. Res. Serv., 1961, 1962.

Brožek, J. Soviet psychology. In M. Marx & W. A. Hillix, *Systems and theories in psychology.* New York: McGraw-Hill, 1963. Pp. 438–455.

Brožek, J. Contemporary Soviet psychology. *Trans. N.Y. Acad. Sci.*, 1965, *27*, 422–438.

Brožek, J. Russian contributions on brain and behavior. *Science*, 1966, *152*, 930–932.

Razran, G. Russian physiologists' psychology and American experimental psychology: A historical and a systematic collation and a look into the future. *Psychol. Bull.*, 1965, *63*, 42–64.

Woodworth, R. S., & Sheehan, Mary R. *Contemporary schools of psychology.* (3rd ed.) New York: Ronald, 1964. Pp. 90–110.

I. M. SECHENOV
Ischlondsky, N. The life and activity of I. M.

Sechenov. *J. nerv. ment. Dis.*, 1958, *126*, 367–391.

Sechenov, I. M. *Selected works.* Moscow: State Publ. House for Biological and Medical Literature, 1935.

I. P. PAVLOV

Gantt, W. H. Pavlov's system. In B. B. Wolman & E. Nagel (Eds.), *Scientific psychology: principles and approaches.* New York: Basic Books, 1965. Pp. 127–149.

Pavlov, I. P. *Selected works.* (Trans. by S. Belsky) Moscow: Foreign Languages Publ. House, 1955.

Pavlov, I. P. *Lectures on conditioned reflexes: twenty-five years of objective study of higher nervous activity (behavior) of animals.* (Trans. by W. H. Gantt) New York: Liveright, 1928.

Pavlov, I. P. A brief outline of the higher nervous activity. (Trans. by D. L. Zyve) In C. Murchison (Ed.), *Psychologies of 1930.* Worcester, Mass.: Clark Univer. Press, 1930. Pp. 207–220.

Pavlov, I. P. *Conditioned reflexes: an investigation of the physiological activity of the cerebral cortex.* (Trans. G. V. Anrep) London: Oxford Univer. Press, 1927.

Wells, H. K. Ivan P. Pavlov. New York: International Publishers, 1956.

REFLEXOLOGY: V. M. BEKHTEREV

Bekhterev, V. M. *General principles of human reflexology.* New York: International Publishers, 1932.

Schniermann, A. L. Bekhterev's reflexological school. In C. Murchison (Ed.), *Psychologies of 1930.* Worcester, Mass.: Clark Univer. Press, 1930. Pp. 221–242.

REACTOLOGY: K. N. KORNILOV

Kornilov, K. N. Psychology in the light of dialectic materialism. In. C Murchison (Ed.), *Psychologies of 1930.* Worcester, Mass.: Clark Univer. Press, 1930. Pp. 243–278.

Razran, G. K. N. Kornilov, theoretical and experimental psychologist. *Science*, 1958, *128*, 74–75.

SOVIET PSYCHOLOGY: 1920–1950

Ananiev, B. Achievements of Soviet psychologists. *J. gen. Psychol.*, 1948, *38*, 257–262.

Borovski, V. M. Psychology in the U.S.S.R. *J. gen. Psychol.*, 1929, *2*, 177–186.

London, I. A historical survey of psychology in the Soviet Union. *Psychol. Bull.*, 1949, *46*, 241–277.

London, I. Psychology in the U.S.S.R. *Amer. J. Psychol.*, 1951, *64*, 422–428.

Luria, A. R. Psychology in Russia. *J. genet. Psychol.*, 1928, *35*, 347–355.

Razran, G. Current psychological theory in the U.S.S.R. *Psychol. Bull.*, 1942, *39*, 445–446.

Schniermann, A. L. Present day tendencies in Russian psychology. *J. gen. Psychol.*, 1928, *1*, 397–404.

Schultz, R. S., & McFarland, R. A. Industrial psychology in the Soviet Union. *J. appl. Psychol.*, 1935, *19*, 265–308.

Viteles, M. S. Industrial psychology in Russia. *Occup. Psychol.*, 1938, *12*, 85–103.

SOVIET PSYCHOLOGY AFTER 1950

Bauer, R. A. (Ed.) *Some views on Soviet psychology.* Washington, D.C.: American Psychol. Ass., 1962.

Bauer, R. A. *The new man in Soviet psychology.* Cambridge, Mass.: Harvard Univer. Press, 1952.

Brackbill, Yvonne. Experimental research with children in the Soviet Union: report of a visit. *Amer. Psychologist*, 1960, *15*, 226–233.

Brožek, J. Current status of psychology in the U.S.S.R. *Annu. Rev. Psychol.*, 1962, *13*, 515–566.

Brožek, J. Recent developments in Soviet psychology. *Annu. Rev. Psychol.*, 1964, *15*, 493–594.

Cervin, V. B. Comparison of psychological curricula at French, Russian, Czech, and Canadian universities. *Canad. Psychologist*, 1964, *5a*, 75–86.

David, H. P. *International resources in clinical psychology.* New York: McGraw-Hill, 1964.

Mintz, A. Recent developments in psychology in the U.S.S.R. *Annu. Rev. Psychol.*, 1958, *9* 453–504.

Mintz, A. Further developments in psychology in the U.S.S.R. *Annu. Rev. Psychol.*, 1959, *10*, 455–487.

Murray, H. A., May, M. A., & Cantril, H. Some glimpses of Soviet psychology. *Amer. Psychologist*, 1959, *14*, 303–307.

O'Connor, N. (Ed.) *Recent Soviet psychology.* New York: Liveright, 1961.

Razran, G. Soviet psychology since 1950. *Science*, 1957, *126*, 1100–1107.

Razran, G. Soviet psychology and psychophysiology. *Science*, 1958, *128*. 1187–1194.

Simon, B. (Ed.) *Psychology in the Soviet Union.* Stanford, Calif.: Stanford Univer. Press, 1957.

Winn, R. B. (Ed.) *Psychotherapy in the Soviet Union.* New York: Philosophical Library, 1961.

16

Psychology in Asia

NO ACCOUNT OF PSYCHOLOGY'S DEVELOPMENT should overlook the progress of psychology in Asia during the post-World War II period. In the past, Western psychologists have explained their inattention to Asian psychology on the basis of its few significant contributions. There was also always the unilateral language barrier. Whereas many Asian psychologists knew English, French, and German, Western psychologists rarely had knowledge of Oriental languages.

After World War II the picture changed. Increased communication between Eastern and Western psychologists—through student exchanges, exchange professorships, and improved transportation facilities—brought East and West closer together. Psychology in Asia began to make progress. Furthermore, the founding of the international journal of the Orient, *Psychologia* (published in English), in 1957 has offered a valuable medium for psychological interchange. Both Oriental and Occidental psychology have profited and been enriched from these closer contacts. While language and cultural barriers have not been completely surmounted, increased understanding and appreciation have resulted.

One noticeable postwar feature is that Western psychology, particularly American psychology, has made a powerful impact in most countries, except China Mainland, where Soviet influence has prevailed. Psychology in Asia in the 1960's is characterized by an emphasis on applied psychology —testing, vocational and educational guidance, educational, clinical, and industrial psychology, and applied social research. Broad, basic research in experimental psychology is not cultivated extensively in Asia. In most Eastern countries, psychological knowledge, imported from the West, is used in the interests of social welfare and social reconstruction. Psychology's assistance has been enlisted in different Asian countries for the solution of diverse problems resulting from democratization, educational reforms, industrialization, and technological changes. The general progress of scientific psychology in Asia, however, can only be understood by examining its development in individual countries.

A survey of psychology in Asian countries reveals several rather universal needs for the field: recognition of psychology as a discipline separate from philosophy and education; improved university training programs; encouragement of original basic research; and an increased number of trained psychologists. In Asian, as in other countries, the demand for psychological services exists; but it cannot be met because of the dearth of trained professional psychologists. Some idea of this deficiency can be obtained from H. C. Lindgren's data on the number of psychologists per million inhabitants in the major countries of Asia (based on the 1958 International Directory of Psychologists) :

China Mainland	.1
China Taiwan	2.0
India	.5
Japan	81.0
Pakistan	.3

From these data it is immediately apparent that, with the exception of Japan, psychology in the Orient is still in its rudimentary stages. While the attainments of these few countries hold promise of extensive future growth, no substantial gains in psychology as science or profession can be achieved unless the ranks of psychologists in almost all the Asian countries are considerably augmented.

JAPAN

Occidental philosophical thought and European findings in anatomy and physiology, which led to Japanese psychology's independent status as a science, first appeared in Japanese writings after the Japanese Revolution (1868). In 1874, A. Nishi (1829-1898) introduced Occidental psychology in his translation of J. S. Mill's *A System of Logic*, followed in 1878 by a translation of J. Haven's *Mental Philosophy*. Eventually translations of Bain, Sully, Wundt, James, and Ladd were also published. The first psychological lectures at the University of Tokyo were given by M. Toyama (1848-1900). S. Nishimura (1828-1902), who emancipated Japanese psychology from religion, urged the Japanese to study Western psychology and its scientific models, but to adapt its concepts to traditional Oriental thinking. Some understanding of traditional Oriental thinking is needed to appreciate the background into which scientific psychology was received in Japan.

BACKGROUND OF JAPANESE SCIENTIFIC PSYCHOLOGY

From ancient times psychology had been cultivated in Japan as a philosophy of mind or as metaphysics by Buddhism and Confucianism. These philosophies together with Shintoism—a religion and national philosophy —created the setting for Japanese importation of scientific psychology in the late nineteenth century. Particularly significant for the new scientific psychology was Zen Buddhism—a blend of Indian Buddhism and Chinese Taoism—which flowered in Japan in the thirteenth century and profoundly influenced Japanese thinking and culture. Zen is an intuitive school of meditation whose goal is to lead the individual to *satori*—or the enlightenment which characterized the Buddha. This enlightenment is a state of lucid awareness of, and openness to, reality. Only an individual with *satori* was believed to be able to lead a satisfying and effective life. The Zen method, which became increasingly popular in Western psychology after World War II, involved self-training to enable the individual to discipline his mind—to grasp intuitively and directly his experiencing of reality, to know the workings of his own mind, and the nature of his own being. The individual must learn to perceive intuitively what he cannot perceive rationally. There is no trance or loss of consciousness. Ordinary cognitive functions are not impaired. Through meditation and concentration, unhampered by distractions and restrictions, each person must simply find this greater awareness for himself. This type of self-reflection was firmly rooted in Japanese culture, together with Confucianism and Shintoism.

As early as 1729, B. Ishida tried to synthesize the philosophies of Buddhism, Confucianism, and Shintoism as a means of clarifying for the layman the instructions of his ethics. Ishida taught that a man must have a clear consciousness of his actions to behave morally. Later, Ho Kamada (1754-1821), who has been called the first Japanese psychologist, organized Japanese thinking into a unique system of psychology. Then during the latter half of the nineteenth century, Western influences crept into Japanese psychological thought from Great Britain, Germany, France, and the United States. Anglo-American and German influences became the principal determinants of later psychological activity in Japan.

FOUNDATIONS OF JAPANESE PSYCHOLOGY

During the last two decades of the nineteenth century, several Japanese students—the nation's later leaders of psychology—studied experimental psychology and conducted researches at foreign universities, chiefly German and American. Two of these students, Y. Motora and M. Matsumoto, became the principal pioneers of scientific psychology in Japan and are generally recognized as the founders of Japanese psychology. Motora, of philosophic mind, was the first systematist and theorist. Matsumoto, an experimentalist, was the father of applied psychology in Japan and a prominent teacher of the early leaders of Japanese psychology.

Yujiro Motora (1858-1912). After receiving his Ph.D. (1888) at Johns Hopkins University under G. Stanley Hall, Motora became the first professor of psychology at the University of Tokyo. His early research on dermal sensitivity in collaboration with Hall was reported in the first volume of the *American Journal of Psychology* (1887). Upon his return to Japan, Motora began a study of Zen. At the Fifth International Congress of Psychology in Rome (1905) he delivered a paper entitled *The Concept of Self in Oriental Philosophy*, which became famous as the first formal introduction of Zen Buddhism to the West. Motora sharply criticized the mechanical character of the British associationists' concept of mind.

Primarily a systematist, Motora presented his theories and views of mind in two works: *Psychology* (1893) and *Essentials of Psychology* (1910). His *Outline of Systematic Psychology* (1915), a posthumous work, offered an exposition of his psychological system in its most mature form. Motora's psychology, pragmatic in character, sought to extend psychological investigations beyond the laboratory to a variety of human activities in society, and to derive psychological laws from them. His influence in Japan is comparable to that of James in the United States or of Stout in England. Motora encouraged Japanese study of scientific psychology through his teaching, through his publications, and through his participation in professional organizations. He was, for example, president of the Society for Child Study (established in 1888).

Matataro Matsumoto (1865-1943). Like Motora, Matsumoto studied experimental psychology in the United States. At Yale University, under Scripture, he conducted research on acoustic space and published his findings in the *Studies of the Yale Psychology Laboratory* (1897). After inspecting American, British, and German laboratories, including Wundt's at Leipzig, Matsumoto returned home in 1900 and designed Japan's first psychological laboratory at the University of Tokyo (1903). Three years later he was appointed professor of psychology at Kyoto University and established the first chair of psychology there as well as a laboratory (1908). The laboratories at Tokyo and Kyoto were the only ones in Japan until 1920. At Motora's death, Matsumoto succeeded him at Tokyo (1913). Since he survived Motora by 31 years, Matsumoto's influence was naturally more extensive.

While Matsumoto borrowed his psychological theory from Wundt, he clearly demonstrated his originality in applied psychology—particularly in his contributions to psychocinematics, the study of psychophysiological behavior. In his book entitled *Psychocinematics* (1914) he formally presented his objective study of purposive bodily movements. His later comprehensive work, *Psychology of Intelligence* (1925)—a milestone in Japanese applied psychology—treated various topics in addition to intelligence: mental work, efficiency, environmental factors, senescence, and military psychology. A sketch of the general development of psychology was also presented together with a summary of studies done by Japanese psychologists under Matsumoto's direction. A special feature of the book is a review of related work by Western psychologists. Versatility characterized Matsumoto's work. An interest in Japanese art led him to write *Psychology of Aesthetic Appreciation of Pictorial Arts* (1926). His emphasis on, and encouragement of, research on the aged made him a pioneer in the psychology of senescence. But above all, Matsumoto's psychocinematics advanced applied psychology in Japan and gained a reputation for him as the Japanese pioneer of objective psychology.

Early Trends. In Japan, as in most countries, scientific psychology progressed slowly at first. Wundtian psychology and American functionalism exerted strong influence since the first Japanese students went to the United States and to Germany for psychological training. From these countries also came the principal psychological textbooks which were translated, widely read, and used in Japan. By the first decade of the twentieth century, experimental studies were undertaken in the psychological laboratories of Tokyo and Kyoto. Students began to study experimental psychology at native universities. Between 1901 and 1917 Japanese psychologists devoted themselves to learning the methods of psychological research.

Although interest in classical experimental psychology ran high, interest in applied psychology also appeared early. Interest in educational psychology was precipitated by the importation of pedagogy from the United States and Germany. In 1882, S. Izawa, recently returned from the United States, published *Pedagogics*. Thereafter, in the early 1900's, numerous books entitled "Educational Psychology" appeared which were little more than general psychology treatises with occasional comments considered useful to teachers. Foreign tests of intelligence—such as the Binet-Simon —and achievement tests were also introduced and adapted for Japanese use. Interest in child study and in educational measurement was fostered by Y. Kubo (1883-1942), who had studied under Hall at Clark University and who founded the Child Study Institute in Japan in 1916. This Institute published annually up to 1937 the *Transactions of the Institute for Child Study*, which was a significant publication for educational psychology in Japan at that time. A pioneer of test studies in Japan, Kubo used the Binet and group intelligence tests. His educational measurement activity also included achievement tests in school subjects, such as reading, writing, arithmetic, and English.

Up to 1910 most of the Japanese psychological work in research and theory was reported in the *Philosophy Magazine*. In 1911 Japanese psychologists published their first journal, *Psychic Study*. The *Japanese Journal of Psychology* was founded by G. Kuroda in 1919. Japanese psychologists also began to write their own textbooks. In addition to the works of Motora and Matsumoto, other important volumes were written— such as K. Ohtsuki's 1,000 page *Experimental Psychology* (1911), which drew heavily on Wundt, Titchener, and on other German and American sources. Various systems and views, such as those of Brentano and the Würzburg school, were explored and studied with interest. As Japanese psychologists were attracted to functionalism and behaviorism, Wundt's psychology and structuralism were sharply criticized.

Behaviorism in Japan. A series of events paved the way for the introduction of behaviorism in Japan. We have already seen that, through his psychocinematics, Matsumoto introduced objective psychology. Narasaki, his student, further extended psychocinematics. Neither of them, however, intended that psychocinematics—with its objective methods—should supplant the traditional psychology which demanded introspection. Furthermore, introduction of the Russian conditioning studies of Pavlov and Bekhterev by Sakuma (1915) and G. Kuroda (1916) also paved the way for behavioristic psychology. Under the influence of American psychologists, the redefinition of psychology as a science of behavior—rather than of consciousness—was proposed by an applied psychologist, Y. Ueno (1911 and 1913). Ueno's early emphasis on behavior, however, was overshadowed by his later criticism of Watson's behaviorism and by his insistence that behavioristic methods were merely auxiliary to introspection.

One year after its establishment in America by Watson, behaviorism was introduced to Japan (1914) by Narasaki and H. Hayami. Narasaki saw in behaviorism a kinship with psychocinematics, because of their mutual emphasis on objectivity. Objective and behavioristic methods, he insisted, were as different from introspection as things were from mind. Accordingly, he demanded that a distinction be made between psychocinematics on the one hand and pure psychology on the other. Hayami recognized that limitation of psychology to the study of consciousness would restrict the development of animal and child psychology. Yet he felt that direct experience could not be studied by behavioristic and objective methods. Although he called attention to behaviorism, Hayami was not one of its protagonists. On the contrary, he inclined toward philosophical psychology and, in particular, toward the views of T. Lipps, Husserl, and Natorp.

Other Japanese psychologists were opposed to reductionistic and physiological theories. While acknowledging the physiological bases of mental phenomena, T. Chiba, for example, argued that these phenomena could not be reduced to mere physiology. M. Imada, who accepted behaviorism as an independent science, nonetheless insisted that its mechanistic principles made it inadequate to analyze concrete experiences. An opponent of the sharp distinction between behaviorism and introspectionism, K. Masuda, called for synthesis of the two systems in 1923. By 1920, however, Gestalt psychology had reached Japan from Germany. Thereafter, the discussions and criticisms of behaviorism were mainly construed in comparison to Gestalt psychology. It became evident that, although Japanese psychologists rather generally favored objective methods, they were reluctant to sever philosophical ties and to abandon consciousness. Perhaps this explains, at least in part, the strong influence of Gestalt psychology in Japan after 1930.

EXPANSION AND DECLINE BETWEEN TWO WORLD WARS

With improved economic conditions in Japan after World War I, the number of colleges and universities increased. New departments of psychology were created. Increased facilities and increased opportunities—academic and professional—attracted more students for psychological training. More attention was directed toward industrial psychology, psychology of crime and delinquency, and to child welfare. With the latter came an increased demand for research on children. Consequently, educational psychology, testing, child study, and guidance were developed rapidly and intensively. At the beginning of the second quarter of the twentieth century, Japanese psychology was set to enter an era of expansion. Between the years 1926 and 1935 Japanese scientific psychology and its applications advanced steadily. Among the more significant developments during this period were: the advent of a new wave of German influence and, particularly, the introduction of Gestalt psychology; the emergence of deliberate concern for original contributions to psychology; the founding of the Japanese Psychological Association; and the cultivation of diverse branches of psychology.

German Influence and Gestalt Psychology. After World War I a new wave of German influence in the form of holistic psychologies reached Japan. We have already seen that these psychologies became prominent in Germany after Wundt's death in 1920. About 1926, the researches of the Leipzig school, including Krueger's *Ganzheitspsychologie,* and the psychology of Stern were imported. In the 1930's German-style eidetic imagery and characterology studies also appeared. However, these psychologies and their related researches apparently exercised a minimal influence in comparison to that of Gestalt psychology.

In 1921, after visits to Germany, several Japanese psychologists described Wertheimer's study of apparent movement and reported on the researches of Stumpf and Köhler. K. Sakuma and U. Onoshima, who studied at the University of Berlin, began the first Gestalt researches in Japan about 1926. Thus, these men became the first Japanese proponents of Gestalt psychology. After 1926, the *Japanese Journal of Psychology* published numerous Gestalt studies. Various Japanese books on this system appeared about 1930, including Onoshima's *Twelve Lectures on the Latest Psychologies* and *Fundamental Problems of the Latest Psychologies*; Kubo's *Gestalt Psychology*; and Sakuma's translation of Köhler's *Gestalt Psychology.* After 1930, the psychological institutes of most Japanese universities trained students along lines of Gestalt research. The volume of Gestalt studies grew, but some failed to support Gestalt theory. However, the Gestalt influence—so evident before World War II in the abundant studies of perceptual space, depth perception, tactile and visual apparent movement—was still discernible in the 1960's.

Search for Identity. At first, Japanese psychologists had been content to import foreign psychology. During their orientation to experimental methods, they were preoccupied with deriving the facts from their own experimentation. As psychology progressed in Japan, however, psychologists were less content merely to import. They wanted to revise traditional psychology in terms of their own Oriental culture and to make original contributions.

It is not surprising that the topic of perennial interest to Japanese psychologists, namely consciousness, provided a basis for formulation of original theories. Between 1920 and 1930 several theories emerged from studies on perception and animal behavior. They were generally developed in terms of the Oriental view of personality. Among such contributions were Chiba's theory of proper consciousness (1927) and Sakuma's theory of basic consciousness as directly experienced (1931). Unique theories were developed by others, such as R. Kuroda (1890-1947), one of the most outstanding Japanese animal psychologists. He insisted that psychology must study behavior and that it must treat unconsciousness as well as consciousness. Kuroda proposed a "psychology of comprehension or stereo-psychology" (1931), based on Buddhist psychology which dichotomized experience into comprehension and consciousness. The struggle for originality and rejection of allegiance to particular schools or "isms" were further evidenced in the publications of this period: Kubo's two volume *Handbook of Experimental Psychology* (1926-1927); Masuda's *Introduction to Experimental Psychology* (1926)—a beginner's manual—and his significant general psychology volume, *Methodology of Psychology* (1934); and Kido's *General Outline of Psychology* (1931).

As Japanese psychologists produced their own research, textbooks, and theories in larger volume, they became increasingly self-conscious and self-critical. They recognized the need to communicate not only with each other but with psychologists of other lands. To implement their aims, they established the Japanese Psychological Association in 1927. The Association's meetings and publications provided opportunities both for communication and for continuing self-scrutiny and self-evaluation. Matsumoto's presidential address of 1933 furnishes evidence of such self-criticism. Three weaknesses of Japanese psychology at that time were cited by him: (1) impetuous adoption of Western psychology without sufficient scrutiny and evaluation; (2) dearth of analytic researches and excessive use of group techniques and questionnaires; and (3) inadequate communication among Japanese psychologists resulting in adequate and ineffective research.

In spite of its weaknesses, however, Japanese psychology continued to progress until 1935, the year of optimal development for psychology in Japan before World War II. A substantial number of important scientific journals were being published, including the *Japanese Journal of Experimental Psychology* (1934), *Tohoku Psychologica Folia* (1933), and *Acta Psychologica Keijo* (1930). Publications representing specialized branches of psychology became available, such as *Animal Psyche, Japanese Journal of Educational Psychology* (1926), and *Japanese Journal of Applied Psychology*. This proliferation of journals attests to the increased productivity of Japanese psychologists during the 1920's and 1930's. Although interest in experimental psychology still predominated, applied psychology also had its advocates, men such as T. Watanabe, K. Tanaka, and Y. Awaji who organized the Japanese Society of Applied Psychology in 1931.

Areas of Research and Application. *Experimental* psychology bore the stamp of Gestalt influence from 1926 to 1939. Sensation and perception were the principal areas of study. Investigations of eidetic imagery, depth perception, apparent movement, perceptual space, size and shape constancy, thinking, and animal behavior were conducted by a few enthusiastic investigators. Researches on human learning were fewer, but they covered various phases of learning and memory. Personality received only limited consideration. T. Watanabe, a pioneer of personality study and a champion of applied psychology, wrote a volume entitled *Prosopology, the Study of Personality*, as early as 1912. But the first systematic researches on personality began in the 1930's under the stimulation of the recently imported German characterology.

In *educational* psychology studies of development, learning, work, fatigue, and personality were conducted. The principal centers for this research were Tokyo and Hiroshima College of Arts and Science. At Tokyo, Tanaka, Narasaki, I. Terazawa, and T. Takemasa wrote textbooks of educational psychology. From 1926 to 1940 they edited a semiprofessional journal, *The Study of Educational Psychology*, which popularized this specialty. Translations of foreign works, such as Thorndike's *Educational Psychology*, also appeared in this period. Studies in *developmental* psychology relevant to education were done at Kyoto University on adolescence (T. Nogami) and on childhood (K. Iwai, M. Kato, T. Sonohara, and M. Moriya). Influenced by Charlotte Bühler's work, Kubo wrote on child psychology, as did K. Hatano—who publicized Piaget's views. An almost exclusive interest in the study of senescence was shown by Tachibana.

Measurement was given impetus by the theoretical studies of tests (Y. Okabe, Tanaka, and S. Otomo). After Otomo, a student of Judd's, published his two volume *Diagnostics of Education* (1928, 1933), intelligence tests were extensively developed and used in Japanese schools and industry. In 1930, standardizations of the Stanford-Binet scale were completed on 10,000 subjects by K. Suzuki, and the Goodenough Draw-A-Man Test was standardized by S. Kirihara. Group intelligence tests (verbal and nonverbal) and achievement tests were designed and widely used. The Rorschach Inkblot Test was introduced by Y. Uchida (1925). A few personality inventories and questionnaires were available, such as the Kirihara revision of the Downey Will Temperament Test (1930) and the Awaji-Okabe Introversion-Extroversion Inventory (1931). The most original personality test of this period was the Uchida-Kraepelin Psychodiagnostic Test (1927), an ingenious adaptation of Kraepelin's continuous addition method.

Mental measurement began to lose favor in the early 1930's. Tests were severely criticized and were eventually suppressed as antagonism toward Western objective measurement mounted. Moreover, the influence of Gestalt psychology, with its emphasis on synthesis, created a distaste for the analytic approach of measurement. With this repudiation of measurement, research studies diminished and progress in educational psychology was almost completely halted. This was particularly true after the outbreak of war with China (1932) when the state took complete control of education. In the 1930's, however, educators and psychologists studied children's behavior problems. Child guidance centers were established, and a few clinics were also affiliated with courts, reformatories, and prisons. These agencies, largely diagnostic in function, gave considerable attention to intelligence testing. Clinical psychology as a professional specialty, however, did not exist formally in Japan before World War II.

Psychoanalysis stimulated some of the first thinking about abnormality and therapy among Japanese psychologists. When it was first introduced into Japan about 1912, Freud's theories were explored simply as novel, interesting ideas, rather than as clinical methods. Treatment of neurosis was exclusively in the domain of the psychiatrist, and not the psychologist's concern. The most powerful advocate of psychoanalytic therapy was K. Marui, who returned to Japan in 1919, after studies with Adolf Meyer, and who became professor of psychiatry at Tohoku University. Marui wrote *Psychoanalytic Therapy* (1928), which encouraged psychiatrists to use psychoanalysis with children as well as with adults. Psychoanalysis had its severe critics, among them S. Morita, who, in 1928, offered his own theory of neurosis and therapy based on Zen thought. In spite of opposition, psychoanalysis aroused enough interest to support two publications in the 1930's: the nonmedical *Journal of Psychoanalysis* and *Beiträge zur Psychoanalyse* ("Contributions to Psychoanalysis"), an influential journal with a clinical emphasis. However, neither academic psychology nor psychiatry took psychotherapy seriously. The strong German influence and emphasis on neurology and psychopathology encouraged the use of somatic therapies. Few psychologists were attracted to clinical treatment of the emotionally disturbed. Two reasons for this disinterest before World War II were the university emphasis on academic experimental psychology and the lack of employment opportunities in clinical psychology.

Social psychology fared somewhat better than clinical. From 1908—when H. Higuchi published the first book on social psychology—until 1920, more than a dozen books on social psychology, group psychology, and racial psychology appeared. Initially social psychology was treated mainly by sociologists and social philosophers, who were influenced chiefly by French sociologists. Their methods of study were speculative rather than scientific. During the first quarter of the twentieth century, however, Wundt's folk psychology and McDougall's social psychology were introduced by Y. Kwata and C. Iritani, respectively. Between 1920 and 1930, Japanese psychologists fashioned a scientific methodology for their social psychology. After 1930, attitude measurement, group psychology, and racial differences were studied. Interest in perfecting methods of social psychology prompted closer scrutiny of American periodicals and publications, such as Murchison's *Handbook of Social Psychology*. In the thirties, various Japanese studies were done on competition, leadership, and friendship. Many of these grew out of incidental interests of experimental psychologists who were primarily concerned with perception or learning. No specialists in social psychology emerged from this activity.

Gradually in the late thirties, the political atmosphere became less and less conducive to the pursuit of social psychology. Tight, powerful militaristic controls, and the risk of political or philosophical misinterpretations, made it perilous to conduct social research, especially on topics such as morale and public opinion. By 1940 the social sciences had practically withered away in Japan. The papers of several psychologists, edited in

1942 by Matsumoto and entitled *Social Psychology* and *Racial Psychology*, may well be considered the last vestiges of Japanese social psychology for this period.

Japanese *industrial* psychology began with the efficiency movement in industry about 1910. A prominent pioneer was Y. Ueno (1883-1957), who published his *Lectures on Increasing Efficiency* in 1912. Translations of various foreign works, including Münsterberg's *Psychology and Industrial Efficiency* (K. Suzuki, 1919) were also published. After World War I, attention was focused on human relations in industry. Various institutes emerged, such as the Kurashiki Institute of the Science of Labor (founded by M. Ohara in 1921) with which Ueno and Kirihara were prominently affiliated. At these institutes systematic studies of human ability and performance were conducted, including job analyses, motion studies, employment testing, and investigations of psychological, physiological, and environmental factors affecting workers' performance. Courses in industrial psychology began to be offered and two journals, *The Science of Labor* and *Management*, were founded. Several books were published during the 1930's and 1940's: Kirihara's *Personnel Management* (1937), *Industrial Psychology* (1938), and *Vocational Guidance and After-Care* (1938); and Ueno's *Industrial Safety* (1942). Industrial psychology, however, did not develop as extensively as experimental and educational psychology before World War II. Not the least significant factor militating against its progress was Japan's overpopulation and the consequent ever-abundant supply of cheap labor. During the war, however, aptitude testing and selection procedures were extensively used in the military service.

Decline after 1935. After 1935 a decline in psychological activity occurred in Japan. This was occasioned by national unrest and by the political and military crises that led to the Sino-Japanese conflict in 1937 and, ultimately, to World War II. New views and new theories were introduced during this period, but they did not arouse the interest and enthusiasm characteristic of the previous decade. Pavlovian conditioning researches failed to elicit interest, as did operationism. Bridgman's new logic of science was studied critically in the early 1940's. It inspired a few investigations, but had minimal influence. The neo-behavioristic studies of Lashley and Tolman, associated with Gestalt psychology, were introduced and received attention principally because the Gestalt influence on experimental psychology persisted.

Personality research, social psychology, and mental measurement were crushed by the rising Japanese militarism and by controls on all social science. During World War II, psychologists in the army and navy did personnel selection and placement studies; but studies of human relations in the service, or of soldier groups, were not permitted. Contributions were made principally to aviation psychology—in which, since the early 1930's, the Japanese had an active research program. During the war, test development yielded place to mere routine processing of candidates for flight training.

Japanese psychology, which gave great promise at the outset, was dealt a final devastating blow by World War II. The number of graduate students in psychology was reduced practically to zero. Psychological research came to a veritable standstill, and the publication of journals was curtailed. By 1945, even the *Japanese Journal of Psychology* was no longer published regularly. The Japanese Society of Applied Psychology merged with the Japanese Psychological Association. Above all, war and its concomitant restrictions isolated Japanese psychologists and prevented them from knowing about psychological developments in other lands.

RENASCENCE OF JAPANESE PSYCHOLOGY

In 1945 the arduous task of postwar reconstruction was begun. Radical social, political, and educational changes accompanied the democratization of Japan. During the Occupation (1945-1952), Japanese psychology slowly but steadily recovered. By the 1960's it was forging ahead toward increased international recognition.

General Aspects of Revival. United States Occupation educational policy not only demanded reform of Japan's educational system; it also influenced academic trends in psychology. After 1946, the number of graduate students in psychology far exceeded prewar levels. At the universities, psychology programs and curricula were developed and expanded. Translations of foreign works continued, but Japanese books appeared in increasing numbers. Old journals resumed publication. New ones were founded; such as the *Japanese Journal of Educational Psychology* (1952); *Japanese Psychological Research* (1954); *Tohoku Journal of Experimental Psychology* (1954); *Japanese Psychological Review* (1957); *Japanese Journal of Educational and Social Psychology* (1960); and *Japanese Annals of Social Psychology* (1960). Increased psychological services in schools, universities, clinics, and in industry provided professional opportunities for psychologists. Membership in the Japanese Psychological Association grew steadily from approximately 700 before the war to more than 2,000 in 1960. Special groups, such as the Japanese Society of Applied Psychology and the Japanese Psychoanalytic Association, were founded or reorganized.

Although some German influences persisted in the emphasis on perceptual research and in the personality studies based on the theories of Kraepelin and Kretschmer, American influence predominated. The frequent citation of American references in contemporary Japanese literature attests to the strong impact of American psychology. Experimental and educational psychology remained important areas of Japanese psychological endeavor, and the previously underdeveloped clinical psychology and social psychology drew more attention. In the succeeding sections postwar trends in the specific branches of psychology in Japan will be noted.

Experimental Psychology. Experimental research on *perception*, mainly visual, continued to predominate, with a concentration on fewer problems than in the past. Numerous studies have been done on figural aftereffects, perceptual constancy, illusions, depth perception, and retinal induction. For his celebrated work in psychophysiology on retinal induction, K. Motokawa has been generally recognized as the most outstanding modern worker on perception. Second only to perception in popularity is *learning* (human and animal). Unlike research in perception, learning research has greatly increased since 1945—with studies on discrimination, incidental learning, inhibition effects, classical conditioning, and schedules of reinforcement. Particularly noteworthy is the heightened interest in the study of animal behavior. Mazes, Skinner boxes, and all kinds of electronic apparatus and recording devices enjoy wide use. The numerous reports of animal research have warranted publication of an *Annual of Animal Psychology* (1943).

Contrasted to that in animal psychology, research on personality as such failed to develop significantly after the war. It was studied incidentally in researches on perception and in investigations of the effects of motives on discrimination. Concern with personality theory has occupied psychologists like K. Sato, author of *Psychology of Personality* (Rev. ed. 1953), whose personality theory is based on both Oriental and Western systems.

Japanese psychologists have scrutinized operationism and explored new methods, such as stochastics and factor analysis. They have introduced hypnotic methods into personality research. Their continued interest in the theory and history of experimental psychology is attested to by their contributions to contemporary literature: T. Yatabe's *A History of Thinking* (1948) and his three volume *Psychology of Thinking* (1948-1954); and the several volumes of a *Handbook of Experimental Psychology*, edited by S. Takagi and M. Kido, which have appeared since 1951.

Educational Psychology, Developmental Psychology, and Measurement. After the war, there were few Japanese educational psychologists, and they were mainly interested in determining the effects of war and postwar upheaval on the intellectual, emotional, and moral development of children and adolescents. As a result of the educational reforms, educational psychology became a requirement in teacher training programs. At many universities educational psychology was made a special course, distinct from general psychology. These changes increased the number of educational psychologists, who then organized their own professional groups, such as the Japanese Association of Educational Psychology and the Japanese Society for the Study of Education, the latter of which published the *Japanese Journal of Educational Psychology*.

In this period, American child study, methods of learning, and educational guidance procedures were introduced. Prominent American psychologists such as A. Jersild, L. D. Crow, and L. J. Cronbach, lectured on educational psychology in Japan. Gradually many Japanese texts on the subject appeared. Some emphasized the humanistic viewpoint in education and others, the social-psychological. Japanese educational psychology research in the 1960's included studies on measurement and evaluation; growth and development; personality and adjustment; exceptional children; and human relations. Studies on the psychology of individual school subjects, more numerous earlier, tended to decline during this period.

Shortly after the war's end, several American texts on developmental psychology—such as those of Jersild and Goodenough—were translated. Soon Japanese psychologists produced their own works on child and adolescent psychology. Only later, and then to a much more limited degree, was attention directed to studies of maturity and senescence. Tachibana, prominent in this branch of developmental psychology before the war, has retained his leadership and continued to urge psychological research on the aged. Experimental studies on learning, thinking, reasoning, and on mental development of children continue to be conducted. Developmental psychology, like educational psychology, has captured the attention of the general public as well as of educators and psychologists. Many popular publications in these areas have appeared in Japan.

Under American influence, the earlier interest of the Japanese in mental measurement was also resurrected. Tanaka, a prewar leader in measurement, remained active in this field until his death (1962). Diagnostic aspects of testing were stressed in schools and guidance centers. Intelligence testing received most attention in the beginning—from 1946 to 1955. The Binet and many American tests, including the Wechsler Adult Intelligence Scale (WAIS) and the Wechsler Intelligence Scale for Children (WISC), were adapted and restandardized for Japanese populations. A large number of group intelligence tests were developed. Techniques such as factor analysis were applied in the construction of tests.

After 1956, attention was directed primarily to construction of intelligence tests for exceptional persons, such as the deaf, feebleminded, and gifted. Research on intelligence and intelligence tests yielded place to the development of personality tests and, particularly, of projective tests. The Rorschach has enjoyed a dominant position and wide use. Although some progress has been made in personality tests and diagnostic aids, Japanese psychologists recognize the need of constructing diagnostic tests and techniques suitable for their own culture. As in other countries, a constant problem for psychologists in Japan has been the restriction of test distribution to qualified personnel. They have not yet been able to establish legal or formal ethical codes to control this serious problem. Another major concern in professional circles is the establishment of qualifications for professional psychometrists.

Clinical Psychology. In the two decades after World War II, clinical psychology developed rapidly and gained status. About one-half of the nation's psychologists in the early 1960's were teaching either educational or clinical psychology or were engaged in clinical practice. Clinical psychologists have their own organization, the Japanese Association of Clinical Psychology and their own periodical, the *Japanese Journal of Clinical*

Psychology. The number of psychological clinics, public and private, increased substantially. By 1955 there were about 110 clinics scattered throughout Japan. These were staffed mainly by psychologists and social workers; rarely by psychiatrists. Clinical psychologists work in schools, universities, colleges, juvenile courts, child centers, and in institutions for the mentally retarded. Japanese adaptations of the Minnesota Multiphasic Personality Inventory, Rorschach, Thematic Apperception Test, Binet revisions, WISC, and WAIS are widely used for psychodiagnosis.

Under American influence, interest in counseling and psychotherapy was stimulated. However, in the early 1960's only a few Japanese clinical psychologists were doing psychotherapy. Most of them prefer the non-directive or Rogerian approach. Private practice of clinical psychology has not developed in Japan as in the United States. Many clinicians are self-trained and function without benefit of supervision by qualified psychotherapists. To meet the pressing academic and social demands, several universities have tried, in recent years, to develop training programs and curricula for clinical psychologists, counselors, and psychotherapists. The principal Japanese research and training center for clinical psychology is the National Institute of Mental Health, established in 1952.

Apart from limited training facilities, however, certain other barriers impede the development of psychotherapy in Japan. Therapy is chiefly practiced by psychiatrists who strongly subscribe to biochemical and biogenetic causes of mental illness. Both they and their patients prefer somatic therapies. In spite of its limited application, psychotherapy has been tried with individuals and groups, with adults and children. Japanese patients are treated with Morita therapy, psychoanalysis, nondirective therapy, and hypnotherapy, as well as with shock and drug therapies. Little interest has been directed to the learning approach to personality changes in counseling and psychotherapy, which is advocated by American psychologists such as O. H. Mowrer.

The two chief types of psychotherapy in use are Morita therapy and to a much lesser extent, psychoanalysis. Morita therapy—a blend of psychotherapy and Zen doctrine—is based on the concept that the patient's illness has made him unduly self-conscious and preoccupied with his physical and mental condition. Bed rest and work treatment are provided as distractions from self, and as a means of developing realistic attitudes toward life. Although client-centered in its stress on self-realization, Morita therapy is essentially directive. Deeply rooted in the traditional Japanese authoritarian climate of the early twentieth century, it appeals to the older generation. Conversely, the younger Japanese, schooled in democracy and awareness of individuality, prefer the nondirective approach. Most Japanese psychiatrists have been trained in Morita therapy and find it difficult to shed its influence. One of the problems for Japanese psychotherapists is the interpretation of Morita therapy from a psychoanalytic viewpoint and vice versa.

Since the renascence of psychoanalysis in 1945, new translations of Freud's works and translations of American psychoanalytic papers have been published. The Japanese Psychoanalytic Association, established in 1953, encourages cooperation among its membership—which includes psychiatrists and psychologists who are not psychoanalysts, as well as those who are. Criticism of Freudian psychoanalysis has continued as in prewar days; but a wider psychopathological viewpoint has become evident. Many Japanese psychologists and psychiatrists favor an eclectic approach. Basically they accept nondirective psychotherapy, but they also recognize the need for directive therapy. Some seek a better background in depth psychology approaches, like the neo-Freudian or existential. Others are anxious to develop their own theory and therapy by blending Oriental and Western psychological thought. Carl Jung, whose works have become better known since World War II, has been seen by many as providing the best link between East and West.

Social Psychology.   Social psychology progressed considerably after 1945 for several reasons: (1) Social science was freed from restraints and controls. (2) Resumption of communications brought new theories, methods, and data from foreign countries—principally from the United States. (3) The upheaval occasioned by the war and postwar reconstruction posed many social problems, solutions for which were sought in social psychology. (4) With the emergence of social psychology as a specialty, social psychologists participated in interdisciplinary research with sociologists and cultural and social anthropologists.

From 1945 to 1964 the foci of research interest in social psychology shifted rapidly. In the immediate postwar period, studies were done on social and cultural phenomena related to the war and its effects, and on group dynamics and interpersonal relationships associated with the democratization of Japan. Later, Japanese social psychologists directed attention to social perception; communication; sociometry; attitude measurement (including factorial studies); further study of group dynamics, culture and personality, public opinion, and market research. In market research, they have employed modern sampling methods and panel techniques. Several research centers have been organized, such as the *Group Dynamics Center* (Kyushu), and the *Center for Ethology* (Kyoto), which promote interdisciplinary research. The development of group dynamics and the study of mass communication have been acknowledged the most striking features of postwar Japanese social psychology. Although there is a wide range of topics investigated, the research on many of them still lacks depth.

In Japan, social psychology has certain disadvantages. At the universities, research facilities are often inadequate, and there are no special training programs for social psychologists. They get their training in departments of sociology and journalism as well as in psychology. Only about ten per cent of the nation's psychologists specialize in social psychology. Many are employed in business, in the mass communications industry, or in social service work. In 1955 they organized their own Society for Social Psychological Study. By 1959, its membership had grown to

200, and in 1960 it began publication of the *Japanese Annals of Social Psychology.*

Numerous texts on social psychology have been written since publication of the first postwar volume by H. Minami, who lived in the United States during the war, and who thus could introduce the new techniques of American social psychology into Japan. Several multivolume Japanese handbooks have been published: *Handbook of Social Psychology; Handbook of Applied Psychology;* and *Handbook of Mass Communication.* Since the war numerous translations of American volumes in social psychology and related areas have been published. On the roster of prominent authors whose works have been publicized in Japan are G. Allport, K. Lewin, G. Lindzey, H. Cantril, T. M. Newcomb, S. Asch, M. Sherif, E. Fromm, T. Parsons, H. D. Lasswell, D. Riesman, and R. Linton.

Industrial Psychology. Postwar industrial psychology continued along its management-oriented and labor-oriented lines as before. Mindful of their scientific and practical missions, Japanese psychologists have pursued studies of employee morale; accidents and safety; fatigue; and working conditions, as well as job analyses; personnel evaluation; marketing and consumer research. There has been increased, although not extensive, application of psychological techniques in personnel selection, placement, evaluation, and training during the 1950's and 1960's.

Only very limited professional opportunities for industrial psychologists have been provided in employment exchanges and in institutes for industrial research. A few chairs of industrial psychology and of vocational guidance have been established at the universities. Of all the Asian countries, Japan has made the most progress in vocational guidance. However, only a few counseling and testing centers are available to the general public. In these, generally, directive counseling and aptitude tests—mostly adaptations of American tests—are used. Almost two decades after the war, industrial psychology remained a minor specialty in Japan. The large labor supply has continued to minimize the need for selection procedures. Continued steady growth of Japanese industry seems to augur well for the increased application of psychology to business and industry in the future.

Japanese Psychology in the 1960's. In summary, Japanese experimental psychology continues to show American influence and to focus on studies of visual perception and learning. Little original research has appeared in social, clinical, personality, or industrial psychology. Since 1945, more emphasis has been given to industrial psychology, but it is still relatively underdeveloped. Clinical and social psychology, on the other hand, have made considerable advance since the war.

Although clinical psychology in Japan has not developed as fully as in the United States, the number of clinics has increased, a variety of diagnostic tests and techniques is being used, and some interest in psychotherapy has emerged. The latter interest is largely academic since clinical psychologists have little opportunity to do therapy, and psychiatrists, who are responsible for therapy, have shown little inclination to accept the dynamic American psychiatry. When they employ psychotherapy at all, they prefer approaches or therapies in the Oriental mode of thought, such as Morita therapy, not psychoanalytic or depth psychological approaches such as existential psychotherapy.

Generally speaking, professional psychology has not reached its full development in Japan. Wider applications of psychology in government, education, and industry are essential if professional opportunities are to be extended in nonacademic settings. Perhaps the most serious problem for Japanese psychology of the 1960's is the lack of sound educational and training programs in the universities and the lack of standardization from university to university. Psychology is variously offered in departments of literature, education, or philosophy. Consigned to the humanities rather than to the natural sciences, psychology as a rule finds itself with poor laboratory facilities and very little research support. The Japanese universities have been slow to establish new chairs of psychology, a factor which has tended to retard the development of clinical psychology. Moreover, Japanese graduate training follows the traditional European pattern. A single professor works with several assistants who serve as apprentices and do some teaching, an arrangement that may continue for many years. The awarding of advanced degrees is contingent not upon completion of a prescribed program within a specified time limit, but rather upon the student's defense of his research and upon the judgment of his professor. It has been charged that the obvious need to maintain the good will of his professor may stifle originality in the student.

These difficulties are further compounded by the fact that universities publish many reports and monographs of their research which are not widely circulated. Hence they are often inaccessible to other Japanese psychologists, who thus remain unaware of researches in their own country. A persistent and larger communication problem for Japanese psychology is its isolation because Western psychologists have had little knowledge of the Japanese language. For this reason, much of Japanese psychology that should have been known went unnoticed for many years. Appendage of English abstracts to articles in Japanese journals has helped Western psychologists a little. A boon to communication between East and West is *Psychologia*, the journal of Oriental psychology, which is published in English and edited by Koji Sato, of Kyoto University, a leading contemporary psychologist in Japan. This publication—together with various intercultural seminars, exchange scholarships, and professorships—has done much to bring Oriental and Western psychologists together in the 1960's.

CHINA

Anticipations of Chinese psychology have been cited from ancient Chinese teachings of Confucius, Lao-tse, and Buddhism and from the philosophical writings of Wing Yang-Ming and others of later periods. However, Chinese scientific psychology is essentially a twentieth century development. It arose in the wake of the new contacts with Western culture, coincident with the establishment of the Chinese republic in 1912. In the early 1900's it passed through the usual period of emancipation from philosophy and through the usual introductory phases, as in other countries: translation of European and American authors such as Wundt, LeBon, McDougall, James, Watson, Dewey, and Woodworth; Chinese students' acquisition of psychological training at foreign universities, mostly American, but some British, German, and French; and the establishment of Chinese departments and laboratories of psychology, and of psychological societies and publications. From the outset, American functionalism exerted a strong influence on Chinese psychology.

Beginnings. Laboratory courses in psychology were first introduced into China at Southeastern University in Nanking (later National Central University), at National Peking University in Peking, and at Fuh Tan University in Shanghai. By 1927, S. K. Chou could report that there were ten departments of psychology in Chinese universities and that most, although not all, had apparatus for demonstrations and elementary laboratory courses. At that time none had a regular laboratory building used exclusively for research in experimental or animal work. The first university alleged to have established adequate laboratories and facilities for psychology was National Tsing Hua University in Peking.

The 1920's, particularly the years from 1922 to 1926, represented a period of much psychological activity, judging by the articles in the *Chinese Journal of Psychology*, founded in 1922 by the Chinese Psychological Society, and in the *Chinese Educational Review*. The range of topics covered—including abnormal, applied, animal, developmental, educational, experimental, industrial, social, systematic psychology, esthetics, and testing—demonstrates the broad scope of interests at the time. Several original works appeared, among them: T. C. Cheng's *Outlines of Psychology*, probably the oldest textbook; Z. Y. Kuo's *Human Behavior*; C. W. Luh's *Psychology*; and S. Liao's *Educational Psychology*. The most prominent Chinese psychologist of this period was Luh. He was well known for his studies on conditions of retention at the University of Chicago (1922). Kuo, the noted animal psychologist who introduced behaviorism to China, had also won distinction for his research (1930) initiating the anti-instinct movement in the United States.

In this early period interest in tests and measurements predominated, largely because psychology and education departments in China were jointly operated. W. A. McCall's arrival in China in 1923 as director of psychological research in the National Association for the Advancement of Education lent further impetus to the test movement. The contributions of Binet, Terman, Thorndike, and Pintner were carefully studied, and soon Chinese adaptations of their tests appeared. In 1930 psychologists and educators founded the Chinese Association of Psychological Testing in Nanking with three objectives in mind: (1) systematization of test preparation; (2) coordination of research programs on psychological and educational testing; and (3) promotion of test use in education, industry, and elsewhere. Progress in measurement was accompanied by increased attention to educational psychology and child study. In 1931, the first child study laboratory was opened at Fu Jen University in Peiping under the auspices of the department of psychology and without any school system affiliation. Here children were tested and observed under laboratory conditions. Child guidance received added stimulation with the founding of the Chinese Association for Mental Hygiene in 1937.

Pre-World War II Status of Chinese Psychology. By 1933, although foreign systems such as Gestalt psychology were still being imported, Chinese psychology had reached a period of independent research. The National Research Institute of Psychology (Academia Sinica) and the departments of psychology of Tsing Hua, Yenching, and Central Universities were all active. Moreover, Chinese psychologists became more self-critical and were trying to improve their science. In 1933, G. H. Wang complained, for example, that Chinese psychologists had gone astray in their overemphasis on testing and studies of maze learning in the white rat. He called for more attention to theory, improved experimental analyses of human and animal behavior, and practical applications of psychology, particularly in industry. While admitting the importance of advancing industrial psychology, Chou urged that experts and sound research should be developed before extensive applications be considered. In view of Chinese industry's infancy at the time, Chou believed that efforts should be concentrated on the betterment of physical working conditions, on problems of administrative and worker efficiency, prior to experimentation and to concern with personnel selection and such problems. At the same time, some psychologists, like I. C. Kuo, emphasized that Chinese psychology should focus on the study of human behavior in a social environment.

Although Chinese psychology made some progress in the early thirties, generally speaking the period was characterized by economic depression and national unrest precipitated by Japanese seizure of Manchuria (1931-1933). Later during a brief peaceful interlude, the Chinese Psychological Association was founded (1937), and Luh and his colleagues, anxious to promote scientific psychology, reestablished the *Chinese Journal of Psychology.* However, just as China seemed to be recovering economically and politically, the Sino-Japanese war erupted in 1937, and Japan seized Peking, Tientsin, and Shanghai. Many universities were appropriated or bombed, and laboratory apparatus was looted or destroyed. As a result, Chinese psychology suffered a sharp setback and eventually came to a virtual halt.

The Sino-Japanese conflict merged into World War II and ended in 1945. But, in the same year Russia, declaring war on Japan, invaded and occupied Manchuria and Korea. Shortly afterwards China was again plunged into turmoil by a Civil War (1946-1949) between the Nationalists and

Communists—a war which culminated in Communist control of the Mainland. In discussing Chinese psychology after 1949, therefore, we must speak separately of its progress on the Mainland and in Taiwan.

China Mainland. Because of political conditions, psychology on the Mainland developed on a theoretical basis different from that of prewar Chinese psychology and that of Taiwan. Patterned after Soviet psychology and dedicated to Pavlovian theory and related researches, it attempted to construct a dialectic materialist psychology. To popularize Russian psychology among the Mainland Chinese psychologists, a special journal which presented selected Russian psychological articles, the *Translation Journal of Psychology* (in Chinese), was published from 1956 to 1958. Preoccupation with theoretical considerations, and with experimental studies of brain activity, and of the physiological bases of various psychological processes, characterized the years between 1949 and 1958. Researches were conducted on human and animal behavior with conditioning and other objective techniques. During this period the applications of psychology to education, industry, and medicine received only slight attention.

After 1957, a period of tremendous advance is said to have occurred. According to S. Pan, director of the Institute of Psychology of Academia Sinica—an important research center in Peking—the Mainland's social reconstruction imposed new tasks and demands upon psychology which initiated a new era of Chinese psychological research. More attention was directed to applied psychology. Although the earlier theoretical interests and experimental researches continued, they were subordinated to educational, industrial, and medical psychology. Educational psychologists studied attention, memory, and related aspects of the learning process, as well as special abilities. Methods of accident prevention, of training workers, of promoting creativity, and of increasing efficiency became important subjects of psychological investigation in industry. Medical psychology devoted itself to the problems of prevention and treatment of mental diseases. Insistence on objective methods and on the materialistic interpretations of psychological processes characterized these investigations of Mainland psychologists.

The 1958 International Directory of Psychologists listed 77 psychologists on the Mainland. Of these approximately 63 per cent were American-educated, about 21 per cent Chinese-trained, and most of the remainder studied in Europe. In 1963 Pan claimed that their ranks had grown markedly, but he failed to provide statistics. Their principal organization is the Chinese Psychological Association (reorganized in 1955), and two of their journals are the *Chinese Journal of Psychology* and *Acta Psychologica Sinica* in Chinese with Russian and English abstracts. Originally Chinese psychologists on the Mainland were engaged chiefly in teaching at universities and teachers' colleges, and in research on physiological, child, and educational psychology. In the 1960's, with the expansion of applied psychology, more nonacademic opportunities became available. However, mental testing and psychoanalysis have been excluded, as they are in Russia. Whether theoretical or practical, Chinese psychology on the mainland bears the unmistakable stamp of the dominant political philosophy.

Taiwan. Psychology in Taiwan dates from 1949 with the establishment of the psychology department at the National Taiwan University by H. Y. Su. After a little more than a decade, it had a counseling center, a child study center, and a graduate program. Its researches on a range of topics including personality, child development, and learning have been published in *Acta Psychologica Taiwanica* (in Chinese with English abstracts), founded in 1958. Taiwan's psychology has built on prewar Chinese psychology, which, as was noted previously, had been influenced chiefly by American functionalism.

Several psychologists in Taiwan hold nonacademic positions in agencies such as the Psychological Research Bureau, created by the Ministry of National Defense (1951). They construct tests and develop classification and selection systems for military personnel. Applications of psychology have not been sufficiently developed in Taiwan to indicate the emergence of professional psychology to any marked degree.

The principal psychological associations in Taiwan are two that were established in prewar China: the Chinese Association of Psychological Testing, with a membership of 245 in 1964, and the Chinese Association for Mental Hygiene, with a membership of 240 in 1964. The former resumed its activities in 1951 and has been publishing its journal, *Psychological Testing* (in Chinese), annually. The Chinese Association of Mental Hygiene reorganized in 1949 and rededicated itself to the promotion of mental health. Supported by school and community, it has made guidance an integral operation of all schools. It publishes a bulletin for its members and disseminates mental hygiene information in the community.

The 1958 International Directory of Psychologists listed 22 psychologists in Taiwan—16 Chinese-trained, five American-trained, and one French-educated. By 1963, when a national psychological association had just been organized, Su, its chairman, reported that the number of psychologists in Taiwan was fewer than 100. Although their researches are sparse because psychologists are few in number, these Chinese psychologists of Taiwan are an active group whose interests run the full gamut of topics investigated by their psychological colleagues around the world.

Hong Kong. Finally the report of Chinese psychology would not be complete without mention of Hong Kong, where there are about a dozen active psychologists, according to a report of E. Kvan in 1963. Most of them are associated with the University of Hong Kong where, either in the department of philosophy or in the department of education, they teach psychology and do research. Because of the small number of psychologists, their activities are limited. Their diverse interests include child guidance, testing, and the psychology of adjustment.

INDIA

Hindu philosophers cultivated psychology as a study of soul for many centuries when India was isolated from European thought. They studied cognition, emotion, personality, and will. They considered meditation important for personality integration and recommended certain Yoga practices for mental health. With the introduction of the British system of education and the establishment of Indian universities in mid-nineteenth century, Western scientific psychology was imported. Both Indian philosophical psychology and modern experimental psychology developed independently, although attempts have been made to integrate them.

Scientific psychology began in India with an essentially British orientation, because most of its pioneers took their graduate training in England or Scotland, where they were nurtured in the statistical and cognitive traditions of Spearman and Thomson. The British emphasis on philosophy, superimposed upon the already strong Indian philosophical tradition, has not made easy the separation of scientific psychology from philosophy in India. Moreover, these influences have tended to preserve the theoretical character of psychology in India and to retard the development of experimentation and applied psychology.

Beginnings. Psychology was introduced into the department of philosophy at Calcutta University in 1906. India's first psychological laboratory and an independent department with a full program of psychology were established there for graduate students in 1916, under the direction of N. N. Sengupta—who had studied at Harvard with Münsterberg. A few years later Mysore University established a department of psychology (1924), and Lucknow University organized a laboratory in 1929. Gradually, psychology courses, particularly those in educational psychology, were introduced into other colleges and universities. At that time psychology was usually taught as a branch of philosophy by philosophers. McDougall's textbooks, *Outlines of Psychology* and *Energies of Men,* were widely used.

The first scientific psychologists concentrated on theoretical aspects of general, educational, abnormal, and social psychology, with special concern for theories of intelligence and mental testing. During the 1920's and 1930's when the schools of psychology were popular, psychologists in India studied and discussed associationism, structuralism, functionalism, behaviorism, Gestalt psychology, hormic psychology, and psychoanalysis. The intense interest in psychoanalysis led to the founding of the Indian Psychoanalytic Society (1922), which fostered investigation of the role of the unconscious in human thought and action, and of the therapeutic aspects of psychoanalysis. In the 1920's, psychology in India attracted enough attention to be included in the Indian Science Congress and to have a section in the Indian Philosophical Congress. While these recognitions signified psychology's progress in India, Indian psychologists were most concerned about promoting the advancement of scientific psychology in India through an organization of their own. Accordingly, in 1926, they

founded the Indian Psychological Association, which had three main purposes: (1) to standardize psychological curricula at the universities;
(2) to coordinate researches from various parts of the country; and (3) to
encourage publication. The latter purpose was almost immediately implemented by the founding of the *Indian Journal of Psychology* (1926).

From 1916 to 1946 the character of scientific psychology in India did
not change radically. Interest in psychoanalysis and mental illness persisted. "Brass instrument" psychology and laboratory psychology patterned after Titchener, Whipple, Drever, and Collins retained popularity.
The importance of psychology in industry was recognized as early as 1931,
but was not developed to any significant degree. Although psychological
testing was introduced into India with some Indian adaptations of American tests in the early 1920's, there were very few workers in psychometrics by 1930. Some impetus to research on testing and vocational
guidance was furnished by the establishment of the Applied Psychology
Section, in the Department of Psychology at Calcutta University in 1938.
The presence of Spearman, Myers, and Jung in India at that time for the
Silver Jubilee of the Indian Science Congress is said to have lent support
to this project. Psychology also found application during World War II
in the study of psychopathic personalities in the army and in the development of selection tests for war technicians. However, little research
was done, and applied psychology made no great strides before 1947, the
year of Indian independence and of the partition of the country.

Later Developments.   After World War II American influence became
apparent in the pronounced shift of interest toward applied psychology.
India's striving for industrialization has stimulated interest in industrial
psychology, with considerable emphasis on human relations in industry.
Studies of fatigue and personnel selection have been instituted. Educational reforms have encouraged psychological testing in the schools—of
intelligence, achievement, and aptitude—and have prompted the establishment of guidance and counseling centers by central and state governments. An interest in clinical psychology has also emerged with emphasis
mainly on the Rorschach and the Thematic Apperception Tests. In addition, applied social research has attracted much attention. Fostered
by United Nations Educational, Scientific, and Cultural Organization
(UNESCO), it has focused on a variety of social psychology problems,
notably on tensions between social groups and classes. At Calcutta University, UNESCO established a center for research on the social aspects
of industrialization in India.

Since 1947, there has been an increased use of psychology for the solution of industrial, social, and cultural problems. While the demand for
psychological services has grown tremendously in the 1950's, the needs
cannot be met adequately. First, there are few professional personnel.
Many who have been rendering services—both clinical and guidance—are
inadequately trained. Better university programs are needed. Although
the industrial psychologist has not yet acquired professional status, and

the job of the clinical psychologist, as such, is unknown, professional psychology has made a beginning and university course offerings must be adjusted accordingly. Second, there is considerable overemphasis on tests. Guidance, for example, is highly test-centered. Yet test research has lagged far behind use. There has been excessive reliance on foreign tests and inadequate development of nonverbal tests. Much more systematic experimentation on tests, mental health, child and genetic psychology is essential to future growth.

In spite of postwar changes, scientific psychology in India has continued to bear the stamp of British influence. As of 1957, 32 of India's 33 universities were teaching psychology as part of education, philosophy, sociology, or social work. Only 15 universities had independent departments of psychology, and psychological training in all of them is restricted entirely to the graduate level. In elementary psychology there is an artificial separation of theory and laboratory practice. McDougall's books are still used for introductory courses. At both undergraduate and graduate levels, almost exclusive emphasis is given to general, abnormal, social, and educational psychology—most often with a theoretical rather than a practical orientation. At few universities are courses available in clinical psychology, industrial psychology, projective techniques, personality theory, comparative psychology, and genetic psychology. The most complete programs are available at Lucknow, Calcutta, Aligarh, Mysore, Baroda, and Bombay. Laboratory psychology has remained inadequate at most universities in terms of equipment, failure to train students in experimental design and basic research, and lack of concern for the modern research areas of learning, motivation, and perception. While some Indian psychologists insist that the traditional Indian philosophical psychology should be taught along with scientific psychology, others have adopted Western psychology and accepted its theoretical formulations uncritically. The majority contend that original researches and new approaches suited to Indian culture should be initiated and developed.

As of 1964, there were about 500 psychologists in India. Of these, about half had academic positions. The rest were engaged in vocational guidance, administration, and research, with a few in public and private institutions and in industry. These psychologists are widely separated geographically from each other, a factor which impedes communication between them. For this reason, the Indian Psychological Association, with headquarters at Calcutta and a branch at Delhi, has been less effective than other national psychological associations. It holds no general conventions, and as of 1963 it had only 95 members. The other national organization, the Indian Academy of Applied Psychology, with headquarters at Madras, has five regional branches. Indian psychologists have made a practice of meeting during the annual sessions of the Indian Science Congress.

Although the research output is small, several psychological journals are published, almost all in English. In addition to the *Indian Journal of Psychology* there are the following: *Samiksa,* a publication of the

Indian Psychoanalytical Society; *Journal of Education and Psychology* (Baroda); and the *Journal of Educational and Vocational Guidance,* an organ of the All-India Educational and Vocational Guidance Association. University publications have also appeared, such as *Manasi,* a bulletin published from time to time at Lucknow University, and *Psychological Studies,* from Mysore. No important research journal in psychology has been published in Indian languages, although in the 1950's these languages began to be recognized as media of higher education. Although written in English, Indian psychological literature has achieved little recognition from Western psychologists, because of its lack of originality and its preoccupation with philosophy.

PAKISTAN

With the partition of the Indian subcontinent, Pakistan became an independent nation in 1947 and its psychology began a separate existence as an offshoot of pre-partition Indian psychology. The latter, as we have just seen, was taught as a branch of philosophy by philosophers, largely from McDougall's textbooks. McDougall's contributions to abnormal and social psychology and Freud's psychoanalysis were well known, while Titchener, Myers, and Whipple were the authorities on experimental psychology. Practically no attention was accorded periodical literature.

Such was psychology's status in the two well-established universities which Pakistan acquired in 1947—the Universities of Punjab (1887) and Dacca (1921), even though the former had a degree course in psychology long before 1947. Pakistan also acquired the newer University of Sind (1946) and subsequently established Peshawar (1950), Karachi (1951), and Rajshahi (1953). In 1959, three of these six universities—Karachi, Punjab, and Rajshahi—offered the M.A. in psychology. At teacher training colleges, educational psychology was a required course for teacher trainees, and social psychology became a frequent requirement for sociology students and for social welfare workers. At Dacca, a child psychology program was opened to women graduate students.

During the 1950's Pakistan psychology began to change, partly because of the influence of foreign-trained psychologists and partly because of the growing recognition of psychology as a separate discipline. However, in tradition-bound Pakistan, the old philosophical orientation persisted. With it came the popularity of general theoretical psychology and the theoretical and speculative treatment of educational, child, and social psychology. Although practical laboratory courses are offered in almost all the universities, they do not stress experimental design or encourage the testing of new hypotheses. The same standard experiments prescribed by Titchener, Whipple, Myers, or Drever and Collins continue to be used. This type of training explains the low research output of most Pakistan psychologists.

The oldest psychological laboratories in Pakistan are at Dacca and Punjab. They are equipped with apparatus for experiments on sensation, association, reaction time, imagery, psychophysics, attention, memory, and elementary studies of emotion and learning. Manuals and equipment for standardized intelligence and personality tests are also available. In the early 1960's the Universities of Rajshahi, Karachi, and Sind started to develop more modern laboratories. Some research on perception, learning, and motivation has been initiated.

Pakistan psychology in the 1960's is still academic and theoretical with almost no concern for basic experimental psychology. Training in experimental techniques and in testing have remained inadequate. At the college level, teaching has continued to be theoretical without benefit of laboratory work. While there has been some application of psychology to selection of military and public service personnel, applied psychology in education, medicine, and industry is underdeveloped. A class of professional clinical psychologists is reported to be growing. There is a pronounced trend toward applied social research which is focused on Pakistan's changing social structure occasioned by the rapid shift from an agricultural to an industrial economy. The future progress of psychology in Pakistan appears to be intimately linked with the practical needs and demands of a new nation.

As of 1964, there were approximately 250 teachers of psychology, but there was no national psychological association, although one is reportedly planned. The psychologists seem content to participate in the annual conferences of the Pakistan Philosophical Congress and the Pakistan Association for the Advancement of Science, each of which has a section on psychology and education. No psychological journals are published in Pakistan, and the research output has not yet created a need for one. Psychological papers are published in periodicals such as the *Pakistan Journal of Philosophy, Pakistan Journal of Science, Punjab Educational Journal,* and the *Proceedings of the Pakistan Philosophical Congress.* An outstanding Pakistan psychologist, S. M. H. Zaidi, of the University of Karachi, has been a frequent contributor to American psychological journals and has presented Pakistan psychology to the West.

PSYCHOLOGY IN OTHER ASIAN COUNTRIES

While psychology in Japan, China, and India has deep historical roots, in some of the smaller Asian countries it has only begun to develop in the second half of the twentieth century. Brief sketches of the status of scientific psychology in these lands are presented in the succeeding sections.

Ceylon. As of 1963, Ceylon had only three or four psychologists, principally British-trained, the best known of whom is J. E. Jayasuriya. At the only university, the University of Ceylon, founded in 1942, there is no separate department of psychology. Psychology is taught in the education, sociology, and philosophy departments. In the Department of Education (established in 1948) it is given prominence, but the emphasis is on psychology applied to educational and social problems, not on pure psychology. Psychological research, although not extensive, has covered the topics of attitude measurement, psychology of school subjects, measurement of aptitudes and interests, intergroup relations, and delinquency. Many studies employ modifications of British and American tests and techniques. Psychological papers are published in periodicals such as the *Journal of the National Educational Society of Ceylon* and in the *University of Ceylon Review*. As of 1960, there was no psychological journal and no national association of psychologists.

Indonesia. In 1952 training of psychologists was begun at the University of Indonesia in Jakarta under the auspices of the Medical Faculty. When an independent Faculty of Psychology was established (1960), it assumed supervision of the program. In 1963, it was admitting about 75 students annually and had a staff of 23 psychologists who had been trained either at home or abroad, or both. Some of the teaching staff are sent, for example, to the United States or Canada for advanced or postgraduate training.

In Indonesia the orientation and approach to psychology, like the university-degree system, are Continental. American textbooks enjoy extensive use. Indonesian psychology, as represented principally by the University Faculty of Psychology, is characterized by eclecticism—with sociocultural and anthropophilosophical emphases, similar to the European schools of phenomenology and existentialism.

According to F. Hassan, secretary of the Faculty at the University of Indonesia, Indonesian psychologists—40 in 1963—were engaged in teaching or in the armed services. They have their own organization, the Indonesian Psychological Association. Psychologists in this country seem to be more interested in professional psychology than in pure experimental psychology. Their applications of psychology have followed closely the pattern of Western psychology. Indonesian psychologists, however, have started to develop clinical, educational, and industrial psychology, according to their own needs.

Philippines. Psychology in the Philippines rather naturally followed the pattern of American psychology from its inception. It has grown steadily since the 1930's when the first psychology students were trained in American universities and returned to teach psychology. Three chief centers of psychological activity emerged: University of the Philippines, Ateneo de Manila, and the Philippine Women's University. American textbooks have always been extensively used because the Filipinos generally—unlike other Asians—know English well, and translations have not been required. Philippine psychology has centered around experimentation, testing, guidance, and cultural studies.

Eager to establish psychology as a profession, to define the role of the psychologist, and to differentiate it from the roles of the philosopher and medical practitioner, Philippine psychologists organized the Psychological

Association of the Philippines in 1962, with S. Padilla as first president. By mid-1963, a membership of 37 was reported, of whom 12 had Ph.D.'s and the remainder, M.A.'s. Apart from regular monthly meetings, the Association held its first convention in 1964 at which a variety of papers was presented. Close cooperation with other scientific groups in the Philippines—such as sociologists and psychiatrists—as well as with psychologists of other countries, is the Association's goal.

Thailand. After World War II, reform and expansion of Thailand's educational system were begun. General and educational psychology, child development, adolescent psychology, and mental hygiene were made required courses in teacher training institutions. For the most part, instruction in psychology was restricted to lectures and was based heavily on foreign textbooks or translations of them.

Almost no psychological research was done until the International Institute for Child Study was established (1955) in Bangkok, through the combined efforts of the Thai Ministry of Education and UNESCO. It was felt that European and American theories of child development might not be applicable to Asian cultures and that Thailand's educational methods and practices would have to be based on understanding the needs and growth patterns of Thai children. From 1953 to 1955 the initial Institute staff was trained by W. Line, professor of psychology at the University of Toronto, Canada. At its opening in 1955, E. E. Boesch, professor of psychology at the University of Saar, Germany, became the first full-time director of the International Institute for Child Study.

The Institute has concentrated its efforts on three areas: (1) *Research*. Investigations of Thai child rearing practices, personality, capacity, emotions, and attitudes have been conducted through use of systematic observation, questionnaires, experimental situations, and sociometry. Attention has been directed to constructing tests of verbal and nonverbal intelligence, psychomotor skills, and educational achievement. The Institute's staff has cooperated with Asians and non-Asians on cross-cultural research. (2) *Teaching*. The Institute's program aims to train research assistants and school psychologists. (3) *Guidance*. Counseling and guidance services are available to children, parents, and teachers, although insufficient staff makes it impossible to render extensive service. This work of the Institute has not only helped to improve Thailand's educational system; it has also given impetus to graduate and postgraduate study of psychology—especially educational psychology and child development.

Two other institutions in Thailand have pioneered in psychological activity, Chulalongkorn University and the Mental Health Clinic administered by the Ministry of Public Health, both in Bangkok. At Chulalongkorn University, the Faculty of Education has a psychological laboratory which serves as a valuable adjunct to courses in general and educational psychology. In 1958, research on child development was initiated here. The Mental Health Clinic, in spite of limited staff, has conducted investigations of child rearing practices, child development, and problems of personality adjustment in Thailand.

Like other Asian psychologists, psychologists in Thailand have adopted and adapted foreign tests and techniques for their own use and have concentrated on applied psychology. Their emphasis of educational and developmental psychology arose from national needs. Although the number of psychologists increased beyond the four listed in the 1958 International Directory of Psychologists, the group was still not large enough in 1963 to warrant having its own national professional association or its own psychological publication. Psychology in Thailand, as in most of the other Asian countries described in this section, is still in its infancy.

ASIAN PSYCHOLOGY—A Summary

Psychology in Asia, with the notable exception of Japan, did not really develop until the middle of the twentieth century. Moreover, in all Asian countries, including Japan, the development was most intense and rapid in the post-World War II period. In all Asian countries which have developed a psychology, the traditional philosophies and cultural beliefs provided not only a milieu in which that psychology grew, but a milieu with which, at times, it had to contend. As in the Occident, the principal sources of Oriental scientific psychology are German and American, with some additional influences from British and French sources. Again with the exception of Japanese, Asian psychology has progressed slowly, and for two principal reasons. First, philosophical and educational traditions have tended to dominate psychological thinking and investigations. Hence attainment of precise identity for scientific psychology has been slowed. Second, and in consequence of this lack of clear identity for psychology, the recruitment and training of psychologists has been retarded. The inevitable effect of the operation of these two factors has been an inadequate number of professional personnel to serve the needs of Asian countries in both experimental and applied psychology.

Japanese psychology is the most fully developed in Asia. This development has its origins in the work of Motora and Matsumoto. The former, primarily a systematist, and the latter, whose primary interest was in applied psychology, were both American trained—at Johns Hopkins and at Yale, respectively. The work which they began before the turn of the century enabled Japanese psychology to maintain a steady growth up to the present time, except during periods of war. The scope of that growth in the past 75 years is indicated by the broad range of its interests: systematic, experimental, behavioristic, educational, Gestalt, developmental, psychometric, social, abnormal, industrial, personality, and clinical psychology. By steady advances in recruitment and training it has attained the level of 81 psychologists per million of population. This is 40 times the number attained by its neighbor, China Taiwan, with the level of 2 per million, and compares with the present American figure of about 120 per million.

Other Asian countries have lagged far behind Japan in range and speed of development. In all other cases, scientific psychology is a strictly twentieth century development. In China, its rise coincides with increased Western cultural contacts following the establishment of the Chinese Republic. A quarter century of progress, during which largely imported systems dominated its course, was slowed by the eruption of the Sino-Japanese War in 1937. World War II and subsequent Civil War divided China into Mainland and Taiwan governments and bifurcated psychological developments in the separate Chinese nations. The initial interests of Chinese psychologists, including physiological, educational, and child psychology, have changed. Mainland China, with a dominating political philosophy in control, has turned its attention to applied areas in the sixties. In China Taiwan there is less control and broader interest. In both nations, professional backgrounds of psychologists include American and European, as well as natively trained. Again, in both cases, the growth of scientific psychology has been hampered by the limited numbers and training of psychologists.

Indian psychology follows the pattern of that in other Asian countries, with philosophical sources being seeded by scientific psychology imported from Western countries. Early scientific psychology interests in India were concentrated on theory—principal investigations being concerned with general, educational, abnormal, and social psychology. Through the thirties and early forties, the main areas of psychology had been probed in India—generally in an unorganized way and after the fashion of European investigations. After World War II, there was a general shift of emphasis to applied psychology—especially in industrial, educational, clinical, and social fields. Development has been slowed however, because of overemphasis of British sources and the traditional fusion of philosophy and psychology. Pakistan was established as a separate nation in 1947. Its cultural, philosophical, and psychological roots are thus substantially the same as those of India. With theoretical and academic interests predominating, activity in experimental psychology has lagged. In other Asian countries, psychology is at an elementary stage of development where it has made its appearance, having mid-twentieth century origins for the most part. Numbers of trained personnel in Ceylon, Indonesia, Thailand, and the Philippines are extremly small in relation to population. Furthermore, their interests are primarily in educational and social areas, with little attention being given to basic research. In all cases, emphases have tended to be intracultural, even when imported theories, techniques, texts, and tests have been used. Principal sources of imported material have been the United States, Britain, and Germany.

Summarily considered, Asian psychology is neither clearly defined nor strongly established. A major obstacle to its definition is the traditional fusion of philosophy and psychology in most Asian countries and consequent confusions of theory, techniques, and objectives. Only in Japan, of all Asian nations, has modern psychology been introduced and developed with marked success. In the other Asian countries, while scientific psychology has been introduced, there has been less enthusiastic and effective response to its possibilities as learning or as a source of practical knowledge.

REFERENCES

ASIAN PSYCHOLOGY

Bentley, M. Experimental psychology in the Orient. *Amer. J. Psychol.*, 1926, *37*, 154.

David, H. P. *International resources in clinical psychology*. New York: McGraw-Hill, 1964. Pp. 101–122.

Sato, K. (Ed.) Psychological activities in Asian countries—Letters from Asian colleagues (in Ceylon, China, Hongkong, India, Indonesia, Pakistan, and the Philippines). *Psychologia*, 1963, *4*, 175–182.

Watts, A. W. Asian psychology and modern psychiatry. *Amer. J. Psychoanal.*, 1953, *13*, 25–30.

JAPAN

Hake, H. W. Japanese experimental psychology viewed from America. *Psychologia*, 1958, *1*, 184–186.

Hirota, K. Development of social psychology in Japan. *Psychologia*, 1959, *2*, 216–228.

Iwahara, S., & Fujita, O. Behaviorism in Japan. *Psychologia*, 1963, *6*, 59–65.

Kaketa, K. Psychoanalysis in Japan. *Psychologia*, 1958, 1, 247–252.

Kido, M. Origin of Japanese psychology and its development. *Psychologia*, 1961, *4*, 1–10.

Kirihara, S. H. Industrial psychology in Japan. *Psychologia*, 1959, *2*, 206–215.

Kodama, H. Personality tests in Japan. *Psychologia*, 1958, *1*, 92–103.

Lloyd, VanV. Psychology in colleges and universities in Japan and the republic of Korea. *J. Psychol.*, 1965, *61*, 183–191.

McGinnies, E. Psychology in Japan, 1960. *Amer. Psychologist*, 1960, *15*, 556–562.

Motoyoshi, R., & Iwahara, S. Japanese studies on animal behavior in the last decade. *Psychologia*, 1960, *3*, 135–148.

Osaka, R. Intelligence test in Japan. *Psychologia*, 1961, *4*, 218–234.

Sato, K., & Graham, C. H. Psychology in Japan. *Psychol. Bull.*, 1954, *51*, 443–464.

Sato, K. Gestalt psychology in Japan. *Psychologia*, 1963, *6*, 7–10.

Tachibana, K. Trends in gerontology in Japan. *Psychologia*, 1959, *2*, 150–156.

Tanaka, Y. Status of Japanese experimental

psychology. *Annu. Rev. Psychol.*, 1966, *17*, 233–272.

Tsushima, T. Notes on trends and problems of psychotherapy in Japan. *Psychologia*, 1958, *1*, 231–236.

Yoda, A., & Hidano, T. Development of educational psychology in Japan. *Psychologia*, 1959, *2*, 137–149.

CHINA

Chou, S. K. Trends in Chinese psychological interest since 1922. *Amer. J. Psychol.*, 1927, *38*, 487–488.

Chou, S. K. The present status of psychology in China. *Amer. J. Psychol.*, 1927, *38*, 664–666.

Chou, S. K. Psychological laboratories in China. *Amer. J. Psychol.*, 1932. *44*, 372–374.

Pan, S. China's recent research on psychology (Mainland). *Psychologia*, 1959, *2*, 193–201.

Su, H. Psychological activities in Taiwan. *Psychologia*, 1959, *2*, 202–205.

Westbrook, C. H. Note on psychology in Occupied Shanghai. *Psychol. Bull.*, 1944, *41*, 304–306.

Westbrook, C. H. Psychiatry and mental hygiene in Shanghai. *Amer. J. Psychiat.*, 1953, *110*, 301–306.

INDIA

Akhilananda, S. *Hindu psychology*. New York: Harper, 1946.

Banerji, M. N. Hindu psychology: physiological basis and experimental methods. *Amer. J. Psychol.*, 1937, *50*, 328–346.

Barnette, W. L. Survey of research with psychological tests in India. *Psychol. Bull.*, 1955, *52*, 105–121.

Bhatt, L. J. Psychology as a profession. *Indian J. Psychol.*, 1956, *31*, 1–13.

Filella, J. Psychology in India. *Amer. Cath. Psychol. Ass. Newsltr.*, Sept. 1961. Suppl. No. 53.

Fletcher, F. M., & Riddle, C. W. The guidance movement in India. *Personnel Guid. J.*, 1962, *40*, 807–810.

Mitra, S. C., & Mukhopadhyay, P. K. Development of psychological studies in India from 1916–1950. *Psychologia*, 1958, *1*, 191–202.

Pareek, U. Psychology in India. *Psychologia*, 1957, *1*, 55–59.

Prabhu, P. H. The state of psychology as a science today. *Indian Psychol. Rev.*, 1964, *1*, 1–11.

Ramadevi, S. T., & Rao, S. K. R. Psychology in India. *Psychologia*, 1957, *1*, 86–91.

Rao, S. K. R. *Development of psychological thought in India*. Mysore, India: Kavyalaya Publishers, 1962.

Sastry, N. S. N. Growth of psychology in India. *Indian J. Psychol.*,1932, *7*, 1–40.

Sastry, N. S. N. Trends of psychological research in India. *Indian J. Psychol.*, 1955, *30*, 25–33.

Sen, I. The standpoint of Indian psychology. *Indian J. Psychol.*, 1951, *26*, 89–95.

Sengupta, N. N. Psychology, its present development and outlook. *Indian J. Psychol.*, 1926, *1*, 1–25.

Sinha, A. K. Planning psychological research in India. *Indian J. Psychol.*, 1958, *33*, 1–20.

PAKISTAN

Zaidi, S. M. H. Psychology in Pakistan. *Psychologia*, 1958, *1*, 187–190.

Zaidi, S. M. H. Problems of human relations in industry in Pakistan. *J. soc. Psychol.*, 1959, *49*, 13–18.

Zaidi, S. M. H. Pakistan psychology. *Amer. Psychologist*, 1959, *14*, 532–536.

Zaidi, S. M. H. On methods of social research in Pakistan. *Psychologia*, 1961, *4*, 48–55.

CEYLON

Jayasuriya, J. E. Psychology in Ceylon. *Psychologia*, 1957, *1*, 127–128.

THAILAND

Saradatta, L., & Miyake, K. Psychology in Thailand. *Psychologia*, 1959, *2*, 120–123.

Part III. Theoretical Psychology

THE PRECEDING PARTS OF THIS HISTORY have been concerned with the beginnings and growth of psychology in Europe, in the United States, and in Asia. In our discussion of the expansion of psychology we may say that the controlling perspective of Part II was geographic. This present section, Part III, will discuss the development of psychological theory. It will survey the principal efforts in various periods of psychology's history to discover and define its own identity—that is, to establish its subject matter, its goals, and its methods. The first organized conception of psychology was that of Wilhelm Wundt. Wundt's theory was effectively formulated in the system of structuralism which was developed and set forth by Titchener, Wundt's student. We shall discuss this system first. Then we shall consider the two American schools which opposed structuralism, namely, functionalism and behaviorism. Next we shall survey two schools of European origin—the Gestalt and the hormic—which stood in sharp opposition to behavioristic psychology, the dominant school in America. The theme of the following chapter is psychoanalysis, a school original and unique in its theory, its methodology, and in the strength of its impact on the science of psychology. Finally, an account will be given of two new approaches in psychology—the phenomenological and the existential—which emerged and crystallized after World War II.

17

Struggle of Schools: Structuralism and Functionalism

THE TERM "PSYCHOLOGICAL SCHOOL" is used several times in this book. Now it is time to explain what psychological school means and to review the major schools of psychology as they developed in the first quarter of the twentieth century. In the history of psychology the word "school" has been used in two senses. In one sense, a school means a group of people—associated with a particular place, usually a university or an institution, or with a teacher or an investigator—sharing common interests or a viewpoint on some specific issue. In this sense we speak of the Nancy school, Würzburg school, Chicago school, or school of C. L. Hull. But traditionally, the term "psychological school" has been used to designate broad systems of psychology. In this sense a psychological school means a general theoretical system seeking to systematize and to provide ultimate explanation for all psychological problems. Such an all-embracing theoretical position attempts to define the nature of psychology and specify its subject matter, aims, and methodology. It usually also shows preference for certain areas of psychology and emphasizes certain topics more than others.

The distinctive characteristic of the evolution of modern psychology was the formation of such schools after the turn of the century. They began to form soon after 1900, crystallized around 1910-1914, and flourished for about 20 years. Major among these schools were structuralism, functionalism, behaviorism, Gestalt, psychoanalysis, hormic psychology or purposivism. Two of these schools, functionalism and behaviorism, originated in America, whereas the others were of European origin. The European schools had not only strong representation in America, but—as it happened—their founders or leaders, with the exception of psychoanalysis, migrated to America and further developed their systems here. Consequently nowhere were the differences between schools and the subsequent cleavage among psychologists as evident as in America. It is then understandable why it was also in America that the debates between schools took place.

The differences between schools were fundamental because they pertained to the issues which were basic to the existence of psychology; its nature, aims, and methods. The leaders and followers of the schools presented and defended their views with vigor and proselytism. The polemics between the schools were often animated and at times acrimonious. The picture of American psychology in the years 1913-1930 was that of division into opposing camps and controversies. There were several psychologies, not one psychology, a situation unprecedented in the history of science. Thus the plural in the titles of books dealing with schools—such as Murchison's *Psychologies of 1925* and *Psychologies of 1930* and Edna Heidbreder's *Seven Psychologies*—was most appropriate.

THE ORIGIN OF SCHOOLS

Each school evolved from certain implicit or explicit presuppositions, rooted in philosophical doctrines. These presuppositions dictated the theoretical premises for the construction of the psychological systems, for the definition of psychology and its orientation. Considering the philosophical substructure of the schools, one can relate them to philosophical doctrines of the past and classify them according to their philosophical foundation. Grouping, though sometimes masking important individual differences, may be useful in pointing out significant common features. The schools, considered from the standpoint of their philosophical derivation, may in general be divided into two groups. One, comprising structuralism and behaviorism, represents the empirical-associationist tradition; the other, comprising functionalism, Gestalt, and hormic psychologies, represents the Cartesian-idealistic tradition. Following G. W. Allport's dichotomy of philosophical tradition in psychology as the Lockean and the Leibnitzian, we find structuralism and behaviorism belonging to the Lockean, and functionalism, Gestalt, and hormic psychologies belonging to the Leibnitzian tradition. The psychoanalytic school possesses elements of both traditions, their relative strengths varying according to the psychoanalytic systems. The ancestry of structuralism and behaviorism includes Hobbes, Locke, Hartley, Mills, Bain, and also Comte, Mach, and logical positivism, and in the natural sciences Newton and Helmholtz. Functionalism, Gestalt, and hormic psychologies are allied with Leibnitz, Kant, Brentano, Husserl, and Windelband.

The classification of psychologies by William McDougall is based on a distinction—made originally by Nietzsche—made with respect to much earlier traditions, namely, two broad contrasting views of the world in Greek thought: the Apollinian and the Dionysian. McDougall thought that this distinction "affords the best clue to a useful classification of psychological theories, since it distinguishes them in respect to their most fundamental features, their inclination towards intellectualism or towards voluntarism." The Apollinian view, according to McDougall, was the parent of European intellectualism which has generated "the allied, though superficially so different, systems of absolute idealism and of Newtonian mechanism," reflected in psychology from Descartes and Locke onward. The Dionysian tradition was expressed in the Scottish school and in philosophers such as Schopenhauer, von Hartmann, Nietzsche, and Bergson. To this tradition, McDougall says, belong hormic psychology and, to an extent, psychoanalysis. We may add that perhaps now McDougall would ally phenomenological, existential, and humanistic trends in contemporary psychology with this tradition. Various dichotomies and contrasting trends have been noted in the history of psychology, each traceable to philosophical doctrines of the past: dualistic-monistic; spiritualistic-materialistic; empirical-nativistic; mentalistic-physicalistic; objectivistic-subjectivistic; atomistic-holistic; static-dynamic; deterministic-indeterministic; nomothetic-idiographic; and many others. Psychological schools, as well as minor theories and viewpoints, can often be described in terms of these dichotomies and categories. For example, structuralism is described as dualistic, empirical, mentalistic, and atomistic; behaviorism as monistic, empirical, physicalistic, and atomistic; Gestalt as nativistic and holistic; hormic as dualistic, spiritualistic, nativistic, and dynamic.

Inherent in each school, even though not explicitly stated or immediately apparent, is a concept or image of man's nature. As Carl Rogers said, "each current in psychology has its own implicit philosophy of man." The implied concept or image of man is closely related to the philosophical underpinning of the school. It transpires especially through the position of the school on the body-mind relationship. It is largely dissatisfaction with the image of man implicit in contemporary psychology which has led in the last two decades to the upsurge of new orientations, such as humanistic and phenomenological-existential.

WUNDT AND THE SCHOOLS

All the psychological schools which originated and flourished during the first three decades of the twentieth century are best understood when viewed in contrast to, and as revolts against, the psychological system of Wilhelm Wundt, the first comprehensive and coherent system of the new psychology. In 1957 a German psychologist, H. von Bracken, said of Wundt that his greatest historical role lay in giving "rise to a productive opposition." Wundt's system—represented in America by structuralism—was based on a parallelistic and associationistic notion of man. Disagreement and dissatisfaction with the various aspects of this system was the starting point of functionalism, behaviorism, purposivism, and Gestaltism. Functionalism disagreed with the Wundtian preoccupation with the "structure of the mind" and stressed instead the functional aspect of mental processes; behaviorism attacked both the subject matter and the method of Wundtian psychology, that is, consciousness and introspection; the Gestalt school rejected its atomistic view of the mind; and hormic psychology objected to the omission of purpose and emphasized purposeful behavior as the proper object of psychological study. Psychoanalysis, which developed outside of academic psychology, shifted attention from the conscious processes to the unconscious motivational forces in man.

STRUCTURALISM

Structuralism, fundamentally, was the continuation of the psychological system of Wundt. The latter system is referred to as *content* psychology, in contrast to *act* psychology, because its subject matter was the contents of consciousness and its task the analysis of these contents. This system had as its most vigorous spokesman on American soil, Wundt's eminent student, E. B. Titchener, one of the giants in the history of psychology. He reformulated the basic principles of the Wundtian system, contrasted this system with American functionalism, defended it as the right kind of psychology against the encroachments of other systems, and followed it faithfully in his research and writings. Structural psychology, so much the product of Titchener and so forcefully put forth by him, might justly be called "Titchenerism."

Titchener's Publications. An early exposition of structuralism and its differentiation from functionalism was given by Titchener in his two articles published in the *Philosophical Review* in 1898 and 1899 and entitled, respectively, *The Postulates of a Structural Psychology* and *Structural and Functional Psychology*. Titchener's later systematic works, like his *Text-Book of Psychology* (1910), also contained expositions of structuralism. He planned to write a multivolume opus on systematic psychology. Undoubtedly he would have presented in it the case for structural psychology even more fully. Very likely he would have dealt with the issues which accrued in the meantime—the issues raised by Gestaltism, behaviorism, and psychoanalysis—and which he followed attentively. This plan did not materialize. His *Systematic Psychology: Prolegomena*, which was published posthumously in 1929, is only a fragment of the intended ambitious work.

Principles of Structuralism. The difference between structuralism and functional psychology is analogous to the difference between anatomy and physiology. Anatomy studies the structure of the organism and all its component parts, while physiology studies the functions of the organism and of its various parts. Anatomy dissects to find what the organism is composed of, and physiology observes the action of the organism to determine the purposes of the various parts. The primary aim of structural psychology, says Titchener, is "to analyze the structure of the mind; to ravel out the elemental processes from the tangle of consciousness, or . . . to isolate the constituents in the given conscious formation." The task of an experimental psychologist, Titchener continues, "is a vivisection, but a vivisection which shall yield structural, not functional results." The constituents of the mental structures, or their elements, are sensations, images, and feelings. Every conscious state of mind or, in other words, every content of consciousness, is to be analyzed and dissected, to determine its constituent parts. The next step is to determine how these parts are combined, how their connection is achieved, and finally to discover the general laws governing these combinations of elements which eventually form the various mental edifices—or structures of consciousness. In this way structural psychology can answer its three basic questions, the *what*, the *how*, and the *why* of mental structures. All these concepts of structuralism are not new to the student acquainted with Wundt's psychology. But they were presented by Titchener in a new form and in contrast to functional psychology. Titchener acknowledged the contributions of functional psychology, but, in his opinion, functional psychology was not *pure* science and its methods could not "lead to results of scientific finality." The scientific status of psychology was Titchener's great concern. He regarded as his mission the preservation of the scientific purity of psychology, which could be achieved, he thought, only within the framework of structural psychology. Only this psychology was the true science of psychology, capable of sustaining and preserving the scientific character of psychology. He said, "the best hope for psychology lies . . . in a continuance of structural analysis." Functional psychology and branches of psychology such as genetic, individual, comparative, applied, and psychometrics do not belong to the science of psychology, at least not as yet. They are premature ventures before the main task had been done, that is, before the structure of the mind had been worked out. Only after this description has been accomplished can such areas as the above be explored and practical uses of psychology be attempted. What Titchener said of functionalism exemplifies his attitude toward other areas: ". . . there is still so much to be done in the field of analysis . . . that a general swing of the laboratories towards functional work would be most regrettable."

Structuralism studied the states of consciousness as experienced by the individual; not the peculiar or unusual states of *an* individual, but the usual states *generally* experienced by the *normal adult* individual. The method for this study was introspection, supplemented by observation and measurement. In structuralism, introspection was the only possible means of access to the conscious experiences. The subjects used in psychological experiments had to be well trained in introspection, and only on this condition could their introspective data be accepted. What could not be investigated through introspection did not belong to psychology. Consequently structuralism rejected data not obtained by introspection and studied but a fraction of what now is regarded as the legitimate scope of psychology. The aspects of consciousness analyzed by structuralism included perception, association, memory, attention, affective states, and thought. To these topics Titchener and his students at Cornell University directed their primary efforts and experiments. But sensation received most attention—which was natural for a psychology permeated by the Wundtian spirit.

Evaluation. Of all the psychological schools, Titchener's structural psychology was the most solidly and consistently built system. A continuation of Wundtian psychology, structuralism was at the same time a continuation of the empirical and associationist tradition. It was also explicitly and thoroughly faithful to psychophysical parallelism. Structuralism was indeed the culmination and the final expression of all these traditions: empiricism, associationism, parallelism, and Wundtism. It can be said that structuralism died with Titchener, its chief and ablest exponent. In 1925 Madison Bentley, writing about structural psychology, said: "I doubt whether we shall find anyone to acknowledge that his own brand is of that kind; though the epithet will often be accompanied by a gesture of indication toward a fellow-psychologist." After Titchener's death in 1927 there was no one to carry on the work of structuralism. And so the system disappeared from the psychological scene. It disappeared not because it was proved explicitly wrong, but because it was superseded by other systems which found it too narrow, too stifling, too philosophical. It was obsolete for a psychological science moving away from its philosophical ancestry, expanding fast, and turning to practical uses. Historically speaking, structuralism made enormous factual and methodological contributions; but as a theoretical system it was left behind to serve as a sort of milestone, which would gauge the distance traveled by the fast-advancing psychology of the following decades.

FUNCTIONALISM

Functional, functionalist, and functionalism have had many different meanings in psychology. C. A. Ruckmick, Titchener's student, made a survey of the meaning of the term *function* as used in 15 American and English textbooks of psychology and published his results in an article, *The Use of the Term Function in English Textbooks of Psychology* (1913). He found that the varied connotations of the word could be reduced to two basic notions. It could mean either mental activity such as perceiving and recalling or a use for some end. The authors of textbooks sometimes employed both meanings. Today we also use the term function in these two meanings when we say that perception is a psychological function or that the function of the eyes is to see.

The term *functional psychology* had a more specific meaning. Usually the term referred to a psychology different from, and opposed to, the psychology which Wundt and Titchener formulated and promoted. In other words, functional psychology signified a protest against the system of psychology concerned primarily with the structure of the mind, and with the dissection of mental contents into their component elements. It was the psychology which instead of dissecting the mind concentrated primarily on the study of the operations of the mind and their role in the adaptation of the organism to environment. For example, whereas structural psychology paid attention to the content of consciousness—such as memory images, functional psychology considered rather the mental process of remembering.

Functional psychology in a *broad sense* was simply a different approach or a different orientation—or, as James R. Angell called it in 1907, "little more than a point of view, a program, an ambition." In this meaning, all psychologies which adopted as their main objective the study of mental acts, processes, operations, or functions—whichever term might have been employed by them—or simply the study of man's activities and their purpose, can be called functional. Consequently, the list of functionalists would include the names of Aristotle, Spencer, Darwin, and Galton. Indeed these names were mentioned by American functionalists as representatives of the functional viewpoint. By the same token, many European psychologists of the older and younger generation can be called functional psychologists—men like Stout, Myers, and Bartlett in England; Ribot, Binet, and Piéron in France; Harald Höffding in Denmark; David Katz, formerly in Germany and later in Sweden; Claparède and Piaget in Switzerland; and Michotte in Belgium. The Austrian-German "act psychology" too was a parallel to functional psychology. The functional approach in psychology emerged naturally and had a stronger appeal than the structural. It is always the activity that we notice more readily and its purpose that arouses our interest more readily. The functional approach corresponded well to the American mentality, which is practical and pragmatic, and to the American temperament, which values action and achievement. This was undoubtedly one of the reasons why a functional orientation was in strongest evidence in America and appeared in the writings of the early American psychologists, even when they had received their training in Leipzig. The consistent preoccupation with function and its adaptive role, together with the practical orientation, characterized all American psychology and clearly expressed its functional nature.

In a *strict sense*, functional psychology, or functionalism, means the psychological school which arose at the end of the nineteenth century in Chicago under the inspiration of John Dewey and James R. Angell. This school dominated the American scene in the first decade of the twentieth century. Many characteristics of the functionalist school were foreshadowed in the views of the American psychological pioneers and in the manner in which they treated and presented psychology in their texts. These pioneers were truly the precursors of the school of functionalism. They included James and Ladd—whose textbooks were written in a functional vein; Baldwin, whose treatment of psychological problems was in the spirit of evolutionism and comprised genetic and social aspects; Hall, with his strong genetic interest; and Cattell, with his mental testing. These approaches—the evolutionary, genetic, and psychometric—were functionalist. Since it was in America that the functional viewpoint orginated, in America that the difference between structuralism and functionalism emerged in sharpest relief, and in America that the tenets of functionalism were most explicitly posed, it is correct to describe functionalism as a distinctly American product.

John Dewey's Role.   At first merely an orientation, a point of view, an approach, functionalism soon crystallized into a formal school. Several significant events contributed to this crystallization. The first important one was an article published by John Dewey (1859-1952) in 1896. A philosopher, but strongly interested in psychology, Dewey wrote the first American textbook for the new psychology, *Psychology*, in 1886. He was then teaching philosophy at the University of Michigan. He moved to the University of Chicago in 1894, and two years later published in the *Psychological Review* his famous article, *The Reflex Arc Concept in Psychology*. Here he voiced his strong opposition to the reflex arc concept—which distinguishes in acts such discrete units as stimulus and response, sensation and movement, and sensory, central, and motor components. He protested against such an elementistic and reductionistic approach. Instead, Dewey argued for a psychology which would not fractionate behavioral acts, but would study them in their entirety and in their adaptive function.

Adaptation to the environment was a central theme of Dewey's psychology and philosophy. His educational theories were a logical result of his concern with man's physical, social, and moral adjustment. His ideas stimulated educational psychology and the study of learning. Dewey's work after 1904—when he moved to Columbia's Teachers College, where he remained until his retirement—was devoted chiefly to philosophy.

James Rowland Angell (1869-1949).   One year after Dewey went to Chicago as the head of the department of philosophy, James Rowland Angell, who had been Dewey's student at Michigan, was appointed, on Dewey's recommendation, assistant professor to teach courses in psychology and to take charge of the laboratory. Angell obtained his M.A. at Harvard where he had studied under James. After Harvard he spent a year in Europe at several universities, met prominent men, among them Ebbinghaus and Helmholtz. The association of Dewey and Angell in Chicago was a significant factor in the development of functionalism. They helped to create the atmosphere which fostered the Chicago school of psychologists, a large group which stood out as a distinct body within American psychology for some time. Two other faculty members, G. H. Mead and A. W. Moore, joined the movement and collaborated with Dewey and Angell. The research program at the Chicago laboratory, inspired by the functionalistic orientation, contributed to the school's consolidation and prestige. In a short time, Angell became the chief spokesman and leader of functionalism while the University of Chicago was not only the cradle but the headquarters of functionalism.

The issue of structuralism and functionalism was discussed publicly by Angell for the first time in a publication in 1903, *The Relation of Structural and Functional Psychology to Philosophy*. His functionalist position was also evident in his successful textbook of 1904, *Psychology*, which bore a characteristic subtitle, "An Introductory Study of the Structure and Function of Human Consciousness." The explicit and the most articulate formulation of functionalism, ten years after its launching by Dewey, was put forward in Angell's presidential address at the meeting of the American Psychological Association in 1906. Called *The Province of Functional Psychology*, this address was published the following year in the *Psychological Review*. In it Angell touched upon the major issues which occupied psychologists of that time. All the basic tenets and aims of functionalism were spelled out clearly. But Angell presented his functionalistic views without pretense of scientific finality. He did not want to be narrow or dogmatic, and he called functionalism simply "a broad and flexible and organic point of view in psychology." Neither did he want to cut off functionalism from philosophy. "But anything," he said, "approaching a complete and permanent divorce of psychology from philosophy is surely improbable so long as one cultivates the functionalist faith."

Angell remained at Chicago until 1919. During his stay there he directed 50 doctoral dissertations. Among his students were John B. Watson, the founder of behaviorism; Walter S. Hunter, leading experimental psychologist and chairman of the department of psychology at Brown University for many years; and Walter V. D. Bingham, known for his outstanding contributions to applied psychology and aptitude testing. Among his colleagues was C. D. Judd, Wundt's former student. Judd was an influential promoter of functionalism and of educational psychology, who published a textbook, *Psychology* (1907). This work was biologically oriented and showed a strong emphasis on motor responses. Angell, two years after having left Chicago, became president of Yale University. He held this position for 16 years, a period described as a "great period in the history of that institution." The departmental chairmanship at Chicago passed to Harvey A. Carr, his former student.

Harvey A. Carr (1873-1954). He succeeded Angell not only as the chairman of the department but also as the leader of functionalism. During Carr's chairmanship (1906-1938) about 150 Ph.D.'s in psychology were granted at Chicago. His area of specialization was comparative psychology. His views were expressed mainly in his textbook, *Psychology* (1925), and in a chapter on functionalism for Murchison's *Psychologies of 1930*. They reflect the state of functionalism 30 years after its inception. Analyzing the stimulus-response relationship, Carr pointed out the need for taking into account the motivating factors in the proper evaluation of a response made by the organism. He thus introduced into the functionalist theory a new conception, that of motivation. At the time of Carr's writings, especially of his 1930 chapter on functionalism—where he argues with Titchener's position—American psychologists were no longer interested in the structuralism-functionalism controversy and many issues associated with it had lost their vitality. Moreover, many of the functionalist concepts had already been absorbed by American psychology and the attention of American leaders was diverted to new issues, while the zest for systematic controversies subsided considerably.

Principles of Functionalism. After this brief history of the functionalist movement, it is appropriate to summarize the main principles and characteristics of functionalism as a school.

1. The *subject matter* of functionalistic psychology was mental operations, or acts, or functions and their ends. The task of psychology was not to study the structures of the mind, but to understand the mind's functions. The "what" of consciousness was not emphasized but the

"what-for." While Angell defined psychology as the science of consciousness or of facts of consciousness, Carr defined it as the "study of mental activity." Mental activity, in Carr's opinion, "is concerned with the acquisition, fixation, retention, organization and evaluation of experiences, and their subsequent utilization in the guidance of conduct."

2. The *method* of functionalism was principally introspection. The functionalists held that the report of the subject's experience was an integral part of the study of a given process—learning, for example— because it added to the understanding of the process. Mere observation would not reveal certain essential aspects involved in the process—for example, the mode of attack in a learning task such as a maze—which could be mastered either on the basis of kinesthetic cues, or through memory of the sequence of turns. Gradually, however, introspection was de-emphasized and used less often in their research by students at Chicago. Objective methods came to be preferred in research.

3. The *principal problem* was the adaptation of the organism to the environment. Consequently, learning through which adaptation is modified was the main area of research. Attention, perception, and intelligence were also stressed because they are significant factors in the adaptive process.

4. *Biological orientation* was a characteristic feature of functionalism from its beginning. Theory of evolution; the heredity-environment problem; the concept of man as an organism; the study of animal behavior; genetic, comparative, and psychophysiological studies—all were expressions or results of this orientation.

5. *Practical applications* of psychology were fostered and sought by functionalists. Many outstanding promoters of applied fields came from the functionalist ranks. One of the first applications—and one in which the influence of the functionalistic school was felt most—was education. Dewey's powerful influence on educational thought, and particularly on so-called progressive education, is well known.

6. Functionalism *increased the scope* of psychology by fostering such areas as differential and social psychology and psychometrics.

7. The interest in the "what-for" of behavioral acts led to the recognition and study of *motivation, purpose,* and *goal,* although this area did not acquire prominent place in functionalist literature.

Robert S. Woodworth (1869-1962). We include Woodworth in this section, under the heading of functionalism, not because he formally belonged to the school of functionalism as did Angell, Judd, and Carr. Placing Woodworth in any school would amount to violating his strong and often expressed dislike for constraints and prescriptions of "isms." But as he was, in Boring's phrase, "the best representative of the broad functionalism that is characteristic of American psychology," it seems appropriate to discuss him here. Woodworth, associated with Columbia University from 1898 to the time of his death, was an extraordinary man who for over seven decades served psychology in the capacities of experimentalist, teacher, textbook writer, and editor. Above all, and in the first place, he was a teacher. Considering his 70 years of teaching—during which he won universal respect and love—and his widely acclaimed, highly successful textbooks, translated into many languages, Woodworth can justly be called the greatest and most influential teacher of psychology America has ever had. His textbooks include the revised edition of Ladd's *Physiological Psychology* (1911); the monumental *Experimental Psychology* (1938), revised with H. Schlosberg in 1954; an introductory text, *Psychology* (1921), in five editions; and *First Course in Psychology* (1944), with Mary R. Sheehan. He also wrote *Contemporary Schools of Psychology* (1931). This excellent work was revised in 1948. A final revision, which Woodworth prepared with Mary R. Sheehan, appeared posthumously in 1964. His views on psychology and contemporary theories were also presented in numerous book reviews, articles, and at length in his *Dynamic Psychology* (1918) and *Dynamics of Behavior* (1958), his last book. The latter, published when Woodworth was 89, has been described as "strikingly modern."

Woodworth was long associated with *dynamic psychology*. Though not the originator of the term "dynamic," he was the first to give it a special meaning and place in his conception of psychology. For him psychology was dynamic because it dealt with causes of thought and action. Woodworth defined it as the study of "cause and effect, motives and processes," or of "the questions 'Why?' and 'How?' focused on human activities and achievements." Dynamic psychology was designed not to be a new system of psychology, but a focus and emphasis. Over the years, as Woodworth found, the qualifier "dynamic" became misleading for his psychology because "dynamic psychology . . . came generally to mean the study of motivation, especially unconscious motivation." Since dynamic psychology, as he conceived it, was not merely and solely concerned with motivation, he entitled his 1958 book—in which he analyzed the dynamic interactions of motivation with perception, learning, and thinking—*Dynamics of Behavior*. The concepts which Woodworth used to explain motivated behavior were drives and mechanisms. Through his dynamic psychology Woodworth sought to synthesize behaviorism with older psychologies. In this program he was careful not to impose methodological restrictions because he felt that dynamic psychology must be free to utilize any data regardless of the methods by which they had been gathered. Resistance to being "fettered" by any dogmatic theoretical dictates characterized Woodworth all his life; it kept him free to "seek light wherever trustworthy information is to be had," as he described his eclectic attitude. During the struggles of the schools, Woodworth's position gave heart to those who, like him, were unwilling to yield to the strictures of systems— mainly those of behaviorism. Thus he encouraged those who despite inadequate methods, wanted to pursue their study of such then unpopular subjects as motivation and personality.

In 1956 Woodworth received the Gold Medal Award of the American Psychological Foundation. On this occasion he was characterized in the

formal citation as an "integrator and organizer of psychological knowledge" and a man who made "unequalled contributions to shaping the
destiny of scientific psychology." Shakow and Rapaport say of Woodworth in their book that he "became the acknowledged dean and elder
statesman of scientific psychology."

Evaluation. Titchener predicted that functionalism, not true science,
would die, while structuralism would triumph. "Functional psychology
. . . ," he said, "is a parasite, and the parasite of an organism doomed to
extinction. . . ." History did not bear this out.

Functionalism, both at Chicago and at Columbia, represented liberation
from the constraints of the atomistic psychology of consciousness, a will
to expand and move forward to new fields, and a desire to make psychology
useful in the life of the individual and society. Functionalism was successful in these three respects. Functionalists made substantial contributions to various fields, particularly to learning theory. As time went on,
some functionalist issues, vital during the structuralism controversy, lost
their significance. Others were overshadowed and lost their prominence
by reason of the new issues which behaviorism or Gestaltism raised.
Moreover, some issues and views lost their identity as functionalist products because they were either incorporated into psychology proper or
assimilated and reinterpreted by other movements. Ultimately functionalism faded away while other schools gained vitality. This was the case
with the Gestalt school and especially with behaviorism, which grew out
of the functionalist movement. These new schools soon drew the attention of American psychologists, and the psychological scene changed.

REFERENCES

PSYCHOLOGICAL SCHOOLS IN GENERAL

Allport, G. W. *Becoming: basic considerations
for psychology of personality.* New Haven:
Yale Univer. Press, 1955.

Mandler, G., & Kessen, W. *The language of
psychology.* New York: Wiley, 1959.

McDougall, W. The hormic psychology. In C.
Murchison (Ed.), *Psychologies of 1930.*
Worcester, Mass.: Clark Univer. Press, 1930.
Pp. 3–36.

McGeoch, J. A. The formal criteria of a syste-,
matic psychology. *Psychol. Rev.,* 1933, *40*
1–12.

For special books on theories and systems
see BIBLIOGRAPHY at the end of this book
under the heading, 3. *Systematic and theoretical.*
For the survey of contemporary theories, highly
recommended are the volumes in the series
Psychology: A Study of a Science (beginning
with 1959) under the editorship of S. Koch and
published by McGraw-Hill.

STRUCTURALISM

Bentley, M. The psychologies called "Structural-
ism": historical derivation. In C. Murchison
(Ed.), *Psychologies of 1925.* Worcester, Mass.:
Clark Univer. Press, 1926. Pp. 383–393.

Bentley, M. The work of the structuralists. In C.
Murchison (Ed.), *Psychologies of 1925.*
Worcester, Mass.: Clark Univer. Press, 1926.
Pp. 395–404.

Boring, E. G. Edward Bradford Titchener:
1867–1927. *Amer. J. Psychol.,* 1927, *38,* 489–
506. Reprinted in E. G. Boring, *Psychologist
at large.* New York: Basic Books, 1961. Pp.
246–265.

Titchener, E. B. The postulates of a structural
psychology. *Phil. Rev.,* 1898, 7, 449–465. Reprinted in W. Dennis (Ed.), *Readings in the
history of psychology.* New York: Appleton-
Century-Crofts, 1948. Pp. 366–376.

Titchener's complete bibliography is to be
found in E. G. Boring, *A history of experimental*

psychology, 2nd ed., p. 435. Other valuable information on Titchener can also be found in this same volume, pp. 410–420, 435–437.

FUNCTIONALISM

Angell, J. R. The relations of structural and functional psychology to philosophy. *Phil. Rev.*, 1903, *12*, 243–271.

Angell, J. R. *Psychology: an introductory study of the structure and function of the human consciousness.* New York: Holt, 1904.

Angell, J. R. The province of functional psychology. *Psychol. Rev.*, 1907, *14*, 61–69. Reprinted in W. Dennis (Ed.), *Readings in the history of psychology.* New York: Appleton-Century-Crofts, 1948. Pp. 439–456.

Boring, E. G. John Dewey: 1859–1952. *Amer. J. Psychol.*, 1953, *66*, 145–147.

Carr, H. A. *Psychology: a study of mental activity.* New York: Longmans, 1925.

Carr, H. A. Functionalism. In C. Murchison (Ed.), *Psychologies of 1930.* Worcester, Mass.: Clark Univer. Press, 1930. Pp. 59–78.

Dewey, J. The reflex arc concept in psychology. *Psychol. Rev.*, 1896, *3*, 357–370. Reprinted in W. Dennis (Ed.), *Readings in the history of psychology.* New York: Appleton-Century-Crofts, 1948. Pp. 355–365.

Harrison, R. Functionalism and its historical significance. *Genet. Psychol. Monogr.*, 1963, *68*, 387–423.

James, W. The Chicago school. *Psychol. Bull.*, 1904, *1*, 1–5.

Miles, W. James Rowland Angell, 1869–1949, psychologist-educator. *Science*, 1949, *110*, 1–4.

Poffenberger, A. T. Robert Sessions Woodworth: 1869–1962. *Amer. J. Psychol.*, 1962, *75*, 677–692.

Ruckmick, C. A. The use of the term *function* in English textbooks of psychology. *Amer. J. Psychol.*, 1913, *24*, 99–123.

Seward, Georgene H. Woodworth, the man: a "case history." In Georgene H. & J. P. Seward (Eds.), *Current psychological issues.* New York: Holt, 1958. Pp. 3–20.

Woodworth, R. S. *Dynamics of behavior.* New York: Holt, 1958.

Autobiographies of American functionalists have been published in C. Murchison (Ed.), *A history of psychology in autobiography.* Worcester, Mass.: Clark Univer. Press, 1930–1936. 3 vols. Judd and Woodworth in Vol. 2, Angell and Carr in vol. 3.

For Woodworth's complete bibliography see Woodworth & Sheehan, *Contemporary schools of psychology.* (3rd ed.) New York: Ronald, 1964. Pp. 391–403. For biographical material see the works by A. T. Poffenberger and by Georgene H. Seward, as cited above. For the presentation of the American Psychological Foundation Gold Medal Award to Woodworth see *Amer. Psychologist*, 1956, *11*, 587–589.

18

Behaviorism

WHEN FUNCTIONALISM AS A SCHOOL began to decline, a new American school, behaviorism, emerged. Its founder was John Broadus Watson, professor of psychology at the Johns Hopkins University. The declaration of behaviorism was made in Watson's article, *Psychology as the Behaviorist Views It*, published in the *Psychological Review* in 1913. From the beginning, behaviorism consciously and explicitly meant to be a revolt. It rebelled against the whole existing psychology, accusing it of utter failure. It set out to build an entirely new science of psychology. Specifically, Watson rejected consciousness and the mind as the subject matter of psychology, and introspection as its method, and made a plea for a truly objective scientific psychology on a par with other natural sciences like physics or chemistry. This new psychology was to be the study of behavior. Watson's stand and program were announced in the opening paragraph of the above-mentioned article:

> Psychology as the behaviorist views it is a purely objective experimental branch of natural science. Its theoretical goal is the prediction and control of behavior. Introspection forms no essential part of its methods, nor is the scientific value of its data dependent upon the readiness with which they lend themselves to interpretation in terms of consciousness. The behaviorist, in his efforts to get a unitary scheme of animal response, recognizes no dividing line between man and brute. The behavior of man, with all of its refinement and complexity, forms only a part of the behaviorist's total scheme of investigation.

Further in the article Watson stated that psychology "failed signally ... during the fifty-odd years of its existence as an experimental discipline to make its place in the world as an undisputed natural science." Since the main reason for this failure was psychology's persistence in adhering to consciousness and introspection, psychology must be redone and rewritten without ever using the terms "consciousness, mental states, mind, content, introspectively verifiable, imagery, and the like." Watson expressed the belief that this rewriting "can be done in terms of stimulus and response, in terms of habit formation, habit integrations and the like," that is, in behavioristic terminology. This could be accomplished, he thought, "in a few years," and his resolution was to devote himself to this task.

J. B. Watson (1878-1958)—Life and Publications. Watson's graduate studies, made at the University of Chicago, culminated with a Ph.D. in 1903. His doctoral thesis, under J. R. Angell and H. H. Donaldson, a neurologist, was on the neurological and psychological maturation of the white rat. He remained at Chicago in charge of animal psychology for five years. While there, he was in contact with John Dewey, Angell,

Jacques Loeb, a zoologist and physiologist, and G. H. Mead. Although exposed to the functionalist atmosphere of Chicago, he rejected functionalism and later attacked it along with structuralism. Of Dewey he said: "I never knew what he was talking about and, unfortunately still don't." In 1908 he became professor of experimental and comparative psychology and director of the psychological laboratory at the Johns Hopkins University, where he stayed for 12 years and where he conceived and developed his system of behaviorism. Originally his research was exclusively in animal psychology. All but one of his 20 publications prior to the famous behaviorist "manifesto" of 1913 were in animal psychology. Later, for a few years, he conducted pioneering experiments on infants and young children. Generally speaking Watson's experimental contributions were neither extensive nor particularly significant.

In 1920 Watson's academic career was abruptly ended, when he had to resign from the university because of adverse publicity resulting from his divorce. He found employment as an executive in an advertising business, in which he was successful. He continued to lecture occasionally and to publish in psychology, but gradually withdrew from active participation in psychology not to be heard from at all during the last 20 years of his life. He died at the age of 80.

The first public exposition of behaviorism was made by Watson in a series of lectures at Columbia University in 1912. His first published account of the system appeared, as mentioned above, in the 1913 article, *Psychology as the Behaviorist Views It*. This was followed the next year by his book *Behavior: An Introduction to Comparative Psychology* and in 1919 by another book, *Psychology from the Standpoint of a Behaviorist*. The latter, in its third edition of 1929, is the best presentation of the system. In 1924-1925 he published *Behaviorism*. This, Watson's last major book, became one of the most controversial of its time. It appeared again in a revised edition in 1930. The style of his works—simple, lucid, and engaging—contributed to their popularity and success.

Sources of Influence. Several sources of influence on Watson and the behavioristic movement can be discerned. Of these the most decisive seem to be animal psychology, evolutionism, functionalism, positivistic philosophy, and, later, the objectivistic psychology of Pavlov and Bekhterev with its key notion, the conditioned reflex. The value of animal studies was recognized early in psychology, as we have seen. Animal psychology posed a number of methodological and theoretical problems. Watson—deeply engaged in animal studies—realized these problems. From his animal research he concluded how useless introspection and various mentalistic concepts were. He became aware that he could study animal behavior without introspection and without any reference to consciousness. Why not dispense with introspection and mentalistic terms in the study of humans? He grew convinced that observation and objective account of human behavior were not only possible but highly desirable. This conviction was consonant with the evolutionary viewpoint which assumed a

ɔlogical continuum, morphological and mental, between species—a view
ɔ which Watson subscribed wholeheartedly. Conditioning, discovered and
developed by Pavlov, provided both a valuable objective method in animal
and in human studies and a useful concept for explaining a large segment
of behavior.

Watson denied any debt to functionalist psychology and fought it
together with the rest of the "old" psychology. Yet the functional atmosphere of Chicago—with its biological orientation, interest in comparative
psychology, and stress on the adjustment of the organism to the environment—must have constituted a favorable milieu for the formation and
growth of his ideas. In a negative sense, functionalism, by its rebellion
against structural psychology, made him realize how futile the struggle
with traditional psychology is, as long as its mentalistic and philosophical
notions are retained.

The questions of whether, which, and how much philosophical systems
influenced Watson's thinking and contributed to the development of behaviorism have been asked often. Watson studied and knew philosophy.
He claimed that explicitly, but he did not invoke any philosophical doctrines in his writings. He, in fact, abjured any philosophy. Nevertheless,
there are implicit, in his system, philosophical presuppositions such as
monism, determinism, mechanism, and positivism. He did more than
simply ignore consciousness and mind; his position actually amounted to
their denial. He saw "no dividing line between man and brute." His
categorical rejection of introspection, his strong plea for objectivism in
psychology, and his acceptance only of observable data as the necessary
conditions for psychology as a science are clearly akin to the positivistic
philosophy of Comte. The implicit philosophical substructure of Watson's
behaviorism was criticized by both his adversaries and supporters. Some
called Watson philosophically naive. His metaphysics was branded by one
critic as "silly." However, the issue of Watson's philosophy was peripheral.
Important historically was his bold program.

The Principles of Behaviorism. It should be realized that behaviorism
in its initial phase was a plea and a program—rather than a complete
system with well-defined methods and concepts supported by adequate
empirical evidence. Many of its claims were undemonstrated, and some
were later disproved. A summary of the tenets and characteristics of
Watsonian behaviorism in its mature form of the 1920's includes:

1. *Definition of psychology:* the science of behavior. Psychology is to
study, exclusively, behavior, which is the reaction of the organism to a
stimulus. Not only human but also infrahuman behavior is to be included
in the scope of psychology. The aim of psychology is not only to describe
behavior but also to predict and control it. All reference to consciousness
must be dispensed with. Therefore mentalistic terms implying consciousness, such as sensation, image, perception, thinking, willing, should be
replaced by objective behavioral terms.

2. *Method.* Introspection, having been declared scientifically worthless, was entirely eliminated. Objective methods of observation and measurement alone were admitted as the means of providing valid data. Concession was made for verbal report because it was a form of behavior. The list of methods proposed by Watson in 1919 included observation with and without instrumental control, conditioned reflex, verbal report, and testing.

3. *Stimulus-response bond.* All behavior, overt and covert, is a response to a stimulus. Complex behavior is composed of simple stimulus-response units or reflexes. The study of the relationship between stimulus and response—or in complex behavior between situation and adjustment—constitutes a fundamental task of psychology. Thus, given the stimulus, psychology will be able to predict the response; or given the response, specify what the effective stimulus was. Responses were classified as learned (or acquired) and unlearned (or innate); explicit (overt) or implicit (the visceral and glandular); and according to the sense organ stimulated (for example, visual, muscular). Because the stimulus-response concept was the core of behavioristic psychology, this kind of psychology was referred to thereafter as the S-R (stimulus-response) psychology.

4. *Learning.* This area has been central in all behaviorism. Watson kept modifying his learning concepts, but he never succeeded in developing a satisfactory learning theory. His views remained associationistic. He came to regard conditioning as a key process in all habit formation. Study of the child Albert, described below, demonstrated to Watson the role of conditioning in the formation of emotional habits.

5. *Feeling and emotion.* What is called feeling of pleasantness or unpleasantness is purely a sensorimotor affair involving specific tissues and muscles. Emotion consists in "profound changes of the bodily mechanism as a whole but particularly of the visceral and glandular systems." Each emotion has its own specific pattern of bodily changes.

Watson studied hundreds of new born babies and came to the conclusion that there are in humans three innate emotions called fear, love, and rage—each with its own specific stimulus situation and response pattern. The existence of this inherited emotional triad was not substantiated by subsequent investigators. Other emotional responses, Watson held, are acquired through conditioning. In a series of experiments Watson's subject—a child, Albert B., the eleven-month-old son of a wet nurse in the hospital where the studies were conducted—was made to fear rats, rabbits, and furry objects. Initially Albert handled a rat or a rabbit without fear. But after a sudden loud noise had been made each time the child reached for the animal, he began to show signs of fear—first, of the animal and then of anything that resembled the animal. The latter reaction Watson called a transfer or spread of conditioned response and believed that this process accounted for many emotional reactions.

6. *Imagery and thinking.* Watson maintained that thinking and imagery—the two notions of strong mentalistic connotation—are not central but peripheral processes consisting of motor responses. Thinking was

called subvocal speech, involving movements of the larynx, tongue, lips, and mouth, which may be neither visible nor audible. This view, since it clashed with the traditional view on thought, stimulated much research and many debates.

7. *Environmentalism*. Watson's concept of stimulus and response led him to extreme environmentalism. "Let us," he said, "forever lay the ghosts of inheritance of aptitudes, of 'mental' characteristics, of special abilities." His strong stress on the environmental influences—as against the hereditary—is well exemplified in his often-cited statement:

> Give me a dozen healthy infants, well-formed and my own specified world to bring them up in and I'll guarantee to take any one at random and train him to become any type of specialist I might select—doctor, lawyer, artist, merchant-chief and, yes, even beggarman and thief, regardless of his talents, penchants, tendencies, abilities, vocations, and race of his ancestors.

Reaction to Behaviorism in America. The seeds of behaviorism fell on ground already well prepared. Disappointment with introspection was keenly felt in the second decade of the present century. Consciousness and mind—concepts handed down by philosophy—were the chief subjects of disagreement among psychologists. At the same time voices clamoring for greater objectivity and for bolstering the scientific character of psychology grew stronger. In such an atmosphere, a daring conception of an entirely objective, aphilosophical psychology was bound to draw immediate attention.

Behaviorism stirred up all American psychology. It was so radical and iconoclastic with respect to basic problems of psychology that no psychologist could remain entirely neutral. It generated enthusiasm and violent opposition. Clark L. Hull, recollecting the reactions for and against behaviorism, wrote: "The zeal of both sides took on a fanaticism more characteristic of religion than of science." Opponents criticized behaviorism both on theoretical and experimental grounds. J. R. Angell in 1915 described Watson's position as "scientifically unsound and philosophically essentially illiterate." But in 1918 he wrote:

> Polemic is now centered about the 'behavioristic' movement, which, with its gospel of objective methods and its crusade against introspection, presents an interesting blend of solid contribution and adolescent exaggeration. Whatever seems to me to be sound in its position, I have adopted.

Titchener criticized behaviorism in a few articles and presented his counterarguments. In 1914 he thought of Watson's behaviorism as a "technology" which can never replace psychology the science. But in 1924 he admitted that behaviorism "has spread over the country in a great wave." As the champion of classical psychology, Titchener was expected to be a more severe critic of behaviorism than he actually was. He and Watson—the guardian of the traditional psychology and the rebel—though poles apart in their theoretical positions, became over the years close and intimate friends. One of the most outspoken and vigorous opponents of Watson and his views was William McDougall, whom we shall consider later. However, the majority of American psychologists acclaimed behaviorism as salutary for psychology, even if they did not agree with some of its aspects. The recognition of Watson by his fellow psychologists was clearly reflected in his election to presidency of the American Psychological Association for the year 1915, at the age of 37, two years after the publication of his first article on behaviorist psychology.

Among the early behaviorists were Max Meyer (b. 1873), author of *The Fundamental Laws of Human Behavior*, published as early as 1911; and Albert P. Weiss (1879-1931), an experimentalist and student of child development, author of *A Theoretical Basis of Human Behavior* (1925); and Edwin B. Holt (1873-1946), a Harvard and Princeton professor with a strong philosophical bent. A little later came Walter S. Hunter (1889-1954), experimentalist in a wide range of problems. Hunter, in his early enthusiasm for behaviorism, suggested a change of the name psychology to anthroponomy (1926). While in this country Z. Y. Kuo (b. 1898), a Chinese behaviorist, advocated extreme environmentalism and fought against the concept of instinct and purposive behavior. Karl S. Lashley (1890-1958), the most outstanding physiological psychologist in America, initially endorsed Watson's behavioristic program. But his experimental findings clashed with some Watsonian views and called for their revision.

The issue of behaviorism was the subject of heated debates for about two decades. Its tenets were continually examined, reviewed, and modified. New formulations were proposed, and thus new varieties of behaviorism developed. The naive behaviorism of Watson, or so-called "muscle-twitch psychology," was replaced by more sophisticated forms. But while the original form of behaviorism gradually declined and differences among behaviorists grew wider, the basic conception of an objective psychology of behavior gained strength and remained the common denominator of various groups. On this important point, it is well to note the words of Walter S. Hunter's *Autobiography:*

> The fundamental issue in behaviorism is not, and never was, the particular speculations of any one behaviorist—of Watson for example. Behaviorism is the point of view in psychology which holds that an adequate account can be given of psychological problems without reference to the term consciousness and introspection.

In this sense it is truly said that American psychology has become behavioristic.

European Reaction to Behaviorism. In Europe behaviorism had a mixed reception. It found friends, but also bitter enemies. On the Continent its adversaries outnumbered supporters. World War I made impossible any immediate or thorough evaluation of behaviorism, but after 1920 more works dealing with this system are found. For example, the Watsonian view on thinking as subvocal speech aroused great interest in Britain. A symposium of the British International Congress of Philosophy and Psychology in 1920 was devoted to this problem. The issue evoked several publications in Britain. One of the major reasons for resistance to behaviorism was perhaps the mechanistic and materialistic bias seen in its violent opposition to all forms of mentalism. Swiss psychologist Edouard Claparède said in 1925: ". . . I fail to see the advantages of the constraint imposed by behaviorists of presenting the simplest facts of psychology in a fashion complicated, hypothetical, artificial . . . practically sterile."

One of the most prominent supporters of behaviorism in Europe was H. Piéron. He wrote favorably on behaviorism and his own system paralleled it closely. Russian psychology of the Pavlov and Bekhterev tradition was sympathetic toward the objective aspect of American behaviorism, but opposed the behavioristic system of psychology. Strong opposition was voiced by proponents of Gestalt psychology. Upon their arrival in the United States, the Gestaltists—like Koffka, for example—started attacking behaviorism. Initially, it seems, they spent more energy fighting it than in presenting their own case. There has been a tendency among European psychologists to separate the theoretical aspects of behaviorism from the methodological. They were willing to accept the objective methods of behaviorism or its emphasis on objectivity, but not the theory— especially its elimination of consciousness and mental processes. The situation changed after World War II. Psychologists in many European countries have shown great interest in behavioristic psychology. Notwithstanding the popularity and influence of phenomenology and existentialism there are signs that behavioristic psychology now has more followers on the Continent than it has ever had.

Evaluation. Some have said of Watson that he was neither unique nor original in his attack against traditional psychology and in his conception of a behavioral psychology. There were psychologists—contemporaneous with Watson or before him—who advocated behavioral psychology. Roback in his *A History of American Psychology* named, as one such man, James Rush (1786-1869), whom he called the first objectivist in America, and who in 1865 had published the *Outline of an Analysis of the Human Intellect.* In this large work Rush advocated a materialistic psychology and study of animal behavior. It is true that several authors independently of Watson were inclined toward behavioristic psychology, spoke in favor of it, and even defined psychology as the study of behavior. Yet none of them made a plea for a new psychology of behavior with equal clarity, vigor, boldness, and skill.

When Watson's *Behaviorism* appeared, a reviewer expressed the opinion that this book marked "an epoch in the intellectual history of man." While this statement was clearly an exaggeration, the historical fact is that Watson indeed opened a new epoch in psychology. Psychology originally was the study of the soul, then it turned to the mind, consciousness, and conscious experience as its subject matter. Functionalism reoriented psychology toward mind and the mind's activity. Behaviorism effected a complete metamorphosis of psychology into an objective study of behavior. After behaviorism, psychology is defined in most textbooks of psychology in America as "the scientific study of behavior." The meaning of behavior, however, is broad, including both overt and covert behavior, movement as well as perception, imagery, and thought.

It matters little whether one calls Watson the promoter, the champion, or the founder of behavior psychology. The important and undeniable historical role of Watson lies in his turning the course of psychology in the direction of objectivity and precision of methodology. "The behavioristic movement," said Harrell and Harrison in 1938 in their article *The Rise and Fall of Behaviorism*, "exerted a tremendous influence for good in changing the whole psychological emphasis away from subjectivity toward objectivized, biologized psychology." In 1957 a citation of the American Psychological Association succinctly summarized the historical significance of Watson when it called his work "one of the vital determinants of the form and substance of modern psychology," and his writings, "the point of departure for continuing lines of fruitful research."

BEHAVIORISTIC PSYCHOLOGY

By 1930 classical, or Watsonian, behaviorism was abandoned by most American psychologists. However, the behaviorist point of view, initiated by Watson, has continued in a new form, often designated as *neobehaviorism*. E. G. Boring and S. S. Stevens, under the influence of operationism, used the term *behavioristics* to describe the physicalistic and monistic tendency of behavioristic psychology. Stevens defined this tendency in these words:

> The notion that all scientific sentences are translatable into a common form—the physical langauge—requires of psychology a behavioristic approach. Psychology so conceived is called *behavioristics*.

But a large number of American psychologists have assimilated the behavioristic point of view without committing themselves to any particular behavioristic theory. Psychology based on a behavioristic viewpoint has been called *behavioristic psychology*, sometimes *S-R psychology*—usually in contradistinction to mentalistic psychology. In the period 1930-1960 several variants or subschools of behavioristic psychology developed. They differed on many issues and often engaged in polemics, but shared reliance on objective methodology, animal experimentation, and emphasis on learning. Some of these variants were identified and designated by names such as molar and molecular, operational, functional, purposive, logical, and deductive behaviorism.

Sigmund Koch distinguished two main phases of the post-Watsonian behaviorism, one from 1930's to mid-forties. This phase he called neobehaviorism, whose main representative was Clark L. Hull. The other, formed in the late 1940's or early 1950's, he termed neo-neobehaviorism. The last phase, according to Koch, has been characterized by extensive modification ("attenuation," "liberalization") of the behaviorist position in respect of its methods and concepts. Moreover, he finds intrinsic to the last phase a concern with problems "formerly bypassed because of the odour of mentalism"—such as perception, for example—and a growing use of introspective methods. This liberalization of behaviorism resulted from the pressures of various intrinsic and extrinsic factors. The important intrinsic factor was behaviorism's inability to realize its theoretical and practical program of the 1930's. Among the extrinsic factors Koch named: "a resurgence of interest in . . . instinctive behavior, perception, complex motivational processes, and thinking; a revivified concern with the physiological basis of behavior . . .; a wider excursion of theoretical ideas . . .; growth in influence of established nonbehaviorist formulations . . .; development of new approaches to behavioral analysis. . . ."

Contributors to Behavioristic Psychology. The most prominent figures in the development of behaviorist psychology during the 1930-1960 period have been: E. C. Tolman (1886-1961), Clark L. Hull (1884-1952), and Edwin R. Guthrie (1886-1959). Burrhus F. Skinner (b. 1904) has been the main exponent of radical behaviorism and the leader of a new form of behavioristic psychology, namely, "operant behaviorism." Behavioristic psychology owes much to the research and theorizing of a large number of psychologists engaged in various fields. Prominent in the field of *learning* and *personality* have been Kenneth W. Spence (b. 1907) and Neal E. Miller (b. 1909)—both of them Hull's students and followers—John Dollard (b. 1900), O. Hobart Mowrer (b. 1907), Harry F. Harlow (b. 1905), and among younger learning theorists, William K. Estes (b. 1919). In *physiological psychology* Donald O. Hebb (b. 1904), Clifford T. Morgan (b. 1915), and Karl H. Pribram (b. 1919) have been outstanding. Charles E. Osgood (b. 1916) and Carl I. Hovland (1912-1962) have also contributed significantly, each in a different way. In the field of pure *logical theory* of behavioristic psychology, Jacob R. Kantor (b. 1888) has been known for his several volumes in theoretical psychology and for a system called by him "interbehavioral psychology" (1958). Kantor is in the process of writing a history of psychology from the behavioristic viewpoint.

The above list of psychologists who have left a mark on behavioristic psychology is by no means exhaustive. Though several of them are discussed in other parts of the book, the description of their views and contributions has been limited by the scope of this volume, and thus is only fragmentary. For greater detail the reader is referred to special works devoted to systems and theories of psychology and to works on theories of learning, personality, and motivation. Among the issues, which have been of particular relevance to behavioristic psychology in the years 1930-1960, are the mediating process and operationism. It is to these issues that we now address ourselves.

The Mediating Process. Early systems of psychology—associationism, structuralism, and functionalism—distinguished more or less clearly among three phases of psychological events—namely, initiating, mediating, and terminating. Behaviorism focused its attention on the terminating phase as a function of the initiating phase, that is, on R (response) in relation to S (stimulus). Early behaviorists, analyzing the behavior process and expressing it by the S-R formula, did not overlook the mediating process or events between initial S and terminal R, but were not primarily concerned with this problem. The mediating events, especially in complex behavior such as thinking, were considered to be mainly verbal. J. F. Dashiell in 1928 referred to "responses . . . that serve in turn as stimuli." "Intraorganic reactions . . . operate as cues," he said. His formulation of this concept was: S implicit R(S)R. According to this formula, stimulus (or a situation) sets up some response in the organism which influences and determines overt behavior. The mediating process or events became a more important issue for behavioristic psychology in the 1930's and 1940's.

Behaviorist psychologists realized that the same S is not always followed by the same R. For instance, presentation of food will bring out a response in a hungry animal different from that in a satiated animal. They felt therefore that an account of events taking place within the organism between the S and the R should be given. R. S. Woodworth proposed the S-O-R formula, in which O stands for the organism and its states. In further elaboration of this paradigm, the formula may be written S-Ox-Rx, where x is the particular state of the organism leading to response Rx. This sequence can be verbalized thus: S elicits Rx when the organism is in x state; for example, presentation of food elicits eating when the animal is hungry; or x elicits Rx in the presence of S, that is, hunger elicits eating when food is presented.

In 1935 Tolman proposed the term and concept of the *intervening variable*, which he subsequently amplified and extensively studied. Between S, which is the independent variable, and R, the dependent variable, there are the intervening variables. Tolman conceived them as hypothesized states or processes or events between five independent variables: (1) environmental stimuli; (2) physiological drive; (3) heredity; (4) past training; and (5) maturity or age, and, the dependent variable, behavior. His original formula was B=f (S, P, H, T, A), where B is behavior, f some function, and the other letters stand for the five independent variables, and it reads: Behavior is some function of S, P, H, T, A. The equation was simplified into B=f (S, A), where S is the situation variables, and A the antecedent variables such as heredity, age, and past experience. The intervening variables arise from the elaboration of the nature of function, and to this elaboration Tolman devoted much attention in his research and writings. He studied the functional relationship of the intervening variables to the stimulus variables (independent variables) and to the behavior variables (dependent variables). Hunger, conceived as a demand for food—an intervening variable—may be related to either the stimulus situation—for instance, to the time from the last feeding—or to the behavior variables, such as speed of eating when food is available.

The concept of the intervening variable initiated much discussion and research among behaviorist psychologists. Voluminous literature exists on this subject. Various intervening variables and their functions have been postulated, particularly for learning behavior. Hull found the notion useful and employed it in the construction of his theory in terms of the hypothetical constructs. In 1948 Kenneth MacCorquodale and Paul E. Meehl in an article, *Operational Validity of Intervening Constructs*, called for a distinction between "intervening variable," defined as constructs which "merely abstract the empirical relationships," and "hypothetical constructs," which are strictly hypothetical with respect to the intervening states or processes—that is, they "involve the supposition of entities or processes not among the observed." The whole notion of the intervening variable—which some regarded as a bridge between behavioristic and nonbehavioristic psychology—and its theoretical context, has undergone considerable modification in the 1940's and 1950's. In recent years the intervening variable paradigm and the theorizing associated with it have been seriously re-examined. In 1959 Tolman described intervening variables as "mere temporarily believed-in, inductive, more or less qualitative generalizations which categorize and sum up for me various empirically found relationships." In view of the vital part the concept of the intervening variable has played in behavioristic psychology since 1935, its history could be conceivably written in terms of this concept.

Skinner and the operant behaviorists have not been concerned with intervening variables or any other "mediators" in the S-R paradigm. Some behavior psychologists preferred to concentrate on the mediation of the physiological processes underlying behavior and sought to establish the neural basis of learning, perception, motivation, and emotion. Their aim was to provide a physiological explanation of behavior. This approach was taken by Karl S. Lashley. Donald O. Hebb also looked for neurophysiological correlates of various aspects of behavior, not shying away from notions unpopular in behavioristic psychology such as set, attitude, attention. As with other psychological processes, so with regard to thought processes he called for "serious, persistent, and if necessary daring, exploration . . . by all available means."

Operationism. One of the influences on American psychological thought and practice in the last three decades, especially on behaviorism, has been operationism, though its effect has gradually diminished. Operationism was not a new school, but a principle calling for definition of concepts in terms of events and operations which can be observed and possibly measured. Such a concept as thirst, for example, could be defined operationally by saying that "an animal is thirsty, if after being deprived of water for 24 hours, he drinks when presented with water." Operationism made the validity of scientific findings and theoretical propositions contingent upon validity of the procedures from which the findings or propositions were derived. Propositions not verifiable by observations were excluded from science as *pseudo-problems.*

Operationism in psychology had two sources, physics and philosophy. In physics, a Harvard physicist and mathematician, and recipient of the Nobel Prize, Percy W. Bridgman, in his *Logic of Modern Physics* (1927), was the first proponent of operational definition of physical concepts. For example, the concept of length, as he said, "involves as much as and nothing more than a set of operations; the concept is synonymous with the corresponding set of operations." In philosophy, logical positivism— rooted in positivistic philosophy, especially in that of Ernst Mach—gained momentum in the 1920's in Vienna. This philosophical movement advocated an approach similar to Bridgman's. A group of scientists and philosophers in Vienna in the 1920's, known as the *Vienna Circle,* used to gather to discuss problems of mutual interest. This group included philosophers Moritz Schlick, Rudolf Carnap, Ludwig Wittgenstein, sociologist Otto Neurath, and physicist Philip Frank, all since distinguished by their influential works.

A segment of American psychologists found operationism advantageous and began to apply it to psychological concepts and research. Among these psychologists, S. S. Stevens (b. 1906), a Harvard professor, became an active supporter and a spokesman of operationism. In his article, *Psychology and the Science of Science* (1939), Stevens gave his view on operationism and presented a list of characteristics of operationism, specifying what operationism is and what it is not. He stressed that operationism was not a school but a technic. Tolman, when he declared his "own brand" of psychology as "operational behaviorism" in 1936, defined operationism as "a science which seeks to define its concepts in such a manner that they can be stated and tested in terms of concrete repeatable operations by independent observers." Edwin G. Boring saw in operationism the "modern phase" of physicalism, which he defined in turn as "the view that consciousness, as an object of observation by science, reduces to the operations by which consciousness becomes known to scientists." In 1944 a symposium on operationism—held at the suggestion of Boring—was conducted by the *Psychological Review* with six participants. One of them was B. F. Skinner who defined operationism "as the practice of talking about (1) one's observations; (2) the manipulative and calculational processes involved in making them; (3) the logical and mathematical steps which intervene between earlier and later statements; and (4) *nothing else.*"

Another symposium, arranged by physical scientists, philosophers, and psychologists, was held in Boston in 1953. It reappraised the status of operationism from various points of view. In the discussion P. W. Bridgman deplored the course operationism took. "I feel," he said, "that I have created a Frankenstein, which has certainly got away from me. I abhor the word *operationalism* or *operationism,* which seems to imply a dogma, or at least a thesis of some kind." He further surprised psychologists, who found comfort and encouragement in his earlier position, when in a later article and a book, *The Way Things Are* (1959), he assigned importance to introspection and value to the introspectional report. It was not the first time that psychology was indirectly rebuked for its physicalistic orientation by a representative of physical sciences, which have constituted the ideal for psychology, and which behavioristic psychology since Watson has tried to emulate. Robert Oppenheimer, the well-known nuclear physicist, in an invited address before the American Psychological Association in 1955, cautioned psychology not "to model itself after physics which is not there any more, which has been quite outdated."

Operationism found adherents among psychologists not only in America but in other countries as well. There has developed, however, strong resistance to operationism both on theoretical and methodological grounds. It has been objected that significant problems are often excluded from psychological study because they cannot meet the requirements of the operational rigors, whereas insignificant issues, more easily accessible to operational techniques, are given preference. Operationism, critics say, has either disregarded such problems as motives, purpose, thought, personality, and the like, or reduced them to merely "verbal shadows." Moreover, operationism produced a social climate, to quote W. C. H. Prentice (1946), "in which the psychological theorist may hesitate to present theories which contain non-operational definitions." On the other hand, many psychologists found the operational approach helpful in clarifying certain issues in psychology and in exploration of various concepts such as, for instance, intervening variables. Operational definitions have often facilitated effective communication.

Burrhus F. Skinner (b. 1904).   The best and most widely known representative and exponent of contemporary behaviorism is B. F. Skinner, a professor at Harvard, to whom we have previously referred on several occasions. After his doctorate in experimental psychology from Harvard in 1931, Skinner taught at the University of Minnesota, then at the University of Indiana, and in 1948 joined the faculty at Harvard. His first book was *The Behavior of Organisms* (1938). He conducted systematic experiments, mainly on the white rat and lately on pigeons, placed in a compartment specially constructed by him and known to every student of psychology as "the Skinner box." In this box the rat learns to press a bar or the pigeon to peck at a disk or a key to receive a food pellet or a piece of grain as a reward. When the animal makes the "correct" response such as pressing a bar, he is rewarded or, in other words, his response is reinforced by food or other means. Such a response is called *operant* behavior, distinguished from *respondent* behavior. Behavior is called respondent when it is *elicited* by a stimulus—for instance a reflex action such as a knee jerk when the knee cap is tapped. This is the classic S-R sequence; knee cap tapping is followed by a knee jerk. In operant behavior the stimulus *emits* the response: accidental pressing of the bar brings a food pellet which subsequently induces a hungry animal to repeat pressing. Food is not the stimulus for bar pressing, but once food is obtained in this way, it will reinforce the action of bar pressing. A dog will learn to sit up and beg, when this behavior is rewarded by food or something else. Here sitting up too is operant behavior.

Skinner set out to measure the rate at which simple operant behavior of experimental animals occurs and to study all the variables affecting this rate. This rate is influenced by reinforcement (reward), which itself may be made to depend on the response rate. The experimenter may employ various *reinforcement schedules*. He may program the food dispenser in the box in such a way that every peck obtains food, that is, is reinforced. Or he may use a *fixed interval* of time, say a minute, for the reinforcement to be given after a peck. Another schedule of reinforcement consists of *fixed ratio*, that is, the animal is reinforced after a series of pecks, for example, once for every five pecks. The interval and the ratio instead of being fixed may be made to vary, thus a *variable* schedule is obtained. The conditions in the boxes and the schedules of reinforcement can now be electronically programmed and controlled, and the responses of the animals automatically recorded. An enormous amount of data can be collected in a relatively short time. The subject of the schedules and the results of numerous experiments are discussed in a book by Skinner and C. B. Ferster, *Schedules of Reinforcement* (1957). The book presents 921 figures which summarize about one-quarter of a billion responses and about 70,000 hours of recorded animal behavior. While studying operant behavior and its various parameters, Skinner is concerned neither with the causal continuity between stimulus and response nor with the intervening variables, but simply with the correlation between S and R. He ignores entirely the mediation—be it psychological or physiological—of the organism. For him the organism is "empty." The variables in which he is interested "lie outside the organism, in its immediate environment and in its environmental history." After the experimenter has determined the environmental variables on which a given behavior is dependent, he can effectively control this behavior, or "shape" it, by manipulating the variables. To do this the experimenter need not know at all the physiological processes involved; even if he knew them, he could not manipulate them to the degree that he can manipulate the environment. When he finds that his methods produce "behavior facts showing a high degree of regularity," the experimenter has no need for any theories in the manner of Tolman or Hull.

If experimentation on operant behavior of animals seems trivial or remote from human conditions, it must be remembered that this kind of experimentation has proved to be a convenient experimental strategy in establishing basic laws and principles of behavior applicable also to human behavior. Knowing these laws, a psychologist can predict and control behavior. Operant behaviorists say that many human activities— both simple, such as routine work on a factory assembly line, and complex, such as music making—can be thought of as operant behavior and studied as such. With regard to animals, operant conditioning techniques have been used with striking success in animal training. Many animal trainers have adopted operant conditioning in their work. There have been many other applications. Pharmaceutical companies have made an extensive use of Skinnerian techniques in measuring effects of drugs, especially of psychoactive drugs. During World War II, Skinner conducted research on the use of pigeons for the guiding of missiles. Skinner and his followers showed how their methods and findings can be extended to various areas of human life, especially to education. Skinner himself has demonstrated how his principles can be incorporated in devices such as teaching machines and chambers for rearing babies. He has applied principles of his psychology to the field of language and thought in his *Verbal Behavior* (1957). Skinner's psychology has far-reaching social and ethical implications for human life. Much aware of these implications, he has pointed to various possible practical uses of operant conditioning in everyday life. He spelled them out in novel form, in *Walden Two* (1948), picturing utopian life similar to that shown by Aldous Huxley in his *Brave New World*. In addition to the works mentioned above, two others have appeared—*Science and Human Behavior* (1953) and *Cumulative Record* (2nd ed., 1961), which consists of 33 reprints of his publications.

Skillful experimenter, clear and persuasive writer, inspiring teacher, enthusiastic scientist, Skinner has become the incontestable leader and champion of behavioristic psychology. The citation accompanying the Distinguished Contribution Award of the American Psychological Association, presented to Skinner in 1958, speaks of the "profound impact" he had on "the development of psychology and on promising younger psychologists." V. Edwin Bixenstine, in his article *Empiricism in Latter-day Behavioral Science* (1964), thinks that "Skinner will emerge historically as one of the most influential behavioral scientists of the mid-20th century." While highly respected and commanding a large following among the younger generation of American psychologists, Skinner, nevertheless, has had enemies and bitter critics. He has been criticized on several accounts. The frequent targets of criticism have been Skinner's atheoretical and aphysiological position; his neglect of statistical analysis of data; his omission of problems such as perception, emotion, motivation and personality; and his exaggerated extrapolation beyond available data. He has dealt with complex psychological problems, but—as Sigmund Koch said—"the mode of his treatment is very seriously limited." Skinner has also been attacked for the narrow scope of his psychology, his ultraempiricism, and his implicitly materialistic philosophy of man.

"Behaviorism at Fifty." In 1963 half a century had elapsed since Watson wrote his historic article and launched behavioristic psychology. This anniversary prompted B. F. Skinner to entitle his article in that year *Behaviorism at Fifty*. The progress of American psychology in these 50 years—particularly in the experimental field—is attributable largely to behavioristic psychology. This psychology has also been the major influence in shaping the character and main orientation of American psychology as we find it today. The hold the behavioristic viewpoint has had on American psychology has been reflected in many ways, as is clear from this and previous chapters. One striking single evidence of the imprint behavioristic psychology has left is our present definition of psychology. The overwhelming majority of textbooks have adopted the behavioristic definition of psychology as "the science of behavior" or "the scientific study of behavior." Some authors, however, are not quite satisfied with this definition and amplify it by adding *"and* of mental life" or *"and* of experience." Allusion to the inadequacy of this widely current definition of psychology as the scientific study of behavior was made by Michael Scriven, a professor in the Department of History and Logic of Science at Indiana University, during the symposium on behaviorism and phenomenology at Rice University in 1963. In the discussion following his paper, the last of a series of six, a member of the audience said: "On behalf of the students of psychology, I should just like to ask this: What is psychology?" Scriven's answer was paraphrased in the protocol of the discussion in this way: "To say 'the scientific study of human behavior' is to include too much physiology and to load the answer in the direction of the behaviorists. The 'scientific study of thought, behavior, feeling, and one or two other things like that' would not be a bad answer. . . ."

As seen now, behavioristic psychology is a heterogeneous movement, consisting of many forms and varying degrees of commitment to the behavioristic prescription. At present its most vigorous form is operant behaviorism. Skinner, its main protagonist, described the position of behaviorism in the opening paragraph of his 1963 article, *Behaviorism at Fifty:*

> Behaviorism, with an accent on the last syllable, is not the scientific study of behavior but a philosophy of science concerned with the subject matter and methods of psychology. If psychology is a science of mental life—of the mind, of conscious experience—then it must develop and defend a special methodology, which it has not yet done successfully. If it is, on the other hand, a science of the behavior of organisms, human or otherwise, then it is part of biology, a natural science for which tested and highly successful methods are available. The basic issue is not the nature of the stuff of which the world is made or whether it is made of one stuff or two but rather dimensions of the things studied by psychology and the methods relevant to them.

In the body of the article Skinner contrasted behavioristic and mentalistic psychology and specified the position of behavioristic psychology on several issues.

In 1964, a symposium was organized to review the current position of operant behaviorism. The participants included E. G. Boring, who gave the introductory paper and chaired the symposium, P. B. Dews, N. Guttman, R. J. Herrnstein, M. Sidman, B. F. Skinner, and P. Teitelbaum. The titles of the papers deliberately bore—but with quotation marks—traditional psychological terms in order to, as Boring said, "emphasize the continuity of psychology in the face of constant change": "Humors," "Experience," "Will," "Anxiety," "Man," and "Appetite." This symposium reflected the wide scope and intensity of research, as well as current views of operant behaviorism on various issues.

The basic behavioristic viewpoint has been increasingly questioned in recent years. It is interesting to note, in this respect, an expression of dissent by Brand Blanshard, professor emeritus of philosophy at Yale, to the views presented at the above-mentioned symposium. In the article, *Critical Reflections on Behaviorism,* published in 1965 in *Proceedings of the American Philosophical Society,* where the symposium papers were also published, Blanshard objected to the rejection of consciousness or to the manner of treatment of this subject by behaviorism. He rejected the goal of behaviorism because, as he bluntly stated: ". . . it makes nonsense of human life." Carl Rogers in his paper *Toward a Science of the Person*, at the previously mentioned symposium on behaviorism and phenomenology in 1963, referred to limitations and inadequacy of behavioristic psychology. His opinion, as cited below, seems to represent well the sentiments of a large segment of nonbehaviorist psychologists in America.

> Valuable as have been the contributions of behaviorism, I believe that time will indicate the unfortunate effects of the bounds it has tended to impose. To limit oneself to consideration of externally observable behaviors, to rule out consideration of the whole universe of inner meanings, of purposes, of the inner flow of experiencing, seems to me to be closing our eyes to great areas which confront us when we look at the human world. Furthermore, to hold to the beliefs, which seem to me to characterize many behaviorists, that science is impersonal, that knowledge is an entity, that science somehow carries itself forward without the subjective person of the scientist being involved, is, I think, completely illusory.

Consciousness. The issue of consciousness reappears in current psychological discussions more often than it has in a long time. It is a frequent subject of debates between behaviorists and nonbehaviorists. A number of contemporary psychologists have voiced their belief of the necessity of the concept of consciousness for psychology. Rex M. Collier in his paper, published in 1963, said that to him there seems "no more challenging need in psychology than to restore to our science a valid and usable concept of consciousness." D. O. Hebb touched upon the matter of consciousness in his presidential address before the American Psychological Association in 1960. He referred in this address to two phases of revolution in American psychology. He said:

> The first [phase] banished thought, imagery, volition, attention, and other such seditious notions. . . . These notions relate to a vital problem in the understanding of man, and it is the task of the second phase to bring them back, brainwashed as necessary. . . . My thesis in this address is that an outstanding contribution to psychology was made in the establishment of a thoroughgoing behavioristic mode of thinking. But this has been achieved, too frequently, only by excluding the chief problem of human behavior. The second contribution must be to establish an equally thoroughgoing behavioristics of the thought process. . . . Mind and consciousness, sensations and perception, feelings and emotions, all are intervening variables or constructs and properly part of a behavioristic psychology.

However, nonbehaviorists find the "behavioristics of consciousness" unsatisfactory. The difference between the behavioristic and nonbehavioristic view is well illustrated in the two articles, one by J. D. Keehn, the other by Cyril Burt, both entitled *Consciousness and Behaviourism* and published in the *British Journal of Psychology* in 1964. The first author argued that Skinner's behaviorism does not deny consciousness and described how it approaches this problem, namely, that it "sets out to show how functional relationship between private experiences (consciousness) and overt behaviour can develop." C. Burt in his reply contrasted his view with that of his opponent in this way:

We are both prepared to accept consciousness as an observable fact. Dr. Keehn, however, regards it as of no scientific interest or importance. I on the contrary hold that, of all the empirical attributes of things that present themselves for observation and research—their position, size, and weight, their energy in its various forms . . . the attribute of consciousness is at once the most distinctive and (in the existing state of knowledge) the most baffling. For that reason, as it seems to me, present-day psychology, instead of evading the problem either by denying its existence or belittling its importance, should once again include within its scope the systematic study of conscious experience.

As will be seen in the chapters on phenomenological and existential psychology, opinions like Burt's are not isolated, and behavioristic psychology has now found strong opposition in various quarters.

Conclusion. The three psychological schools, structuralism, functionalism, and behaviorism, reviewed in the preceding and in this chapter, represent the evolution of psychological thought in America. Functional from its very beginning, American psychology made its formal break with Wundtian psychology through the school of functionalism. But the decisive turn into an entirely objective direction was achieved by behaviorism. Although behaviorism attacked functionalism together with structuralism, this school was actually only a more radical expression and culmination of tendencies which had existed in American psychology and which had contributed to the rise of functionalism. As Harrell and Harrison said in their article *The Rise and Fall of Behaviorism* in 1938: "Whereas functionalism was only a partial and somewhat half-hearted movement away from a structural analysis which was too sterile and academic, behaviorism completed that evolution which moved slowly out of intellectual and speculative psychology through introspective analysis to the study of mental function and ultimately to the study of behavior." Because of the combined effect of both schools—but principally because of behaviorism—American psychology has drifted further away from philosophy and closer to natural sciences. It has become more quantitative than qualitative, more practical than theoretical, and more concerned with the control and prediction of behavior than with its understanding. Having become the dominant orientation in American psychology after half a century of hegemony, behavioristic psychology—although still vigorous, especially in operant behaviorism—is being challenged and confronted with new theoretical alternatives.

When Wundt's psychology emerged from philosophy as a separate science, it was looked upon as the truly "new" psychology, the *scientific* psychology, in contrast to the "old" psychology, the *philosophical* psychology. When functionalism came, and especially when Watson's behaviorism originated, it was behaviorism which was regarded as the new and more scientific psychology than Wundt's system. Now operant behaviorism is referred to as the "new" psychology. Boring wrote in 1964: ". . . in America just now the new psychology is this operant behaviorism." It is conceivable that this process of new orientations springing up while systems of yesteryear decline will continue and that what is new and vigorous now will be old another day. In the following chapter two other schools—which originated almost at the same time as behaviorism and which came to America simultaneously—both strongly hostile to behaviorism, will be considered. These schools are those of Gestalt and hormic psychologies—one still alive, the other, though no longer represented in contemporary psychology, not entirely forgotten.

REPRESENTATIVES OF BEHAVIORISM

Classical or early behaviorism (1913–1930)
John B. Watson (1878–1958), founder.
John F. Dashiell (b. 1888)
Edwin B. Holt (1873–1946)
Max Meyer (b. 1873)
Albert P. Weiss (1879–1931)
Walter S. Hunter (1889–1954)
Z. Y. Kuo (b. 1898)

Later behaviorism, neobehaviorism
Edward C. Tolman (1886–1961)
Clark L. Hull (1884–1952)
Edwin R. Guthrie (1886–1959)
Kenneth W. Spence (b. 1907)

Operant behaviorism, radical behaviorism
Burrhus F. Skinner (b. 1904)

Behavioristic viewpoint in theory and/or method
Karl S. Lashley (1890–1958)
S. Smith Stevens (b. 1906), operationism
Neal E. Miller (b. 1909)
Donald O. Hebb (b. 1904)
Harry F. Harlow (b. 1905)
O. Hobart Mowrer (b. 1907)
Charles E. Osgood (b. 1916)
Jacob R. Kantor (b. 1888), theorist, interbehaviorism

REFERENCES

BEHAVIORISM

Beach, F. A., Hebb, D. O., Morgan, C. T., & Nissen, H. W. (Eds.), *The neuropsychology of Lashley.* New York: McGraw-Hill, 1960.

Bergmann, G. The contributions of John B. Watson. *Psychol. Rev.*, 1956, *63*, 265–276. Reprinted in J. Scher (Ed.), *Theories of the mind.* New York: Free Press of Glencoe, 1962. Pp. 674–688.

Carmichael, L. Karl Spencer Lashley, experimental psychologist. *Science*, 1959, *129*, 1409–1412.

Erickson, R. W. An examination of the system of Professor K. S. Lashley. *J. gen. Psychol.*, 1950, *42*, 243–260.

Harrell, W., & Harrison, R. The rise and fall of behaviorism. *J. gen. Psychol.*, 1938, *18*, 367–421.

Hunter, W. S. Psychology and anthroponomy. In C. Murchison (Ed.), *Psychologies of 1925.* Worcester, Mass.: Clark Univer. Press, 1926. Pp. 83–107.

Hunter, W. S. Anthroponomy and psychology. In C. Murchison (Ed.), *Psychologies of 1930.* Worcester, Mass.: Clark Univer. Press, 1930. Pp. 281–300.

Koch, S. Behaviorism. *Encyclopaedia Britannica*, 1961. Vol. 3, 326–329.

Larson, C. A., & Sullivan, J. B. Watson's relation to Titchener. *J. Hist. behav. Sci.*, 1965, *1*, 338–354.

Lashley, K. S. *Brain mechanisms and intelligence.* Chicago: Chicago Univer. Press, 1929.

Meyer, M. *The fundamental laws of human behavior.* Boston: Badger, 1911.

Roback, A. A. *Behaviorism and psychology.* Cambridge, Mass.: Univer. Bookstore, 1923.

Roback, A. A. *Behaviorism at 25.* Cambridge, Mass.: Sci-Art, 1937.

Schlosberg, H. Walter S. Hunter: pioneer objectivist in psychology. *Science*, 1954, *120*, 441–442.

Skinner, B. F. John Broadus Watson, behaviorist. *Science*, 1959, *129*, 197–198.

Watson, J. B. Psychology as the behaviorist views it. *Psychol. Rev.*, 1913, *20*, 158–177. Reprinted in W. Dennis (Ed.), *Readings in the history of Psychology.* New York: Appleton-Century-Crofts, 1948. Pp. 457–471.

Watson, J. B. *Psychology from the standpoint of a behaviorist.* Philadelphia: Lippincott, 1919. 3rd ed,. 1929.

Watson, J. B. *Behaviorism*. New York: Norton, 1925. Rev. ed., 1930.

Watson, J. B., & McDougall, W. *The battle of behaviorism*. New York: Norton, 1929.

Weiss, A. P. Relation between structural and behavioral psychology. *Psychol. Rev.*, 1917, *24*, 301–317; 353–368.

Weiss, A. P. *A theoretical basis of human behavior*. (2nd ed.) Columbus, Ohio: Adams, 1929.

Woodworth, R. S. John Broadus Watson: 1878–1958. *Amer. J. Psychol.*, 1959, *72*, 301–310.

C. Murchison (Ed.), *A history of psychology in autobiography*. Worcester, Mass.: Clark Univer. Press. It has autobiographies of Watson (Vol. 3) and Hunter (Vol. 4).

BEHAVIORISTIC PSYCHOLOGY

General

Blanshard, B. Critical reflections on behaviorism. *Proc. Amer. Phil. Soc.*, 1965, *109*, 22–28.

Boring, E. G. The trend toward mechanism. *Proc. Amer. Phil. Soc.*, 1964, *108*, 451–454.

Burt, C. Consciousness and behaviourism: a reply. *Brit. J. Psychol.*, 1964, *55*, 93–96.

Collier, R. M. Selected implications from a dynamic regulatory theory of consciousness. *Amer. Psychologist*, 1964, *19*, 265–269.

Diserens, C. M. Psychological objectivism. *Psychol. Rev.* 1925, *32*, 121–152.

Frank, P. G. (Ed.) *The validation of scientific theories*. Boston: Beacon, 1956.

Goss, A. E. Early behaviorism and verbal mediating responses. *Amer. Psychologist*, 1961, *16*, 285–298.

Hebb, D. O. The American revolution. *Amer. Psychologist*, 1960, *15*, 735–745.

Kantor, J. R. *Interbehavioral psychology*. Bloomington: Principia, 1958.

Keehn, J. D. Consciousness and behaviourism. *Brit. J. Psychol.*, 1964, *55*, 89–91.

MacCorquodale, K., & Meehl, P. E. On a distinction between hypothetical constructs and intervening variables. *Psychol. Rev.*, 1948, *55*, 95–107.

Oppenheimer, R. Analogy in science. *Amer. Psychologist*, 1956, *11*, 127-135.

Stevens, S. S. Psychology and the science of science. *Psychol. Bull.*, 1939, *36*, 221–263. Also in M. H. Marx (Ed.), *Psychological theory: contemporary readings*. New York: Macmillan, 1951. Pp. 21–54.

C. H. Hull

Hull, C. L. *Principles of behavior*. New York: Appleton-Century-Crofts, 1943.

Hull, C. L. *A behavior system: an introduction to behavior theory concerning the individual organism*. New Haven: Yale Univer. Press, 1952.

Koch, S. Clark L. Hull. In W. K. Estes, *et al.* (Eds.), *Modern learning theory*. New York: Appleton-Century-Crofts, 1954. Pp. 1–176.

Autobiography of Hull is to be found in E. G. Boring, *et al.* (Eds.), *A history of psychology in autobiography*. Vol. 4. Worcester, Mass.: Clark Univer. Press, 1952. Pp. 143–162.

Operationism

Ayer, A. J. (Ed.) *Logical positivism*. Glencoe, Ill.: Free Press, 1959.

Bergmann, G. Sense and nonsense in operationism. *Sci. Monthly*, 1954, *79*, 210–214.

Bridgman, P. W. *The logic of modern physics*. New York: Macmillan, 1927.

Bridgman, P. W. Remarks on the present state of operationalism. *Sci. Monthly*, 1954, *79*, 224–226.

Bridgman, P. W. *The way things are*. Cambridge, Mass.: Harvard Univer. Press, 1959.

Israel, N., & Goldstein, B. Operationism in psychology. *Psychol. Rev.*, 1944, *51*, 177–188.

Margenau, H. On interpretations and misinterpretations of operationalism. *Sci. Monthly*, 1954, *79*, 209–210.

Prentice, W. C. Operationism and psychological theory: a note. *Psychol. Rev.*, 1946, *53*, 247–249.

Stevens, S. S. The operational basis of psychology. *Amer. J. Psychol.*, 1935, *47*, 323–330.

The papers presented at the 1944 Symposium on Operationism were published in *Psychol. Rev.*, 1945, *52*, 241–294.

E. C. Tolman

MacCorquodale, K., & Meehl, P. E. Edward C. Tolman. In W. K. Estes, *et al.* (Eds.), *Modern learning theory*. New York: Appleton-Century-Crofts, 1954. Pp. 177–266.

Tolman, E. C. *Purposive behavior in animals and man*. New York: Appleton-Century-Crofts, 1932.

Tolman, E. C. Operational behaviorism and current trends in psychology. *Proceedings Twenty-fifth Anniversary Celebrating Inaug. Grad. Stud.* Los Angeles: Univer. of Southern California Press, 1936. Also in M. H. Marx (Ed.), *Psychological theory: contemporary readings*. New York: Macmillan, 1951. Pp. 87–102.

Tolman, E. C. Principles of purposive behavior. In S. Koch (Ed.), *Psychology: a study of a science*. Vol. 2. New York: McGraw-Hill, 1959. Pp. 92–157.

Autobiography of Tolman is to be found in E. G. Boring, *et al.* (Eds.), *op. cit.* Vol. 4. Pp. 323–339. For Tolman's complete bibliography and a biographical sketch see *Amer. Psychologist*, 1958, *13*, 155–158.

E. R. Guthrie

Mueller, C. G., Jr., & Schoenfeld, W. N. Edwin R. Guthrie. In W. K. Estes, *et al.* (Eds.), *Modern learning theory*. New York: Appleton-Century-Crofts, 1954. Pp. 345–379.

For the citation of the American Psychological Foundation Gold Medal Award see *Amer. Psychologist*, 1958, *13*, 739–740.

B. F. Skinner

Bixenstine, V. E. Empiricism in latter-day behavioral science. *Science*, 1964, *145*, 464–467.
Skinner, B. F. The operational analysis of psychological terms. *Psychol. Rev.*, 1945, *52*, 270–277.
Skinner, B. F. *Walden two*. New York: Macmillan, 1948.
Skinner, B. F. *Science and human behavior*. New York: Macmillan, 1953.

Skinner, B. F. *Verbal behavior*. New York: Appleton-Century-Crofts, 1957.
Skinner, B. F. Teaching machines. *Science*, 1958, *128*, 969–977.
Skinner, B. F. A case history in scientific method. In S. Koch (Ed.), *Psychology: a study of a science*. Vol. 2. New York: McGraw-Hill, 1959. Pp. 359–379.
Skinner, B. F. *Cumulative record*. (Rev. ed.) New York: Appleton-Century-Crofts, 1961.
Skinner, B. F. Behaviorism at fifty. *Science*, 1963, *140*, 951–958. Also in T. W. Wann (Ed.), *Behaviorism and phenomenology*. Chicago: Chicago Univer. Press, 1964. Pp. 79–108.
Skinner, B. F., & Ferster, C. B. *Schedules of reinforcement*. New York: Appleton-Century-Crofts, 1957.
Verplanck, W. S. Burrhus F. Skinner. In W. K. Estes, *et al.* (Eds.), *Modern learning theory*. New York: Appleton-Century-Crofts, 1954. Pp. 267–316.

For a Skinner bibliography see *Amer. Psychologist*, 1958, *13*, 735–738.

19

Schools of European Origin:
Gestalt and Hormic

THE TWO SCHOOLS to be discussed in this chapter—the Gestalt and hormic
—originated in Germany and England, respectively. While both attacked
structuralism and both turned against behaviorism, they differed considerably from each other in their philosophical bases and in the problems
to which they addressed themselves. Gestalt psychology began with a
phenomenological study of visual perception and developed as a system
based on the holistic view of mental and behavioral processes. Hormic
psychology was a system built on the assumption that the essential character of all activity, human and animal, is purposefulness. Gestalt psychology gained many adherents and supporters, received wide recognition
for its contributions, and survived to the present age. Hormic psychology,
on the other hand, in its short life did not enjoy popularity, and its tenets
were either ignored or vigorously attacked.

GESTALT PSYCHOLOGY

The Gestalt school originated in Germany in the second decade of the
twentieth century as a protest against the elementism of Wundt's psychology. It was Dilthey's "understanding psychology" which was the first
effective and influential opposition—on philosophical grounds—to the
atomistic character of the early German psychology. Gestalt school was
the first German psychological movement which—on experimental grounds
—successfully challenged Wundt's psychology by demonstrating the existence of perceptual phenomena unaccountable in the terms of Wundtian
elementism. Their main argument was that psychological facts do not
"consist of unrelated inert atoms" and, hence, that a holistic approach is
necessary for their study. They held that perception is not an unorganized
mosaic of elements, which are subsequently associated into meaningful
contents in the mind. Instead they viewed perception as an organized
structured entity—a configuration or, in the term adopted by the school,
a *Gestalt*. This German noun, *Gestalt*, is usually translated into English
as "shape" or "configuration." Gestalt, as a term, both designates the
school and provides its central concept. It underscores clearly this school's
opposition to the elementistic or atomistic approach in psychology and its
emphasis of the holistic approach. Application of the Gestalt concept
to visual perception of motion was the actual beginning of the new
school.

The "Phi Phenomenon."   In presenting their theory the Gestaltists appealed to logic and epistemology. But the main strength of their offensive and the secret of their success lie principally in the results of their experimental investigations. The historically important events in the launching of the school were Max Wertheimer's experiments on the perception of movement at Frankfurt in 1910-1912 and the publication of his results in a paper, *Experimentelle Studien über das Sehen von Bewegung* ("Experimental Studies on the Viewing of Motion") in 1912.

Max Wertheimer (1880-1943) was born in Prague, studied under Külpe, and received the doctorate at Würzburg in 1904. In 1910 he began a series of experiments on the illusion of motion at Frankfurt. Using instruments such as the stroboscope and tachistoscope, he presented to his subjects in succession simple objects, a line or a stripe, for example, and noted their resulting visual impressions. One of his experiments was to present a vertical line, first in one position (*a*) and then in quick succession in a different position (*b*), either to the right or left of the first position. Then he would return the line to the *a* position. He continued to present the line in the rapidly alternated positions—*ababab*. At a certain time interval between presentations or exposures, the observer saw a line move from *a* to *b* and from *b* to *a*. But when the time interval was further reduced, the observer saw, not the line, but *something* moving from one position to the other. In such an experiment, an optimal time could always be found under given conditions of observation for the subject to see clearly *motion* alone without perceiving the object, its shape or color. This was a phenomenon of pure motion, which Wertheimer termed *phenomenal* motion or the *phi* phenomenon. "The psychic state of affairs," Wertheimer wrote in his 1912 paper, "can be called a-phi-b. . . . Phi designates something that exists outside the perceptions of *a* and *b*; what happens between *a* and *b*, in the space interval between *a* and *b*; what is added to *a* and *b*." The *phi* phenomenon breaks down, if the interval between presentations is further shortened or, in other words, when the rate of alternating presentation of the line is speeded up. The observer then sees two lines side by side instead of pure motion. Various parameters were explored in these experiments by Wertheimer and later by other investigators, who introduced new spatial and temporal arrangements and different colors and shapes. It was found that under proper conditions the *phi* phenomenon always appeared, regardless of the position, shape, or color of objects. The observers in Wertheimer's original experiments were Wolfgang Köhler, Kurt Koffka, and Koffka's wife. "It proved to be unnecessary," Wertheimer wrote, "to obtain a large number of subjects, since the characteristic phenomena appeared in every case unequivocally, spontaneously and compellingly. . . ."

The historic importance of the discovery of the *phi* phenomenon lay in the fact that this phenomenon was an experimentally verifiable case of a dynamic whole which could neither be reduced to simple sensory elements —for it was as elementary as sensation—nor be explained as a sum or succession of sensations. The *phi* phenomenon thus constituted a challenge to the "old" atomistic psychology. Wertheimer made effective use of this and of other visual phenomena when he attacked atomistic psychology in his subsequent writings.

Leaders of the Gestalt Movement. Wertheimer remained in Frankfurt from 1910 to 1916. During this time, and also later when he moved to Berlin, Wertheimer, the oldest of the three, was closely associated with Köhler and Koffka, a decisive factor in the formation of the Gestalt school. The three men, with the help of Kurt Goldstein and Hans Gruhle, who were neurologists and psychopathologists, founded in 1921 a journal, *Psychologische Forschung*. This journal, which existed until 1938, was not only a recognized organ of the Gestalt school but was also regarded as one of the best psychological periodicals. After several years at the Berlin University, Wertheimer returned to Frankfurt in 1929 as full professor. Compelled to leave Germany because of the political situation, he came to the United States in 1933 and joined the faculty of the New School for Social Research in New York. He taught there until his death in 1943. Wertheimer was a brilliant thinker of wide interests and a careful experimenter. His only book in English, *Productive Thinking*, a result of his study of thinking, appeared posthumously, in enlarged edition in 1959.

Kurt Koffka (1886-1941) was born in Berlin, where he studied and took his doctorate in 1908 with Stumpf. He came to America in 1924 and was appointed professor at Smith College in 1927. He remained there until 1941, the year of his death. Koffka's first major work was on developmental child psychology (1921). It was translated into English as *The Growth of the Mind* (1st ed., 1924; 2nd ed., 1928). In 1922 Koffka introduced Gestalt theory to American psychologists in an article in the *Psychological Bulletin*. He amplified his exposition of the Gestalt psychology in a book, *Principles of Gestalt Psychology* (1935).

Wolfgang Köhler (b. 1887) was born in Reval, Estonia. Like Koffka he received his Ph.D. at Berlin under Stumpf, in 1909. After a stay in Frankfurt from 1909 to 1913, Köhler went to study anthropoid apes on Tenerife, the largest of the Spanish Canary Islands. The results of his research and their interpretation along the lines of the Gestalt theory are reported in his well-known and historically important book *The Mentality of Apes* (1st German ed., 1917; English transl., 1925). This book introduced the Gestalt concept of *insight* learning. It was often cited in arguments against trial-and-error theory. This book was followed by *Die physischen Gestalten in Ruhe und im stationärem Zustand* ("Physical Gestalten in Rest and in Stationary State," 1920), whose thesis was that there are formlike holistic systems in the physical world. This work added a broader perspective to the Gestalt theory by postulating the basic unity of the physical and psychological realms. Isomorphism, the Gestalt psychophysical theory based on this assumption, holds that there is correspondence between the physical forms or Gestalten, the physiological forms in the brain, and the forms ascertained phenomenologically. In his theory of isomorphism and in his general discussion of psychological facts,

Köhler—who was Max Planck's student and had a thorough knowledge of physics—often drew upon physical concepts, especially on those from electromagnetism. In 1922 Köhler was appointed Stumpf's successor to the important chair at Berlin. In the following year he published his research on time-error, a notable contribution to psychophysics. Köhler visited the United States in 1925-1926 and lectured at Clark and Harvard. Soon after this visit Köhler gave a systematic exposition of the Gestalt viewpoint in English, *Gestalt Psychology* (1929). In 1934 Köhler left Berlin and took up permanent residence in America. In 1935 he was appointed professor of psychology at Swarthmore College, where he remained until his retirement.

After coming to America, Köhler continued to experiment and write. In his research here, he was alert to new developments in neurophysiology and worked to elucidate the relationship between perceptual processes and the nature of the cortical processes in the brain. The growth and success of the Gestalt viewpoint in psychology are largely attributable to Köhler's research and writing. Köhler made numerous significant and lasting contributions to psychology both as an experimentalist and as a theorist. He received the Distinguished Contribution Award from the American Psychological Association in 1956. The award citation states that Köhler's contributions to perception "have substantially modified the scientific understanding of perceptual processes and have supported a new conceptualization of brain function."

The Phenomenological Method.   For the Gestaltists, psychology was the study of direct (or immediate) experience of the whole organism. But they did not use the classical introspection of structural psychology. In his *Gestalt Psychology* Köhler stated that ". . . psychology, so far as it deals with direct experience by the method of introspection, has not only been a complete failure; it has also become boresome for all those who are not professionally connected with it." Köhler agreed with the behaviorists in their main criticism of introspection. "Indeed," he said, "much of current introspection seems to be rather sterile and, in an odd contrast to its ambitions, to lead research away from the more urgent problems." On the other hand, Gestalt psychology violently disagreed with behaviorism's rejection of the study of direct experience and criticism of the unscientific character of such a study. In response to behaviorists, Köhler argued that observation, even in physics, involves observation of direct experience and that "the physicist and the psychologists are in exactly the same situation in this respect." And he continued:

> It does not matter at all whether I call myself a physicist or a psychologist in observing a galvanometer. In both cases my observation is directed towards the same "objective experience." The procedure works in physics. Why not in psychology? There must be some cases in which my observation of direct experience does not disturb the observed facts seriously.

The principal method adopted and practiced by Gestalt psychology was phenomenology, that is, observation and description of phenomena directly experienced by the individual. Since in Gestalt psychology the conditions of the phenomenological exploration of the observers' experiences are controlled as much as possible, this kind of phenomenology has been called *experimental phenomenology*. The history and features of the phenomenological method are detailed in the chapter on phenomenological psychology. Phenomenology in the hands of the Gestaltists proved to be most fruitful for the purpose for which they employed it, that is, a full exploration of experience. David Katz in his *Gestalt Psychology* states: ". . . the critique which Gestalt psychology directs against the older psychology, and its own positive contributions as well, stand or fall on the merits of the phenomenological method."

The Gestalt. To understand Gestalt psychology is to understand its central concepts, among which the principal ones are *Gestalt* and *field*. The German noun *Gestalt* has been translated into English as form, configuration, structure, shape, or pattern. The precursor in the use of Gestalt both as a term and a concept was *Christian von Ehrenfels* (1859-1932), a professor at Prague University, who in 1890 proposed the notion of form-quality, in German *Gestaltqualität*. The Gestalt school extended the meaning of von Ehrenfels' concept beyond the mere perception of form. Gestalt to them means any integrated organized whole or totality, in contrast to a mere summation of units or parts. Gestalt possesses properties of its own not derived from individual parts or their relation. Gestalt can be experiential or behavioral, static or dynamic. It can also be classified according to its realm of existence into: phenomenal, that is, in our experience; physiological, that is, in living organisms; physical, that is, in inorganic nature; and logical, that is, in systematic thinking. The Gestalt concept is applied to perception (visual, auditory, tactual, and the like), to learning, thinking, motivation, acting. A pattern of dots or lines is a Gestalt, so is a melody, a particular taste, a sentence spoken or heard, a swimmer's dive.

The Laws of Gestalt. The Gestalt school explored not only the various types of Gestalten, but studied the laws or principles governing them. The literature on these laws is extensive. It is possible to enumerate over 100 different "laws of Gestalten" postulated in the literature. The most intensively explored have been visual Gestalten and the factors operating in the organization of the visual field. Several factors aiding in the organization or patterning of the parts of the visual field have been determined and named—such as nearness and similarity of the units seen, familiarity or set of the viewing observer, and "closure." The latter is a natural tendency to overlook small gaps in figures (for instance, a gap in a circle), to "close up" such gaps and perceive the figure as complete and normal. Similar to closure is the principle of *Prägnanz* ("pregnance"), that is, the tendency of a figure to assume to the observer the most characteristic shape for its kind, or the best possible Gestalt.

Some of these laws have been generally recognized and incorporated into textbooks of psychology. Among the best known are the law of constancy and the law of transposition. The constancy law refers to the tendency of a form to retain for the observer its proper or usual shape, size, brightness, and color. The law of transposition means that a Gestalt can be preserved even if its components are changed or rearranged. This law was already postulated by von Ehrenfels and was illustrated by him in an example of a tune. A tune can be played in different keys, on different instruments, can be rearranged in various ways and yet remain the same recognizable tune. But separate the notes of the tune, play each of them individually, and you will have tones but no tune. On the other hand, one can use the same sets of notes and compose a variety of different tunes as children, using the same wooden blocks, can build many different structures.

The organization of discrete elements into a Gestalt is characteristic of experience and behavior. This characteristic manifests itself in men and animals alike. It is primitive, direct, spontaneous, and mostly unlearned. Gestalt research showed that animals respond not to a mosaic of elements but to organized wholes. It has been demonstrated that laws of Gestalten, such as the law of transposition, work also in animals. Suppose that an animal is presented visually with a pair of circles having diameters of one foot and one-half foot, respectively, and that he is trained to react only to the one-foot circle. When the habit is well established, one can change the diameters of the circles. The previously "correct" circle of one-foot diameter is now paired with a two-foot circle, or the "incorrect" half-foot circle with a quarter-foot circle. The animal will respond invariably to the larger of the two circles and not to the previously "correct" one-foot circle. This result shows that the animal—as the Gestaltists say—"endowed the pair of circles with a form quality which is transferred from one pair to the other." Similar transference or transposition functions in other conditions.

Gestalt theories and hypotheses inspired a variety of experiments within and outside the Gestalt school. Such experimentation augmented the repertoire of new findings and perceptual phenomena and provided a great deal of relevant material for the Gestalt school. At the same time they reinforced and popularized the Gestalt movement. Among the various studies which fitted Gestalt conceptualization well were: the figure and ground research by *Edgar Rubin*; phenomena of color and touch by *David Katz*; laws of apparent movement by *A. Korte*; finished and unfinished tasks by *Bluma Zeigarnik*; neurophysiological cases studied by *Kurt Goldstein*; and studies of behavioral phenomena of ravens, jay birds, and bees by *Mathilde Hertz*.

Field. The exponents of Gestalt psychology made extensive use of the word and concept "field." Field can simply mean "area," and in this sense we speak in psychology of "visual fields" or "field of touch." But for the Gestalt school, "field"—even a "visual field"—has a dynamic connotation and is used in such combinations as "dynamic field," "field of force," "psychological or phenomenal field," "cortical field." The concept is borrowed from physics, where one speaks of the "magnetic" or "electric field." A wire conducting an electric current or a magnet will create a field of force. The field of force of a magnet will be seen in the characteristic arrangement of iron filings around it. The essential property of a field is its dynamic aspect. In a dynamic field there is interaction between all of its parts so that, as Kurt Lewin put it, "the state of any part of this field depends on every other part of the field." Another important aspect of a dynamic field is its equilibrium. Again Gestalt psychology drew upon physics in developing this concept of equilibrium, which to Gestaltists is one of the most fundamental concepts for explaining psychological phenomena. The dynamic equilibrium of a field has the natural tendency to maintain itself. Because of this tendency a disturbance of the equilibrium by another force is only temporary; the equilibrium is soon again restored and stabilized. Percepts manifest this property because they tend to stabilize themselves and to remain stable if not disturbed. In his motivational theory, Lewin spoke of the disequilibrium brought about by arousal of needs and explained motivated behavior in terms of a tendency of the organism to restore a state of equilibrium.

The concept of the dynamic field has been applied by Gestalt psychology to perception—"perceptual field"; to the environment as perceived by the individual—"psychological field"; and to the cortical processes in the brain underlying perceptual phenomena—"cortical fields." The work of Köhler in the 1940's and 1950's was precisely concerned with the relationship of auditory and visual phenomena to the dynamics of cortical fields. Together with *Hans Wallach* (b. 1904), of Swarthmore College, Köhler proposed the "satiation" hypothesis—a temporary obstruction in the cortical tissue caused by a prolonged fixation of a figure—to account for the observed phenomena. Because the field concept has been so characteristic of the Gestalt school, the Gestalt theory has been referred to as a "field theory." In this respect it is contrasted to "association theories," such as structuralism and behaviorism, which emphasize analysis of complex units into simpler ones.

Lewin's Field Theory. The field concept in the system of Kurt Lewin is a pivotal one and is closely integrated with his other important concept of "life-space." Kurt Lewin (1890-1947) was born in Mogilno, Poland and studied at various universities in Germany. His Ph.D. was from the University of Berlin (1914), where he subsequently taught for several years. While in Germany, he came under the influence of the Gestalt school, but later his research and theories showed much originality and independence. He migrated to the United States in 1932. For ten years (1935-1945) he was professor of child psychology at the University of Iowa, where he developed the Child Welfare Research Center. The last two years of his life were devoted to a new research venture, a study of group dynamics. In 1945 he founded and directed the Research Center for Group Dynamics at the Massachusetts Institute of Technology, a project which was moved after his death to the University of Michigan. Lewin's research, highly imaginative and productive, was focused on child psychology, personality theory, motivation, and social dynamics. In order to give a more precise mathematical formulation to his ideas and hypotheses, he took time to study a special branch of higher mathematics dealing with transformation properties of geometric configurations—topology—and a branch of physics, namely, vector analysis. These studies are reflected in Lewin's formulations of his concepts such as repulsion and attraction and life-space. The latter concept denotes the person and his psychological environment, that is, environment as perceived and conceived by the person and as related to his needs. Lewin's formula, $B=f$ (P, E)—behavior is a function of interaction of the person and the environment—expresses the importance Lewin attached to the interaction between the two poles of the dynamic relationship, the individual and his psychobiological environment. *A Dynamic Theory of Personality* (1935) and *Principles of Topological Psychology* (1936) were Lewin's major books. Many of his theories and experimental research were presented in articles, some of which were collected in book form, *Field Theory in Social Science* (1951). Lewin was highly respected by American psychologists, even by those who did not share his views.

Reactions to Gestalt Psychology.   Initially the greatest direct impact of the Gestalt theory was felt in Germany, generating much research there, especially in the field of perception, and stimulating many theoretical discussions. After a dormant period during the Nazi regime, interest in Gestalt psychology was revived in postwar Germany. Some of the earlier followers of the Gestalt theory have gained prominence in the academic life of Germany and have resumed their work in the spirit of this theory. Gestalt psychology is now represented at several German universities, such as Berlin, Leipzig, Frankfurt, Münster, and Tübingen, and is applied to many fields such as cognition, personality, social psychology, and psychophysics. For other details the reader is referred to the chapter on German psychology.

Anglo-American psychology became directly acquainted with the Gestalt school for the first time through its German representatives who participated in the International Congress of Psychology in Oxford in 1923, the first such congress after the First World War. In America, the lectures given by the founders of the Gestalt school, Koffka and Köhler, during their visits here, provided the occasion for an encounter with the new movement. Among the earliest American supporters of the Gestalt psychology was R. M. Ogden (1877-1959), of Cornell, who had studied in Germany and had taken his Ph.D. under Külpe in Würzburg in 1903. Ogden discussed Gestalt psychology in a paper at the annual meeting of the American Psychological Association in 1922, the year that Koffka published an article in the *Psychological Bulletin* (at the persuasion of Ogden). E. C. Tolman was first introduced to Gestalt psychology, when he spent a summer month with Koffka in 1912. Although, as he reported in his autobiography, he "sensed only vaguely what it was all about," this visit prepared him "to be receptive to Gestalt concepts." In the fall of 1923 he went back to Koffka "for a couple of months to learn more."

The initial response to the Gestalt psychology in America was mixed, and when favorable, it was far from enthusiastic. There were many reasons why Gestalt psychology did not evoke much interest among American psychologists. One of them was the fact that American psychology was already far removed from the atomistic psychology to which most of the Gestalt argument was addressed. Second, behaviorism was the center of interest and discussions, and the majority of American psychologists were moving in the behavioristic direction. The Gestalt trend did not have enough attraction for American psychologists to stem their behavioristic trend. Several reviews of Gestalt psychology appeared in American psychological journals in the 1920's and 1930's. Among them the most comprehensive—and sympathetic—were those written by Harry Helson (b. 1898), now of Kansas State University, in the *American Journal of Psychology* in 1925 and 1926 and in the *Psychological Review* in 1933. Other early reviewers of the Gestalt theory were G. W. Allport (1924) and Mary Calkins (1926).

Gradually Gestalt psychology became much better known to American psychologists, and Gestalt research and concepts more appreciated as significant contributions. Various fields of psychology absorbed many of these concepts and research data. Gestalt principles were applied to education and psychotherapy. Psychological theory of personality and learning showed also the influence of the Gestalt psychology. Tolman's learning theory is but one instance. Several psychologists at various universities carry on research in the Gestalt theoretical framework. Among them are psychologists such as *Fritz Heider* (b. 1896), former associate of Koffka at Smith, and now professor at the University of Kansas, working on social perception and interpersonal interactions; *Mary Henle* (b. 1913), of New School for Social Research, in the field of motivation and thinking, who is also interested in systematic problems of psychology; *Solomon Asch* (b. 1907), of Swarthmore College, author of *Social Psychology* (1952); and *Rudolf Arnheim* (b. 1904), of Sarah Lawrence College, known for his work in esthetics and his book, *Art and Visual Perception* (1954).

The influence of Gestalt psychology was greatly felt in Japan, as our survey of Japanese psychology showed. According to Koji Sato, of Kyoto University, Japan was the country where Gestalt psychology's domination was stronger than in "any other country in the world." This domination was particularly evident in the 1930's, but the influence of Gestalt psychology on psychological research in Japan was still much in evidence in the 1960's.

Evaluation.   The founders of the Gestalt school, Wertheimer, Koffka, and Köhler, were ingenious experimenters, original thinkers, and capable writers. Each of them concentrated, although not exclusively, on a special field of research; Wertheimer on visual perception and thinking; Koffka on developmental psychology; Lewin on motivation and social psychology;

and Köhler initially on psychophysics and learning. Köhler became the systematizer and the main spokesman of the school. His research since the 1940's has been devoted to figural aftereffects and to the cerebral currents underlying perceptual phenomena.

The Gestalt school was at first principally a revolt against the prevailing atomistic and associationist psychology, which the Gestaltists called "brick and mortar psychology." Proceeding from the holistic viewpoint, Gestalt psychology also attacked behaviorism—as well as any S-R psychology—especially for its reductionism. Complex behavior, the Gestalt school held, cannot be explained in terms of accumulation of stimulus-response bonds. They pointed to the data of experience, which are not mosaics but organized wholes. They derived their first arguments and evidence from an experimental study of perception. Subsequently they expanded the scope of their investigations and contributions to fields such as memory, learning, thinking, motivation, social psychology.

The Gestalt psychology gradually developed from a mere opposition to atomistic psychology into a general systematic theory embracing almost all major problems of psychology. Its principal method has been phenomenology, that is, observation and description of direct experience. Its subject of study has been man's direct experience; its central concepts, Gestalt and dynamic field; its basic psychophysical viewpoint, isomorphism. The theory of isomorphism assumes the unity of the physical and psychological systems. Thus psychological phenomena in their spatial and temporal relations and their dynamic aspects are said to correspond exactly to the underlying cerebral fields and their dynamics.

The school has been criticized for its too radical rejection of analysis, philosophical character, philosophical presuppositions, lack of clearness of some of its central concepts, and for too much reliance on the phenomenological method. Some of the views of Gestalt psychology have been questioned on experimental grounds, others on a theoretical basis. However, it is generally agreed that Gestalt psychology has made substantial contributions, factual and conceptual, to several fields of psychology— especially to psychology of perception. As an all-embracing psychological theory Gestalt psychology has had little unequivocal support and has attracted a limited following. Nevertheless, Gestalt theory constituted an intellectual force which compelled re-examination of many psychological issues and effected revisions and reformulations within rival theories. Several postulates and concepts of the Gestalt theory—or more specifically, of Köhler's theory—such as isomorphism, for example—have been accepted without commitment to the theory as a whole.

HORMIC PSYCHOLOGY

Hormic psychology is identified principally with William' McDougall, a British psychologist, who came to America and spent the last 18 years of his life here. McDougall gave this psychology its name and was its chief exponent. This hormic system of his grew out of his challenge to nineteenth century psychology. McDougall was the first to oppose seriously and successfully the concept of psychology as the science of consciousness. Also he was the first to propose the definition of psychology as the study of behavior. This definition appeared in 1905 in McDougall's *Physiological Psychology*. The systematic exposition of his hormic psychology was first presented in his *Introduction to Social Psychology* in 1908. Chronologically then, hormic psychology preceded both the Gestalt school and behaviorism. Moreover, it was formulated before psychoanalysis became known outside Vienna and was recognized as a psychological school. Although at first received enthusiastically by certain circles in psychology and by social scientists, hormic psychology has never become a movement equal in influence to other schools.

Though no longer represented in contemporary psychology as a system, hormic psychology is worth our attention for various reasons. First of all, hormic psychology was an original theory of historical significance. It rebelled against both the mentalistic and mechanistic exaggerations in psychology. Moreover, it brought into sharp focus the dynamic and purposive aspects of behavior, which thus far had not been of serious concern to psychologists. Yet these very aspects—as history proved—became the central problems of modern psychology of motivation. Another reason for considering hormic psychology is that its originator, William McDougall himself, is one of the ablest and most productive minds in the history of psychology. Since he played a significant part in this history—first in Britain and then in the United States—his views cannot be overlooked. Still another reason for reviewing hormic psychology is the recent renewed interest in McDougall. To borrow the term of an article published in 1965 —McDougall is now being "revisited."

Life of William McDougall (1871-1938). It has been said that no other psychologist has ever come to psychology as thoroughly prepared academically as McDougall. Born in Chadderton, the industrial suburb of Oldham, Lancashire, England, he first attended the local school. At the age of 14 he was sent to a school in Weimar, Germany, for one year. Deciding on a career in pure science, he entered the University of Manchester, at the age of 15. After graduation with honors in 1890, he studied at Cambridge, specializing in physiology, anatomy, and anthropology. After four years at Cambridge during which he earned the highest honors, McDougall received a scholarship for medical studies at St. Thomas Hospital in London. He had no intention of becoming a practicing physician, but thought that medicine was "a desirable part of a thorough education, especially for one who aspires to work in any of the sciences concerned with man." An additional reason was that, as he said, "there is no other way in which the student can bring himself into the most intimate touch with human nature in all its aspects." During his medical studies he read William James's *Principles of Psychology*, which had been published just a few years earlier. This work of James was a decisive factor in McDougall's turning to psychology. Twenty-five years later, as a successor of James in the chair of psychology at Harvard, McDougall dedicated his *Outline of Psychology* (1923) "To the honored memory of William James, great philosopher, great psychologist, and great man."

After four years at the University of Manchester, four years at Cambridge, and four years of medical studies in London, McDougall, at 27, was still much interested in broadening as much as possible, his "basis for the study of man." Invited to join the Cambridge Anthropological Expedition to the Torres Straits (the straits between New Guinea and Australia), McDougall accepted "with enthusiasm." As a member of this expedition he became involved in the study of sensory capacities of the natives living on the islands of the Torres Straits. Soon after, at the invitation of Dr. Charles Hose, a political leader in Sarawak, he joined in a study of the tribes in the interior of Borneo. The result of this study was the publication, with Hose, of a two volume work, *The Pagan Tribes of Borneo* (1912). After visiting Java, China, and India, McDougall returned to London. Now his attention was occupied with further pursuit of his psychological studies. When he had read a great deal in the field, he decided to make first-hand acquaintance with psychology and psychologists in Germany. He chose Göttingen and spent a year there studying under G. E. Müller. When McDougall returned to England, he was appointed to the Department of Psychology at the University College, London, in 1900. After four years, he accepted a lectureship of "mental philosophy" at Oxford, where he remained until World War I. At both London and Oxford McDougall did a great deal of experimental research in physiological psychology, especially in vision. In 1920 McDougall accepted a chair of psychology at Harvard, coming to America "with good hopes and intentions." After seven years at Harvard he moved to Duke University in 1927. There he remained until his death in 1938, serving as a professor and chairman of the Psychology Department.

Although McDougall did not regret his decision to leave Great Britain, where his influence was described as "immense," and to plunge into the American "adventure," as he called it, his position here was far from a conquest. His basic beliefs and views in psychology appeared entirely out of step with American psychology which was moving in the behaviorist and positivist direction. By vigorous attacks upon the deterministic and mechanistic tendencies in psychology, by affirming the existence of the soul in *Body and Mind* (1911) and the freedom of the will, and by proposing his hormic psychology and advocating the instincts, McDougall was a freakish phenomenon on the American scene. He was looked upon as a spokesman of the old psychology, which was considered long buried and happily done with. His interest in, and support of, psychical research further contributed to his unpopularity. Moreover, certain of McDougall's personality characteristics—especially an intellectual "arrogance"—which McDougall himself recognized and deplored—and the acerbity of his criticisms intensified animosity toward him. He was often involved in controversies and debates not only with the behaviorists, but with Gestaltists, Freudians, and others as well.

McDougall's Work. From his student years McDougall realized his intense interest in "the art and theory of the internal life of man." His life goal was soon crystallized and expressed by him as the uncovering of "the secrets of human nature." It appeared to him that the best way to implement this plan was to study the nervous system. In the brain, he thought, "were locked the secrets of human nature." But reading James's *Principles of Psychology* showed him that the study of the nervous system was "not the only road to the uncovering of those secrets." He then realized—as he reports in his autobiography—that those secrets "should be approached from two sides, from below upwards by way of physiology and neurology, and from above downwards by way of psychology, philosophy, and the various human sciences." This two-directional approach constituted McDougall's scientific program. The early phase of his scientific career was dedicated to the first approach, that is, specifically to physiological psychology. This phase included his researches on vision, attention, fatigue, the effects of drugs, the emotions. He studied also the chemical basis of temperament, especially of extroversion-introversion. These researches resulted in his developing neurophysiological hypotheses to account for the various processes. Among them was his "drainage hypothesis." This theory postulated a hypothetical secretion in the nervous system, termed "neurin," which he thought to be flowing from areas of high potential to areas of lower potential—much like water in a system of interconnected tanks and pipes. On the basis of this hydrostatic analogy, McDougall tried to explain various psychological processes. He explained inhibition, such as observed in behavior, as drainage of energy b one active area of the nervous system at the expense of other areas. Th physiological phase of McDougall's work was concluded by his publicatio of *Physiological Psychology* in 1905.

In the second phase of McDougall's career he constructed his system of *hormic*, or "purposive," psychology. His most important books of thi period, which highlighted his intellectual evolution, were: *Introduction t Social Psychology* (1908) and its sequel *The Group Mind* (1920); the two systematic outlines, *Outline of Psychology* (1923) and *Outline of Abnormal Psychology* (1926); and *The Energies of Men: A Study of the Fundamentals of Dynamic Psychology* (1932). He also published books on philosophical and political subjects during this period. In all, McDougall was the author of 24 books and 167 articles and notes. Of his works, the most successful was his book *Introduction to Social Psychology*, which appeared in 23 editions, and which has been reprinted 30 times, the last printing in 1960. *His Body and Mind* (1911) has also been frequently reprinted. The 1961 reprint was prefaced by Jerome S. Bruner, of Harvard, McDougall's former student, who called the book "a handsome and impassionate piece of scholarship." *The Outline of Psychology* was one of the three important systematic expositions of psychology in the first quarter of the twentieth century, the other two being Titchener's and Watson's. *The Outline of Abnormal Psychology* was the product of McDougall's clinical experiences with "shell-shock" cases in World War I, while in the Royal Army Medical Corps. In this book McDougall proposed his theory of personality.

Characteristic of McDougall was his inclination and ability to systematize every area of psychology in which he was working—physiological, abnormal, social, and general. He always tried to present a complete and exhaustive picture of the problems involved and to form theories to explain them. His theories were criticized for their speculative character and lack of factual substantiation. Keeping abreast with current psychological literature as well as with new developments in science, McDougall gave prompt notice to material relevant to his theories. In response to these new developments and ideas he at times modified his formulations or adopted new ones. If he disagreed, he stated his opposition directly and frankly. His bluntness and occasional sarcasm in polemics were found highly offensive by some of his adversaries.

McDougall never lost faith in his chosen life goal, "to uncover the secrets of human life." As one obituary described his dedication to this goal, he "lived" psychology. Despite his accomplishments, however, McDougall grew more skeptical of the success of his efforts. Three years before his death he said: "Even now, after some forty-five years of sustained effort, I am not sure that I have made any progress, have learnt anything of human nature."

The Lamarckian Experiment.   Before giving an account of McDougall's hormic theory, and of the principles of his psychology, we turn our attention to an experiment which McDougall considered extremely important and which has often figured prominently in the evaluation of his career. Soon after arriving in America, McDougall began a long-range experiment designed to support the Lamarckian hypothesis on transmission of acquired characteristics. To this experiment, first conceived in the 1890's and begun in 1920, McDougall gave all "the time and energy" he had available. His personal description of this venture is of particular interest because it reveals both the purpose of the experiment and the motivation of the experimenter:

> . . . with a small group of graduate students, I set out on this fool's experiment. Yet not altogether foolishly, for, even though the issue might be entirely adverse to the Lamarckian hypothesis, a clear-cut negative issue of a well-planned and long-continued experiment would be not altogether without value. . . . And, in any case, the question at issue seemed to me the most important question yet formulated by the mind of man and clearly susceptible of solution by experimental procedure. And a positive answer indisputably established by experiment would not only give us a working theory of biological evolution, but would be a heavy blow to the mechanistic biology. It would place mind at the very heart of the evolutionary process, instead of leaving it as a byproduct of that process, an unintelligible excrescence upon life.

The experiment consisted of white rats trained to select the correct escape platform in a water tank. The tank had three parallel alleys. The rat, placed in the central alley, had to swim its length and then turn either to the right or to the left alley. In both side alleys an escape platform was provided, one illuminated and the other dark. The animal, to escape from the water and avoid drowning, had to climb one of the platforms. The correct platform was the dark one, whereas the illuminated one gave an electric shock. One generation of rats after another was trained to climb the correct platform and to avoid the lighted one. The average number of errors was carefully recorded for each generation. Writing about this experiment in 1930—when it was in its tenth year and 24th generation—McDougall expressed the belief that it seemed "to promise a clean-cut and indisputable proof of the reality of Lamarckian transmission." When McDougall died, the experiment was in its 17th year and 50th generation. The average error was now less than one-fifth of the original score, and the rats seemed to have acquired "photophobia" in the water tank.

This long and costly experiment created wide interest. Because of the issue involved, two independent investigations repeated McDougall's experiment in its major features. Both of them failed to corroborate McDougall's results. The investigators rejected the Lamarckian explanation of these results. They suggested alternative explanations for the improvement in the performance of the succeeding generations of rats in McDougall's experiment. The principal criticisms of the experiment were focused on the experimental procedure and the selective breeding of the rats. The whole Lamarckian affair undoubtedly weakened McDougall's position in the eyes of his adversaries.

Nature of Psychology. From the beginning of his career as a psychologist, McDougall was not satisfied with the current state of psychology. He thought of it as "sterile and narrow," feeling that it was preoccupied exclusively with consciousness to the neglect of behavior. For him psychology was "the science of conduct or behavior," a definition which he gave in 1905 in *Physiological Psychology* and reiterated in 1912 in *Psychology, the Study of Behavior*. He regarded this definition as logically the best. But later—when behaviorism also defined psychology as the study of behavior—McDougall, a vigorous antagonist of behaviorism, preferred to drop the word "behavior" to avoid the mechanistic implications attached to it by behaviorists. To preclude any association with the behavioristic interpretation of behavior, McDougall defined psychology as "the positive and empirical science of the human mind." If this shift from "behavior" to "mind" is surprising, it is well to consider McDougall's reasons as given in his *Outline of Psychology*. The "old-fashioned" word "mind" meant "that *something* which expresses its nature, powers, and functions in two ways: 1) the modes of individual experience; 2) the modes of bodily activity, the sum of which constitutes the behavior of the individual." He defines the mind further by saying that it "is that which expresses itself" in experience and behavior, and that "we have to build up our description of the human mind by gathering all possible facts of human experience and behavior and by inferring from these the nature and structure of the mind." By "structure" he meant the characteristics peculiar to each individual, whereas "nature" of the mind signified to him those qualities which are shared by all individuals. But what is the nature of the mind? What is McDougall's justification for making the mind the subject of psychology? The following citation from the *Outline of Psychology* provides the answer and at the same time an example of McDougall's argumentation:

> The mechanist psychologists will say: What you call "the mind" is just what I call "the brain." Why go out of your way to set up this vague, mysterious, purely hypothetical *something* which, as you admit, no one has ever seen or handled or can hope to see or handle, while all the time you have the brain, as solid and as real as a lump of cheese, which we positively know to be concerned in all experience and in all behavior, and about which the labor of thousands of expert workers has built up an immense mass of knowledge? To this I would reply: I do not underrate the value of this physiological knowledge and research; but I assert that, in the present state of science, it is not profitable to substitute the brain for the mind. To do so limits unduly our freedom of thought; it ties us down to one kind of explanation, leads us to absurd consequences (of the kind we have noticed), and, worst of all, is apt to blind us to facts of observation, and biases our interpretation of other facts.

Compared to the other two systematists of psychology, Titchener and Watson, it is clear that McDougall occupies an intermediate position. He was opposed to the structuralists' concept of psychology as the study of consciousness, on the one hand, and to the behavioristic psychology as the study of behavior—mechanistically and atomistically interpreted—on the other. McDougall asked for a psychology which would study both experience and behavior. But, in McDougall's understanding the essential and distinct feature of behavior, whether animal or human—and the feature which psychology must recognize—is that it is purposive. Arguing this issue in an essay *Men or Robots*—and contrasting his view with that of mechanists—he referred to the two assumptions which, in his opinion, the mechanistic position in science implied: (1) "that all processes in the world are fundamentally of one kind only"; and (2) "that all these processes are of the kind commonly assumed by the physical sciences in their interpretations of inorganic nature; namely mechanistic, or strictly determined and therefore strictly predictable, events." "It may well be," he continued, "that the former assumption is true, but that the latter is false. And, if we accept the former assumption as a working hypothesis and reject the second, we can hope to avoid the absurdity which . . . inevitably results from accepting both assumptions." His own stand McDougall summarized in the last paragraph of this same essay:

> . . . at present we stand to gain no advantage by assuming that men are Robots, mere pieces of machinery. Without presuming to assert that men are, or are not, Robots, let us continue to use the working hypothesis that they are not; let us cheerfully go on assuming that men are what they seem to be, namely purposive intelligent agents, striving with some success to improve themselves and the conditions of their life in this strange world. And let us continue to assume that children and animals exhibit in their lower degrees the same principles of action. For that is the profitable way, the way of progress in psychology.

With respect to the method of psychology, McDougall's position again is intermediate between the introspection of the structuralist and the total rejection of introspection by the behaviorist. He recognized introspection's "peculiar difficulties and limitations," but also saw its usefulness when combined with experimental observation. Introspection can achieve,

McDougall maintained, "a generalized description of types of experience." Experience—especially experience of our own purposive actions—was for McDougall a vital part of psychological study. Introspection, he insisted, needs to be supplemented by observation and description of the conditions or occasions under which the experiences appear. Another type of observation is that of external conduct. The observed modes of behavior should be correlated with modes of experience. While he stressed the need and value of objective methods in the study of behavior, he thought that without the use of introspection behavior would appear only as a mechanical activity.

Hormic Theory. The term *hormic* comes from the Greek word, *hormé*, meaning "onset" or "impetus." McDougall borrowed this term from Percy T. Nunn, a distinguished British educationalist and scholar. Hormé, according to Nunn, is an internal "drive" or "urge" which moves the organism toward an end or purpose. Hormic activity, as McDougall explains it, is an energy manifestation which always involves cognition or awareness; it is a striving initiated and governed by cognition, and it results in satisfaction or dissatisfaction.

The basic proposition of hormic psychology is that all behavior is purposive or goal-seeking. For man it means that, as McDougall expressed it, "from cradle to the grave, his life is one long round of purposive strivings, of efforts to attain, to make real, those things which he imaginatively conceives to be good or desirable." In the *Outline of Psychology* Mc-Dougall listed the specific marks of purposive behavior: (1) A certain spontaneity of activity, that is, activity initiated within the organism and not merely brought about by external forces. (2) "Persistence of activity independently of the continuance of the impression which may have initiated it." (3) "Variation of direction of persistent movements," exemplified by the varying directions of a running rabbit, which tries to dodge its pursuer until it finds a safe place. (4) Termination of activity as soon as it brings about a particular change—for example, a rabbit stops running, when it reaches a safe place. (5) "Preparation for the new situation toward the production of which the action contributes." A cat waiting in preparation for the spring upon its prey may serve as an example. (6) Improvement in the effectiveness of activity, when it is repeated under similar circumstances. (7) Activity is a total reaction of the organism. The processes of all the parts of the organism "are subordinated and adjusted in such a way as to promote the better pursuit of the natural goal of the action."

Further light on the hormic theory is provided in McDougall's article, *The Hormic Psychology*, written for Murchison's *Psychologies of 1930*. In this article McDougall discussed the main features of hormic theory and its "advantages" for psychology. Not to lose their characteristic flavor, it is well to hear the main points made by McDougall in his own words:

> Hormic theory enables us to sketch . . . an intelligible, consistent, and tenable story of continuous evolution. . . .

The hormic psychology . . . does not pretend to know the answers to the great unsolved riddles of the universe. It leaves to the future the solution of such problems as the relation of the organic to the inorganic realm, the origin or advent of life in our world, the place and destiny of the individual and of the race in the universe . . . it makes for the open mind and stimulates the spirit of inquiry, and is hospitable to all empirical evidence and all legitimate speculations. . . .

The hormic theory is radically opposed to intellectualism. . . . It recognizes fully the conative nature of all activity and regards the cognitive power as everywhere the servant and the guide of striving. Thus it is fundamentally dynamic and leads to a psychology well adapted for application to the sciences and practical problems of human life. . . .

It recognizes that the fundamental nature of the hormic impulse is to work towards its natural goal and to terminate or cease to operate only when and in so far as its natural goal is attained. . . .

It regards all experience as expressive of a total activity that is everywhere hormic, selective, teleological. . . .

It is able to render intelligible account of the organization of the affective or emotional-conative side of the mental structure . . . which remains a closed book to all psychologies of the intellectualistic mechanistic types. . . .

The hormic theory projects a completely systematic and self-consistent psychology on the basis of its recognition of the whole of the organized mind of the adult as a structure elaborated in the service of the hormic urge to more and fuller life. . . .

Perhaps it is unfair to McDougall to present his hormic theory by citing these selective excerpts without his supportive explanation and argumentation, but the intention here is simply to indicate what the salient issues of this theory are.

Theory of Instincts.   Associated closely with hormic psychology is McDougall's theory of instincts.   This theory provoked heated arguments among psychologists and sociologists and became one of the major reasons for the unpopularity and rejection of hormic psychology in the 1920's and 1930's.   The theory of instincts was first presented in 1908 in the *Introduction to Social Psychology*, which—as will be remembered—intended to provide a system of psychology which would be meaningful and useful for the social sciences.   While the author's intention was appreciated, his theory of instincts became a stumbling block to acceptance of his system. McDougall realized, as he wrote about it in 1930, that instincts were "out of fashion" and that to write of them "without some such qualification as 'so-called' betrays a reckless indifference to fashion amounting almost to indecency."   Yet, he thought that the word "instinct" was "too good to be lost to our science" and that it expressed his ideas better than any other word.   However, a few years later, to obviate the difficulties associated with the word, he preferred to use the term *propensity*.   "Recognizing now," he wrote in the *The Energies of Men* (1932), "clearly as I believe, and only now for the first time, the crux of this difficulty and of this divergence of opinion, I propose to avoid the use of the term 'instinct' in defining the constitution of man, and to content myself with the term innate or native propensity."

McDougall taught that both animals and men are endowed with a number of innate instincts.   These instincts, in his definition, are the innate or hereditary tendencies or "psychophysical dispositions" which impel the organism to act in a specific mode to attain an end or goal natural to the species. Among the basic or primary instincts are food-seeking, escape, and sex. McDougall endeavored to identify all major instincts and drew up a list of them. In 1908 he proposed 12 major human instincts. But in 1932—after several revisions—his list contained 18 instincts or propensities. Every major instinct, in his view, is coupled with its own characteristic emotion, which is its integral part and is essential to its functioning. Thus McDougall looked for the emotions correlated with each instinct. Instinct of escape, for instance, is coupled with the emotion of fear; repulsion with disgust; curiosity with wonder; pugnacity with anger; and so on. It was sometimes difficult or impossible for McDougall to identify and describe the characteristic emotion of every instinct. For example, the emotion accompanying the parental instinct was difficult to verbalize; McDougall called it simply "tender emotion." In addition to the affective or emotional aspect of instincts, McDougall recognized a cognitive or sensory aspect, namely a predisposition to perceive certain stimuli, such as is manifest in our noticing food when we are hungry. In sum then, instincts have three logically distinguishable—but in reality inseparable—aspects: (1) The cognitive or sensory; (2) the conative or motivational; and (3) affective or emotional.

Sentiments.   Some instincts or propensities are primary and universal. Others may be secondary, that is, composed of several basic propensities. The secondary propensities may function differently in different environments. Although innate, the instincts are modifiable by learning and experience. When several instinctive tendencies become combined and attached to the same object, they form what McDougall called *sentiments*.

A sentiment is an acquired tendency "to experience certain emotions and desires in relation to some particular object." Love and hate are typical examples of sentiments. Friendship and patriotism are also sentiments, combining several different instinctive tendencies and emotions. Sentiments are "the main sources of all our activities." They give consistency, continuity, and order to our behavior. When they become organized harmoniously in one larger comprehensive system, they form, according to McDougall, *character*.

The sentiment which is of particularly vital significance in McDougall's scheme is *self-regard*. This term, "self-regard," McDougall applies to the process which integrates various sentiments that relate or have reference to the self. They include self-respect, pride, ambition, and others such as those expressed in personality characteristics and described as vanity and humility, selfishness and altruism, aggressiveness and meekness. The conduct of the individual depends on the nature and strength of his self-regard. This sentiment is, moreover, "the main source of some of our most vivid emotional experiences, of our most intense and sustained efforts and of our most acute satisfactions and sufferings." McDougall illustrates this in an example of an ambitious man, who in his desire of personal distinction sacrifices the happiness of his life, his children, and himself. For him there is no greater pleasure than praise and adulation of the public, and no keener pain than failure, disgrace, or contempt. The concept of self-regard resembles other concepts proposed by various theorists and known by such names as "ego-ideal," "creative-self," "idealized self-image," or "self-concept." Cofer and Appley remark in their book *Motivation* (1964) that "McDougall's discussion of this sentiment has a modern, although usually unacknowledged, ring and resembles several theories in which notions about the self play a central role."

In his construction of personality theory McDougall did not stop at sentiments and their hierarchy. He attempted to give an account of all the components of personality. He discussed disposition, temper, temperament, character, and intellect. These were the terms that he employed to describe the fundamental components—or "factors" in his terminology —of personality. But he warns that personality should not be thought of as "the mere sum" of these factors. Though it is convenient to consider each factor separately, he maintained that the organic whole of personality must be borne in mind.

Reactions to McDougall. British and American reactions to McDougall differed sharply. In Britain McDougall enjoyed respect and prestige. His systematic books were widely used at British universities. No other author rivals his influence on the generation of British psychologists developing in the first three decades of this century. But even in Britain his influence eventually waned. In America—consistently and clearly—McDougall and his views were unpopular. He was severely criticized for his theories and found no strong following. One of the severest single attacks against McDougall was made by J. McK. Cattell at the International Congress of Psychology in New Haven in 1929. It seems that the inherent basic premise in the criticism and rejection of McDougall's theory is to be sought in the then-generally accepted concept of science and in the accepted criteria of what is scientific and what is not. Judged by the then-current criteria of science, McDougall's views seem grounded in assumptions which are purely speculative and unscientific or which lack scientific evidence. The reaction was the same with regard to McDougall's broad theoretical system, as well as to some specific doctrines, such as that of purpose and instinct.

While the concept of purposive or goal-seeking behavior eventually found its way into psychology—though not principally through McDougall —the instinct theory, even the concept of instinct, was for a long time rejected by the majority of psychologists and constituted the primary target of attacks against hormic psychology. Among sociologists, one of the strongest criticisms against instinct theory was marshalled by L. L. Bernard in his book, *Instinct, A Study of Social Psychology* (1924). Bernard pointed to social environment as more powerful than innate tendencies in molding human behavior. The arguments of psychologists against instincts revolved mostly around the validity of the concept itself. It was argued that this concept was redundant and circular. It did not provide any explanation of behavior at all. To say that a bird's ability to build a nest is instinctual is providing a word but not an explanation. As to complex human behavior, it was viewed as principally the result of learning, rather than of heredity. Even if this behavior contained innate elements, they would be difficult if not impossible to disentangle from the learned elements. Perhaps McDougall's adversaries failed to notice the role that he ascribed to experience in the adaptation of instinctive behavior. Moreover, they did not always seem to recognize that for McDougall it was not the instinctual behavioral pattern itself that was important, as much as was the "motive power" supplied by the innate instinct, for thought and action. The power of the instinct and its direction were innate, but the behavioral patterns—by which the instinct expressed itself —were not. It was precisely because of the confusion of the two distinct ideas—the instinctual behavior patterns and the instinctual motive—that McDougall started to use the word "propensity" instead of "instinct." In any event, the concept of instinct has since been redefined and is at present discussed increasingly in textbooks of psychology. Even a behaviorist such as Walter S. Hunter defended McDougall's notion of instincts in 1947. The renewed attention to instinct and the reappearance of the term in psychological literature is to be ascribed—among other factors—to the rise of a new science called *ethology*, the study of the environmental-physiological relationships in the behavior of animals during their entire life. One of the foremost ethologists, Nikolass Tinbergen, reintroduced the term "instinct" in 1951.

Other developments in psychology and science in general in the decades following McDougall's death tended to put some of his theories in a more favorable light, which even his opponents recognized. E. Guthrie in his address before the Division of General Psychology of the American Psychological Association in 1949 stated that, to his notion, two psychologists, Janet and McDougall, "made valuable suggestions toward psychological models which have remained unexploited." He referred to McDougall's "attempt to describe man as an energy system." On the experimental side, Lashley's research—for example, on the serial order in behavior such as fast piano playing—provided evidence against the mechanistic chain-reflex explanation of complex behavior, which McDougall vehemently and frequently attacked. Even the concept of teleology has become not as objectionable in the eyes of theorists and experimentalists. Scientists working with digital computers referred to this concept in connection with negative feedbacks. Also computer simulation of personality provides notions which parallel McDougall's notion of sentiments. McDougall's personality theory received support by factorial analysis of personality structure both in America and England. Particularly, R. B. Cattell's multivariate factorial analysis of personality seems to vindicate some of McDougall's theoretical propensities. Hall and Lindzey in their *Theories of Personality* (1957) regard McDougall as "a theorist of great importance" and think that "his contemporary impact is largely mediated by more recent theorists who have borrowed features of his theory." Eysenck and his collaborators revived interest in McDougall's theory of extroversion and introversion and in the supposed differential effect of drugs in extroverts and introverts. In brief, McDougall's theories in the 1960's do not appear as "outlandish"—the word that McDougall used when referring to what his critics thought of them—as they did 40 or 30 years ago.

Evaluation.   The dislike and criticism of McDougall's theories notwithstanding, McDougall, the man, was paid a high tribute by many prominent psychologists. He was respected and admired for his intellectual powers, for his devotion to his work and ideals, and for his contributions to psychology—even by those who repudiated his theories. There have been some who rank him as one of the giants in the history of psychology for his inquisitive spirit, his relentless effort to fathom man's nature, and for the breadth of his approach. A. A. Roback in his *A History of American Psychology* declares that "McDougall has been and will remain, perhaps for a long time yet, the foremost English-speaking psychologist, with no exception." Though there are those who disagree with this opinion, most psychologists concede that McDougall has contributed to the initiation of social psychology, has given impetus to dynamic psychology, and has introduced the problem of purpose into scientific psychology. The scope of McDougall's experimental and theoretical work was broad— extending from physiological psychology to social and abnormal psychology.

The philosophical substructure of McDougall's theories was the main obstacle to his playing a stronger role in the psychological developments of his time. As *Contemporary Schools of Psychology* by Woodworth and Sheehan expresses it: "McDougall's influence has been probably greater than he thought, but it has been limited by his insistence that psychologists follow him beyond the boundaries of what they consider scientific into regions that are the province of philosophy." This insistence was doubtless one of the chief obstacles to McDougall's winning a wider circle of disciples and enthusiastic followers, always an essential condition for survival of schools. Lack of support for his theories—not surprising at the time of behavioristic triumph—was a strong factor in the early eclipse of McDougall's system. But, if one does not allow oneself to be put off—as Margaret A. Boden expressed it in her 1965 article *McDougall Revisited*— by McDougall's frequent use of "metaphysical" language and argument, one finds the content of his message more acceptable now than it was in the past, as the examples cited above testify. "If we can see through the archaism of his language," says the author, "we shall see that McDougall is a purveyor of surprisingly new wine in misleading old bottles." Viewed from the vantage point of the psychology of the 1960's, McDougall's psychology is found to be more compatible with the present day psychological thought than with that of the twenties and thirties. Not only are parallels to modern theories of personality found in McDougall's writings, but more psychologists seem to agree that the most fundamental "mark of behavior" is purposive striving. It appears, in conclusion, that this "much maligned psychologist," as R. B. MacLeod called McDougall in 1957, is being exonerated in some of his theories and that hormic psychology is not a dead issue in psychology.

SCHOOLS IN RETROSPECT

The main schools or systems of psychology, reviewed in the last three chapters, were structuralism, functionalism, behaviorism, Gestalt, and hormic psychology. These schools originated within academic psychology. Another school—psychoanalysis—which developed outside of academic psychology, will be treated separately in the following chapter. A synoptic table of all the six schools is provided at the end of this chapter. It is to be noted that these schools do not represent the only systematic positions that developed in the history of psychology. They simply represent the major and the most influential streams of psychological thought. In addition to these systems there have been many other more or less extensive psychological theories. Textbooks concerned with psychological theories differentiate these various theoretical positions and group them usually under such headings as organismic, personalistic, field, holistic, and S-R theories.

The Role of Schools. The first three decades of this century, from about 1900 to 1930, constitute the period of the great debates among the schools. The controversies among these schools revolved mostly around the body-mind problem and the subject matter and methods of psychology. At first the controversy was between structuralism and functionalism. After 1910 other systematic positions crystallized: behaviorism, hormic, Gestalt, and psychoanalysis. In the 1920's the debates were intensified and reached their peak. The differences grew sharper and divided American psychologists into opposing camps. Many psychologists, and also outside observers, witnessing this division, took a pessimistic view of psychology and its future. It appeared that the ambition of psychology to be a science—and a science on a par with natural sciences—could never be realized. Mary Calkins, speaking before the Ninth International Congress of Psychology in New Haven in 1929, called the division of psychology "one of the scandals of contemporary science." E. Claparède in 1930 called the schools "a nuisance." However, looking back at this period of schools, we recognize that the schools were a phenomenon of normal growth. Considering the philosophical roots of psychology, the schools were inevitable. A new science, born from philosophy, dealing with elusive and complex problems of man's "psychic life," groping to specify its subject matter and methodology, could not be monolithic. Such a science quite naturally tended to formulate a variety of theoretical constructions. Psychological schools then are to be looked upon as important milestones of the development of psychological thought. They both signified and stimulated progress of psychology. They fulfilled the function expressed in Alfred N. Whitehead's words: "A clash of doctrines is not a disaster—it is an opportunity. . . . The clash is a sign that there are wider truths and finer perspectives. . . ." McDougall had a similar thought when he said in 1932:

> Psychologists are still divided in many schools. This state of affairs has many drawbacks; but it has, I hold, this advantage: the great issues in dispute, if they are sharply pointed up, stimulate the student to think and challenge him to strive toward decisions while, at the same time, he gets a glimpse of the extent of our ignorance and of the magnitude of the tasks that lie before us. So treated, psychology, as a provocative to thinking, has, it seems to me, no rival among the academic disciplines.

Viewed historically, each school made some specific contribution—either by adding new empirical facts, by offering new insights and speculations, or by correcting and mitigating the propositions of the other school or schools.

Disappearance of Schools.   After 1930 the struggle among the schools subsided, and the cleavage of systems began to disappear. The basic issues were not resolved, and the differences of opinion remained. Controversies also continued. But the acerbity and aggressiveness and dogmatism of the schools were all gone. Consequently hostility and division among American psychologists were dissolved, and tolerance and respect for different viewpoints took their place. Several factors were responsible for this change in the psychological scene in America. Some of them can be easily identified.

One of these factors was the death, or withdrawal from the debates, of some of the schools' great protagonists. Especially significant in this regard was the death of Titchener in 1927. After his death there was no one of the same stature and acumen to represent structuralism or to take to task its opponents. Boring described the effect of Titchener's passing in these words:

> The death of no other psychologist could so alter the psychological picture in America. Not only was he unique among American psychologists as a personality and in his scientific attitude, but he was a cardinal point in the national systematic orientation. The clearcut opposition between behaviorism and its allies, on the one hand, and something else, on the other, remains clear only when the opposition is between behaviorism and Titchener, mental tests and Titchener, or applied psychology and Titchener. His death, thus, in a sense, creates a classificatory chaos in American systematic psychology.

Among other factors in the dissolution of cleavage were, on one hand, the doctrinal differentiation within the schools, and, on the other, mutual recognition of respective contributions, conceptual and methodological. As the discussions continued, differences within schools such as functionalism and behaviorism began to accrue and to destroy the solidarity among their members—thus diminishing the effectiveness and impetus of the schools. Furthermore, in face of the empirical data and experimental successes of rival schools—exemplified, for instance, in animal experimentation of behaviorists and studies in perception by the Gestaltists—the schools had to acknowledge contributions made by one another. The once seemingly divergent and irreconcilable lines of thought and research began to approach and converge. Titchener himself remarked in 1921 that "functional" and "structural" as qualifications of psychology were "obsolete terms." In 1930 Woodworth wrote of the schools that they had "more in common than would at first appear" and that the "curious cleavage into schools . . . must be less fundamental than it seems." And S. Rosenzweig in 1937 saw a "complementary pattern" in the schools; he argued that the schools of psychology were more complementary than antagonistic. Some concepts and postulates of the initial declarations of the schools were absorbed and became part of the common fund of psychology. Functional approach, study of behavior rather than of consciousness, emphasis on the whole and the field, recognition of the unconscious, consideration of purpose, adoption of objective and quantitative methods—these became the distinctive characteristics of most American psychologists.

Controversies among schools and the division of American psychology discouraged psychologists at large from siding with schools or systems, even from all theorizing. The "isms" were seen as too dogmatic and restrictive. It was felt that global theorizing and construction of final and closed systems—at a time when many facts were not yet established and many relationships not yet studied—were premature. Thus most psychologists preferred to remain unfettered by the confines of schools and became eclectic with regard to theories, methods, and concepts. This attitude was favored in circles which gave primary consideration to practical applications of psychology. The demands of society, government, and industry on the science of psychology for services increased. Many psychologists turned their attention away from theoretical issues to practical fields where the value of psychological research and findings was immediately demonstrated. What W. S. Hunter said in 1947 illustrates the attitude many psychologists had shared for some time:

> Today there are no "psychologies of 1947" to distract us. It no longer matters so much as formerly it did what one's systematic position is. There is urgent work to be done in laying bare the fundamental principles of human behavior. . . . This is the task to which the psychologists of all lands must contribute their united efforts.

Return of Theory. It is obvious that theorizing is indispensable in the life of science. Theory systematizes accumulated data, interprets them, and indicates lines of productive research. Consequently, a renewal of interest in theoretical issues—after the passionate polemics died out—was to be expected in American psychology. But when serious theorizing began—in the late 1940's and 1950's—it followed a pattern different from that of the 1920's. The new theories no longer attempted to encompass all psychology. Rather they concentrated on restricted areas such as learning, perception, emotion, personality, and motivation. The restriction of theorizing went even further—to single functions or processes. Although often the thought of the traditional large systems is echoed in the smaller and limited theories, theorizing is applied not to a wide range of psychological problems, but to narrow and precisely delineated fields. These small theories or systems dealing with single fields or specific groups of problems have been referred to as *miniature* theories or systems—in contrast to the large comprehensive systems of the past. Global theories, grounded in

SYNOPSIS OF SCHOOLS

NAME	APPROX. DATE OF ORIGIN	FOUNDERS LEADERS	SUBJECT MATTER	PRINCIPAL METHODS	PRINCIPAL AREAS OF INTEREST AND RESEARCH	RELATED SYSTEMS AND REPRESENTATIVES
STRUCTURALISM	1879 / 1898	Wundt (Germany) at Leipzig / Titchener (U.S.A.) at Cornell	Immediate experience / Contents of consciousness	Introspection	Sensation / Images / Feelings / Psychophysics	None
FUNCTIONALISM	1896 / 1904	Dewey (U.S.A.) at U. of Chicago / Angell (U.S.A.) at U. of Chicago	Mental activity in its adaptive significance	Introspection and objective observation	Learning / Mental testing / Child psychology	Judd / Carr / Woodworth (dynamic psychology)
BEHAVIORISM (classical)	1913	Watson (U.S.A.) at Johns Hopkins	Behavior without reference to consciousness / S-R connection	Only objective experimental methods / Conditioning (classical)	Motor responses / Animal behavior / Learning	Hunter / Lashley
HORMIC PSYCHOLOGY	1908	McDougall (England) at Oxford	Purposeful behavior	Introspection and objective observation	Purposive behavior / Instincts / Sentiments / Social psychology	None
GESTALT	1912	Wertheimer / Köhler / Koffka at U. of Frankfurt (Germany)	Consciousness and behavior as unified wholes	Experimental phenomenology	Perception / Thinking	Lewin (field theory / Goldstein (organismic psychology)
PSYCHOANALYSIS	1895	Freud (Austria)	The unconscious	Dream analysis / Free association	Diagnosis and treatment of neuroses	Jung (analytic psychology) / Adler (individual psychology) / Neo-Freudians
NEOBEHAVIORISM	1930's	Hull (U.S.A.) / Tolman / Guthrie	Behavior in S-R framework	Objective methods / Conditioning	Animal learning	N. E. Miller / Spence

philosophical presuppositions, ambitiously attempting to provide explanation of all human nature or of all psychology have been all but abandoned. We have now specific theories attempting to integrate and explain established facts in a circumscribed field, such as verbal or motor learning; attitude; concept formation; neurophysiological basis of emotion; or decision making. These miniature systems employ hypothetical constructs and models. An example of this approach is the so-called hypothetico-deductive method. C. L. Hull's research on rote learning follows this method.

The model-making approach has attracted psychologists because of its flexibility; it does not demand commitment to any particular theory. Many find that model construction helps greater precision of research and allows for higher accuracy of prediction. Of course, model construction and miniature theories are only stages of theoretical psychology—not its ultimate goals. As more data are collected and more complex relationships are established, models and theories can be expanded to incorporate knowledge acquired. Eventually, smaller or miniature systems may be integrated into a larger system and thus may provide explanation for a larger body of facts and relationships. In the 1950's the interest in theoretical issues steadily increased in American psychology, as did also willingness to examine critically the whole status of psychology. In 1959, Sigmund Koch, commenting on the views expressed by the contributors to *Psychology: A Study of a Science*, made the following observations:

> There is longing, bred on perception of the limits of recent history and nourished by boredom, for psychology to embrace—by whatever means may prove possible—problems over which it is possible to feel intellectual passion. The more adventurous ranges of our illimitable subject matter, so effectively repressed or bypassed during recent decades, are no longer proscribed.
> *For the first time in its history, psychology seems ready—or almost ready—to assess its goals and instrumentalities with primary reference to its own indigenous problems.* It seems ready to think contextually, freely, and creatively about its own refractory subject matter, and to work its way free from a dependence on simplistic theories of correct scientific conduct.

In conclusion, it may be said that psychology has achieved a quality of poise in the 1950's and 1960's. During this very productive period, a widespread eclecticism, dedicated to the refinement of viably delimited areas and techniques has replaced commitments to relatively generalized and rigid systems and methodologies. Differences persist, but conversation has tended to replace confrontation in discussions of them.

REFERENCES

GESTALT PSYCHOLOGY

Asch, S. E. Max Wertheimer's contribution to modern psychology. *Soc. Res.*, 1946, *13*, 81–102.

Ellis, W. D. *A source book of gestalt psychology.* New York: Harcourt, Brace & World, 1938.

Estes, W. K. Kurt Lewin. In W. K. Estes, *et al.* (Eds.), *Modern learning theory.* New York: Appleton-Century-Crofts, 1954. Pp. 317–344.

Hartmann, G. W. *Gestalt psychology.* New York: Ronald, 1935.

Helson, H. The psychology of Gestalt. *Amer. J. Psychol.*, 1925, *36*, 342–370; 1926, *37*, 25–62; 189–223.

Helson, H. The fundamental propositions of gestalt psychology. *Psychol. Rev.*, 1933, *40*, 13–32.

Henle, Mary (Ed.) *Documents of gestalt psychology.* Berkeley: Univer. California Press, 1961.

Katz, D. *Gestalt psychology.* New York: Ronald, 1950.

Katz, D. Edgar Rubin—1882–1951. *Psychol. Rev.*, 1951, *58*, 387–388.

Koffka, K. Perception: an introduction to Gestalt-Theorie. *Psychol. Bull.*, 1922, *19*, 531–585.

Koffka, K. *Principles of gestalt psychology.* New York: Harcourt, Brace & World, 1935.

Köhler, W. Kurt Koffka. *Psychol. Rev.*, 1942, *49*, 97–101.

Köhler, W. Max Wertheimer, 1880–1943. *Psychol. Rev.*, 1944, *51*, 143–146.

Köhler, W. *Gestalt psychology: an introduction to the new concepts in modern psychology.* New York: Liveright, 1947. Paperbound edition by The New American Library (Mentor).

Köhler, W. Gestalt psychology today. *Amer. Psychologist*, 1959, *14*, 727–734.

Köhler W. Gestalt psychology in 1962. *Psychologia*, 1963, *6*, 3–6.

Metzger, W. Zur Geschichte der Gestalttheorie in Deutschland. *Psychologia*, 1963, *6*, 11–21.

Ogden, R. M. Gestalt psychology and behaviorism. *Amer. J. Psychol.*, 1933, *45*, 151–155.

Prentice, W. C. H. The systematic psychology of Wolfgang Köhler. In S. Koch (Ed.), *Psychology: a study of a science.* Vol. 1. *Sensory, perceptual, and physiological formulations.* New York: McGraw-Hill, 1959. Pp. 427–455.

Sato, K. Gestalt psychology in Japan. *Psychologia*, 1963, *6*, 7–10.

Spitz, H. The present status of the Köhler-Wallach theory of satiation. *Psychol. Bull.*, 1958, *55*, 1–28.

The most useful sources of information on the theory and experimentation of Gestalt psychology are the books of Hartmann and Katz. Source material, excerpts from original works, are to be found in Ellis' and Henle's books. A large part of the original Wertheimer's 1912 paper on the perception of motion is available in T. Shipley's *Classics in Psychology* (1961), pp. 1032–1089. Excerpts from Köhler, Koffka, and Lewin are also found in this volume. Köhler's bibliography and a short biography are in *Amer. Psychologist* 1957, *12*, 131–133. He expressed his view on Gestalt psychology in his presidential address in 1959, subsequently published in the *Amer. Psychologist*, 1959, *14*, 727–734. For Helson's bibliography and a biographical sketch see *Amer. Psychologist*, 1962, *17*, 895–898.

HORMIC PSYCHOLOGY

Agar, W. E., Drummond, R. H., & Tiegs, O. N. Third report on a test of McDougall's Lamarckian experiment on the training of rats. *J. exp. Biol.*, 1948, *25*, 103–122.

Boden, Margaret A. McDougall revisited. *J. Pers.*, 1965, *33*, 1–19.

Bruner, J. S. Preface. William McDougall, *Body and mind.* Boston: Beacon, 1961.

Burt, C. The permanent contributions of McDougall to psychology. *Brit. J. educ. Psychol.*, 1955, *25*, 10–22.

Cofer, C. N., & Appley, M. H. *Motivation: theory and research.* New York: Wiley, 1964.

Crew, F. A. E. A repetition of McDougall's Lamarckian experiment. *J. Genet.*, 1936, *33*, 61–101.

Drew, G. C. McDougall's experiments on the inheritance of acquired characteristics. *Nature* 1939, *143*, 188–191.

Guthrie, E. R. The status of systematic psychology. *Amer. Psychologist*, 1950, *5*, 97–101.

Langfeld, H. S. Professor McDougall's contribution to the science of psychology. *Brit. J. Psychol.*, 1940, *31*, 107–114.

MacLeod, R. B. Teleology and theory of human behavior. *Science*, 1957, *125*, 477–480.

McDougall, W. *An introduction to social psychology.* (14th ed.) London: Methuen, 1919. Paperbound edition-London: Methuen; New York: Barnes & Noble, 1960.

McDougall, W. Men or robots? In C. Murchison, (Ed.), *Psychologies of 1925.* Worcester, Mass: Clark Univer. Press, 1926. Pp. 273–305.

McDougall, W. The hormic psychology. In C. Murchison (Ed.), *Psychologies of 1930.* Worcester, Mass.: Clark Univer. Press, 1930. Pp. 3–36.

McDougall, W. *Outline of psychology.* New York: Scribner, 1923.

Smith, M. Obituary. William McDougall. *Brit. J. med. Psychol.*, 1939, *18*, 105–111.

For McDougall's bibliography and brief biographical outline see: Robinson, A. L. *William McDougall, M.B., D.Sc., F.R.S.: A bibliography, together with a brief outline of his life.* Durham: Duke Univer. Press, 1943. McDougall's autobiography is to be found in C. Murchison (Ed.), *A history of psychology in autobiography.* Vol. 1. Worcester, Mass.: Clark Univer. Press, 1930. Pp. 191–223.

SCHOOLS IN RETROSPECT

Allport, G. W. The fruits of eclecticism—bitter or sweet? *Psychologia*, 1964, 7, 1–14.

Boring, E. G. Psychology for eclectics. In C. Murchison (Ed.), *Psychologies of 1930*. Worcester, Mass.: Clark Univer. Press, 1930. Pp. 115–127.

Guthrie, E. R. The status of systematic psychology. *Amer. Psychologist*, 1950, 5, 97–101.

Hunter, W. S. Some observations on the status of psychology. In *Miscellanea Psychologica Albert Michotte*. Louvain: Institut Supérieur de Philosophie, 1947. Pp. 39–48.

Klein, D. B. Eclecticism versus system-making in psychology. *Psychol. Rev.*, 1930, *37*, 488–496.

Koch, S. Theoretical psychology, 1950: an overview. *Psychol. Rev.*, 1951, *58*, 295–301.

Zubin, J. On the powers of models. *J. Pers.*, 1952, *20*, 430–439.

20

Psychoanalysis

THE SCHOOL OF PSYCHOANALYSIS differs from other psychological schools in many respects. It originated outside the academic field of psychology. It was first espoused and propagated as a method of therapy by medical men—neurologists and psychiatrists. Its point of departure was not experimental findings but clinical observations. It does not encompass the whole of psychology but only certain areas such as motivation and personality. Psychoanalysis was initially intended to be a method of therapy and did not seek to replace or attack any contemporary theories of psychology. Eventually it developed into a theory which revolutionized psychology and greatly affected its future course—principally because it presented a new image of man. By reason of the fact that this image was so radically different from that universally accepted, psychoanalysis affected not only psychology, but many other areas of man's thought and life—in particular, such areas as literature, art, education, ethics, sociology, anthropology, and theology. Psychoanalysis has been said to have altered man's conception of himself to a degree equalled only by the Copernican and Darwinian theories. As Copernicus destroyed the illusion of the earth's and of man's central position in the universe, and Darwin destroyed the illusion of man's uniqueness in living nature, Freud dealt a lethal blow to man's perhaps greatest illusion—that of being the master of his thoughts and actions.

In the present account of psychoanalysis, we shall concentrate on the history of the psychoanalytic movement rather than on a detailed exposition of its theories and methods. The particular topics of our presentation will include Freud's life, a summary of his views, the relation of these views to the development of psychology, the reactions to psychoanalysis in Europe and in America, and a review of other important psychoanalytic orientations.

Life of Freud (1856-1939). Sigmund Freud lived 83 years, 78 of which—apart from his frequent travels—were spent in Vienna. Born in Freiberg, now Příbor in Czechoslovakia, he came with his family to Vienna at the age of four. He studied medicine and took—in his own words—a "somewhat belated" doctorate in medicine in 1881. Freud delayed his medical studies for two principal reasons. First of all, he was not particularly eager to practice medicine. Furthermore, he became interested in the histology of the nervous system while working in the laboratory of the famous physiologist, Ernst Brücke. After taking his doctorate and during his residence in medicine he continued his research in neuroanatomy and published several papers in this field. One of these papers dealt with the analgesic properties of cocaine. In time Freud became a competent neurologist,

interested more and more in neurological diseases. At first his attention
was directed to organic neurological disorders. But he soon discovered
that many so-called nervous diseases were not organic in origin, but had
a psychological background. This observation aroused Freud's interest in
psychoneuroses, which were to become his main area of study. Generally
regarded, nineteenth century psychiatry was closely linked to neurology
and had a distinctly organic orientation. It was the historic role of Freud
to show that mental illness is not necessarily the result of brain pathology.
He introduced instead the concept of "functional" disease as opposed to
"organic" disease, and he worked to develop a special therapy for this
functional form of disease.

Consequential for the development of Freud's theory was his association
with the Viennese physician *Josef Breuer* (1842-1925), who began in 1880
to treat a 21-year-old girl, Anna O., suffering from a variety of neurotic
symptoms. Working with Breuer in the treatment of this case, Freud
observed many facts which alerted him to the link between childhood
experiences and neurotic symptoms. In addition, he saw the curative
potential of such procedures as free association and catharsis, that is, the
relief from emotional tension by "talking out" troubled emotions. Now
deeply interested in the neuroses, Freud decided to go to France to study
with J. M. Charcot, famous for his investigations of hysteria and for his
practice of hypnosis. This study was made possible through a fellowship
which he received, following his appointment as a lecturer in neuropathology in 1885. After almost five months in Paris, and a few weeks in
Berlin, Freud returned to Vienna to resume his medical practice and
research. He married in the same year (1886). In treating neurotics,
Freud used hypnosis initially, but he was not always successful with this
method. To increase his knowledge of hypnosis and improve his hypnotic
techniques, he visited another French center of hypnotic studies, Nancy,
in 1889. There—as he says in his autobiography—Freud "received the
profoundest impression of the possibility that there could be powerful
mental processes which nevertheless remained hidden from the consciousness of men." Eventually Freud abandoned *hypnotherapy*, substituting
for it the procedure which was to become a standard accompaniment of
psychoanalytic therapy: a patient lying on a couch relaxed and freely
associating and a psychiatrist taking notes and observing the patient.

The collaboration with Breuer resulted in their joint publication of
Studien über Hysterie ("Studies on Hysteria," 1895), which was Freud's
first book related to psychoanalysis. The year of its appearance—1895—
is usually considered the birth year of psychoanalysis. Breuer and Freud
eventually parted because of differences in point of view on issues such as
the therapist-patient relationship, or transference, a phenomenon more
fully explored by Freud later. On his own, Freud proceeded to develop
the ideas presented in the *Studies on Hysteria*. Other books followed,
each adding a new dimension to the theory and method of psychoanalysis:
in 1900 *Die Traumdeutung* ("The Interpretation of Dreams"); in 1904
Zur Psychopathologie des Alltagslebens ("The Psychopathology of Every-

day Life"); and in 1905 *Drei Abhandlungen zur Sexualtheorie* ("Three Essays on the Theory of Sexuality"); and *Der Witz und seine Beziehung zum Unbewussten* ("Wit and Its Relation to the Unconscious"). With the last two books the main framework of psychoanalysis was completed. Freud, then 49 years old, was known and discussed both in Vienna and abroad. His psychiatric practice was substantial. Many physicians, interested in his theories, wrote to him; several came to study with him. Gradually the psychoanalytic movement began to take shape. In 1908 the International Psychoanalytic Association was founded, with Freud as its president. This association grew and organized congresses, at which important issues pertaining to psychoanalysis and the psychoanalytic movement were debated.

In 1909 Freud was invited to the United States by G. Stanley Hall to participate in the twentieth anniversary celebration of Clark University in Worcester, Massachusetts and to deliver a series of lectures on psychoanalysis. This event was important for Freud personally because it encouraged—as he described it—his "self-respect in every way." It was also an event of considerable consequence for the psychoanalytic movement in America and for the rapprochement of psychoanalysis and psychology. The occasion brought together a number of prominent people. Among the outstanding psychologists attending were William James, E. B. Titchener, J. McK. Cattell, and E. B. Holt. There were also Adolf Meyer, the psychiatrist; James J. Putnam, professor of neurology at Harvard; Franz Boas, an anthropologist; and H. S. Jennings, a biologist. Among the associates and followers of Freud at the Clark meetings were Carl G. Jung, Sandor Ferenczi, Ernest Jones, and A. A. Brill. The five lectures presented by Freud were translated into English and printed in the *American Journal of Psychology* in the following year. It is interesting to note that 40 years later—at the 60th anniversary of Clark—Freud's daughter Anna was the main speaker.

As the psychoanalytic movement grew, sharp differences arose between Freud and its members. In 1911 Alfred Adler, and in 1913 Carl Jung, who was expected to be Freud's successor, broke with the master and went their separate ways, founding their own schools. In the 1920's several other close associates of Freud—even members of a specially created committee, who formed the inner circle of the psychoanalytic movement— left Freud and initiated new psychoanalytic trends to the dismay and disapproval of the founder. This was to be the fate of the psychoanalytic movement—a diffusion into many divergent streams, each flowing its own course, often markedly different from the one charted by Freud.

The year 1923 proved to be of particular significance for Freud as a person and for the history of psychoanalysis. The book which Freud published in that year, *Das Ich und das Es* ("The Ego and the Id"), constituted a new and important development because it presented the Freudian concept of personality in terms of the ego, the id, and superego. The same year also marked a tragic turn in Freud's personal life when it was discovered that he had cancer of the jaw and underwent the first of 33 operations for this condition during the remaining 16 years of his life. The cancerous condition steadily deteriorated, and Freud suffered increasingly from pain, discomfort, and various impairments. He had difficulty in eating, smoking, talking, and hearing. Another blow struck Freud later in that year: the death of his beloved grandchild, four and a half-year-old Heinz. Jones wrote that "it was the only occasion in his life when Freud was known to shed tears" and that the boy's death "had a profound effect on Freud's spirits for the rest of his life." Despite all these physical and emotional pains, Freud continued working. In 1926 he published *Hemmung, Symptom und Angst* ("Inhibition, Symptom and Anxiety"), the last of his important clinical works. His subsequent larger works dealt with nonclinical topics. The last published book in his life was his *Moses, sein Volk und die monotheistische Religion* (published in English as "Moses and Monotheism," 1938).

In 1938 the Nazis, who had been attacking Freud for some time because of his Jewish origin and had publicly burned his books, occupied Vienna. But with the intervention of his friends, Freud was saved from the Nazis and brought to London in June, 1938. There he died the following year, on September 23, 1939.

Freud as a Person. Freud's conduct and personality have often been subjected—by both his friends and enemies—to a thorough scrutiny and analysis aimed at finding clues to the genesis of his theories. Without any pretension to our own psychoanalysis of Freud, we shall mention a few of his characteristics which seem to be particularly relevant to the understanding of his historical stature. A significant starting point is the matter of Freud's motivation in choosing a medical career and in specializing in mental diseases. In his autobiography Freud wrote:

> Neither at that time [that is, before entering the university], nor indeed in my later life, did I feel any particular predilection for the career of a physician. I was moved, rather, by a sort of curiosity, which was, however, directed more towards human concerns than towards natural objects.

The main driving force in Freud's life was not the desire to cure or improve people, but rather the curiosity of a philosopher or psychologist seeking to understand man and his nature and especially the *why* of human behavior.

In this pursuit Freud was greatly helped by his natural inquisitiveness —demonstrated in his anatomical and neurological studies—and by his gift of observation, clearly evidenced in his clinical writings. This gift is apparent in his letters in which he describes people, places, nature, or works or art. Another great asset of Freud—a powerful factor in his success, though interpreted by some as an escape from his own neurosis and a kind of occupational autotherapy—was his capacity for work. Freud worked hard all his life to his last days, regardless of personal trials and tribulations and despite his age and the tortures he suffered from the cancerous condition of his face. Still another significant asset was Freud's lucid and captivating writing style.

Much has been written about Freud's faults and deficiencies, but no one can deny that Freud was an extraordinary man in his tenacity to his principles and in his courage. Freud had the courage to study the strangest and darkest elements of the human mind—which others were reluctant to study—and he held his courage in the face of isolation, ostracism, personal disappointments, and in moral and physical pain.

PSYCHOANALYSIS AS A THEORY AND AS A THERAPY

Psychoanalysis can be viewed in three different ways: as a theory of personality and motivation; as a therapeutic method; and as a method of investigation. Some writers have held that these three aspects are so closely interwoven that they are inseparable. Others have maintained that these aspects are not interdependent and that they can be considered separately—in other words, that it is possible to practice psychoanalytic method without subscribing to psychoanalytic theory; similarly that it is possible to accept the theory but reject the method. The fact is, that the distinction between the psychoanalytic doctrine and psychoanalytic therapy has been consistently made by many psychologists and psychiatrists.

Psychoanalytic therapy consists of intensive and extensive exploration of the patient's unconscious, in the attempt to reach the earliest infantile experiences. Its aim is to bring into consciousness the inner conflicts, troubled emotions, and repressed experiences of the patient and to analyze them in the light of reason and life realities. The primary techniques used are free association, dream analysis, and analysis of such mechanisms as resistance and transference. *Resistance* is the inability or unwillingness of the patient to reveal certain ideas, experiences, or wishes. *Transference* is a process by which the patient attaches feelings experienced toward another person, usually a parent, to the therapist.

Theory. As to Freud's psychoanalytic theory, a brief survey cannot do justice to all its facets. We shall describe here only the major features. But first a general observation is in order about the development of Freud's theory. This theory was not conceived at once, but developed gradually. In the span of 40 years—beginning with the publication of the *Studies on Hysteria* (1895), in which he laid down the fundamental principles of his system—Freud kept improving, modifying, and even changing his ideas. Changes and innovations introduced by Freud sometimes caught his loyal followers by surprise and provoked protests and disagreements. This is precisely what happened, when Freud, for example, introduced for the first time in 1920 the notion of *Thanatos* or the *death instinct.* Because the evolution of Freud's thought extended over so many years and referred to diverse problems, a full and accurate understanding of Freudian theory requires familiarity with most of his writings. This is a demanding task when one considers that they total 24 volumes in English translation.

Freud was not averse to considering other theories and was receptive to some of them. Nevertheless, he was intransigent when suggestions to modify his views on infantile sexuality were offered, even when they came from his closest friends. The theories proposed by Freud were based on clinical observations. He thought that clinical evidence was not only sufficient, but that it had greater validity than experimentation. Hence he did not attach much significance to attempts at experimental verification of psychoanalytic assertions.

The Unconscious. Historians of the psychoanalytic movement have often speculated about the antecedents of Freud's concepts, especially about the concept of the unconscious. Was Freud influenced by others or was he original in his views on the unconscious? Several authors have shown that the idea of the unconscious can be traced to medieval and even ancient thinkers. In the eighteenth and nineteenth centuries many philosophers and scientists were aware of the existence of the unconscious and made references to it. But there is no evidence that Freud was influenced by any particular writer. It is likely that his philosophical studies prepared him and sensitized him to the understanding and appreciation of the unconscious. However, the real influence on Freud's thinking came from his own observations of hypnotic phenomena, of catharsis, of amnesia, as well as from dream analyses, and likely from the self-analysis which he undertook in 1897. The true significance of Freud lies not in his "discovering" the unconscious. Rather it is in his finding and demonstrating the importance of the unconscious in human motivation and in devising a method for reaching and studying the unconscious.

Freud taught that our psychic life consists of conscious, preconscious, and unconscious levels. As far as our motivation is concerned, the unconscious is the most important of the three levels. The *unconscious* is that part of our psychic life of which we have no immediate awareness, but which determines our thinking, feeling, and action. Some mental material, although not directly conscious to us, can be brought easily to consciousness. This level Freud called *preconscious*. Unlike the preconscious, the unconscious material is buried deeply within us and can be brought to consciousness, if at all, only with difficulty. Many events and experiences, fears and unfulfilled desires, because they are painful or shameful to us, may be banished from our consciousness and relegated to our unconscious. This process, if voluntary, is called *suppression*; if involuntary, *repression*. The repressed material remains active and influences all our conscious life. It motivates our feelings, thoughts, and actions without our awareness of being so motivated. The repressed content from time to time appears in our dreams, in words or ideas that come to our mind in free association, in our tongue slips, mistakes, or accidents. The repressions may sometimes become troublesome and disrupt our thinking and behavior and may lead to neurotic symptoms. According to Freud's theory, to be freed from this disrupting influence of the repressed unconscious, it is necessary to uncover the troublesome elements and to bring them into the open. By this he meant that they should be brought to consciousness and be subjected to conscious and rational examination. The uncovering of the unconscious is one of the essential ingredients of the psychoanalytic therapy. One of its principal techniques is dream analysis, which Freud called "the royal road to the unconscious." Freud's book, *The Interpretation of Dreams*, is generally considered one of the most momentous works in the history of psychoanalysis. There are two types of content in dreams, the *manifest* and the *latent* (or hidden) content. The manifest content is that which we remember upon awakening. For psychoanalysis the important content is the latent, because through it the unconscious can be reached. Repressed elements such as wishes and impulses intolerable to the individual's conscious mind are transformed in dreams in various ways so that they are rendered tolerable. They may appear, for instance, in symbolic ways. The task of the analyst is to interpret the dreams and thus to reveal the repressed material.

The Instincts. The keynote to Freud's motivational theory is the concept of instincts—a concept repeatedly revised by Freud. The German term which Freud used was *der Trieb*, more accurately rendered in English as "drive." But the term "instinct" has been the term commonly used in psychoanalytic literature written in English. Instincts are the biological forces of the organism, releasing mental energy and causing certain activity. They are distinguished by their source, aim, and object. Their *source* is a stimulation in some part of the body such as the "erotogenic zones," that is, the parts of the body capable of generating erotic sensations; their *aim* is the allaying of the stimulation by activity such as sex satisfaction; their *object* is that which brings satisfaction. Freud's initial groups of basic instincts were the ego-instincts (self-preservation instincts) and the sexual instincts (race-preservation instincts). Later Freud proposed a more general grouping: *Eros*, or life instinct, and *Thanatos*, or death instinct. Eros was understood as the force underlying all life and included such specific instincts as hunger, thirst, and sex. Thanatos was the destructive force, directed either toward oneself or others. These two instincts were said by Freud to coexist within each individual and to account for the conflicts continuously arising in the lives of men.

A concept central to Freud's theory is that of the *libido*, which in the past was often misinterpreted—largely because of Freud's earlier writings. Freud described libido in various ways. In one text, libido is defined as "that force by which the sexual instinct is represented in the mind . . . analogous to the force of hunger, or the will to power, and other such trends among the ego-tendencies." Other texts imply that libido is not only the mental aspect, but also the bodily aspect of the sex instinct—that is, both an erotic thought and a sex activity. But later libido denoted the energy of all the life instinct as contrasted to the energy of death instinct. Thus not only pleasurable activities, but also all self-preservative activities, were considered by Freud as erotic in his sense of the term. The notion of the pervading role of the libido in human life is known as Freudian *pansexualism*. It is this aspect of Freud's theory which provoked most opposition and dissension among his followers.

As is well known, Freud attached great significance to infantile sexuality and its development as determinants of personality and adjustment. As a clinician, Freud became convinced that the origin of neuroses could be traced to the experiences of early childhood—particularly to the sexual development of the child. He believed that sex perversions arose from disturbances of this development, that is, from a failure to achieve normal sexual maturity. On the basis of the sources of libidinal gratification, Freud distinguished the following consecutive stages of psychosexual development: in the first five to six years of age—the oral, the anal, and the phallic phases; in adolescence—the genital phase. Between age six and adolescence is the latent period. During this period the sex instinct is dormant, and the child prefers to be with children of the same sex. For this reason Freud characterized this phase as "homosexual." The sexual life of adults is determined by the way they had passed through the stages of normal sexual development. If the libidinal impulses, in childhood or adulthood, cannot be satisfied directly, the individual uses various defense mechanisms, one of which is *sublimation*. This mechanism consists of vicarious gratification by channelling the sex drive into activities which are acceptable to the individual and society. One type of sublimation, according to Freud, is the creative arts.

The Structure of Personality. The Freudian concept of personality has been one of the most influential concepts in the psychology of personality. According to Freud, personality has three components: the id, the ego, and the superego. The *id* represents the basic and primitive aspect of personality. It is the constitutional and animalistic substratum of personality, where all the instincts and all energy are located. It is unconscious, blind, amoral, and irrational. It demands satisfaction of its impulses and needs at any cost. It follows the pleasure principle, one of the two basic principles postulated by Freud, the other being the reality principle.

The *ego* is the conscious and rational part of personality; it follows not the pleasure, but the reality principle. This means that the ego, in satisfying the demands of the id, considers the realities of existence, the conditions, the rules and laws of the world, and also past experiences. Ego has the role of the chief executive. It makes decisions and takes action, using the energy derived from the id. Freud's conception of the ego fluctuated widely. At times he saw it as relatively weak and at other times as a more powerful force. Its role and importance were radically re-evaluated by Freud's daughter Anna, and by all his heirs, including both the "orthodox" and the "neo-Freudians."

The *superego* has the role of a critic or a censor, who observes, evaluates, and judges everything in reference to all the moral and idealistic standards acquired by the individual throughout life. These standards are adopted especially in early childhood and are derived mostly from parents. The superego represents the supreme ideal which the ego is supposed or expected to achieve.

A simple example may illustrate the differences and the relations between these three components of personality. A young man meets an unknown but attractive girl for the first time. His id may urge him to take her in his arms and kiss her; but the superego declares that such an action is immoral and shameful; the ego then resolves this by a behavior which satisfies both the id and superego, but which at the same time is socially proper; the result is a smile, a cheerful "hello," or a warm handshake. Although Freud himself often used anthropomorphic terms when describing these three components, they should not be thought of as three separate entities—almost like three "little men" living within us and continuously fighting. Rather, they should be understood as symbolic terms for three personality processes whose interaction constitutes the core of the dynamics of the person. These dynamics may be summarized in this way: The ego is placed between the urgent demands of the id and the strictures of the superego forbidding satisfaction of these demands. Should the ego yield to the id, it will be punished by the superego with a feeling of guilt or inferiority. And yet, action is necessarily consonant with the requirements of the environment. Caught between the demands of the id and the demands of the superego on one hand, and the demands of reality on the other, the "poor ego"—as Freud described it—is in conflict. It is in a conflict analogous to that of a man in a court of law. He could be freed by a lie, but his ethics forbid a lie. He would rather say nothing, but the court demands that he plead or else be presumed guilty. Freud taught that in its conflicts the ego uses certain defenses. These defenses are special modes of behavior which relieve the person from tensions arising from conflicts. Among these defenses—or as he called them "defense mechanisms"—are repressions, regressions, rationalizations, and fantasies. Sublimation, described above, is also one of them because it discharges the urges of the id in a manner which is satisfactory to the superego and to society.

FREUD AND PSYCHOLOGY

Was Freud influenced in the construction of his system by the scientific psychology of his time? What did he think of this psychology? Soon after Freud began his medical studies in 1873, the two great works of the new psychology appeared, Wundt's *Physiological Psychology* and Brentano's *Psychology from an Empirical Standpoint*. We do not know if Freud read these books, but one of the authors, Franz Brentano, who was then at the Vienna University, became his professor in philosophy. Philosophical courses were no longer required of medical students, but Freud took several courses under Brentano. Undoubtedly Brentano, who was highly respected as a person and a teacher, contributed substantially to Freud's philosophical formation. There is no evidence, however, that the contact with Brentano was a significant factor in the origin and development of Freud's theories.

As to the academic psychology, which so rapidly developed in Freud's time and of whose development he was well aware, it was clearly of little interest to him. Freud was interested in psychology as such. He tried to develop a system of psychology of his own, which he called *metapsychology*. But doing so, he ignored academic psychology. Freud's negative attitude toward academic psychology and its achievements was noted and criticized by contemporary psychologists. In his writings Freud referred occasionally to Helmholtz, Hering, Lipps, and especially to Fechner. The latter, according to Ernest Jones, was "the only psychologist from whom Freud ever borrowed any ideas." Freud himself said in his autobiography: "I was always open to the ideas of G. T. Fechner and have followed that thinker upon many important points." One of these points, specifically mentioned by Freud, was Fechner's "tendency to stability." Freud applied it to the pleasure and unpleasure relation; the tension of the unpleasant leads to the release which is pleasant. Regarding Wundt, Freud read his *Völkerpsychologie* when he worked on *Totem and Taboo*, his own book in this field. He remarked in a letter in 1912: "Wundt makes me furious. To have to read such balderdash after eleven hours at analysis is a hard punishment."

The system of psychology which Freud attempted to develop was named by him *metapsychology* to signify his intention to transcend psychology— to go "beyond" it in a way similar to that in which Aristotle's metaphysics went "beyond" physics. Metapsychology meant "a method of approach" to the study of mental processes in their dynamic attributes, topographical features, and economic significance. This seemed to Freud to "represent the furthest goal that psychology could attain." Freud's intention in his metapsychology was to provide a theoretical system which would assist psychoanalysts in the interpretation of clinical observations. Freud used the term metapsychology for the first time in 1896. When he completed his essays on metapsychology in 1915, he felt that he could go no further. He thought then that his life work was accomplished and that whatever else he might add would be only complementary and of minor importance. Freud's later work on the psychology of the id, ego, and superego, and on the death instinct proved otherwise.

REACTIONS TO PSYCHOANALYSIS

Freud's theory generated much enthusiasm but also great hostility. There was as well much ambivalence of opinion about Freud's system. In considering these reactions one must distinguish between those of the lay public and of the literary circles, and those of the scientists, especially of psychiatrists and psychologists. But the latter groups were often affected by the effects the Freudian thought had on the general public and by the pressure of current public opinion.

The effect of the Freudian theory on psychiatry must be viewed in reference to the state of this branch of medicine at the time of the publication of the *Studies on Hysteria*. It must be remembered that psychiatry then subscribed to the theory that mental disease was brain disease. With this orientation, psychiatry was unable, despite its persistent efforts, either to demonstrate organic correlates of psychoses or to develop any rational therapy for psychoses. As to the neuroses, the nineteenth century psychiatry could offer neither a theory nor a therapy for them. Psychoanalysis with its functional and biographical approach held a promise both of explaining and treating neuroses and other mental disorders. This was the main reason why psychoanalysis revolutionized psychiatric thinking and methods, even though many of its tenets were rejected.

The strongest opposition and the sharpest criticism have been directed from various quarters against Freud's theory of sex—or against what has been called Freudian pansexualism. As we have already observed, this was the main cause of division within the psychoanalytic movement. Another object of attack, this one based not on empirical data but on philosophical considerations, was Freud's *psychic determinism*—that is, the theory inherent in his system that every human action, thought, and feeling, and all psychic phenomena are determined by definite causes, in the same way as physical phenomena are determined by physical causes.

Psychoanalysis in Europe. Reactions to Freud differed in various countries. The earliest and most important recognition and serious support of Freudian theories outside Austria came from a distinguished Swiss psychiatrist, *Eugen Bleuler* (1857-1939), in 1904. He applied Freud's concepts to the interpretation of psychotic symptoms, especially of schizophrenia. His assistants at the mental clinic at Burghölzli were Karl Abraham (1877-1925), later one of the members of Freud's Committee and one of his most influential followers, and Carl G. Jung, to whom more attention will be devoted in another part of this chapter.

In general, the *Anglo-American* world was much more receptive to psychoanalysis than other countries. Marie Bonaparte, a close friend of Freud, said that it was easier for the Anglo-Saxons to understand psychoanalysis because of their "strongly realistic turn of mind" and their "courage in the face of facts." The *French*, on the other hand, possess certain features, Marie Bonaparte stated, which made this understanding more difficult. Freud himself observed in 1927 that France was "for so long refractory" to psychoanalysis. Indeed, Freud's name, with a few exceptions, was almost unknown in France before 1914. Translations of Freud's works began to appear in 1921. They caused a stir, but not so much in psychiatry as in literary circles. French psychiatrists began to pay attention to psychoanalysis, when *Eugenia Sokolnicka*, who had been analyzed by Freud and strongly recommended by him, arrived in Paris in 1922 and gave demonstrations in psychoanalytic therapy. She was a cofounder of the Psychoanalytic Society in Paris in 1925. Among French psychologists who drew upon Freudian concepts in their work was *Daniel Lagache* (b.

1903), a professor at the Sorbonne. He applied these concepts—though he modified them considerably—to the study of child development and the formation of personality. Psychoanalysis in France seems to have prepared a favorable ground for the reception of existentialist psychiatry in the 1940's. To some degree psychoanalysis played the same role in other countries, attuning psychology and psychiatry to the existentialist concepts. In *Italy* there was much opposition to psychoanalysis as a theory dangerous to morals. The first systematic and sympathetic treatment of psychoanalysis there was given by *Enzo Bonaventura* (1891-1948), a professor at the University of Florence, in his book *La Psicoanalisi* ("Psychoanalysis") in 1948. In *Austria,* the country of its origin, and in *Germany,* psychoanalysis progressed only slowly. The foundation of the Berlin Institute of Psychoanalysis in 1920, followed by the foundation of similar institutes in Vienna and Budapest, contributed to the advance of psychoanalysis in Germany, Austria, and Hungary. In 1927 Freud remarked that German psychiatry was undergoing "a kind of 'peaceful penetration' by analytic views."

The first systematic presentation of psychoanalysis in *England* was the work of *Ernest Jones* (1879-1958), a British physician and surgeon—*Papers on Psychoanalysis* (1912), a successful book, many times revised and republished. Jones, who practiced medicine in London, became interested in psychoanalysis and personally acquainted with Freud in 1908. He remained the closest and most loyal friend to the very end of Freud's life. Jones published the most detailed and authoritative biography of Freud, in three volumes. It is largely because of Jones's writings and activities—he organized a psychoanalytic society in Britain—that psychoanalytic concepts became known early to British psychologists. Another influential figure in the recognition and dissemination of psychoanalytic concepts in Britain was Jones's friend *Bernard Hart* (b. 1879). Hart was a physician, who wrote *The Psychology of Insanity* (1912), which was reprinted 20 times in 40 years. Characteristic of British psychology was its early recognition of psychoanalysis and its sympathetic reaction to psychoanalytic concepts. As early as 1913 psychologists *T. H. Pear* (b. 1886) and *William Brown* (1881-1951), who had a medical degree, gave papers on Freudian theories. In the following year a symposium, attended by both psychologists and psychiatrists, was held on Freud's theory of forgetting. Proceedings of this symposium were published in the *British Journal of Psychology*. The pioneer of experimental psychology in Britain, *W. H. R. Rivers,* M.D. (1864-1922), became familiar with Freud's concepts in the latter part of his career. He discussed some of the psychoanalytic concepts such as the unconscious, repression, and instinct, offering his own interpretation of them. It is noteworthy that the British psychologists who showed greatest interest in psychoanalysis, and who published most on this subject, held medical degrees. *William McDougall* (1871-1938), who also had a medical degree and some medical practice, gave much attention to psychoanalysis. He even decided to undergo—for the experience—psychoanalysis under Jung. He said afterwards in his autobiography that he "made an effort to be as open-minded as possible; and came away enlightened, but not convinced." There are parallels between Freud's theory of motivation and McDougall's hormic psychology. Freud rather reinforced McDougall's views than influenced their formulation. McDougall appreciated Freud's contributions to psychology—even called them the greatest since Aristotle—but expressed reservations on some specific Freudian views and criticized them.

The influence of Freud eventually crystallized itself in British psychology in the form of what has been called "depth psychology." This has been an eclectic orientation, which assimilated some psychoanalytic concepts not only from Freud but also from other psychoanalysts such as Jung and Adler. However, depth psychology rejected certain concepts—principally the libido theory and psychic determinism. However a minor segment of British psychology remained closely allied with Freudian psychoanalysis. Among those who were identified with psychoanalytic theory was *J. C. Flugel* (1884-1955), of London University. It was he who was invited by Carl Murchison to be the spokesman for psychoanalysis in *Psychologies of 1930*, a review of psychological theories at that time. *R. W. Pickford* (b. 1903) also showed much interest in psychoanalysis, probably more than other contemporary experimental psychologists in Britain.

To conclude our review of psychoanalysis in Britain, we must mention the daughter of Sigmund Freud, *Anna Freud* (b. 1895), who made her home in England. She carried on the work of psychoanalysis through writings—among which her *The Ego and the Mechanisms of Defense* (1946) is the most notable—by lectures in various countries, by professional activity at the Hempstead Child Clinic, and as a coeditor of *The Psychoanalytic Study of the Child*, established in 1945. Also prominent in child psychotherapy in England was *Melanie Klein* (1882-1960). Born in Vienna and well trained in psychoanalysis, she came to England at the invitation of Jones in 1925 and spent the rest of her life in Britain. She wrote *The Psychoanalysis of Children* (1932), a book which found a sympathetic reception in Britain and elsewhere.

Psychoanalysis in America.   Apparently, the first notice of Freud's work in America came from William James who in the *Psychological Review* in 1894, referred briefly to an "important paper" of Breuer and Freud, published in a neurological journal in 1893. In the years immediately following, references to Freud appeared in other journals. The word "psychoanalysis" was used for the first time in a psychological journal, in an article by James J. Putnam in the *Journal of Abnormal Psychology* in 1906. Putnam, a neurologist on the staff of the Harvard Medical School, is thought to have been the first in America to use psychoanalytic treatment on his patients (1904). After meeting Freud at Clark University in 1909, Putnam publicly endorsed psychoanalysis as a method of treatment in his paper read before the American Neurological Association in 1910. Putnam's prestige was a strong factor in the sympathetic reception of psychoanalysis by American psychiatry. Freud realized this when he said in his autobiography that Putnam "threw the whole weight of a personality that was universally respected into the defence of the cultural value of analysis and the purity of its aims."

In 1911 Ernest Jones organized the American Psychoanalytic Association with Putnam as its first president. Earlier in the same year *Abraham A. Brill* (1874-1948), a psychiatrist in New York, founded the New York Psychoanalytic Society. Brill received his medical degree from Columbia University. To acquaint himself with the new European trends he went to Burghölzli in Switzerland in 1907, and thence to Austria, where he visited Freud. Upon his return to New York he began private practice of psychoanalysis in 1908, thus initiating a new specialty in America. Brill was the first translator of Freud into English, publishing *Selected Papers on Hysteria and Other Psychoneuroses* in 1909. After Freud's death Brill wrote an appraisal of Freudian influence on psychiatry, entitled *Freud's Contributions to Psychiatry* (1944). Among other American psychiatrists who supported psychoanalysis, and figured prominently in the history of psychoanalysis in America, were *William A. White* (1870-1937), associated for 34 years with the St. Elizabeth Mental Hospital in Washington, D.C., and *Smith Ely Jelliffe* (1866-1945), who is regarded as the founder of psychosomatic medicine in this country. It is chiefly because of Jelliffe that American psychosomatic medicine assumed from the beginning a distinctly psychoanalytic orientation. While a professor at Fordham University Medical School, he invited Carl Jung to give a series of lectures at Fordham in 1911 and 1912. Both White and Jelliffe founded the first psychoanalytic journal in the English language, the *Psychoanalytic Review,* which has appeared since 1913. In the 1920's and 1930's the psychoanalytic movement in America gathered further momentum with the arrival and activities of prominent European psychoanalysts, such as Hanns Sachs, Karen Horney, Erich Fromm, Franz Alexander, and Otto Rank. In 1931 the New York Institute of Psychoanalysis was established. A similar institute was organized in Chicago by Franz Alexander in 1932. In the following years other such institutes were established. The success of psychoanalysis in scientific circles, especially in psychiatry, and its popularity among the general public, have been greater in America than in any other country. In 1925, when Freud appraised the status of psychoanalysis in America, he described psychoanalysis here as being "extremely popular among the lay public" and "recognized by a number of official psychiatrists as an important element in medical training." But he complained that psychoanalysis in America "has suffered a great deal from being watered down." Freud also made reference to the conflict of psychoanalysis and behaviorism in America.

American Psychology and Freud. Thus far, our survey of American reactions to Freud has been limited chiefly to psychiatry. Let us now briefly examine the effect of psychoanalysis on American academic psychology. An assessment of this effect—as any assessment of historical influences—

is an intricate task demanding careful selection of criteria for measuring this influence. The danger of a personal bias—unconscious or conscious—always lurks in the selection of these criteria and in the weight assigned to them. This danger is perhaps intensified in the evaluation of psychoanalysis because of the ego-involvement that is so often present in such an undertaking. Several psychologists have reviewed and discussed Freudian influence on American psychology as a whole and on some of its fields. The interested reader is referred to their accounts, whose list is provided at the end of this chapter. Here, we shall point out only those general and salient effects of Freud's influence that are almost universally recognized.

In evaluating Freud's influence in America one must again refer to the historically important visit of Freud to Clark University in 1909, where he addressed—as never before or after—an audience of so many leading psychologists of one country. This visit gave American psychologists an opportunity to learn about psychoanalysis—at this relatively early stage of its development—from the founder himself. Moreover, it occasioned the translation of his lectures, which were made available in the following year in the *American Journal of Psychology*, a widely circulated American journal. Among American psychologists who met Freud at the Clark University celebration was Edwin B. Holt (1873-1946). Holt was the first American psychologist to espouse Freudian concepts in a book. This work was *Freudian Wish and Its Place in Ethics*, published in 1915, and probably the first book by a professional psychologist presenting and endorsing Freud's theory. Holt did not accept all of Freud's ideas but selected only those which fitted into his own theoretical scheme, consisting of a combination of both behavioristic and dynamic elements.

The influence of Freudian theories and the penetration of psychoanalytic concepts into American psychology steadily increased. Surveys made in the 1940's and 1950's showed that Freud was the most quoted author in all areas of psychology—with the exception of physiological psychology and intelligence—and that his name was at the head of the lists of persons named by American psychologists as their major influences. Obviously, this does not mean that Freud's influence extended to all psychologists with the same strength. The opinions of American psychologists varied widely, ranging from favorable to hostile, and in individual cases changing from unfavorable to favorable, or vice versa. In general, however, these opinions concur in one respect, namely, that psychoanalysis was a significant development for psychology. But with respect to the value of psychoanalysis as a general psychological theory or to the validity of specific psychoanalytic concepts, opinions differed. While few rejected psychoanalysis in its entirety, few embraced it unequivocally. The prevailing attitude in America was eclectic—accepting some ideas, rejecting others. Certain psychoanalytic concepts, nevertheless, have gradually gained universal approval, even though other aspects of psychoanalysis were rejected. Among the accepted were, for instance, the importance of the unconscious elements in motivation; the crucial role of childhood experiences, sexual or otherwise, in the formation of personality and adaptive behavior; operation of various defense mechanisms, such as repression, displacement, rationalization, and sublimation. Not all of the accepted psychoanalytic concepts were of Freudian origin; they also came from other psychoanalytic writers. Adler's inferiority feeling is one of such generally accepted concepts. These concepts were eventually assimilated by psychology; they seeped into textbooks, especially those of abnormal psychology; and finally they have become part and parcel of American psychological thinking. This is a tangible and indisputable measure of the Freudian influence.

Other clear expressions of Freud's influence have been strong interests in motivation, personality, and in the theory and practice of psychotherapy —all evident in the last few decades. Other theoretical and experimental trends concerned with purposive and dynamic aspects of behavior, although not of Freudian inspiration, have been greatly reinforced by psychoanalytic thought. Child psychology has also greatly benefited by the stimulation of psychoanalytic theory. Moreover, psychoanalysis contributed to the acceleration of the professionalization of psychology in this country. From the point of view of research, both clinical and experimental, psychoanalytic concepts inspired many investigations. The research of E. C. Tolman, R. R. Sears, and the Yale group of experimental psychologists, headed by John Dollard and N. E. Miller, to cite just a few, exemplifies the effect of the psychoanalytic concepts in the field of experimental psychology. These concepts served as hypothetical constructs, which were subjected subsequently to experimental study and verification.

Evaluation.   In 1925, Freud concluded his autobiography with this statement:

> Looking back, then, over the patchwork of my life's labours, I can say that I have made many beginnings and thrown out many suggestions. Something will come of them in the future, though I cannot myself tell whether it will be much or little. I can, however, express a hope that I have opened up a pathway for an important advance in our knowledge.

This statement sums up well the historical significance of Freud as a trail blazer. Freud opened up a new pathway to the knowledge of human nature by demonstrating—convincingly and artfully—the importance of the unconscious processes, of sex, and of childhood experiences to the understanding of human motivation and personality characteristics. It is true that many of Freud's specific concepts and theories on the operation of these factors in motivation and personality development have been seriously challenged, undermined, or rejected—even by those who admired him most and understood him best. Moreover, it must be recognized that Freud's methods have seldom survived in the precise form conceived by him. But, historically speaking, Freud's pointing to the unconscious roots of human behavior and initiating their study have proved an enriching contribution both to general psychology and to psychiatry. Specifically, Freud deserves the credit for demonstrating the significance of sex in normal and abnormal behavior and thus for pointing up the need for the psychological study of sex.

It is unlikely that any single theory will ever be so all-inclusive as to explain the totality of human nature and to provide all the keys to the complexity of human behavior—and the Freudian theory is no exception. Like other theories, Freud's theory ought to be viewed as one more effort —a very significant one as judged from historical perspective—to shed light on the complicated human problem and one more approach to its study. D. Shakow and D. Rapaport, in their book *The Influence of Freud on American Psychology* (1964), expressed it in these words:

> What use are *psychologists*—all those professionally involved with human nature— to make of Freudian thinking? The answer lies essentially in the recognition that Freudian thinking is part of man's conquest of nature—the understanding of human nature. Psychoanalysis . . . is part of the heritage which great men provide. As the discipline most directly involved, it is up to psychology to understand, develop, and build on this heritage, making the changes that imagination coupled with careful observation and experiment indicate.

OTHER ANALYTICAL THEORIES

Several other analytical orientations developed both during Freud's life and after. Some of them, building on Freud's fundamental concepts, sought to develop Freud's theories further or to complement them. Others deviated considerably from Freudian theory or methods. Still other psychoanalysts, after initial friendship and collaboration with Freud, broke with him and even attacked his system, giving rise to new analytical schools. In the last category were Carl G. Jung, one of Freud's severest critics, and Alfred Adler, one of the bitterest enemies of Freud. Jung became attracted to Freud's theories of neuroses while working as a young psychiatrist at the Burghölzli Psychiatric Clinic. He corresponded with Freud and then went to visit him at Vienna in 1907. Together they founded the International Psychoanalytical Association in 1910, with Jung as its first president. Three and a half years later Jung left Freud because he could not accept Freud's sexual theory of libido and Freud could not agree with Jung's theory of the collective unconscious. Jung went his own way and developed a system, known as *analytical psychology*. Adler, born in a suburb of Vienna, studied medicine at the Vienna University, as did Freud, and obtained his M.D. in 1895. He became associated with Freud and the psychoanalytic movement in 1902. But his views clashed with those of the master, and the two parted in 1911. Adler formed his own system and movement, known as *individual psychology*. We shall outline the main features of the Jungian and Adlerian systems and shall also mention later a few other analytical orientations, which became known and found followers in America.

Carl Gustav Jung (1875-1961). In the early phase of his career, and before he joined Freud, Jung began research from which developed the word association test. This test, familiar to psychologists, consisted of the presentation of significant stimulus words to which the subject responded with any word as quickly as possible. Jung found this test useful in detecting conscious lies and conscious or unconscious mental complexes. Among the "complex indicators" operating during the test, Jung listed: long reaction time, repetition or misunderstanding of the stimulus word, behavioral reactions, and change in the electric resistance of the skin. Another of Jung's early contributions to psychology, which stirred up much interest and provoked an enormous amount of research, was the concept of introversion and extroversion. To the distress of Jung, some of the subsequent research on the extrovert-introvert typology often departed from the basic Jungian concept or misinterpreted its meaning. Most of Jung's attention and boundless energy in later years was turned to other fields, principally to the study of religion and history of alchemy. The study of these subjects was considered by him the best approach to the understanding of the human *psyche*. Understanding the "depths and heights of our psychic nature," as Jung expressed it, became the dominant passion of his life.

The most characteristic concept of Jung's psychology is his notion of the *collective unconscious*. Like Freud, Jung held that human motivation is founded in the unconscious. But in opposition to Freud, he distinguished two layers or levels of this unconscious foundation. According to Jung, in every man, besides his individual unconscious—consisting of personal repressions—there is also a race or group unconsicous—that is, an unconscious shared by a group or a whole race. This collective unconscious "conceals an untold abundance of images which have accumulated over millions of years of living development and become fixed in the organism." In the collective unconscious are deposited *archetypes*, that is, instinctual forms, which—in a quasi-Lamarckian sense—represent the inherited behavior potentials. Discussing the concept of the archetypes in 1957, Jung observed that this concept "has been frequently misunderstood as denoting inherited patterns of thought or as a kind of philosophical speculation." Archetypes, he said, "belong to the realm of the activities of the instincts and in that sense they represent inherited forms of psychic behaviour." In other words, archetypes determine and express themselves in our psychological functioning and behavior patterns in a way similar to that of the biological instincts in animals. Collective unconscious and its archetypes cannot be a subject of direct observation. They can be reached only through symbols appearing in dreams, fantasies, and also in the hallucinations and delusions of psychotics. They can be clarified most effectively through the study of myths, religions, creative works, and the history of alchemy.

Medieval alchemy—the striving for the discovery of the secret of transforming base elements into the noble element, gold—symbolizes and dramatizes, Jung held, the striving of the psyche to unify its base (unconscious) and the noble (conscious) elements. This is the essential process of the psyche, which Jung called *individuation*. He viewed this process of individuation as an innate striving for "selfhood" or "self-realization." Through this process of striving, embedded in the human psyche, all man's potentialities are brought to fruition and stable "psychic wholeness" is established. Since neuroses, in his view, were disturbances of individuation, Jung's psychotherapy was focused on rectifying the natural course of this process. Jung practiced his therapy for over 40 years, during which time he attracted people from all parts of the world. Many people of international renown came to him to seek help and advice.

The voluminous writings of Jung are among the most difficult to comprehend. Erudite, philosophical, abstract, sometimes almost mystical, they met with greater success in literary and philosophical circles than among academic psychologists. A number of outstanding contemporary thinkers have acknowledged their debt to Jung. Some psychologists have criticized Jung's method as unscientific and his conclusions as mere speculations. But Jung insisted that he proceeded from empirical facts which anybody can verify and that his method is more effective in understanding "the infinite variety and mobility of individual psychic life" than the so-called scientific methods of academic psychology. Despite the various objections levelled at Jung and the resistance to his theories, there have been signs of increased interest in Jung in America in recent years.

Alfred Adler (1870-1937). In several respects, Adler represents a sharp contrast to both Freud and Jung. Unlike Freud, Adler de-emphasized sex in personality dynamics and stressed man's orientation towards the future, instead of his early past, as critical in the formation of personality. Moreover, he advocated the notion of the unity of the self, instead of the fractionation of the self in terms of the id-ego-superego triad. He also took greater cognizance than Freud of man's relation to society and the role of social forces in motivation. Compared to Jung's, Adler's writings were more intelligible and his arguments easier to follow. In his works Adler appealed to everyday experiences and common sense. He made an ostensible effort to reach and win wide circles rather than a small group of the intellectual elite. He visited America for the first time in 1926. This visit was followed by many others. He lectured at Columbia in 1927, wrote an article on his theories for Murchison's *Psychologies of 1930*, and in 1932 became professor of medical psychology at Long Island University, the first such appointment in the United States. He made America his permanent home in 1934. He died while on a lecture tour in Scotland in 1937. His daughter, Alexandra Adler, and his son Kurt Adler, a psychiatrist, have carried on their father's work in this country.

None of the numerous books of Adler contains a systematic exposition of his theories. His writings deal with a diversity of subjects which appealed at various times to his active mind. His natural inclination was not so much to build a coherent conceptual system as to provide a body of knowledge of immediate practical value. In the first place Adler was not a theorist—like Freud—but a therapist concerned with people and their individual psychological problems. He has been criticized for neglecting to deal with some important aspects of personality and for not going deeply enough into problems which he did discuss. However, several of Adler's concepts won wide acceptance, some of them having been adopted by clinical psychology. Notable among these are the feeling of inferiority and insecurity; compensation and overcompensation; striving for superiority and self-assertion; and style of life.

The foundation of Adler's psychology, as he himself said in 1930, was "the belief that *all psychical phenomena originate in the particular creative force of the individual and are expressions of his personality.*" This creative force in man stems from his feeling of inferiority, which leads to the compensatory striving for superiority. The feeling of inferiority arises from the realization of inferiority of body organs and of their inadequacy to cope with nature. This was Adler's thesis, expressed in his first major work, *Studie über Minderwertigkeit der Organe und die seelische Kompensation* ("A Study of Organic Inferiority and Its Psychical Compensation," 1907). This view, accepted by Freud as a contribution to psychoanalytic thought, was to become the cornerstone of Adler's individual psychology, a rival system to that of Freudian psychoanalysis.

According to Adler, the child, seeking to overcome his inferiority feeling and to satisfy his striving for self-assertion during the first five years of life, gradually develops his *style of life* that subsequently guides his thoughts and actions throughout life. The striving for superiority and the endeavors to overcome inferiority feelings result either in a successful compensation, in overcompensation, or in a retreat into illness. Successful compensation is a wholesome reaction which is reflected in satisfactory adjustment to life's three main aspects: society, work, and sex. Overcompensation—an exaggerated reaction to inferiority feeling, exemplified by the unusual and extraordinary accomplishments of great men reacting to some organic defects—may lead to various forms of maladjustment. Sometimes, an individual, in his attempt to free himself from the feeling of inferiority, develops a neurosis—either as a means of escape from situations that might disclose his particular inferiority or as a device of dominating others by gaining their sympathy or protection. Because of the stress in our civilization on masculinity and identification of strength and power with masculinity, on the one hand, and underestimation of femininity and feminine role in society on the other, women may acquire a strong feeling of inferiority and react to it by "will to conquer all difficulties of life in the masculine fashion." This reaction Adler called the *masculine protest* of women.

The main objective of Adlerian psychotherapy is to detect the individual's style of life. This is done through the study of his family relations in childhood, of his likes and dislikes, occupations, games and habits, as well as through dream analysis. The therapist-patient relation in the Adlerian therapy is more direct and personal than in the Freudian type of psychoanalysis. The treatment does not require a couch, a prolonged delving into the remote past of the patient, or transferences, and it is less time consuming. The Adlerian psychotherapy has been found to be particularly helpful with children. Several Adlerian clinics for the treatment of children, as well as adults, were established both here and in Europe.

Other Developments. To complete our review a few other notable derivatives of psychoanalysis will be mentioned, and some concluding remarks will be made. Our intention in citing these other psychoanalytic trends is not so much to depict their features and differences as to underscore the fact of evolution and proliferation of psychoanalytic thought. The various neo-Freudian and post-Freudian schools, as they have been called, were usually concerned with both the psychoanalytic theory and with therapy. They aimed at complementing or modifying some aspects of psychoanalytic theory or at perfecting therapeutic techniques to increase their effectiveness and scope. The evolution of psychoanalytic thought is particularly notable in two areas: in the psychology of the ego and in the study of the effect of environmental—that is, social, cultural, and economic—factors on the development of personality, both normal and abnormal.

Otto Rank (1884-1939) was among the early members of the psychoanalytic movement, who, like Jung and Adler, rebelled against Freud's views and proclaimed their own. Rank's innovation was the concept of *birth trauma*—that is the psychological consequences of the separation of the child from the mother's womb. On this concept Rank based his interpretation of anxiety—the "separation anxiety." His novel therapeutic techniques, which in structure and aims differed radically from classic psychoanalysis, and which he preferred to call simply psychotherapy, were also based on this concept. Even though therapists may not accept Rank's birth trauma theory, they find his clinical observations about the "separation anxiety" useful.

Among the second generation of psychoanalysts who sought to develop further some aspects of the Freudian theory was *Heinz Hartmann* (b. 1894). In 1939 he published a work dealing with ego psychology, *Ich-Psychologie und Anpassungsproblem* ("Ego Psychology and the Problem of Adaptation," 1958). This work was well received by Anna Freud and exerted influence in Europe and America. Further exploration of the problem of the ego appeared well justified in view of the fluctuation of Freud's thought on the role of the ego and his own warning not to draw sharp dividing lines between ego, superego, and id, but rather to allow "what we have separated to merge again." Today ego psychology is one of the central problems of the psychoanalytical theory. In addition to Anna Freud's work, *The Ego and the Mechanisms of Defense* (1946), and to Hartmann's writings, important contributions to ego psychology were made by *Ernst Kris* (1901-1957), *David Rapaport* (1911-1961), and *Erik Erikson* (b. 1902). Rapaport, well known for his book *Organization and Pathology of Thought* (1951), is especially notable for his contribution to greater rapprochement between psychoanalysis and academic psychology.

Another aspect which drew special attention of several psychoanalysts was the problem of interpersonal relations and social factors. One of the prominent representatives of this trend in America was *Karen Horney*

(1885-1953). She practiced psychoanalysis as an orthodox Freudian in Berlin for 15 years and taught at the Berlin Psychoanalytic Institute. In the United States, where she spent the last 20 years of her life, she was first associated with the Chicago, and then with the New York Psychoanalytic Institute. Eventually she moved away from Freudian orthodoxy, left the Institute, and formed her own group, known as the American Institute of Psychoanalysis. Karen Horney challenged the biological assumption of Freudian theory and stressed instead the social factors in the development of neurosis. The very concept of neurosis, she maintained, is closely related to social and cultural background. Behavior, considered neurotic in one culture, may be normal in another. There are, however, two distinct features shared by all neurotics: rigidity of reactivity—that is, inability to adapt adequately to changes in the environment—and discrepancy between the individual's potentialities and accomplishments. This discrepancy is most acutely reflected at the level of the self, when conflict arises between the idealized self-image and the real self. This conflict is the focal point of the neurosis. Therefore, in the therapy of the neuroses, it is necessary to understand not only the patient's past experiences, but also his present situation in terms of his cultural background. Karen Horney's books, written for the most part for the layman, gained popularity in America. In memory of Karen Horney a special type of clinic was founded in New York in 1955 and named *Karen Horney Clinic*. Its idea was to provide psychoanalytic treatment, based on Horney's principles, to a large number of people at low cost by a staff of qualified analysts.

Another former Freudian who accorded great significance to social factors has been *Erich Fromm* (b. 1900), a practicing lay psychoanalyst associated with the William Alanson White Institute in New York. For him the fundamental problem of psychology is man's relation to the world. Unable to explain the universe and his own existence in it, and confronted with his existential aloneness, man feels helpless. Oppressed by this feeling, some men (neurotic) try to escape from themselves and their freedom by establishing relations with the world and people that are distorted because of their attempts to deny this aloneness. In his book, *Man For Himself* (1947), Fromm discusses the mechanisms by which man has attempted to satisfy his need for relatedness in various epochs of cultural and social history. Fromm described four different forms of these mechanisms—or, as he called them, dynamic *orientations* of personality—which characterize man's relations. The most recent of these orientations is *marketing*—in Fromm's terminology—which is the product of the capitalistic structure of society. In this orientation personality qualities are only as good as they are useful—or, we may say, as they are "marketable." This orientation deepens man's sense of emptiness and futility according to Fromm.

Associated with the William Alanson White Foundation—as its founder, its president for ten years, and as an influential member—was a Washington psychiatrist, *Harry Stack Sullivan* (1892-1949). He, too, paid much attention to social factors and man's adaptability to environment. Since he believed that behavior patterns of individuals result from the interpersonal relationships—as they develop from infancy to adulthood—his theory is called *interpersonal*. He conceived of schizophrenia as a disturbance in interpersonal relations. Sullivan analyzed the various aspects and the psychological effects of interpersonal relations such as those of the child to his mother, his home, his peers, his teachers. In therapy the interpersonal relationship of the therapist and the patient is also an essential factor. The therapist, to be successful, must develop empathy toward his patient and become emotionally involved in his patient's problems. Sullivan's therapeutic method focused on concrete human transactions, rather than on dreams and other classic psychoanalytic devices. As such, this method is viewed by some therapists as more appropriate in helping the severely disturbed. Sullivan is thus credited with making psychotherapy available to the severely disturbed, when it had been all but dismissed for such cases by classic psychoanalysis.

Abram Kardiner (b. 1891) concentrated on the effect of cultural factors on personality development. He made a cross-cultural study of child-rearing practices and their influence in shaping personality. A former professor of clinical psychiatry and director of the Psychoanalytic Clinic at Columbia University, he is now research professor at Emory University. His major book is *The Individual and His Society: The Psychodynamics of Primitive Organization* (1939).

Among psychologists who contributed to the interpretation and evaluation of psychoanalytic thought in America have been *Ruth Munroe* (1903-1963), the author of the useful work, *Schools of Psychoanalytic Thought* (1955); and *Robert W. White* (b. 1904), a professor of clinical psychology at Harvard since 1958. As an influential teacher of psychoanalysis and psychiatry, *Clara Thompson* (1893-1958) deserves notice. She received her M.D. from Johns Hopkins in 1920. Trained in psychoanalysis by S. Ferenczi, she was later associated for many years with H. S. Sullivan and E. Fromm. She taught at various universities and institutions.

Conclusion. As we have seen, psychoanalysis during the 70 years of its existence has undergone a substantial metamorphosis. No other school preserved its identity for such a long period and evolved in so many directions as psychoanalysis. Nor had any school generated so many new strands. Even Freud's own theory in his own hands changed considerably between 1895, the publication date of *Studies on Hysteria*, and 1926, the date of *Inhibition, Symptom and Anxiety*, his last significant clinical work. In the hands of his disciples it has undergone even greater transformation. It has split into groups. They are usually broadly classified into "orthodox" Freudians and neo-Freudians. The neo-Freudians are characterized by their willingness to incorporate knowledge from all social sciences into psychoanalysis, by readiness to revise psychoanalytic concepts and techniques in the light of current research, and by their stress on ego psychology. However, because of the interaction of various influences on psycho-

HIGHLIGHTS IN THE HISTORY OF PSYCHOANALYSIS

1856   Freud born.

1885   Freud's visit to France (Paris).

1889   Freud's second visit to France (Nancy).

1894   William James refers to an article by Breuer and Freud.

1895   *Studies on Hysteria* published by Breuer and Freud.

1908   First International Psychoanalytical Congress (Salzburg, Austria).
       A.A. Brill visits Freud.

1909   Freud's visit to America. Lectures at Clark University.
       First English translation of Freud's selected works.

1910   Founding of the International Psychoanalytic Association.
       James J. Putnam endorses psychoanalysis in a paper before the American Neurological
       Association.

1911   Foundation of New York Psychoanalytic Society by A.A. Brill.
       Foundation of American Psychoanalytic Association by Ernest Jones.
       Alfred Adler parts with Freud.

1912   First book on psychoanalysis in English by E. Jones.

1913   Carl G. Jung breaks off with Freud.

1923   Freud's first operation for cancer.

1925   Freud publishes his autobiography.

1931   New York Psychoanalytic Institute founded.

1937   Death of Adler.

1939   Death of Freud.

1950   Anna Freud visits America and lectures in several cities.

1961   Death of Jung.

PSYCHOANALYTIC MOVEMENT

Members of the "Committee," initiated in 1912, organized in 1919: Sigmund Freud
(1856–1939), Karl Abraham (1877–1925), Max Eitingon (1881–1943), Sandor Ferenczi
(1873–1933), Ernest Jones (1879–1958), Otto Rank (1884–1939), Hanns Sachs (1881–1947).

REVISIONISTS	FREUDIANS	SECESSIONISTS
Neo-Freudians	Anna Freud (b. 1895)	Carl Jung (1875–1961) (analytical psychology)
Emphasis on social and cultural factors in personality development: Karen Horney (1885–1953) Erich Fromm (b. 1900) Harry Stack Sullivan (1892–1949) Abram Kardiner (b. 1891)	Melanie Klein (1882–1960) Heinz Hartmann (b. 1894) (ego psychology)	Alfred Adler (1870–1937) (individual psychology) Otto Rank (1884–1939) (birth trauma)

analytic thought, the criteria of identification of various groups have become difficult to define. The comment on this subject by Woodworth and Sheehan in their *Contemporary Schools of Psychology* (1964) is worth citing:

> It is significant that it is becoming more and more difficult to draw a firm line of demarcation between orthodox or "classical" Freudianism and the movements which may or may not be regarded as schismatic. It would appear that in this area as well as in current learning theory the rigid boundaries of the past have become more permeable, allowing a chance for greater diffusion of ideas that have proved of value. Any theory—unless it be perfect—must allow such assimilation to take place. Without alteration or repair, by virtue of its own internal consistency it may be able to stand by itself, but like great-grandmother's wedding gown, it will go more and more out of fashion and will no longer fit the figure of the modern age. Keeping this in mind we can see that neo-Freudians and "neo-classical Freudians," however they may disagree with Freud or with one another, are alike in representing the harvest of a great man's thought, and in assuring its preservation by adaptation rather than by embalming.

The continuous metamorphosis of psychoanalysis can be largely explained in terms of the cultural changes that have taken place in the twentieth century. As a movement closely related to its cultural milieu, it could not but react to new discoveries in sociology, anthropology, psychology, and neurophysiology. Clara Thompson described the effect of multiple and complex cultural changes in her *Psychoanalysis: Evolution and Development* (1950) in these words:

> It is not unimportant that analysis in its short life has lived through momentous changes in European culture. Beginning in the Victorian era it has seen emancipation of women, momentous economic changes, wars, unemployment and depression, and a very great weakening of the power of religion. These changes have produced new problems for man and some of the older ones have become less important. The difficulties attendant on repressed sexuality were a more prevalent preoccupation in the 1890's than they are today.

To the effect of the changes in European culture, one must add the impact of the socioeconomic pattern of the United States, to which many of the psychoanalytical thinkers, educated in Europe in the orbit of Freud's personality, were subjected. This impact has also left an imprint on their thought and at least partly accounts for its direction.

REFERENCES

Literature on psychoanalysis is more extensive than on other psychological schools. The references have been selected as the most significant from the historical viewpoint or the most relevant to the topics covered in this chapter.

FREUD AND THE PSYCHOANALYTIC MOVEMENT
The most extensive and authoritative biography of Freud is:

Jones, E. *The life and work of Sigmund Freud.* New York: Basic Books, 1953–1957. 3 vols.

There is an abridgment of this work in one volume published by Doubleday.
Freud's autobiography:

Freud, S. *An autobiographical study.* (Authorized translation by J. Strachey) New York: Norton,

1963. (First German ed., 1925.)

Complete edition of his original works:

Gesammelte Werke. Chronologisch geordnet. London: Imago, 1940–1952. 18 vols.

Edition of his works in English translation:

The standard edition of the complete psychological works of Sigmund Freud. (Translated and edited by J. Strachey) London: Hogarth Press and The Institute of Psychoanalysis, 1953. 24 vols.

Selected writings. New York: International Psychoanalytical Library, 1924–1925, 1950. 5 vols.

Collected papers. London: Hogarth Press and The Institute of Psychoanalysis, 1924–1950. 5 vols. First American edition: New York: Basic Books, 1959. 5 vols.

The basic writings of Sigmund Freud. (Translated and edited by A. A. Brill) New York: Random House, 1938.

A concise introduction to psychoanalysis, especially recommended for its clarity and readability, is:

Hall, C. S. *A primer of Freudian psychology.* Cleveland: World Publishing, 1954. Available in paperbound edition as a Mentor Book.

A survey of various psychoanalytic theories:

Munroe, Ruth L. *Schools of psychoanalytic thought.* New York: Dryden Press, 1955.

For a systematic presentation of major psychoanalytic theories of personality:

Hall, C. S., & Lindzey, G. *Theories of personality.* New York: Wiley, 1957.

For history of psychoanalysis in America:

Oberndorf, C. P. *A history of psychoanalysis in America.* New York: Grune & Stratton, 1953. In paperbound edition: Harper Torchbook, 1964.

A thorough study of the influence of Freud on American psychology:

Shakow, D., & Rapaport, D. *The influence of Freud on American psychology.* New York: International Univer. Press, 1964. (*Psychological Issues.* Vol. IV, No. 1. Monograph 13).

Complete bibliographical lists of psychoanalytic literature:

Rickman, J. *Index psychoanalyticus, 1893–1926.* London: Hogarth Press, 1928.

Grinstein, A. (Ed.) *The index of psychoanalytic writings.* New York: International Univer. Press, 1956–1966. 9 vols. This is a complete listing of psychoanalytic literature in 21 languages from its inception through 1960.

The Yearbook of Psychoanalysis. New York: International Univer. Press. Appearing since 1945 under the editorship of Sandor Lorand and others.

The annual survey of psychoanalysis. New York: International Univer. Press. Vol. 1, 1950. Vol. 8 appeared in 1964 under the editorship of J. Frosch and N. Ross.

Allers, R. *The successful error.* New York: Sheed & Ward, 1940.

Arlow, J. A. & Brenner, C. *Psychoanalytic concepts and the structural theory.* New York International Univer. Press, 1964.

Dalbiez, R. *Psychoanalytical method and the doctrine of Freud.* (Trans. by T. F. Lindsay) New York: Longmans, 1941. 2 vols.

Bailey, P. The great psychiatric revolution. *Amer. J. Psychiat.,* 1956, *113,* 387–406.

Alexander, F., & Ross, Helen (Eds.) *The impact of Freudian psychiatry.* Chicago: Chicago Univer. Press, 1952.

Barclay, J. R. Franz Brentano and Sigmund Freud. *J. Existentialism,* 1964, *5,* 1–36.

Bruner, J. S. Freud and the image of man. *Amer. Psychologist,* 1956, *11,* 463–466.

Burnham, J. C. The beginnings of psychoanalysis in the United States. *Amer. Imago,* 1956, *13,* 65–68.

Burnham, J. C. Sigmund Freud and G. Stanley Hall: exchange of letters. *Psychoanal. Quart.,* 1960, *29,* 307–316.

Choisy, Maryse. *Sigmund Freud: a new appraisal.* New York: Philosophical Library, 1963.

Freud, M. *Sigmund Freud: man and father.* New York: Vanguard Press, 1958.

Heidbreder, Edna. Freud and psychology. *Psychol. Rev.,* 1940, *47,* 185–195.

Jahoda, Marie. Some notes on the influence of psychoanalytic ideas on American psychology. *Human Relations,* 1963, *16,* 111–129.

Klein, D. B. Psychology and Freud: an historico-critical appraisal. *Psychol. Rev.,* 1933, *40,* 440–456.

Nelson, B. (Ed.) *Freud and the 20th century.* New York: Meridian, 1957.

Nuttin, J. *Psychoanalysis and personality.* New York: New American Library, 1962.

Park, D. G. Freudian influence on academic psychology. *Psychol. Rev.,* 1931, *38,* 73–86.

Skinner, B. F. Critique of psychoanalytic concepts and theories. *Sci. Monthly,* 1954, *79,* 300–305.

Stendler, C. B. New ideas for old: how Freudism was received in the United States from 1900 to 1925. *J. educ. Psychol.,* 1947, *38,* 193–206.

Stoodley, B. H. *The concepts of Sigmund Freud.* Glencoe, Ill.: The Free Press, 1959.

Thompson, Clara. *Psychoanalysis: evolution and development.* New York: Nelson, 1950.

Thurstone, L. L. Influence of Freudism on theoretical psychology. *Psychol. Rev.*, 1924, *31*, 175–183.

Walker, N. A new Copernicus? In B. Nelson (Ed.), *Freud and the 20th century.* New York: Meridian, 1957. Pp. 22–30.

JUNG

A complete collected edition of Jung's works in English translation has been undertaken in America by the Bollingen Foundation. Some of the works, previously published, have been revised textually and newly translated. The edition, when completed, will consist of 20 volumes. Most of them have already appeared. Publishers: New York: Pantheon Press; London: Routledge and Kegan Paul.

There are a number of selections of Jung's writings. Among them in paperbound editions:

Psychological reflections. Selected and edited by Jolande Jacobi. New York: Harper, 1953.

Psyche and symbol. Edited by Violet S. de Laszlo. Garden City, N.Y.: Doubleday, 1958.

Douglas, W. Carl Gustav Jung: 1875–1961. *Amer. J. Psychol.*, 1961, *74*, 639–641.

Dry, A. M. *The psychology of Jung: a critical interpretation.* New York: Wiley, 1961.

Evans, R. I. *Conversations with Carl Jung.* Princeton, N. J.: Van Nostrand, 1964.

Fordham, Frieda. *An introduction to Jung's psychology.* (New ed.) Baltimore, Md.: Penguin, 1959.

Jacobi, Jolande. *The psychology of C. G. Jung.* (6th rev. ed.) New Haven: Yale Univer. Press, 1962.

New York Association for Analytical Psychology. *Carl Gustav Jung: 1875–1961. A memorial meeting: New York, December 1, 1961.* New York: Analytical Psychology Club of New York, 1962.

Selesnick, S. T. C. G. Jung's contributions to psychoanalysis. *Amer. J. Psychiat.*, 1963, *120*, 350–356.

ADLER

Adler, A. Individual psychology. In C. Murchison (Ed.), *Psychologies of 1930.* Worcester, Mass.: Clark Univer. Press, 1930. Pp. 395–405.

Ansbacher, H. L., & Ansbacher, Rowena (Eds.) *The individual psychology of Alfred Adler.* New York: Basic Books, 1956.

Orgler, Hertha. *Alfred Adler: The man and his work.* New York: Putnam, 1965.

OTHER PSYCHOANALYTIC THEORIES AND AUTHORS

Alexander, F., & Ross, H. (Eds.) *20 years of psychoanalysis: a symposium in celebration of the twentieth anniversary of the Chicago Institute for Psychoanalysis.* New York: Norton, 1953.

Brown, J. A. C. *Freud and the post-Freudians.* Baltimore: Penguin, 1961.

Freud, Anna. *The ego and the mechanisms of defense.* New York: International Univer. Press, 1946.

Hartmann, H. *Essays on ego psychology: selected problems in psychoanalytic theory.* New York: International Univer. Press, 1964.

Horney, Karen. *The collected works of Karen Horney.* New York: Norton, 1963. 2 vols.

Rapaport, D. Structure of psychoanalytic theory. In S. Koch (Ed.), *Psychology: a study of a science.* Vol. 3. *Formulations of the person and the social context.* New York: McGraw-Hill, 1959. Pp. 55–183.

Ruitenbeek, H. M. (Ed.) *Psychoanalysis and contemporary American culture.* New York: Dell, 1964.

Salzman, L., & Masserman, J. H. (Eds.) *Modern concepts of psychoanalysis.* New York: Philosophical Library, 1962.

Segal, Hanna. *Introduction to the work of Melanie Klein.* New York: Basic Books, 1964.

21

Phenomenological Psychology

IN THE FIRST HALF OF THE TWENTIETH CENTURY two new and original philosophical movements appeared: first, phenomenology and, later, the second—closely related to phenomenology historically and conceptually— existentialism. Developing and spreading rapidly, these movements belong now to the most influential philosophies of this century. Their influence transcended philosophy to fields such as literature, art, sociology, law, anthropology, theology, and notably psychology and psychiatry. Their effect on continental European psychological thought manifested itself in the form of a trend which has been called phenomenological, existential, or phenomenological-existential. The Anglo-American world and its psychology remained indifferent to the phenomenological and existential movements for some time. In the late 1940's, however, phenomenological and existential philosophy began to attract the attention of American psychologists. Gradually the phenomenological-existential approach in psychology aroused wider interest. By the end of the 1950's it had won so much support that some designated it as the "third force in American psychology," in addition to the two established forces, namely, behaviorism and psychoanalysis. Publications and organized discussion on phenomenology and existentialism have reflected this increased interest. In 1959, at the annual convention of the American Psychological Association in Cincinnati, the first American symposium on existential psychology was held. Similar symposia followed in subsequent years. In 1963 a special symposium was organized at Rice University under the title "Behaviorism and Phenomenology: Contrasting Bases for Modern Psychology." This meeting signaled that the phenomenological approach had sufficient importance to be confronted with behaviorism. Since this new phenomenological-existential trend has been of great consequence for psychology on the Continent and, recently has become of interest in America, students of psychology will want to understand its meaning and historical development. This is the main reason why more attention is devoted in this part of the present volume to the phenomenological and existential movements than to other psychological schools and systems. There are several books on the latter, while there is little systematic information on the former movements in current psychological textbooks. Some time ago David Katz, a prominent European psychologist, whose contributions will be discussed later in this chapter, said that "comprehension of contemporary psychology necessitates an understanding of the phenomenological method." The present chapter will attempt to explain this method and the concepts associated with it. The next chapter will deal with existential psychology. But as such movements become intelligible only when traced to their theoretical foundations, a brief exposition of these foundations will serve as a preamble to both chapters.

PHENOMENOLOGY AS PHILOSOPHY

The etymology of the term *phenomenology* derives from the Greek words *phenomenon* (plural, *phenomena*) and *logos*. *Phenomenon* literally means appearance, that is, that which shows itself. In psychology, phenomena are commonly defined as data of experience which can be observed and described by the experiencing subject at a given time. In philosophy this word assumed a variety of meanings. In general, however, phenomena meant appearances of things as contrasted with things themselves. Kant made this contrast a cornerstone of his philosophy, when he taught that our mind cannot ever know the thing in itself, or the *noumenon*, as he expressed it, but only as it appears to us or the *phenomenon*. The theory, which states that our knowledge is restricted only to appearances of things or to phenomena, is called *phenomenalism*. The latter is not to be confused with phenomenology.

The term *phenomenology* was coined in the middle of the eighteenth century. But when Edmund Husserl used it at the beginning of the twentieth century, he gave it his own definition. For him, phenomenology was a science of phenomena, that is, of all the data of consciousness. Husserl was the founder and most prominent exponent of phenomenology. But it would be erroneous to identify all phenomenology exclusively with his philosophy, even as it would be equally wrong, for example, to confine psychoanalysis to the system of Freud. For, with the passage of time, various divergent orientations of phenomenology developed, some of which have gone beyond, or even contrary to, Husserl's thought. The diversity of phenomenological systems today renders a single general definition of phenomenological philosophy impossible. Phenomenology is not a school or doctrine in the sense of a body of definite tenets. It is more appropriate to designate it as a movement encompassing various doctrines around a common core. This common core of the movement, or the common denominator that unites the various systems and justifies the phenomenological designation, is its identical point of departure—the phenomenological method. Before describing this method, however, we must first acquaint ourselves with its eminent representative and proponent, Edmund Husserl.

Husserl's Life. Edmund Husserl (1859-1938) was born in Moravia, then part of the Austro-Hungarian empire, but now in Czechoslovakia. When he began his academic studies, his main interest lay in mathematics and the natural sciences. He went first to Leipzig, in 1876, where he attended the lectures of Wilhelm Wundt, the founder of experimental psychology. However, Wundt did not make any special impression on him. After two years Husserl went to Berlin, where he studied mathematics mainly, and then to Vienna, where he wrote a dissertation on a mathematical problem and received the Ph.D. degree in 1883. After serving briefly as an assistant in mathematics at the University of Berlin, he returned to Vienna in 1884 to study philosophy under Brentano. The latter was to influence Husserl in more ways than one. It was because of Brentano that Husserl chose philosophy as his life work. Moreover, it was Brentano's teaching that fertilized Husserl's mind and directed it to the development of phenomenology. Since Brentano's philosophical ideas were the seed of this new philosophy, Brentano is called the forerunner of the phenomenological movement. Husserl acknowledged his indebtedness to Brentano, referring to him as "my one and only teacher of philosophy." Brentano's personality had an equally strong effect on Husserl. Like his master, Husserl also felt that he had a mission to fulfill in his life. Eventually the two men parted intellectually, for Brentano frowned upon some of Husserl's ideas and perhaps failed to appreciate others; yet they remained friends. Their last meeting took place in Florence in 1907, when Brentano was 69 years old and blind. Husserl also studied with Brentano's student, Carl Stumpf, in Halle, and their relations were friendly too. In fact, Husserl dedicated his book, *Logische Untersuchungen* ("Logical Investigations," 1900), to Stumpf "in admiration and friendship."

Husserl's academic career in philosophy began at the University of Halle in 1887, when he became a Dozent after completing his qualifying or so-called habilitation thesis on the concept of number. He lectured there for 14 years. In 1901 he moved to Göttingen as an associate professor and remained there for 15 years, until 1916. His colleague at the University was the great pioneer of experimental psychology, Georg E. Müller, who had an active laboratory, as will be remembered, and whose students also attended Husserl's lectures. Among the Göttingen students Husserl found followers who formed a special group to discuss phenomenology. A similar group was organized at the University of Munich. At this early stage of the phenomenological movement, wide differences among the members of these groups already emerged. In 1916 Husserl was appointed full professor at the University of Freiburg in Breisgau, a post he held until his retirement in 1929. During this period and after his retirement, as well, he lectured on phenomenology at other universities—in London, Prague, Vienna, and Paris. His assistant in Freiburg was Martin Heidegger, who later became his successor in the chair. Husserl died in Freiburg, in 1938, at the age of 79. He was active to the end in developing his system. At the time of his death phenomenology had become a powerful movement, and Husserl won recognition as one of the keenest intellects and one of the most influential philosophers of the century.

Husserl's Major Works. The list of Husserl's works is not yet complete because there are still numerous unpublished manuscripts deposited in the specially founded Husserl Archives at the University of Louvain. His early work, *Philosophie der Arithmetik* ("The Philosophy of Arithmetic," 1891), was not yet explicitly concerned with phenomenology. The beginning of his phenomenology is to be found in the *Logische Untersuchungen*, in two volumes (1900-1901), which was revised and published in three volumes in 1913. The central theme of this work was the foundation of logic. In the book entitled *Ideen zu einer reinen Phänomenologie und phänomenologischen Philosophie* ("Ideas Concerning a Pure Phenomenology and Phenomenological Philosophy," 1913), he presented phenomenology as an objective method to be applied to all philosophy and science. *Vorlesungen zur Phänomenologie des inneren Zeitbewusstseins* ("Lectures on the Phenomenology of Inner Awareness of Time," 1928) is of particular interest to psychologists studying time perception. The book *Formale und transzendentale Logik* ("Formal and Transcendental Logic," 1929) and the posthumous *Erfahrung und Urteil* ("Experience and Judgment," 1939) marked the further development of Husserl's phenomenology. The last book published before his death contained his Paris lectures and appeared first in French as *Méditations cartésiennes* ("Cartesian Meditations," 1931). Several other volumes were published from his manuscripts after his death.

Husserl's Philosophy. In reviewing Husserl's philosophy we shall be selective and mention only features relevant to the understanding of phenomenological psychology. Therefore, this presentation will include: the basic assumptions of phenomenology; the essential characteristics of the phenomenological method; the concept of intentionality; and Husserl's views on psychology. Husserl's thought underwent continuous modifications. Historians of the phenomenological movement point to the difference between Husserl's early and later thought, particularly to his later novel conceptions which came to light only through posthumous publications of his manuscripts. One of these later concepts was the *Lebenswelt* (the life world, that is, the world of experience of everyday life), which has received considerable attention in contemporary phenomenological and existential writings.

One approach to understanding phenomenology is to view it with reference to the oldest and most fundamental problem of philosophy: What is the relationship between the objective reality existing outside the mind, and the thought which we have of it? How are these two worlds, the world of thought and the world of objective reality, to be reconciled? All philosophies attempt to answer this question. Phenomenology also made such an attempt. Its point of departure is the affirmation that (1) philosophical inquiry cannot begin with anything else but with phenomena of consciousness because they are the only givens accessible to us, the only material at our immediate disposal; (2) only phenomena can reveal to us what things, essentially, are. The latter proposition is grounded in the concept of intentionality, which will be explained later. Taking this stand, phenomenology avoids the subject-object dilemma and "the cleavage between subject and object," which, especially since Descartes, to use Rollo May's phrase, "has bedeviled Western thought and science." The only possible approach to the knowledge of things, according to Husserl, is through the exploration of human consciousness. Thus phenomenology is principally a *systematic* and *full* exploration of consciousness. The phenomena of consciousness are numerous and manifold: things, persons, events, experiences, memories, feelings, moods, thoughts, images, fantasies, mental constructs, and the like. Phenomenology enlists them all and explores them through a method especially adapted for this purpose, known as the phenomenological method. Husserl was not its inventor or the first philosopher to employ it. But he refined this method, specified its conditions and object, and raised it to a status of a fundamental philosophical procedure. The method became the keystone of his entire philosophical system. Through its use Husserl hoped to reform philosophy and to establish—and this was the guiding motive of Husserl's entire philosophical work—a rigorously scientific philosophy, which could provide a firm basis for all other sciences. Husserl's first step in this direction was to demonstrate the fallacy of *psychologism,* a theory which held that mathematics and logic are dependent on psychological laws. Husserl showed that logical laws are not psychological laws and are not contingent on psychological processes, but are self-evident, universal, and eternally true.

The Phenomenological Method. This method consists of examining whatever is found in consciousness, or in other words, the data or phenomena of consciousness. Its primary concern is not the act of consciousness, but the object of consciousness, that is, for instance, all that is perceived, imagined, doubted, or loved. The ultimate goal is to reach and grasp the essences of things appearing in consciousness. The method is practiced in a systematic way, proceeding through various steps or techniques. Spiegelberg in his *Phenomenological Movement* (1960) distinguishes seven separate steps in the phenomenological method. Not all of them are used by all phenomenologists. The most fundamental of them, used extensively also by psychologists, is the phenomenological description. According to Spiegelberg's interpretation and terminology, three phases of this technique can be differentiated: *phenomenological intuiting, analyzing,* and *describing.* Intuiting means an intense concentration on, or attentive internal gaze at, the phenomena; analyzing is finding the various constituents of the phenomena and their relationship; describing is an account of the intuited and analyzed phenomena in such a manner that they can be understood by others. Another step is called *Wesensschau,* which has been translated from German as *intuition of essences, insight into essences, experience* or *cognition of essences.* Spiegelberg prefers the term "intuiting" to avoid the vague and possibly mystical connotation of "intuition." Intuiting of essences is also called *eidetic intuiting.* The word *eidetic* comes from *eidos,* meaning essence, borrowed by Husserl from Plato. The function of this technique is to seize or apprehend the essences of things through the phenomena. This apprehension is accomplished usually by surveying a series of particular instances exemplifying something more general—as, for instance, surveying various shades of red or colored objects leads to the apprehension of redness or color. This procedure of getting to the essences themselves, Husserl called *eidetic reduction.*

The basic prerequisite for the successful practice of the phenomenological method is freeing oneself from any preconceptions or presuppositions. It is imperative that in the exploration of consciousness all biases, theories, beliefs, and habitual modes of thinking be suspended or "bracketed," that is, put between "brackets," as Husserl described this process, using an expression familiar in algebra. This suspension of all judgments Husserl called *epoché*, a Greek word meaning abstention. Only when *epoché* is accomplished can fruitful exploration of phenomena be expected, because only then are they not obscured or distorted by a person's individual idiosyncrasies. *Epoché* is similar in some respects to the Cartesian doubt, but differs from it in that it never ceases in the phenomenological exploration; it differs also in that the existence of things is not doubted but simply not considered. This latter characteristic of the *epoché*, that is, the suspension of judgment as to the existence or nonexistence of things, obtains ultimate reduction—the *transcendental reduction*, in which only the stream of pure subjective consciousness is revealed. The phenomena, completely purified, without even the admixture of existential elements, are now ready to be intuited, analyzed, and described. Since transcendental reduction was not sufficiently explained by Husserl, it lent itself to different interpretations and implications, and it is this aspect of Husserl's phenomenology, which created deviations from him and dissension among his followers.

The practice of phenomenological method is laborious and requires considerable training. In his *Ideas* Husserl stated: "That we should set aside all previous habits of thought, see through and break down the mental barriers which these habits have set along the horizons of our thinking . . . these are hard demands. . . . To move freely along this new way . . . to learn to see what stands before our eyes, to distinguish, to describe, calls . . . for exacting and laborious studies."

Intentionality. Paramount to the phenomenological theory is the notion of intentionality. The reasonableness of phenomenology's goal to get at things themselves through the study of consciousness, as well as its claim of the validity of the knowledge thus acquired, rest upon this notion. Husserl learned of intentionality from Brentano, who took it from scholastic philosophy and gave it a new interpretation.

The term *intentionality* comes from the Latin word *intentio* or *intendere*, the latter meaning "to stretch forth." The scholastics—especially Thomas Aquinas—taught that intellect, in the act of cognition of objects, "stretches forth" to the objects and draws them into itself, as it were. Thus the object is said to exist in the mind intentionally; mental phenomena, then, are always related to real objects. Presupposed in this scholastic notion of intentionality is the assertion of the real existence of the physical world. Brentano extended the concept of intentionality to all consciousness and spoke of *intentional inexistence* (in German *Inexistenz*), which meant existence in, or indwelling of the object in consciousness. For him, consciousness is intentional, that is, it always tends to something, has a rapport with the object. Husserl seized upon this concept and adapted it to his own thought. For him, as for other phenomenologists, consciousness is always consciousness of something. All the acts of consciousness are naturally related or point to something. There is no love without someone or something loved, no desire without something desired, no perception without something perceived, and the like. Knowing the contents of consciousness is knowing the object itself. Since the object can be accessible only in consciousness, the sole way to knowledge of things is the examination of consciousness, for in consciousness, as Maurice Merleau-Ponty said, the universe resides. The purpose of the phenomenological method is to make this examination effective so that we can arrive at the knowledge of things themselves without being entangled in solipsisms.

Husserl's Views on Psychology. The issue of psychology and the place to be assigned to psychology in the phenomenological system occupied Husserl seriously all his life. Psychology for him was an important discipline to which, he believed, phenomenology could and should contribute much, but from which it could also derive considerable benefit. The phenomenological method, Husserl recognized, need not be as radical in its reduction in psychological inquiry as in philosophical inquiry. Rather it ought to be adapted to the objectives of psychology. The goal of psychology, in his conception, is the study of consciousness in its meaningful structure and function. Phenomenological method would furnish a basis and orientation for this study. Experimentation would perform a useful function as an aid and complement to the phenomenological investigation. Such being his views, Husserl was opposed to the positivistic and mechanistic tendencies in psychology as he was to the other extreme, psychologism. Irreconcilable with Husserl's view also was the empiricist and associationist notion of consciousness. The publication of Husserl's lectures on phenomenological psychology from his manuscripts will shed further light on his position (Husserl's *Phänomenologische Psychologie*, edited by W. Biemel, 1962). The reader will find very helpful the concise but illuminating analysis of Husserl's phenomenology and its relevance to psychology in S. Strasser's recent article *Phenomenologies and Psychologies* (1965).

Husserl's Following. Many were influenced by Husserl as a person and as a philosopher, but few accepted his philosophy to the letter. The phenomenology, initiated by him, soon broke up into several streams, each following its own course. Husserl's close associate for several years, and the expected successor of his philosophical work, *Martin Heidegger* (b.1889), departed radically from the master. Although he succeeded Husserl in the chair of philosophy at Freiburg, his philosophy took a new and original direction which eventually became the main inspiration for the existential movement. Heidegger's intellectual estrangement was a painful disappointment to Husserl.

The other most important representative and propagator of the phenomenological movement was *Max Scheler* (1874-1928). He applied the phenomenological approach to new fields and problems, notably to religion and ethics. There was much vacillation in his views, especially with respect to religion. His deep concern with the human person and human values makes his writings especially interesting to psychologists. One of his books, in English translation entitled *The Nature of Sympathy*, contains a phenomenological analysis of sympathy, love, and hatred, illustrating the manner in which the phenomenological method can be utilized in dealing with psychological problems of this nature. In emphasizing the emotional aspects in cognition and interpersonal relations, Scheler moved beyond Husserl. For some, his philosophy became a bridge from phenomenology to existentialism.

The phenomenological movement, confined at first mostly to Germany, began to penetrate into France, where it soon showed a new vigor and began to merge with the existential current. The most prominent representatives of this development, about which more will be said in the next chapter, were Gabriel Marcel, Jean-Paul Sartre, Paul Ricoeur, and Maurice Merleau-Ponty.

While phenomenology was growing and winning new adherents in continental Europe, it was little known in America. Husserl's works were not available in English translation (with the exception of the *Ideas*, which appeared in 1931, translated by an Australian scholar). There were few studies before that date. Only in the later 1930's, Americans who had studied philosophy in Europe, and European phenomenologists, who immigrated to America, began to acquaint the American public with phenomenology. An American pioneer in bringing Husserl to the attention of the public in this country was the philosopher Marvin Farber (b. 1901), Husserl's student, on whose initiative an International Phenomenological Society was organized in 1939 and a quarterly, *Philosophy and Phenomenological Research,* was founded in 1940. This journal, although not confined solely to phenomenology, has been the main platform for discussions on phenomenological philosophy in this country. Farber edited a book of essays on Husserl in 1940 and published his own work on Husserl's phenomenology, *The Foundation of Phenomenology,* in 1943 (second edition in 1962). The latter book was the first extensive exposition of Husserl's phenomenology in America. Although sympathetic to Husserl's philosophy, Farber was never entirely committed to it and remained critical of some of its aspects. A comprehensive presentation of Husserl's phenomenological philosophy was given by J. Quentin Lauer in his book *The Triumph of Subjectivity* in 1958. In 1960 Herbert Spiegelberg published a two volume work, *The Phenomenological Movement,* which is the most competent survey and evaluation of this philosophical current.

Among the European-trained phenomenologists in America, Aron Gurwitsch (b. 1901) is to be singled out, because his writings display familiarity with contemporary psychological thought and concern with basic psychological problems. Consciousness is the field to which he has devoted special attention in articles and in a book—first published in French in 1957 and then in English in 1964—under the title *The Field of Consciousness.* This book has been well received in Europe and praised as a distinguished work in phenomenological psychology.

Evaluation. Historians of philosophy agree that Husserl's phenomenology was a decisive break from the philosophical past and that it is of great consequence for philosophy and other domains of thought. The intention of phenomenology was to provide a methodology which would serve not only philosophy, but all fields of inquiry. According to Anna-Teresa Tymieniecka's *Phenomenology and Science in Contemporary European Thought* (1962), the phenomenological method has been adopted by almost all European philosophers and has been successfully applied to various subject matters. Phenomenology has affected psychology profoundly both in theory and in practice. Its influence on psychology will be discussed more explicitly in the next section. The Anglo-American world, whose philosophical thought has followed the naturalistic, neopositivistic, and analytical trend, was not receptive to phenomenology. To the Anglo-American mind, phenomenology appeared too ambiguous, and too speculative to be of any significant value in science—psychology included.

PHENOMENOLOGY AND PSYCHOLOGY

Before the connection between phenomenology and psychology is discussed, one misconception must be dispelled; namely, that phenomenology in psychology has resulted solely from Husserl's influence or that it is directly a product of phenomenological philosophy. As much as it is true that Husserl profoundly influenced psychology, and we shall consider this influence in detail later, the phenomenological approach in psychology had existed long before him. What Merleau-Ponty observed about phenomenological philosophy can also be applied to psychology. "The opinion of the responsible philosopher must be," he said, "that phenomenology can be practiced and identified as a manner or style of thinking, that it existed as a movement before arriving at complete awareness of itself as a philosophy." The phenomenological approach in psychology also existed before crystallizing itself in the form which we today call phenomenological psychology. The following pages will be concerned with the development and manifestations of this approach in the history of psychology.

The most frequent terms denoting the relation between phenomenology and psychology have been *phenomenological psychology* and *psychological phenomenology*. It is with the distinction and definition of these terms that we shall begin.

Psychological Phenomenology. This term refers to phenomenology as a method applied to psychological problems or employed at the psychological level of inquiry. In this context, *psychological phenomenology* is to be distinguished from *philosophical* or *transcendental* phenomenology, which, as noted above, is a procedure of philosophy directed toward the essences of things and the knowledge of ultimate reality. Psychological phenomenology is a more restricted and specific procedure designed to explore man's immediate consciousness and experience. It may be defined as a systematic observation and description of the experience of a conscious individual in a given situation. Karl Jaspers defined it as "the completest and most careful description possible of what is experienced by healthy or by sick people." The exploration of consciousness refers to both acts and contents of consciousness and to their objects and meanings. The phenomenal data to be explored include perceptions, feelings, images, memories, ideas, and everything else that appears in consciousness. They are accepted and described as they are experienced without any presuppositions or transformations. Past knowledge, modes of thinking, theoretical biases must be kept in abeyance or "bracketed out," as the phenomenologists would say, in order to view the phenomenal world in all its richness and purity. Robert B. MacLeod calls this "an attitude of disciplined naïveté."

Phenomenology and Introspection. Psychological phenomenology is different from the classical introspection of Wundt and Titchener in many respects. In fact, phenomenologists attacked introspection as a biased and only fragmentary exploration of consciousness. Wolfgang Köhler, the Gestaltist, voiced the phenomenologists' criticism in his *Gestalt Psychology* (1929), pointing out the limitations and weaknesses of introspection as a method in psychology.

In the classical introspection, a well-trained observer upon receiving a stimulus, relates his impressions and attempts to reduce them to the simplest mental elements, that is, to sensations, feelings, images; and to find their attributes, such as quality, intensity, and duration. In a phenomenological study no assumption concerning the composition or attributes of impressions is allowed. Moreover, whereas in an introspective report objects and meanings are excluded, in a phenomenological study they are essential. The phenomenologist is interested in the meaning that stimuli or situations have for the observer. Presented with a tactual stimulus, a sheet of paper, for example, Titchener's subject was not asked what the object was. Rather he was asked to analyze his impressions in terms of the classical fourfold elements of touch, namely, pain, warmth, cold, and pressure, and to report any other sensory elements that might have been experienced, such as kinesthetic sensation. In a phenomenological experiment the subject reports, in a similar situation, that the presented stimulus is a sheet of paper, if he had so identified it, that it feels smooth or rough, hard or soft, large or small. A good example of the contrast in methodology and results is found by comparing the experiments performed by Titchener's students at Cornell University on so-called touch blends with the phenomenological studies of touch by David Katz (1925) and Géza Révész (1938). In his study of clamminess in 1933 Zigler, Titchener's student—interested in determining the sensory components of this touch blend—found that it could be reduced to cold, softness, movement, and unpleasant imagery. Katz's studies on tactual impressions concentrated not on the combination of the sensory elements, but on the richness of tactual experiences. They revealed different modes of appearances of touches. Katz was able to classify these modes into several meaningful categories.

Titchener, writing on introspection in 1912, referred to phenomenology and conceded that a phenomenological account may be "useful or even necessary as the starting-point of a truly psychological description" or "as an additional check" after the introspective description; but in itself it had no scientific value. However, phenomenologists proved so successful in the use of their method, through which they made numerous contributions to the field of sensation, perception, and other fields, that by 1930 the phenomenological method virtually displaced introspection.

Phenomenological Psychology. Phenomenological psychology is not a school or theoretical system, such as associationism, Gestalt psychology, or psychoanalysis. It is an attitude, an approach, an orientation in the psychological study of man. As such, it appeared early in the history of psychology and expressed itself in various ways before it found its more substantial and explicit form in the twentieth century, largely due to the influence of phenomenological philosophy.

The following characteristics have manifested themselves and bespeak the nature of the phenomenological psychology and its relationship to other trends in psychology:

1. Its basic *method* is the phenomenological method as described above.
2. Its *goal* is understanding man in all his facets.
3. Its primary *interest* lies in human experience and in its qualitative exploration.
4. It rejects any philosophical assumptions concerning the nature of consciousness, and it especially opposes the empiricists' tabula rasa concept of consciousness, the associationistic view, and all reductionist tendencies.
5. It is opposed to the exclusive restriction of the subject matter of psychology to behavior.
6. It favors and stresses the holistic approach to the study of psychological problems.

The above characteristics are not present to the same degree in all phenomenologists, but they tend to underlie, at least implicitly, their views and utterances. The phenomenological approach has not been limited to one field, but has been applied to various areas of psychology, theoretical, experimental, and clinical. Phenomenological psychologists insist that their psychology is not a closed system, but an ever-growing and expanding orientation. One of its newer directions is the existential, which is blended together with the phenomenological in a number of psychologists. Thus there is frequent reference now to the phenomenological-existential trend.

Phenomenological Tradition. Examples of a phenomenological approach can be found in all periods of the history of psychology. An early outstanding example of this approach is the fourth century autobiography, the *Confessions*, in which its author, Augustine, gave a deep and sincere account of his experiences, emotions, memories, desires, and other feelings and thoughts. Many contemporary phenomenological writings refer to Augustine and quote him. Husserl himself, in his lecture in Paris, cited Augustine's statement, "Turn into yourself: truth dwells inside man."

In the seventeenth century, Descartes began his philosophical quest with doubt, resolved in the celebrated *Cogito, ergo sum,* as a basis of his philosophy. His radical dualism, and his psychology built on the assumption of a dichotomy of the thinking mind and mechanical body, favored the phenomenological method as appropriate for the study of a spiritual entity, the mind. Being a psychology of mind, Cartesian psychology fostered and strengthened the phenomenological approach. Consequently the phenomenologists of the twentieth century have discussed Cartesian philosophy extensively. Descartes has been the reference point with which they contrast or compare their own views.

The first systematic and effective use of phenomenology was in the study of visual phenomena. The studies of Goethe and Purkinje at the beginning of the nineteenth century are often cited for their use of the phenomenological method in this field. Goethe studied systematically and in detail many subjective color phenomena, among them afterimages and effects of contrasts on color perception. His investigations and the rich inventory of various color phenomena were described by him in his two volume *Zur Farbenlehre* ("On Colors," 1810). After him, many other distinguished investigators including Hering, Stumpf, G. E. Müller, David Katz, Wertheimer, Ach, and Michotte, pursued studies of various sensory and perceptual phenomena. Whereas Goethe mistrusted experimentation and obstinately rejected experimental evidence in favor of purely phenomenological verification, his successors in these investigations undertook laboratory experimentation and used experimental data. These data complemented phenomenological observations and were related to data of physics and physiology. Such constructs as color solid, smell prism, and taste tetrahedron are products of phenomenological research of this kind. Although, in the second half of the nineteenth century, the emphasis in sensory and perceptual research shifted to physiological and psychophysical aspects, phenomenological studies continued. Prominent physiologists and psychophysicists—among them Johannes Müller and Gustav T. Fechner—also conducted phenomenological studies. Ewald Hering, particularly, made extensive use of phenomenology in his studies of vision and based his theories, which clashed with those of Helmholtz, on phenomenological material. The Hering-Helmholtz controversy illustrates the two approaches—experimental and phenomenological—with their merits and shortcomings. Stumpf, who practiced both approaches in his studies of tones, regarded phenomenology as a preparatory stage of psychology and for this reason called it the "propaedeutics" of psychology. At the beginning of the twentieth century the scope of phenomenology was extended to other problems. The Würzburg and Göttingen laboratories studied learning, thought, and will. The French used the phenomenological method in their studies of affective states and psychopathological conditions. Ribot's study of the experiences involved in mechanical invention was also principally phenomenological. Finally Katz and Wertheimer inaugurated a new era of phenomenological psychology when they launched their systematic experimentation on color perception and apparent movement, respectively. Their research incorporated both the phenomenological method and laboratory techniques—a combination which has been called *experimental phenomenology*. The findings obtained through this new methodology provided the basis for the Gestalt school. The success of this school in the psychology of perception was largely due to its skillful use of experimental phenomenology. It gained new adherents to phenomenology and inspired further phenomenologically oriented research, especially on the Continent—where the phenomenological tradition was stronger than in America or England.

Husserl's Influence. Husserl's philosophy gave identity, name, and both philosophical justification and framework to the already existing phenomenological approach in psychology. It also reinforced it, and occasionally inspired new areas of inquiry. Its effect was more direct in the circles within the orbit of Husserl's personal influence. These included the students and faculty at the University of Göttingen, where Husserl taught. Many studies in the psychological laboratory of Göttingen, and several at the Würzburg laboratory, owed their inspiration to Husserl. Karl Bühler, for example, was much impressed by Husserl, and this undoubtedly was a factor in his interest in and research on thought processes at Würzburg (1907-1908). Boring thinks that Bühler might even have introduced Husserl to Külpe, who later showed vivid interest in phenomenology. Husserl's philosophical ideas were enthusiastically received by Wilhelm Dilthey and left a mark on his "understanding psychology," which, as we have seen, had considerable success in Germany.

Gestalt psychology, on the other hand, in its early stage, did not show dependency on Husserl. Only in America in the late 1920's did the Gestaltists begin to make explicit references to Husserl. Structuralism remained impervious to phenomenology. In 1912 Titchener declared that "no form of phenomenology . . . can be truly scientific." Realizing the "profound influence upon current psychological thought" of Husserl, Titchener decided in 1917 to study Husserl "less for his own sake, than for the way in which psychologists have understood him." But he did not alter his original position with respect to Husserl's phenomenology.

David Katz (1884-1953). In the twentieth century, experimental phenomenology found its first and prominent exponent in David Katz. The contributions which he made to this field during a scientific career spanning more than half a century, exemplify the phenomenological-experimental trend at its best. Three influences interacted in the formation of David Katz as a phenomenologist and psychologist: the phenomenological tradition represented by Hering; Husserl's phenomenology; and the experimental spirit of the Göttingen laboratory. Katz was interested in Hering's work and theories, visited his laboratory at Leipzig, and later, after his investigations, sent him his book on color perception, which evoked favorable comment from Hering. As to Husserl, Katz stated in his autobiography: "To me phenomenology, as advocated ... by Edmund Husserl, seemed to be the most important connection between philosophy and psychology. None of my academic teachers with the exception of G. E. Müller has more deeply influenced my method of work and my attitude in psychological matters than Husserl by his phenomenological method." For 14 years Husserl and Katz were at the same university. Husserl took "an ardent interest," as Katz said, in his work on color and touch. Max Scheler, who became Katz's friend, was also interested in his research. Stumpf, too, showed much concern with Katz's academic career. Katz was associated for 18 years with the Göttingen laboratory, known for its strong experimental orientation. He studied at Göttingen, received his Ph.D. there in 1906, and from 1907 to 1919 was Müller's assistant. His wife, who later collaborated with him on several research projects, was a former Göttingen student.

With this background of phenomenology—the old (Hering) and the new (Husserl)—and excellently trained in experimental methods, Katz was well prepared to become the best exponent and promoter of phenomenological psychology. Another factor in his serious engagement with this psychology was his interest in the Gestalt school and his "cordial relations," as he termed them, with its members and sympathizers. His highly successful book *Gestalt Psychology* (1943) was a concise, clear appraisal of the school. In its preface he declared that although his "views are close to those of the Gestalt psychologists in many, perhaps even in most respects," he does "not agree with them completely" and does "not believe that all psychological facts are in accord with the Gestalt viewpoint." In addition to this volume, Katz wrote *Der Aufbau der Tastwelt* ("The World of Touch," 1925); *Gespräche mit Kindern* (1927, English translation, *Conversations with Children*, 1936), in collaboration with his wife; *Hunger und Appetit* ("Hunger and Appetite," 1932); and the book best known in American circles, *The World of Colour* (published in English in 1935 from a 1930 German edition). He also published numerous articles and monographs on topics related mostly to his experimental research.

Katz left Göttingen in 1919 to become professor in Rostoek, where he remained until 1933 when the Nazis made his stay impossible because of his non-Aryan origin. He left Germany and went to England, where he conducted research for four years until he was called to a professorship in Stockholm. Katz was a visiting professor in the United States in 1929 and in 1950.

Katz's Phenomenological Research. The phenomenological approach, which Katz pursued all his life, manifested itself in his first published research on children's drawings in 1906, where he touched upon the phenomenon of color constancy, that is, the persistence of colors despite change of illumination. Later he studied this phenomenon more extensively. Troubled by the paucity of psychological treatment of visual phenomena compared to the abundance of physiological studies and complaining that the latter—frequently conducted by psychologists—"could be handled just as well or even better by a sensory physiologist," he started research on the psychology of color. This research, done in 1911, preceded Wertheimer's discovery of the *phi* phenomenon and is cited as the beginning of experimental phenomenology. It was continued and culminated in the publication of *The World of Colour*. Through skillful experiments, Katz demonstrated for the first time, new, and up to then, unknown or unexplored, color phenomena. His results proved convincingly that simple attributes of hue, brightness, and saturation are inadequate to account for all color experiences and that it is necessary to go beyond the dimensions related to the physical properties of the stimulus. The same color can appear, Katz found, in different modes such as a surface color, or film color, or as bulky, shiny, transparent, or luminous—categories now well known to students of color. The chromatic or achromatic objects, Katz showed, tended to be perceived as being of the same color even when their illumination changed. Equally, the normal apparent brightness of the objects tends to remain the same although the intensity of their illumination is increased or decreased. For example, the whiteness of a sheet of paper is perceived to be the same in spite of dimmer or brighter light falling on the paper. This constancy of color or brightness is destroyed, if the observer views the object isolated from the rest of the visual field and thereby deprived of certain cues. This is the case when the object is observed through a "reduction screen," that is, a small hole. The latter finding demonstrated the effect of the total field in the perceptual process. Katz's subsequent studies amplified many of his findings and substantiated his theoretical views.

It was characteristic of Katz to be fascinated by unexplored fields and to venture into them with enthusiasm. Some lines of research charted by him are still waiting to be pursued further. He moved from the exploration of color phenomena to tactual sensations; from problems of child psychology to the study of animal behavior; from the psychology of mathematics instruction to the psychology of hunger and appetite. His studies included such divergent areas as: proprioception; taste; vibratory sense; formation of composite photographs; temporal measurement of phases of writing; drug effects; and even occult phenomena. In the last decade of his life he became seriously interested in the reaction of the human and animal organism to exceptional conditions. Averse to laboratory experimentation of trivial and superficial matters, which, in his opinion, produces little meaningful information for psychology, despite expenditure of much time and energy, Katz preferred to concentrate on processes basic to understanding the organism.

Katz is seen as the first experimentalist who systematically and consistently applied the phenomenological method to a wide array of psychological problems. He was able to collect rich data, experimentally sound, which challenged the atomistic and associationistic viewpoints. He also demonstrated the value of the holistic approach in psychological investigations and the need to consider the dynamic interplay between environmental and subjective variables in understanding perception and adaptive responses.

His work generated much interest on the Continent and found followers in many laboratories.

Other Phenomenologists. Phenomenological research in a vein similar to Katz's was often instituted in European laboratories by students from Göttingen and Würzburg. The Danish psychologist Edgar Rubin, known for his research on figure and ground, pursued this course in Copenhagen; Géza Révész in his native Hungary; Narziss Ach in Königsberg; Karl Bühler in Vienna; Gemilli in Milan; Michotte in Louvain. In turn their students, when appointed to chairs and laboratories, extended the phenomenological spirit to new places. It will be remembered that the two founders of Gestalt psychology, Wertheimer and Koffka, were students at Würzburg, and that Wertheimer received his Ph.D. under Külpe. Much research in Germany in the years 1910-1940 was phenomenological, often stimulated by problems posed by the Gestalt school. In addition to the Berlin school where Gestalt psychology flourished, a prominent center of phenomenological research continued to be Göttingen. Leipzig became the third center, when Wundt's successor, Felix Krueger, turned to the study of personality and emotions. Although perception had the largest share in these investigations, other areas were also intensively explored, such as volition, thought, expressions, esthetics, and language. New problems are constantly being added to the repertoire of phenomenological studies. It must be noted, however, that phenomenology, although the major single force in continental psychology in the years 1910-1940, found also strong critics and opponents in Germany and elsewhere.

But the phenomenological trend was not confined exclusively to experimentation. It also expressed itself in theory. The data continually amassed demanded a theoretical framework which would structure them and render them meaningful. Several theories on emotions, personality, and adjustment, conceived in Europe, bear the phenomenological trademark. Continental psychologists develop hypotheses and theories, which frequently are based on, or are supported by, evidence too scanty to convince their American colleagues. They are, however, often effective as a motivating drive and a guiding principle in research.

Among the outstanding European phenomenological psychologists, two have gained particular renown: a Belgian, Albert Michotte, for his systematic experimental studies; and a Dutchman, F. J. J. Buytendijk, chiefly for his theoretical contributions. Both were influenced directly by Husserl, but Buytendijk, more than Michotte, worked in continued close association with phenomenological and existential thought. Quite a unique position in contemporary phenomenology is held by the French philosopher Maurice Merleau-Ponty, once professor of child psychology at the Sorbonne. He effected a confrontation of psychological and philosophical problems within the phenomenological framework and discussed them systematically in two books on behavior and perception. Some authors count the eminent Swiss psychologist, Jean Piaget, as a phenomenologist, particularly for his studies in child psychology. His work has a phenomenological tint, but Piaget has not identified himself with phenomenology. The works of some British psychologists in the 1920's and 1930's were of phenomenological character. Honoria Wells' *The Phenomenology of Acts of Choice* (1927) may be cited as an example.

Albert Edouard Michotte (1881-1965). Born in Brussels, Albert Edouard Michotte van den Berck studied at the University of Louvain. He also worked at Leipzig and Würzburg laboratories. In 1905 he started his teaching career at the University of Louvain, with which he was associated until his retirement in 1946. An avid and skillful experimentalist, Michotte devoted his best efforts to the Louvain laboratory, which he directed for 25 years. Students from many countries studied under him and conducted research under his supervision. A strong believer in the value of scientific "cross-stimulation," as he called it, he maintained lively contacts with psychologists in many countries and frequently attended international congresses of psychology. He served as president of the International Union of Scientific Psychology and the Fifteenth International Congress of Psychology in 1957. Michotte won admiration, respect, and friendship to a degree rarely encountered, from students and colleagues, for his work and personal qualities.

Three periods can be distinguished in Michotte's research career: from 1905 to 1914, from 1920 to 1939, and from 1939 to his death. In the first period the research was similar to that of the Würzburg school in that it focused on volition. The second period included problems of perception, movement, rhythm, and learning. The investigations after 1939 on the perception of causality were the most original and attracted widest attention. New ingenious experimental techniques were used for the first time in these studies. The experiments consisted of observation of relations of moving objects and description of observers' impressions. In one series of experiments, circular spots were projected on the screen and made to move. In a variation of this series, object A moved toward object B and when both were joined, A was stopped and B moved in the direction of A's previous motion. The impression of all the observers was that A gave impulse to, or hurled, B. In another variation, A, after having approached B, continued to move together with B. In this case the observers had the impression that A carried, pushed or took away B with itself. In a different series of experiments, rectangles were moved along a horizontal slot at various speeds and in different relative positions. The spatial and temporal parameters determining the impressions reported by the observers were systematically explored. The methods and results of the experiments were described in a 1946 book, which appeared in English translation as the *Perception of Causality*, in 1963. Of this book David Katz said that it is "not only one of the most important contributions to experimental psychology in recent years, it will take its place among the classical works of psychology."

From the findings of this research, Michotte concluded that the perception of causality is like any other perception, such as that of color or tone.

It is a primary experience, not a secondary interpretation of experience, and has a quality of a Gestalt, similar to the *phi* phenomenon, occurring invariably under certain conditions. Further experiments on causality and allied problems, conducted in the 1940's and 1950's, provided additional information about these perceptual phenomena and permitted some generalizations. This phase of experimentation is presented by Michotte and several of his collaborators in a volume published on the occasion of his 80th birthday, *Causalité, permanence et réalité phénoménales* ("Phenomenal Causality, Permanence and Reality," 1962). In his analysis of the perceptual phenomena of causality, Michotte was careful to specify that this was mechanical causality, avoiding thereby a commitment to any philosophical theory of causality.

This extensive research on causality and related problems, conducted at Louvain for over 25 years, constitutes a significant chapter of phenomenological psychology. Although Michotte has been linked either with the Gestalt school or the school of functionalism, he and his research cannot be categorized in terms of schools. For Michotte, opposed to theoretical biases, remained free from school bonds and was primarily concerned with giving full and impartial attention to the phenomena themselves. This does not mean that Michotte was not interested in theoretical issues or in the theoretical implications of his experimental findings. However, it implies that he preferred to give priority to experimentation rather than to theorizing.

F. J. J. Buytendijk (b. 1887).   Buytendijk was born in Holland. Although he obtained a medical degree in 1910, he did not practice medicine; instead he chose an academic career. University appointments took him to Amsterdam, Groningen, Nijmegen, and Utrecht. At Groningen he was professor of physiology and director of the Physiological Institute. Until he was almost 50 years of age, his research was exclusively in physiology, zoology, and comparative psychology. Gradually he turned to psychology and philosophy. Impressed profoundly by the French existential philosophy, he directed his attention to phenomenological and existential problems. Most of his works were published in Dutch, but many were translated into other languages. His work *Pain* (first Dutch publication in 1943), which was dedicated to Michotte "in token of friendship," has been available in English since 1962. In 1957 a commemorative collection of articles in phenomenological psychology and psychopathology was published in honor of Buytendijk on his 70th birthday. The bibliography of Buytendijk, included in this publication, contains 245 items.

After several years of research on the physiological basis of animal and human behavior, Buytendijk found the physiological account of man inadequate. As he stated: "Behavior can never be reduced to physiological processes and explained as a result of the integration of reflexes." He did not dismiss the physiological approach, but sought to integrate it with the phenomenological study of man. Such an integration was attempted in his 1948 work, *General Study of the Posture and Motion of Man as the Connection and Contrast of Physiological and Psychological Views*. He maintained that psychology must focus its attention on man as a being existing in the world. In his opinion we are indebted to Husserl for the development of psychology as "a science of the human being and of the world of man." His phenomenological studies included research on the psychology of women, artistic expressions of man, pain, feelings and emotions, also on dance and sports. Out of his studies of human relations came the concept of *encounter*, which is now a popular and much discussed term in phenomenological literature. Basically, encounter refers to a meeting or a meaningful communication between people. In the last two decades in the Netherlands, there has been great interest in phenomenology and existentialism as evidenced by numerous scholarly studies on these subjects. Buytendijk has been caught by the wave of this interest, but in turn he also has been responsible for stimulating it further. If it is true that "nowhere else than in the Netherlands has the phenomenological method been used so expertly and with such an ingenious originality for the renewal of psychology and psychiatry," as W. A. Luijpen said in his *Existential Phenomenology* (1960), Buytendijk has had a substantial part in it. Among the French existentialists, to whose popularity in the Netherlands Buytendijk contributed, is Merleau-Ponty.

Maurice Merleau-Ponty (1907-1961). Even in his thirties, Maurice Merleau-Ponty was widely acclaimed as one of the ablest philosophers of contemporary France. His philosophy was regarded as the most original and most successful integration of phenomenology and psychology. Much was expected from him, but premature death at the age of 54 abruptly terminated his brilliant career.

He was born in Rocheford-sur-Mer, on the west coast of France. A succession of university appointments attests to his recognition: professorship of philosophy first at the University of Lyon, then at the Sorbonne, and finally the chair at the Collège de France, the most distinguished position for a philosopher in France. For a time he was closely associated with Jean-Paul Sartre as friend, cofounder, and coeditor of *Les Temps Modernes* —a notable existential magazine. Philosophical and political differences which gradually arose between the two led to their estrangement. Merleau-Ponty was much impressed by Husserl, especially by the last phase of Husserl's thought—still buried in unpublished manuscripts—which he studied in the Husserl Archives in Louvain.

Remy C. Kwant in his *The Phenomenological Philosophy of Merleau-Ponty* states that "One who wants to make a philosophical study of our world can hardly avoid a confrontation with Merleau-Ponty's thought. . . . His eyes are wide open to the fundamental facts of our period and he is full of the spirit of our era. His philosophy most strikingly mirrors both the light and the shadows of our time." He also had a knowledge of modern psychology and an appreciation of its problems. Even though his commitment was to philosophy, and his discussions of psychological matters served him only as a stepping stone in his philosophical discourse, there is much relevance and thought-provoking material for psychologists in his writings. Of special interest to psychologists are his two major works: *Structure du comportement* (1942; 2nd ed., 1949; translated into English as *The Structure of Behavior*, 1963) and *La Phénoménologie de la perception* (1945; translated into English as *Phenomenology of Perception*, 1962). Both of these books have been much discussed by European psychologists. Familiar with psychological schools, with various fields of psychology, and also with neurology and psychopathology, he made copious references to them and used them to illustrate some of his points.

In the first sentence of *The Structure of Behavior*, Merleau-Ponty expressed the aim and program of his inquiry: "to understand the relations between consciousness and nature." By "nature" he understood all external events in their causal relationship. There is a fundamental difference between nature and consciousness, because the latter is not subject to causality. He reached this conclusion after studying various forms of behavior, including consciousness, which he approached from the behavioristic viewpoint—that is, also as a specific form of behavior. Behavior is always structured and the methods used in psychology, he held, are inadequate to study it as such. The appropriate method for studying behavior is systematic phenomenology of perception. Human behavior consists of three levels: the physical, the vital (biological), and the human (psychical). Each possesses its own dynamic form. The highest, and specifically human, is the third level, which, however, is dependent in its emergence on the integration of the two lower levels.

In the *Phenomenology of Perception* his main purpose was not the systematic analysis of perception for its own sake, but the derivation of a firm basis from it for his philosophical synthesis. Why did he choose perception as a foundation of his philosophy? Merleau-Ponty wanted to understand the essential feature of man, which is, in his opinion, the dialectic— that is, the dynamic relationship and interchange—between consciousness and reality. This dialectic is achieved and reflected in the perceptual process. To him perception is man's primordial contact with the world: "It opens a window onto things," and as such it should be a starting point for the study of man and the world.

The sequence of topics in *Phenomenology of Perception* reflects the author's course of reasoning to achieve his aim. After a succinct exposition of his view on phenomenology, whose task, as he put it, is to "reveal the mystery of the world and of reason," he proceeds first to remove "traditional prejudices," which stand in the way of fruitful phenomenological exploration. These prejudices are the elementistic and associationist views of consciousness. The next task is to explore man's phenomenal field. The first part of this exploration is focused on the body or bodily being, the second on the world as perceived by man. In the first part the author shows how the physiological and psychological accounts of the body are inadequate. He considers various aspects of bodily being, such as the body image, the body in terms of space, body as moving, body as sexual being, and finally body as expressing itself in gestures and speech. It is in these discussions that he makes extensive use of psychopathology and neurology to illustrate or support his statements. The second part deals with perception and analyzes the sundry facets of the perceptual process. The third part is speculative and closely related to Merleau-Ponty's main philosophical theme. The title of this part is "Being-for-Itself and Being-in-the-World."

One of the concepts stressed by this great French philosopher is *Lebenswelt*. He found this concept in Husserl's unpublished manuscripts. *Lebenswelt*, variously translated, sometimes as "life-world," or "world of everyday life," and sometimes as "world of lived experiences," was assimilated by other phenomenologists, as we have mentioned earlier. Moreover, it has received various interpretations in phenomenological-existential literature. But in general it refers to the world as experienced, or as perceived subjectively, by an individual person.

THE AMERICAN SCENE

During the first two decades of the twentieth century, while Husserl was writing his books and while his phenomenology was becoming widely known, and winning interest and support on the Continent, America was scarcely aware of this new movement. William James, who maintained close and friendly relations with Stumpf, was familiar with the latter's concept of phenomenology and commented favorably on it. But there is no evidence that he was familiar with Husserl's philosophy. Husserl, on the other hand, not only knew James's psychology, but was impressed with it and acknowledged his debt to James more than once. Titchener, always abreast of developments in Germany, knew of Husserl, read him—it will be remembered—but did not find in the latter anything useful for psychology in his understanding of the word. Neither the intellectual climate nor the course of events in American psychology was conducive to giving phenomenology an impartial hearing. American psychology was moving away from German psychology and developing its own functional character. Soon behaviorism appeared on the scene and captured American attention. Rejection of introspection, emphasis on objective methods, quantification, rigorous experimentation, and abandonment of consciousness as the subject of psychology became the dominant trends—trends difficult to reconcile with the phenomenological approach. A factor particularly antagonistic to phenomenology was the intentional and radical dissociation of American psychology from philosophy. In Europe, where psychology kept close quarters with philosophy and was resistant to the behavioristic trend, phenomenology had a better chance to exert its influence on psychological thought. It was not until the 1920's and 1930's when the Gestaltist studies found favorable reception in America, that the phenomenological method, as practiced by the Gestalt psychologists, met with a more sympathetic reaction. Still, few American psychologists were willing to undertake phenomenological research and not much attention was paid to such research being conducted in Europe. After World War II the situation changed, and European phenomenological thought began to attract more attention. Phenomenological research in America and American reactions to the phenomenological approach will be summarized presently.

Robert MacLeod (b. 1907). Among American psychologists, MacLeod was the one who showed an early interest in psychological phenomenology and consistently pointed to its methodological values. He became familiar with German phenomenology during his studies in Frankfurt and Berlin. He met David Katz personally and, with C. W. Fox, translated Katz's book, *The World of Colour*. His article on the phenomenological approach in social psychology, published in the *Psychological Review* in 1947, elicited favorable comments here and abroad. In this article MacLeod described the phenomenological approach and outlined its potential contributions to social psychology. MacLeod's position on phenomenology both as theory and method was never extreme. In the above-mentioned article he stated that phenomenology is not to be a substitute for psychophysics and psychophysiology. Sixteen years later, at the symposium on behaviorism and phenomenology in 1963, he reiterated his moderate position, when he spoke of phenomenology not as an exclusive approach, but as one which in certain areas might be more useful and appropriate than in others, and which in general might enrich psychology. He specified the experimental areas in which this approach may prove particularly fruitful. He also expressed the belief that "what in the old, prescientific days, we used to call 'consciousness' still can and should be studied." But is such a study scientific? The concept of science and views on what is not science underwent a considerable revision in the present century. In MacLeod's formulation, to be a scientist "is to have boundless curiosity tempered by discipline." In other words, there is no justification in branding phenomenology as unscientific.

MacLeod's view that phenomenology is one of the acceptable and useful approaches in psychology, and reconcilable with other trends, including the behavioristic, is in marked contrast to some extreme opinions for or against phenomenology. The extremists in support of phenomenology hold that the phenomenological approach is the only correct and justifiable method in psychology; whereas those against phenomenology, deny it any place in psychological inquiry and consider its data scientifically worthless.

Individual Behavior. *Donald Snygg* (b. 1904), in a 1941 article entitled "The Need for a Phenomenological System of Psychology," in the *Psychological Review,* called for a psychology developed from the phenomenological viewpoint. This was the first voice in an American psychological journal which clearly supported a phenomenological approach to psychology. Without any reference to philosophical phenomenology, Snygg postulated that "behavior is completely determined by and pertinent to the phenomenological field of the behaving organism." Only a psychology developed along phenomenological lines could accurately predict individual behavior, he declared. Eight years later he and *Arthur W. Combs* (b. 1912) presented such a psychology in the book *Individual Behavior: A New*

Frame of Reference for Psychology—the first such venture in American psychological literature. A revised edition appeared in 1959 with the revised subtitle, *A Perceptual Approach to Behavior*. While recognizing the contributions of objective psychology, which studies behavior from "the outside," the authors find such an approach inadequate for the study of individual behavior. They developed their system of psychology on the assumption that the key to understanding and prediction of individual behavior is the world within the individual himself or within his phenomenal field. The term *phenomenal field* is used in the book synonymously with "perceptual field," that is, "the entire universe including himself, as it is experienced by the individual at the instant of action."

In the first part of the book the perceptual frame of reference is applied to the basic problems of psychology—such as learning, emotions, and personality. The second part is devoted to the application of the perceptual approach to sociology, education, and clinical situations. The principal concept, permeating this system of psychology, is the concept of the phenomenal self, called also the perceived self. The phenomenal self is discussed in various aspects—such as its origin, development, characteristics, relation to the environment, and role in behavior. The basic need of human beings is the maintenance and enhancement of the phenomenal self. The book has had a good reception.

The Phenomenological Problem. The increased attention to the phenomenological approach by American psychologists was reflected in the republication in 1959 of 14 articles which had appeared in ten different American journals during the years 1939-1957. Each article deals with matters discussed from a viewpoint sympathetic to, and compatible with, the phenomenological approach. The articles appeared in a book entitled *The Phenomenological Problem* (1959). As Alfred E. Kuenzli, the editor of the book, explained, its purpose was to clarify the meaning of the phenomenological emphasis in modern psychology.

Another expression of this emphasis—in the clinical field—is the book by Joseph Lyons (b. 1918), *Psychology and the Measure of Man* (1963) with the subtitle *A Phenomenological Approach*. Lyons was well qualified to write this book by his extensive examination of phenomenological and existential literature. In this new book he attempts—in his own words— "to outline a phenomenological psychology of clinical problems." Based on European phenomenological and existential thought, this outline is addressed to American clinicians. It is not a new method or system that Lyons offers, but a re-evaluation of some basic clinical problems in the spirit of phenomenology and existentialism. The second chapter of Lyon's book is devoted to the relationship between phenomenology and psychology. In it he sets forth his phenomenological position and differentiates it from other approaches in psychology. A reviewer in *Contemporary Psychology* called the book "a significant milestone in the development of an 'authentic' psychology" and one which should be "a minor classic in contemporary psychological theorizing."

Phenomenology of Perception. The phenomenological approach in the experimental study of perception found a few followers in America. An eminent example of this is the work of *James J. Gibson* (b. 1904). After several years of research on visual problems and extensive experimentation on visual phenomena, he published *The Perception of the Visual World* (1950), which is an analytical description of how man sees the world. This book deals with a question to which all visual phenomenologists repeatedly return, namely, the correlation of the visual field (what is exactly represented in, or impinged on, the sensory visual system—for example, the railroad tracks converging in the distance) and the visual world, that is, the objects as perceived (for example, the tracks perceived as equidistant). Gibson's description of the dependence of the visual world on the visual field contributes novel and original insights to the phenomenology of vision.

Several European scientists, who settled in America in the last 20 years or so, have made contributions to American phenomenological literature either by publishing their older works in English translation or by reports on results of new research conducted here. Some of them initiated fresh and ingenious methodologies. *Erwin W. Straus* (b. 1891), a psychiatrist who had won recognition in Europe as an outstanding phenomenologist, emigrated from Germany and became an effective promoter of phenomenology in this country, especially in the field of psychiatry. Thanks to his efforts, two international conferences of phenomenology were organized in Lexington, Kentucky. The Second Lexington Conference, held in 1964, was attended by philosophers, psychologists, and psychiatrists. We mention him in this section because his book, *The Primary World of Senses*, published in English translation in 1963, covers a wide spectrum of perceptual problems from a phenomenological point of view.

An active researcher in visual perception has been *Mercedes Gaffron* (b. 1908). She received her Ph.D. in Berlin and M.D. in Munich and is now associated with Duke University. Her work on Rembrandt's etchings, published in German in 1950, brought out new methods and avenues of approach in the study of esthetics. Her subsequent work in America dealt with phenomenological experiences evoked by pictures presented in systematically varied spatial orientations. These new excursions in the world of perceptual phenomena provided a basis for a critical look at the existing perceptual theories and led her to reformulate some of the fundamental issues concerning the perceptual process. Her strong emphasis has been on the scientific significance and validity of experiential properties of human perceptual activity. Noteworthy work in this area has also been done by *Karl E. Zener* (b. 1903), independently and in collaboration with Dr. Gaffron.

Current Situation. As already mentioned, phenomenological psychology began to attract serious attention of American psychologists only after World War II. Increased intellectual communication between America and Europe, more frequent personal contacts between psychologists of various countries, and the immigration of European phenomenologists to

America were factors contributing to a better acquaintance with the phenomenological trend. But the strongest single factor in arousing this new interest of American psychologists in phenomenology was the introduction of the phenomenological method, together with existentialist concepts, into clinical practice and theory. This blending of both the phenomenological and existential elements was effective in stimulating interest. The phenomenological-existential approach appealed first to a certain segment of American clinicians, who saw in it new promise for better understanding of the patient and more effective psychotherapy. At first the so-called third force began to be felt in clinical psychology, but gradually other branches of American psychology showed interest in the phenomenological-existential approach. Owing to the increased number of English translations of classical phenomenological literature and critical discussions at special conferences, American psychology is becoming more and more familiar with phenomenological and existential thought and is beginning to take issue with this new approach. Reactions to phenomenology vary from enthusiastic to hostile. A sympathetic response has come from those American psychologists who, independently, had developed similar viewpoints. The new approach is being confronted with orientations firmly embedded in American psychology such as behaviorism or operationism. The symposium of 1963, "Behaviorism and Phenomenology," mentioned at the beginning of this chapter, was one such confrontation. The inroads made by the phenomenological-existential trend in America and American reactions to it will be further discussed in the next chapter.

SUMMARY

In the first part of this chapter we reviewed phenomenological philosophy and the contributions of its founder, Edmund Husserl. In the second part we viewed the phenomenological tradition, which had existed before Husserl, and the phenomenological trend in psychology. Special attention was given to experimental phenomenology. Several European phenomenologists and their contributions to psychology were enumerated. The relation of American psychology to phenomenology was the topic of the last part of the chapter. The following is a brief recapitulation of the main points discussed in the text.

PHENOMENOLOGICAL PHILOSOPHY

Precursor: Franz Brentano (1838–1917)

Founder and principal exponent: Edmund Husserl (1859–1938)

Definition: Phenomenology is principally a method of: (a) direct intuition as the primary source of knowledge; (b) intuitive study of essences. This method is adopted by various philosophical orientations which are collectively referred to as the *Phenomenological Movement*.

PHENOMENOLOGICAL PSYCHOLOGY

Definition: An approach or orientation in psychology consisting of unbiased exploration of consciousness and experience. The phenomena are intuited, analyzed, and described as they appear in consciousness without any preconceptions.

Early practice: Goethe (1810); Purkinje (between 1819–1825), Hering (1834–1918)

Phenomenology as propaedeutics to psychology: Carl Stumpf (1848–1936.)

Experimental phenomenology: Göttingen and Würzburg Schools

David Katz (1884–1953)

Gestalt School

Albert E. Michotte (1881–1965)

Theoretical orientation: Maurice Merleau-Ponty (1907–1961)
    F. J. J. Buytendijk (b. 1887)
American representatives of the phenomenological approach:
    Robert MacLeod (b. 1907)
    Donald Snygg (b. 1904) and Arthur W. Combs (b. 1912)
    Joseph Lyons (b. 1918)
    Various investigators of the phenomenology of perception.
First American symposium on behaviorism and phenomenology was held at Rice University in 1963.

REFERENCES

Phenomenological Philosophy

Drüe, H. *Edmund Husserls System der phänomenologischen Psychologie.* Berlin: De Gruyter, 1963.

Farber, M. *The foundation of phenomenology.* (2nd ed.) New York: Paine-Whitman, 1962.

Husserl, E. *Ideas.* (Trans. by W. R. Boyce Gibson) New York: Collier, 1962. (First German edition, 1913; first English edition, 1931).

Husserl, E. *Phänomenologische Psychologie; Vorlesungen Sommersemester 1925.* Haag: Nijhoff, 1962.

Husserl, E. *Phenomenology and the crisis of philosophy.* (Trans. with notes and an introduction by Quentin Lauer) New York: Harper Torchbook, 1965.

Johann, R. O. The return to experience. *Rev. Metaphysics,* 1963–64, *17,* 319–339.

Lauer, J. Q. *The triumph of subjectivity: an introduction to transcendental phenomenology.* New York: Fordham Univer. Press, 1958.

Luijpen, W. A. *Existential phenomenology.* Pittsburgh: Duquesne Univer. Press, 1960.

Spiegelberg, H. *The phenomenological movement: a historical introduction.* Haag: Nijhoff, 1960. 2 vols.

Strasser, S. *Phenomenology and the human sciences.* Pittsburgh: Duquesne Univer. Press, 1963.

Straus, E. W. *Phenomenology: pure and applied.* Pittsburgh, Pa.: Duquesne Univer. Press, 1965.

Tymieniecka, Anna-Teresa. *Phenomenology and science in contemporary European thought.* Toronto-New York: Farrar, Straus & Cudahy, 1962.

Phenomenological Psychology

Buytendijk, F. J. J. The phenomenological approach to the problem of feelings and emotions. In M. L. Reymert (Ed.), *Feelings and emotions.* New York: McGraw-Hill, 1950, Pp. 127–141.

Buytendijk, F. J. J. Die Bedeutung der Phänomenologie Husserls für die Psychologie der Gegenwart. La signification de la phénoménologie Husserlienne pour la psychologie actuelle. In H. L. van Breda (Ed.), *Husserl et la pensée moderne.* Haag: Nijhoff, 1959. Pp. 78–98 and 98–114.

Combs, A. W., & Snygg, D. *Individual behavior: a perceptual approach to behavior.* (Rev. ed.) New York: Harper, 1959.

Gaffron, Mercedes. *Die Radierungen Rembrandts, Originale und Drucke.* Mainz: Kupferberg, 1950.

Gibson, J. J. *The perception of the visual world.* Boston: Houghton Mifflin, 1950.

Gurwitsch, A. *The field of consciousness.* Pittsburgh: Duquesne Univer. Press, 1964.

Katz, D. *Gestalt psychology: its nature and significance.* (Trans. by R. Tyson) New York: Ronald, 1950.

Katz, D. Autobiography. In E. G. Boring, *et al.* (Eds.), *A history of psychology in autobiography.* Vol. 4. Worcester, Mass.: Clark Univer. Press, 1952. Pp. 189–211.

Kuenzli, A. E. (Ed.) *The phenomenological problem.* New York: Harper, 1959.

Kwant, R. C. *The phenomenological philosophy of Merleau-Ponty.* Pittsburgh: Duquesne Univer. Press, 1963.

Landsman, T. Four phenomenologies. *J. indiv. Psychol.,* 1958, *14,* 29–37.

Langan, T. Maurice Merleau-Ponty: in memoriam. *Phil. & Phenomenological Res.,* 1962–63, *23,* 205–216.

Lyons, J. *Psychology and the measure of man: a phenomenological approach.* Glencoe, Ill.: The Free Press of Glencoe, 1963.

MacLeod, R. B. Phenomenological approach to social psychology. *Psychol. Rev.,* 1947, *54,* 193–210; also in A. E. Kuenzli (Ed.), *op. cit.* Pp. 149–181.

MacLeod, R. B. David Katz, 1884–1953. *Psychol. Rev.,* 1954, *61,* 1–4.

May, R. (Ed.) *Existence: a new dimension in psychiatry and psychology.* New York: Basic Books, 1958.

Merleau-Ponty, M. *Phenomenology of perception.* New York: Humanities, 1962. (First French edition, 1945).

Merleau-Ponty, M. *The structure of behavior.* Boston: Beacon, 1963. (First French edition, 1942).

Michotte, A. Autobiography. In E. G. Boring, *et al.* (Eds.), *A history of psychology in autobiography.* Vol. 4. Worcester, Mass.: Clark Univer. Press, 1952. Pp. 213–236.

Michotte, A., *et al. Causalité, permanence et réalité phénoménales.* Louvain: Publications Universitaires, 1962.

Mischel, T. Merleau-Ponty's phenomenological psychology. *J. Hist. behav. Sci.,* 1966, *2,* 172–176.

Rencontre, encounter, Begegnung: contributions à une psychologie humaine dédiés au professeur F. J. J. Buytendijk. Utrecht: Uitgeverij Het Spectrum, 1957.

Robinet, A. *Merleau-Ponty, sa vie, son oeuvre avec un exposé de sa philosophie.* Paris: Presses Universitaires de France, 1962.

Snygg, D. The need for a phenomenological system of psychology. In A. E. Kuenzli (Ed.), *op. cit.* Pp. 3–27.

Strasser, S. Phenomenological trends in European psychology. *Phil. & Phenomenological Res.,* 1957–58, *18,* 18–34.

Strasser, S. Phenomenologies and psychologies. *Rev. existential Psychol. Psychiat.,* 1965, *5,* 80–105.

Walker, K. F. A critique of the phenomenological theory of behavior. *Aust. J. Psychol.,* 1957, *9,* 97–104.

Wann, T. W. (Ed.) *Behaviorism and phenomenology: contrasting bases for modern psychology.* Chicago: Chicago Univer. Press, 1964.

Wellek, A. The phenomenological and experimental approaches to psychology and characterology. In H. P. David and H. von Bracken (Eds.), *Perspectives in personality theory.* New York: Basic Books, 1957. Pp. 278–299.

Winthrop, H. Some considerations concerning the status of phenomenology. *J. gen. Psychol.,* 1963, *68,* 127–140.

Zener, K., & Gaffron, Mercedes. Perceptual experience: an analysis of its relations to the external world through internal processings. In S. Koch (Ed.), *Psychology: a study of a science.* Vol. 4. New York: McGraw-Hill, 1962. Pp. 515–618.

22

Existentialism and Psychology

CLOSELY RELATED to the effects of the phenomenological movement on psychology is the impact of the existentialist movement on psychological thought. Like the phenomenological movement, this movement also grew out of a philosophy—existential philosophy. Thus it is in order to consider first, if only generally, the origins, the basic concepts, and chief exponents of this philosophy. The seeds of existentialism are to be found in the middle of the nineteenth century in the writings of the Danish religious thinker, Sören Kierkegaard. Its crystallization as a philosophical movement, however, took place between the two World Wars in continental Europe. The principal founders of existential philosophy were the Germans, Martin Heidegger and Karl Jaspers. In France, notable representatives of this philosophy have been Gabriel Marcel, Jean-Paul Sartre, Maurice Merleau-Ponty, Paul Ricoeur, and Simone de Beauvoir. In Spain José Ortega y Gasset is the best known exponent. In America, an early exponent of existential thought was a prominent theologian, Paul Tillich. World War II intensified interest in existentialism. After the war, existentialism developed into a powerful cultural movement with repercussions felt in virtually all aspects of contemporary life and culture. Maurice Friedman in his *The Worlds of Existentialism* described existentialism as "a powerful stream, welling up from underground sources, converging and diverging, but flowing forward and carrying with it many of the most important intellectual tendencies and literary and cultural manifestations of our day." Vigorous in its expansion on the continent for some time, the movement has now captured the attention of the Anglo-American world and gained sympathetic audiences in various fields, including psychology. "For good or ill," William Barrett (1964) said, "existentialism has taken an acknowledged place among the more significant modes of thought within the modern world."

EXISTENTIALISM AS PHILOSOPHY

Husserl provided much of the initial stimulation for existentialist philosophers such as Heidegger, Sartre, and Merleau-Ponty, but the main stream of existential philosophy turned to a direction different from that charted by him. It will be remembered, that Husserl's philosophy was concerned with the essences of things, whereas the main theme for existentialists has become *existence*. For many contemporary existentialists, phenomenology was the starting point and the first phase of their philosophical evolution. Some, notably the French existentialists, have retained closer association with phenomenology than others such as the German. All of them, however, have accepted the phenomenological method as a basic, valid method. In this sense it can be said that existentialists are phenomenologists, but not vice versa. Although the historical origin of existential philosophy owes much to phenomenology, its essential inspirations are to be sought elsewhere, in the thought of the already mentioned Kierkegaard, and of Friedrich Nietzsche (1844-1900), and of even earlier thinkers. It is noteworthy that this new movement sprang up simultaneously and yet independently in various countries and that it spread rapidly. The similarity of the intellectual climate and the simultaneous existence of common coincidental factors and conditions explain the origin of existentialism and its wide appeal in so many countries.

Complexity of Existential Philosophy. Existential philosophy—also called existentialist philosophy or philosophy of existence—is not a homogeneous doctrine. It is a philosophical movement, comprising philosophies divergent in assumptions, conceptualization, and scope of problems. In fact, the differences among these philosophies, even to a higher degree than among phenomenological philosophies, exceed their similarities. They have, however, a common basic preoccupation, namely, existence. Existence is the reason for the common existentialist label, that is, existence as experienced by man as an individual. The label, *existentialist*, first appeared in the 1920's, but, as a designation of the philosophy of existence, it did not come into general use until the 1940's. The French existential philosophers, such as Sartre, and the early Marcel, accepted this designation. However, the Germans, such as Heidegger and Jaspers, rejected it.

Popular notions often associate existentialism with the Parisian bistros or with bohemians. Some think of it as a rebellion against contemporary culture or social order, or as an expression of a radical break with tradition. Whatever the motive in individual cases, the essence of existentialism and the key to its comprehension, lies in its conceptual substrate, that is, in existential philosophy itself. This philosophy, it must be emphasized, is a highly technical and complex philosophy, which can be neither easily summarized nor readily grasped. Its chief spokesmen, especially Heidegger and Sartre, are professional philosophers whose philosophical works are intellectually accessible only to those who are trained in abstract and speculative discourse, and who are also thoroughly schooled in the history of philosophy. For example, Sartre's major work, *L'Être et le néant* ("Being and Nothingness") has been described as a difficult one even for those well versed in philosophical literature. It is mostly because of his novels, plays, and essays—media which render his philosophy somewhat intelligible to the average reader—that Sartre enjoys his popularity and influence. An additional source of difficulty for readers of existential writings is their unusual language, abounding in neologisms. Reading philosophical works of the existentialists may be, therefore, a discouraging experience. "If one reads the existentialists without exasperation one is almost certainly misreading them," observed the translators of Bocheński's *Contemporary European Philosophy*. The length of some of these works, as exemplified by Jaspers' *Philosophische Logik* ("Philosophical Logic")—whose first volume consists of 1,103 pages—also makes the reading of existentialist literature an arduous task.

In view of the diversity and complexity of existentialist thought, a summary, which is attempted in this chapter, is bound to be both fragmentary and incomplete. Facing the dilemma of either omitting altogether an account of existential philosophy or giving an elementary—hence oversimplified—version of it, the authors chose the latter course. The reason for their choice is the hope that a summary of existential thought will serve as an introduction to further study of existentialism and will, at least, call attention to those of its ideas relevant to psychology.

Departure from the Philosophical Past. Like any new philosophical movement, existentialism is best understood when examined in relation to the doctrines it has opposed. The *raison d'être* of every new philosophical doctrine lies primarily in dissatisfaction with other doctrines. Existentialism, particularly, is best comprehended if viewed as a vigorous and passionate attack against the entrenched views and main directions of the entire Western philosophical tradition.

Existentialism reacted against the rationalism of Hegel (1770-1831), bringing out instead the nonrational aspects of human nature. It rejected also positivism, materialism, and pragmatism. It opposed the Newtonian concept of an orderly, predictable world governed by immutable laws— a concept which left out entirely the human person and his specific problems. At the same time, it repudiated scientism, which conceived the world as being composed of parts that could be identified and separately analyzed, and which are subject to the law of cause and effect. Above all, existentialism directed its attention not to the essence of things—thus far the main focus of science and philosophy—but to existence, to man's individual existence, in particular. While proceeding in this direction, existentialism also intentionally bypassed or overcame the distinction of subject and object—a distinction inherent in all modern Western philosophy and a perennial source of its debates and division.

Existence. Although philosophy has distinguished between essence and existence and has been concerned with the essence-existence relationship, its principal interest has been traditionally in essence, that is, in what things are, rather than in their being or in existence as such. Essence has been described as "that which makes things what they are." Essence determines all characteristics and properties of things, gives them their existence and stability. Existentialists—Sartre is especially emphatic about this—deny that essence is primary and that it precedes existence. True, in human creations essence may precede existence as in the case of a table made by a cabinet maker. He has to have a concept of a table, of its dimensions and properties. According to this concept, he constructs the table. Here the essence precedes and determines existence. But when it comes to all nature, and particularly to the individual man, his being in the world and his individual characteristics are not determined by a prior idea. He does not *possess* existence like the table does, he *is* his existence. All his characteristics and properties are the consequence of his existence. It is his existence that is to him the only real concrete thing—everything else being only an abstraction. This notion of human existence as experienced subjectively by man is the core of existential philosophy. If existentialist philosophers go beyond the experienced existence to engage in the metaphysics of existence—as Heidegger did—their point of departure and reference is nevertheless always human existence.

Human Experience. Existentialists interpret existence in accordance with the etymology of this word. The Latin word *exsisto,* I exist, is composed of *ex* and *sistere,* meaning literally to stand out, or to become, to emerge. That is how the existentialists understand human existence, not as merely static being, always the same, but as becoming, continually changing, developing. Man is said to be thrust in the world and necessarily and irrevocably bound to it. This notion is the basic axiom of existential philosophy. This notion also points to the root of man's *existential* problems, analysis of which is the central subject of existentialist writings.

The two main problems of man's existence are "the other man" and God. Man is constantly in some regard, or in relation, to other men, upon which his being, according to some existentialists, is contingent. Heidegger describes this relatedness to others as "togetherness" (*Mitsein*); Jaspers as "communication"; and Marcel as the "I" and "thou" relationship. Marcel sees men bound by love and communion with one another. Sartre describes the "other" man as enemy and his regard as menacing and degrading. The last words of Sartre's play *No Exit* are: "Hell it's the others." With respect to God there are wide differences among existentialists. While Sartre is unequivocally atheistic, Marcel is positively theistic, and others are ambivalent or ambiguous. Martin Buber (1878-1965) brings together the two notions, God and the other man, when he says that "the love of God is unreal unless it is crowned with love for one's fellow men." The pages that follow will present the specific views of the chief exponents of existential thought.

Sören Kierkegaard (1813-1855). The life of this Danish thinker was short—merely 42 years, but of far-reaching consequences, when we consider that he stirred up the minds and hearts of many great men of many countries and that he is still widely read and discussed. A well-to-do man, he acquired a thorough training in philosophy, which he studied in Berlin at the time of Hegel. He engaged in journalism for a time, and then spent the rest of his life in solitude, meditating and writing. His books— the outstanding among which are, in their English titles, *Either/Or, The Concept of Dread* and *The Sickness unto Death*—became famous only after 1909 when they were translated into other languages. Kierkegaard thought of himself as a "religious author," yet he was admired, not so much for his theological ideas as for his penetrating analysis of man's inner experiences, or—to put him in relation to existential thought—man's existential problems. He was, in fact, perhaps the first to use the term "existence" in the sense that existentialists are using it now.

The main theme of Kierkegaard's works is man and his conflicts. He views man as constantly desiring eternity, to be as eternal as God Himself, but yet clearly realizing that his existence is temporal and finite. He wants to escape from his finitude, but cannot. He then defends himself from the thought of eternity. He tries to forget it by desperately occupying himself with trivialities and temporal things, so that his mind will not have time to think about eternity and God. The conflict between these two opposing forces, toward eternity and toward temporality—the conflict arising from the finite man confronting infinite God—stirs in man torment, anguish, dread. The Danish philosopher gave an account of this experience in his *Concept of Dread*. It has been said that nothing comparable to this genuine, moving, and profound account can be found in any literature.

Martin Heidegger   (b. 1889) owed his philosophical formation to several thinkers, but principally to Husserl and Kierkegaard. His association with Husserl was mentioned in the previous chapter. After he left the chair of philosophy at Freiburg, Heidegger retired to a remote place in the Black Forest to devote himself entirely to his philosophical work. He is recognized as an original and brilliant thinker. At the same time, however, he is perhaps the most difficult contemporary philosopher to read and follow because of his unusual terminology comprised of German, Latin, and Greek words. His chief work, *Sein und Zeit* ("Being and Time," 1927), has been of particular significance for psychology and psychiatry. Several existential psychologists and psychiatrists in Europe have drawn upon it as they did upon Heidegger's published lecture *What is Metaphysics?* (1929) and a *Postscript* to it written 18 years later.

Human existence (*Dasein*), Heidegger teaches, is tied inseparably to the world (*being-in-the-world,* as the English translators render this idea) and with other human beings. Of all beings only man is aware of his existence. He realizes that his existence is not of his making or a consequence of his choice, but that it has been thrust upon him, and it will be his lot until his death. Finding himself thrown into this incomprehensible and threatening world, as Heidegger describes it, and among strange people, and discovering his life oriented toward inescapable death, man experiences dread, anguish. This experience Heidegger describes in great detail. Man tries to overcome dread, Heidegger says, by camouflaging it with life which is conventional and "inauthentic." His thoughts, acts, and speech conform to the conventional modes of thinking, acting, and speaking. He thinks and does what "one" usually thinks or does. He thinks, for instance, that "one has to die," but he does not allow himself to think that it is he himself who has to die. But there is a price man has to pay for evading the realities of his being, for this camouflaging. It is a feeling of guilt which pervades his entire being. Thus only by accepting the inevitability of death and nothingness can man be true to himself, that is, have an authentic existence and be genuinely free. Only few succeed in living an authentic existence, and those who do have to defend it constantly against the clutches of the conventional, inauthentic modes of existence. It is this concept that some psychiatrists—particularly the Swiss psychiatrist, Ludwig Binswanger—elaborated and applied to the field of psychotherapy.

Jean-Paul Sartre (b. 1905). None of the existentialist philosophers is better known than Sartre. It is mainly because of his novels, plays, and articles which popularized his ideas that, to some, existentialism was synonymous with Sartre's philosophy. Before World War II Sartre was a teacher of philosophy. During the war, he served in the French army, was taken prisoner by the Germans, and when released, joined the French underground movement. After the war his activities have been varied, including journalism, editorship of a magazine, politics, and, most important, publication of philosophical books, novels, and plays. Sartre stirred up public opinion when he refused the Nobel Prize for literature in 1964. Sartre's first publications were concerned with psychological subjects, imagination and emotions. The book which established his place in philosophy was *L'Être et le néant* ("Being and Nothingness," 1943).

The central question for Sartre has revolved around the meaning of man's existence. What is this meaning? Sartre's striking answer is that man's and world's existence have no meaning at all. No reason can be found, he says, to explain why the world and man in it should be at all. If God existed, such an explanation would be possible, but there is no God; according to Sartre, there is not even the possibility of God. The very concept of God, Sartre considers a contradiction. Thus the world with all the beings has no justification, no sense; it is absurd. Of all the beings, man is the most inexplicable on account of his consciousness, which is an undeniable reality and yet incomprehensible as to its origin and continuity. What characterizes man best is his freedom and capability of choice. This freedom is not merely a quality, an attribute, that he possesses, but he *is* freedom, and therefore he has to choose and decide all the time. Since he inevitably has to bear all the consequences of his decisions, his freedom is an awesome yoke. As Sartre puts it, man is condemned to be free. Man is what he decides to make of himself; his mode of existence is of his choice. If he tries to escape his freedom, he is gripped by nausea, anxiety, forlornness, and despair.

The springboard of Sartre's philosophy was phenomenology. The subtitle of his *Being and Nothingness* is characteristic: "An Outline of Phenomenological Ontology." The phenomenological approach is evident in Sartre's psychological discussions, especially in his study of imagination and emotion. Finding the existing theories on imagination unsatisfactory, he called in *L'Imagination* ("Imagination," 1936) for a phenomenological analysis of this process. Later he undertook this analysis in *L'Imaginaire:*

psychologie phénoménologique de l'imagination (1940, translated into English as "Psychology of Imagination"). Emotions were another subject of his phenomenological analysis. In *Esquisse d'une théorie des émotions* (1939, in English, "The Emotions: Outline of a Theory") he discussed their nature and significance. Emotions are "a certain way of apprehending the world," he said. Their purpose is to transform the real world, when it becomes too difficult to handle in certain situations, into an unreal one, into a magical world, conferring on it qualities which it actually does not possess. In his description of fear, for example, he speaks of fainting from fear as "a refuge." "Lacking the power to avoid the danger, I denied it" by fainting or fleeing away.

In *Being and Nothingness* there is an extensive chapter on existential psychoanalysis. This is not the Freudian psychoanalysis, but Sartre's own method of finding the value system adopted by the patient. This value system can be found by the analysis of a patient's behavior. Since, as Sartre teaches, each individual chooses what he wants to be and since as a man he is a unified whole, he expresses his choice in every aspect of his behavior. An analysis of his behavioral acts should therefore reveal what his original choice had been. When this choice is revealed to the patient, he will usually recognize it. The patient may, however, deceive himself; he may be, as Sartre calls it, "of bad faith" and may not acknowledge his original true choice. It is then up to the psychoanalyst to reveal to the patient what his choice had been and also the fact of his being in "bad faith."

This brief account of Sartre's views has been selective. Sartre has dealt with many other problems of man and society. His thought on various issues is still evolving, however. Occasionally he modifies or reformulates his earlier views. He obviously has not yet said his final word, but the effect of his philosophy has already left a deep mark on contemporary thought.

Gabriel Marcel (b. 1889). Unlike most existentialist philosophers, Marcel has developed his philosophy independently of Husserl and other phenomenologists. He put forth existentialist concepts as early as 1914. He shares many features with other existentialist thinkers such as Heidegger and Jaspers, but the tone of his philosophy—hopeful and optimistic—and his theism, are in striking contrast with theirs, in particular with Sartre's. Like Sartre, he is also a playwright and a literary critic and has found a wide and receptive audience in France and elsewhere. For a time he called himself a "Christian existentialist," but he emphatically renounced existentialist designation of his philosophy in 1951.

Marcel has not written any systematic exposition of his entire philosophy. He preferred to deal with single issues separately. His major book, *Journal métaphysique* ("Metaphysical Diary," 1927), contains analysis of several problems. Books such as *Homo Viator* ("Man the Wayfarer," 1945) or *The Mystery of Being* (1951) are devoted to analyses of a variety of human experiences and to meditations on topics such as art, technology, and fatherhood. The realm of thought for which Marcel is best known pertains to man-to-man relationship. The key word to the understanding of his thought on this subject is *being-by-participation*. Man comes into his individual being, Marcel says, by communion with other men through love, hope, and faithfulness. The other man must not be a mere "It" or just "somebody," but "Thou," known and loved. Only through the relationship with man as "Thou" does the "I" find his freedom and fulfillment. Loving others, man transcends his own limited self. Without love man's existence is isolated and reduced. God is the absolute "Thou" who cannot be demonstrated by rational discourse, but is only encountered in man's personal engagement with Him.

Karl Jaspers (b. 1883).   He was a practicing psychiatrist before he gave himself entirely to philosophy. In 1913, as a psychiatrist, he wrote a large systematic volume on general psychopathology, which was well received and gained for him recognition in psychiatry. In this work Jaspers emphasized the need of a detailed description of the patient's subjective experiences for a correct diagnosis, and of empathy with the patient's feelings for a successful therapy. His work *Die Psychologie der Weltan-schauungen* (" Psychology of Personal Views on Life," 1919) signalled his turning to philosophy. Jaspers held a chair of philosophy at Heidelberg one time, and since 1948 he has been professor of philosophy at the university in Basel, Switzerland. He presented his philosophical views in a systematic manner in his three volume *Philosophie* ("Philosophy," 1932). The number and scope of his publications surpass those of his contemporary existentialists. He has also been the most consistent and comprehensible of all the existential philosophers.

Jaspers has been concerned with all great traditional philosophical problems, but especially with all aspects of being. His aim has been to provide a philosophy which would encompass the entire spectrum of problems related to man's existence. He distinguished three forms or modes of being, *being-there, being-oneself,* and *being-in-itself*. Being-there is the objective empirical world, which we come to know through observation and experiment. Being-oneself is the personal existence, depending on our awareness of ourselves and of our liberty, and on our assertion of ourselves by choice and decisions. The third form is the world in its transcendence. Philosophy has to keep these forms distinct and explore them through appropriate methods, but man can participate in all three at once. But even then, man can never fathom the entire meaning of existence.

Man is continually self-becoming through realization of his liberty and through his decisions. He is, Jaspers maintains, confronted with inescapable situations such as death, suffering, struggle, and guilt, and he has to deal with them all alone. Yet he is not isolated from the rest of the world, but is in constant communication with other existences. This communication is constitutive of his own existence, that is, he exists because he is in communication with others. There are various forms of communication such as discussion, social intercourse, ruling and serving, and political relations. Communication between systems of thought is essential for philosophy, because no philosophical system can possess entire and ultimate truth.

General Comments.   The above outlines are too brief to do justice to the entire spectrum of existential thought. They are intended to exemplify the main and general feature of existentialism, namely, its genuine concern with the question of human individual existence and its ultimate meaning. But existentialism, it is clear enough, has not offered one comprehensive answer to this question. There are as many answers as there are forms of existential thought.

Existentialism is an attempt to deal seriously and squarely with problems, which philosophy had thus far neglected. Traditional Western philosophy has concentrated almost exclusively on the metaphysics of being, on essences, and on the external objective world. Thus it has bypassed man's burning questions of the meaning of life, of suffering, and of death. The individual man, with his unique individual problems of everyday existence, and all the basic existential problems shared by all men, has been left out of philosophical inquiries. Existentialism, reacting to this deficiency, centers its attention on man as existing in the world, on his relation to the world and to his fellow men. This reaction, as we have already noted, appeared in various countries and in many fields simultaneously, and yet independently. Such a phenomenon may be explained in terms of common conflicts and anxieties, which have arisen in the Western world in the last 100 years and which have been intensified by the global wars and the threat of annihilation by nuclear explosion. These conflicts and anxieties are also believed to account for the upsurge in the Western world of interest in some Oriental philosophical and religious systems such as Lao-Tzu and Zen Buddhism, systems which contain elements akin to existentialism. Apparently the Western man finds or hopes to find—be it in such Oriental movements or in existentialism—ideas and answers, which could allay his anxieties, give him understanding of himself, and make it possible for him to discover the meaning of life.

Existentialism as a philosophy has put itself in opposition to materialistic reductionism, to idealism, and to rationalism. In attacking these doctrines, however, existentialism has perhaps gone too far in the opposite direction and has left by the wayside the objective and scientific elements of philosophy. Some critics say that if the proposition of some existentialists, namely, that there are no universal truths or laws, were correct, construction of science would be impossible. Other objections leveled at existential philosophers include: excessive subjectivism—reliance on personal subjective experiences as the basis for conclusions without any attempt of proof or demonstration—categorical tone of existentialist pronouncements, and uncommunicative esoteric language. The latter has been the object of vehement criticism of neopositivists, who insist on precision of expression and definitions. They deride the vague and peculiar parlance of some existential writers. Their special target has been Heidegger—for such expressions as, for example, "nothingness makes nought" (*das Nichts selbst nichtet*).

The above characteristics of existentialism have been partly the reason why American philosophers and psychologists too, were indifferent for many years to existentialist philosophy. The intellectual climate of America, where neopositivism and pragmatism have dominated, and where rigorous scientific methodology has been demanded, was not conducive to the study of existentialism and contributed to the delay of this study. But the situation has changed, and in the 1960's existentialism is being increasingly studied, discussed, and acknowledged here.

There is a general agreement in nonpartisan circles that, whatever its exaggerations and deficiencies, existentialism has opened new horizons for philosophical inquiry and awakened man's reflection in a new and vital direction. It has succeeded in forcing philosophers and psychologists to re-examine their notions about man and his nature and to take a stand with regard to man's existential problems. It is also generally agreed, on the other hand, that it would be an exaggeration to contend that existentialist thinking is the only legitimate approach in philosophy and the existential issues the only issues worthy of philosophical study. The specific influence of existentialism on psychology will be the subject of the following section.

EXISTENTIAL PSYCHOLOGY

In Europe there have always existed favorable conditions for the penetration of novel philosophical ideas into psychology, as we have pointed out before. The two disciplines, philosophy and psychology, have traditionally remained in close contact. An average European intellectual has some training in philosophy because university curricula demand it from most students. Also, characteristically, he is interested in new philosophical currents. This is particularly true of psychologists who, as a rule, are better versed than the average educated person in philosophy, especially in the history of philosophy. It is then understandable that such a powerful and psychologically oriented movement as existentialism readily influenced European psychological thought, especially in quarters where phenomenology had already prepared the ground for such an influence. Phenomenologically minded psychologists were attuned and well disposed to existentialism; thus they were the first to espouse existentialist concepts and weave them into their psychologies.

Existential psychology, as it began to emerge in Europe, did not aspire to be an all-exclusive new form of psychology, nor even a new theory or branch of psychology. Rather it viewed itself as a new orientation or a new perspective, essentially idiographic, as opposed to the nomothetic tendencies of other forms of psychology. Its intention has been not to abolish the existing tendencies and approaches of modern psychology but to complement them by introducing another viewpoint and new themes and methods, which were either missing altogether in traditional psychology or up to now had not been given sufficient attention. A factor contributing to the emergence of existential psychology was dissatisfaction with the course which psychology had followed for the last 50 years. This dissatisfaction was referred especially to the image of man which modern psychology had constructed. This image was considered only partial, incomplete, and one-sided. It was felt that psychology, particularly the behavioristic psychology, became "dehumanized"—that, although spectacularly successful in certain areas, it failed to contribute much to the understanding of man and his existential condition. Existential psychology seeks to turn the tide toward "humanization" of psychology.

Characteristics of Existential Psychology. The existential approach in psychology is still historically new and variable and not sufficiently systematized to permit a comprehensive account of its development or its precise definition. The following points are made in an attempt to specify those of its characteristics that apply rather to the movement as a whole than to its individual representatives. They should be regarded as tentative formulations of viewpoints expressed by various writers on different occasions.

1. Existential psychology is not a school but a *movement,* inspired by existential philosophy, which focuses its inquiry on man as an individual person as being-in-the-world. It seeks to bring into psychology a new viewpoint, new themes and methods.

2. Several basic theses or presuppositions to underlie this movement:
    (a) Every man is unique in his inner life, his perception and evaluation of the world, and his reaction to it. (b) Man as a person cannot be understood in terms of the functions or elements that make him up. Neither can he be explained in terms of physics, chemistry, or neurophysiology. (c) Psychology, modeled after physics—employing exclusively objective scientific methods, working solely within the stimulus-response framework, and focused on functions such as sensation, perception, learning, drives, habits, and emotional behavior— is incapable of contributing significantly to the understanding of the nature of man. (d) Neither the behavioristic nor the psychoanalytic approach is completely satisfactory.

3. Existential psychology attempts *to complement,* not to replace or suppress, other existing orientations in psychology.

4. Its *aim* is the development of a comprehensive concept of man and the understanding of man in his total existential reality. Its approach in working toward this aim is basically idiographic—that is, it deals not with generalities applicable to any human person, but with problems peculiar to this or that individual person. Its concern is with this person's consciousness, feelings, moods, experiences related to his individual existence in the world and among other men. But its ultimate goal is to discover the basic force, theme, or tendency in human life which would provide a key to the understanding of human nature in its entirety.

5. Its frequent *themes* are man-to-man relationship, freedom and responsibility, individual scale of values, meaning of life, suffering, anxiety, death.

6. Its chief *method* is the phenomenological method, described in the previous chapter, consisting in the exploration of man's consciousness and subjective experiences. Existential psychology is trying to develop specific methods to be able to study meaningfully various dimensions of individual experiences.

7. The *contributions* which existential psychology has so far made are principally in the field of personality theory, psychotherapy, and counseling.

There is much conceptual and methodological overlapping and communality of aims between the existential and the phenomenological approach. The intermingling of the phenomenological and existential philosophies may be so complete in many instances that distinction and classification with regard to the two categories cannot be made. Since these two approaches are so closely blended together, they are often designated as the phenomenological-existential approach, a favorite expression in some circles. Some groups, which do not ally themselves explicitly with any particular philosophy—although sharing many features with both phenomenological and existential psychologies—adopted the name *humanistic psychology*. We shall say more about this psychology later.

European Existential Psychologists. Now we shall proceed to enumerate, without pretension of being exhaustive, first those in Europe and next those in America who have been more or less closely associated with the existential approach either in psychology or psychiatry—fields which are sometimes difficult to separate in individual cases. The existential approach to psychology developed on the European continent into a distinct movement in the 1940's, almost simultaneously with the philosophical movement. It grew steadily more articulate and influential. Confined for a while to continental Europe, and noticed in America only when it was well advanced, this movement has quickly become international. It now has followers among psychologists and psychiatrists in every western European country. It is to be noted, though, that existential psychology in Europe is far from homogeneous in its character and orientation. Its representatives show wide differences in conceptualization, interests, and emphases. Of all the countries in Europe, the Netherlands has had a particularly active and productive group of phenomenologically and existentially oriented psychologists. The two trends, phenomenological and existential, are closely knit there. Phenomenological-existential publications of Dutch scholars are promptly translated into other languages and enjoy popularity on the Continent. Several of these works are available in English. To a large extent these publications have been responsible for dissemination of the existential approach in America. Visits to the United States and lectures by Dutch existentialists here have also contributed to a closer acquaintance with this approach. A prominent role in this regard has been played by a Dutch-born psychologist, *Adrian van Kaam*, of whom we shall speak later.

The foremost leader of the phenomenological-existential approach in psychological theory and research in the Netherlands has been *F. J. Buytendijk*, whom we have already discussed in the previous chapter. He described existential psychology as being based "on the primordial fact of human existence" and consisting "first and foremost" in the analysis of the meaning-structures of the personal world toward which all activity is directed." In his opinion the best way to know man is "to study the dialogue of man with objects and with his fellow-men." "It is impossible to know an individual," he says, "without taking his personal world into account."

English translations of Stephan Strasser's books have acquainted Americans with other aspects of the existential approach. Born in Vienna in 1905, Stephan Strasser studied at the Universities in Vienna and Dijon and later lectured at the University of Louvain. In 1947 he was nominated professor of philosophical anthropology at the University of Nijmegen in Holland. In 1957 he was in the United States as a visiting professor of philosophical psychology at Duquesne University. Strasser's first book translated here was *The Soul in Metaphysical and Empirical Psychology* (1950; English translation 1957). In 1963 *Phenomenology and the Human Sciences* appeared, subtitled "A Contribution to a New Scientific Ideal." In this book Strasser reviewed critically the basic characteristics and tendencies of modern science. He proposed in it a new concept of science which includes a psychology based on phenomenological principles and insights. His recent article, *Phenomenologies and Psychologies* (1965), is an excellent concise review of the relations between various forms of phenomenology and psychology.

Among other active Dutch existentialists are *J. Linschoten* and *D. J. van Lennep*. Linschoten, director of the Psychological Laboratory at the University of Utrecht, advocates the notion that experimental research in psychology can be exact and fruitful only if the object of this research is first subjected to phenomenological study. He also wrote a book on William James from an existential viewpoint. Van Lennep is the director of the Institute of Clinical and Industrial Psychology in Utrecht. Active in the field of projective techniques, he developed a projective test, the Four Picture Test, which in its rationale, use, and interpretation is based on existentialist concepts.

In France the notable contributions to existential psychology came from the existential philosophers. *Merleau-Ponty* with his two books on behavior and perception, respectively, is a prominent example. Another example is the close follower and collaborator of Sartre, Simone de Beauvoir (b. 1908), who wrote an existential psychological study of woman and femininity, entitled in the English translation *The Second Sex* (1953). Polish born, French psychiatrist *Eugène Minkowski* (b. 1885), has become the eminent spokesman for the existential approach in psychiatry. In Germany, existential psychology—especially the field of personality—

has had its representative in *Albert Wellek,* professor of psychology and director of the Psychological Institute at the University of Mainz.

EXISTENTIAL PSYCHOTHERAPY

The influence of existentialism is also strongly evident in psychiatry, psychodiagnostics, in theory of mental disorders, and most particularly in psychotherapy. This influence is understandable in the light of the genuine concern for the human condition and subjective experience of the individual shared by both existential philosophy and psychotherapy. Moreover, the psychotherapist discovers in existential philosophy a frame of reference particularly well suited for the therapeutic situation. Hendrik M. Ruitenbeek expressed this in his introduction to *Psychoanalysis and Existential Philosophy* (1962), a book edited by him, in these words:

> Existential philosophy . . . provides the analyst with a set of principles which can serve as guidelines in a broad general interpretation of clinical material. For existentialism approaches man's life directly. By using its concepts, the analyst can press on to the bedrock of man's existence and so establish a more immediate and fruitful relation with his patients.

New and vigorous psychotherapeutic systems and concepts, constructed on phenomenological and existential principles, emerged, some of them opposing and seriously challenging the psychoanalytic system in its method and theory.

Existential Analysis. The most widely known—and undoubtedly the most influential—existential concept in psychiatry is that of the Swiss psychiatrist *Ludwig Binswanger* (b. 1881), who has termed it *Daseinsanalyse,* or existential analysis, a term borrowed from Heidegger. Originally a Freudian, Binswanger departed substantially from Freud when he incorporated into his concepts elements from phenomenology and existentialist philosophy, particularly from Heidegger. Existential analysis is neither a new system nor a new technique, but a new concept —Binswanger calls it "a psychiatric-phenomenologic research method" —which envisages man as being-in-the-world. As such, it is not satisfied with the mere phenomenological exploration of the patient's subjective experiences, but probes into his "existential modes." This means that the patient is to be understood in terms of the relationships that his "self" establishes with the world (*Umwelt*), with his fellowmen (*Mitwelt*), and himself (*Eigenwelt*). In existential analysis, the therapist does not direct, guide, or correct the patient according to some preconceived notions; rather, he simply helps him become his own authentic self or, in other words, to achieve a degree of self-realization capable of preserving his integrity. The psychotherapist, as Binswanger says, allows the patient "to find his way back from his neurotic or psychotic, lost, erring, perforated or twisted mode of existence and world, into the freedom of being able to utilize his own capacities for existence."

Binswanger found many enthusiastic followers in Europe. Outstanding among them are *Medard Boss* and *Roland Kuhn,* both Swiss. But there are also opponents and critics of Binswanger's existential analysis. The most objectionable aspect of Binswanger's *Daseinsanalyse* seems to be its heavy philosophical substructure and its close linkage with Heidegger's philosophy. Jaspers, who introduced phenomenology into psychiatry, finds in Binswanger's view "a philosophical and scientific error."

Other Psychotherapeutic Approaches.   There are several derivations of Heidegger's or Binswanger's *Daseinsanalyse.* "Existential analysis" covers now a number of psychopathologic and psychotherapeutic schools of thought, closely or loosely allied with Heidegger's philosophical system. There are also approaches which are not allied at all with any particular existential philosopher, but only with the general core of the existential thought. One of the common features of these various approaches is the emphasis on complete exploration of patient's consciousness and experiences. On this basis the therapist tries to arrive at a meaningful reconstruction of his patient's mind and to establish the underlying unifying bond of its various states. It is essential for him to find what his client's original or basic choice was that led to his maladjustment. Most existential therapists believe that the neurotic is not realizing fully his potentialities; therefore he must be helped to come back to the full experience of his existence.

The effort on the part of the therapist to enter into his patient's inner world, to experience what the patient experiences, is the distinctive feature of the existential approach to psychotherapy. The understanding of this inner world of the patient (especially his *Eigenwelt*) guides the clinician in the selection of therapeutic measures. There is no standard therapeutic technique specific to the existential approach. In fact, representatives of this approach hold that overemphasis on technique is one of the main obstacles to the understanding of the patient. It is not the understanding that follows technique, but the technique that follows understanding. However, several therapeutic methods and even specific techniques have been developed. They are not practiced, however, rigidly or indiscriminately. Their use depends on the individual patient, on the therapeutic situation, and other considerations. There is a large group of existential psychiatrists and psychotherapists, each representing a specific viewpoint with respect to the psychotherapeutic process: in France there is *Eugène Minkowski* (b. 1885); in Germany, *Victor E. von Gebsattel* (b. 1883); in the Netherlands, *J. H. van den Berg* (b. 1914); and in the United States, *Erwin W. Straus* (b. 1891)—who until 1938 practiced in Germany. *Igor A. Caruso* (b. 1914), a practicing Austrian psychiatrist, formulated a concept of "personalistic psychotherapy," which considers analysis as only the first step to the more important phase of the therapeutic process, a synthesis in which religious and moral values of the patient play an essential part. His book *Psychoanalyse und Synthese der Existenz* (1951), in which he argues in favor of such a synthesis, was translated into English in 1964—unfortunately, with the grossly misleading title, *Existential Psychology: From Analysis to Syn-*

thesis. It is noteworthy that some of the existential European literature in psychiatry and psychotherapy has strong religious overtones, which reflect the beliefs of the authors, Jewish, Catholic, or Protestant.

Logotherapy. A much discussed existential approach to psychotherapy has been the *logotherapy* of *Viktor E. Frankl* (b. 1905), professor on the medical faculty of the University of Vienna and director of the Neurological Poliklinik in Vienna. The basic thesis of logotherapy, which is referred to as the "Third Viennese School of Psychotherapy" (after Freud and Adler), is that man's most fundamental drive is to understand the meaning of his own existence. Frankl calls this drive the "will-to-meaning." If this drive is not fulfilled, frustration follows—"the existential frustration," which may result in a neurosis whose characteristic feature is escape from freedom and responsibility. The task of the therapist is not to provide an authoritative answer to the question "What am I for?," but to help the patient to discover for himself the meaning of his personal existence and to encourage him to put it to full realization. In doing this, psychotherapy restores in the patient freedom and responsibility, the two distinctive human characteristics. Underlying logotherapy is a concept of man as a spiritual being whose existence has an intrinsic meaning. This meaning, which is individual for every person, man has to find and to realize in his life.

It is not Frankl's intention to replace other forms of therapy but to supplement them. With regard to Freud he does not reject him but seeks to complement him. In his highly successful and well-known book, *Man's Search for Meaning* (new English edition, 1963)—which contains his autobiographical account of his experiences in a Nazi concentration camp, as well as the fundamental concepts of logotherapy—he tells of his answer to a question ". . . what is the difference between psychonanalysis and logotherapy?" Before answering, Frankl asked the man who posed the question to him: " . . . but in the first place, can you tell me in one sentence what you think the essence of psychoanalysis is?" The answer was: "During psychoanalysis, the patient must lie down on a couch and tell you things that sometimes are very disagreeable to tell." "Whereupon I immediately retorted," tells Frankl, "with the following improvisation: 'Now, in logotherapy the patient may remain sitting erect, but he must hear things that sometimes are very disagreeable to hear.'" Logotherapy found followers and sympathizers both in Europe and America. A certain amount of research has been done here to test some of the theses proposed by Frankl. A psychometric instrument has been devised, the PIL (Purpose in Life), designed to measure the degree to which the subject has found meaningful goals around which he integrates his life.

THE AMERICAN SCENE

The terms *existential psychology* and *existentialism* were used in America as early as the beginning of this century, but in a meaning entirely different from present connotation. Titchener applied these terms to his structural psychology in order to contrast it with act and functional psychology. His system of psychology considered contents of consciousness as the subject matter of psychology. The mental contents were to be studied as bare "existential realities," that is, devoid of meaning, value, or function, for which reason the adjective "existential" seemed to Titchener appropriate for such a system of psychology. But "existential psychology," in the present meaning, as previously delineated, came to be known in America in the late 1940's as a European product. The following section will deal with the reactions to, and interpretations of, this European existential psychology in America. But first a comment on William James in whose views and concepts some writers find close resemblances to existential concepts.

William James and Existentialism. It will be remembered that Husserl was impressed and influenced by James's ideas and felt indebted to James. Several authors in recent years, such as Alfred Schuetz, Aron Gurwitsch, Paul Tillich, Rollo May, and Johannes Linschoten, pointed to the parallels between some of James's ideas and phenomenological-existential ideas. Linschoten devoted an entire book to James as the one who in many ways anticipated the phenomenological-existential approach. In this book, published in Dutch, *Toward a Phenomenological Psychology*, with subtitle "Psychology of William James," he contends that James's psychology was oriented toward phenomenological psychology. Indeed, when one reflects on James's concepts such as "stream of consciousness," "immediacy of experience," "sense of reality," "union of thought and action," and many others, one perceives their affinity to some existential concepts. Perhaps most of all it is the spirit of James's psychology and his concern with man and his nature that strike us as being akin to the existential approach. Moreover, Jame's open-mindedness and willingness to try any avenue promising to lead to a better understanding of man bring him close to the existentialist movement. Rollo May finds a parallel to the existential psychologists in James's "humaneness and his great breadth as a human being," which "enabled him to bring art and religion" into his thought "without sacrificing his scientific integrity."

Introduction of the Existential Approach to America. Translations of existentialist works into English, and American studies of the existential movement began to appear in the 1940's. In 1944 Paul Tillich (1886-1965) published an article on existential philosophy. Tillich was born and resided until 1933 in Germany. After he came to the United States he was a professor of philosophical theology at Union Theological Seminary in New York for 22 years. From 1955 to 1962 he was a professor at Harvard Divinity School. He then moved to the University of Chicago Divinity School. His numerous books, widely read, have aroused interest in existential thought and won many sympathizers especially for existential psychotherapy. He has been a vital link between European existential thought and American. One of the early publications, judged by some as the best introduction to the subject·in the English language, was William Barrett's 1947 series of articles "What is Existentialism," expanded into a book in 1964. In 1958 Barrett published a study in existential philosophy, *Irrational Man,* which was well received and has been widely read. As to psychologists or psychiatrists—perhaps because of their long estrangement from philosophy—they at first did not show, generally speaking, interest in the new philosophical movement and did not see its implications for their domains. What seems to have been the first public sign of interest in the movement on the part of psychiatry was the article by H. L. Silverman in the *Psychiatric Quarterly Supplement* in 1947 under the title "The Philosophy and Psychology of Existentialism." This article was highly critical of existentialism.

There were, however, psychologists in America who were familiar with the existentialist movement and whose views were influenced by existential thought. This is evidenced in the presentation in 1950 of a psychological system, bearing for the first time the designation "existential." It was *Values and Personality: An Existential Psychology of Crisis* by *Werner Wolff* (1904-1957). The author was born and educated in Europe, where he also became acquainted with existential philosophy. He realized that his existential psychology, as proposed in his book, was only indirectly related to existential concepts, but he felt that its designation "existential" is justified because, as he said, "the frame of reference for this psychological approach is man's existence." He defined existential psychology in the following words:

> Man's behavior considered in terms of his individual value system; the psychology of man as far as he questions his existence. Its object is the personal inner experience of the individual; the focus upon the moment when he, consciously or unconsciously, takes his existence into his hands; the focus upon his intent rather than upon his apparent behavior.

One-fourth of the book is devoted to the theory of existential psychology, which is contrasted with other theoretical positions in psychology. In this part the author offers a number of novel concepts and postulates related to personality theory. The orientation of the book is clinical, centered around a specific form of neurosis, named by the author "existential neurosis," and its therapy. As Wolff relates, he developed the concept of existential neurosis on the basis of his observations with patients whom he treated in the years 1929-1933 in Berlin. Existential neurosis, in his definition, is

> a disturbance of creativeness, that is, of the freedom of self-expression, in whatever area of living caused by an Existential Conflict, which is based upon an individual's direct experience of having lost his connection with the world at large through a disillusion by key figures such as father, mother, beloved, friend.

An "existential conflict" is the conflict experienced by man, when he "realizes his freedom of decision and suffers from the burden of his responsibility." The book did not generate much interest among American psychologists. In view of the lack of interest in existentialism here at that time, the message of the book was perhaps too premature to be noticed, much less to generate any discussion.

Existential Analysis in America.   At this point something should be said about American psychiatry in relation to European developments in the field of psychotherapy and psychiatry. In the 1950's American psychiatrists began to take serious cognizance of European existential analysis. A book, which was probably the first discussion of European existential psychotherapy in this country, Ulrich Sonnemann's *Existence and Therapy,* subtitled "An Introduction to Phenomenological Psychology and Existential Analysis," appeared in 1954. The author, a clinical psychologist, born and trained in Europe, has since lectured on and practiced psychotherapy in America. Ideas presented in the book, still relatively foreign here at that time, novel and unorthodox, evidently bewildered a reviewer of this book, who confessed that they appeared to him as almost defying "any purely intellectual comprehension," and to be like "double-talk." Existential analysis found, however, a sympathetic response among psychotherapists and psychiatrists here. The appearance of books and periodicals devoted to existential analysis attests to the existing interest in and support of this new approach to psychotherapy. In 1960 the *Journal of Existential Psychiatry* made its appearance and in 1964 *The Existential Analyst,* a newsletter of the New York Institute of Existential Analysis. There are a number of psychiatrists in the United States who are declared supporters and practitioners of existential analysis. Among the psychiatrists writing on the subject of existential psychotherapy in this country have been, to mention a few, Clemens E. Benda, Leslie H. Farber, Eugene Kahn, and W. Van Dusen.

Wider Interest in Existentialism.   It was not until the late 1950's that the word "existential" became familiar to a wider circle of American psychologists. Because of the challenge presented by existential analysis to psychoanalysis, it is not surprising that the first among American psychologists who began to study and evaluate the existential movement were clinical psychologists. There had been among them—as well as among personality theorists—some who, independently of European existentialism, were already for some time concerned with the existential problems. Finding parallels between existential concepts and their own thinking, they turned to a serious study of the existential movement and by their writings awakened interest in it among other psychologists. A prominent role in arousing this interest in existentialism has been played by *Rollo May* (b. 1909).

In 1958 a book appeared, *Existence,* edited by Rollo May and containing his own interpretation of existential thought. This volume was the first sympathetic presentation of existentialism as a relevant movement for psychiatrists and psychologists. Although addressed primarily to psychotherapists, the book attracted the attention of many American psychologists. A year later, 1959, a symposium on existential psychology was organized in conjunction with the annual convention of the American Psychological Association in Cincinnati. This was the first time that existential psychology was put on the convention's official program. The papers read at this symposium were published in a 1961 book under May's editorship, *Existential Psychology*. It was hoped, as May said in the foreword, that this book "may serve as a stimulus to students who are interested in the field and that it may suggest topics and questions to be pursued." The contributors to this volume were Gordon Allport, Herman Feifel, Joseph Lyons, Abraham Maslow, and Carl Rogers. As a clinician and practicing therapist, Rollo May was interested chiefly in the value of the existential approach from the clinical viewpoint, but he viewed this approach from a broader perspective. He confronted it with the prevalent tendencies of contemporary psychology in America. May observes in *Existential Psychology*:

> The existential approach is not a movement back to the armchair of speculation, but an endeavor to understand man's behavior and experience in terms of the presuppositions that underlie them—presuppositions that underlie our science and our image of man. It is the endeavor to understand the nature of this man who *does* the experiencing and to *whom* the experiences happen.

The presuppositions, to which May refers in the above quotation, are, in his opinion, of crucial importance for psychology, for they touch upon the most fundamental issue, the nature of man and the nature of his experience. They guide and give meaning to the empirical data gathered in psychology. But his crucial area has almost always been bypassed in psychology. "We tend to assume uncritically and implicitly," he says, "that our particular method is true for all time." May cautions against "absolutizing or dogmatizing" presuppositions. The existential approach calls for a continual analysis and clarification of the basic presuppositions of psychology. In the book he defends the existential approach from the criticism that it is unscientific. He also points out the new dimensions which the existential approach introduces to psychology, its emphasis on will, decision, and problems of the ego. But he also warns about its exaggerations and limitations. Cognizant of its inherent good and bad points, May believes that in existential psychology there is "the demand for and the guiding principles toward a psychology that will be relevant to man's distinguishing characteristics as man."

Reactions to Existential Psychology. After having been introduced to American psychology, the existential approach began to be better and more widely known. It also began to elicit from psychologists opinions and reactions. While it would be interesting to have a survey of these opinions and reactions among contemporary American psychologists, no such a survey has been made. But various publications and papers and utterances at psychological meetings indicate that the opinions about existential psychology range over a wide spectrum. Critics of the existential approach object to its obscure thought and still more obscure language, its exaggerated subjectivism, its dogmatic tone, and its unscientific character. Sympathetically disposed psychologists see in existential concepts and theories a new challenge and a valuable potential for enriching the whole of psychology. This does not mean that they uncritically accept all existential notions. On the contrary, they too have reservations about some features of the existential movement. There are no American psychologists, so it appears, who are entirely committed to one particular existential system or to existentialism in general. The prevailing tendency seems to be eclectic, that is, to extract only certain elements from the varieties of existential thought, and perhaps to synthesize them with other theories, rather than to subscribe to a single existential system. One aspect of existential psychology, however, seems to have met with wide approval among favorably disposed American psychologists, namely, its decisively humanistic orientation.

In an article in the *American Psychologist*, in 1960, *Lawrence A. Pervin* (b. 1936) outlined some of the basic elements of existentialism and gave his evaluation of the new trend. While he thought that it would be "foolhardy to accept or reject" existentialism and existential analysis "in their entirety," he admits that they are potentially useful and "worthy of serious attention and investigation." The article ended with this conclusion: "They represent possible suggestions for further study by psychology. If approached in this light, I think that existentialism may have much to offer and psychology considerable to gain."

Abraham Maslow (b. 1908) expressed perhaps the feeling of many American psychologists, when he posed the question "What's in existential psychology for us?" which was the title of his paper presented at the A.P.A. symposium in 1959 and published in the book *Existential Psychology* (1961). In this paper he expressed the belief that existential psychology would enrich psychology and that "it may also be an additional push toward the establishment of another *branch* of psychology, the psychology of the fully evolved and authentic self and its way of being."

Gordon Allport (b. 1897), who voiced his opinion about existentialism on several occasions, thinks that existentialism "prepares the way (for the first time) for a *psychology of mankind*." He explains this notion in the following statement taken from *Existential Psychology:*

A series of facts unites mankind—all mankind. The human being is born of a father and mother, ordinarily conceived and nurtured in love. He pursues certain biological goals; but he also pursues other goals which require him to establish his own identity, to take responsibility, to satisfy his curiosity concerning the meaning of life. He usually falls in love and procreates. He always dies alone. Along the way, he experiences anxiety, longing, pain, and pleasure.

This series of events is universal; but psychology has never before gone about its task with this sharpened perspective. For this reason our store of concepts and methods and our points of emphasis are defective in handling many items in this series. Existentialism invites us to fashion a universal psychology of mankind.

Carl Rogers (b. 1902) aligned himself, as he said, with those psychologists in America who "are concerned with the whole spectrum of human behavior and that *human* behavior is, in some significant ways, something more than the behavior of our laboratory animals." At the 1963 symposium on "Behaviorism and Phenomenology" he said that the phenomenological-existential view in psychology "carries with it a new philosophical underpinning for psychological science, which is, I believe, more fruitful and more human than the presently held philosophies."

There are psychologists who do not agree with the opinions cited above. They are skeptical of the value of the existential approach; indeed, they perceive in it dangers for psychology. *Sigmund Koch* (b. 1917), for example, speaking at the symposium in 1963, said that he is somewhat worried "by the style of the current interest in existentialism in American psychology." It seems to him that there is

> a disposition to accept in advance an intellectual object the properties of which have hardly been cognized. And there are indications that existentialism is tending to be viewed, in some global sense, as an *external source of authority* for whatever ideas the viewer already owns that he feels to be unconventional.

And Koch added:

> If existential philosophy is to be of concrete significance for the problems of a psychology of experience, this remains to be *established*. The slogans per se (e.g., "existence precedes essence") are not especially illuminating, whatever comfort they may give. My guess, though limited by very slight contact with existentialist literature, is that even if the conditions for *responsible* exploitation were met, there might not be a great contribution to psychology forthcoming.

Adrian van Kaam. The most active interpreter and exponent of phenomenological-existential psychology among psychologists in America has been Adrian van Kaam. Born in the Netherlands in 1920, he studied philosophy, theology, and psychology in his native country. Subsequently he held various teaching and counseling positions. Well acquainted with the European phenomenological-existential movement, he came to America to continue his studies in psychology. In 1958 he obtained a Ph.D. in psychology at Western Reserve University. In 1962 he joined the faculty of Duquesne University as associate professor. At Duquesne, now the principal center of studies in existentialism in America, he has given courses and organized seminars on existential psychology. In addition to teaching, he has lectured extensively on existential psychology in the United States and Canada and has participated in symposia devoted to phenomenology and existential psychology. Having studied in Europe and in the United States, van Kaam has gained familiarity with European as well as American trends and viewpoints in psychology. This familiarity gives him an obvious advantage in his promotion of the existential approach. He is the author of numerous articles, reviews, and books. He is also cofounder and chief editor of the *Review of Existential Psychology and Psychiatry*. This *Review*, according to the editorial policy, "seeks to advance the understanding of human existence by encouraging the dialogue between the behavioral sciences and the phenomenology of man, and to point toward the integration of the theories and data of psychology and psychiatry into a science of man based on increasing knowledge of his essential nature."

Promoting the phenomenological-existential viewpoint in psychology and psychotherapy, van Kaam hopes to expand the horizons of these fields. He does not place himself in opposition to the existing trends, but he would like to add another trend in order to bring psychology closer to the ideal of being a true science of man, man in all his dimensions. It is a case of augmenting the old with the new. Van Kaam calls existential psychology "a comprehensive scientific theory which attempts to integrate the contributions of the various behavioral sciences." This integration, he believes, cannot be achieved without a comprehensive conceptual framework concerning the nature of man. Such a framework is provided by existential philosophy. However, a psychologist in accepting this framework is not concerned with its ontological or epistemological aspects, nor does he have to presuppose the scientific validity of its concepts. These existential concepts serve him as "hypothetical constructs from which testable propositions can be deduced and put to the empirical test." If they do not pass this test, they are to be dismissed and other propositions are formulated. "The ultimate criteria of existential psychology," van Kaam says, "are the results obtained by strict observation and research by different specialists in the various areas of psychology. . . . " Van Kaam has just completed a book entitled *Existential Foundations of Psychology* (1966).

The "Third Force."   The designation "the third force," for the new orientation in American psychology—the third in addition to the two other orientations, behaviorism and psychoanalysis—originated with Abraham Maslow and Anthony Sutich in 1958. It has since been applied to phenomenological psychology, existential psychology, and humanistic psychology, respectively or collectively. Perhaps this appellation is rather intended to refer to the distinguishing common feature of the three movements together, than to any of them alone. This common feature or core seems to be principally the emphasis on man as a person, on his unique subjective problems, and on the use of any methods capable of advancing our knowledge of man; or simply, to cite J. F. T. Bugental, the emphasis on "the functioning and experience of a whole human being." A comparison of the postulates and aims of these movements reveals indeed close parallels between them. The *Articles of Association* of the American Association for Humanistic Psychology describe humanistic psychology in these words:

> Humanistic psychology is primarily an orientation toward the whole of psychology rather than a distinct area or school. It stands for respect for the worth of persons, respect for differences of approach, open-mindedness as to acceptable methods, and interest in exploration of new aspects of human behavior. As a 'third force' in contemporary psychology it is concerned with topics having little place in existing theories and systems: e.g., love, creativity, self, growth, organism, basic need-gratification, self-actualization, higher values, being, becoming, spontaneity, play, humor, affection, naturalness, warmth, ego-transcendence, objectivity, autonomy, responsibilty, meaning, fair-play, transcendental experience, peak experience, courage, and related concepts.

Bugental, in his presidential address at the meeting of the American Association for Humanistic Psychology in 1963, gave these postulates as basic for humanistic psychology: "Man, as man, supersedes the sum of his parts; Man has his being in a human context; Man is aware; Man has choice; and Man is intentional."

In the light of the existing parallels between phenomenological-existential psychology and "humanistic psychology," it is understandable that the American psychologists associated with one of these movements also often support the other. Thus some of them contribute articles to both journals, the *Review of Existential Psychology and Psychiatry* and the *Journal of Humanistic Psychology,* and also to the *Journal of Existential Psychiatry.* The former two were established in 1961, while the latter appeared in 1960. Its present title is *Journal of Existentialism.* Humanistic psychology, a younger movement, is sensitive to the viewpoints and concepts of phenomenology and existentialism. As Henry Winthrop, one of the editors of the *Journal of Humanistic Psychology,* wrote: "This sensitivity is an inescapable, professional perspective for the Third Force which seeks a balance of understanding between the demands of the logico-empirical tradition and the humanistic and philosophical emphases and needs which recognize the importance of the subjective and intuitive in mediating much of human behavior."

Existential Psychology as "Third Force."   How justified is this designation "the third force," specifically with regard to existential psychology as we see it developing here? Is it a "force" in a true sense? A categorical answer is obviously impossible. One notes, however, signs of increased interest in existential psychology and of its influence on American psychology. As we have already seen, a number of prominent American psychologists, among them authors of established renown, declared their support or sympathy for the existential cause. It cannot be denied that this approach has been steadily gaining new adherents, attracting attention of talented minds, and appealing to a wide segment of the young generation of American psychologists. Psychology teachers at universities notice lively interest in existential psychology among their students. Perusal of *Psychological Abstracts* of the last few years reveals a steady numerical growth of articles and books representing the existential viewpoint and dealing with psychological problems from this viewpoint. Existential psychology has to its credit the introduction of new topics and the stimulation or amplification of research in novel directions.

It appears that a significant factor in this increasing interest in existential psychology is the spreading feeling and conviction that psychology has for too long studied functions of man exclusively while consistently missing man himself; that it has concentrated on the secondary and peripheral, while neglecting the primary and the essential. Such a feeling is reinforced by the reading of the 1964 volume by B. Berelson and G. A. Steiner, *Human Behavior: An Inventory of Scientific Findings.* The authors admit, after having reported 1,045 scientific findings about human behavior, that the image of man as it emerges from these findings, is "incomplete." They say:

> Indeed, as one reviews this set of findings, he may well be impressed by another omission perhaps more striking still. As one lives life or observes it around him (or within himself) or finds it in a work of art, he sees a richness that somehow has fallen through the present screen of the behavioral sciences. This book, for example, has rather little to say about the central human concerns: nobility, moral courage, ethical torments, the delicate relation of father and son or of the marriage state, life's way of corrupting innocence, the rightness and wrongness of acts, evil, happiness, love and hate, death, even sex.

It is the omission of these very problems by modern psychology that seems to be turning young psychologists toward existential psychology. Through it they hope to find a way of pursuing these problems and thereby to acquire a fuller understanding of man. John Cohen, professor of psychology at the University of Manchester, England, who disavowed the existing orientation of presentday psychology, especially its reductionism, expressed the same feeling when he called for reorientation of psychology in his book, *Humanistic Psychology* (1958). As he summarized his position: "the subject matter of psychology is distinctively human; it is not the mere 'lining of physiology.' Our first step should therefore be to study what is characteristic of man, the blossom rather than the root."

On the other hand, there are those among American psychologists who have serious reservations about "the third force." To this group belongs, it seems, Sigmund Koch, previously cited. At the Rice Symposium, already mentioned, he called "the third force" a metaphor which "is becoming a little bit overabused." The protocol of the discussion at this symposium summarizes Koch's views—which are worth reflecting upon—in the following way:

> Insofar as he can see, the third force "is an extraordinarily loose congeries of people who are very much concerned about the constriction of problematic interests in American psychology . . . who are eager to embrace some kind of alternative." To speak of "this as a force is the bad use of a metaphor . . . because it is *not* a third force, it is a group of a large number of individuals who . . . would have considerable difficulty communicating with each other and who stand for nothing focal other than a feeling of disaffection from the emphases of recent American psychology." While he does not reject it, he does not look on it as "some wave of the future" which can "rescue psychology."

Whether the existential approach eventually will become a genuine force, and whether it will enrich psychology significantly, remains to be seen. But whatever its fate and contributions may be in the future, there seems to be little doubt that existential psychology in America in its themes, orientation, and methods will be different from that in Europe. Like other psychological imports from the European continent, existential psychology can also be expected to take on the American idiom—to become, as it were, Americanized. Some differences between the two versions of existential psychology are already evident. For one thing, American existential psychology is more communicative and less esoteric than the European has been. Moreover, since American psychologists abhor all "isms," the existential psychological movement here is less philosophical and abstractive, less tied to specific existential philosophies, and is free from the pessimistic undertones present in the European movement. The strong scientific, objectivistic, quantitative, and practical tendency, which has traditionally characterized American psychology, will undoubtedly be preserved and reflected in the further development of existential psychology in this country. For existential psychology clearly wants to co-exist with other trends and to complement them rather than combat them; to enter into a dialogue with other approaches and theories, rather than to ignite polemics and controversies that could lead to division instead of integration. The Association of Existential Psychology and Psychiatry in its *Review of Existential Psychology and Psychiatry* states that "Existential psychology and psychiatry is not a new school or professional interest group, but a joint attempt by representatives of various fields and schools to deepen the foundations of their own area of scientific specialization by means of the dialogue between the human sciences and the phenomenology of man."

SUMMARY

Existential psychology grew out of two philosophical movements, phenomenology and existentialism. In this chapter are sketched, first, the main features of existentialism as a philosophy, and its founders and leading representatives are introduced. In the second part of the chapter the effect of existential thought on psychiatry, psychotherapy, and particularly psychology is pointed out. We outlined the character of existential psychology by specifying its presuppositions, aims, themes, and methods. In reviewing the reactions of American psychology to existential psychology, we cited opinions and attitudes found here in this regard. In closing the chapter, we considered the prospects of existential psychology becoming the third force in American psychology. The following is a brief recapitulation of the main points discussed in the text.

EXISTENTIAL PHILOSOPHY
> *Founder:* Sören Kierkegaard (1813–1855)
> *Chief representatives:* In Germany—Martin Heidegger (b. 1889) and Karl Jaspers (b. 1884); in France—Gabriel Marcel (b. 1889) and Jean-Paul Sartre (b. 1905).
> *Definition:* Since existentialism comprises various disparate philosophies with few common characteristics, and an extensive range of themes, any brief definition cannot be but a gross oversimplification. In this oversimplified sense, existential philosophy is to be thought of as a movement composed of various philosophies which rest on similar foundation, primarily phenomenological, and which share the same object of inquiry, that is, *existence* as a peculiarly human mode of being. Its focus is on man and his subjective consciousness of being-in-the-world.

EXISTENTIAL PSYCHOLOGY
> *Definition:* Not a school or system, existential psychology declares itself as a new approach and attitude which seeks to complement other trends in psychology. Its basic presuppositions about the nature of psychology and its orientations have been inspired by existential philosophy. Its *aim* is to understand man in his total existential reality, especially in his subjective relationship to himself, to his fellow men, and to the world. It employs all *methods* available, particularly, however, the phenomenological method as the most appropriate one in the exploration of the individual's inner experience. But it also endeavors to develop new methods suited for its areas of investigation. Existential psychology originated in Europe in the 1940's. It began to be studied and discussed in America in the 1950's.

Developments in America:
The first *system of psychology* based on existential principles was proposed by Werner Wolff (1904–1957) in 1950.
The book *Existence*, edited by Rollo May (b. 1909), appeared in 1958.
The first *symposium* on existential psychology was held at the annual meeting of the American Psychological Association in 1959. Papers presented at this symposium were published in book form in 1961, under the title *Existential Psychology*, with Rollo May as editor.
Journals founded— *Journal of Existential Psychiatry* in 1960 (now *Journal of Existentialism*); *Review of Existential Psychology and Psychiatry* in 1961. The latter is edited by one of the chief exponents of existential psychology in this country, Adrian van Kaam (b. 1920).

REFERENCES

EXISTENTIAL PHILOSOPHY

Barrett, W. *Irrational man: a study in existential philosophy.* New York: Doubleday, 1958.

Barrett, W. *What is existentialism?* New York: Grove Press, 1964.

Benda, C. E. Existentialism in philosophy and science. *J. existential Psychiat.*, 1960, *1*, 284–314.

Blackham, H. J. *Six existentialist thinkers.* New York: Macmillan, 1952.

Collins, J. D. *The existentialists: a critical study.* Chicago: Regnery, 1952.

De Beauvoir, Simone. *The second sex.* New York: Knopf, 1953.

Ewijk, T. J. M. van *Gabriel Marcel: an introduction.* (Trans. by M. J. van Velzen) Glen Rock, N. J.: Paulist Press, 1965.

Friedman, M. (Ed.) *The worlds of existentialism.* New York: Random House, 1964.

Kaufmann, W. A. (Ed.) *Existentialism from Dostoevsky to Sartre.* New York: Meridian, 1956.

Olson, R. G. *An introduction to existentialism.* New York: Dover, 1962.

Sartre, J. P. *The emotions: outline of a theory.* New York: Philosophical Library, 1948.

Sartre, J. P. *The psychology of imagination.* New York: Philosophical Library, 1948.

Sartre, J. P. *Existential psychoanalysis.* New York: Philosophical Library, 1953.

Wild, J. *The challenge of existentialism.* Bloomington, Ind.: Indiana Univer. Press, 1959.

EXISTENTIAL PSYCHOLOGY

Berelson, B., & Steiner, G. A. *Human behavior: an inventory of scientific findings.* New York: Harcourt, Brace & World, 1964.

Bieliauskas, V. J. Existential philosophy and psychoanalysis. In R. W. Russell (Ed.), *Frontiers in psychology.* Chicago: Scott, Foresman, 1964. Pp. 17–24.

Bixler, J. S. The existentialists and William James. *Amer. Scholar*, 1959, *28*, 80–90.

Coleman, J. C. Conflicting views of man's basic nature. In F. T. Severin (Ed.), *Humanistic viewpoints in psychology: a book of readings.* New York: McGraw-Hill, 1965. Pp. 54–60.

Dempsey, P. J. R. *The psychology of Sartre.* Cork, Ireland: Cork Univer. Press, 1950.

Kronfeld, A. Die Bedeutung Kierkegaards für Psychologie. *Acta Psychol.*, Hague, 1935, *1*, 135–156.

Linschoten, J. *Auf dem Wege zu einer phänomenologischen Psychologie. Die Psychologie von William James.* (Trans. from the Dutch by F. Mönks) Berlin: De Gruyter, 1961.

Maslow, A. H. A philosophy of psychology: the need for a mature science of human nature. *Main currents in modern thought*, 1957, *13*, 27–32. Reprinted in F. T. Severin (Ed.), *Humanistic viewpoints in psychology.* New York: McGraw-Hill, 1965. Pp. 17–33.

Maupin, E. W. Zen Buddhism: a psychological review. *J. consult. Psychol.*, 1962, *26*, 362–378.

May, R. (Ed.) *Existence: a new dimension in psychiatry and psychology.* New York: Basic Books, 1958.

May, R. (Ed.) *Existential psychology.* New York: Random House, 1961. (Contains "A bibliographic introduction to phenomenology and existentialism" by Joseph Lyons).

Muuss, R. Existentialism and psychology. *Educ. Theor.*, 1956, *6*, 135–153.

Nath, P. Existential trends in American psychology. *Psychologia*, 1963, *6*, 125–130.

Pervin, L. A. Existentialism, psychology, and psychotherapy. *Amer. Psychologist*, 1960, *15*, 305–309.

Strasser, S. Phenomenologies and psychologies. *Rev. existential Psychol. Psychiat.*, 1965, *5*, 80–105.

Van Kaam, A. L. Assumptions in psychology. *J. indiv. Psychol.*, 1958, *14*, 22–28.

Van Kaam, A. L. *The third force in European psychology—its expression in a theory of psychotherapy.* Greenville, Del.: Psychosynthesis Research Foundation, 1960.

Van Kaam, A. L. The impact of existential phenomenology on the psychological literature of Western Europe. *Rev. existential Psychol. Psychiat.*, 1961, *1*, 63–92.

Van Kaam, A. L. Existential psychology as a comprehensive theory of personality. *Rev. existential Psychol. Psychiat.*, 1963, *3*, 11–26.

Van Kaam, A. L. *Existential foundations of psychology.* Pittsburgh: Duquesne Univer. Press, 1966.

Wann, T. (Ed.) *Behaviorism and phenomenology.* Chicago: Chicago Univer. Press, 1964.

Wolff, W. *Values and personality: an existential psychology of crisis.* New York: Grune & Stratton, 1950.

EXISTENTIAL PSYCHOTHERAPY

Allers, R. *Existentialism and psychiatry.* Springfield, Ill.: Thomas, 1961.

Binswanger, L. *Being-in-the-world.* New York: Basic Books, 1964.

Braaten, L. J. The main themes of "existentialism" from the viewpoint of a psychotherapist. *Ment. Hyg., N.Y.*, 1961, *45*, 10–17.

Caruso, I. A. *Existential psychology from analysis to synthesis.* (Trans. from the 1951 German edition of *Psychoanalyse und Synthese der Existenz* by Eva Krapf) New York: Herder & Herder, 1964.

Frankl, V. E. *Man's search for meaning: an introduction to logotherapy.* New York: Washington Square, 1963.

Riese, W. Phenomenology and existentialism in psychiatry: an historical analysis. *J. nerv. ment. Dis.*, 1961, *132*, 469–484.

Ruitenbeek, H. M. (Ed.) *Psychoanalysis and existential philosophy.* New York: Dutton, 1962.

Silverman, H. L. The philosophy and psychology of existentialism. *Psychiat. quart., Suppl.*, 1947, *21*, 10–16.

Sonnemann, U. *Existence and therapy: an introduction to phenomenological psychology and existential analysis.* New York: Grune & Stratton, 1954.

Van den Berg, J. H. *The phenomenological approach to psychiatry.* Springfield, Ill.: Thomas, 1955.

HUMANISTIC PSYCHOLOGY

Bugental, J. F. T. Precognitions of a fossil. *J. humanistic Psychol.*, 1962, *2*, 38–46.

Bugental, J. F. T. Humanistic psychology: a new break-through. *Amer. Psychologist*, 1963, *18*, 563–567.

Bugental, J. F. T. *The search for authenticity; an existential-analytic approach to psychotherapy.* New York: Holt, Rinehart & Winston, 1965.

Cohen, J. *Humanistic psychology.* New York: Collier, 1962.

Severin, F. T. (Ed.) *Humanistic viewpoints in psychology: a book of readings.* New York: McGraw-Hill, 1965.

23

Conclusion: Retrospect and Prospect

THIS BOOK HAS CONSIDERED THE ROOTS OF PSYCHOLOGY, its growth in various countries, and the major systems of psychology. We have seen that, in its prescientific phase, as part of philosophy, psychology was preoccupied primarily with the soul. In this initial stage, psychology relied mainly on philosophical methods, that is, on speculation and deduction. This early psychology proceeded from a philosophical premise of dualism, assuming that man is composed of two different elements, the soul and the body. Until the seventeenth century, psychology concentrated on the study of the metaphysical nature of the nobler element, the soul, and of its relation to the lower element, the body. One of its chief inquiries was how man acquires knowledge of external objects. Interest in this problem led psychology to the study of the senses and their functioning, which required observation and assimilation of whatever information on sensation other disciplines could provide. The study of perception was to remain a basic and principal concern of psychology.

In the seventeenth century the focus of psychology shifted from the soul to the mind, its nature, and its functions. This development was due largely to the influence of Descartes, who equated the soul with the mind, but who also carried the dualistic principle to its extreme. During the eighteenth and early nineteenth centuries, psychology was a philosophical study of the mind. It was increasingly influenced by physical sciences—especially by Newtonian physics—and also by biological sciences when they began to develop. The culmination of this evolution was the separation of psychology from philosophy in the second half of the nineteenth century. Beginning its new phase of development, psychology had a resolute program to construct a science similar to physics or chemistry. The subject matter of the new psychology remained the mind and the nature of consciousness and experience. Thus its principal method could not be any other but introspection. Moreover, its entire conceptualization was deeply rooted in philosophy. Initially, the main feature which differentiated the new psychology from the old philosophical psychology was its investigation of the relation of mental processes and phenomena to bodily functions and its adoption of experimental methods from physiology. Hence the initial name of the new psychology: *physiological psychology*. It was chiefly in psychophysics that the developing psychology first implemented its scientific program, by using the methods made available by Fechner and by setting up experimental laboratories.

At first, scientific psychology focused its efforts on sensation and perception. But the scope of psychology expanded rapidly, moving further away from philosophy and closer to natural sciences. Critical for the subsequent development of psychology was the origin and influence of two powerful movements, behaviorism and psychoanalysis. They altered the course and character of psychology. Behaviorism proceeded to implement fully the original program of psychology, namely, to be entirely independent from philosophy and to develop as a science. Watson's stated purpose was to make psychology "a purely objective, experimental branch of natural science." Consequently, behaviorism repudiated all mentalism. While rejecting introspection, it declared behavior the subject matter of psychology, to be studied with objective scientific methods. Under the influence of psychoanalysis, a new orientation originated, that is, exploration of man's unconscious and study of motivation and personality. Behaviorism studied man's behavior from the outside and directed its attention to observable responses. Psychoanalysis probed the inside of man and looked into his unconscious for explanations not only of his actions, but also of his thoughts and feelings. Each of these two orientations grew in strength within its respective orbit of interest and activity. Behavioristic psychology effected significant advances in experimental psychology and applications in industry and other fields. Psychoanalysis fostered clinical orientation of psychology and stimulated the growth of dynamic psychology, psychology of personality, and abnormal psychology.

How Psychology Grew. Like the growth of other sciences, the growth of psychology resulted from the interaction of multiple factors—cultural, socioeconomic, and political. Some of these factors helped the progress of psychology, while others were a hindrance. World Wars I and II, for example, slowed down or halted the advance of psychology in theoretical areas. In certain practical areas, however, these wars were a powerful stimulus to acceleration. But reflection upon the origin and growth of psychology reveals characteristics not found to the same degree in the history of other sciences. Unlike other sciences, psychology grew at an irregular pace and in an unordered manner. The growth curve of psychology, if we would attempt to plot one, would prove to be full of plateaus and sudden spurts. For psychology has not developed through steady addition or accretion, analogous to construction of a building, where one brick is added to another until stage by stage the building is completed. Some historians, referring to the manner in which psychology grew, describe it as a series of theses and antitheses leading to a synthesis. Others compare it to a pendulum swinging from one direction to another, from one extreme to another. Numerous examples substantiate both metaphors. It seems, however, that the most striking aspect of the history of psychology has been the recurrence of identical problems, but in each instance in a novel form or in a new context. R. S. Crutchfield and D. Krech used the analogy of a spiral to describe this phenomenon, that is, the growth of psychology reveals, in their words, the "recurrence of older conceptions but at a more advanced level of complexity and sophistication." "It is not only concepts and theories," they say, "that show this spiraling phenomenon; experimental *methods* do so too." They give these examples:

research on intelligence revealing a limited number of fundamental factors "brings us back—though in a far more complicated form—to the much earlier and subsequently discredited notion of mental 'faculties'"; "in the work on cortical localization of function there was a continuous spiraling from the notion of specificity to the notion of generality." More instances of such historical spiraling readily can be found in other areas. The body-mind problem, explanation of perceptual processes, instinct theories, and typologies are all topics recurring persistently throughout the history of psychology, and each time in a more complex formulation. The use of introspection demonstrates strikingly the spiraling phenomenon. Once categorically rejected by behaviorism, introspection is again found useful, if not indispensable, in certain areas of contemporary research such as psychopharmacology. Moreover, it can be seen that old theories, once discarded, reappear in new interpretations; that theorists, once repudiated, are exonerated and are discussed anew and re-examined in the light of more recent advances. At the beginning of this century Wundtian psychology was accused of being "sterile and narrow" (McDougall) because of its exclusive preoccupation with consciousness and neglect of behavior. Fifty years later consciousness is being reintroduced into psychology. Demands are voiced that psychology "should once again include within its scope the systematic study of conscious experience" (C. Burt, 1964), that it ought to "restore . . . a valid and usable concept of consciousness" (R. M. Collier, 1964). It is behavioristic psychology which is now accused of being sterile and narrow.

The spiraling phenomenon demonstrates the value of a historical study of psychology both for the researcher and the theorist. As with all other human efforts, genuine progress in chosen areas of psychology may depend significantly on knowledge of what had been done or said in the past on topics related to the study of these areas. Knowledge of the previous achievements or failures may provide vital clues not only for further progress, but for avoidance and perpetuation of errors. At the same time realization of the spiraling in the history of psychology will encourage intellectual humility and forestall intellectual arrogance.

National Differences. We have often observed the varied backgrounds of scientific psychology and the indigenous patterns of cultural and socioeconomic forces which mold the character of this psychology in various countries. We have seen the effect of these factors on psychology in the countries discussed in this book. This effect is reflected in the rate of growth of psychology; in its philosophical underpinning; in its dominant emphases; in the position it occupies in society; and in its relation to other sciences. We have noted these differences in Europe, in America, and in Asia. We have noted, for instance, the powerful influence of philosophy on German psychology; the combination of philosophical and biological factors in the formation of British psychology; the dominant role of psychopathology in the development of French psychology; the strong behavioristic and applied orientation of American psychology; the restricting effect of the imposed political system on psychology and psychologists in Soviet Russia; and the steadfast interest in, and concern with, the inner life of man of Oriental psychology. However, as we follow the growth of psychology in these and other countries, we cannot fail to note how the national differences gradually diminish and how psychology in one country begins to resemble—rather than differ from—the psychology of another country. Eventually, it may be expected, psychology will be less differentiated and more homogeneous, regardless of geographical and cultural differences. Undoubtedly, peculiar geographic, cultural, economic, and ideological influences will continue to play a role in the manner of investigation, selection of problems, and emphases in psychology. But these influences—judging from the changes that have already manifested themselves in various countries—will be rather limited, incidental, and secondary as compared to the major forces.

Historical Trends.   A historical grasp of the growth of a science in its entirely often reveals to the student of that science dominant and especially significant forces or trends. Such insights help to interpret historical events and often provide some logical unity to seemingly disparate phenomena. In the history of psychology several of such forces or trends, also termed traditions, have been recognized and their roles studied by historians. They usually appear first in philosophy and then continue to be reflected in psychological concepts and theories. On several occasions in this book we have referred to such broad and usually contrasting trends and traditions. We have mentioned, for example, the Lockean and the Leibnitzian traditions, the monistic and dualistic traditions, and the phenomenological tradition. We have also alluded to the distinction between the Apollinian and Dionysian traditions, discussed by McDougall. A frequent result of broad dichotomous traditions is the formation of antinomies such as empiricism and nativism, atomism and holism, structuralism and functionalism, physicalism and purposivism, and others. From a contemporary perspective, the dominant trends and antinomies, the viewpoints or tendencies which have thus far prevailed in American psychology are not too difficult to identify. Joseph Lyons in his book *Psychology and the Measure of Man* (1963) summarized them in these words: ". . . psychology today may be described as positivist and empiricist in its bases, behaviorist in its origin, and physicalistic and quantitative in its emphases."

Robert I. Watson in his article on the national trends in American psychology (1965) analyzed the dominant "prescriptions." Prescriptions in his definition are the ". . . prevailing inclinations or tendencies to behave in a definable way." "A prescription," he observes, "when deeply ingrained, tends to be unverbalized and utilized as a matter of course, unless circumstances force one to see its inapplicability." In Watson's opinion, the dominant prescriptions characteristic of American psychology—in addition to "determinism, naturalism, physicalism and monism" —are operationalism, quantitativism, hypothetico-deductivism, and environmentalism. But Watson notes the appearance of new prescriptions which run counter to the dominant prescriptions. His summary view is as follows:

> Determinism, naturalism, physicalism and monism, although very much operative, are judged to incite relatively little opposition. Functionalism, operationalism, quantification, hypothetico-deductivism, environmentalism, and nomotheticism are likewise dominant, but there are counter-prescriptions which tend to oppose them. . . .Serving as counter-prescriptions to those dominant in psychology are those calling for increased complexity in theorizing, for an increased attention to philosophical matters, for general acceptance of phenomenology, for increased attention to existential psychology and in a somewhat amorphous way almost all of the areas of personality theory calls for counter-prescripitions of one sort or another.

The Emergence of New Trends. Several authors have noted the emergence of new trends in contemporary American psychology. Among them —unless we misread the signs or take for reality what is only wishful thinking—two interdependent trends seem to stand out and to be most striking. One is of negative, the other of more positive nature. The negative is the unwillingness to surrender to any one specific theory or methodology. The positive consists of the willingness to re-examine entrenched positions and readiness to consider new propositions and judge them on their merits rather than on their origin. Several factors contributed to this outlook. Some of them are endogenous, that is, operating within psychology itself. Others are exogenous: they originate in other sciences and in philosophy and influence psychology only indirectly. One of the latter external factors is the currently changing concept of science. In the past—to use the phrase of Michael Polanyi, the philosopher of science at Manchester University in England—any human thought could have been "discredited by branding it as unscientific." In psychology, certain topics and methods were discredited precisely because they were branded unscientific. But the nineteenth century concept of science is no longer popular. The traditional ends and means of science have greatly amplified and the definition of "scientific" is now much more liberal. Polanyi expresses the changing attitude toward the image of science, when he urges that:

> . . . the abuses of the scientific method must be checked, both in the interest of other human ideals which they threaten and in the interest of science itself, which is menaced by self-destruction, unless it can be attuned to the whole range of human thought.

The result of these endogenous and exogenous influences is a broadening of the thematic and conceptual scope of psychology and of its approaches. Additional comments and opinions of contemporary authors specify further this new aspect of the evolution of psychology.

Psychologists today, in contrast to psychologists of the past, are unwilling to subscribe to one exclusive viewpoint, to take an "either-or" or "all-or-none" position. They are more self-critical and seem to be willing more than ever before to listen to other viewpoints and to explore any and each promising avenue opened to them. There is greater awareness of the complexity of psychology and therefore clearer recognition that such a complex domain demands many approaches. A. A. Roback observes in his *A History of American Psychology* (1964) that "mental life or behavior is too complex and comprehensive to be seen through one window, even if it be a bay window." Sigmund Koch, commenting on the views of 34 authors who contributed to the first three volumes of *Psychology: A Study of a Science* (1959), notes "a far more open and liberated conception of the task of psychology, the role of its investigators and systematists, than we have enjoyed in recent history." Referring to the same phenomenon, Shakow and Rapaport in their *The Influence of Freud on American Psychology* (1964) note that psychology

> . . . seems to be developing more positive qualities. These include a readiness to face substantive aspects of problems, with insistence upon only the degree of rigor necessary to protect the substance; an appreciation of the psychologist's personal motivations for entering the field . . . , and an appreciation of the stage of psychology's scientific development . . . a readiness to participate in a group commitment to a field where tolerance for tentativeness needs to be great; above all, an ability to recognize the value of a variety of approaches to psychology, even if one's personal commitment is to one particular approach. These are the qualities of mature psychologists who have to work with an inevitably adolescent psychology.

Broadening of Perspectives.   Examples of the recognition of "the value of a variety of approaches to psychology" and calls to broaden psychologists' viewpoints and perspectives have been appearing in current literature with increasing frequency and urgency. Gardner Murphy, in his article *The Psychology of 1975: An Extrapolation* (1963), speaks of "a dialectical movement by which psychology will get more rigid, orderly, scientific, correct, and afraid of saying 'boo' to any of the experiences not yet codified. But at the same time, these experiences not yet codified will push and kick until they somehow or other create enough discomfort to prevent rigor mortis from setting in." It appears that psychology is now, in Murphy's phrase, "loosening," "reaching," and "reopening questions." Gordon W. Allport at the American Psychological Association annual meeting in 1965 said he saw evidence that the tide was turning away from "itsy-bitsy empiricism" and that "the concern with broader issues, with philosophical problems, is returning."

Representatives of allied sciences have also occasionally expressed a desire for a broader and more comprehensive psychology. An eminent British neurologist, W. R. Brain, at the meeting of the American Association for the Advancement of Science in 1964, suggested a conception of man which should include

> . . . the primacy of the private, personal, subjective, individual experience over any public account which science can give. This means that persons are to be regarded as values in themselves, and not reducible to either physico-chemical systems or bundles of psychological trends or impulses.

Richard W. Coan, in his article *Theoretical Concepts in Psychology* (1964), defended private, individual inner experience as a legitimate subject for scientific investigation. He says in the conclusion of the article:

A restriction of subject matter has been widely advocated by behaviourists. This may lead to respectable research; yet it runs counter to the general course of science. It is commonly defended on grounds of repeatability and verifiability. But the extension of such criteria to the choice of subject matter is unjustified. Overt movement, physiological processes, and inner experience constitute three sources of observation, and three realms of subject matter. Each warrants scientific investigation and an attempt at explanation.

New Vistas. Examples of voices postulating broadening of psychological inquiry and signs of actual broadening in contemporary psychology can be multiplied. They are cited here not to create the impression of an imminent radical reorientation of the whole field of psychology. They are brought out merely to indicate that in our day there are psychologists and other scientists who urge a wider spectrum of psychological inquiry. It is incumbent upon students of psychology that they be alert to these new perspectives and trends in psychological inquiry.

While some psychological theorists have specified the problems that this wider spectrum ought to include, others have voiced their opinions in more general terms. Carl Rogers (1964) spoke of the trend which "will attempt to face up to *all* of the realities in the psychological realm. Instead of being restrictive and inhibiting, it will throw open the whole range of human experiencing to scientific study." Among the more specific suggestions for augmentation of psychology, the most common seem to be: that man be studied not merely in the S-R framework, but in all his behavioral *and* experiential aspects; that human experience be recognized as a legitimate scientific datum; that the variety of human experience be not merely catalogued but thoroughly investigated; that appropriate methods and hypotheses for such an investigation be developed; and that psychology ultimately strive genuinely to contribute to the understanding of human nature in all its aspects. Abraham Maslow, in his *A Philosophy of Psychology: The Need for a Mature Science of Human Nature* (1957), cited a number of specific "musts" which he feels "are essential if psychology is to mature as a science and accept its full responsibilities." In summary form, Maslow's requirements for future psychology include the notions that:

> Psychology should be more humanistic, that is, more concerned with the problems of humanity, and less with the problems of the guild. . . .
> Psychology should turn more frequently to the study of philosophy, of science, of aesthetics, and especially of ethics and values. . . .
> American psychology should be bolder, more creative; it should try to discover, not only to be cautious and careful in avoiding mistakes. . . .
> Psychology should be more problem-centered, and less absorbed with means or methods. . . .
> Psychology ought to become more positive and less negative. It should have higher ceilings, and not be afraid of the loftier possibilities of the human being. . . .
> Psychology should study the depths of human nature as well as the surface behavior, the unconscious as well as the conscious. . . .
> Academic psychology is too exclusively Western. It needs to draw on Eastern sources as well. It turns too much to the objective, the public, the outer, the behavioral, and should learn more about the subjective, the private, the inner, the meditative. Intro-

spection, thrown out as a technique, should be brought back into psychological research. . . .

Psychologists should study the end experiences as well as the means to ends—the pragmatic, the useful, and the purposive. What does man live for? What makes living worthwhile? What experiences in life justify the pains of existence?

Psychology should study the human being not just as passive clay, helplessly determined by outside forces. Man is, or should be, an active autonomous, self-governing mover, chooser and center of his own life. . . .

Intellectuals tend to become absorbed with abstractions, words and concepts, and to forget the original real experience which is the beginning of all science. In psychology, this is a particular danger. . . .

The lessons of Gestalt psychology and of organismic theory have not been fully integrated into psychology. The human being is an irreducible unit, at least as far as psychological research is concerned. Everything in him is related to everything else, in greater or lesser degree. . . .

Psychologists should devote more time to the intensive study of the single unique person, to balance their preoccupation with the generalized man and with generalized and abstracted capacities. . . .

Finally, as we begin to know more about legitimate wants and needs for personal growth and self-fulfillment, that is, for psychological health, then we should set ourselves the task of creating the health-fostering culture. . . .

A program like Maslow's or other similar programs may appear utopian or at least not feasible at present. However, the authors of such programs or prescriptions feel that psychology by its very nature is committed to full study of the "phenomenon of man," and therefore its goals cannot be other than ambitious. Maslow emphasized psychology's responsibility in this respect when he said in the article cited above:

I believe that psychologists occupy the most centrally important position in the world today. I say this because all the important problems of mankind—war and peace, exploitation and brotherhood, hatred and love, sickness and health, misunderstanding and understanding, happiness and unhappiness—will yield only to a better understanding of human nature, and to this psychology alone wholly applies itself.

The Prospect. What does the future hold for psychology? No crystal ball or special wisdom is needed for the rather general, but safe prediction that psychology will grow in importance and content in both of its two dimensions—as a science and as a profession. Such a prediction is somewhat inevitable on both logical and historical grounds. The rapid and spectacular growth of psychology in the past 100 years; its expansion in many directions; its increasingly precise awareness of its nature and goals; and the burgeoning of its services in the community, government, education, business and industry, and in mental health—all these developments forecast a propitious future for psychology both in theoretical and practical areas. Even if its achievements in some areas are disappointing, one must concede that the potentialities of psychology are vast and intriguing and that there is no substantive reason why they should not be realized. Contemporary psychological trends, recorded above, foreshadow a future psychology richer in contents and more varied in approaches and methods than that of the past. It is not at all improbable—in the light of these new trends when they are viewed against the background of psychology's entire history—that psychology will become that catalytic force which ultimately will effect the synthesis of mankind's two great interests and challenges—the scientific and the humanistic.

REFERENCES

Brain, W. R. Science and antiscience. *Science*, 1965, *148*, 192–198.

Brunswik, E. Historical and thematic relations of psychology to other sciences. *Sci. Mon.*, 1956, *83*, 151–161.

Coan, R. W. Theoretical concepts in psychology. *Brit. J. statist. Psychol.*, 1964, *17*, Part II, 161–176.

Collier, R. M. Selected implications from a dynamic regulatory theory of consciousness. *Amer. Psychologist*, 1964, *19*, 265–269.

Immergluck, L. Determinism-freedom in contemporary psychology: an ancient problem revisited. *Amer. Psychologist*, 1964, *19*, 270–281.

Kahn, T. C. Evaluation of United States of America psychology by the "four-years-absent" method. *Amer. Psychologist*, 1962, *17*, 706–708.

Koch, S. Epilogue. In S. Koch (Ed.), *Psychology: a study of a science*. Vol. 3. New York: McGraw-Hill, 1959. Pp. 729–788.

Koch, S. Psychological science versus the science-humanism antinomy: intimations of a significant science of man. *Amer. Psychologist*, 1961, *16*, 629–639.

Koch, S. Psychology and emerging conceptions of knowledge as unitary. In T. W. Wann (Ed.), *Behaviorism and phenomenology*. Chicago: Chicago Univer. Press, 1964. Pp. 1–45.

Maslow, A. H. A philosophy of psychology: the need for a mature science of human nature. *Main currents in modern thought*, 1957, *13*, 27–32. Reprinted in F. T. Severin (Ed.), *Humanistic viewpoints in psychology*. New York: McGraw-Hill, 1965. Pp. 17–33.

Murphy, G. The psychology of 1975: an extrapolation. *Amer. Psychologist*, 1963, *18*, 689–695.

Murray, H. A. Prospect for psychology. *Science*, 1962, *136*, 483–488.

Nuttin, J. *Tendances nouvelles dans psychologie contemporaine*. Louvain: Publications Universitaires de Louvain, 1951.

Polanyi, M. Scientific outlook: its sickness and cure. *Science*, 1957, *125*, 480–484.

Rogers, C. R. Toward a science of the person. In T. W. Wann (Ed.), *Behaviorism and phenomenology*. Chicago: Chicago Univer. Press, 1964. Pp. 109–133.

Royce, J. R. Psychology in mid-twentieth century. *Amer. Scientist*, 1957, *45*, 57–73.

Scriven, M. Views of human nature. In T. W. Wann (Ed.), *Behaviorism and phenomenology*. Chicago: Chicago Univer. Press, 1964. Pp. 163–190.

Watson, R. I. The historical background for national trends in psychology: United States. *J. Hist. behav. Sci.*, 1965, *1*, 130–138.

BIBLIOGRAPHY FOR THE HISTORY OF PSYCHOLOGY

This bibliography contains only major works published after 1900. It is divided into (1) general history; (2) psychology in America; (3) specific, that is, dealing with the history of a country or specific historical period; (4) systematic and theoretical; (5) readings in the history of psychology; and (6) histories written in German and French, not translated into English.

The more important ones and those particularly recommended are indicated by an asterisk (*). The letter "P." after a reference indicates that one or more paperbound editions are available.

1. General

Baldwin, J. M. *History of psychology.* London: Watts, 1913. 2 vols.

Boring, E. G. *Sensation and perception in the history of experimental psychology.* New York: Appleton-Century-Crofts, 1942.

*Boring, E. G. *A history of experimental psychology.* (2nd ed.) New York: Appleton-Century-Crofts, 1950.

Boring, E. G. *History, psychology, and science: selected papers.* (Edited by R. I. Watson and D. T. Campbell) New York: Wiley, 1963.

Brennan, R. E. *History of psychology from the standpoint of a Thomist.* New York: Macmillan, 1945.

Brett, G. S. *A history of psychology.* London: Allen & Unwin, 1912, 1921. 3 vols.

Brett, G. S. *Psychology, ancient and modern.* New York: Longmans, 1928.

Brett, G. S. *A history of psychology.* (Edited and abridged by R. S. Peters) New York: Macmillan, 1953. 2nd ed. Cambridge: Massachusetts Inst. Tech., 1965. P.

Dessoir, M. *Outlines of the history of psychology.* New York: Macmillian, 1912.

Esper, E. A. *A history of psychology.* Philadelphia: Saunders, 1964.

Flugel, J.C. *A hundred years of psychology.* (New edition with an additional Part: 1933–1963 by D. J. West) New York: Basic Books, 1964.

*Garrett, H. E. *Great experiments in psychology.* (3rd ed.) New York: Appleton-Century-Crofts, 1951.

Hall, G. S. *Founders of modern psychology.* New York: Appleton-Century-Crofts, 1912.

Heidbreder, Edna. *Seven psychologies.* New York: Appleton, Century-Crofts, 1933. P.

Hulin, W. S. *A short history of psychology.* New York: Holt, 1934.

Kantor, J. R. *The scientific evolution of psychology.* Vol. 1. Chicago-Granville, Ohio: Principia, 1963.

Klemm, O. *History of psychology.* New York: Scribner, 1914.

Mercier, D. *The origins of contemporary psychology.* London: Washbourne, 1918.

Miller, G. A. *Psychology: the science of mental life.* New York: Harper & Row, 1962.

Misiak, H. *The philosophical roots of scientific psychology.* New York: Fordham Univer. Press, 1961.

Moore, J. S. *The foundations of psychology.* Princeton: Princeton Univer. Press, 1933.

Müller-Freienfels, R. *The evolution of modern psychology.* New Haven: Yale Univer. Press, 1935.

Murchison, C. (Ed.) *A history of psychology in autobiography.* Worcester, Mass.: Clark Univer. Press, 1930–1936. 3 vols. Volume 4 of the same series was edited by Langfeld, Boring, Werner, and Yerkes; it appeared in 1952.

Murchison, C. (Ed.) *Psychological register.* Worcester, Mass.: Clark Univer. Press, 1929–1932. 3 vols.

Murphy, G. *Historical introduction to modern psychology.* (Rev. ed.) New York: Harcourt, Brace, 1949.

Pillsbury, W. B. *The history of psychology.* New York: Norton, 1929.

Postman, L. (Ed.) *Psychology in the making.* New York: Knopf, 1962.

Roback, A. A. *History of psychology and psychiatry.* New York: Citadel, 1961. P.

*Spearman, C. E. *Psychology down the ages.* London: Macmillan, 1937. 2 vols.

Villa, G. *Contemporary psychology.* New York: Macmillan, 1903.

*Watson, R. I. *The great psychologists from Aristotle to Freud.* New York: Lippincott, 1963.

Williams, R. D., & Bellows, R. W. *Background of contemporary psychology.* Columbus: Hedrick, 1935.

Zilboorg, G. *A history of medical psychology.* New York: Norton, 1941.

2. American

Cattell, J. McK. *Psychology in America.* New York: Science, 1929.

Clark, K. E. *America's psychologists.* Washington, D. C.: American Psychological Assoc., 1957.

Fay, J. W. *American psychology before William James.* New Brunswick, N.J.: Rutgers Univer. Press, 1939.

*Roback, A. A. *A history of American psychology.* (Rev. ed.) New York: Collier, 1964. P.

3. Specific

Akhilananda, S. *Hindu psychology.* New York: Harper, 1946.

Bauer, R. (Ed.) *Some views on Soviet psychology.* Washington, D. C.: American Psychological Assoc., 1962.

Hearnshaw, L. S. *A short history of British psychology 1840–1940.* New York: Barnes & Noble, 1964.

Misiak, H., & Staudt, Virginia M. *Catholics in psychology: a historical survey.* New York: McGraw-Hill, 1954.

Rao, S. K. *Development of psychological thought in India.* Mysore, India: Kavyalaya Publishers, 1962.

Stratton, G. M. *Theophrastus and the Greek physiological psychology before Aristotle.* New York: Macmillan, 1917.

Walker, Helen M. *Studies in the history of statistical method.* Baltimore: Williams & Wilkins, 1931.

Warren, H. C. *A history of association psychology.* New York: Scribner, 1921.

Winn, R. B. *Soviet psychology.* New York: Philosophical Library, 1961.

4. Systematic and theoretical

*Chaplin, J., & Krawiec, T. S. *Systems and theories in psychology.* New York: Holt, Rinehart & Winston, 1960.

Ellis, W. D. *A source book of gestalt psychology.* New York: Harcourt, Brace & World, 1938.

Hartmann, G. W. *Gestalt psychology.* New York: Ronald, 1935.

Henle, Mary (Ed.) *Documents of gestalt psychology.* Berkeley, Calif.: Calif. Univer. Press, 1961.

Katz, D. *Gestalt psychology.* New York: Ronald, 1950.

Köhler, W. *Gestalt psychology.* New York: Liveright, 1947. P.

Levine, A. J. *Current psychologies.* Cambridge: Sci-Art, 1940.

Marx, M. H. (Ed.) *Psychological theory.* New York: Macmillan, 1951.

Marx, M. H. (Ed.) *Theories in contemporary psychology.* New York: Macmillan, 1963.

Marx, M. H., & Hillix, W. A. *Systems and theories in psychology.* New York: McGraw-Hill, 1963.

May, R. (Ed.) *Existential psychology.* New York: Random House, 1961. P.

Miller, G. A. *Psychology: the science of mental life.* New York: Harper & Row, 1962.

Murchison, C. (Ed.) *Psychologies of 1925.* Worcester, Mass.: Clark Univer. Press, 1926.

Murchison, C. (Ed.) *Psychologies of 1930.* Worcester, Mass.: Clark Univer. Press, 1930.

Oberndorf, C. P. *A history of psychoanalysis in America.* New York: Grune & Stratton, 1953. P.

Shakow, D., & Rapaport, D. *The influence cf Freud on American psychology.* New York: International Univer. Press, 1964.

Titchener, E. B. *Systematic psychology: prolegomena.* New York: Macmillan, 1929.

*Wann, T. (Ed.) *Behaviorism and phenomenology.* Chicago: Chicago Univer. Press, 1964. P.

Wolman, B. B. *Contemporary theories and systems in psychology.* New York: Harper, 1960.

*Woodworth, R. S., & Sheehan, Mary R. *Contemporary schools of psychology.* (3rd ed.) New York: Ronald, 1964.

5. Readings

Dennis, W. *Readings in the history of psychology.* New York: Appleton-Century-Crofts, 1948.

Drever, J. (Ed.) *Sourcebook in psychology.* New York: Philosophical Library, 1960.

*Herrnstein, R. J., & Boring, E. G. (Eds.) *A source book in the history of psychology.* Cambridge, Mass.: Harvard Univer. Press, 1965.

Mandler, Jean M., & Mandler, G. *Thinking: from association to gestalt.* New York: Wiley, 1964. P.

Rand, B. *The classical psychologists.* New York: Houghton Mifflin, 1912.

Shipley, T. (Ed.) *Classics in psychology.* New York: Philosophical Library, 1961.

Wolman, B. B., & Nagel, E. (Eds.) *Scientific psychology: principles and approaches.* New York: Basic Books, 1965.

6. German and French

Foulquié, F. *La psychologie contemporaine.* Paris: Presses Universitaires de France, 1951.

Hehlmann, W. *Geschichte der Psychologie.* Stuttgart: Kröner, 1963.

Holzner, B. *Amerikanische und deutsche Psychologie.* Würzburg: Holzner, 1958.

Hoyos, C. *Denkschrift zur Lage der Psychologie.* Wiesbaden: Steiner, 1964.

Mueller, F. L. *Histoire de la psychologie de l'antiquité à nos jours.* Paris: Payot, 1960.

Reuchlin, M. *Histoire de la psychologie.* Paris: Presses Universitaires de France, 1963.

Appendix

International Congresses of Psychology

THE FIRST SUGGESTION for an international congress of psychology was made as early as 1881, but it took eight years for such a congress to convene. Since the purpose of congresses is the exchange on information and ideas, international congresses of psychology are a valuable historical index of prevailing trends and currents in psychological thought, as well as of psychological activity at the time of their meeting.

The First International Congress. It was in 1889, ten years after the establishment of the first psychological laboratory, that the First International Congress met—a convincing indication of the rapid growth of the new science. The place of this meeting was not Germany, and the congress was not presided over by Wundt, as one might expect. It convened in Paris under the presidency of J. M. Charcot and T. Ribot. There were 203 delegates from 20 different countries, among them Wundt and Helmholtz from Germany, Bain and Galton from England, James and Jastrow from the United States, and Janet and Binet from France. It is worth noting that many leading neurologists and philosophers also participated in this congress. In his inaugural address, Ribot declared that the primary intention of the congress was to make psychology a pure science which would base its future progress on observation and experimentation. The topics discussed covered a wide range, but the predominant interests were hypnotism and heredity. Enthusiasm and optimism characterized this first international meeting of psychologists.

Other Congresses. Since 1889 there have been 18 international congresses, the last one in 1966 in Moscow, Russia. The titles of the first congresses testify to the gradual change in psychology's orientation. The first one in 1889 was a congress of *physiological psychology;* the second, in 1892, of *experimental* psychology; the fourth, in 1900, was simply called an international congress of *psychology,* a title which has endured. Paris was the scene of three congresses (1889, 1900, 1937); Great Britain of three (London in 1892, Oxford in 1923, and Edinburgh in 1948); Germany of two (Munich in 1896 and Bonn in 1960); United States of two (New Haven in 1929 and Washington, D.C. in 1963); other countries of one: Italy (Rome in 1905); Switzerland (Geneva in 1909); The Netherlands (Groningen in 1926); Denmark (Copenhagen in 1932); Sweden (Stockholm in 1951); Canada (Montreal in 1954); Belgium (Brussels in 1957); and Soviet Union (Moscow in 1966). The resolution of the International Committee of Congresses was to hold congresses every three years, but the two World Wars caused lapses of 14 and 11 years, respectively.

INTERNATIONAL CONGRESSES OF PSYCHOLOGY

NUMBER	PLACE	YEAR	PRESIDENT	ATTENDANCE
I	Paris	1889	J. M. Charcot, honorary T. Ribot	203
II	London	1892	H. Sidgwick	300
III	Munich	1896	C. Stumpf	450
IV	Paris	1900	T. Ribot	430
V	Rome	1905	L. Bianchi, honorary G. Sergi	475
VI	Geneva	1909	T. Flournoy	600
VII	Oxford	1923	C. S. Myers	200
VIII	Groningen	1926	G. Heymans	200
IX	New Haven	1929	J. McK. Cattell J. R. Angell, vice-president	826
X	Copenhagen	1932	H. Höffding (designated but died before the meetings) E. Rubin	over 200
XI	Paris	1937	P. Janet, honorary H. Piéron	592
XII	Edinburgh	1948	J. Drever (ill) G. Thomson, acting	658
XIII	Stockholm	1951	D. Katz	658
XIV	Montreal	1954	E. A. Bott E. C. Tolman, co-president	1021
XV	Brussels	1957	A. Michotte	1183
XVI	Bonn	1960	K. Bühler, honorary W. Metzger	1833
XVII	Washington, D.C.	1963	E. G. Boring	1902
XVIII	Moscow	1966	A. N. Leontiev	

The proceedings of the congresses indicate the prevailing trends of psychology and sometimes also reflect the political situation of the world at the time. The first congress gave much attention to hypnotism and even more characteristically to spiritism, with the leading figures of the spiritistic movement present and with the demonstration of various spiritistic media. The congress of 1896 in Germany brought up the problem of psychophysical parallelism. The congress of 1905 in Rome was preoccupied with the measurement of intelligence and with mental diseases. In the congress of 1923 the Gestalt school was the novelty. At the congress of 1937 in Paris there were addresses and papers which treated the issues provoked by the political currents then prevalent in Europe, Nazism, Fascism, and Communism. The first congress in the United States, in

INTERNATIONAL CONGRESSES OF APPLIED PSYCHOLOGY

NUMBER	PLACE	YEAR
I	Geneva	1920
II	Barcelona	1921
III	Milan	1922
IV	Paris	1927
V	Utrecht	1928
VI	Barcelona	1930
VII	Moscow	1931
VIII	Prague	1934
IX	Bern	1949
X	Gothenburg	1951
XI	Paris	1953
XII	London	1955
XIII	Rome	1958
XIV	Copenhagen	1961
XV	Ljubljana	1964

New Haven in 1929, revealed the numerical and qualitative strength of American psychology. It also presented a cross section of the theoretical and practical trends existing in American psychology at that time. It showed that America had matured and had overtaken other countries in psychological productivity. The next congress on the North American Continent, in Montreal in 1954, which convened a good representation of European psychologists, offered an opportunity to note contrasts in approaches and view on some issues between American and European psychologists. Among the most active participants at the congresses were the French psychologist Henri Piéron, who was present at every congress from 1900 to 1957, and the Swiss psychologist Edouard Claparède, who served as a secretary general of the International Committee of Congresses, the organizing body, for many years.

The congresses were often occasions both for the assessment of psychology's progress and for critical examination of the various current issues and views. This function was well reflected in the inaugural address at the Paris congress of 1937, delivered by the dean of French psychologists, Pierre Janet. He had assisted in organizing the first congress, had been secretary of the fourth in 1900, and finally achieved the honor of presiding at the Eleventh Congress in 1937. His experience of witnessing the growth of psychology for half a century gave his keynote address special significance and made this one of the more interesting of the psychological congresses. Janet referred to the hopes of those psy-

chologists who in the initial phase of psychology's existence, 50 years
ago, cherished an overoptimistic ambition of solving all the problems of
man through physiological psychology. Conceding that those hopes were
not fulfilled, and that the problems proved more difficult than anticipated,
he appealed to the new generation of psychologists to employ new means,
and added efforts in their study of man and thus to contribute to man's
greater happiness.

American Participation. The participation of American psychologists
in the international congresses was rather modest up to the Oxford congress in 1923, which had a large delegation from the United States.
William James attended four congresses: the first two, the fourth, and
the fifth. At the Fifth Congress in Rome in 1905 he delivered a provocative paper on consciousness which was enthusiastically debated by the
participants of the congress. All the congresses from 1923 forward were
actively supported and attended in ever-increasing numbers by Americans.
At the congress in Bonn, Germany, in 1960, psychologists from the United
States contributed 46 per cent of the papers and addresses, whereas Germany, the host of the congress, and Britain contributed ten per cent each;
France, seven; Italy, four; and other countries together, 23 per cent.

International Union of Scientific Psychology. Since 1951 the International Congresses of Psychology have been organized by the International
Union of Scientific Psychology (IUSP). Founded at the Thirteenth International Congress in Stockholm in 1951, this body is described in its
Statutes as "an organization uniting those National Societies and Associations whose aim is the development of scientific psychology, whether
biological or social, normal or abnormal, pure or applied." Its primary
purpose is "To develop the exchange of ideas and scientific information
between psychologists of different countries, and in particular to organize
International Congresses and other meetings. . . . " IUSP has a consulta-
tive status with UNESCO and receives from it an annual subvention.
Twenty-nine countries are offically represented in the IUSP. Affiliated
with it are the Association de Psychologie Scientifique de Langue Française, the Interamerican Society of Psychology, the International Association of Applied Psychology, and the International Council of Psychologists.

IUSP is governed by the Assembly, which elects every three years a
president, a vice-president, and an executive committee. Thus far presidents of the IUSP have been: Henri Piéron (1951-1954), Jean Piaget
(1954-1957), Albert Michotte (1957-1960), Otto Klineberg (1960-1963),
and James Drever (1963-1966). The first executive secretary was H. S.
Langfeld. After Langfeld's death, O. Klineberg was elected, and after him
Roger W. Russell.

Other International Bodies. In addition to the general International
Congresses of Psychology there are special international organizations
of psychologists which sponsor their own congresses. Among them is

The International Association of Applied Psychology which sponsors international congresses of applied psychology. The organization was founded in 1920 through the efforts of Edouard Claparède, who served as president of the first and the second congress. There have been altogether 15 of these congresses, convened in different counties. A list of these congresses appears on page 473.

The Interamerican Society of Psychology, founded in 1951 in Mexico City, seeks to provide direct communication among psychologists in North and South America. It has sponsored annual or biennial congresses convened mostly in the Latin American countries. The Society has fostered a number of projects aiming at better interchange between the United States and Latin America.

There are additional special international groups of psychologists which hold meetings on an international scale on subjects such as psychoanalysis, Rorschach,parapsychology, psychosomatics, and psychodrama. The American Psychological Association has created a committee, Committee on International Relations, which promotes and coordinates international contacts between psychologists of the United States and other countries.

REFERENCES

American Psychological Association. Reciprocal influences in international psychology. *Amer. Psychologist*, 1960, *15*, 313–315.

Kelman, H. C., & Hollander, E. P. International cooperation in psychological research. *Amer. Psychologist*, 1964, *19*, 779–782.

Langfeld, H. S. Note on the history of the International Congresses of Psychology. *Amer.*

Psychologist, 1954, *9*, 91.

MacLeod, R. B. A note on the International Congress. In H. P. David & H. von Bracken (Eds.), *Perspectives in personality theory.* New York: Basic Books, 1957. Pp. 419–424.

Piéron, H. Histoire succincte des Congrés Internationaux de Psychologie. *Année psychol.*, 1954, *54*, 397–405.

■ SYNOPSIS ■

of 1 Philosophical and Scientific Roots of Psychology
2 Transitional Period
3 Pioneers in Germany, Britain, France, and United States
4 (a) Theoretical and Thematic Growth
(b) Philosophical and Scientific Influences on Psychology in the 20th Century.

LEGEND: PHILOSOPHY   PSYCHOLOGY   SCIENCE

Transition

Beginning (19th c.)

Growth (20th c.)

1

Aristotle

Christian: Tertullian, Augustine	Galen
Scholastic: Thomas Aquinas	Roger Bacon
Renaissance: Vives	Galileo
Descartes	Newton
Leibnitz	Galvani
Empirical: Locke, Berkeley, Hume	Purkinje
Enlightenment: Condillac, LaMettrie, Cabanis	Phrenology—Reaction time in Astronomy
Associationism: Hartley, James Mill, J. S. Mill	Hypnotism—Psychiatry

2

Kant	Bain	Fechner	Lotze	Weber—J. Müller
Herbart	**3** Wilhelm Wundt			Helmholtz—Hering
Spencer	James	Külpe	Brentano	Neuroanatomy: Bell, Magendie, Flourens, Rolando
Comte	Galton	Ebbinghaus	G. E. Müller Stumpf	Neurology: Broca, Wernicke
Taine	Ward	Hall	Titchener Ribot	Darwin
Trenoelenburg	Sully	Ladd	Baldwin Binet	Bernard
Mach	Myers	Cattell	Witmer Janet	Statistics: Pearson

4a

Bergson	Structuralism	Physiological	Sherrington	**4b**
Husserl	Functionalism	Animal	Pavlov	
Dilthey	Behaviorism	Abnormal	Adrian	
Neopositivism	Psychoanalysis	Psychometrics	Cannon	
Neo-Kantism	Hormic	Dynamic	Berger	
Pragmatism	Gestalt	Personality	Magoun—Jasper Lindsley—Penfield	
Marxism	Operationism	Social	Cybernetics	
Neoscholasticism	Phenomenogical-Existential	Clinical	Ethology	
Existentialism	Humanistic	Industrial	Psychopharmacology	

Index of Names

Abraham, K., 388, 401
Abt, L. E., 223
Ach, N., 47, 91, 98, 99, 100, 106, 112, 117, 416, 420
Adams, J. F., 125
Adler, Alexandra, 396
Adler, A., 111, 116, 374, 380, 390, 393, 394, 396–398, 401, 404, 447
Adler, K., 396
Adrian, E. D., 42
Agar, W. E., 376
Akhilananda, S., 312, 470
Albee, G. W., 177
Albrecht, F. M., 152
Alcmaeon, 18
Alexander, F., 391, 403, 404
Allen, F., 211
Allers, R., 403, 459
Allesch, J. v., 92, 115, 116
Allport, F. H., 158, 177
Allport, G. W., 28, 30, 107, 152, 156, 157, 158, 167, 170, 172, 176, 232, 297, 316, 326, 357, 376, 451, 452, 465
Ames, A., Jr., 168
Ananiev, B. G., 273, 276, 279, 280
Anastasi, Anne, 63, 158
Anaxagoras, 5, 9
Ancona, L., 252
Andrews, T. G., 63
Angell, F., 55, 56, 83, 87, 97, 148, 151
Angell, J. R., 46, 56, 74, 135, 136, 148, 150, 151, 152, 153, 320, 321, 322–323, 324, 327, 328, 332, 374, 472
Anger, H., 123
Angermeier, W. F., 125
Anokhin, P. K., 274
Anrep, G. V., 280
Ansbacher, H. L., 404
Ansbacher, Rowena, 404
Appicciafuoco, R., 257
Appley, N. H., 177, 368, 376
Aquinas, T., 4, 8, 9, 10, 15, 26, 410, 469
Ardigò, R., 247, 255

Aristotle, 4, 6–7, 8, 9, 10, 13, 15, 19, 21, 26, 37, 85, 89, 91, 94, 134, 321, 387, 390, 469, 470
Arlow, J. A., 403
Arnheim, R., 357
Arnold, W., 117, 123
Arps, G. F., 85
Artemov, V. A., 276
Arthur, Grace, 156
Asch, S., 297, 357, 375
Atkinson, R. C., 63
Augustine (Bishop of Hippo), 8, 415–416
Awaji, Y., 288, 289
Ayer, A. J., 347

Bacon, F., 9, 127
Bailey, P., 256, 403
Bain, A., 14, 15, 22, 24, 26, 29, 129, 133, 225, 232, 234, 236, 255, 282, 316, 471
Bakan, D., 63
Baldwin, J. M., 56, 57, 66, 130, 142, 145, 146, 148, 149, 150, 151, 153, 207, 321, 469
Banerji, M. N., 312
Banissoni, F., 252, 255
Barclay, J. R., 103, 403
Bard, P., 134
Barnette, W. L., 312
Barrett, W., 432, 449, 458
Bartlett, F. C., 171, 226, 228, 229, 230, 255, 256, 321
Bartley, S. H., 177
Basov, M., 272
Bauer, R. A., 280, 470
Beach, F. A., 346
Beare, J. I., 10
Beaunis, H., 57, 239
Beauvoir, Simone de, 432, 444, 458
Beers, C., 132, 199, 221
Bekhterev, V. M., 34, 57, 87, 262, 264–267, 269, 271, 272, 278, 279, 280, 285, 329, 334
Bell, C., 32, 44

Bell, H., 156
Bellows, R. W., 157, 469
Belsky, S., 280
Benda, C. E., 450, 458
Bender, H., 123
Beneke, F. E., 69
Bennett, C. C., 63
Bentley, M., 125, 147, 312, 319–320, 326
Benussi, V., 248, 257
Berelson, B., 455, 458
Berg, J. H. van den, 446, 459
Bergius, R., 123
Bergmann, G., 346, 347
Bergson, H., 236, 316
Beritov, I. S., 274
Berkeley, G., 15, 17, 18, 22, 29, 30, 127, 128
Bernard, C., 41–42, 44, 258, 260
Bernard, L. L., 368
Bernheim, H., 71
Bernreuter, R., 156
Bernstein, J., 33, 44
Bertalanffy, L. v., 15, 30
Bertrand, F. L., 256
Bessel, F. W., 72
Beuchet, J., 256
Bhatt, L. J., 312
Bianchi, L., 472
Bieliauskas, V. J., 458
Biemel, W., 411
Binet, A., 28, 57, 61, 62, 67, 71, 100, 108, 144, 156, 196, 203, 205, 208, 221, 222, 237, 238, 239–241, 244, 245, 248, 255, 256, 285, 289, 294, 299, 321, 471
Bingham, W. V., 176, 178, 192, 193, 323
Binswanger, L., 437, 445, 446, 459
Bixenstine, V. E., 9, 342, 348
Bixler, J. S., 458
Blackham, H. J., 458
Blake, R. R., 168, 177
Blank, L., 223
Blanshard, B., 343, 347
Bleuler, E., 388
Blonsky, P., 272
Boas, F., 380

477

Index of Subjects

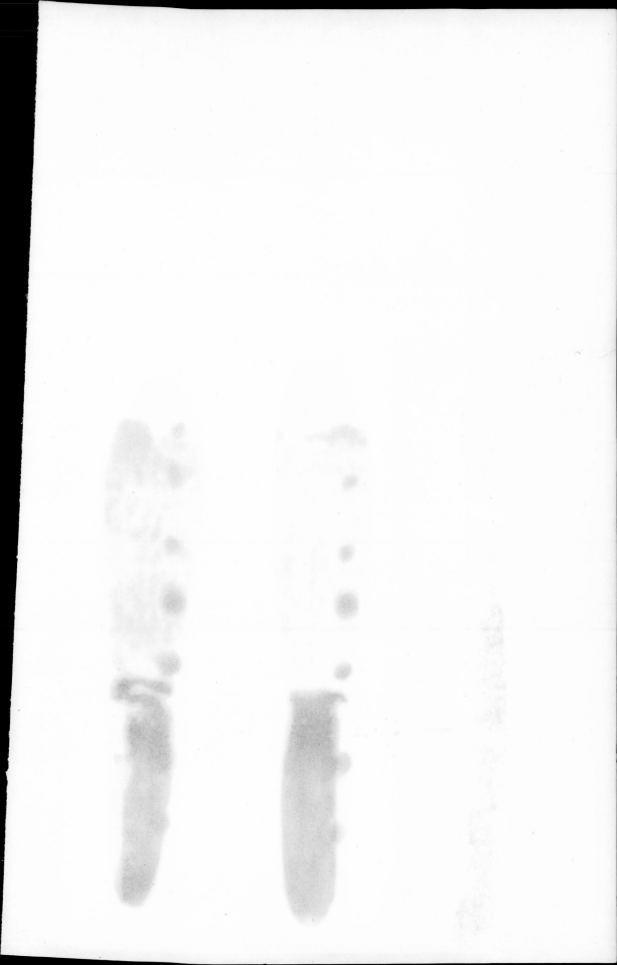

DATE DUE	
OCT 1 9 1994	
NOV 1 1994	
OCT 2 6 1999	
OCT 3 0 2002	
MAR 2 0 2003	

GAYLORD   PRINTED IN U.S.A.